Kohitan

DS
.H68

DS/195/H68 HOVANNISIAN, R ARMENIA ON THE ROAD TO IN

BERGEN COMMUNITY COLLEGE LIBRARY

BERGEN COMMUNITY COLLEGE LIBRARY
100 PARAMUS ROAD
PARAMUS, N.J. 07652

Return postage guaranteed.

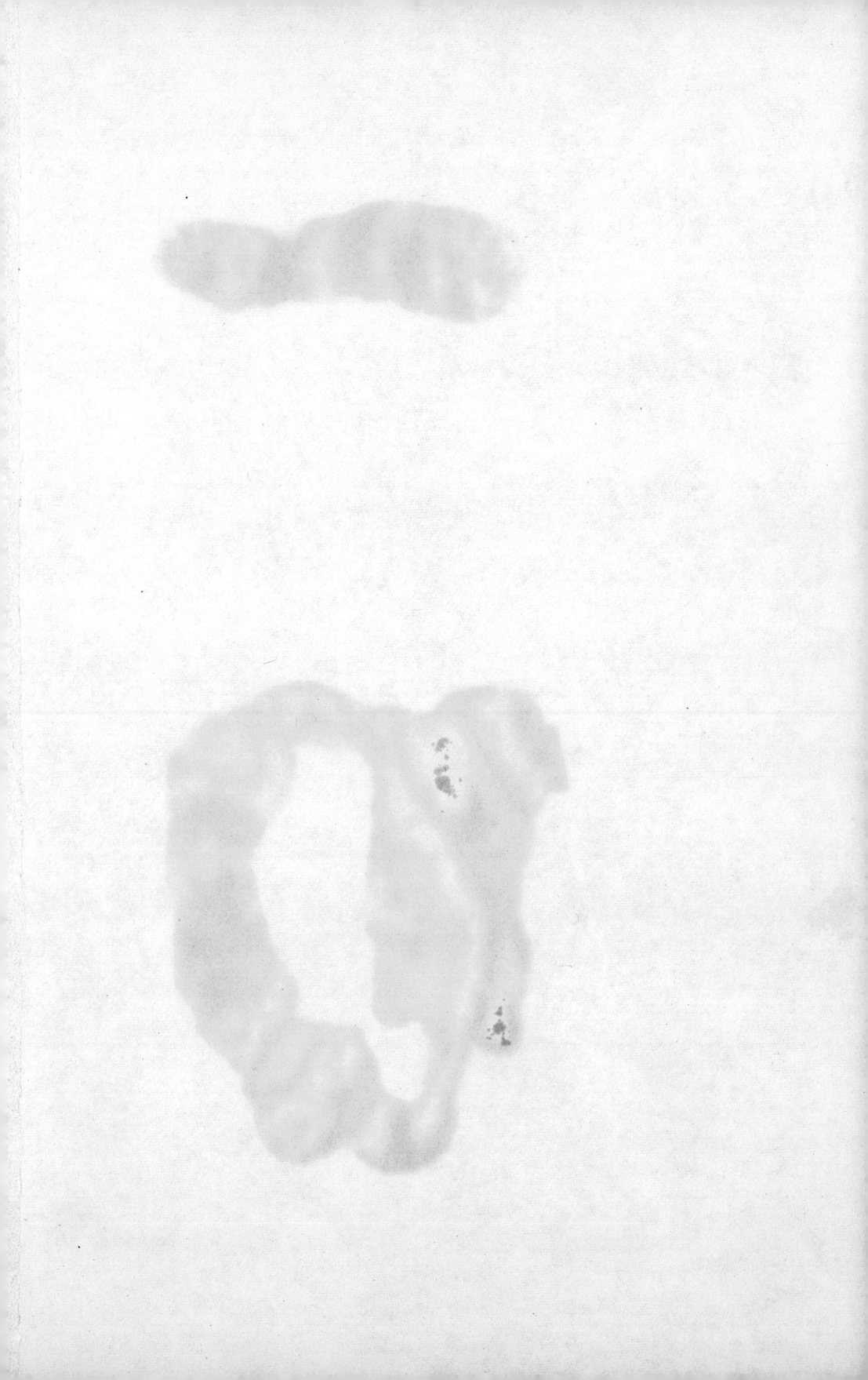

Armenia
on the Road to Independence

Published under the auspices of the
NEAR EASTERN CENTER
University of California, Los Angeles

Armenia
on the Road to Independence
1918

By Richard G. Hovannisian

University of California Press
Berkeley, Los Angeles, London

University of California Press
Berkeley and Los Angeles, California

University of California Press, Ltd.
London, England

© 1967 by The Regents of the University of California
Third Printing, 1974
ISBN: 0-520-00574-0
Library of Congress Catalog Card Number: 67-13649
Designed by Betsy Davis
Printed in the United States of America

To
*a Generation Whose Ideals
Continue To Inspire*

Preface

The road to Armenian independence, spanning an entire century, culminated during the turbulent years of World War I and the Russian revolutions. Emerging from the dissolution of the Romanov Empire and from the fragmentation of Transcaucasia, Armenia strove from 1918 through 1920 to join the family of sovereign states. The object of this study is to present and analyze the numerous complex factors that led to the establishment of an Armenian government for the first time in more than five hundred years.

This book is based primarily on documents deposited in the National Archives in Washington, D.C., and in the Archives of the Armenian Delegation to the Paris Peace Conference. Many published documents and relevant works were also found in the Library of Congress, the Hoover Institute, the Public Library of New York City, and the Alexander Miasnikian State Library in Erevan, Armenian SSR.

The Armenian titles are transliterated in a simplified form not necessitating the use of diacritical marks. For Russian titles, the Library of Congress system is used, with diacritical marks omitted, although several proper names, both in Russian and Armenian, are given, not in conformity with the adopted system of transliteration (see Key, pp. 255–256), but in keeping with the generally accepted English spelling. Moreover, for the sake of clarity, all dates, except where noted, are according to the Gregorian calendar, which in the twentieth century is thirteen days ahead of the Julian calendar, used in Russia and Transcaucasia until 1918.

In completing this study, I have incurred indebtedness to the staffs of the libraries of the University of California, particularly to Ann T. Hinckley of the Interlibrary Loan Service, to the Hoover Library and Institute, and to the Academy of Sciences of the Armenian SSR. The Armenian Revolutionary Federation (Hai Heghapokhakan Dashnaktsutiun) placed at my disposal the archives of the party as well as those of the Armenian delegations to Berlin and Constantinople in 1918 and to the Paris Peace Conference in 1919–1920. These archives, now housed in Boston, Massachusetts, are among the most extensive and valuable primary sources for the history of the Armenian Republic.

Certain individuals inspired or aided me in the development of this work. Simon Vratzian, former premier of the Republic, provided me with insights that could not have been gained from the pages of any publication. To professors Raymond H. Fisher and Hans Rogger I owe thanks for their encouragement and for their abilities as historical critics. I am also very thankful to Marilyn A. Arshagouni, who read the manuscript and made valuable suggestions concerning form and style. The maps were prepared with the expert assistance of Grigor G. Kotcholosian and Dwight E. Williams. The inclusion of photographs was made possible through the cooperation of Harvard University Press, Richard Pipes, Akaki Ramishvili, Zahid Khan-Khoysky, and Vahan Afrikian. I am especially grateful to the Near Eastern Center of the University of California, Los Angeles, and to its director, Professor G. E. von Grunebaum, for facilitating the publication of this book. Finally, there is the debt that can not be measured or repaid. That is to Vartiter, who, besides inspiring self-confidence and assisting in the gathering of relevant material, shared with me every experience and emotion of the following pages.

R. G. H.

Contents

I. *The Antecedents*	1
II. *Russian Armenia*	7
III. *Turkish Armenia*	24
IV. *"The Fateful Years" (1914–1917)*	40
V. *"Hopes and Emotions" (March–October, 1917)*	69
VI. *The Bolshevik Revolution and Armenia*	94
VII. *Transcaucasia Adrift (November, 1917–March, 1918)*	106
VIII. *Dilemmas (March–April, 1918)*	131
IX. *War and Independence (April–May, 1918)*	157
X. *The Republics of Georgia, Azerbaijan, and Armenia*	186
XI. *The Suppliants (June–October, 1918)*	216
XII. *In Conclusion*	243
Appendix: The Allies and Armenia	247
Transliteration Key	255
Notes	257
Bibliography	317
Index	345

Maps

1. Historic Armenia   3
2. The Caucasian khanates of Persia   9
3. Provinces of Transcaucasia   12
4. Administrative subdivisions of Transcaucasia   14
5. The six Armenian vilayets   35
6. The planned partition of the Ottoman Empire   61
7. The Caucasus front, 1914–1917   65
8. The Turkish offensive, February–May, 1918   136
9. The battles of May 16–30, 1918   192
10. Territorial losses of Transcaucasia   200
11. The struggle for Baku, June–September, 1918   226

I

The Antecedents

THE ARMENIAN PEOPLE, subjected for centuries to foreign domination, experienced a cultural and political renaissance during the eighteenth and especially the nineteenth centuries. The growth of national consciousness was manifested in literary movements, in the establishment of hundreds of schools throughout the Ottoman and Russian empires, and in the emergence of societies striving for Armenian self-administration. The focus of concern was the great Armenian Plateau in eastern Anatolia. On this land the Armenian nation had taken form in the first millennium before the Christian era.[1] It was there that Armenian kings had reigned and a distinct native culture had developed.

The northern and southern frontiers of the Armenian Plateau are well defined by the Pontus and Taurus mountain chains, the former dividing the Black Sea littoral, and the latter the plains of Mesopotamia from the highland. The Pontic Alps lose their massive character at their eastern extremity where they splinter into several secondary subranges, separating the Plateau from the Georgian lowlands. The unambiguous character of the border is resumed in the northeastern reaches of the Plateau where minor ranges skirt Lake Sevan and extend southeastward to the Araxes River. This area, commonly referred to as Mountainous Karabagh, contrasts sharply with the steppes of Mughan and Karabagh, which, several thousand feet below, fan out toward the east.[2] Natural borders in the west and the southeast are much less pronounced. The western Euphrates from the Taurus Mountains to the river's abrupt turn eastward and the volcanic agglomerations from that point to the Pontic Alps are often identified as the western limits of the Plateau.[3] The most imperceptible gradation occurs in the southeast between the Araxes River and Lake Urmia, as the Iranian tableland converges with the Armenian highland. On the Plateau rise the headwaters of the Tigris and the Euphrates, flowing southward toward the Persian Gulf, the Araxes and the Kur, winding eastward to the Caspian Sea, and the Chorokh, following a shorter course to the Black Sea.[4]

All the Plateau was included within Greater Armenia, the term applied historically to the fifteen provinces east of the Euphrates.[5] To the west of the river, three other provinces which centered around Sebastia (Sivas) formed Lesser Armenia. The two regions were unified under a single dynast only for short periods. Separate native princes and, more often, foreign powers dominated Lesser Armenia, which invariably was among the first of the Armenian-populated areas to be affected by external political and cultural currents.[6] Together, Greater and Lesser Armenia encompassed an area of between 120,000 and 140,000 square miles, whereas the Republic created in 1918 began its existence on a twentieth part of that land.[7]

The strategic geographic position of the Plateau has contributed to the turbulence that characterizes its history. As a major crossroad, a land of rich natural resources, and an excellent base for military operations against enemies in the surrounding lowlands, it has been coveted by powerful empires. Often, the possession of Armenia was the key to supremacy over much of Western Asia. Understandably then, the Plateau has served as the arena for countless rivalries and wars, its peoples have been subjected to many foreign lords, and its land has been repeatedly devastated. From the west have come the armies of the Macedonian, Roman, and Byzantine empires; from the east, the armies of the Persian, Turkic, and Mongol empires; from the south, the armies of the Seleucid, Arab, and Mamluk empires. Yet the tribulations of the Armenians produced sturdy stock, people who throughout the generations retained many of their national characteristics, repeatedly restored the prosperity of their homeland following years of havoc, and, after the invaders had been swept away, reestablished native rule.

The tradition of self-government was well known to the Armenians long before the Christian era. They had moved onto the Plateau as Indo-European conquerors and extended their hegemony over the indigenous peoples, whom they eventually assimilated. Then, after a period of submission to the Achaemenids and the Seleucids, they regained independence under a dynasty that wielded authority throughout the two centuries before Christ. During the reign of Tigranes of that royal Artaxiad family, the Armenians even formed the dominant element in an empire stretching from the Caucasus Mountains and Caspian Sea to Cilicia and from the Pontus to Mesopotamia and Syria.[8] From the first century to the beginning of the fifth century A.D. Armenia was ruled by the Arsacid dynasty, which, though caught between the rivalries of East and West and subjected to vassal status during much of its existence, maintained the tradition of self-government. Under the Arsacids, Armenia accepted Christianity in approximately A.D. 301 and, just over a century later, adopted its own alphabet, an event that ushered in the Golden Age of Armenian literature.[9]

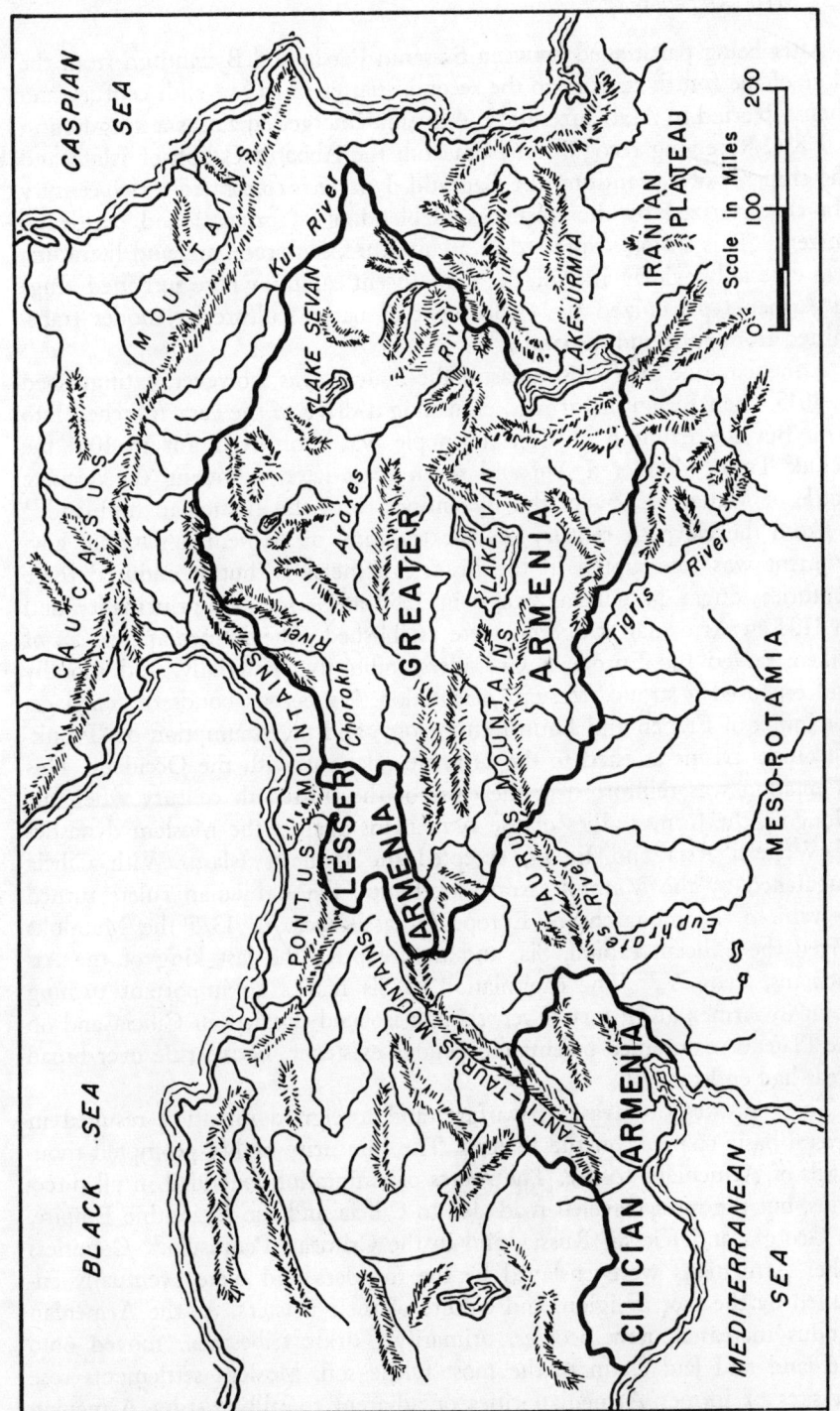

Map 1. Historic Armenia

After being partitioned between Sassanid Persia and Byzantium from the close of the fourth century to the second quarter of the seventh century and then subjected to Arab suzerainty, Armenia emerged again as a kingdom in A.D. 886. Receiving recognition from both the Abbasid Caliph of Islam and the emperor of Byzantium, the Bagratid dynasty inaugurated a two-century era characterized by the unsurpassed blending of oriental and occidental currents. This fusion, expressed in architecture, sculpture, art, and literature, was especially evident in Ani, the magnificent capital, where turbaned kings of Armenia patronized the enrichment of native culture by modes transmitted from surrounding lands.[10]

Armenian rule over most areas of the Plateau was, however, extinguished in 1045 when Byzantine armies, climaxing a drive to the east, marched into Ani. But the triumph of Constantinople was short-lived, for in 1064 the Seljuk Turks plundered Ani and seven years later, following the decisive battle of Manzikert, swept the Byzantines from the Armenian highland.[11]

From the eleventh century on, the tradition of Armenian national government was interrupted in the historic homelands, but it endured three centuries longer in Cilicia, where in 1080 an Armenian principality and in 1198 an Armenian kingdom were established. The Armenian princes of Cilicia served the European Crusaders militarily, materially, and morally and espoused a strong Western orientation. Numerous bonds of marriage, the influx of French and Latin terminology, and the assumption of "Frankish" mannerisms attested to the intimate relations with the Occident. This orientation was reinforced at the close of the thirteenth century when the Mongols, the former allies of the Armenians against the Moslem dynasties of Western Asia and Egypt, accepted the faith of Islam. With Cilicia threatened by the Mamluk armies of Egypt, the Armenian rulers turned in vain to the monarchs of Europe for assistance. In 1375 the Mamluks seized the Cilician capital, Sis, and took captive the last king of the Armenians, Leon V.[12] The capitulation of Sis marks an important turning point in Armenian history. Even though isolated districts in Cilicia and on the Plateau maintained a semiautonomous existence, native rule over broad areas had ended.

The centuries of invasion, warfare, and foreign domination resulted in several basic changes on the Plateau. The insecurity of life prompted thousands of Armenians to flee. The routes of emigration extended in all directions, but the most traveled roads led to Cilicia and the Byzantine Empire, to Georgia and Kievan Russia, and to the Crimean Peninsula.[13] Countless other Armenians were enslaved by the invaders and were eventually engulfed by the race, religion, and culture of their masters. As the Armenian exodus increased, new peoples, primarily Turkic tribesmen, moved onto the land and laid claim to the most fertile soil. Moslem settlements rose on sites of former Armenian cities or adjacent to still existing Armenian villages. The process of ethnic transmutation gradually led to Turkic-Moslem dominance on the Plateau. One aspect of that change was the conversion of extensive irrigated fields into pasturelands, which were essential to the conquerors' mode of living. Of those Armenians who remained on the Plateau after the downfall of the Bagratid kingdom, most eventually lost their lands to notables of the military-feudal states that embraced the region, and then assumed the status of tenant farmers or sharecroppers. Accompanying loss of government, ethnic alteration, and economic regression was intellectual, cultural, and moral decline. Armenia descended into abjection, indifference, and humiliation. Society receded toward autarky; localism and particularism were the inevitable results.[14]

With the loss of Armenian independence, successive Mongol and Turkic dynasties battled one another for possession of the Plateau. During the sixteenth century Persia and the already powerful Ottoman Turkish Empire emerged as the rivals. By 1520 the western and central sectors of the Plateau had come under Ottoman sway and in 1639, after more than a century of recurrent ravaging warfare, the Safavid Shah of Persia acquiesced in a settlement that awarded most of the remaining disputed territories to the Ottoman Sultan.[15]

Thus, into the Ottoman state structure were incorporated Cilicia, Lesser Armenia, and most of Greater Armenia. Provincial boundaries were redrawn to form *eyalet*s or *pashalik*s, which in turn were subdivided into *sanjak*s or *liva*s. The eyalet of Van, comprising thirteen sanjaks along the Persian frontier, was contiguous to Erzerum, one of the largest eastern provinces of the Ottoman Empire. Combining twelve sanjaks, the Erzerum eyalet extended from Shabin Karahisar in Lesser Armenia to Lake Van and the Kars pashalik. East of the Erzerum eyalet the provinces of Kars and Akhaltsikh (Childer) bordered on the domains of Persia and Georgia. Of the other former Armenian districts, most of Lesser Armenia fell within the Sivas eyalet, whereas Cilicia was apportioned among the provinces of Marash, Cyprus, and Aleppo.[16] Most of that sector of the Armenian Plateau retained by Persia was included within the *khanate*s of Erevan and Nakhichevan.[17] The highlands on the eastern border, Mountainous Karabagh, were added, however, to the khanate of Ganja,[18] while the northernmost districts of historic Greater Armenia remained in the Georgian Bagratid kingdom.[19]

This division of what once had been Armenia prevailed until the Russian armies flanked the Caucasus Mountains and, in the first three decades of the nineteenth century, annexed nearly all Persian territory north of the Araxes River. When to this land Russia added border districts won from the Ottoman Empire, the geographical-political entity of Transcaucasia encompassed the area from the Caspian to the Black Sea and from the Caucasus Mountains to the Araxes River. For the Armenians, the entrance of Russia into the sphere of Western Asian politics, coupled with their own cultural renaissance, was to point the way to a national revival but was also to occasion new disillusionments and tragedies. The Western orientation of the Armenians was reawakened, but the response of Europe was insufficient to justify the wisdom of that orientation.

II

Russian Armenia

THE CONQUEST of Transcaucasia by the expanding Russian colossus was an important step toward Armenian independence. To most Armenians of Turkey and Persia, Romanov Russia symbolized an advanced civilization and society, a champion of Christendom against Islam, and the hope for emancipation. There was some validity to this belief, for much of the Armenian Plateau was eventually liberated by the Russian armies. Many of the aspiring Armenian youth were allowed to study in the universities of Russia, and some succeeded in entering the ranks of the civil and military elite of the Empire. The masses, however, did not rise from their inferior status, as the Romanov motto, "Orthodoxy, Autocracy, and Nationality," precluded equality for the subject minorities.[1] The Moslems, Georgians, and Armenians of Transcaucasia, like Poles, Jews, and religious dissenters in other areas of the Empire, were subject to numerous restrictions. Thus, when conspirators and utopians of nineteenth-century Russia schemed against the Romanov dynasty in order to inaugurate representative government and the era of the new society, they were joined by many intellectuals of the minority groups. Of the latter, some sought the severance of their native provinces from the Empire, but Armenian opposition to the tsars was never a manifestation of separatist tendencies. On the contrary, Russia, before and after her annexation of Transcaucasia, was considered by the Armenians as the most auspicious means to a profound national revival.

Russian Conquest of the Caucasus

Long before the Russian annexation of Transcaucasia, adventurous Armenian champions of liberty and more than one Catholicos, the supreme religious prelate of the Church of Armenia, had petitioned the Romanov rulers to deliver the area from the Moslem masters.[2] It is doubtful that the tsars were overly concerned with the fate of the Armenians, but it is certain that they welcomed the prospect of territorial expansion. The southward drive of Peter I (1682–1725) was resumed in earnest by Catherine II (1762–1796), who seized rich strategic Ottoman lands along the entire northern coast of the Black Sea and compelled the Sultan to recognize Russia's right to intercede on behalf of his Christian subjects. In 1783 when Catherine, by treaty arrangement with Iraklii II of Georgia, extended her protection over his Caucasian realm, Imperial Russia approached the northern limits of the Armenian Plateau. Tsar Paul (1796–1801) continued his mother's expansionist policies and, violating the agreement with Iraklii II, annexed eastern Georgia.[3] His successor, Alexander (1801–1825), seized the remaining Georgian provinces of Mingrelia, Imeretia, Guria, and Abkhazia between 1803 and 1812 and, in the Treaty of Bucharest, obliged Turkey to relinquish its claim to these regions.[4]

Alexander's armies moved into Persian territory during those same years and in 1813 constrained the Shah to renounce his pretensions to eastern Georgia and to surrender the northeastern section of the Armenian Plateau as well as several *khanate*s extending from Ganja and Karabagh to Kuba and Baku.[5] The peace that was established by this settlement, the Treaty of Gulistan, was short-lived. The interregnum following Alexander's death, the "Decembrist" uprising, and Moslem rebellions in Russia's newly acquired Caucasian provinces convinced Persian Crown Prince Abbas Mirza that he could regain the ceded khanates. In 1826 the Persian Army crossed the frontier demarcated in the Treaty of Gulistan. Only after months of bitter contest did the Russian forces, assisted by hundreds of Armenian volunteers, succeed in expelling the invader.[6] Tsar Nicholas' Caucasian Army, commanded by General I. F. Paskevich, then pushed toward Erevan and in October, 1827, captured that fortress city, which for decades had stood as the most imposing symbol of Persian domination on the Armenian Plateau. Leaving the Armenian volunteers to police the area, regular Russian units advanced across the Araxes River to the village of Turkmanchai, where the Qajar dynasty of Persia capitulated and, in a treaty of peace, not only recognized Russian sovereignty over the territory lost in 1813 but also yielded two more provinces, the khanates of Erevan and Nakhichevan.[7] Moreover, Armenian inhabitants of North Persia were to be permitted to resettle north of the Araxes River, the newly designated international boundary. During the following months, nearly fifty thousand availed themselves of that opportunity.[8]

The negotiations at Turkmanchai had just been concluded when Russia became embroiled in war with Turkey. Ready for combat, Paskevich's army drove westward into the Armenian Plateau as far as the great citadel of Erzerum. Along the entire route, Armenians welcomed the Russian troops as liberators and rejoiced that the day of deliverance was at hand. Such optimism was shattered by the peace treaty signed in September, 1829,

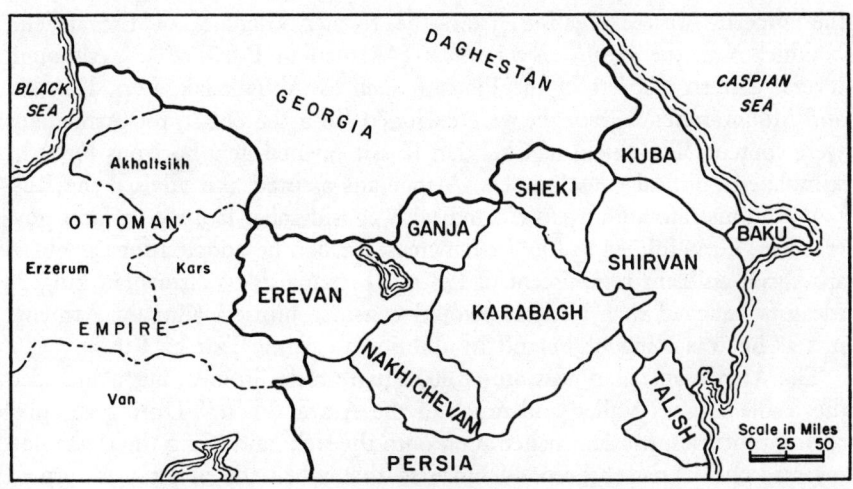
Map 2. The Caucasian khanates of Persia

at Adrianople. There, the Russians agreed to clear their forces from the *eyalets* of Erzerum and Kars, in return for which the Ottoman Sultan withdrew his claim to territories along the eastern littoral of the Black Sea and ceded most of the *pashalik* of Akhaltsikh.[9] Because they had welcomed the Russian advance, many Armenians in Kars and Erzerum feared Moslem reprisals; others bewailed the prospect of restored Ottoman jurisdiction. For them the Treaty of Adrianople offered an alternative. Within eighteen months they could quit their native villages, pass beyond the new frontier, and become the subjects of Tsar Nicholas I. Conversely, Moslems in Akhaltsikh were given the privilege of moving west of the established boundary. By the end of 1830, approximately one hundred thousand Armenians from the plains of Erzerum and Alashkert followed the example of those who had emigrated from North Persia to Transcaucasia.[10] Most of these Turkish Armenians settled in the abandoned Moslem areas of Akhalkalak, part of the former pashalik of Akhaltsikh.[11] No one could then have known that this action was to contribute to an Armeno-Georgian conflict nearly a century later. In 1918, the Armenian Republic was to demand Akhalkalak on geographic and ethnic principles, while the Republic of Georgia was to assert its historic and economic rights to the district.[12]

The Armenian Oblast

An outgrowth of the Romanov conquest of Transcaucasia was the formation of Russian Armenia. Geographically, the term was applied to that portion of the Plateau included within the Russian Empire, while all Armenian subjects of the tsars became known as Russian, or Eastern, Armenians. In a sequel to the Treaty of Turkmanchai, Tsar Nicholas issued the imperial decree creating, from the former khanates of Erevan and Nakhichevan, the *Armianskaia oblast* ("Armenian Province").[13] Although several eastern districts of the Plateau, such as Akhalkalak, Lori, Kazakh, and Mountainous Karabagh, were excluded from the oblast, the Armenians were content. The shield of Christian Russia opened new horizons for their stimulated political consciousness. Armenians assisted and advised the Russian administrators and participated with considerable latitude in local government. Gratefulness to the Tsar increased when he adopted for the oblast an official emblem reminiscent of the royal standards of Armenian kings.[14] Idealists believed that Nicholas would consider himself King of Armenia just as he was King of Poland in addition to being Tsar of Russia.

The Armenian oblast was only 8,000 square miles in area, but it included the fertile Araxes Valley and much of the Ararat Plain.[15] During the preceding centuries, Moslem penetration onto the rich land along the rivers had reversed the Christian preponderance so that when the oblast was formed barely a third of the population was Armenian. In 1838, however, after the influx of immigrants from Persia and Turkey, the Armenians constituted one-half of the province's 165,000 inhabitants. Moreover, in the remainder of Transcaucasia lived more than 200,000 Armenians, some of whom, by moving subsequently to Erevan-Nakhichevan, contributed to the reestablishment of a Christian majority in the province.[16] But the principal source of increment remained the continual trickle of Turkish Armenian refugees.

Provincial Reorganizations in the Caucasus

The conviction that Russian patronage would assure the revival of Armenian governmental life was shaken in 1840 when orders from St. Petersburg did away with the special status of the Armianskaia oblast.[17] The initial favorable Russian attitude toward the Armenians had soon given way to apprehension of their deepening national sentiment. Influential civic and religious leaders were neutralized or required to leave Transcaucasia.[18] Tsarist policy for the Caucasus was now aimed at replacing the diversities in administration with a system uniform throughout most of the Empire.[19] Often, separatist tendencies in particular regions were discouraged by combining contrasting geographic entities into new provinces with unnatural boundaries and heterogeneous populations. Abolition of the oblast in 1840 and consolidation of all Transcaucasia into two provinces, the Georgian-Imeretian *guberniia* and the Caspian oblast, were the outgrowth of these administrative principles. In the new apportionment, the former Armenian oblast, along with Akhalkalak and Lori in the northern reaches of the Plateau and a portion of the former khanate of Ganja, renamed Elisavetpol, were included within the Georgian-Imeretian guberniia. Mountainous Karabagh was attached to the Caspian oblast, which encompassed eastern Transcaucasia.[20]

The territorial reorganization did not yield the desired results but instead inspired resistance. Moslem mountaineers of the Caucasus, aroused by their heroic chieftain Shamil, refused submission to Russia.[21] To cope with the problem, Nicholas consolidated the *Kavkazskii krai* (Transcaucasia and the northern mountains) into a single administrative unit in 1844 and appointed Prince M. S. Vorontsov to the newly created post, Viceroy for the Caucasus.[22] Commissioned to pacify the region, Vorontsov attempted to establish firmer control by partitioning the Caucasus into smaller provinces. Doing away with the Georgian-Imeretian guberniia and the Caspian oblast, he formed the guberniias of Kutais, Tiflis, Shemakh, and Derbend. These in turn were subdivided into counties (*uezd*s) and districts (*uchastok*s). Most Armenian-populated areas were included in the Tiflis guberniia.[23] In 1849, however, in order to win the confidence of the Armenians and to deal with certain economic, fiscal, and military problems, Vorontsov created the Erevan guberniia, the fifth province of Transcaucasia. Though it was not known as the "Armenian Province," the Erevan guberniia was considered by many as an indemnification for the loss of the former oblast. Indeed, the entire area of the oblast, as well as the Alexandropol uezd minus the Akhalkalak district, was incorporated into the Erevan guberniia.[24]

Other Transcaucasian administrative innovations were made by Vorontsov's successors. The Shemakh and Derbend provinces were redrawn and renamed Baku and Daghestan, and in 1868 the geographically and ethnographically artificial Elisavetpol guberniia was formed by combining the easternmost mountains of the Armenian Plateau with the Steppe of Karabagh below.[25] The Tiflis, Erevan, and Baku guberniias relinquished land for the creation of the province of Elisavetpol, possession of which was to be bitterly contested by the twentieth-century Georgian, Armenian, and Azerbaijani republics. Another dispute was to center on the district of Lori, which in 1862 was detached from the Alexandropol uezd of the Erevan guberniia and consolidated with the Tiflis guberniia.[26] Considered an integral part of the Plateau by Armenians, who made up more than three-fourths of its population, Lori extended from the vicinity of Karakilisa northward to the Khram River. In 1880 this district and a tract of land north of the Khram were joined to form the Borchalu uezd of the Tiflis guberniia. In the Erevan guberniia, the final internal partition occurred in 1875 when two additional uezds were formed from territories of the original five. The boundaries of the Etchmiadzin, Alexandropol, Erevan, Novo Bayazit, Sharur-Daralagiaz, Nakhichevan, and Surmalu uezds then remained unchanged until the disintegration of the Romanov Empire.[27]

Russian Annexation of Kars, Ardahan, and Batum

As a result of the Russo-Turkish War of 1877–1878, adjacent regions of the Armenian Plateau were added to Transcaucasia. During the campaigns,

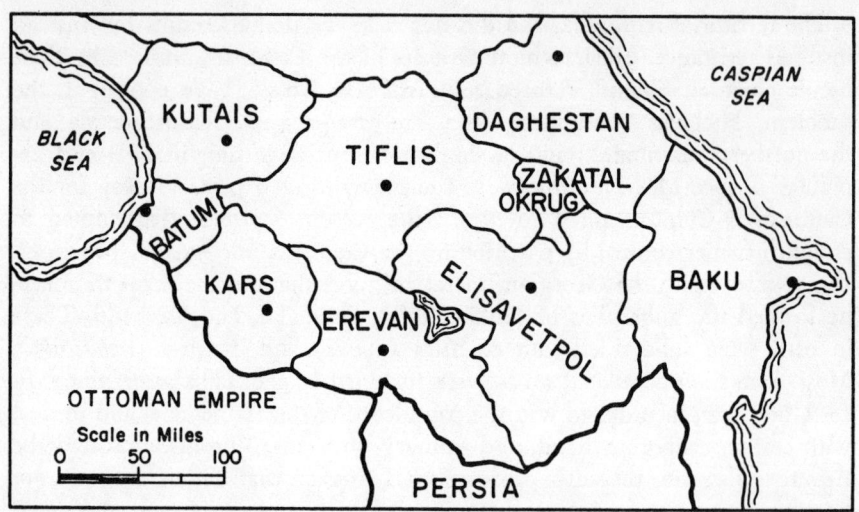

Map 3. Provinces of Transcaucasia

generals M. T. Loris-Melikov, A. A. Ter Gukasov, and I. I. Lazarev, Armenians in tsarist service, successfully stormed the fortress of Kars and advanced into Erzerum, while other Russian armies pushed down through the Balkans to the village of San Stefano, just outside Constantinople. By the Treaty of San Stefano in March, 1878, the Ottoman Empire ceded its eastern provinces of Kars, Ardahan, Batum, and Bayazit and the Plain of Alashkert. The Armenians, having found a champion in Count N. P. Ignatiev, former Russian ambassador to Constantinople (1864–1877), felt rewarded by the provision that stipulated that tsarist armies would occupy the remainder of the Plateau until the Sultan had executed reforms to guarantee the security of the native Christian population.[28] The aftermath of the Treaty of San Stefano is familiar to the student of European history. Tsar Alexander II yielded to the pressure of Western Europe, particularly Great Britain, and in July accepted a revised settlement negotiated at the Congress of Berlin. On Turkey's eastern border, Bayazit and the Plain of Alashkert were restored to Sultan Abdul Hamid II, and no longer was evacuation of Russian troops made contingent on the implementation of effective reforms.[29] Embittered Armenians watched Russian troops withdraw from the Plain of Erzerum for the second time in half a century. In a new exodus, approximately twenty-five thousand Ottoman Armenians accompanied the army of Loris-Melikov beyond the revised borders of Transcaucasia.[30]

Though the proceedings at Berlin humiliated Russia, they did not nullify all provisions of the Treaty of San Stefano. Alexander annexed Kars, Ardahan, and Batum, forming the Kars oblast from the first two districts and establishing Batum as a separate oblast.³¹ In 1878 three-fourths of the inhabitants of the Kars oblast were Moslem, but in the following two years approximately seventy-five thousand of them sought refuge within the Ottoman Empire. Their abandoned lands were repopulated by Russian religious dissenters and Turkish Armenians who continued to filter across the border. An Armenian plurality was gradually established in the two southern *okrug*s ("counties") of the oblast. By 1916, 37 percent of the residents in the Kars okrug and 42 percent in the Kaghisman okrug were Armenian.³² The national composition of the oblast's four okrugs by that date was as follows:³³

Okrug	Total population	Armenian	Turco-Tatar	Kurd	Other (primarily Greek and Russian)
Kars	192,000	81,000	54,000	11,000	46,000
Ardahan	89,000	5,000	50,000	25,000	9,000
Kaghisman	83,000	35,000	6,000	27,000	15,000
Olti	40,000	5,000	27,000 (incl. Kurds)		8,000

Armenians, Georgians, and Moslems of Transcaucasia

The addition of the Kars and Batum oblasts to the Empire increased the area of Transcaucasia to over 130,000 square miles. The estimated population of the entire region in 1886 was 4,700,000, of whom 940,000 (20 percent) were Armenian, 1,200,000 (25 percent) Georgian, and 2,220,000 (45 percent) Moslem. Of the latter group, 1,140,000 were Tatars. Paradoxically, barely one-third of Transcaucasia's Armenians lived in the Erevan guberniia, where the Christians constituted a majority in only three of the seven uezds.³⁴ Erevan uezd, the administrative center of the province, had only 44,000 Armenians as compared to 68,000 Moslems. By the time of the Russian Census of 1897, however, the Armenians had established a scant majority, 53 percent, in the guberniia; it had risen by 1916 to 60 percent, or 670,000 of the 1,120,000 inhabitants. This impressive change in the province's ethnic character notwithstanding, there was, on the eve of the creation of the Armenian Republic, a solid block of 370,000 Tatars who continued to dominate the southern districts, from the outskirts of Erevan to the border of Persia.³⁵

If national compactness may be taken as an indication of strength, the Georgians, concentrated in the Kutais and Tiflis guberniias, commanded the most favorable position, while the Armenians, scattered throughout every province of Transcaucasia, held the least favorable. According to Rus-

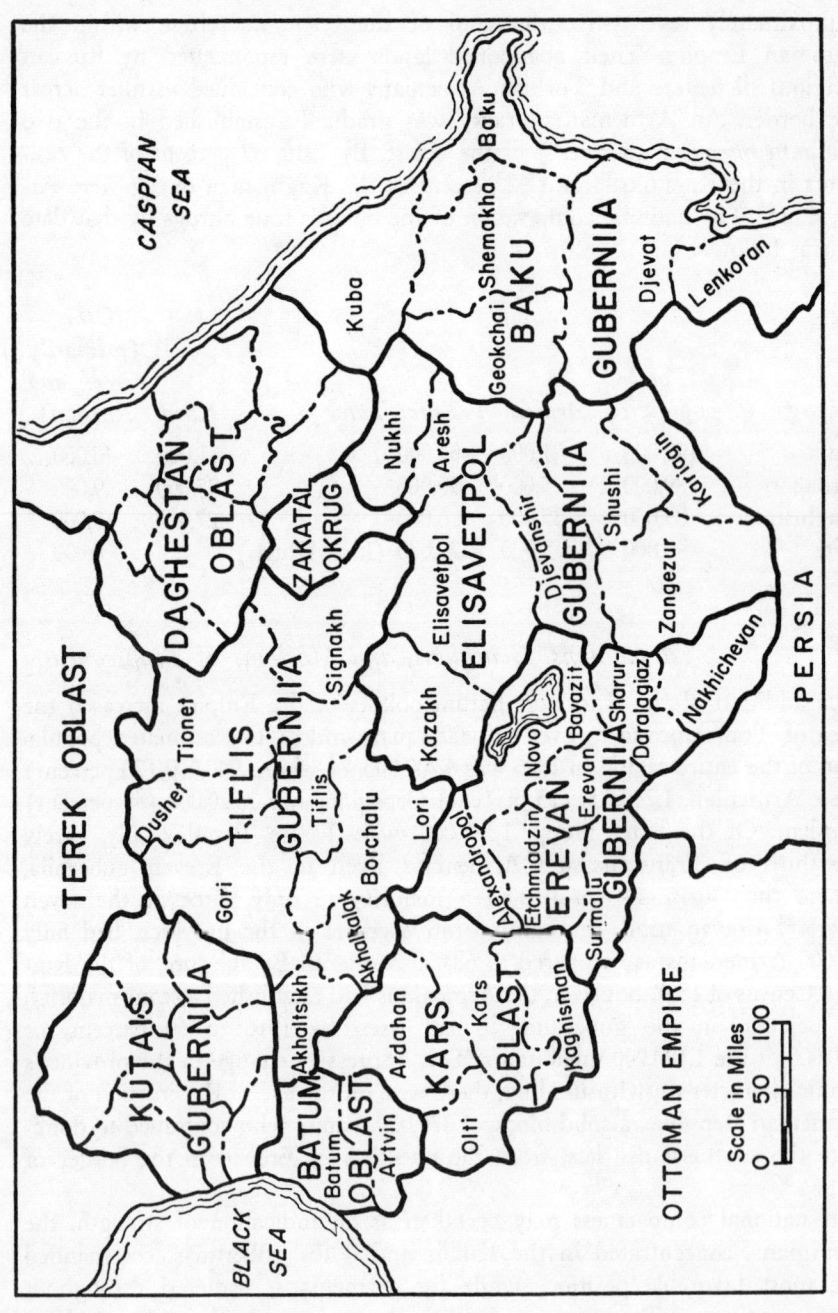

Map 4. Administrative subdivisions of Transcaucasia

sian population statistics of 1917, 1,783,000 Armenians, 22 percent of Transcaucasia's 7,500,000 inhabitants, were distributed as follows:

Province	Armenians[36]	Percentage of total population[37]
Erevan	669,000	60
Kars	119,000	30
Tiflis	415,000	28
Elisavetpol	419,000	33
Baku	120,000	9
Batum, Kutais, Daghestan	41,000	

The growth of Armenian political awareness led to increased dissatisfaction with the administrative subdivisions of Transcaucasia. Bordering on the Erevan guberniia but included in other provinces were several districts populated preponderantly by Armenians. Opportunity to express discontent and to propose rectifications was afforded the Armenians in 1905 by the Viceroy, Count I. I. Vorontsov-Dashkov, who summoned a conference of indigenous leaders to consider the possibility of introducing *zemstvos*, agrarian districts with assemblies that were permitted limited economic, cultural, and educational initiative.[38] Previously few non-Russian areas of the Empire had been granted the zemstvo system, and even this 1905 conference and a later one in 1909 failed to extend that institution to Transcaucasia. Nonetheless, participation in these deliberations motivated the Armenian politicians to crystallize their proposals for altering the provincial boundaries. They insisted that the area of jurisdiction of each zemstvo should correspond with that of a given province, which should be as ethnically homogeneous as possible. The Armenians would have three zemstvo-provinces, together encompassing the entire Erevan guberniia, the two southern okrugs of the Kars oblast, the Akhalkalak uezd and Lori uchastok of the Tiflis guberniia, and the mountainous regions of the Elisavetpol guberniia.[39] That the Georgians and Moslems rejected the Armenian plan is significant, for the disputes concerning Kars, Akhalkalak, Lori, and Mountainous Karabagh were carried over into the period when Transcaucasia was divided into three separate states.[40]

The Armenian Literary Movement and Subsequent Emergence of Political Societies

Although the formation of Russian Armenia did not culminate in the anticipated autonomy under the aegis of a Christian power, Romanov rule in Transcaucasia afforded the Armenians sufficient economic, social, and physical security to enhance their national, political, and cultural renaissance.

From emerging industrial bourgeois centers such as Tiflis and Baku and from South Russia, scores of Armenian youths enrolled in the universities of the Empire and abroad, became engulfed by the egalitarian and socialist currents sweeping over the Continent, participated in international organizations campaigning against arbitrary government, and then directed their attention to the problems of their native people. As adherents of the Russian revolutionary movement, they considered the bureaucracy and the Romanov tsars symbols of tyranny, but when they shifted their concern to the Armenians of Turkey, the evils of the Russian state faded before the harshness of the Ottoman ruling system.[41]

Initially, Armenian self-perception was developed through the evolving literary movement. The Lazarian Academy in Moscow, the Nersisian in Tiflis, and later the Gevorgian in Etchmiadzin, helped to inculcate nationalism into the young authors, who, following the European pattern, passed through stages of classicism, romanticism, and realism. In each phase they accentuated in a distinct style the woes of the fatherland and the exigency of reviving its political existence. The classicists rediscovered the epic heroes of Armenia and sang the praises of the eternal ideals of justice and freedom. With emotion and sentimentality the romanticists glorified patriots of bygone eras, bewailed the bitter fate of the homeland, and disparaged the intrusion of inferior, barbarous peoples onto the sacred soil. By the last quarter of the nineteenth century, the school of "romantic-realists" was exhorting the nation to arms. The "new hero" of the popularized novel defied death to resist oppression.[42] Russian advances into the western portions of the Plateau, the *erkir* ("homeland"), though crowned with disappointments, incited vigorous public enthusiasm, which indicated that the Armenians had awakened from their long political slumber.

The Armenians of the nineteenth century were not prepared, however, to propose independence. Physical security, unhindered cultural development, and regional autonomy were deemed the maximal and ideal conditions for which they should strive. For the eastern Ottoman provinces, most Armenian leaders considered self-administration within the framework of the Turkish Empire as the most desirable improvement. Of the several political and revolutionary societies organized during the last quarter of the century, only the Hnchakist, a Marxist organization initiated in 1887 at Geneva, advocated outright separation from the Ottoman Empire. The influence of this party, dedicated to the reestablishment of an Armenian state within the structure of the future socialist world society, was felt strongly in Constantinople and Cilicia, less in the eastern provinces, and least in Transcaucasia. Its views were assessed by most Armenian leaders in the Russian Empire as impracticable and utopian.[43]

In Transcaucasia and the eastern Ottoman vilayets, the platform of Hai Heghapokhakan Dashnaktsutiun ("Armenian Revolutionary Federation") gained greater acceptance. Founded in 1890 at Tiflis, the Federation became by the first years of the twentieth century the most powerful and comprehensive Armenian political organization.⁴⁴ Its initial program, adopted in 1892, propounded the administrative and economic freedom of Turkish Armenia. More specifically the platform called for

1) creation of a popular-democratic government based on free elections;
2) security of life and the right to work;
3) equality of all nationalities and religions before the law;
4) freedom of speech, press, and assembly;
5) distribution of land to the landless;
6) taxation according to ability to pay;
7) elimination of compulsory and uncompensated labor;
8) abolition of the military exemption fee and replacement of it with equal conscription;
9) establishment of compulsory education and promotion of national intellectual progress;
10) reinforcement of communal principles as a means to greater production and distribution.⁴⁵

To effect these aims and to defend the peaceful population, Dashnaktsutiun would, when necessary, organize fighting units, arm the populace, operate an espionage network, propagandize to raise the revolutionary spirit of Armenians, and, in particular, resort to the terrorization of corrupt officials, traitors, and exploiters. The methods adopted by Dashnaktsutiun were similar to those of the Russian Narodnaia Volia and its successor, the Social Revolutionary party, both of which maintained close contact and ideological bonds with the Armenian leaders.⁴⁶

Until the first years of the twentieth century, the focus of Armenian revolutionary activities lay within the Ottoman Empire.⁴⁷ Dashnaktsutiun made a conscious and concerted effort to avoid active involvement in the Russian opposition movement. Despite the fact that tsarist bureaucrats harassed and imprisoned Armenian political leaders and ordered the border patrols to kill or arrest the armed bands that attempted to slip into Turkey, Dashnaktsutiun, imposing strict party discipline, forbade retaliation. Engrossment in a struggle on two fronts would only dissipate the organization's limited strength. The undesirable occurred, however, in 1903 when, in addition to Abdul Hamid and his *Hamidiye* cavalry units, the Russian bureaucracy became the object of Armenian terrorism. What had provoked Dashnaktsutiun to alter its strategy?

The Armenian Church Crisis, 1903–1905

The reaction following the assassination of Tsar Alexander II in 1881 was characterized by attempts to Russify the minority groups of the Empire. Russian colonists were sent to the border regions to weaken the cohesiveness of the respective nationalities. Limitations were imposed on the educational privileges of the non-Russians, whose schools, after being closed for a time, were obliged to adopt a Russian-style curriculum. In the Caucasus the Governor-General, having superseded the Viceroy and possessing greater military prerogatives, intensified measures for assimilation. At that post, Prince Grigorii Golitsyn[48] counseled Tsar Nicholas II to confiscate the properties of the Church of Armenia and to take from its jurisdiction the established network of schools. The national wealth and influence concentrated in the Church would be shattered; schools, placed under state supervision, would accelerate the process of Russification, thus depriving the revolutionaries of their primary source of strength. Golitsyn anticipated little resistance from the aged Catholicos.[49] The exhortations of the Governor-General convinced Nicholas of the wisdom of the project. In June, 1903, the Tsar decreed that all goods and properties not essential to the performance of religious services were to be expropriated and transferred to the ministries of Agriculture, State Properties, and Interior. In return the Ministry of Interior would provide sufficient funds for the operation of Armenian schools and churches.[50]

The Armenian reaction was immediate and overwhelming. Golitsyn had miscalculated, for the decree inspired greater nationalism and incited thousands who previously had remained aloof from the revolutionary movement to turn toward Dashnaktsutiun in the expectation that it would provide direction for the expression of public indignation. Socialist societies, including Marxist groups, deviated from their anticlerical tradition to rise in defense of the Armenian Church, so frequently criticized by them. Dashnaktsutiun took charge of the Central Committee for Self-Defense and, in conjunction with the Catholicos, organized mass protest demonstrations in nearly every Armenian community of the Russian Empire. In a bloody reign of violence which lasted two years, hundreds of Russian bureaucrats fell before the bullets, knives, and bombs of Armenian "terrorists." Golitsyn himself was critically wounded.[51] Nevertheless, during the first year of unrest, Minister of Interior V. K. Plehve, the influential collaborator of Golitsyn, prevailed upon the Tsar to remain resolute and uncompromising. As the fate of the national properties lay in the balance, the General Congress of Dashnaktsutiun in 1904 responded officially to the Russian challenge. Revising its program, the party declared that, although amelioration of the unbearable conditions in Turkish Armenia remained the basic concern, oppression within the Russian Empire could be ignored no longer. Dashnaktsutiun pledged itself to defend the basic rights of all Armenians, whether in the realm of sultan or tsar.[52]

Other socialist-oriented circles also condemned the tsarist confiscations but utilized the opportunity to attack Dashnaktsutiun as well. Marxist Social Democrats mocked the decision of that nationalist party. Tsarist suppression was not new; why had Dashnaktsutiun only in 1904 raised its voice in opposition? The Marxists answered their own query by postulating that Dashnaktsutiun, by combining the questions of Turkish and Russian Armenia and assuming socialist phrases, was attempting to deceive the masses in order to divert them from the mainstream of the Russian revolutionary movement.[53] However, the Armenian Marxists, few and divided, had little influence upon those masses. Not until 1903 had they been able to form a Social Democrat group in the Erevan guberniia, although in 1899 Stepan Shahumian, later a close associate of Lenin, had initiated a Marxist study group in neighboring Lori.[54] Moreover, while some Marxists belonged to the multinational Caucasian Union of the Russian party, others founded their own Social Democratic Workers Armenian Organization. The latter, referred to as the "specifist," contended that the realities of the Armenian situation were quite different from those affecting the general proletariat, and that, therefore, the "specific" disparities warranted particular consideration. Consequently this group represented itself as the only true spokesman for the Armenian toilers and advocated the principles of federative government, national-cultural self-determination, and, within the Marxist movement, regional party autonomy.[55]

The more orthodox Marxists, guided by Shahumian, exposed and denounced the nationalistic tendencies of the specifists and accused them of being contaminated by the "infectious ideology" of Dashnaktsutiun. In their aversion to nationalism, orthodox Armenian Marxists often aspired to be more Russian than the Russians themselves. Shahumian favored compulsory use of the Russian language, condemned the hypothesis that each people has a "mystique," and argued that nations are formed as the result of economic concentrations during the capitalistic stage of social development. In more precise terms, Shahumian and his associates vociferously attacked embroilment in the Turkish Armenian question, for, they held, the struggle should not inflame race against race, but instead class against class.[56] Though critical and active, the Armenian Marxists were unable to destroy the national-political monopoly of Dashnaktsutiun. Only in 1920, when the Republic of Armenia was supplanted by the Soviet Socialist Republic, would they be rewarded for their long, sometimes seemingly hopeless struggle against their implacable foes.

During 1904, those foes, while directing the resistance in Transcaucasia, sought to solidify their bonds with other discontented elements of Russia. These, along with Dashnaktsutiun, applauded when a Russian Social Revolutionary bomb pulverized Plehve, a cardinal enemy of the minority groups. Collaboration among the various revolutionary and opposition societies was attained in December when seventeen delegates representing Russian, Finnish, Latvian, Armenian, Georgian, and Polish organizations convened in Paris. Of divergent political and economic persuasions, all were united in their condemnation of tsarist nationality and minority policies and in their conviction that the autocracy would be superseded by a democratic, constitutional regime for all Russia.[57]

Probably few participants in the Paris convocation would have believed then that even before they returned to Russia the St. Petersburg militia would fire on a group of workers petitioning Tsar Nicholas II and that this event on "Bloody Sunday" would mark the beginning of the 1905 Revolution.[58] The Russian failures in the war with Japan and mushrooming domestic unrest created a critical situation. The Caucasus united with all Russia to express its discontent through strikes and violence.[59] Armenians used the occasion to enunciate their refusal to consent to the sequestering of their national properties. If Nicholas were to survive the tempest, he had to yield and compromise. In Transcaucasia this entailed the recall of Prince Golitsyn and the restoration of the Viceroyalty for the Caucasus. To quell the wave of revolution and to regain the loyalty of the multinational region, Nicholas appointed Count I. I. Vorontsov-Dashkov to the post.

The Viceroy, who retained the title for ten years, has become the subject of heated controversy. Many adherents of Dashnaktsutiun and nearly all Soviet students of the period accuse Vorontsov-Dashkov of hypocrisy, deceit, and perfidy. Golitsyn's open expression of contempt for the peoples of Transcaucasia was assertedly transformed into a shrewd, calculated policy of divide and rule. At times feigning tolerance and even benevolence, the Viceroy pursued the aims of his predecessor in a more deliberate manner. In fairness to Vorontsov-Dashkov, it is necessary to point out that, although he employed stringent measures against dangerous revolutionary groups and quite naturally considered the interests of the Romanov dynasty above all else, he adopted a tactful, astute, and, in general, conciliatory operational code.[60] In relation to the Armenians, he reasoned that the most effective weapon to discredit the revolutionaries was the restoration of traditional prerogatives to the national Church. Having regained privileges, goods, and properties, the clergy would then revert to its customary conservatism, and the populace, forsaking the radicals, would pledge fealty once again to the Romanov dynast. If, however, the impasse were not rapidly surmounted, the agitated Russian Armenians might begin to clamor for the same type of autonomy they proposed for the Turkish Armenians, and, spurred on by revolutionary dispositions, they would then demand the unification of the eastern and western branches of their nation, so artificially divided. The consequences of such ferment were unpredictable, but one need not be a prophet to recognize the evil omens. Vorontsov-Dashkov wisely counseled his monarch to annul the controversial edict, which had aroused the Russian Armenians even more than the bloody activities of Abdul Hamid. In August, 1905, Nicholas heeded the words of admonition, rescinded the offensive decree of 1903, and expressed affection for his Armenian subjects.[61] The maneuver yielded immediate results. Hundreds of thanksgiving messages were received by Vorontsov-Dashkov and Nicholas. Spontaneous demonstrations of rejoicing, gratitude, and fidelity surged through many Transcaucasian cities and villages. Significantly, even some members of Dashnaktsutiun participated in these manifestations.[62] The crisis precipitated by the confiscation of Church properties was overcome. Vorontsov-Dashkov was satisfied, and so was Dashnaktsutiun, whose prestige, instead of diminishing, soared.

The Armeno-Tatar Conflict and the Revised Platform of Dashnaktsutiun

Despite settlement of the issue, however, Transcaucasia was not pacified, for the Russian Revolution continued and, even more momentous, strife between Armenians and Tatars engulfed the entire region. The Russian bureaucrats were accused by their many enemies of instigating interracial enmity, of provoking Armeno-Tatar conflicts so that both peoples would be distracted from the current of revolution. Testimony of the participants in the hostilities and of tsarist officials themselves indicates that the indictment against the bureaucracy is not without validity. Much bloodshed could have been avoided if the representatives of the Tsar had used the power at their disposal to halt the spreading violence. But not until 1907, after the Russian Revolution had run its course, did they and regular Russian military contingents take measures to terminate the holocaust. However, it cannot be proved, as some attempt to do, that the full responsibility rested with the Russian bureaucracy, for, although the psychology of divide and rule was certainly prevalent, bases for interracial hostilities already existed. National, religious, economic, and social incompatibilities separated the two neighboring peoples. In the electrified atmosphere of 1905–1907, mutual suspicions, jealousies, and rivalries exploded into fierce combat.[63] Thousands of casualties and property losses amounting to over forty million rubles were the result of two years of anarchy.[64] Yet when the Armeno-Tatar clashes were evaluated, when the dead were counted and the material losses assessed, Armenian political leaders seemed not entirely unhappy. National consciousness had advanced another step. A moral victory had been won, for the myth of Moslem invincibility had been dispelled; Armenians had once again learned to fight. Nor were the results entirely negative for the Tatars. Intensified distrust of the Armenians, who had long dominated the middle-class professions, provided added impetus for the Moslems to develop their own artisan and bourgeois class, from which would stem a more progressive educational system, several Turkish language journals, and a network of philanthropic-cultural societies. The political-social mind of the Moslems of Transcaucasia was taking shape.

The stirring incidents that began with the confiscation of Church properties were among the items considered by the Fourth General Congress of Dashnaktsutiun, which convened at Vienna in 1907. The radical wing of the party had been reinforced by the Caucasian disturbances. After bitter debates concerning the proposed revision of the organization's program, the Congress overruled the objections of the conservatives and adopted an explicit socialist platform. In the same year, despite vigorous Bolshevik opposition, the party was granted membership in the Second Socialist International.[65] The nationality plank of the 1907 platform reiterated liberation of Turkish Armenia as the primary goal of Dashnaktsutiun. Such emancipation would entail delimitation, within the Ottoman Empire, of an autonomous Armenian region that would be guaranteed initiative in local affairs; representative assemblies elected by secret, direct, equal, and proportional suffrage; freedom of press, assembly, and speech; separation of church and state; free, universal education; and communal ownership of land. The Congress also advocated a similar arrangement for all Transcaucasia, which, as a member of the future federated democracy of Russia, would provide for national-cultural progress of all its constituent peoples.[66] The strategy of Dashnaktsutiun was to combine nationalism and socialism, but the latter was always subordinate. Party theoreticians reasoned that, by serving his nation, the individual assisted humanity toward its ultimate aim—socialism. An Armenian who was not a dedicated patriot could not be a true socialist.

The Years of Reaction, 1907–1912

The influence of Dashnaktsutiun, however, like that of all revolutionary societies in Russia, waned after 1907. The Romanov dynasty had emerged, shaken but intact, from the Revolution and the war with Japan. Emboldened by the disunity among the opposition groups and the failure of new strike movements, the secret police again arrested, imprisoned, or exiled thousands of suspected political enemies. In Transcaucasia, the Armenian populace recoiled after the sensational events of 1903–1907. The political pendulum moved rapidly toward the right as the first years of the Russian reaction began. Dashnaktsutiun was deprived of much of its vigor because of internal splintering and mass arrests, while weaker organizations such as the Armenian Marxist groups became inactive. P. A. Stolypin, the inexorable enemy of the revolutionaries and President of the Russian Council of Ministers, struck ruthlessly at the Armenian political and civic leaders.[67] Many languished in tsarist prisons until brought to trial before the Russian Senate early in 1912. Alexander Kerensky, future premier of Russia, and Pavel Miliukov, influential politician, historian, and journalist, were among the defenders of the accused, only fifty-two of whom were finally sentenced, most to amazingly light terms.[68] This was the final manifestation of the Stolypin reaction, for soon the Balkan wars, considerations of Russian foreign policy, and the prospect of a new Russo-Turkish conflagration transformed the Romanovs and Dashnaktsutiun into collaborators.

During the century of Russian domination in Transcaucasia, the Armenian political mind had been molded and solidified. Despite the fact that tsarist protection did not fulfill initial Armenian expectations, the influences of the relatively advanced Russian culture stimulated the growth of Armenian national consciousness. It was, however, not official Russia but the oppositional movement of Russia which was strongly reflected in the political, administrative, social, and economic views of the Armenians. By the end of the century, this people had definite aspirations. It was not independence that was sought but local native administration and the redivision of Transcaucasia into distinct ethnic provinces. For the first time in centuries, Armenians constituted a majority in the territory around Erevan, but this was not enough to satisfy them. Their gaze was upon the peripheral areas of the Plateau. That the intensification of such views led to further misunderstandings with the other Transcaucasian peoples needs little explanation.

Yet the Armenians of Russia did not limit their concern to the Caucasus. The land on which they lived often seemed much less significant to them and warranted less attention than the "real homeland," Turkish Armenia. It was in the zeal to liberate this area that the political comprehension of the Armenians revealed its greatest naïveté and weakness. The entire nation was easily aroused by the prospect of foreign intervention in the affairs of the Ottoman Empire. Thus, the memories of the disappointments of 1828–1829, 1877–1878, 1894–1896,[69] of Europe's repeated ineffectiveness in compelling Ottoman reforms, and of the reactionary domestic policy of the Romanov tsars were repressed in 1912, when the Armenians turned once again to St. Petersburg and the other capitals of Europe for the realization of their most sacred goal—freedom and autonomy for Turkish Armenia.

III
Turkish Armenia

ARMENIAN LIFE in Transcaucasia did not develop in isolation. Political, social, and cultural currents among the Russian Armenians were influenced by and in turn affected those which were emerging across the border. The Turkish Armenians, too, arose from their political torpor to beseech and to demand. As in the experience of the Armenians of Russia, intellectual revival nurtured opposition to arbitrary government. Moved by the egalitarian principles of the French Revolution, this Christian minority of the Ottoman Empire came to feel itself deprived of the inherent rights of individuals and of nationalities. Disillusioned with the several reform acts promulgated but not enforced during the nineteenth century, the Armenians increasingly turned to the nations of Europe, which, they believed, had the power to determine the fate of the entire Empire.[1] But on the eve of World War I, frustrated by European diplomacy, they looked to Russia as the champion of their cause. These events were to constitute an important stride toward Armenian independence.

The Armenians of the Ottoman Empire

By 1520, most of the Armenian Plateau had been included in the Ottoman realm. In the following decades, thousands of Armenians left the Plateau to settle in Constantinople and the western Anatolian Peninsula, particularly along the seacoasts. There, as interpreters, merchants, artisans, and traders, their importance exceeded their numerical strength. Some reached the higher levels of the administration and enjoyed the company of the reigning sultan. Most Ottoman Armenians, however, lived in the Empire's eastern *pashalik*s, where, from generation to generation, they tilled their fields. Although usually at peace with their Moslem neighbors and subservient to the Ottoman officials, the Armenians, as Christians, could not expect equality. Islamic law included special provisions concerning them, the *dhimmi*—the protected nonbelievers. In return for the privilege of professing their religion openly, they were required to pay special taxes and to submit to personal and collective limitations. Though some Christians surmounted this inferior status by converting to Islam, most Armenians held tenaciously to their native dialects and religion.

The ability of the Armenians to maintain their national identity throughout centuries of Turkish domination can be attributed in part to the administrative structure of the Empire. When Mehmed II made Constantinople the Ottoman capital in 1453, the Turkic-Moslem element formed a minority in many areas of his domains. The Sultan reduced his administrative problems by according internal autonomy to the non-Moslem communities. In return, the religious superior of each group was responsible for maintaining order among his people and for collecting the required community levies. The Armenian bishop of Brusa was invited to Constantinople in 1461 and elevated to the rank of Patriarch of all non-Orthodox Christians. His community, the *Ermeni Millet,* and the Greek Orthodox and Jewish millets became the three official non-Moslem establishments within the framework of the Empire.[2] The millet system proved workable and beneficial for the Armenians. Even though the Church lacked its former luster and was weak in intellectual pursuits, it safeguarded the identity of the Armenians by preserving their loyalty to the national faith.

Pronounced religious antagonisms in the Ottoman domains were of relatively late development. As long as Europe was considered culturally, politically, and militarily inferior, and as long as the subject nationalities performed their special obligations, there was little purpose in upsetting the established balance. During the seventeenth century, however, rebellions by Moslem chieftains, corruption in the administrative system, and the European threat to the security of the Empire fostered the growth of intolerance. The following century brought in its wake large Ottoman territorial losses and intensified unrest among the Balkan Christians, who were eventually to be assisted in their drives toward liberation by the diplomacy and arms of Europe.

It was unfortunate for the Armenians that the resurgence of their political consciousness lagged behind that of the Balkan peoples. The Armenian Plateau, distant from Western Europe, was not given the same attention by the Continental powers as were the Balkan provinces. By the time the Armenians had formulated their programs for reform, self-rule, and even political autonomy, the Ottoman Empire was entrenched in a period of reaction. To the Turkish government, threatened with the final partition and dissolution of the Empire, Armenian demands were embarrassing, disloyal, and dangerous. Each supplication to Europe aroused more Turkish antagonism and suspicion. Every protest from Europe further sensitized the Ottoman rulers to the Armenian problem. If the Armenians were to follow the Balkan example, the entire Plateau would be lost.

Internationalization of the "Armenian Question"

In 1876, the failure of projects for general reforms in Turkey, the Armenian protestations against devastating incursions of Moslem tribesmen, and, above all, contagious Balkan revolts, elicited strong European pressure on the Sublime Porte.[3] Apparently in an attempt to eliminate the grounds for foreign intervention in Ottoman affairs, Sultan Abdul Hamid II promulgated a liberal constitution, which, if properly applied, should have satisfied not only the Armenians but all the subject peoples of the Empire.[4] That the constitution was soon suspended and the parliament instituted by it prorogued indicated, however, that Abdul Hamid's maneuver would prove no more advantageous for the Armenians than had the earlier reform measures. Consequently the Armenians welcomed the Russian advance of 1877, and the Patriarchate, thrusting aside its normal conservatism and Russophobia, begged tsarist officials to protect the Ottoman Armenians. Article 16 of the Treaty of San Stefano seemed to provide for such protection, but its force was swept away by Article 61 of the Treaty of Berlin, which stripped Russia of her coercive power and placed the responsibility for compelling the Sultan to carry out reforms upon the entire European Concert of Nations. Thus, as the influential Duke of Argyll later declared, "What was everybody's business was nobody's business."[5] Despite this setback, Patriarch Nerses Varzhapetian could still report to the representatives of his people that the solution to its problems was not hopeless, but simply delayed. As the spokesman for the Turkish Armenians, he reiterated his loyalty to the Sultan and insisted that any changes be initiated within the framework of the Ottoman administration.[6] At the time that the Balkan states were being awarded independence, Armenian separatist tendencies were still negligible.

The Treaty of Berlin elevated the so-called Armenian question to the level of international diplomacy. Whether any benefits were derived from this is debatable, but that reforms remained unimplemented is not. From the eastern provinces, European diplomatic representatives kept their respective superiors informed about the aggravated misery of the Armenians and the injustices of Ottoman officials.[7] Neither the British proposals for reform, the increase in the number of European consuls on the Plateau, nor the subsequent notes of protest and warning from the six-nation European Concert improved the situation.[8] By 1881 Austria expressed the view that continued collective action was unnecessary, and Germany urged that further consideration of the Armenian problem be postponed until the involved Ottoman-Greek boundary dispute was settled.[9] Active European participation on behalf of the Armenians thus entered a period of dormancy lasting more than a decade.

Massacres, Reform Plans, Massacres, 1894–1896

When the Armenian was abandoned, he turned to extralegal means to attain his goals. The societies of the 1870's, weak in structure, local in character, and influencing but few, were superseded by the better organized, more extensive and popular Hnchakist and Dashnakist political parties. While the Patriarch in Constantinople continued his supplications to the Sublime Porte, the exponents of the new political mentality preached resistance and retribution. Under such influence, the rugged villagers of Sassun in the Bitlis *vilayet* refused to pay the extortionary "protection tax" to Kurdish chiefs. In 1894, when the Kurds were unable to subdue their former underlings, they appealed to the Ottoman government, accusing Sassun of sedition. Regular Turkish units joined the irregular *Hamidiye* cavalry corps and, after weeks of combat, forced the Armenians to submit. Amnesty was promised, but instead the Sassunites were massacred.[10] The European consuls in the eastern provinces were joined by many Christian missionaries in crying out against these violations. The press of America and Europe once again bewailed the sufferings of the Armenians and clamored for action. The diplomats of the Continent turned to the complex problem for the second time in one generation. A European commission of inquiry reported that the Armenians of Sassun had acted in self-defense, while Ottoman officials maintained that they were rebels whom it was necessary to suppress.[11]

The Sassun problem revived the question of reforms, but, unlike their involvement in 1878, Germany, Austria-Hungary, and Italy abstained from the proceedings. The Triple Alliance had no intention of antagonizing the Ottoman Sultan, and among the three remaining powers unanimity was often lacking. Nevertheless, by the spring of 1895, representatives of Britain, France, and Russia presented a plan of reforms to the Sublime Porte. The project provided that the "Armenian provinces" of the Empire would be consolidated, nomination of governors confirmed by the European powers, Armenian political prisoners granted amnesty, émigrés allowed to return, reparations accorded to victims of Sassun and other unfortunate areas, forced converts to Islam restored to their original faith, a permanent control commission established in Constantinople, and a high commissioner appointed to execute the reform provisions. Moreover, nomadic Kurds were to move only under governmental surveillance and were to be encouraged to adopt a sedentary mode of life. The Hamidiye corps, to be disarmed and without uniforms during peacetime, would be attached to regular army units if activated.[12] Diplomatic exchanges continued throughout the summer and autumn of 1895 until at last, in October, Abdul Hamid succumbed to European pressure and promulgated reforms based on, but not as inclusive as, those proposed by the European ambassadors. On behalf of their governments, the representatives of Russia, France, and Britain expressed satisfaction and gratitude to the Sultan.[13]

Recent historians of Ottoman reform movements emphasize that many sincere officials attempted to bring progressive change to the Empire and that all imperial decrees were not mere "paper reforms." This view undoubtedly has validity, but it is difficult to substantiate in the Armenian experience. European intervention unsustained by force added to the tragedy of the Armenians. Even before the proclamation of the reform act of October, 1895, massacres had begun in Trebizond. In the following months, the Armenian Plateau met with the same fate.[14] Abdul Hamid's actual response to European meddling was the extirpation of between one and two hundred thousand Armenians during 1895–1896. Thousands more suffered material ruin or fled abroad.[15] Once again, the nations of Europe, now involved in the struggle for empire, turned away from the tragedy to which they had contributed.[16] Nor could the Armenians any longer find solace in Russia. Her new foreign minister, B. A. Lobanov-Rostovskii, expressed in definite terms his Armenophobia and loathing for the revolutionary societies. The Romanovs had already experienced the ingratitude of Bulgaria, which had been granted near independence through Russian efforts. Lobanov-Rostovskii did not want another Bulgaria on the border of Transcaucasia. His solution was an "Armenia without Armenians."[17] Such views were naturally shared by Prince Golitsyn, the proponent of confiscating the properties of the Armenian Church.

The Armenian revolutionaries were not as successful in their battle against Abdul Hamid as they were in their campaign against Golitsyn. In the decade following 1896, disillusion and disappointment were widespread among the populace. It was, however, too late to retreat. Attention was turned from the evils of the system to the culpability of the Sultan. Dashnaktsutiun, ascribing importance to the role of the individual in history, plotted to eliminate Abdul Hamid.[18] Kristapor Mikayelian, one of the party's founders, directed a group of conspirators to carry out the verdict in 1905. By a quirk of fate, the plans were foiled; Abdul Hamid lived, but Mikayelian died from the explosives intended for the Sultan.[19] Significantly, participants in the plot were of several nationalities, for, by the turn of the century, Dashnaktsutiun had accepted the tactic of collaboration with other groups struggling against the common oppressor.

The "Young Turks" and the Coup of 1908

Armenians were not alone in their opposition to the Sultan. In Geneva, Paris, and other émigré centers, the "Young Turks" formed societies, drafted programs for change, and envisaged a new, improved state structure for their homeland. Patriotic Turkish leaders like Ahmed Riza believed that only the institution of efficient, just government could save the Ottoman Empire from dissolution.[20] In 1902 the first congress of Ottoman liberals, attended by Turkish, Arab, Greek, Kurdish, Armenian, Albanian, Circassian, and Jewish representatives, convened in Paris. Though united in condemnation of Abdul Hamid, the congress split on the issue of inviting the European nations to intervene on behalf of the abused peoples of the Empire.[21] Riza denounced the Armenian-sponsored majority resolution calling for intervention and opposed any form of regional-national self-rule. In his view, "Autonomy is treason; it means separation."[22]

The anti-Hamidian currents were spurred on by army officers who revived the opposition within the Empire during the first years of the twentieth century. In 1907 these groups, whose strength was concentrated in the headquarters of the Ottoman Macedonian Army, merged with Ahmed Riza's "Young Turk" faction to found Ittihad ve Terakki ("Committee of Union and Progress"). As the party's chief representative, Riza then attended the second congress of Ottoman liberals, convoked primarily on the initiative of Dashnaktsutiun. The congress, meeting in Paris, pledged to overthrow Abdul Hamid's regime by the swiftest means, not barring revolution.[23] Already events within the Empire were leading toward mutiny. When Ittihadist conspirators in the Macedonian Army were in danger of being exposed, they marched on Constantinople and demanded that the constitution be restored. With little alternative, Abdul Hamid yielded on July 24, 1908, and agreed to play the role of a constitutional monarch. A cabinet dominated by Ittihadists assumed the helm of government.[24]

The Armenians had not participated in the actual coup, but they rejoiced at the victory of the army and its Ittihadist commanders. Yet, with the Empire immediately beset by foreign threats, these patriotic officers subordinated liberalism to nationalism. Austrian annexation of Bosnia-Herzegovina, Bulgarian declaration of complete independence, Cretan proclamation of union with Greece, Italian invasion of Tripolitania (Libya), and, finally, the Balkan wars drove the Ittihadist leaders toward extremism. During those trying years Dashnaktsutiun remained loyal, urging the populace to support the government and exhorting the Armenian units in the Imperial Army to fight bravely in defense of the Empire.[25]

The Counterrevolution and the Ascendancy of the Ittihadist Triumvirate, 1909–1913

The setbacks during the first months of Ittihadist rule provided impetus to the forces of reaction. In 1909, conservative Turkish elements, inspired by the supporters of Abdul Hamid, attempted to overthrow the new government. The constitution again was endangered, but Ittihad ve Terakki was saved by the "Army of Deliverance," which moved into Constantinople and crushed the counterrevolution. Abdul Hamid was dethroned and exiled.[26] Meanwhile, the interlude of the Hamidian reaction brought tragedy for the Armenians. Traditionalist Moslem elements, joined by Turks imbued with the new nationalism, massacred between fifteen and twenty thousand Armenians in Cilicia.[27] Though partisans of Ittihad ve Terakki were implicated in the carnage, that party moved to soothe the raging passions by condemning the incident, ascribing it to Hamidian henchmen, and conducting a public memorial service for both Turkish and Armenian citizens who had sacrificed their lives "in defense of the revolution." Enver Bey, the future Minister of War, delivered the eulogy.[28]

The attempted coup prompted Ittihad ve Terakki to declare a state of siege in Constantinople. The normal guarantees of the constitution were suspended until 1912. During the intervening years, Talaat Bey, later an influential cabinet member, came to the conviction that there could be no equality in the Empire until all citizens were "Ottomanized." To Talaat, Ottomanization signified Turkification.[29] By 1911, dissension within the Ittihad party resulted in the formation of a splinter group, the Liberal Union, which in the following year succeeded in establishing a cabinet of moderates, pledged to the principles of the original revolution. Unfortunately, continued military failures on the Balkan front and the demands by the victors for territorial concessions, especially Adrianople, contributed to the Ittihadist countercoup of 1913, which culminated in the ascendancy of the dictatorial nationalist elements of Ittihad ve Terakki. The actual functions of government were seized by the triumvirate of Enver, Minister of War; Talaat, Minister of Interior and later, in 1916, Grand Vizier; and Jemal, Military Governor of Constantinople and subsequently Minister of the Marine. The party and the government were theirs until the end of 1918.[30]

Russia and Armenian Reforms, 1912–1914

The plight of the Ottoman Armenians was not mitigated after 1908, for governmental directives did not affect the armed, mobile Kurdish bands in the eastern provinces, where Ottoman officials reportedly assisted the marauders. The situation was aggravated when Armenian military contingents left their native districts to participate in the first Balkan War. The dispatches of English, French, and Russian consuls described the unbearable anarchy which had become the rule rather than the exception.[31] As in the reign of Abdul Hamid, the Patriarch's pleas to the government received sympathetic responses and pledges, but effective measures did not ensue. The clamor of protest again extended beyond the borders of the Empire.[32] Armenian communities and Armenophile societies throughout the world called for European intervention. In 1912 Balkan Armenians responded by forming a volunteer unit to assist the Bulgarians against Turkey, while

Armenians of Transcaucasia again agitated for Russian involvement in Ottoman affairs. Their cries no longer fell on deaf ears. The Tsar of Russia and his Viceroy for the Caucasus now expressed concern over the injustices to which Ottoman Armenians were subjected. Obviously, by 1912 the foundations of Russian foreign policy had changed radically from the days of Lobanov-Rostovskii.

Paradoxically, the years of reaction following the Russian Revolution of 1905–1907 were characterized not only by the suppression of subversive societies but also by certain measures to pacify the subject nationalities. In Armenian life the latter trend became obvious at the beginning of 1912, when most of the political leaders tried by the Senate in St. Petersburg were acquitted and freed. There were important reasons in 1912 for satisfying the Armenians. By reviving the Armenian question in Turkey, the Tsar not only would regain the loyalty of his Armenian subjects but also would strike a blow against possible anarchy in Transcaucasia.[33] Russian Foreign Minister S. D. Sazonov wrote subsequently:

> A revolt of the Armenians in the vilayets of Asia Minor, bordering upon Transcaucasia, was always possible in view of the intolerable conditions of life there. Such a rising threatened to set fire to our own border provinces. . . .
> These observations will make it clear that, apart from a purely humanitarian interest in the fate of an unfortunate Christian people, the desire to maintain order in the most restless of our border provinces obliged the Imperial Government to take the initiative in negotiating for the introduction of radical reforms in the Armenian vilayets.[34]

More tangible elements in shaping the new Russian policy were Middle East considerations. In 1907, Britain had come to terms with its old Russian rival by concluding an Eastern settlement. One provision divided Persia into zones of influence, with most of the northern provinces awarded to Russia. To protect her interests in this sphere and to plan for possible future expansion, Russia needed a loyal Transcaucasia and a peaceful Turkish Armenia.[35] Moreover, St. Petersburg feared German economic penetration onto the Armenian Plateau. The Tsar's advisers reasoned that, should the Ottoman government be compelled to introduce Russian-supervised reforms into Turkish Armenia, the Germans would be excluded from the provinces adjacent to Transcaucasia. Nicholas, his Foreign Minister, Sazonov, and his ambassador at Constantinople, M. N. Giers, were therefore prepared, after fifteen years of silence, to resurrect the Armenian question.

In Transcaucasia, the new Russian outlook was reflected in amazing curtailment of censorship and in greater freedom of Armenian expression. Newspapers printed morbid descriptions of conditions across the border. Conservative clergy, bourgeois Constitutional Democrats, compatriotic-philanthropic-educational societies, and socialist Dashnakists and Hnchakists united to demand immediate intercession. Even the Marxist Social Democrats, who had consistently condemned "national-cultural autonomy" and had charged that the problem of Turkish Armenia was being exploited by the enemies of the proletariat, now sought means to defend the Armenians of the Ottoman Empire.[36]

In October, 1912, Catholicos Gevorg V petitioned for Russian intervention in Turkish Armenia and applied to Viceroy Vorontsov-Dashkov for permission to travel to St. Petersburg to plead in person. The Viceroy discouraged such a journey but assured the prelate that his supplications would be conveyed immediately from Tiflis to the Imperial Palace. Vorontsov-Dashkov fulfilled his promise. In a lengthy letter to the Tsar, the Viceroy reviewed the course of Russian policy in relation to the Armenians. He pointed out that this people had long associated its most ardent hopes with the benevolence of the Russian Crown. Vorontsov-Dashkov regretted the Armenophobia of Lobanov-Rostovskii and the ill-advised deeds of Golitsyn. He urged Nicholas to revive the question of reforms for Turkish Armenia, since such action would add to the prestige of the Tsar in that region and would strengthen the Russian orientation of the Armenians.[37]

Encouraged and assisted by Vorontsov-Dashkov, Armenian leaders arranged for a conference of representatives from many communities throughout the Romanov Empire. Convening in Tiflis in November, 1912, the meeting concerned itself primarily with Turkish Armenian problems and elected a permanent bureau

1) to assist the Catholicos in his efforts to mitigate the distress of Turkish Armenians;
2) to establish contact and coordinate activities with Armenian communities abroad;
3) to propagandize among Russian public and official circles to ensure a favorable settlement.[38]

Catholicos Gevorg then appealed to Nicholas to include the subject of reforms on the agenda of the London Conference, which had been summoned to establish peace in the Balkans.[39] At the same time, the primate ceremoniously enjoined Boghos Nubar, son of a former Armenian premier of Egypt,[40] to advance the national cause by utilizing his influential European contacts.[41] Gevorg was notified through Vorontsov-Dashkov that placing the Armenian problem before the entire Concert of Europe was unwise, especially as unanimity was not expected at the London Conference and the consequences would be unfavorable to the Armenians.[42] For the time being, Russia apparently wished to maintain her monopoly in the question.

The Negotiations

Meanwhile, Ottoman Armenian leaders, enthused by revived Russian interest, composed petitions and memorandums. A commission of the Armenian National Assembly, the governing body of the Apostolic Christians of the Empire, examined the Patriarchate's archives, tax ledgers, and parish reports to prepare statistics on the Armenian population and its geographic distribution. Another committee selected by the National Assembly drafted what it considered a suitable and applicable reform measure. The resulting project was then submitted to André Mandelstam, chief dragoman of the Russian Embassy at Constantinople.[43] The main provisions of the plan were later incorporated into a Russian scheme, which was relayed in mid-1913 to the embassies of Great Britain, France, Germany, Austria-Hungary, and Italy. Russia's action drew sharp German protests, and soon the six major powers of Europe were again entangled. Though German Ambassador Hans von Wangenheim, bolstered by his colleagues of the Triple Alliance, vehemently objected to Russian intervention, he was compelled to accept the proposal that the six ambassadors at Constantinople discuss the question. The summer residence of the Austrian ambassador became the usual site for the meetings.[44] There, in June and July, the ambassadors and their appointed commission haggled over the Russian suggestions, which provided for the

1) unification of the six Armenian vilayets, with the exclusion of certain peripheral districts, into a single province;
2) selection of an Ottoman Christian or European governor for the province;
3) establishment of an administrative council and a provincial assembly consisting of both Moslem and Christian elements;
4) formation of a mixed Moslem-Christian gendarmerie commanded by European officers in Turkish service;
5) dissolution of the former Hamidiye Kurdish cavalry units;
6) publication of official decrees in Turkish, Kurdish, and Armenian, with permission to use those languages in legal proceedings;
7) extension of the franchise only to sedentary elements;
8) right of each nationality to establish and administer private schools for which special taxes might be levied on members of that community;
9) selection of a special commission to investigate the extent of Armenian losses caused by usurpation and to supervise restitution in the form of currency or land;
10) exclusion from the province of Moslem refugee-immigrants;
11) institution of similar improvements outside the province for areas inhabited by Armenians, particularly Cilicia;
12) obligation of the European Powers to ensure the enactment of the program.[45]

The Ottoman government, excluded from the preliminary negotiations, attempted to counter the Russian project by declaring general reform measures for the entire Empire. The Turkish maneuver was rejected by the representatives of the Franco-Russo-British Entente, who were, however, unable to convince the ambassadors of the Triple Alliance to accede to the Russian proposals.[46] Because of the stalemate, Giers for the Entente and von Wangenheim for the Triple Alliance agreed to continue talks, which lasted throughout the remainder of 1913. At last, after numerous impasses and the exchange of voluminous correspondence between the Constantinople ambassadors and their respective foreign ministries, a Russo-German compromise was attained, which, with several modifications, was accepted under duress by the Ittihadist government as the Reform Act of February 8, 1914.[47]

Statistical Controversies

Prior to discussing the modifications incorporated into the final agreement, it is apropos to define the term "Armenian vilayets" and to consider the racial-religious composition of their inhabitants. The battle of statistics is pertinent to the controversies preceding and following the World War. After Ottoman expansion onto the Armenian Plateau, administrative boundaries fluctuated considerably, but the term *Ermenistan* was used to refer to most of the region. In the last half of the nineteenth century, administrative revisions abolished the *eyalet* and instituted instead the vilayet.[48] By the end of the century, the borders of the Erzerum, Van, Bitlis, Mamuret-ul-Aziz (Kharput), Sivas, and Diarbekir vilayets had been stabilized. These were the provinces commonly referred to as Turkish Armenia. Together, they encompassed all the Plateau included within the Empire and most of historic Lesser Armenia.

Armenian sources, with reasonable historical justification, stress that when the Plateau was annexed during the sixteenth century, much of it was placed within the Erzerum eyalet. This fact was recorded by the sixteenth-century geographers, Nicholas du Daulphine and Pierre Belon.[49] Hammer-Purgstall, in his classic history of the Ottoman Empire, drew repeated attention to the importance of Erzerum, undoubtedly the largest province of the Plateau.[50] On the 1848 map of geographer Levasseur, the Erzerum eyalet continued to embrace most of the Plateau.[51] Consequently, it is claimed that Ottoman rulers of the nineteenth century, alarmed by the encroachments of the European powers and the separation of the Balkans, reorganized the vilayets in the east so that the Armenians would constitute a minority in each province. From Erzerum were sheared several districts of Armenian concentration, while at the same time surrounding Moslem-populated regions were joined to the eastern provinces: Hekkiari to Van, Seert to Bitlis, districts south of Malatia to Kharput, and other lands in the west and south to Sivas and Diarbekir.[52] An 1895 memorandum of the French, Russian, and British ambassadors at Constantinople drew attention to the frequent territorial reorganizations in the eastern provinces, and,

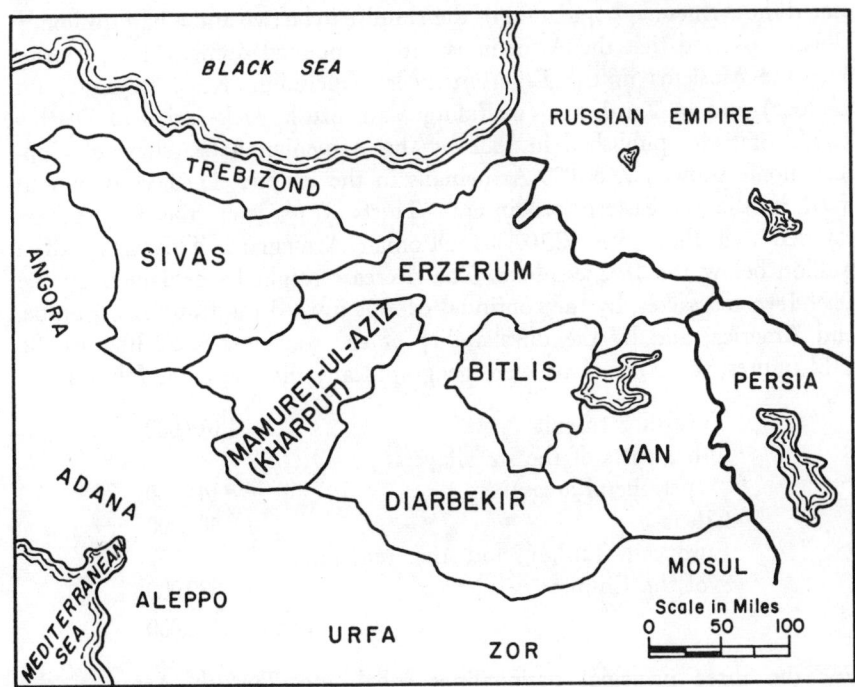

Map 5. The six Armenian vilayets

though the motivation for such action may be subject to debate, the Armenian charge that peripheral regions were incorporated into the provinces on the Plateau can be substantiated.[53]

Armenians have also claimed that for many years the *muhajir* ("emigrant") Moslems were resettled on the Plateau in a conscious effort to dilute the Armenian majority. Not only did these elements emigrate from Akhaltsikh, Kars, Ardahan, Batum, and the North Caucasus, but thousands of them were Balkan Moslems who, since 1878, had been streaming into Anatolia. In 1917, Hamdi Bey, chief of the Ottoman immigration bureau, reported that over 850,000 Moslems had found refuge in the Empire between 1878 and 1904.[54] A study of the several European reform projects that included provisions to end *muhajir* settlement on the Plateau supports the contention that the Ottoman government directed many of the immigrants toward the Plateau.

Accurate statistics concerning the population of the Ottoman Empire do not exist. The reliability of one set of figures is challenged by another. There is general agreement that the proportion of Armenians in the eastern part of the Empire had decreased since the area was annexed, but there is no concurrence on the degree of that decline. In the mid-nineteenth century, the statistician and traveler Ubicini and the Armenologist Dulaurier estimated the Armenian population of the Empire to be two and a half million.[55] Ubicini asserted that the Armenians still maintained numerical superiority over the Moslems in the Erzerum eyalet (including Kars, Bayazit, and Childer) and in Kurdistan (including Van, Mush, Hekkiari, and Diarbekir).[56] Statistics published in 1882 by the Armenian Patriarchate of Constantinople showed 2,660,000 Armenians in the Empire, 1,630,000 of whom lived in the six eastern provinces.[57] Thirty years later, the Patriarchate claimed that there were 2,100,000 Ottoman Armenians. This was half a million below the 1882 estimate. The decrease might be explained by the 1894–1896 massacres, by the continual exodus toward the Caucasus, Europe, and America, and by the unreliability of the statistics. According to the 1912 figures, the Armenians were geographically distributed as follows:[58]

Turkish Armenia	1,018,000
Other parts of the six vilayets (peripheral areas)	145,000
Cilicia	407,000
European Turkey and the remainder of the Empire	530,000
Total	2,100,000

For the three principal nationalities inhabiting Turkish Armenia, the Patriarchate gave the following statistics:[59]

	Turks	Kurds	Armenians
Erzerum	240,000	75,000	215,000
Van	47,000	72,000	185,000
Bitlis	40,000	77,000	180,000
Kharput	102,000	95,000	168,000
Diarbekir	45,000	55,000	105,000
Sivas	192,000	50,000	165,000
Percentage of total population	25.4	16.3	38.9

It was also claimed that in these provinces Christians constituted a plurality:[60]

Moslems		Christians		Other religions	
Turks	666,000	Armenians	1,018,000	Kizilbashes	140,000
Kurds	424,000	Nestorians	123,000	Zazas	77,000
Others	88,000	Greeks, etc.	42,000	Yezidis	37,000
Total	1,178,000	Total	1,183,000	Total	254,000
Percentage of total population	45.1		45.2		9.6

In advancing these figures, the Armenians might be charged with manipulation by excluding the predominantly Moslem southern and western border districts. Even at that, to establish an Armenian plurality it was necessary to list individually the several Moslem peoples, and only by including such heterodox Moslems as the Kizilbash in the category of "other religions" was it possible to establish a scant Christian numerical superiority. Finally, it is likely that the figures relating to the Armenians were exaggerated while those pertaining to the Moslems were minimized.

Turkish figures seem even more distorted. They show that the Armenians constituted a minority even at the time of the Ottoman conquest of the Plateau. It is claimed that on the eve of the World War there were only 660,000 Armenians in the six eastern provinces, or less than 17 percent of the total inhabitants, as compared to 3,000,000 Moslems, 79 percent, and that in the entire Empire there were 1,295,000 Armenians, 7 percent of the population.[61] Thus a difference of 800,000 Armenians exists between Ottoman and Patriarchate contentions.[62] Turkish authors have attempted to substantiate their assertions by utilizing the study of Vital Cuinet, *La Turquie d'Asie,* which shows that only in the vilayet of Bitlis did the Armenians constitute more than 30 percent of the population.[63] The Armenians, refuting these figures, have pointed out that Cuinet's work is riddled with discrepancies and inconsistencies. For example, Cuinet gave only four thousand as the number of Armenians in the entire district of Marash in Cilicia, whereas that figure actually pertained only to those who no longer adhered to the Armenian Apostolic faith. Moreover, Cuinet himself had confessed that his statistics were unreliable and complained that Ottoman officials had refused to make available much pertinent information.[64]

Obviously, somewhere between these contrasting figures lies the true ethnic distribution. It can be deduced with relative certainty that there were more than one and a half million but fewer than two million Armenians in all Turkey. Yet, even if the maximal figures of the Patriarchate are accepted as accurate, there is conclusive evidence that the Armenian population in the eastern province did not represent a majority. There were at least as many Moslems as Christians. This fact was to pose a major obstacle to the Armenian Republic, which, after World War I, strove to convince the European peacemakers that it should be awarded the entire Plateau. On the eve of the war, however, there was not the slightest indication that an independent Armenia would be established. Armenians continued to think in terms of cultural-national autonomy under the supervision of the European nations. By the compromise reform measure of February 8, 1914, it seemed as if realization of this goal was at hand.

The Compromise Reform of February 8, 1914

The final accord for Armenian reforms, though sanctioned by all six European nations, was signed only by the Ottoman Vizier and Foreign Minister, Said Halim, and by the Russian chargé d'affaires, K. N. Gulkevich, acting in the absence of Ambassador Giers. Among the numerous modifications of the original Russian plan was the creation of two Armenian provinces, one incorporating the Trebizond, Sivas, and Erzerum vilayets, and the other the Van, Bitlis, Kharput, and Diarbekir vilayets. A foreign inspector-general, the supreme civil authority, was to be selected for each province. The division of Turkish Armenia into two separate areas and the reduction of the Armenians' proportional strength by the inclusion of all peripheral areas as well as the Trebizond vilayet were obvious concessions to the Ottoman government. Moreover, no mention was made of restitution for Armenian losses, the exclusion of muhajirs, the extension of the reform measure to Armenians living beyond the two inspectorates, or the obligation of the European powers to guarantee the execution of the program. While the terms "Armenian" and "Christian" were used repeatedly in the original Russian project, neither was employed in the compromise settlement. Instead, "ethnic elements" and "non-Moslems" were substituted as an additional concession to the Ittihadist rulers. The agreement did not formally pertain to "Turkish Armenia," but to "Eastern Anatolia." [65] The act of February, 1914, did not fulfill all Armenian expectations, but it did represent the most viable reform proposed since the internationalization of the problem. Many Armenian leaders were content, but the Geneva organ of Dashnaktsutiun, while not repudiating the measure, warned:

> . . . before placing trust in diplomatic reforms, the Nation must subject itself to basic renovations; it must extirpate the curse of cowardly passiveness; it must be inspired by the healthy and redeeming principle of self-assistance; it must arm and be prepared! [66]

The February reform act was not implemented immediately, for the choice of suitable inspectors-general occasioned considerable disagreement and negotiation among the European ambassadors as well as between them and the Porte. Nevertheless, by April, 1914, Westenenk, chief provincial administrator in the Dutch East Indies, and Major Hoff of the Norwegian Army were selected. They arrived in Constantinople a few weeks later to receive instructions before departing for the interior.[67] Their rights and duties included

1) traveling freely to supervise administration in all districts of the inspectorate;
2) preparing monthly reports for the government;
3) enforcing all laws and directives;

4) appointing special committees for matters of local concern;
5) inaugurating measures to settle the nomads;
6) promoting interracial harmony;
7) conducting a census;
8) guaranteeing just legal proceedings and prohibiting bribery;
9) simplifying methods of tax collection;
10) suggesting needed improvements to the central government;
11) observing educational and law enforcement agencies in order to assure each religious community its own schools as well as representation in the gendarmerie;
12) utilizing sufficient administrative staff, including interpreters, to perform properly and efficiently all of these delegated functions.[68]

By the summer of 1914 Hoff was already in Van, his administrative center, and Westenenk was about to depart for Erzerum. But at this moment of triumph, when the strivings of the nineteenth-century Armenian political mind seemed in large part gratified, when national-cultural autonomy was in sight, all was obliterated with a single stroke. And even when that blow fell, there was hardly a person who imagined that it was to exterminate the Turkish Armenian. For this people, the tragic effects of World War I cannot be exaggerated.

IV
"The Fateful Years"
(1914–1917)

RUSSIAN AND TURKISH entanglement in World War I emerged as a key factor in the establishment of the Armenian Republic. It was from the ruins of these two empires and from the remnants of their own people that the Armenian leaders created a new political entity. The hopes based on the February, 1914, accord for reforms in the eastern provinces of the Ottoman Empire were shattered by the surprise Turkish attack on Russia in October of the same year. That blow not only annulled the reform plan but also initiated the most devastating calamity in the turbulent history of the Armenian people. The experiences of Turkish and Russian Armenians from the outbreak of war to the abdication of Tsar Nicholas II in 1917 constitute a vital chapter in the saga leading to independence.

The Turkish Decision for War

Secret German-Turkish negotiations were concluded on August 2, 1914, by a pact signed at Constantinople by Ambassador von Wangenheim and Grand Vizier Said Halim in the presence of War Minister Enver and Interior Minister Talaat. It was agreed that, if German assistance to Austria in the Serbian crisis led to war with Russia, Turkey would enter the conflict. In return, Germany pledged to protect any Ottoman territories threatened by Russia.[1] Moreover, contact between the Moslems of Turkey and of Russia was to be secured through certain frontier rectifications.[2] Since the agreement was signed a day after the German declaration of war against Russia, Ottoman involvement was a fait accompli. Led by Enver Pasha, the militant faction of Ittihad ve Terakki triumphed. Mobilization was ordered immediately, and two months later, on October 22, Enver relayed the following instructions to Admiral Wilhelm Souchon, a German in command of the Ottoman Black Sea Fleet: "The Turkish fleet will gain naval supremacy in the Black Sea. Seek the Russian fleet and strike it without a declaration of war, wherever you find it."³ A week later the Turkish Navy bombarded the Russian installations at Sevastopol, Odessa, Theodosia, and Novorossiisk, and returned victoriously to Constantinople.⁴ On November 4, Russia responded with the anticipated declaration of war.⁵

Enver's expectations were great. His Pan-Turanic views were expressed through circulars distributed on November 12 by Ittihad ve Terakki, calling for destruction of Russia, expansion of the natural frontiers, and unification with all Turkic peoples in the Moslem world's struggle for liberation from the infidel oppressors.⁶ Aware that the realization of his aspirations was dependent on a powerful military force on the eastern front, Enver added a third division each to the IX, X, and XI corps of the Third Army, based at Erzerum. With jurisdiction extending from Van and Kharput northward to the Black Sea coast, that army, by the end of 1914, consisted of over two hundred thousand regulars and fifteen to twenty thousand Kurdish tribesmen, *ashiret*s.⁷ The Armenian Plateau was fortified.

The Erzerum Congress

Throughout the summer of 1914 the Armenians fearfully considered the probable involvement of Turkey in the impending war. The Eighth General Congress of Dashnaktsutiun, convening in Erzerum at the same time that the Serbian problem threatened to engulf the whole of Europe, sought to avert Ottoman ensnarement in the conflict. Peace was requisite for the implementation of the February reform measures and for the welfare of the Armenians, most of whom inhabited a natural theater of war on both sides of the Russo-Turkish border. Though critical of the accentuated narrow nationalism of the Ittihadists and the alarming hostility toward non-Turkic elements of the Empire, Dashnaktsutiun pledged to collaborate with the government in all efforts to avoid war. Before deliberations on the crucial question had been concluded, however, the delegates learned of the order for general mobilization. Alerted by the ominous significance of Enver's move, the Congress appointed a committee to formulate the party's policies in conformity with the unfolding course of events and then promptly adjourned.⁸

As the delegates hastened to their respective countries or provinces, authoritative members of Ittihad ve Terakki arrived in Erzerum to negotiate with Dashnaktsutiun. Dr. Bahaeddin Shakir, Omer Naji, and Hilmi Bey, accompanied by an international entourage of peoples from the Caucasus, proposed to the Armenian liaisons, Arshak Vramian, Rostom (Stepan Zorian), and E. Aknuni (Khachatur Malumian), that, in the event of Russo-Ottoman hostilities, Dashnaktsutiun incite rebellion among the Russian Armenians who, by harassing the tsarist armies, would facilitate Turkish conquest of Transcaucasia. The Ittihadist representatives, disclosing that similar schemes already had been approved by Georgian and Moslem spokesmen from Russia, promised, in return for collaboration, an autonomous state comprising Russian Armenia and several *sanjak*s of the Erzerum, Van, and Bitlis *vilayet*s. The three Armenian conferees, respected in Ottoman governmental circles, rejected the feasibility of such a plot and reiterated their party's plea for a sane policy—neutrality. If, however, despite their earnest endeavors, the conflagration should envelop Turkey, the Ottoman Armenians would defend the fatherland and perform all obligations as faithfully and conscientiously as during the Libyan and Balkan crises of 1911-1913. But provoke revolts within the Russian Empire they could not.[9] The Armenian reply, considered prudent by some, has been judged by others as contributory to the subsequent national cataclysm. The dissatisfied Turkish mission departed from Erzerum without having achieved its objective.[10]

When Ottoman participation in the World War became a reality, the apprehensive Armenian leaders strove to convince the Ittihad government of their fidelity and patriotism. The Patriarch instructed the prelates of all dioceses within the Empire to perform religious services for the victory of the Ottoman homeland.[11] *Azatamart,* the influential organ of Dashnaktsutiun, exhorted the Armenians to act as exemplary citizens and to avoid friction with other elements of the Empire. Aknuni and several other leaders of Dashnaktsutiun depended on their personal friendship with Enver and Talaat to persuade the ruling clique of Turkey that the Armenians were resolved to protect the integrity of the common fatherland.[12] Although most Armenians maintained a correct attitude vis-à-vis the Ottoman government, it can be asserted with some substantiation that the manifestations of loyalty were insincere, for the sympathy of most Armenians throughout the world was with the Entente, not with the Central Powers. By autumn, 1914, several prominent Ottoman Armenians, including a former member of parliament, had slipped away to the Caucasus to collaborate with Russian military officials. Such acts provided the Ittihadist Triumvirate with the desired excuse to eradicate the Armenian problem and eliminate the major racial barrier between the Turkic peoples of the Ottoman and Russian empires.

Russian Armenian Preparations

Whereas the Armenians of Turkey promised to fulfill their duties, those of Russia begged Tsar Nicholas II for the opportunity to undertake more than their normal obligations. War fever once again stirred Transcaucasia to extraordinary vivacity. Tiflis, the intellectual, cultural, and financial center of the Russian Armenians, became the site of pronounced anti-Turkish agitation. Anticipating war in a near festive atmosphere, the National Bureau, which had been formed in 1912 to pursue the problem of Ottoman reforms, attempted to coordinate Armenian strategy. Already in August,

1914, through the Bureau's initiative, Catholicos Gevorg had appealed to Nicholas to take under his benevolent wings the suffering Turkish Armenians, to protect their lives and property, and to guarantee the implementation of the reform project.[13] Count Vorontsov-Dashkov, acting as intermediary, informed the Catholicos in September that the government was determined to introduce into the eastern Ottoman provinces the measures envisaged in the original Russian plan of 1913 and to make no compromises on the Armenian question. The Viceroy continued:

> I feel obliged, however, to warn you that at the present moment Armenian activity both on our side and beyond the border must be in complete conformity with my directives, for because of the existing strained relations between Turkey and Russia, from the point of view of general policy shared by our allied governments, it is imperative that the occasion for war be given by Turkey itself and not by any action of ours. Thus, it is very undesirable and even dangerous to instigate a revolt among the Turkish Armenians.[14]

Vorontsov-Dashkov concluded by requesting the Catholicos to keep his flock prepared to act in case of armed conflict.

The Viceroy for the Caucasus maneuvered skillfully to gain the loyalty of Dashnaktsutiun, which, since 1904, had been at war with the Russian bureaucracy. Pursuing this goal, he coaxed Nicholas to appease the Armenians by responding favorably to an appeal of the Catholicos to liberate the many members of Dashnaktsutiun still in prison or exile. In his petition, the Catholicos had defended the patriotism of the party, whose antagonism to the Russian government he ascribed to the misguided and harmful policies of Vorontsov-Dashkov's predecessors. In addition to a general amnesty, the prelate requested the immediate release of a hundred and eighty specifically named civic and political leaders.[15] The voice of the Armenians seemed now to reach the Imperial Palace, for the Tsar accepted the advice of his Viceroy and returned the prisoners of the "Stolypin era" to Transcaucasia.

Vorontsov-Dashkov followed closely the debates of the Armenian National Bureau, regional assemblies of Dashnaktsutiun, and numerous special conferences relating to the formation of volunteer contingents. Such units had assisted the Russian armies in 1827–1828, 1855–1856, and 1877–1878, but on each occasion the Armenians had felt insufficiently compensated for their sacrifices. Soon after the German declaration of war, Vorontsov-Dashkov conferred with Bishop Mesrop of Tiflis, Alexandre Khatisian, mayor of the city, and Dr. Hakob Zavriev, active both in Dashnaktsutiun and Russian public circles, and suggested that the Armenians initiate the creation of volunteer corps.[16] Later, through his military staff, the Viceroy offered to provide the necessary weapons, matériel, and money to outfit four separate groups, which would be commanded by popular revolutionary heroes. The enemies of the Tsar were to become his officers.[17]

Most Armenians needed little prodding. Even before the final decision was reached, volunteers gathered in every part of Transcaucasia. But the enthusiasm of the national leaders was not unanimous, for there were "voices in the wilderness" that strove unsuccessfully to convince the Armenians of Transcaucasia of the possible deleterious consequences. It is noteworthy that Hovhannes Kachaznuni and Simon Vratzian, the first and the last premiers of the future republic, warned that the Ittihadist rulers of Turkey would utilize the existence of volunteer units, composed partly of former Ottoman subjects, to justify violent measures against the Turkish Armenians.[18] The minority opinion, however, was in direct opposition to the prevailing psychology of the Russian Armenian masses, who considered the time for words past and the moment of redeeming action at hand.

Having agreed to the proposal of Vorontsov-Dashkov, the National Bureau selected a special committee to supervise the operations of the volunteer corps. Functioning from Tiflis, Alexandropol, and Erevan, the committee began its activities by assigning enlistees to the four authorized units, all of which were immediately filled to capacity.[19] The military role of the volunteers, insignificant in number when compared with the total Russian strength on the Caucasus front, was primarily to scout, to guide the Russian armies over the rugged terrain of the Plateau, and to fulfill the perilous assignments of the avant-garde.[20] The first group, over 1,000 men, was led by Andranik, an experienced revolutionary who had participated in the Balkan wars as commander of an Armenian contingent in the Bulgarian Army. Andranik's unit joined the Russian forces in North Persia, while the other three advanced toward the Turkish border. Dro, assisted by the former Ottoman parliament member, Armen Garo, directed the second group, which, moving over Igdir in the Erevan province, poised for an offensive against Van. The third and fourth units, commanded by Hamazasp and Keri, took advance positions along the western border of the Kars *oblast,* from Sarikamish to Olti.[21] When the Turkish battleships bombarded the Russian coast in October, the Armenian volunteers were already supplied and prepared to violate the boundaries of the Ottoman Empire. That the commitment to form volunteer units was above and beyond the call of duty is evidenced by the fact that already serving in the regular Russian armies were nearly 150,000 Armenians, most of whom had been transferred to the European front.[22]

Nicholas II in the Caucasus

War between Turkey and Russia sealed the rapprochement between Dashnaktsutiun and Tsar Nicholas, who appealed to his Armenian subjects to join in the defense of the Empire. The unpleasantness of the past was not mentioned—only the great love of the Tsar for his Armenian children. As an expression of his sincerity, Nicholas made a personal inspection tour of the Caucasus front and conferred with Armenian political and religious leaders. Those who had cursed the Tsar ten years earlier now knelt offering homage and dedicating themselves to the triumph of Holy Russia.[23] Samson Harutunian, President of the National Bureau, declared:

> From all countries, Armenians are hurrying to enter the ranks of the glorious Russian Army, with their blood to serve the victory of Russian arms. . . . Let the Russian flag wave freely over the Dardanelles and the Bosporus. Let, with Your will, great Majesty, the peoples remaining under the Turkish yoke receive freedom. Let the Armenian people of Turkey who have suffered for the faith of Christ receive resurrection for a new free life under the protection of Russia.[24]

Catholicos Gevorg V spoke of the benevolence shown the Armenians by Russian monarchs since the time of Peter the Great and of the leading role that Nicholas' government had assumed in the recent negotiations for reforms in Turkish Armenia. Changes to be implemented through the channels of the Turkish government, however, invariably had remained dead letters: "The salvation of the Turkish Armenians is possible only by delivering them definitively from Turkish domination and by creating an autonomous Armenia under the powerful protectorate of great Russia."[25] Nicholas performed well on the emotional occasion as he exclaimed to the Catholicos, "Tell your flock, Holy Father, that a most brilliant future awaits the Armenians."[26] Though soothing and comforting to the political mind of the Armenians, such statements disturbed the few who feared that the declarations would only deepen the suspicion of the Ittihad government toward its Armenian subjects.

Enver's Disastrous Winter Campaign of 1914

While the Tsar and the Armenians of Transcaucasia wooed one another, Enver Pasha traveled to Third Army headquarters in Erzerum and then proceeded to the front lines in December of 1914 to direct personally the military operations against the Caucasus. His strategy was to outflank the Russian forces, cut their lines of communication with the main supply base at Kars, and retrieve the territories ceded to Russia in 1878. Occupation of Kars, Ardahan, and Batum would facilitate the planned revolt of Caucasian Moslems against Russia and open the routes to Tiflis and beyond. To realize this goal, the XI Corps of the Third Army, along with Kurdish ashirets, was to strike in a frontal attack against the major border fortress, Sarikamish. Simultaneously the IX Corps, passing over Barduz, would hit the Russian positions from the rear, while the X Corps, crossing the border at Olti, would move toward Ardahan and Kars, sever the railway connections with Sarikamish, and participate in the outflanking maneuver.[27] The timing for such an operation seemed propitious, for the Russian High Command had transferred its most experienced divisions from Transcaucasia to the imperiled front in Europe.[28]

The Turkish attack began on December 22, and five days later, despite heavy losses, Enver's forces had interrupted rail communication between Kars and Sarikamish and had nearly encircled the latter city. The Russian commander, General Myshlaevskii, fearing the complete annihilation of the Caucasus Army, fled to Tiflis and ordered a full retreat. That several other Russian generals refused to comply ultimately proved fortunate for the tsarist war effort.[29] In the last days of December, the opposing forces fought in pitched battles for possession of Sarikamish. Enver, with nearly half his army already on the casualty list, was still certain of success and planned his strategy to vanquish the great bastion of Kars and to seize Tiflis.[30]

Partly justified in his appraisal of the disorganization and inexperience of the Russian Army, Enver failed, nevertheless, to take precautions against the severe winters of the Armenian Plateau. The poorly uniformed and meagerly supplied Turkish soldiers succumbed en masse to the freezing weather. The Turkish War Minister denied his forces rest, insisting that the major objectives were in sight and should not be jeopardized by unnecessary halts.[31] When epidemics of typhus and cholera augmented the heavy casualties from exposure and combat, entire divisions of the IX and X corps vanished. By the start of the new year, the initiative passed to the Russian Command. Generals Przhevalskii, commander at Sarikamish, Kalitin, at Ardahan, and Iudenich, facing the XI Turkish Corps, led the counteroffensive all along the front.[32] The Ottoman Army dissolved, and Enver, despite his yearning for rapid victory in the Caucasus, relinquished his command to Colonel Hakki Bey. Then, "on the 7th, Enver left for Erzerum en route for Istanbul, abandoning to the Armenian winter the shattered remnants of his 'Pan-Turanian' army."[33] By January 12 the Russian troops had regained the prewar boundary. Hakki Bey, unable to stem the rising tide of disaster, narrowly avoided capture, and, leaving behind additional thousands of dead, prisoners, and stragglers, also fled toward Erzerum. A week later the tsarist armies had advanced several miles into Ottoman territory to the positions held prior to the ill-fated "Sarikamish Operation."[34] That campaign cost the Third Army dearly. General Otto Liman von Sanders, chief of the German Military Mission in Turkey, estimated that, of the ninety thousand men lost, only twelve thousand were taken prisoner.[35] According to Joseph Pomiankowski, the Austrian military attaché in Turkey, Enver's hundred-thousand-man force dwindled in two weeks to less than 15 percent of its original strength.[36]

Effects of the Campaign in Transcaucasia

Many Armenians were among the thousands of casualties suffered by the Russian Caucasus Army. The four volunteer units, impatient to face the

Turks, participated in the fiercest battles from Olti to Sarikamish and Persian Azerbaijan. By the end of the campaign a third of the volunteers had been killed or wounded.[37] The Armenian combatants felt adequately rewarded, however, when service medals and certificates of commendation were showered upon their units by Russian officials and generals.[38] Public statements of praise printed in papers around the world strengthened the conviction of the Russian Armenians that the future prosperity of the nation was dependent upon the success of the tsarist armies. The rapport between government and subjects was evidenced again during 1915 when the Armenians were authorized to organize three more volunteer groups, led by Vardan, Avsharian, and Arghutian.[39] Though all units were subject officially to the general directives and strategy of the Russian Caucasus Army Command, immediate contact and orders emanated from the special Armenian committee in charge of volunteer activities. The Armenians were gaining administrative experience. Yet because the committee and its parent organization, the National Bureau, were accused of complete subservience to the dictates of Dashnaktsutiun, the sixth corps of volunteers, composed primarily of Hnchakists and enlistees from America and the Balkans, operated independently.[40] Though disputes among the various units and their respective commanders were numerous, all were united in their attitude toward the Ottoman government and Turkish Armenia.

The Russian victories of January, 1915, had averted the immediate threat to Transcaucasia, but the crisis had left its scars. Nearly seventy thousand Armenians uprooted from the battle zone had fled toward Erevan and Tiflis. The influx of these refugees further aroused the Transcaucasian Armenians, who created numerous relief societies and solicited public contributions for the unfortunate victims. Originally, both natives and refugees believed that only temporary relief measures were necessary, for with the expected occupation of the entire Plateau by Russian troops the Armenians from the border area could return home to rebuild with confidence and security.[41]

The effect of the Sarikamish operation on the mutual relations of the Transcaucasian peoples was of a different nature. During the first days of the Turkish offensive, the loss of the entire region seemed imminent. Families of Russian officials evacuated to safer areas and governmental establishments prepared to withdraw to the North Caucasus. The Armenian populace was struck with horror, for little compassion was expected from Enver Pasha.[42] In the midst of the turmoil, Armenian, Moslem, and Georgian political leaders conferred in Tiflis. The Armenians advocated active popular resistance to the invaders and urged their Transcaucasian neighbors to organize militias. Although the Moslem representatives professed loyalty to Russia, they remained noncommittal, while the Georgians overtly opposed the strategy suggested by Dashnaktsutiun. Noi Ramishvili, an influential Social Democrat and future premier of Georgia, agreed to the formation of a militia charged with maintaining law and order after the anticipated Russian evacuation but considered a defensive stand both illogical and impossible. The only way to save Transcaucasia from destruction was to welcome the Turks and to simulate submission to the conqueror. To allay Armenian misgivings, Ramishvili pointed out that Enver Pasha was German-trained and thus naturally imbued with the enlightened European attitudes toward the conduct of war.[43] Fortunately, the subsequent Turkish fiasco at Sarikamish permitted the Transcaucasians to evade the necessity of reaching a decision, but, significantly, the episode had exposed their fundamentally divergent concepts.

Armenian suspicions increased when rumors of Georgian and Moslem collaboration with the enemy spread. Actually, Georgian émigrés in Germany and Turkey had offered to form volunteer units to fight for the liberation of Georgia from Russian domination. The action was somewhat parallel to the institution of Armenian units against Turkey. Georgian volunteers expected from the Central Powers the restoration of a national government with jurisdiction over the territories included within the eighteenth-century realm of Iraklii II as well as the surrounding provinces. However, the Georgian contingent participated in few campaigns, was distrusted by the Turkish Command, and was ignored by almost all Georgians, whose loyalty to the multinational Russian homeland was impeccable.[44] Moslem sympathy for Turkey was more natural. While the Turkish First Expeditionary Force occupied Persian Azerbaijan during the first months of 1915, Halil Pasha, commander of the group and uncle of Enver, conferred with Aslan Khan Khoiskii, nephew of a later premier of the Azerbaijan Republic. The military accord they concluded entailed a Moslem insurrection in North Persia and Transcaucasia against Russia in return for Ottoman assistance in creating an independent Azerbaijan, which would encompass Persian Azerbaijan in addition to the *guberniias* of Erevan, Baku, and Elisavetpol. Enver sanctioned the project, which nonetheless remained unexecuted.[45] Russian pressure in North Persia and Armenian armed activities at Van, to the rear of Halil's division, compelled the Ottoman commander to evacuate Persian Azerbaijan, thus severing the direct link between the Moslems of Transcaucasia and the Turkish forces.[46]

Deportation and Massacre of the Turkish Armenians

Several authors assert that Armenian resistance at Van constituted a key factor in the Turkish evacuation of Persia and motivated the Ittihadist leaders to annihilate the Turkish Armenians. The question of responsibility for the massacre or deportation of nearly all Ottoman Armenians has evolved into a polemic. Hundreds of books, articles, and documents have been published to describe the horrifying scenes of violence and death. Many writers, such as the British Bryce and Toynbee, French Pinon, German Lepsius, American Morgenthau and Gibbons, have insisted that the massacres were premeditated and ruthlessly executed. They have refuted the Ottoman government's official publications and justifications by substantiating that anti-Armenian measures were deliberated by the Ittihadists even before the outbreak of war.[47] The fact remains that an estimated eight hundred thousand to over a million Armenians perished within a few months, and several hundred thousand more succumbed in the following years to the ravages of disease, famine, and refugee life. Unknown numbers of women and children were converted forcibly to Islam, possessed by Turkish men, or adopted by Moslem families.

That the disaster occurred is indisputable, but the reasons for it remain as controversial as ever. In 1959, the press attaché of the Turkish Embassy in Washington, D.C., wrote:

> Turkish response to the Armenian excesses was comparable, I believe, to what might have been the American response, had the German-Americans of Minnesota or Wisconsin revolted on behalf of Hitler during World War II.

And further:

> The non-Turkish elements of the empire continued to press for separatism and sought the support of the major powers. They were apprehensive that a real reformation might delay the division of the spoils, and turned a cold shoulder to the overtures of the earnestly pro-Western "Young Turks."[48]

Talaat Pasha, one of the originators of the cataclysm, stated in his memoirs:

> I admit that we deported many Armenians from our eastern provinces, but we never acted in this matter upon a previously prepared scheme. The responsibility for these acts falls first of all upon the deported people themselves. . . .
> These preventive measures were taken in every country during the war, but, while the regrettable results were passed over in silence in the other countries, the echo of our acts was heard the world over, because everybody's eyes were upon us.[49]

Most Turkish sources claim that deportations were wartime measures necessary for the security of the state, and that they were adopted only after evidence of Armenian treachery was conclusive. Proof of malevolence included the formation of volunteer units in the Caucasus, the participation of Turkish subjects in these groups, threats and antagonism expressed in Armenian journals abroad, and preparations for armed insurrection. During the course of the war, the Ottoman government issued several publications that included secret conspiratorial correspondence of Armenian revolutionaries as well as numerous photographs of arms caches and confiscated weapons. The Armenians were charged with a nationwide plot.[50] Turkish authors have particularly stressed that no official action was taken against the Armenians until they had rebelled. Thus, when on April 24, 1915, Armenian civic, political, and intellectual leaders in Constantinople were arrested, deported, and subsequently executed, a revolt allegedly had already begun.[51] On May 26 Minister of Interior Talaat Pasha sent to the Grand Vizier a communiqué concerning Armenian deportations:

> Because some of the Armenians who are living near the war zones have obstructed the activities of the Imperial Ottoman Army, which has been entrusted with defending the frontiers against the country's enemies; because they impede the movements of provisions and troops; because they have made common cause with the enemy; and especially because they have attacked the military forces within the country, the innocent population, and the Ottoman cities and towns, killing and plundering; and because they have even dared to supply the enemy navy with provisions and to reveal the location of our fortified places to them; and because it is necesary that rebellious elements of this kind should be removed from the area of military activities and that the villages which are the bases and shelter for these rebels should be vacated, certain measures are being adopted, among which is deportation of the Armenians from the Van, Bitlis, Erzerum vilayets; the *livas* ["counties"] of Adana, Mersin, Kozan, Jebelibereket, except for the cities of Adana, Sis, and Mersin; the Marash sanjak, except for Marash itself; and the Iskenderum, Beylan, Jisr-i Shuur, and Antakya districts of the Aleppo vilayet, except for the administrative city of each. It is being announced that the Armenians are to be sent to the following places: Mosul vilayet except for the northern area bordering the Van vilayet, Zor sanjak, southern Urfa except for the city of Urfa itself, eastern and southeastern Aleppo vilayet, and the eastern part of the Syrian vilayet.[52]

Four days later, on May 30, the Ottoman Council of Ministers confirmed the necessity of deportations but gave to the law a semblance of fair play by approving provisions

1) to safeguard the person and possessions of the deportees until they had reached their destination and to forbid any form of persecution;
2) to compensate the deportees with new property, land, and goods necessary for a comfortable life;
3) to permit Moslem refugees to inhabit the abandoned villages only after having officially recorded the value of the homes and land and making clear that the property still belonged to the legal owners;
4) to sell or rent those fields, properties, and goods not settled by Moslem refugees and to keep in the treasury, in the owner's name, an account of the derived income, after first deducting administrative expenses;
5) to authorize the finance minister to create special committees to supervise these transactions and to publish circulars pertaining to the compensations for the properties and their protection;

have concluded that the deportations and massacres were calculated, irresponsible, and brutal crimes. Utilizing scores of documents and the testimony of many European witnesses, these critics have insisted that the overwhelming majority of the Armenians fulfilled every obligation of Ottoman citizenship during the first months of war. Exhortations of the Patriarch, the revolutionary organizations, and many other societies urging the Turkish Armenians to maintain a correct attitude have been cited. Moreover, the dedication of Armenian soldiers was acknowledged by Enver himself, who, upon returning from the Sarikamish debacle, informed the Patriarch and other high-ranking clergy of the unsurpassed bravery of these troops.[63]

The gravest Turkish accusation involved Armenian rebellion during time of war; the "Revolt of Van" became the classic charge. The Lepsius-Toynbee school of critics labeled the indictment as fabrication. The city rose in self-defense only after the deportations and massacres had begun in Cilicia and after Jevdet Bey, brother-in-law of Enver and Armenophobe *vali* ("governor") of Van, had ordered the destruction of Armenian villages in the outlying districts.[64] If, as Turkish sources claim, the revolt were premeditated, why would Ishkhan, popular leader of the Van Armenians, leave the city at the behest of the vali to restore peace between feuding Moslems and Christians in an isolated upland of the vilayet? Only after the treacherous murder of Ishkhan, the imprisonment of Arshak Vramian, a member of the Ottoman parliament, and the siege of the Armenian quarter by Jevdet's forces did Van rise in self-defense, barricade the streets, and inaugurate in the last half of April, 1915, the monthlong obdurate resistance. This sequence of events was substantiated by testimony of American eyewitnesses.[65]

Turning from the question of Van, the castigators of Turkish policies then negated the other contentions. The hopeless battles in the interior of Turkey at Shabin Karahisar, Urfa, and Cilicia were not indications of an Armenian revolution fermenting throughout the Empire, but simply reflected the resolution of a condemned people to fall fighting rather than be slaughtered. That the Armenians possessed weapons was not astounding; they had carried arms for decades to defend their homes and fields from depredation. Among the photographs published by the Ittihadist government were pictures of bombs and grenades, but these explosives belonged to the era when both Turkish and Armenian opposition groups were struggling against Abdul Hamid II. Since the attempted Hamidian coup of 1909, when Ittihad leaders had requested that these weapons be used against the forces of reaction, they had not been touched by the Armenians.[66] To the charge that Ottoman subjects, as volunteers in the Russian Army, viciously attacked the Empire, Arnold Toynbee drew an analogy to the Polish units, which, joining the Austro-Hungarian forces, battled against the tsarist armies. If the entire Armenian nation could be condemned for the activities of several hundred or even several thousand men, then should not Russia, on the same basis, annihilate the millions of Poles within its borders?[67]

Analyzing the real motivations for Ittihad measures against the Armenians, Johannes Lepsius first summarized the Ottoman charges:

1) Garegin Pasdermadjian (Armen Garo), member of the Ottoman parliament, had deserted to Russia and joined the volunteers.
2) English and French naval commanders had sent agitators into Cilicia where the population was engaged in sabotage and espionage.
3) Armenians in Zeitun had resisted the commands of the military authorities.
4) Turkish opponents of the Ittihadists had contrived against the government and used as accomplices several members of the Hnchakist party.
5) The Armenians of Van had taken up arms against the government.
6) The combatants of Shabin Karahisar had barricaded themselves in the ancient citadel and fought against Turkish troops.[68]

Even if the accusations were true, exclaimed Lepsius, to construe an Armenian revolution from them was fantastic. Not Armenian treachery but the ideology adopted by the Ittihadists was the foundation for the government's action. Nationalism as understood by the "Young Turks" on the eve of the World War necessitated the "Turkification" of all elements of the Empire. As long as there were Armenians, foreign intervention, as experienced during the latest episode of the reform question, would pose a constant threat to the sovereignty of Turkey. Moreover, eradication of the Christian Armenian element from Anatolia and the eastern provinces would remove the major racial barrier between the Turkic peoples of the Ottoman Empire, Transcaucasia, and Transcaspia.[69] Enver's dream of a Pan-Turanic empire would be a step closer to realization.[70]

German implication in the Armenian tragedy is similarly subject to acrid disputation. Certainly part of the German press bewailed the suffering of the Eastern Christians. The German General Staff and members of the Military Mission to Turkey condemned the radical measures of the Ittihadist dictators, for the depopulation of vital farmland and the elimination of the most important professional and artisan classes caused immeasurable harm to the war effort of the Central Powers.[71] Nevertheless, most official publications in Germany repeated Turkish charges against the Armenians and asserted that involvement in the internal affairs of an ally during time of war was imprudent.[72] Ambassador Johann Bernstorff in Washington echoed these views and noted that the Armenians had brought the tragedy upon themselves.[73] The Germans have been accused of direct complicity in the deportations, for the Berlin government had both the influence and the force to restrain its Turkish partner. When a German economic project in southern Anatolia was threatened because of the deportations, Kaiser Wilhelm's officials exerted sufficient pressure to spare the Armenian laborers until completion of the work. The Ottoman Empire was economically and militarily dependent on Germany; the Kaiser's threats to withdraw that aid would have moderated Ottoman tempers.[74] To those who, in defense of Germany, cited the several protest notes delivered to the Sublime Porte, critics retorted that the messages were too late and too formalistic to convince the Ittihadists of their sincerity.[75]

Besides referring to the protests from Berlin, the exonerators of German moral integrity have documented the abnegation, perils, and deprivations suffered by many German missionaries, officials, and civilians, who, while in Anatolia and Syria, attempted to diminish the anguish of the deportees. Numerous dispatches from German consuls assailing the abhorrent Turkish action and begging for immediate relief have been published.[76] Pomiankowski, while denouncing the brutality and disastrous consequences of Ittihad tactics, lashed out at the critics of Germany and Austria-Hungary, maintaining that the deportation arrangements were so shrouded in secrecy that the diplomatic corps was ignorant of the proceedings for many days after their inauguration. The Austrian military attaché also implicated the United States, for if Ambassador Morgenthau were aware of the impending tragedy, as he claimed, his government was obligated to take stern measures. The Armenians might have been spared had the United States threatened the Turkish leaders with war, but instead, throughout the entire deportation operations, diplomatic relations were maintained with the Sublime Porte, which finally, in April, 1917, took the initiative upon itself to sever the ties.[77] It has been noted already that Pomiankowski and other citizens of the Central Powers have attributed the massacres in part to Enver's defeat at Sarikamish and Halil's forced evacuation of Persian Azerbaijan. Those failures together with the "Revolt of Van" were crippling blows to the fulfillment of the Pan-Turanic mission.

Deliverance and Evacuation of Van

As the caravans of deportees trudged toward the Syrian desert and Jevdet Bey attempted to crush the rising at Van, the Russian Armenians wavered between optimism and pessimism. They were not yet fully aware of what had befallen the Turkish Armenians, but, believing the latter imperiled, clamored for Russian occupation of the entire Plateau. When news of the fighting at Van reached Transcaucasia, the demand for immediate action burgeoned, and the IV Corps of the Russian Caucasus Army launched an offensive toward Van and Manzikert.[78] Participating in the operation were the second, third, fourth, and fifth volunteer battalions combined under the command of Vardan into the Legion of Ararat. Departing from Erevan on April 28, 1915, the Legion joined General Nikolaev's regular divisions, which passed over the prewar boundary on May 4.[79] Two weeks later the Armenian units, followed by the Russian troops, were greeted joyously by the insurgents at Van, while Jevdet Bey retreated along the southern shore of the lake toward Vostan.[80] The Armenian volunteers were showered with praise by IV Corps Commander General Oganovskii, who, through the person of the Catholicos, informed the Armenian people of the valor of their Legion.[81] Russian military authorities appointed Aram Manukian, who had coordinated the Armenian defense of Van, governor of the occupied region. Armenian political consciousness again was stimulated, for the promised reward, an autonomous Armenia under Russian protection, was within sight.[82] Already native administration, militia, and police were established in the cradle around Lake Van, where the Armenian nation had been molded more than two thousand years before.[83]

At the end of June, the Armenian Legion, now attached to the special forces of General Trukhin, was entrusted with the task of expelling the Turks from the entire southern shore of the lake in preparation for a concerted Russian drive into the Bitlis vilayet, where nearly a hundred thousand beleaguered Armenians awaited deliverance.[84] Impatient to reach the Plain of Mush and the mountains of Sassun, the Legion, joined by Andranik's unit, attained the southwestern extremity of the lake by mid-July and garnered the laudations of General Trukhin. However, when Russian divisions advanced toward Bitlis, they met the vigorous counteroffensive of Abdul Kerim's strongly reinforced Special Army Group, whose blows were directed north of the lake against the main concentration of the IV Caucasus Corps near Manzikert.[85] To avoid encirclement, Trukhin's group was commanded to withdraw to Van, but upon arriving there the general found the entire region already evacuated by the remainder of the IV Corps. Thus, on July 31, 1915, the native inhabitants were ordered to abandon their homes and move toward the Russian border.[86] The panic was indescribable. After the monthlong resistance to Jevdet Bey, after the city's liberation, after the establishment of an Armenian governorship, all was blighted. Fleeing behind the retreating Russian forces, nearly two hundred thousand refugees, losing most of their possessions in repeated Kurdish ambushes, swarmed into Transcaucasia.[87] Providing for this multitude, coping with their impatience to return home, and assuaging their complaints against their Russian Armenian neighbors were among the many serious problems inherited by the future republic.

If the evacuation of Van occasioned much discontent and grief, the failure of the march toward Bitlis resulted in tragedy. The welcome sound of Russian artillery heard by the Armenians of Mush and Sassun had faded away as Turkish divisions, having repulsed the foreign enemy, concentrated upon their internal foes. It was only after the few survivors of the blood bath had straggled into Transcaucasia that the full impact and significance of the Turkish Armenian annihilation was delivered.[88] When the IV Corps and Armenian units reoccupied Van in September, 1915, captured Vostan in October, and advanced into Mush in February and Bitlis in March, 1916, there remained no one to liberate. Russian victory then occasioned little rejoicing among the volunteers or Armenian populace of Transcaucasia.[89]

Revelation of Actual Tsarist Attitudes

While the Russian armies occupied most of the Armenian Plateau during the winter and spring of 1916, Armenian leaders were most apprehensive. Apparent respect of tsarist officials for Armenian political-civic bodies and volunteer groups had changed into expressions of sarcasm and distrust. As early as the first half of 1915, disquieting reports from Russian junior officers, accusing the volunteers of lawlessness and looting, had reached Tiflis. Publication of such dispatches elicited sharp protests to Vorontsov-Dashkov from the Armenian National Bureau. Subsequently, the Viceroy informed members of the Bureau that an investigation had proved the detrimental news unfounded, and he promised to publicize this report. That he did not was significant.[90] The National Bureau also complained that in the occupied territories the Kurds, instead of being disarmed, were allowed freedom of action. While these "enemies of yesterday" continued their violations against the sedentary population, tsarist officials confiscated the weapons of the Armenian peasantry. A deputation composed of Bishop Mesrop, Mayor Khatisian, and Samson Harutunian requested that Vorontsov-Dashkov authorize the Armenian refugees to carry arms for protection and to settle in deserted Moslem villages.[91] Though the Viceroy reassured the delegation of the government's benevolence, Armenian leaders could not ignore the ascendance of traditional bureaucratic views toward the minorities. What the National Bureau did not know was that representatives of the Romanov sovereign were earnestly negotiating the partition of Turkey with the other members of the Entente. Moreover, Russian designs to annex the eastern vilayets included no provisions for Armenian autonomy.[92]

Correspondence of ranking tsarist officials was indicative of the Russian retrenchment. In April, 1915, before the Van offensive, General N. N. Iudenich, Field Commander of the Caucasus Army, reported to Vorontsov-Dashkov about the Alashkert Plain and Bayazit Valley:

> The Armenians intend to have their refugees occupy the lands abandoned by the Kurds and Turks in order to benefit from that territory. I consider this intention unacceptable for the reason that, after the war, it will be difficult to reclaim those lands seized by the Armenians or to prove that the property does not belong to them, as was the case after the Russo-Turkish War [of 1877–1878]. I consider it very desirable to populate the border regions with a Russian element. . . .
> It has already pleased Your Excellency to affirm my recommendation for

the immediate expulsion, to beyond the Turkish lines, of all those Kurds of the Alashkert, Diadin, and Bayazit valleys who have shown us any kind of resistance, and in the future, when these valleys enter within the bounds of the Russian Empire, to populate them with colonists from the Kuban and Don and in that way to form a Cossack region along the border.[93]

A memorandum in a similar vein was relayed to Foreign Minister Sazonov in March, 1915, by Minister of Agriculture A. V. Krivoshein:

> The success of our military activities on the Turkish front gives reason to think that, more or less, in the near future, we will have the opportunity to rectify our Caucasian boundary and to round out our possession of Asia Minor and Armenia.

After considering the agricultural prospects of the Black Sea coastal area, he continued:

> ... the other region, which falls southeast of the former, is the basin of the upper currents of the Araxes and Euphrates, which is generally called Armenia (Erzerum and Van vilayets as well as part of Bitlis vilayet). This region is mostly high above sea level and is completely suitable for Russian colonists.[94]

Wartime documents published by the Bolshevik government cast a good deal of light upon the foreign policy fostered by Nicholas II and his ministers. That the Armenians were dupes and pawns in the game of international politics is glaringly exposed in these records.[95] An exchange of notes between Sazonov and A. P. Izvolskii, ambassador to France, touches on a special mission of Hakob Zavriev. After the outbreak of war, the Armenian politician had conferred with the Russian Foreign Minister and, having received certain assurances, departed for Paris to gain the blessings of the French government for an autonomous Armenia. On May 17, 1915, Izvolskii informed Sazonov:

> Dr. Zavriev, who has come here, has presented a memorandum to me about the results of his talks in our Ministry of Foreign Affairs. In this note, among other things, it is said that Russia intends to propose to the governments that within the Turkish boundaries there be created an autonomous Armenia, under Turkish suzerainty and the protection of the three governments, Russia, England, and France. Supposedly, Armenia's lands are to encompass not only all of the Armenian provinces, except for a few border districts, but also Cilicia with a seaport on the Mediterranean Sea, at Mersin. ... The point in relation to Cilicia is, I feel, especially delicate, because France has already expressed to us her ambitions concerning the area.[96]

On the following day, Sazonov replied, "Our talks with the Armenians have had a completely academic character." [97]

The Secret Entente Agreements

While conducting "academic" talks with Dr. Zavriev, the Russian Foreign Ministry and other Entente governments were busily planning to partition the Ottoman Empire. In March, 1915, Foreign Minister Sazonov impressed upon British Ambassador George Buchanan and French Ambassador Maurice Paléologue that a lasting postwar settlement required Russian possession of "the city of Constantinople, the western shore of the Bosporus, Sea of Marmora, and Dardanelles, as well as southern Thrace up to the Enos-Midia line," and "a part of the Asiatic coast between the Bosporus, the Sakarya River, and a point to be determined on the shore of the Bay of Ismid." He requested the benevolence of Britain and France in this matter, promising in return that "the Allied governments may be assured that they will meet, on the part of the Imperial Government, the same sympathy for the realization of plans which they may have in regard to other regions of the Ottoman Empire and elsewhere." [98] Through diplomatic exchanges of the next few days, the London and Paris governments received guarantees regarding commercial privileges at Constantinople and passage through the Straits. In addition, Britain requested, among other things, that Arabia and the Holy Lands be made a separate Moslem state,[99] and France expressed the desire "to annex Syria, including the province of the Gulf of Alexandretta, and Cilicia to the Taurus Range." [100] With the provisions approved, the Constantinople–Straits Agreement was sealed on April 10, 1915.[101] Two weeks later, on April 26, other negotiations in London climaxed in Italy's promise to enter the war against Austria-Hungary in return for numerous territorial gains, primarily along the eastern coast of the Adriatic, and against the Ottoman Empire in return for the Dodecanese Islands and, in the event the Empire were partitioned, the Adalia vilayet on the mainland.[102]

Several months later, at the end of 1915, the British and French governments found it advisable to reach an understanding regarding their plans for Western Asia. The resulting Sykes-Picot accord was the most comprehensive secret agreement of the Entente. By February 10, 1916, Sir Mark Sykes, British Foreign Office Near East expert, and Georges Picot, former French Consul-General of Beirut, had arrived at a provisional arrangement that gave France "direct or indirect" rule over Lebanon, the Syrian coastline, Cilicia, and territory protruding onto the Anatolian highlands and along the Taurus Mountains as far as the Persian border. Mesopotamia, from the environs of Baghdad to the frontier of Persia and to the Persian Gulf, and the Mediterranean ports of Acre and Haifa were included within the British zone of domination. Most of the remaining areas, the desert regions, were divided into spheres of British and French influence.[103]

Now in accord, the Anglo-French partners turned to the touchy task of winning Russia's approval. Sykes and Picot traveled to Petrograd,[104] where they revealed the provisions of the agreement and assured Sazonov that no objections would be raised were Tsar Nicholas to decide to annex the vilayets of Erzerum, Van, and Bitlis and portions of the vilayets of Trebizond, Sivas, and Kharput—that is, the Armenian Plateau.[105] When Sazonov opposed the deep French penetration into Diarbekir and the Taurus lands, the British proposed a compromise whereby the eastward thrust of France would be broken at the Tigris River, in return for which Paris would be awarded the Sivas vilayet, formerly reserved for Russia.[106] A memorandum prepared by Sir Mark in support of this compromise was a contorted appraisal of the Armenians and their aspirations. He began by asserting that, because of the recent Turkish atrocities, the Armenians could never again be left under Ottoman bondage. Indeed, scores of Allied declarations to that effect had been published the world over. According to Sykes, the future of the Armenian people could be resolved in one of four ways:

1) *The formation of an Armenian government under Turkish suzerainty.* This would, however, lead either to the creation of a second Bulgaria spinning plots in the Caucasus or to an unworkable arrangement, for the Armenians could not compete (militarily) with the Kurds.
2) *The creation of an Armenian government with international protection.* This would expose the area to continual intrigue, from which Germany would benefit sooner or later.
3) *The inclusion of all Armenia in Russia.* This would burden the Tsar with a country overflowing with revolutionary syndicalists who maintained close bonds with subversives in Persia and the Caucasus. As a matter of fact, an Armenian revolutionary had once informed Sykes that the annexation of all Armenia to Russia would be ideal, for it would allow conspiratorial societies of the Caucasus, Azerbaijan (North Persia), and Turkey to unite and to create the unrest vital to their dominance.
4) *The partition of Armenia so that France would acquire former Roman or Lesser Armenia, while Russia would annex the remaining portions of the Armenian Plateau.* This was the best solution![107]

In advancing the fourth alternative, Sir Mark noted that it would encumber Russia with a minimum number of Armenians since Kurds and Lazes constituted the overwhelming majority on the Plateau. Armenia, as Sykes understood the term, would, under French administration, become the center of Armenian national sentiment. This would be especially advantageous for Russia, for, while the Armenians of the Caucasus and eastern vilayets were "anarcho-socialists," those of Lesser Armenia were imbued with religious, conservative tendencies which would foster moderate administrative ideologies. Sykes emphasized that historic Zeitun, Hadjin, Diarbekir, and Sivas had entered the domains of the Kingdom of Cilician

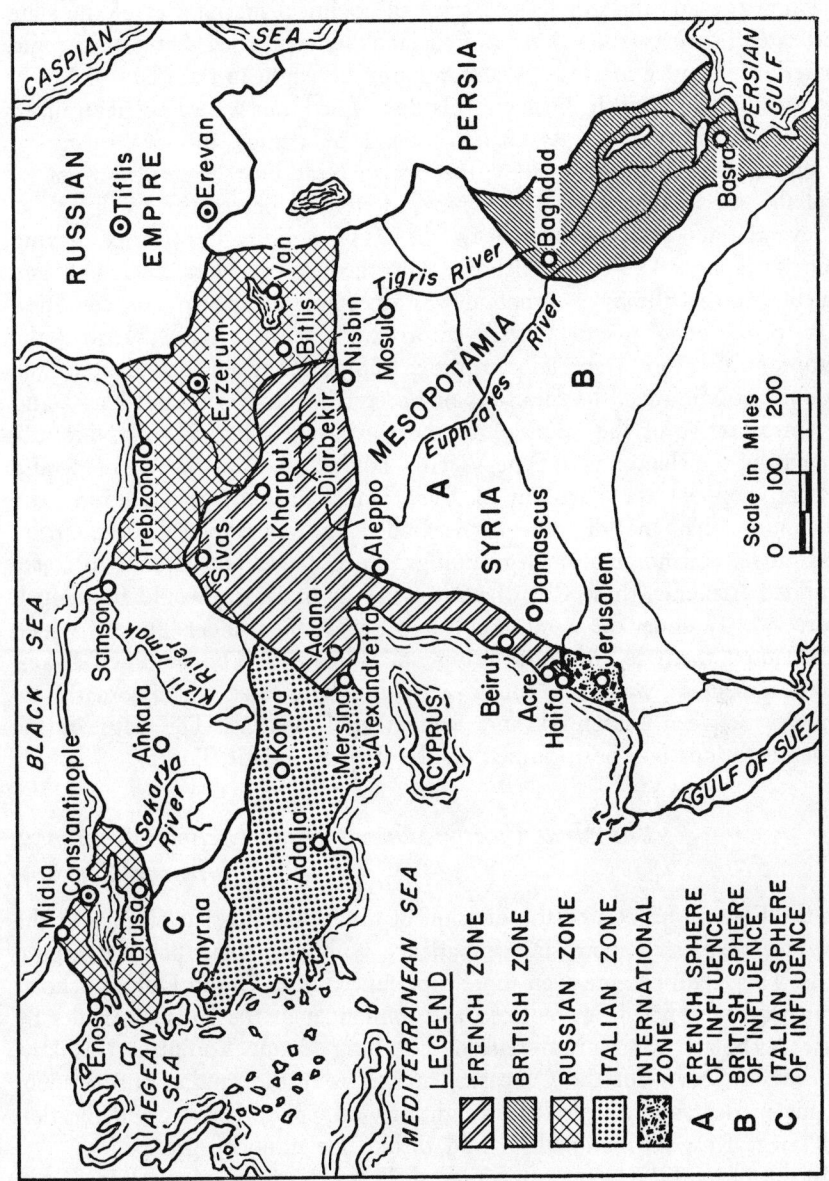

Map 6. The planned partition of the Ottoman Empire

Armenia, and that the inhabitants of those areas had little in common with the Armenians of the Plateau. If all Armenia were annexed by the Romanovs, however, the natural administrative center would be Erzerum, enabling the anarcho-socialists to seize the political mechanism of the state and extend their tyranny as far as Cilicia. Sykes concluded that Russia could spare herself much anguish by also waiving her right to the Plain of Mush, for as a part of French Armenia this den of sedition would be neutralized and the Caucasus and Azerbaijan would be denied this wellspring of revolutionaries.[108] Unfortunately, the British Near East "expert" did not reveal the source that inspired his most interesting observations.

Several days later, on March 17, the Russian Foreign Minister, having won the approval of Tsar Nicholas, informed ambassadors Buchanan and Paléologue that the Sykes proposal was acceptable in principle on condition that the Straits Agreement were enforced.[109] Sazonov then defended the compromise before a special committee composed of the President of the Council of Ministers, the ministers of Foreign Affairs, War, and Navy, and a representative of the Viceroy for the Caucasus. When N. V. Nikolskii, director of the chancellery of the Viceroy, advised that the Armenians would violently oppose the partition of their lands, Sazonov reiterated Sykes's contention that the division corresponded to topographical peculiarities and religious denominational groupings. Since it was not possible to create a united Armenia, those Christians left outside of Russia would find much more security under the wing of cultured France than under Turkey, which had caused them so much suffering and sorrow.[110] The modified Sykes-Picot agreement was then confirmed through a series of diplomatic exchanges between March 31 and September 1, 1916.[111] The flags of the Entente nations had been pinned on the map of Asiatic Turkey.

The New Viceroy, Grand Duke Nicholas Romanov, in the Caucasus

As the Entente negotiated the division of the spoils, Russian officials in the Caucasus expressed increasing impatience with Armenian political aspirations. This trend became even more pronounced after Grand Duke Nicholas Romanov, who had been replaced as commander of the Russian armies by Tsar Nicholas, was sent to relieve the ailing Count Vorontsov-Dashkov. The new Viceroy for the Caucasus, casting aside the caution and wisdom of his predecessor, adopted a straightforward policy based on dedication to "Great Russian" nationalism and dislike for minority groups.

In October, 1915, soon after Grand Duke Nicholas' arrival in Tiflis, Khatisian and Harutunian, reporting on the Armenian volunteers, informed the Viceroy that during the preceding year nearly five hundred men had sacrificed their lives and over twelve hundred had been wounded or were missing in the Russian war effort.[112] Yet the official attitude toward the Armenian units worsened, and in December the Supreme Command of the Caucasus Army ordered the National Bureau to liquidate the volunteer contingents, which would then be reorganized into regular rifle battalions of the Russian Army.[113] Implications of this change stung the political sensitivity of the Armenians, for as integral units of the regular army the new companies could be dispatched to any front. More disconcerting was the thought that motivation to eliminate the special status of the volunteer groups stemmed from tsarist opposition to a special status for Turkish Armenia. During the first quarter of 1916, over three thousand volunteers, each refusing to become a *russkii soldat*, were discharged. Andranik's large unit was completely dissolved, while the men remaining in the other groups were transferred to six Armenian rifle battalions, commanded by regular officers of the Russian Caucasus Army. Grand Duke Nicholas Nicholaevich reimposed strict censorship on the Armenian press and proscribed discussion of the volunteer movement and other vital national questions.[114]

In Petrograd, Pavel Miliukov, speaking for the liberal faction of the State Duma, questioned the Armenophobe policy of the government and reported that General Nicholas Ianushkevich, Chief of Staff and a close associate of Grand Duke Nicholas, had encouraged Kurds to adopt a sedentary way of life at the expense of the Armenians, whose families had been murdered by those same ashirets. "We are more friendly to them than to our old friends," complained Miliukov.[115] The official government view, however, was expressed in the June 27 letter of Sazonov to Grand Duke Nicholas. Discussing the future administration of Turkish Armenia, the Foreign Minister postulated that Russia might satisfy the Armenians by granting full autonomy as envisaged in the prewar reform scheme or else try to replace the Armenians with Moslems and relegate the political significance of the former to zero. But neither alternative was desirable or beneficial for Russia. Autonomy was impractical since Armenians had *never* constituted a majority in the area and, as the result of the recent tragedy, now represented barely a fourth of the total population. Under such conditions, "Armenian autonomy will result unjustly in the minority enslaving the predominant element." On the other hand, favoritism should not be shown the Moslems, for this would make conditions for the Armenians more unbearable than under the Ottoman regime and would certainly drive them to cast glances of envy at their compatriots in the French-controlled districts. "Thus, the Armenians in certain areas might exercise educational and ecclesiastical freedoms, be permitted to use their mother tongue, and be granted municipal and rural self-government. . . ." The same should apply to non-Christians.[116] Grand Duke Nicholas was in full accord as he replied on July 16 that there was absolutely no Armenian question at present and that mention of such a question should not even be allowed. Of course, the Turkish Armenians should be granted ecclesiastical and educational liberties and the opportunity for cultural development.[117] Obviously this was not "an autonomous Armenia under Russian protection."

Occupation and Administration of the Armenian Plateau, 1916

In January, 1916, General Iudenich ordered an offensive along the entire Turkish front. The IV Corps and attached Armenian groups advanced steadily toward Bitlis and Mush, while the other major Russian column struck from Kars toward Erzerum. Hasankala, gateway to Erzerum, was occupied in mid-January, but the Russians did not besiege the fortress city until the beginning of February when artillery support arrived from Kars.[118] The Third Army, having lost, in one month alone, sixty thousand men and two-thirds of its effective strength, could not with the remaining eighteen thousand troops withstand the Russian divisions, which entered Erzerum on February 16.[119] Turkish Commander Mahmud Kiamil retreated hastily toward Erzinjan, where he attempted to regroup his shabby, demoralized forces. When Kiamil was replaced in March by General Mehmed Vehib Pasha, the Russian forward lines extended from a point west of Rize on the Black Sea southward across the main routes between Erzerum and Baiburt-Mamakhatun and then curved to the southeast, passing below Mush and along the southern shore of Lake Van into North Persia.[120]

Alarmed by the Russian threat, Enver Pasha transferred the ten divisions of the Second Army to the Malatia-Diarbekir-Kharput area, the staging ground for a powerful counteroffensive.[121] This army, led by Ahmed Izzet Pasha, former Minister of War and Commander in Chief, was high-spirited after its participation in the heroic Gallipoli defense, which had foiled Entente schemes to vanquish the Ottoman Empire by capturing Constantinople.[122] Enver now planned to recover Erzerum and expel the Russians from the Plateau by a coordinated operation of the Second and Third armies, but, repeating the mistake of the Sarikamish campaign, he gave insufficient consideration to logistics. Because motored transport was totally inadequate, movement of the Second Army consumed weeks of valuable time, and because the Armenians of these regions had been deported or massacred, Ahmed Izzet's forces were deprived of essential local economic resources. Thousands of Turkish troops died of famine and exposure in this ravaged land. Furthermore, collaboration between the two Ottoman armies was impeded by formidable mountain ranges.

Understanding the purpose of the Turkish concentration, General Iudenich seized the initiative by ordering a new offensive toward Trebizond. Capture of that vital seaport by General V. Liakhov's two divisions on April 18 allowed the Russian fleet to supply and bolster the land forces more effectively.[123] Because of the Russian assault, Vehib Pasha was unable to delay his operations until the Second Army was prepared to move and therefore countered the enemy offensive with a drive aimed at Erzerum. After four

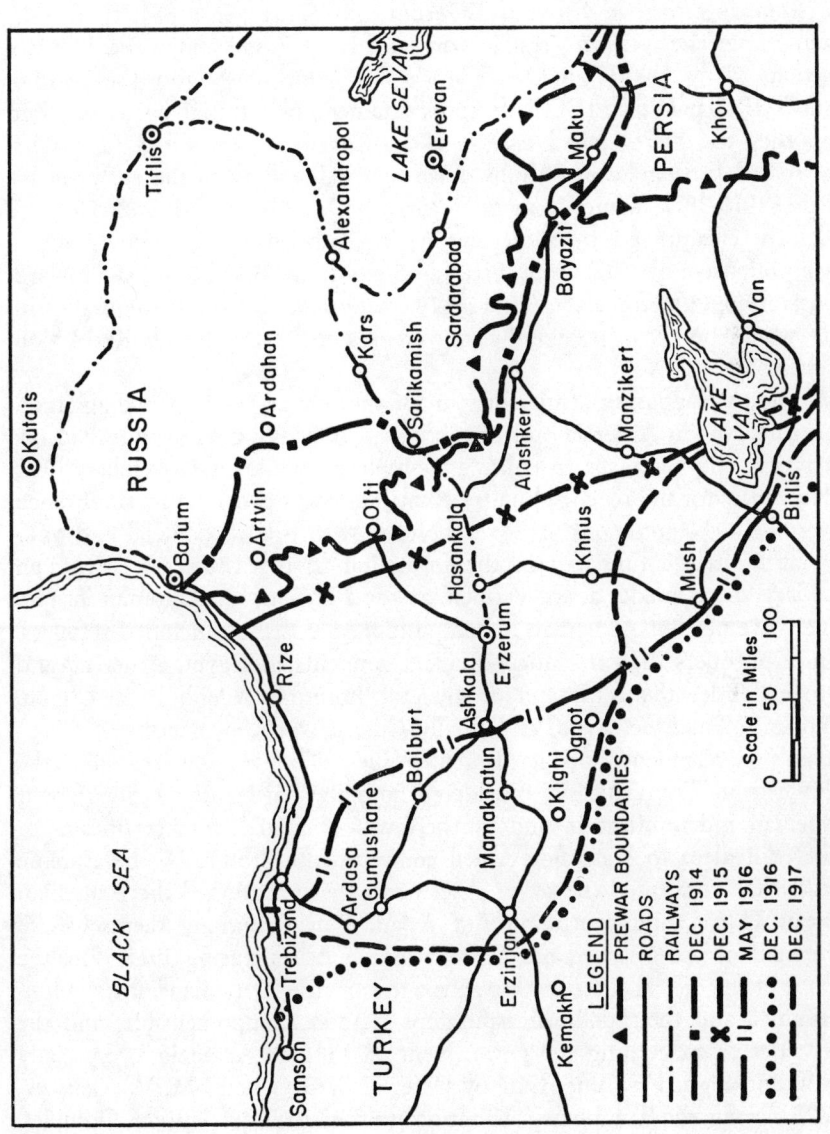

Map 7. The Caucasus front, 1914–1917

weeks of bloody pitched battles, however, he was forced to yield in the face of a hundred thousand enemy troops. The Russian I Corps, including the First Armenian Rifle Battalion, advanced over Mamakhatun into Erzinjan on July 24 and occupied the western areas of the Armenian Plateau and the strategic crossroad between Erzerum and Sivas (Sebastia).[124]

Only after the rout of Vehib's Army did Izzet Pasha attack the Russian positions along the Kighi-Ognot-Mush line. During August the Second Army's II, III, IV, and XVI [125] corps attained their initial objectives, but then they too were stalled and repelled. Enver's strategy had failed; he was spared further losses only by a Russian halt owing to the early snows of the 1916–1917 winter season.[126] Grand Duke Nicholas and General Iudenich, encouraged by successes on the Turkish front, planned for a spring offensive over Kharput, Sivas, and along the Black Sea coast toward Constantinople to force the Ottomans to capitulate. Such an eventuality in 1917 would not have been unlikely were it not for the March Revolution in Russia.

As the two opposing armies dug in for the winter, Turcophobe agitation by Armenians in America and Europe swelled. Many men already had departed for the Caucasus to enlist as volunteers, while in November, 1916, a new outlet for the revenge-hungry Armenians was provided by the French government. Negotiations of Boghos Nubar with French political and military authorities culminated in the formation of the Légion d'Orient, an auxiliary force made up of Armenians and Syrians of Ottoman origin. Ninety-five percent Armenian in composition, the Légion included refugees, former prisoners of war, and permanent residents of Egypt, America, and Europe. Under the command of General Edmund Allenby, the Légion, fighting in Palestine, Syria, and finally Cilicia, won the plaudits of Clemenceau's government and its Entente allies. The légionnaires, like the volunteers in Transcaucasia, considered both the official declarations about Armenian indemnification and the bestowal of medals and certificates of valor equivalent to bona fide Allied commitments. Ironically, the Entente already had confirmed the secret agreements that partitioned the Armenian Plateau, Cilicia, and much more of Asiatic Turkey among themselves.[127]

In light of the guarded negotiations of the Allies during 1915–1916, the change of the official Russian disposition toward the Armenians, their volunteer units, and their political aspirations is more comprehensible, and the tsarist decree concerning the government of Turkish Armenia is especially significant. Signed in June, 1916, by Chief of Staff General M. V. Alekseev, the "Rules for the Temporary Administration of Areas of Turkey Occupied by the Right of War" transformed the eastern provinces of the Ottoman Empire into a military governor-generalship for the purpose of maintaining order and assisting the war effort. The governor-general, his chief assistants, and the administrators of the various territorial subdivisions were all to be officers of rank, while minor regional posts might be filled by civilians of rank. Use of confiscated enemy goods and lands, which were at the disposal of the governor-general, was reserved solely for the military forces. "Armenia" or "Armenian" were terms not found in the decree, which was worded so that it might apply to any territory occupied in time of war.[128] In place of the autonomy envisaged by the Armenians, the eighth article of the "Rules" instructed the officials of the governor-generalship

> ... to reestablish and uphold law and order, to protect the life, honor, property, religious-civil liberties of the inhabitants, to consider all nationalities equal before the Russian government, and to guarantee these inhabitants the possibility of free and tranquil labor, on condition that they submit in toto to the suzerainty of Russia.[129]

Appointed governor-general in the summer of 1916, General Peshkov began preparations for the direct and unconditional annexation of the Armenian Plateau to the vast Romanov Empire.[130]

Renewed Russian Armenian Activity

The year 1916 was a black one for the Russian Armenians. The full extent of the blow that had struck from Constantinople to Bitlis was only then clearly comprehended. Russian occupation of Erzerum and Trebizond would have elicited delirious celebrations throughout Transcaucasia in 1914, but in 1916 it was greeted with silent interest, for the tsarist armies had occupied "Armenia without Armenians," the ideal not only of Enver and Talaat but also of the former Russian Foreign Minister, Lobanov-Rostovskii. With the tsarist order to disband the volunteer units, the Russian Armenians entered a period of shock, disillusionment, and dismay. It was the plight of the refugees which jolted them back into action. By the end of 1916, nearly three hundred thousand Ottoman Armenians had sought safety in Transcaucasia, where nearly half were destined to die from famine and disease.[131] The revitalized National Bureau, philanthropic societies, and populace attempted to mitigate the suffering of the Turkish Armenian survivors by contributing over 5 million rubles for relief activities. Armenians from every corner of the Russian Empire participated in this newest of "all-national" efforts.[132]

After several delays and obstacles, the Russian government, in May, 1916, authorized Armenian leaders to convene in Petrograd on the condition that the agenda include only relief measures. Joining the delegates from the influential Armenian communities of Moscow and Petrograd were representatives from Transcaucasia, South Russia, and the United States, as well as spokesmen for the refugees from Turkey. The spectrum was broad, for among the more than a hundred delegates were the two Armenian members of the Russian State Duma, both Constitutional Democrats; ranking Dashnakists, Social Democrats, and Social Revolutionaries;[133] several eminent scholars; and representatives of numerous philanthropic, social, cultural, and religious organizations. Officials of the Russian bureaucracy were also in attendance so that forbidden topics might not be broached. Though the tangible results of the deliberations were negligible, the Armenians were afforded a new and broader experience, the exchange of opinions by actual or potential leaders from widespread areas and with divergent ideological views.[134] During these sessions, Duma member M. S. Ajemian, who had intimate contacts in the Russian Foreign Ministry, confided to a member of Dashnaktsutiun that the Armenian political future was endangered by secret Entente plans to partition Turkey. When Dr. Zavriev, Dashnaktsutiun's most experienced international diplomat, was informed of the rumor, he dismissed it as useless gossip.[135]

Though the tsarist government proscribed discussion of certain subjects, it was compelled to recognize the inevitability of broader public participation in the defense effort, for the Russian bureaucracy had proved incapable of effectively gearing the nation to war. Among the several conferences sanctioned at the end of 1916 was the All-Russian Congress of Cities. Alexandre Khatisian, as mayor of Tiflis and president of the Caucasus Union of Cities, represented Transcaucasia at the Moscow meeting. There the future premier of Armenia spoke of the progressive role played by Russia in the Caucasus and testified that, severed from the Empire, Transcaucasia would be bled white. While in Moscow and Petrograd, however, Khatisian witnessed growing public discontent and impatience with the protracted war.[136] Yet on his return to Tiflis he reported to a secret session of the Armenian National Bureau that conditions at the front and in the government were relatively stable. Though there were indications of corruption and inefficiency, the Empire was not imperiled. Nor did he consider the reigning sovereign endangered by revolutionary organizations, for, especially since the assassination of the scoundrel Rasputin, the prestige of the Romanovs had risen. Optimistically, Khatisian stressed that the successful conclusion of war would ensure realization of the basic Armenian aspiration—autonomy for Turkish Armenia under Russian or Entente protection. Paradoxically, the Georgians were also informed of governmental stability by a member of the State Duma and leader of the Menshevik Social Democrats, N. S. Chkheidze.[137] These appraisals, made only a few weeks before the Russian Revolution, indicated that the Armenian politicians had not learned to analyze symptoms accurately. During the first months of 1917, they were not alone in that shortcoming.

V

"Hopes and Emotions"
(March–October, 1917)

The March Revolution

"NEVER, Never! has the future seemed so beautiful, victory so near, as now, in these dreamlike days of hope and emotion. . . . Thrones are shattered and chains broken, while crowned bandits tremble before the merciless judgment of the world."[1] Such, in spring, 1917, was the opinion of *Horizon,* Dashnaktsutiun's Tiflis organ and one of the most widely circulated papers in Transcaucasia. The unexpected, the seemingly impossible had occurred when the Romanov dynasty was overthrown. On March 8, thousands of angry citizens, rioting in Petrograd because of the bread shortage, were joined by mobs of striking and locked-out workers, as well as by many women commemorating a feminist-movement holiday. Thus, the spontaneous rising yearned for by the Russian Populists of the 1870's materialized in 1917. On March 12, the Volinskii Guard Regiment joined the demonstrators, now turned insurgents, and the representatives of labor and the army established the Petrograd Soviet[2] of Workers' and Soldiers' Deputies, under the chairmanship of Georgian Menshevik N. S. Chkheidze. At the same time the State Duma refused to comply with an order to disperse and instead formed the Temporary Committee, which, after appealing in vain for concessions from the Tsar, demanded his abdication. In the midst of chaos, Nicholas II abdicated on March 15 in favor of his brother Michael, who had the sense to reject the honor until the people of Russia, through a national assembly, had expressed their desires. On the same day, the Petrograd Soviet and the Duma's Temporary Committee sanctioned the creation of the Provisional Government, headed by Prince G. E. Lvov, prominent Constitutional Democrat and president of the Zemstvo Union. Among his cabinet members were P. N. Miliukov, Foreign Affairs; A. I. Guchkov, War and Navy; and A. F. Kerensky, Justice.

This government of liberals was readily accepted by Russia's wartime allies. The "Democratic Revolution" was manifest.[3]

M. V. Rodzianko, President of the Duma and its Temporary Committee, notified Grand Duke Nicholas Nicholaevich of the Petrograd events and requested that the Viceroy for the Caucasus cooperate with the acting administration by immediately eliminating press censorship. The Viceroy's assistant, Prince Orlov, in a circular dated March 16, 1917, informed all officials in the Caucasus of the political change and appealed for the maintenance of order. The Grand Duke himself issued a similar request, advising the populace to comply with the directives of Prince Lvov's Provisional Government.[4]

News of the Petrograd revolution electrified Transcaucasia. Delirious demonstrations of rejoicing burst forth from the occupied territories of Turkish Armenia to Baku and from the Caucasus Mountains to North Persia. The malicious, the "divide and rule" tsarist regime had been smashed. Sidewalk orators excited the masses by painting scenes of a promising future. Georgians, Moslems, and Armenians together proclaimed their loyalty to the Provisional Government and emphasized the firm belief that in their brotherhood was the assurance of a democratic, progressive Transcaucasian region within the new Russian Republic. The Tiflis headquarters of Dashnaktsutiun was the site of festive celebrations, as the leaders and unknowns of that revolutionary society were captivated by the emotions and hopes of the moment. There were, however, a few who did not share the enthusiasm of their comrades. Rostom Zorian, one of the party's founders and a seasoned foe of tsarism, bewailed the abdication of Nicholas II as he exclaimed to his friends, "You don't understand what is happening; revolution during the time of war! That is death for the Armenian people."[5] Events of the following months were to bear out the accuracy of that statement.

Formation of Soviets in Transcaucasia

Even before the ecstatic popular outbursts had subsided, liberal and socialist political elements responded to the possibility of greater governmental participation. On the day of Nicholas' abdication, the Tiflis City Duma recognized the jurisdiction of the Petrograd Temporary Committee and petitioned that body to proclaim a general amnesty, guarantee the inviolability of the basic rights of all citizens, and restore freedom of expression to the press.[6] A week later, the Executive Committee of the Tiflis Duma selected N. Zhordania, Georgian Menshevik theorist, A. Khatisian, mayor of the city, and D. Popov, representative of the Russian Army of the Caucasus, to assume the administrative functions of the recalled Grand Duke.[7] Similar measures to assure the continuity of local government were taken by other Transcaucasian cities as well. On March 19, the Baku Soviet of Soldiers' Deputies established liaison with the Petrograd Soviet and Provisional Government. Like action was approved on the following day by the Soviet of Workers' Deputies, which elected Stepan Shahumian, just released from exile and en route to Baku, chairman. Attesting to the irresistible popularity and awe which Shahumian commanded even among his political opponents was the fact that only four of the fifty-two voting delegates were Bolsheviks.[8]

Socialist parties in Tiflis, the Transcaucasian capital, also organized a workers' soviet, and in the following weeks local councils of workers, soldiers, and peasants sprang up in every province. To coordinate the activities of the many groups, regional bodies were instituted. All followed the formulas prescribed by the central Petrograd Soviet. Though councils emerged in the Erevan *guberniia* as well, these had little representation or influence in the regional soviets, all of which met in Tiflis. For example, during the May session of the Regional Soviet of Workers' and Peasants' Deputies, there were from the Erevan guberniia no villagers and only six workers, five of whom spoke for the railway employees of Alexandropol.[9] Usually the soviets heard reports on the "current moment," accepted resolutions demanding an "honorable peace without annexations or indemnities," and recognized the critical need for agrarian reform, but evaded the potentially explosive nationality question. While advocating unhindered cultural development and even the principle of self-determination, they circumvented the main issues by declaring that the forthcoming Constituent Assembly of Russia alone was vested with the powers to formulate a nationality policy. Especially averse to discussing the question was the Regional Soviet of Soldiers' Deputies, overwhelmingly Social Revolutionary and Russian in composition. Moreover, the military representatives, though pledging to defend the front, demanded that the Provisional Government publicly repudiate the imperialistic designs of the tsarist regime.[10]

The Position of Georgian, Armenian, and Moslem Parties

Not only the soviets but also the dominant political parties in the Caucasus affirmed their loyalty to the central government and their dedication to mutual cooperation. Noi Zhordania, as the Menshevik spokesman, condemned those who wished to raise controversial international and interracial issues. He charged that nationalism was a weapon of the bourgeoisie, which desired to seize control of the administration, and of the aristocracy, which was struggling to dispel the threats to its social and governmental monopoly. Furthermore, the welfare of the workers and peasants did not necessitate national self-rule, which the former classes coveted, but only cultural autonomy. Radically divergent from the postulations he was to assert several months later, Zhordania now rejected federation as a solution to the nationality question, for it corresponded to neither the economic nor the administrative needs of the Transcaucasians. There should be, instead, one united Russian republic based on cultural and regional autonomy.[11]

Opposing Zhordania, the weaker Georgian National Democrats demanded national political autonomy. They advocated the convocation of an assembly, elected on the basis of direct, equal, secret suffrage, with proportional representation, to draft a constitution for Georgia, which should be independent in all matters except war and peace, foreign relations, and the general budget.[12] Fascinating for the student of the Georgian Mensheviks is the process that gradually transformed these international socialists into champions of the policies outlined by their National Democrat rivals. That metamorphosis was completed in May, 1918, when the Mensheviks declared the independence of the Republic of Georgia.

The national consciousness of the Moslems of Transcaucasia was just beginning to stir. The Musavat ("Equality") party, composed mainly of intellectuals, was most representative of this developing political thought.[13] Organized during the Balkan wars when the tenets of Pan-Turanism spread rapidly throughout the Turkic-Islamic world, the organization adopted the slogan, "Turkism, Islamism, and Modernism."[14] The Moslem Democratic Party Musavat, in an introduction to its program, decried the decadence and oppression to which Moslems were now subjected, after having in bygone years dominated the expanse from the Pacific to the Atlantic oceans. The Musavatists, vowing on the Holy Koran, pledged themselves to the resurrection and unity of the Islamic world. Important points in the party's platform called for

1) unification of all Moslems, regardless of nationality or sect, to defend their mutual interests;
2) revival of subjected Moslem states and assistance to those peoples struggling for independence;
3) maintenance of liaison with societies dedicated to the progress of Moslems and all humanity;
4) improvement and development of the economic life of Moslems;
5) extension of the organization and program to all parts of Russia.[15]

The Azerbaijani Bolshevik Huseinov has accused the Musavat of becoming absorbed into the Turkic Federalistic Party, an organization of feudal landlords. The unification of the two societies in mid-1917 to form the Turkic Federalistic Party of Musavat assertedly subjected progressive Baku to the will of reactionary Ganja (Elisavetpol), stronghold of the Tatar aristocracy.[16] The similarities between the original platform of the Federalistic Party and the program of the Musavat are, however, much more striking than the differences.

Even before the merger of the two parties, the basic views of both were expressed at Baku in April, 1917, by the Transcaucasian Conference of

Moslems. Mehmed Emin Rasul-Zade, a founder of the Musavat,[17] proposed the formation of a Russian federative republic in which broad national-religious autonomy would be guaranteed. Accepting this thesis, the Conference also emphasized the indispensability of establishing an Islamic administrative center with legislative prerogatives to protect the Moslems of Russia. Echoing the decisions of many other Transcaucasian meetings, this gathering also adopted resolutions demanding peace without annexations or indemnities and pledging cooperation with all peoples of the Caucasus.[18]

The impact of the Revolution momentarily jolted the Caucasian Armenian mind so forcefully that the primary objects of concern, Turkish Armenia and the maintenance of a strong military front, were subordinated to internal regional and Russian affairs. In every *uezd* of Erevan and throughout many districts of the Tiflis, Elisavetpol, and Baku guberniias, assemblies of Armenian peasants discussed the future form of government and repeated the trite-sounding resolutions of loyalty and interracial harmony. Memory of the 1905 Revolution and the subsequent Armeno-Tatar clashes was fresh; all hoped that the unfolding democratic movement would foster better relations. While Moslems met in Baku, the Villagers' Congress of Erevan Guberniia, expressing the expectations of the Armenian peasantry, proposed

1) establishment of a democratic Russian republic;
2) adoption of the federative principle, which alone was applicable in such a multinational country;
3) governmental support for economic and cultural development;
4) internal partition of Transcaucasia into cantons and preparation by the Provisional Government of sound suggestions for provincial reorganization along geographic-economic-ethnographic lines, to be submitted to the Constituent Assembly for consideration;
5) immediate adoption of local languages by administrative-judicial organs and the appointment of officials competent in those tongues;
6) implementation within three months of a curriculum in native languages in all elementary schools;
7) institution of the zemstvo for all Transcaucasia as soon as new administrative boundaries had been determined.[19]

The Congress called upon the Transcaucasian intelligentsia dispersed throughout Russia to return to assist in regional and national endeavors.

The program suggested by the Erevan Villagers' Congress reflected the views of Dashnaktsutiun, for that organization enjoyed the same authority in the rural Armenian areas of Transcaucasia as did its allied Social Revolutionary party in the hamlets of Russia. Paradoxically, the political platform of the Armenian bourgeoisie was not radically dissimilar. Formerly belonging to the Russian Constitutional Democrat (Kadet) party or its Armenian affiliate, these middle-class representatives created in March, 1917, a separate organization, Hai Zhoghovrdakan Kusaktsutiun ("Armenian Populist Party"). With membership drawn primarily from the intellectual, professional, and industrialist classes of Tiflis, the Populists maintained close bonds with the Russian Kadets. In its initial manifesto,[20] dated April, 1917, the Zhoghovrdakan party

1) pledged support to the Provisional Government;
2) adopted the Russian Kadet program of general reforms;
3) recommended Armenian territorial-political autonomy within the Russian state;
4) suggested that the boundaries of the autonomous areas of Transcaucasia be determined along ethnic lines and that cultural freedom of the minorities in each region be guaranteed;[21]
5) proposed that the independence of the Armenian Church be restored in full and that a national clerical synod be convened to effectuate necessary religious-administrative reforms.[22]

The "Specifist" Armenian Social Democrats (not to be confused with Armenian members of the Russian Bolshevik organization) and the Armenian Social Revolutionaries found themselves in a quandary. Both favored the uncompromised unity of Russia and censured those programs suspected of fostering separatist tendencies. Yet neither organization, each composed of a small circle of intellectuals, could emancipate itself from the enthusiasm elicited by suggestions for local rule and national-cultural development. Inconsistencies and internal disagreements often neutralized the little popular influence each party commanded.[23]

The "April Theses" and the Armenian Bolsheviks

Armenian Bolsheviks, as members of the Russian organization, loyally followed the dictates of the party's Central Committee. Accordingly, during the initial days of Provisional Government rule, they were reserved in their criticism of the Petrograd administration. Assessing the March Revolution as the bourgeois-democratic interlude that, according to Marxist precepts, was to precede the proletarian victory, the Bolsheviks often collaborated or united into a single organization with their fellow Social Democrat Mensheviks. Most of the Bolshevik Central Committee, including I. V. Stalin, believed that the second stage of the revolution, the proletarian rising, was not imminent.[24] Such an appraisal was bitterly denounced by Lenin (Vladimir Ulianov) soon after his return from Swiss exile. In his famed "April Theses," Lenin condemned the duality in administration shared by the Provisional Government and the Petrograd Soviet, rejected the coalition tactic, mocked collaboration with the Mensheviks, demanded the creation of a true revolutionary socialist coordinating body, the Third

International, lashed out against continuation of the capitalistic-imperialistic war, and insisted that the time was at hand to progress to the second stage of the revolution—dictatorship of the proletariat. "All Power to the Soviets" was the slogan that best expressed Lenin's "Theses."[25] Despite opposition from many Bolshevik leaders who considered the program untimely and unorthodox, Lenin skillfully maneuvered it to adoption by the All-Russian Bolshevik Conference at Petrograd in May, 1917.[26]

The Armenian Bolsheviks, led by Shahumian, Anastas Mikoyan, Askanaz Mravian, Sargis Khanoyan, and others,[27] adapted their activities to the "Theses." But because the Mensheviks were the masters of Social Democrat politics in the Caucasus, it was the Bolsheviks who were compelled to withdraw from the already established party committees and editorial boards. Among the Bolshevik membership considerable indecision developed, for in some areas their numbers were so few that separation from the Mensheviks seemed thoroughly impractical. Nevertheless, even in local organizations such as in Kars, where there were only four Bolsheviks, the division was finally effected.[28] When Shahumian learned that the "April Theses" had been adopted, he introduced in the Baku Soviet a motion of no confidence in the Provisional Government, but the non-Bolshevik majority balked. It was Shahumian who received the no-confidence vote, resulting in his being replaced as chairman of the Soviet.[29] Undaunted, he engrossed himself in ceaseless party activity. With Mikoyan, he edited *Sotsial-Demokrat,* an Armenian-language Bolshevik newspaper with a reported circulation of four thousand.[30] In June, Shahumian was in Petrograd to participate in the First All-Russian Congress of Soviets.[31] On his return to the Caucasus, he encouraged his comrades in Tiflis, the den of Menshevism, to withdraw from the staff of *Paikar* ("Struggle") and publish their own journal, *Banvori krive* ("The Worker's Battle"). In Alexandropol, Shahumian assisted the editors of *Nor kiank* ("New Life"), the first Bolshevik-oriented Armenian newspaper to appear in Erevan guberniia.[32] The Armenian Bolshevik press attacked the nationalistic policies of Dashnaktsutiun, demanded assumption of power by the soviets, and defamed those who supported continuation of the war. The Russian soldier, impatient to return home, was exhorted to rise against his commanders.[33]

The Ozakom

While local and regional soviets sprang up throughout Transcaucasia, Prince Lvov's Provisional Government acted to fill the administrative vacuum occasioned by the dismissal and departure of Viceroy Nicholas Romanov. The Osobyi Zakavkazskii Komitet ("Special Transcaucasian Committee"), better known by the abbreviation Ozakom, was created on March 22. The collegial body was entrusted with the civil administration of Transcaucasia as well as the occupied Ottoman territories.[34] In September the prerogatives of the Ozakom were clarified and limited by a directive bearing the signatures of A. Kerensky, Minister-President of Russia, and V. Nabokov, Commissar for Caucasian Affairs. The Special Committee was

1) to be directly subordinate to the Provisional Government;
2) to constitute the supreme local administration;
3) to exercise the powers of an executive, having no legislative initiative;
4) to assume the rights and duties of the former Viceroyalty, but without jurisdiction over the North Caucasus;
5) to confer with the pertinent governmental ministries about the appointment of officials whose realm of activities included other regions in addition to Transcaucasia;
6) to manage finances by the existing procedure and to petition the government for additional appropriations;
7) to deny state support to party, professional, and other public organizations or to individuals, unless employed by the central government or the Ozakom.[35]

Serving on the Ozakom were Chairman V. A. Kharlamov, Russian Kadet; A. I. Chkhenkeli, Georgian Menshevik; Prince Kita Abashidze, Georgian Social Federalist;[36] M. Iu. Jafarov, nonpartisan Moslem; and M. I. Papadjanian, Armenian Kadet.[37] Chkhenkeli also acted as the Petrograd Soviet's envoy to the Caucasus and thus served as a liaison between the Ozakom and the socialist societies in Tiflis.[38]

Even before its arrival in Transcaucasia, the Ozakom was criticized by the Executive Committee of the Tiflis Duma. Zhordania complained that nearly all Ozakom members, especially Kharlamov and Papadjanian, were ardent nationalists and that the time was inopportune to inflame passions with the nationality question. He recommended that the Executive Committee protest to the Petrograd government about the lack of common ground between the appointed body and the masses of Transcaucasia. The Duma's Executive Committee, continued Zhordania, expressed the will of the people much more realistically.[39] But while the Georgians were partly compensated by the appointment of Chkhenkeli and the Moslems by that of Jafarov, the Armenians, represented by Dashnaktsutiun, were thoroughly dissatisfied with the choice of Papadjanian. A member of the small but influential Tiflis-Baku bourgeoisie, the Kadet party, and the Russian State Duma, he was thought unlikely to defend the interests of the Armenian peasants and workers. Moreover, when Ozakom portfolios were distributed, Papadjanian received what Dashnaktsutiun labeled an insignificant and nonstrategic department, Judicial Affairs, while Chkhenkeli was awarded the highly influential Ministry of Interior and Jafarov the Ministry of Communications.[40]

Despite the misgivings of the major political parties, many people regarded the arrival of the Ozakom on March 31 as a symbol of the new era. It was to heal the wounds inflicted by the old regime, relieve the critical shortage of food, dispel national antagonisms, reinforce the military front, and foster a new and just administration. But the expectations were too great, for the Ozakom had not the means, the will, or the support to undertake such a comprehensive program. Not only was the Special Committee restricted in operational latitude by the Petrograd government but it also was scrutinized closely by the suspicious revolutionary organizations. An uneasy truce with the soviets endured throughout the spring and summer of 1917, but by autumn the Social Democrats demanded the replacement of the Ozakom's "counterrevolutionary" members by socialists. The liberal parties could be trusted no longer.[41]

On arriving in Tiflis, where it occupied the residence of the former viceroy, the Ozakom appealed to the peoples of Transcaucasia for support and outlined its objectives:

1) to guarantee the freedom of religion;
2) to reorganize municipal self-government;
3) to institute the zemstvo system with broad local jurisdiction;
4) to provide for the election of judges;
5) to improve routes of transportation and means of communication as well as to protect the populace from brigands;
6) to study the problems of education, military service, and other vital issues.[42]

Avoiding commitments on the crucial land reform and redistribution question, the Ozakom assured the peasantry that the forthcoming Constituent Assembly would satisfy their needs, but that until that time they should desist from seizing the fields, should combat anarchy, and should perform all previously established obligations, including the payment of taxes.[43] In April, the Ozakom appointed the Temporary Committee for Land Affairs to "plan the liquidation of the last vestiges of serfdom," but in July it again warned the peasantry to respect the inviolability of the land until a final solution had been adopted, for the legal government of Russia would recognize no sequestering.[44] The unheeding villagers of Transcaucasia, like those of all Russia, refused to await the decrees of the still unconvened Constituent Assembly. As tillers of the soil, they reasoned that the land and the right to confiscate it from the parasitic gentry were theirs. In its logic and spontaneity, the peasantry of Russia was unconditionally supported only by the Bolshevik party.[45]

Not only the agrarian but also the administrative measures of the Ozakom were deemed inadequate by most of the citizenry of Transcaucasia. In April, regional branches of the Special Committee were formed, but the entrenched tsarist mechanism of government was difficult to supplant.[46] From Bayazit in Turkish Armenia came complaints that former Romanov officials continued to oppress and disarm the populace, while Kurdish tribesmen went unhindered in their raids upon Christian villages.[47] Other Armenian peasants repeatedly petitioned for the return of their property deeds, confiscated by order of General Ianushkevich in 1916. Both Moslems and Christians of the Daralagiaz district of Erevan protested the appointment of a former tsarist agent, Vekilov, to the post of uezd commissar.[48] From Shushi and Elisavetpol it was reported that the Revolution had brought no administrative changes except in the highest echelons and that the food crisis was assuming dangerous proportions.[49] Conversely, landlords and even the authorities of the Armenian Church complained bitterly to the Ozakom about the anarchy of the peasantry and the illegal seizure of land.[50] Papadjanian, alarmed by such reports, requested the governor of Erevan and the commissar of Lori to take decisive measures against the lawless villagers.[51] However, neither the Provisional Government, the Ozakom, nor even the soviets could keep pace with the demands of rural Russia so aptly expressed in the adopted Bolshevik slogan, "Peace and Land."

The First Congress of Western Armenians

Even though the Ozakom's activities—or, more accurately, lack of activities—were criticized by nearly every stratum of society, the air of freedom in Transcaucasia after March, 1917, contrasted sharply with the restrictive atmosphere of Grand Duke Nicholas' administration. Nearly three hundred thousand Turkish Armenian refugees also experienced the difference. Having found shelter in the Caucasus, they had, nonetheless, been abused and disarmed by tsarist officials, allowed no corporate societies, and usually prevented from returning to their Russian-occupied native districts unless they possessed property deeds, a requirement few could satisfy. Their primary concerns following the Revolution, unlike those of the Eastern (Russian) Armenians, remained repatriation and defense of the front. Taking advantage of the easing of restrictions, an interparty council summoned the First Congress of Western Armenians to meet at Erevan in May, 1917. Of the eighty delegates, fifteen came from occupied Turkish Armenia, twenty-seven from the refugee communities in the Caucasus, fourteen from various societies, eight from political parties, and three from the press. The remainder were invited national leaders.[52] Critical of the uncoordinated relief efforts, the Congress called for the immediate creation of a single executive body to supervise these activities. To secure the physical existence of the Turkish Armenians, revive their disrupted economy, rebuild their homeland, and provide a progressive academic and civic education for their maturing generation, a network of auxiliary societies was to be organized both in the Caucasus and in the native provinces and the cooperation of the Eastern Armenians was to be solicited.[53] The Congress entrusted the program to the Western Armenian Council, eight of whose members were Dashnakist, three Ramkavar,[54] two Hnchakist, and one Social Democrat.

The body's Executive Bureau included Vahan Papazian, Chairman, and Garo Sassuni (Dashnakists); Artak Darbinian, Hakob Ter Zakarian, and Avetis Terzipashian (Ramkavars); and Hrand Galikian (Hnchakist).[55] By autumn, considerable success was evidenced as scores of local branches were activated. The relief efforts of the Caucasian Armenian Benevolent Society, the Armenian Agrarian Society, the Brotherly Aid Committee, the Moscow Committee, and other groups were unified. A number of elementary schools were opened in Turkish Armenia to serve the refugee population that streamed homeward. At winter's end, twenty-five primary schools were in operation in the Van area alone.[56] By that time, approximately a hundred and fifty thousand natives of Van, Bitlis, Erzerum, and Trebizond *vilayet*s had repatriated.[57] This apparent Armenian resurgence had been sanctioned and supported by the Petrograd Provisional Government.

The "Provisional Government's Arrangement about Turkish Armenia"

Soon after the March Revolution, Dr. Zavriev, utilizing his close association with members of Prince Lvov's cabinet, requested that the new Russian administration nullify the 1916 tsarist act, which reeked with Armenophobe overtones.[58] The gratifying response to Zavriev's appeal was the appearance in the official organ, *Vestnik Vremennago pravitel'stva,* of the "Provisional Government's Arrangement about Turkish Armenia," dated April 26 [May 9], 1917, and signed by Minister-President Lvov and Foreign Minister Miliukov:

I. The land of Turkish Armenia, insofar as the civil administration taken over by the Russian forces is concerned, is removed from the jurisdiction of Caucasian administrative bodies and of the military authorities of the Caucasus front, and is subject directly to the Provisional Government.

II. The powers mentioned in Article I, as well as the prerogatives granted the governor-general for the administration of these Turkish Armenian regions by the temporary law of June 5 [18], 1916, are entrusted by the Provisional Government to its appointed General Commissar for Turkish Armenia.

III. The General Commissar of Turkish Armenia will have an assistant to deal with civil affairs.

IV. The General Commissar, in pursuance of a report from his assistant for civil affairs, will immediately submit to the Provisional Government his proposals for desirable additions to or changes in the June 5 [18], 1916, temporary law concerning the administration of the Turkish Armenian regions.[59]

For the realization of Armenian aspirations, the decree was an impressive victory. The occupied territories were to be removed from the arena of

Ozakom and Transcaucasian rivalries and administered directly by the central government. Though not specifically mentioned, the appointment of Dr. Zavriev as the civil assistant to the General Commissar had already been approved in Petrograd. Soon after publication of the decree, that choice as well as the selection of aged and amiable General P. Averianov to the post of General Commissar received official confirmation. The new administrators of Turkish Armenia divided the area into the provinces of Van, Erzerum, Bitlis, and Trebizond, retaining whenever possible the already established internal boundaries. Now the Armenians enjoyed a taste of officialdom, for they assumed most civil positions created by the Commissar or his assistant. The government of Van and Bitlis was without exaggeration an Armenian monopoly. Because appointed superior Russian officials rarely left Tiflis, the Western Armenians were granted even greater opportunities to gain from the ruling experience.[60] If the military front could be stabilized and the war advantageously concluded, the revival of the Plateau seemed at hand.

The Caucasus Front and American Consul F. Willoughby Smith

During the weeks that followed the March Revolution, the Caucasian front remained relatively firm. The Turkish Third Army defended a line extending from Tireboli on the Black Sea down to Kemakh, southwest of Erzinjan, while the Second Army held positions from Kighi to the southwest of Lake Van. Winter conditions claimed many victims. Lack of adequate provisions augmented the already alarming number of both sick and deserting. Fifty thousand soldiers are reported to have fled from the Third Army alone,[61] adding to the nearly half-million Turkish desertions since the beginning of the World War.[62] Third Army Commander Vehib Pasha attempted to consolidate his undermanned contingents by altering the structure of the V, IX, X, and XI corps.[63] By combining the three divisions of each into single units and by adding two other divisions, he created the I and II Caucasian corps, consisting of the 9th, 10th, 36th and the 5th, 11th, 37th divisions, respectively.[64]

To better coordinate activities along the front, Enver, in March, 1916, combined the Second and Third armies into the Caucasian Army Group, commanded by Izzet Pasha and headquartered at Kharput. Mustafa Kemal replaced Izzet as head of the Second Army.[65] Taking advantage of the Russian soldier's reluctance to fight after the March Revolution, he directed a limited Turkish advance which resulted in the reoccupation of the Bitlis region as far as Mush.[66] The rapid termination of this May maneuver was due in part to the inability of Kemal's army to conduct a major campaign. It might also be attributed to the request made to Enver by German Quartermaster General Erich von Ludendorff that further Ottoman military initiative on the Caucasus front be avoided in order to impress upon the Russian government that the German allusions to the desirability of peace were sincere.[67]

The Russian Caucasus Army, though in men and matériel superior to the Turkish forces, also suffered from the effects of the harsh winter. Even more damaging, however, was the malignancy of demoralization and unrest. Soldiers' soviets often refused to comply with orders, insulted ranking officers, and expressed impatience with the Petrograd government for not concluding immediately a "no annexations—no indemnities" peace settlement. General Iudenich, Commander of the Front since the March Revolution, was suspected of tsarist sympathies and discredited because of the Russian evacuation of the Bitlis-Mush area. With the approval of the clamoring revolutionary societies, he was replaced in June by General Przhevalskii, veteran of the 1914 Sarikamish campaign.[68]

Mustafa Kemal's maneuver at Mush and the widespread disaffection among the Russian troops alarmed the repatriated Western Armenians. On their behalf, Zavriev, Armen Garo, and members of the Moscow-Petrograd Armenian committees conferred with the Provisional Government. They attempted to convince Kerensky, first in his capacity as Minister of War and later as Minister-President, of the importance of maintaining a solid Caucasus front and requested transferral of thousands of Armenian soldiers in Europe to the Armenian Plateau.[69] The withdrawal of these men from the European theater would have no significant repercussions on that front, but their presence in Turkish Armenia would be a decisive factor in the retention of Russian-occupied territory. Kerensky accepted the proposal but attempted to effect the move inconspicuously so that this action would not establish a precedent for similar requests by other peoples of the Empire.[70] On the eve of the Provisional Government's collapse in November, 1917, an indeterminate number of Armenian troops, at least thirty-five thousand, had received orders to transfer to the Caucasus. Only several thousand, however, had actually departed. Of the latter, most traveled the primary southern routes as far as Baku, whence they were to entrain to Tiflis and the military lines.[71] Unfortunately, by that time the tensions between the Baku Soviet and most Tatars of the guberniia had reached dangerous proportions. The Moslems, controlling most of the territory through which the Baku-Tiflis railway passed, often forbade trains to proceed until they were checked for undesirable elements. As the Ottoman orientation of the Transcaucasian Moslems increased, the Armenian troops moving toward the front were labeled as undesirable and denied transit. Throughout the remainder of the year and most of 1918, this force remained stranded in Baku, where, under the direction of the Armenian Council, it assisted the city's Soviet administration.[72]

While the troops from Europe trickled into Baku, the six Armenian Rifle battalions, which had superseded the volunteer units in 1916, remained along the front lines. In North Persia, the only theater of combat during the summer, the VII Caucasus Corps, to which the 4th and 6th Armenian battalions were attached, penetrated deeper to the southwest of Lake Urmia in an attempt to link up with the British Mesopotamian forces. Again, messages of felicitation, congratulation, and praise were showered upon the Armenian participants.[73] The value of these soldiers grew in direct proportion to the increasing unreliability of the Russian troops. General Przhevalskii, commending the national units, authorized the conversion of the Armenian battalions into regiments in July, 1917.[74] The order brought a step closer to realization the Armenian aspiration to have a distinct division and ultimately an entire corps.[75]

F. Willoughby Smith, the American consul in Tiflis, was an ardent proponent of reinforcing the front with national units. To Ambassador David Francis in Petrograd, Smith often repeated his conviction that only a native Transcaucasian Christian force could successfully rebuff a Turkish offensive. On October 2 he pleaded for American material assistance,[76] and later in the month objected to Francis' position that advising the Provisional Government to send more Armenian and Georgian troops to the Caucasus was interference in the affairs of Russia.[77] On another occasion Smith warned, "No time should be wasted in carrying out these plans, particularly in regard to the Armenian troops on whom full reliance can be placed. Delay will allow the Turks to concentrate on the Mesopotamian and Syrian fronts." Hoping to prod his superior into action, the Tiflis Consul enclosed a letter from the Russian Deputy Minister of War, Boris Savinkov, who, in reference to the threatening military disintegration, had written, "Only the Armenian units are not touched and maintain combative capacity and a firm attitude." Savinkov proposed augmenting the Armenian strength to eight regiments, each with three battalions.[78] Ernest Yarrow of an American relief committee reported subsequently that in August, 1917, Smith, General Offley Shore of the British Military Mission, and G. F. Gracey, later a captain in British intelligence, conferred with Andranik, who assured them that he could raise a national force of ten to twenty thousand men. The experienced guerrilla fighter was certain that, in the event of Russian abandonment, a joint Armenian-Georgian army could defend the territory from Van to Trebizond. All four men were agreed that success of the plan was contingent on receipt of financial assistance and trained officers from the British Mission.[79] Though the project did not materialize, Smith's support for such quixotic schemes evoked the undisguised irritation of the American ambassador to Russia.

Russia in Crisis, July–November, 1917

Smith's evaluation of the crisis in Russia and on the front was accurate. The Provisional Government was unable to rule, and the socialist parties that dominated the Petrograd Soviet would not rule. Most orthodox Marxists and SR's continued to postulate that immediate assumption of full power was incompatible with the "two-stage revolution" formula. To check the mounting popular dissatisfaction with the government and to rally public support, Kerensky advocated a successful military campaign. Reminiscent of Plehve's desire on the eve of the 1904 conflict with Japan for a "victorious little war," Kerensky's exuberance lead to the July 1 offensive along the Austrian front. After initial success, however, the unenthused soldiery balked. Instead of complying with orders to advance, the military soviets engaged in polemics, attempting to define the point at which "defensive war" transformed into "aggressive war." While Russian soldiers attended mass rallies and listened to professional agitators, the German Army struck a potent blow that shattered the enemy and multiplied Russian desertions, disorder, and impatience.[80] Angry mobs swarmed through the streets of Petrograd on July 16–17, demanding that the Executive Committee of the Soviet seize power. Russia was saturated with the ineffectiveness of governmental duality; the only body considered capable of ruling, the Petrograd Soviet, was now pressured to accept the responsibility. The Bolsheviks joined the spontaneous movement and led the familiar chant, "All Power to the Soviets." Still, the Executive Committee refused to yield to the popular manifestation. Instead, the Provisional Government, releasing a rumor that Lenin was a German agent, called in loyal troops, who dispersed the demonstrators and, on July 18, destroyed the Bolshevik headquarters and the offices of *Pravda*.[81] The episode of the "July Days" forced Lenin underground and prompted another modification in Bolshevik tactics. In August, the sessions of the party's Sixth Congress no longer rang with the tumultuous cry, "All Power to the Soviets," for it was those same soviets that had just betrayed the Revolution.[82]

Prince Lvov's cabinet did not survive the "July Days." Suppression of the Bolshevik-supported demonstrations was followed by formation of a new coalition government in which Kerensky assumed the ill-fated post of Minister-President.[83] Transcaucasia again remained loyal to the Provisional Government and the Petrograd Soviet. On July 20, the executive committees of the several regional soviets at Tiflis jointly announced news of the liquidation of the "July Days" and summoned all Transcaucasians to preserve order. In their resolutions reaffirming fidelity to the central government and condemning all activities not authorized by the soviets, Social Revolutionaries, Mensheviks, Armenian Social Democrats, Dashnakists, Moslem leaders, as well as some Bolsheviks were unanimous.[84]

Although temporarily discredited, the Bolsheviks were again swept to the foreground as a result of the September affair known as *Kornilovshchina*. A feud between Kerensky and the Commander in Chief of the Armed Forces, General L. G. Kornilov, climaxed in the latter's march on the capital "to save the country from anarchy and maximalism." The General was arrested and the responsibilities of his post were assumed by the Minister-President, but the attempted putsch so alarmed Kerensky and the Petrograd Soviet that imprisoned Bolsheviks were released, armed, and enrolled in the "Red Guard," which was formed to defend the Revolution. Russia now edged leftward politically as numerous soviets passed under the spell of the Bolshevik-Left Social Revolutionary coalition. Enjoying more popular support than ever, the Bolsheviks again gave their approbation to the slogan, "All Power to the Soviets." [85] Adoption of Bolshevik-sponsored resolutions in those soviets was no longer a rarity. From Kornilovshchina to the November Revolution, the national crisis intensified; disintegration of the army, anarchic encroachments by peasants, lockouts and strikes in labor, an unbearable inflation—all contributed to the crescendo of radicalism. The Provisional Government was held responsible for the misfortunes, and because both Mensheviks and Social Revolutionaries now participated in the coalition cabinet, they, too, were implicated. The Russian people began to wonder if, after all, the Bolsheviks did not offer the correct solution to the dilemma.

Reflecting the psychology of the rest of Russia, the lands beyond the Caucasus Mountains also swayed toward the left. To combat "counterrevolution," the dictatorial Committee for Public Safety reared its head in Tiflis, while in the Regional Center of Soviets Zhordania demanded the expulsion of the Kadets from the Petrograd government and the substitution of the discredited coalition with a pure socialist cabinet. The Tiflis City Duma and most of the revolutionary societies echoed the Menshevik orator's ultimatum. On the regional administrative level, the Ozakom was now attacked openly. Numerous Soviet and Public Safety meetings, all dominated by the Mensheviks, insisted that Ozakom membership include socialist, democratic, revolutionary, but not national elements and that Mensheviks and Social Revolutionaries control the reconstituted body, whose jurisdiction, they proposed, would extend to the North Caucasus and the occupied territories of the Ottoman Empire. Representatives of Dashnaktsutiun, having little influence in these gatherings, and even Armenian Mensheviks were wary of the Georgian proposals. When Zhordania and E. P. Gegechkori advised noncompliance with Kerensky's order to disband the special safety and revolutionary committees formed during the Kornilov "mutiny," they were criticized by their Armenian political comrades, Zohrabian and Nazarov, who suggested moderation. The Armenian Mensheviks attempted to disguise their alarm about the radical tendencies of their Georgian colleagues by postulating that the preservation of revolutionary order necessitated a single administrative organ—the Ozakom. By mid-October, passions had subsided sufficiently to permit a compromise. No longer did the Mensheviks attempt to exclude from Ozakom membership the representatives of Moslem organizations or Dashnaktsutiun. Furthermore, to avoid duality in government, it was agreed that the Committee for Public Safety, campaigner against anarchy, would serve as a commission subordinate to the Ozakom.[86] The compromise remained on paper, however, for the November Revolution directed the current of Transcaucasian administrative concern into another channel.

The First Regional Conference of Caucasian Bolshevik Organizations

While the soviets of Transcaucasia discussed Kornilovshchina and reorganization of the Ozakom, two other assemblies that were to affect the course of Armenian history convened. One, the First Regional Conference of Caucasian Bolshevik organizations, was directed by an Armenian Social Democrat; the other, the Armenian National Congress, was controlled by the leaders of Dashnaktsutiun. After the "July Days," Bolshevism was discredited in Transcaucasia even more than in other parts of Russia, but the resilience of Lenin's disciples was amazing. Their local press chastised those who spoke of retribution against participants in the Petrograd demonstrations and lashed out with acerbic attacks against the leading parties of Transcaucasia. These organizations' support of coalition government, condoned by the Petrograd Soviet prior to Kornilovshchina, was ridiculed by Shahumian and his comrades. Elected to the Bolshevik Central Committee by the party's Sixth Congress, Shahumian labored with superhuman energy to place Transcaucasia under the banner of Bolshevism.[87]

When the Regional Conference of Bolsheviks convened at Tiflis on October 15, the Petrograd Soviet had already accepted several Bolshevik-sponsored resolutions.[88] Assured of victory, Shahumian exhorted the delegates to prepare for the armed revolution decreed by the party Congress. He rebuked those local Bolsheviks who continued to preach collaboration and compromise with the Mensheviks. During the five-day meeting, his resolutions proposing nationalization of the land and its immediate transferral to the peasantry were adopted.[89] As the climax to a bitter debate, and yielding to the insistence of Shahumian and Mikoyan, the Conference also agreed that the party should participate in the Constituent Assembly, if only to appease the masses and let them see for themselves that the Assembly would be unable to solve the nation's basic problems. A slate of thirty-six Transcaucasian candidates was prepared for the approaching elections; significantly, most were from the Caucasus Army, indicating the primary sphere of Communist influence.[90]

Solution of the perplexing nationality question was of vital concern to the peoples of Transcaucasia. The resolution of the Conference

1) condemned the Provisional Government's perpetuation of tsarist "divide and rule" schemes in the border lands;

2) repeated the claim that only the Bolsheviks could solve the nationality question;
3) denounced the Armenian and Georgian bourgeois-nationalist parties for endeavoring to weaken the bonds between the Russian proletariat and the masses of Transcaucasia;
4) pledged active opposition to suggested bourgeois programs;
5) chastised the Petrograd rulers for not proclaiming the right of all peoples to self-determination up to complete separation from Russia;
6) favored local cultural autonomy, education in native languages, a regional assembly (*seim*), but opposed administrative divisions based on nationality;
7) qualified the party's position on self-determination by asserting that separation from Russia or establishment of a federative state was not in the interest of the masses;
8) insisted that the inhabitants of Western (Turkish) Armenia, Lazistan, and Persian Azerbaijan were alone to determine the form of government for those areas, in whose reconstruction all nations should participate;
9) proclaimed that only with the assistance of the Russian proletariat could these goals be attained.[91]

In such a declaration, one could seek and find whatever he desired.

In addition to adopting resolutions, the Conference heard reports of party activity in the several provinces. Anastas Mikoyan announced that his Haghpat-Alaverdi district of Lori was the only area in which the landless Armenian villagers had accepted the leadership of Social Democracy. Unfortunately, however, the claws of Dashnaktsutiun were implanted deeply into the flesh and mentality of most Armenian peasants.[92] Then, before adjourning, the delegates elected a Regional Committee to direct the activities that would culminate in armed rebellion. The international composition of that body—S. G. Shahumian, P. A. Japaridze, F. I. Makharadze, G. N. Korganov, M. D. Orakhelashvili, M. G. Tskhakaia, H. Nazaretian, A. A. Mravian, I. T. Feoletov, and S. I. Kavtaradze—adequately reflected the Bolshevik stand on the nationality question.[93] Immediately after the Conference, Shahumian traveled to Alexandropol, where he urged the large military garrison and many railway workers to turn their weapons against the perfidious Petrograd government. Then he hurried to Baku to direct the party's efforts in the most advanced proletarian and industrial center of all Caucasia.[94]

The Russian Armenian National Congress

The Bolshevik conference was short and calm in comparison to the charged, boisterous sessions of the Armenian National Congress, which opened on

October 11 in the Artistic Theater of Tiflis. Initiative for the meeting belonged to the National Bureau, which in April had invited civic leaders, the interparty council, and representatives of the former volunteer units to consider the situation in Petrograd and at the front. All agreed that a broader assembly of Russian Armenians should convene in Erevan within two months to express more democratically the national will. The interparty council was charged with supervising the elections, which were to be based on equal, secret, direct suffrage and proportional representation, with one delegate per ten thousand of the Empire's two million Armenians.[95] Plans to implement democratic procedures were overly optimistic, for soon it was learned that the holding of elections on the stated principles was a near impossibility in the existing chaotic conditions of Russia. Moreover, the opponents of Dashnaktsutiun complained that in direct elections their numbers would be so insignificant that the proposed meeting would simply evolve into a party gathering rather than a national congress.[96] Therefore, democratic ideals gave way to imposing realities. The established method of selecting representatives from the various cultural, economic, professional, benevolent, religious, and political societies was employed once again.[97] Not only election procedures but also the final selection of the meeting site was determined by actualities. True, Erevan was the heartland of the Armenian provinces, but this overgrown village with dirty, winding streets did not offer the comfort, convenience, or attraction of Transcaucasia's largest and most beautiful city, Tiflis. Rural Armenia yielded once again to the Armenian-dominated capital of Georgia.

Over two hundred delegates from Armenian communities scattered throughout Russia presented their credentials at the opening session. Political affiliation was as follows:[98]

Dashnakist	113
Populist	43
Social Democrat	9
Social Revolutionary	23

The Congress, which lasted a fortnight, was the most comprehensive Eastern Armenian gathering since the Russian conquest of Transcaucasia. Only the Bolsheviks were missing, although they had sent a statement of their views.[99] They had refused to participate, repeating the declaration of their party's Tiflis committee, which alleged that the Congress would be a bourgeois-clerical assembly, ignoring the interests of the workers and peasants, and that, in its counterrevolutionary capacity, it would intrigue to deceive the Armenian people and to prolong their subservience to capitalism and imperialism. The attempt to solve current problems through a national organization was treachery, for only the Russian and Caucasian proletariat and revolutionaries striving together could attain that goal. The Bolsheviks appealed to the Armenian masses to deny support to the Congress.[100] Of a similar nature was the proclamation of the Temporary Executive Committee of *Spartak,* a Marxist youth organization, which cursed Dashnaktsutiun and the Populists for attempting to estrange the Transcaucasian peoples from one another.[101] In 1917, however, the popular influence of the Armenian Bolsheviks was so slight that their absence from the National Congress seemed to perturb no one.

At the inaugural session, the chairman, Stepan Mamikonian, active civic leader from the Moscow Armenian Committee, called for cooperation among the numerous politically opposed delegates in order to formulate a workable national policy. On the following day, Simon Vratzian, member of Dashnaktsutiun's Bureau, the party's supreme body, analyzed the situation in Russia. Drawing attention to the general demoralization, anarchy, and economic and military collapse, he proposed that a strong central coalition government liquidate the major source of evil—war. But he added that although "war to a decisive victory" was folly, peace without the agreement of the other Entente members was impossible. Therefore, until the workers of Western Europe could compel their respective governments to halt the bloodshed, the peoples of Russia would support only a "defensive war."[102] Obviously the views of Dashnaktsutiun on war and peace were identical with those expressed by most soviets throughout the spring and summer. Representatives of the other organizations agreed in essence with this policy, but, while accepting coalition, the SD's and SR's chastised the bourgeois parties of Russia and their Armenian counterpart. Kristapor Vermishian of the Populists denied the bourgeois character of his party and testified to its "classless" nature. Supporting the proposal for a strong coalition government, he reminded his colleagues that coalition necessitated compromise and that the moderate elements should not be expected to make all the concessions.[103]

Turning from the problems of all Russia to the issues particular to Transcaucasia, the majority of the delegates favored the program presented by Dashnaktsutiun, which proposed

1) to organize without delay the democratic Armenian elements;
2) to foster harmonious relations with the Georgian and Moslem workers, for regional progress and peace depended on international cooperation;
3) to revise the administrative boundaries of Transcaucasia according to geographic, ethnic, and economic factors and then to adopt the zemstvo;
4) to create within Armenian life a representative national body with membership from all political-social currents but in proportion to the popular support enjoyed by each.[104]

There was little to dispute in the first three points, but the fourth was the subject of much oratory and private negotiation.

Records of the Congress indicate that the Ozakom was the primary topic of at least three sessions. All agreed that Transcaucasia had been given "rulers" but not "rule." Hambardzum Arakelian, a Populist, proposed that the Ozakom be reorganized into a seven-man Kadet-socialist coalition with four members appointed by the central government and one each by the Georgians, Armenians, and Moslems of Transcaucasia. Nikol Aghbalian, a theoretician of Dashnaktsutiun, accepted the suggestion but insisted that the Armenian representative should express the will of the people. The barb was aimed at the Kadet Papadjanian, the current member. Aghbalian regretted that the Ozakom had become the arena for the intensification of Transcaucasian rivalries and jealousies. He accused the Georgian Mensheviks of pursuing nationalistic aims under the guise of socialism, as was apparent when, during discussions on revamping the Ozakom, Zhordania and his followers, asserting that Dashnaktsutiun was not a true socialist society, attempted to exclude it from membership. If the Mensheviks had their way, the Armenian people would be deprived of legitimate representation. According to Aghbalian, the Armenians were not above reproach, for the reawakening of their national consciousness lagged behind that of their neighbors. The historic causes for that shortcoming could be summarized as follows:

1) The Armenian people were not a compact element in their native lands but lived in the midst of other peoples, each with distinct aspirations. Constant friction with those neighbors had hindered Armenian progress.
2) The Armenian tradition of government had been severed in the eleventh century, after which no social class coveting political domination existed. Conversely, the Georgians and Tatars had aristocratic elements which, down to the present, were accustomed to rule and received the patronage of the Russian government.
3) Living for centuries under foreign lords, each more abhorrent than the other, the Armenians had come to associate government with evil. Even when presented the opportunity to rule, they shunned the responsibility and suspected any of their own people who attempted to rise in the administrative hierarchy. The psychology of the Armenians, in sharp contrast with that of the Georgians and Tatars, was that of a subject people.
4) The Armenian intellectuals had not been concerned with Transcaucasian affairs, for they had concentrated all their attention on the problem of Turkish Armenia. Moreover, imbued with strong nationalistic tendencies, they had not produced individuals of all-Russian and international significance. Again, the Georgian Mensheviks stood in contrast.
5) The recent massacres and flight of the Ottoman Armenians detracted further from interest in Russian administrative and revolutionary activity, and the struggle for physical self-preservation hampered the development of national consciousness and unity.[105]

The Congress mirrored the anarchy that had engulfed all Russia when the Menshevik, Simeon Pirumian, in his condemnation of the Ozakom, also vilified Dashnaktsutiun and its "bandit chiefs." The commotion in the Artistic Theater nearly disrupted the National Congress, but the situation was saved when Aramayis Erzinkian apologized for the unkind epithets of his Menshevik comrade and conceded that the Armenian representation on the Ozakom properly belonged to Dashnaktsutiun. Papadjanian took the podium to defend his activities and to attribute the deficiencies of the Ozakom to the lack of cooperation from the local revolutionary societies. Nonetheless, he agreed that the new Ozakom should be a socialist body, for conditions had so deteriorated that only the socialists could possibly induce the masses of Transcaucasia to respect law and order.[106]

During its final session, the Congress selected a thirty-five-member National Assembly to act as the legislative body for the Armenians of Russia, and a smaller body of fifteen members, the National Council, to assume the executive functions.[107] Distribution of places on the Council according to political affiliation caused considerable discord until a compromise allotted six seats to Dashnakists, two each to SR's, SD's, and Populists, and three to nonpartisans. Ascribing great importance to the Council, the Armenian political parties selected their elite to serve:[108]

Dashnaktsutiun	Avetis Aharonian (Chairman)
	Aram Manukian
	Nikol Aghbalian
	Ruben Ter Minasian
	Khachatur Karjikian
	Artashes Babalian
Populist	Samson Harutunian
	Mikayel Papadjanian
Social Democrat	Misha (Mikayel) Gharabekian
	Ghazar Ter Ghazarian
Social Revolutionary	Haik Ter Ohanian
	Anushavan Stamboltsian
Nonpartisan	Stepan Mamikonian
	Tigran Bekzadian
	Petros Zakarian

As the Russian political crisis deepened, the role of the National Council increased. Assuming the functions of an unofficial Armenian government through the turbulent months from November, 1917, to May, 1918, this was the body destined to proclaim the independence of Armenia.

Proposals for the Provincial Reorganization of Transcaucasia

Prior to adjournment, the National Congress had also considered the administrative redivision of Transcaucasia. Stepan Kamsarakan, a nonpartisan, proposed that the most satisfactory solution would be the creation of a large

Transcaucasian Armenian province comprising fifteen counties, ten with absolute Armenian majorities. The province, with its administrative center at Erevan, would have 2,033,000 inhabitants, of whom 60 percent, or 1,220,000, would be Armenian. This territory would include, besides the existing Erevan guberniia, the contiguous Lori-Akhalkalak districts of Tiflis, the mountainous part of Elisavetpol, and a portion of the Kars *oblast*.[109] It is significant that the area proposed by Kamsarakan corresponded almost identically to that segment of Transcaucasia claimed by the subsequent Armenian Republic. But even this ideal plan, annexing to the Erevan guberniia only those districts that seemed advantageous, was a precarious venture, for a third of the inhabitants of the new province would be Moslem, while nearly a half-million Transcaucasian Armenians, as well as the centers of Armenian cultural, economic, and political life, Baku and Tiflis, were to be excluded.

Statistical experts Gevorg Khatisian[110] and Avetik Shahkhatuni, though acknowledging the desirability of a single Armenian province, reasoned that the proposed solution would elicit immediate opposition and suspicion from the central government and the other peoples of Transcaucasia. Khatisian advocated instead a plan to form three Armenian districts, Gandzak, Shirak (Alexandropol), and Erevan, together encompassing the same areas suggested by Kamsarakan. In advancing the three-province formula, which had been adopted by the regional meeting of Dashnaktsutiun at the end of 1916, Shahkhatuni argued that this solution would benefit the other Transcaucasian peoples as well. Russian governmental statistics for 1916 revealed that fewer than 44 percent of the Tiflis guberniia inhabitants were Georgian. If, however, the province were relieved of its southern districts, Lori-Akhalkalak, the Georgian preponderance would rise to 68 percent. Moreover, since the inhabitants of the mountainous areas of Elisavetpol were nearly 70 percent Armenian while those of the plains were 90 percent Moslem, the separation of these two contrasting sectors was not unjust. If, as was logical and equitable, the plains of Elisavetpol were united to the Baku province, from which they originally had been shorn, the population of "Tataria" would be 76 percent Moslem.[111]

SD and SR delegates to the Congress loudly protested this plan, for it would engender added Georgian and Moslem antagonism. A more realistic settlement was considered to be the division of the entire Caucasus into cantons, all subject to a single administrative center, Tiflis. Erzinkian accused the authors of the single- and triple-province projects of chauvinism and separatist inclinations.[112] Thus the Armenian politicians, dissonant concerning the details, were unanimous on the need for some type of provincial reorganization and redistribution. The complications inherent in the formation of national-territorial subdivisions stemmed from the massive intermixture of indigenous populations. This pertained particularly to the Moslems and Armenians, as shown by 1916 Russian statistics:[113]

Province	Total population	Turco-Tatar		Armenian	
Tiflis[114]	1,473,000	106,000	7.0%	411,000	28.0%
Baku	1,290,000	877,000	68.0%	120,000	9.3%
Elisavetpol	1,276,000	783,000	61.4%	419,000	32.8%
Erevan	1,120,000	374,000	33.3%	670,000	59.7%
Kars	404,000	130,000 [115]	33.2%	125,000	31.0%

Though the topic of internal boundaries and zemstvo introduction had been discussed in conferences summoned by Count Vorontsov-Dashkov and Grand Duke Nicholas, no governmental action had been taken. The issue was revived by the Provisional Government in the summer of 1917, when delegates from all Russia gathered in Petrograd to arrange for the elections to the Constituent Assembly. Taking advantage of the presence of many Transcaucasian leaders, Boris Veselovskii, director of the Interior Ministry department dealing with regional affairs, requested that, before leaving the capital, Georgian, Armenian, and Moslem representatives propose a plan on the administrative-territorial reorganization of their provinces.[116] A prominent Georgian professor, Zurab Avalov, presided over the committee meetings. There, Ramishvili and Zhordania, announcing that the Social Democrat party was a champion of self-determination, conceded that Lori and Akhalkalak rightfully should enter the Armenian zemstvo areas. Despite the objections of the Georgian National Democrats, who insisted that at the time of the 1783 Russo-Georgian treaty the territories in question were either part of the Georgian realm or were promised to King Iraklii by Tsarina Catherine, the general outlines of the Armenian scheme to form relatively large zemstvo districts were approved by the Ministry of Interior and forwarded to the Ozakom for consideration and approval.[117]

In Tiflis, the Ozakom appointed a fifteen-member committee, with five men from each of the three dominant peoples, to finalize the project. The three sessions held by the committee were presided over by Zhordania, Chkhenkeli, and Ramishvili, respectively.[118] Speaking for the Moslems, Akber Sheikh-ul-Islamov agreed that administrative-territorial alterations were an indication of progress but insisted that the ideal solution would be the creation of small cantons. In that event, four of Erevan's seven districts would be predominantly Moslem. This system offered Moslems the best security, for the Armenian areas would be limited in size and would be surrounded and neutralized by Islamic cantons.[119] Turco-Tatar control of all southern and eastern Transcaucasia would thus be guaranteed. No agreement was reached between the Moslem and Armenian delegates, but the Armenians were gratified that the Mensheviks had reconfirmed the decision to follow the ethnic principle in Lori-Akhalkalak, where less than 10 percent of the population was Georgian.[120] Again, no official action was taken, since, before a final solution could be worked out and endorsed by the

Ozakom, the Provisional Government was overthrown and the Bolshevik Soviet government inaugurated. The discussions and arguments of Armenians, Georgians, and Moslems during 1916 and 1917 were not useless, however, for they clarified the territorial aspirations of each people, who, unknowingly, were racing toward independence. When that momentous event occurred, the Tatars and Georgians were still those who had, and the Armenians those who wanted.

Indeed, the months March through October, 1917, were permeated with Armenian hopes and emotions. The Revolution was acclaimed by all Transcaucasia, which began its organizational activities at a phenomenal rate. The soviets, the Ozakom, the political conferences, the national sessions—all added to the gradual maturation of the Armenian mind. Though beset by internal rivalries and entangled in misunderstandings with their neighbors, the Eastern Armenians were more active and organized than for nearly a millennium past. Their aspirations were relatively clear: to develop freely in the political, social, economic, and cultural realms while remaining an integral member of the federated Russian state. For Western (Turkish) Armenia, autonomy, or perhaps unification with the Armenian region of Transcaucasia, was the envisaged solution. The March Revolution eliminated the tsarist restrictions and gave the Armenians the opportunity to gain valuable experience in the administration of occupied Turkish Armenia. Their hopes seemed closer to realization than ever before.

Yet the emotions of March–October, 1917, had not all been elicited by joy and expectations, for the Revolution brought with it many perils. Political chaos threatened the security of the entire state, while demoralization among the exhausted soldiers particularly jeopardized the Armenian hopes tied to the emancipation of Turkish Armenia and the progress of Transcaucasia. Every event in Petrograd sent out its radiating ripples. By October, 1917, the ripples had become waves and the Armenians, still filled with hopes and emotions, were swept by the tide toward a new mark on their way to independence.

VI

The Bolshevik Revolution and Armenia

Revolution, the Sovnarkom, and Self-Determination

THE INABILITY of Kerensky's Provisional Government to cope with the military, economic, and social crises was climaxed by the Bolshevik Revolution on November 7, 1917. The so-called Democratic Conference and Pre-Parliament, which had been assembled in the preceding weeks, also failed to satisfy the demands of the war-weary soldiers and the land-hungry peasants. Determined to remain loyal to democratic procedures during such unpropitious times, the moderate socialist elements reserved for that illusionary panacea, the Constituent Assembly, all major policy decisions. Meanwhile, Lenin gathered enough party support to convince the Central Committee on October 23 that the time for the uprising was at hand. Against the bitter opposition of Lenin's old associates, L. B. Kamenev and G. E. Zinoviev, who argued for victory through legal means, the meeting declared:

> So, recognizing that armed insurrection is inevitable, and that the time is quite ripe for it, the Central Committee proposes to all Party organizations to be guided by this and solve all practical problems . . . from this standpoint.[1]

The Bolshevik-Left Social Revolutionary coalition of the Petrograd Soviet was prepared to follow Lenin's directives. On November 2, L. D. Trotsky was named to command the Military Revolutionary Committee, which intensified antigovernmental agitation among the Petrograd garrison. The great arsenal within the Peter-Paul fortress was occupied by Trotsky's men on November 5. Kerensky responded by declaring a state of siege on the following day, but the Pre-Parliament, while denouncing the insurrection, nonetheless indicted him for the critical state of affairs. Belatedly, the socialists demanded immediate transferral of the land to the peasantry, and decisive measures to end Russian involvement in the war. Such resolutions, however, were worthless, for within a few hours the Bolshevik militia had occupied the strategic points in the capital and shortly after midnight moved into the Winter Palace, Provisional Government headquarters. Kerensky, in search of loyal soldiers, had already fled the city. By the morning of November 7, news of the nearly bloodless Bolshevik coup was broadcast to the world.[2]

The Second All-Russian Congress of Soviets convened that same day. In contrast with the First Congress in June, it was controlled by the Bolshevik-Left SR coalition. The assembly called for a "just and democratic" peace without annexations or indemnities and repudiated secret diplomacy, especially the Entente agreements apportioning the spoils of war.[3] On November 8 the new cabinet, Council of People's Commissars (Sovnarkom), was confirmed, with Lenin as Chairman, Trotsky as Foreign Commissar, and Stalin (I. V. Djugashvili) as Commissar for Nationalities.[4]

Among the first acts of the Sovnarkom was the publication of the "Declaration of Peoples' Rights," which guaranteed equality to all peoples in Russia, offered each nationality self-determination up to and including complete separation and establishment of independent states, abolished all privileges and restrictions based on religion or nationality, and promised all minority groups of Russia unhindered development.[5] Apparently Lenin, by subscribing to "national self-determination," had altered the orthodox Marxist tenet that nations and nationalities were vestiges of the *ancien régime* and would be swept away by the formation of an international army of working peoples. It has been asserted that Lenin utilized the principle of self-determination whenever it might further the goal of world revolution or lead to the destruction of anti-Soviet governments. Nationalism, long the object of Bolshevik curses, now was fostered in order to win the confidence of the oppressed minorities and to enervate the opponents of communism.[6] While offering the peoples of Russia the right to secede, Lenin nevertheless consistently advocated the unity of all the former Romanov Empire.

The views of the Commissar for Nationalities were not so dichotomous. Bluntly criticizing the borderlands for severing their bonds with Soviet Russia, Stalin contended:

> All this points to the necessity of interpreting the principle of self-determination as the right to self-determination, not of the bourgeoisie, but of the working masses of the given nation. The principle of self-determination should be a means in the struggle for socialism and should be subordinated to the principles of socialism.[7]

His views could not be misconstrued when he declared, "So, the interests of the peoples masses dictate that the demand for secession of the border regions at this stage of the revolution is profoundly counterrevolutionary."[8]

With no qualms, the Commissar championed the cleavage of India, Arabia, Egypt, Morocco, and other colonies from the European imperialists but steadfastly rejected the separation of the Russian border provinces. The first would bring liberation from oppression, whereas the latter would result in capitalistic enslavement.[9]

It is clear that Bolshevik success stemmed partly from the sagacity to adapt to the psychology of the people. In 1917–1918 the masses cried not only for peace and bread, but also for the scarcely understood right of self-determination. Carried to the extreme, that principle could have led to the complete dissolution of the Empire, so painstakingly pieced together during the preceding centuries. By making the right of self-determination contingent upon what would benefit "the working masses," however, the Sovnarkom had contrived a formula that allowed for proclaiming democratic ideals while resisting separatism. "Voluntary union" was the Leninist motto, but most non-Russians were not captivated by the phrase. Stalin later found it necessary to admit that the Soviet government had been incapable of counteracting "the inevitable process of temporary disintegration."[10]

The Armenian interpretation of self-determination was quite clear—regional autonomy for Transcaucasia and national-territorial autonomy for Turkish Armenia. The most recent modification of these gradually developed concepts was the widespread conviction that the latter territory should not, in any way, revert to Ottoman suzerainty. The Provisional Government's administrative arrangement for Turkish Armenia indicated that the despised Ottoman would never again be permitted to set foot on the Plateau. The November Revolution thus compelled Armenians on both sides of the 1914 border to appraise the nationality policies of the Bolsheviks. Naturally, there was no Armenian proclivity toward independence, for separation under the existing conditions was equivalent to self-destruction. Only in a federated Russia could the provincial boundaries of Transcaucasia be redrawn to correspond to the Armenian notion of self-determination. More important, only with the protection of powerful, united Russia could the fruit of victory in Turkish Armenia be retained and autonomy assured. Consequently, the leading Armenian political currents were permeated with skepticism toward certain Bolshevik declarations, especially those which, in the name of self-determination, demanded Russian evacuation of the occupied portions of Persia and the Ottoman Empire.

Lenin's Declarations about Armenia

In articles contributed to *Pravda* in the spring of 1917, Lenin painted a dismal picture of the suffering in Turkish Armenia, the victim of imperialistic rivalries. Members of the Provisional Government, especially Foreign Minister Miliukov, were attacked for advancing plans to annex the area and for continuing tsarist practices toward such subject peoples as the Poles and the Armenians.[11] In May, Lenin complained that "the Russian capitalist government holds part of Galicia, Turkish Armenia, Finland, the Ukraine, etc."[12] He also asserted:

> The annexation of Belgium, Serbia, etc., will not cease being annexation because the German Kadets have replaced Wilhelm, just as the annexations of Khiva, Bukhara, Armenia, Finland, the Ukraine, etc., did not stop being annexations by the substitution of Nicholas by Russian Kadets, the Russian capitalists.[13]

During the same month, at the May, 1917, Bolshevik conference that called for "All Power to the Soviets," Lenin again accused Lvov's cabinet of selfishly continuing the imperialistic, predatory war, and assailed the government's confirmation of the shameful tsarist secret treaties, which "promise the Russian capitalists freedom to rob China, Persia, Turkey, Austria, etc."[14] While discussing the nationality question, he exclaimed, "if the Soviet seizes power tomorrow . . . we shall then say: Germany, out with your armies from Poland; Russia, out with your armies from Armenia—otherwise, it will be a lie."[15]

The voice of Lenin reached relatively few at the Bolshevik conclave, but several hundred delegates from all parts of Russia heard him on June 22 as he addressed the First Congress of Soviets. Execrating the Entente annexationist agreements, he shouted:

> If we publish these treaties and clearly say at meetings to the Russian workers and the Russian peasants, especially in each remote little village: this is what you are fighting for, for the Straits, for the retention of Armenia, then everyone would say: we do not want such a war.[16]

Proceeding a step further, Lenin made the following suggestion:

> There is our army on the Turkish front; its size I do not know. Let us assume it is about three million. If this army, now kept in Armenia and carrying out annexations which, while preaching peace without annexations to other people, you tolerate, even though you have the power and the authority—if that army turned to this program, if it made Armenia into an independent Armenian republic, and gave it the money that is being taken from us by the Anglo-French financiers, that would be much better.[17]

Such statements elicited a negative response from most Armenian leaders. Kadets and Populists, Social Revolutionaries and Mensheviks, added their voices to those of the Dashnakists, who ridiculed the "adventuristic" maneuvers of the Bolsheviks. If Russian armies were withdrawn, there would not be "an independent Armenian republic," but a Turkish offensive into Transcaucasia. Soviet historian B. A. Borian has contended that, though realizing evacuation would place the Armenians before the threat of new massacres, Lenin was more intent on inciting international revolution. Retention of Ottoman territory would expose the Soviet government to the charge of hypocrisy. Only by renouncing pretensions to Armenia could Russia convince the Asian peoples of her sincere desire for peace without annexations. Assured of that, the oppressed masses of the East would unite with the Soviets to strike a deadly blow against the imperialistic, colonialist governments of the Occident.[18] In this light, the December 3 Sovnarkom "Appeal to the Moslems of Russia and the East" is particularly significant. One of the pledges reads, "We declare that the treaty for the partition of Turkey, which was to deprive her of Armenia, is null and void." [19]

As the prestige of Bolshevism increased in many parts of Russia, Lenin continued to hammer forth his demands. A month before the November coup, in his "Aims of the Revolution," he explained:

> Then it is our duty immediately to satisfy the demands of the Ukrainians and the Finns, to guarantee them, as well as all other nationalities in Russia, complete freedom, including freedom to secede, and to apply the same to the *whole* of Armenia, undertaking to evacuate it as well as the Turkish lands occupied by us, etc.[20]

This position was clarified two weeks later:

> Having assumed power we would naturally recognize immediately this right [of separation] of Finland, the Ukraine, Armenia, and any other nationality which has been oppressed by tsarism (and by the Great Russian bourgeoisie). But we, on our part, do not at all desire that separation. We want the largest possible state, the closest possible union, the largest possible number of nations who are neighbors of the Great Russians. . . .[21]

Of the Transcaucasian peoples, only the Armenians were mentioned specifically in these representative statements. Even to the Bolsheviks, the future of the Armenians seemed to warrant special consideration. It was indeed enigmatic that the cherished goal of the Armenian revolutionaries—autonomy and self-determination—was being offered by the Bolsheviks but now spurned and suspected by the veterans of the Armenian liberation movement.

The Decree "About Turkish Armenia"

Upon its formation, the Sovnarkom took measures to free Russia from the imperialistic war and to recall the occupying armies from Persia and the Armenian Plateau. The term "self-determination" was utilized repeatedly in both instances. Armenian Bolsheviks hailed the Leninist declarations. For half a century, European diplomacy had only added to the oppression and misery of the Ottoman minorities, whereas the Sovnarkom now repudiated secret, traditional diplomacy and offered self-determination instead. But even in their praise, the Armenian followers of Lenin were unable to disguise their concern completely. Soon after the November Revolution, Lenin, at his Smolny Institute headquarters, received Vahan Terian, youthful, talented poet, and Sargis Lukashin, party activist. After preliminary discussions, Lenin requested that his comrades prepare a brief on the Armenian situation and submit drafts for a suitable proclamation for use by the Commissariat for Nationalities. Terian, assuming the responsibility, promptly presented the work to Lenin and Stalin. After describing the untold suffering of Armenians under the Ottoman yoke, the poet-Bolshevik assailed the tsarist-Kerensky machinations, which were intended to prevent the revival of devastated Armenia. Unfortunately, he continued, Dashnaktsutiun, having captured the mind of the masses during the preceding decades, had led the people down the path toward destruction. Terian extolled the nationality policy of the Soviet government but earnestly requested that Russian troops remain in Turkish Armenia until its sovereignty was guaranteed and arrangements for honest, unhindered referendums, solid governmental order, and local militia had been made.[22] Even Stepan Shahumian, appointed Extraordinary Commissar for the Caucasus by the Sovnarkom on December 29, was not immune to feelings of doubt. A bitter enemy of all forms of nationalism and, like Lenin, convinced that only rapid Russian disengagement from the war could save the country, Shahumian comprehended, nonetheless, that recalling the armies on the principle of self-determination without first securing the safety of the inhabitants might correspond to the letter but certainly not to the spirit of Bolshevik ideals.[23]

The question of the Caucasus front and Turkish Armenia was often included on the Sovnarkom's agenda during December, 1917. The decree drafted by Terian for the Nationalities Commissariat was studied and altered, but its adoption was delayed until January 11, 1918, seemingly because of discord among government members. Signed by Lenin and Stalin, the declaration "About Turkish Armenia" appeared in *Pravda* two days later.[24] In the same issue, the Commissar for Nationalities wrote:

> So-called "Turkish Armenia" is the only country, it seems, that Russia occupied "by right of war." This is that "little corner of paradise" which for many years has served (and still serves) as the object of the voracious diplomatic appetites of the West and the bloody administrative exercises of the East. Pogroms and massacres of Armenians, on the one hand, and pharisaic "intercession" of the diplomats of all countries, as a cover for new massacres, on the other, and as a result a blood-soaked, deceived, and enslaved Armenia. . . .
>
> The sons of Armenia—heroic defenders of their native land, but by no means farsighted politicians, who have allowed themselves to be deceived time and again by the beasts of imperialist diplomacy—cannot fail to see that the old path of diplomatic scheming does not point the way to the liberation of Armenia. It is becoming clear that the path of liberation for oppressed peoples lies through the workers' revolution that was started in Russia in October. . . .

> Let everyone know that the imperialist policy of national subjugation is countered by the Council of People's Commissars with the policy of complete liberation of the oppressed peoples.[25]

As a declaration of principles, the decree "About Turkish Armenia" complimented the righteousness of Bolshevism, but as a course of action its benefits were nullified by the first of the following conditions on which self-determination was to be based:

> 1. The withdrawal of the troops from the boundaries of "Turkish Armenia" and the immediate formation of an Armenian militia to secure the safety of person and property of the inhabitants of "Turkish Armenia."
> 2. Unhindered return to "Turkish Armenia" of refugee Armenians as well as expatriate Armenians scattered in various countries.
> 3. Unhindered return to the bounds of "Turkish Armenia" of Armenians forcibly exiled into the interior of Turkey during the war by Turkish authorities, on which the Sovnarkom will insist at the peace negotiations with Turkish officials.
> 4. Creation of a Temporary People's Administration of "Turkish Armenia" in the form of a Soviet of Deputies of the Armenian people, elected by democratic procedures.
>
> Extraordinary Temporary Commissar for Caucasian Affairs, Stepan Shahumian, is entrusted to cooperate in every way with the population of "Turkish Armenia" in the task of realizing points 2 and 3, as well as to embark upon creation of a mixed commission for the establishment of a deadline and the method of withdrawal of troops from the bounds of "Turkish Armenia" (point 1).[26]

The decree was confirmed in late January:

> The Third Congress of Soviets welcomes the policy of the Council of People's Commissars, which has proclaimed the absolute independence of Finland, has commenced the withdrawal of troops from Persia, and has given Armenia the right to self-determination.[27]

Unfortunately, neither the Sovnarkom, its Extraordinary Commissar, nor the Congress of Soviets had the means to implement points 2, 3, and 4. In discussing the decree, war correspondent Henry Barby asked, "Was it the naïveté, ignorance or cynicism of Lenin and the Commissar for Nationalities?"[28] Purged Soviet historian Borian seems to have answered:

> Consequently, it was necessary to abandon tsarist Russia's policy toward Turkey, Persia, and Afghanistan and to prove the logical nature of Soviet policy by demonstrating that it actually does not pursue imperialistic aims. The withdrawal of Soviet troops from Persia and Turkish Armenia served as the proof of this. The Armenian question thus became the means and not the end.[29]

The most tangible effect of the entire episode was the added momentum given Russian soldiers streaming homeward. But in fairness to the Sovnarkom it must be stated that with or without the document in question the Caucasus front would have been denuded. Desertions had reached massive proportions prior to the Bolshevik coup, and there was probably no existing force that could have halted the movement. Moreover, the Caucasus did not recognize the government of People's Commissars, and the military command in South Russia was still dominated by anti-Bolshevik generals. Nonetheless, nearly all Armenian politicians blamed the Sovnarkom for subverting native attempts to stabilize the front and retain the occupied territories.

The Sovnarkom Seeks Peace

In Soviet efforts to end the state of war with or without the approval of the former Entente partners, the term "Armenia" was used once again. On November 21, two weeks after Kerensky's flight, the Sovnarkom instructed the Commander in Chief, General N. N. Dukhonin, to arrange an immediate armistice with the Central Powers.[30] Refusing, Dukhonin was lynched, and the obligation devolved on N. V. Krilenko of the Commissariat for Military and Naval Affairs. Unit commanders were immediately ordered to communicate with the opposing forces to arrange a cease-fire. Then Soviet negotiators traveled to the Polish village of Brest-Litovsk, German Eastern Front Headquarters, where, on December 15, after extolling the magical terms "self-determination," "no annexations," and "no indemnities," they concluded a preliminary armistice, to take effect two days later.[31] On that occasion the Commissariat for Foreign Affairs appealed to the toilers of Europe to pressure their respective governments:

> Belgium, Serbia, Rumania, Poland, the Ukraine, Greece, Persia, and Armenia can only be liberated by the workers in all belligerent and neutral countries in the victorious struggle against all imperialists, and not by the victory of one of the imperialist coalitions.[32]

Peace negotiations began on December 22 with A. A. Ioffe leading the Sovnarkom delegation, while an assorted array of militarists and diplomats represented the German, Austro-Hungarian, and Ottoman empires and the Bulgarian kingdom. During the first plenary session, Ioffe announced the Soviet bases for peace. There was to be

1) no forceful appropriation of territories taken during the war; withdrawal of all occupying armies;
2) restoration of political independence to nationalities deprived of this since the outbreak of war;

3) choice for nationalities hitherto not independent of either independence or unification with other states;
4) safeguarding of minorities in multinational territories;
5) imposition of no indemnities;
6) settlement of colonial questions in accordance with points 1 through 4.[33]

A few days later a specific suggestion was presented regarding point 1:

> Russia will withdraw its troops from all parts of Austria-Hungary, Turkey, and Persia which it occupies, while the Powers of the Quadruple Alliance will withdraw theirs from Poland, Lithuania, Courland, and other regions of Russia.[34]

The Soviet government was quite prepared to relinquish Russian advantages on the Caucasus front in return for restoration of her western provinces. Of course, German militarists, represented by General Max von Hoffman, refused to consider such proposals seriously and advanced plans to shear from Russia some of her most fertile, populous regions. At the same time the Ottoman delegate at Brest-Litovsk, General Zekki Pasha, adjutant to the Sultan and military envoy to Berlin, attempted to prod the German allies to demand the reestablishment of the 1877 Russo-Turkish boundary. Von Hoffman and his associates received the suggestion coldly, insisting that, at least for the present, recovery of the eastern provinces was adequate compensation for the Turks.[35]

By the beginning of 1918, the annexationist ambitions of Germany were made painfully clear. On January 1, the Central Executive Committee of the All-Russian Soviet appealed to the peoples of Europe and protested that, although accepting the principles of a no annexations–no indemnities settlement, the German militarists still had not renounced imperialistic designs. The Executive Committee earnestly urged that "you will not allow the German and Austrian imperialists to carry on war against revolutionary Russia so that they can enslave Poland, Lithuania, Courland, and Armenia."[36] Von Hoffman was unmoved. Trotsky, who had replaced Ioffe as chief Soviet delegate, returned to Petrograd in mid-January to report on the German territorial demands. The humiliating terms hopelessly split the Bolshevik Central Committee. Some demanded "revolutionary war"; others, including Lenin, insisted on peace at any price. Finally Trotsky's formula carried—"no war, no peace."[37] Returning to Brest, the Foreign Commissar declared on February 10 that Russia had withdrawn from the war but could not sign the proposed peace terms:

> ... in refusing to sign a peace of annexation, Russia declares, on its side, the state of war with Germany, Austria-Hungary, Turkey, and Bulgaria as ended. The Russian troops are receiving at the same time an order for a general demobilization on all lines of the fronts.[38]

The German Offensive and the Treaty of Brest-Litovsk

Trotsky's strange maxim did not impress the German High Command. Within a week the German armies advanced along the entire front. All of European Russia and the North Caucasus were imperiled by the Berlin war machine. The Sovnarkom was unable to wage a "revolutionary war," and, on February 23, the Central Executive Committee received and accepted a German ultimatum dated two days earlier. The Armenians were affected by point 5: "Russia shall do everything in her power to guarantee a speedy and orderly return of the East Anatolian provinces to Turkey."[39]

A more conventional diplomat, G. V. Chicherin, replaced the disillusioned Trotsky as Foreign Commissar and scurried to Brest with a new delegation to sign the peace. But where the demands of Enver's delegates had earlier been held to a minimum, the interlude of renewed hostilities now altered the situation. Immediately following Trotsky's "no war, no peace" speech, General von Ludendorff informed the Ottoman Chief of Staff, General Hans von Seeckt, that Germany would welcome a strong Turkish offensive against the Caucasus.[40] Thus when, on February 27, Enver Pasha directed Ismail Hakki, diplomatic envoy to Berlin and delegate at Brest-Litovsk, to demand the provinces of Kars, Ardahan, and Batum in addition to the restoration of the eastern *vilayets*, Germany yielded to the insistence of her ally.[41] Furthermore, on March 1, von Seeckt informed the German High Command that Russia should be compelled to recognize the existence of a separate Transcaucasian state, to pledge nonintervention in the affairs of that nation, and to guarantee the right of self-determination to the Moslems of Kazan, Orenburg, Turkestan, and Bukhara. The Enver-Talaat regime requested the benevolent support of Berlin in these matters.[42]

When Chicherin's delegation arrived at Brest, it waived discussion of the details and offered to sign the peace without further ado. Any terms placed before the Soviet delegates would be signed, for this was not a voluntary but a dictated settlement. By refusing to review the treaty, the Sovnarkom representatives wished to dramatize the compulsory character of the proceedings. Furthermore, only after reaching Brest-Litovsk did Chicherin learn of the last-minute Turkish demand for part of Transcaucasia.[43] Once again the Soviet delegation bowed before the reality that dictated peace at any price or else death to the newly established order. Nonetheless, while accepting the terms on March 3, 1918, the Russian delegation declared:

> In the Caucasus, plainly violating the conditions of the ultimatum of 21 February drawn up by the German Government itself, and ignoring the real wishes of the population of the districts of Ardahan, Kars, and Batum, Germany detaches these areas for the benefit of Turkey, whose armies had never conquered them.[44]

With complete absence of pomp, the treaty was signed.

That portion of the Brest-Litovsk settlement pertaining to Transcaucasia and Turkish Armenia vitally conditioned subsequent events in those territories. Article IV included two important provisions:

> Russia will do all within her power to insure the immediate evacuation of the provinces of Eastern Anatolia and their lawful return to Turkey.
>
> The districts [*sanjak*s] of Ardahan, Kars, and Batum will likewise and without delay be cleared of Russian troops. Russia will not interfere in the reorganization of the national and international relations of these districts, but leave it to the population of these districts to carry out this reorganization in agreement with the neighboring states, especially Turkey.[45]

One needs only to compare the decree "About Turkish Armenia" with Article IV to comprehend the wrath of the political leaders and populace of Turkish Armenia and Transcaucasia.

But Article IV was not the full extent of the injury. The Brest-Litovsk treaty made provision for additional separate conventions between Russia and each of the Central Powers. The first two articles of the Russo-Turkish bilateral agreement detailed the time limit and procedure for Russian evacuation from Turkish Armenia, Kars, Ardahan, and Batum. The Soviet government pledged that within eight weeks no Russian soldier would be found in these districts, and that no vengeance would be taken on the land or populace during the withdrawal. Not more than one Russian division was to remain in the entire Caucasus and, in the event internal security demanded more than that number, the Central Powers were to be informed in advance.[46] The Armenians, who, despite the Brest negotiations and Russian desertion, had endeavored to man the front, were especially stung by Article I, paragraph 5 of the additional treaty:

> The Russian Republic assumes the responsibility to demobilize and dissolve the Armenian bands, composed of Russian and Turkish subjects, which are found in Russia as well as in the occupied Turkish provinces, and will completely disperse these bands.[47]

Other clauses provided for the establishment of commissions to determine the prewar boundary and the territorial limits of Kars, Ardahan, and Batum.

The Fourth All-Russian Congress of Soviets, meeting in Moscow,[48] ratified the Treaty of Brest-Litovsk on March 15. The breathing spell gained by signing this "Tilsit Peace" cost Russia over a million and a quarter square miles and sixty million people.[49] According to Leninist logic, the inevitable communist revolution would soon engulf Germany and the West and thus automatically nullify the humiliation of Brest. Lenin expounded this view at the Russian Social Democrat Bolshevik Seventh Congress, which, besides condoning the government's policy at Brest, adopted Lenin's proposal to rename the organization the Russian Communist Party (RKP).[50]

The Treaty of Brest-Litovsk humbled and weakened Russia, but it crushed Transcaucasia, where a temporary anti-Bolshevik administration had been formed. On the day before the treaty was signed, Lev M. Karakhan, secretary of the Soviet delegation at Brest, enumerated in a wire to the Tiflis government the latest Russian concessions to Turkey. The information left Transcaucasia dumbfounded.

VII

Transcaucasia Adrift

(November, 1917–March, 1918)

THE STIRRING EVENTS from the Bolshevik coup to the Treaty of Brest-Litovsk threw Transcaucasia into turmoil. Repeatedly expressing their dedication to the ideal of a united, democratic Russia, the Transcaucasian leaders believed initially that the creation of an interim regional administration until "liquidation of the Communist adventure" was sufficient. As the weeks slipped by, however, the Bolsheviks continued to master the central government, thus driving the border regions to pursue an ambivalent political course permitting independent action, but without entailing separation from Russia. This dichotomy only deepened the dilemma of Transcaucasia, which, bewildered by its own double-talk, was finally compelled in April, 1918, to proclaim independence. During this five-month interval, Transcaucasia was beset by the intertwined problems of Russian politics, conditions on the Turkish front, organization of a transitory local government, and internal national-religious strife.

The Transcaucasian Commissariat

In opposing the new Russian government, Transcaucasia was nearly unanimous. On the day the Bolsheviks raised their banner over the Winter Palace, D. Donskoi, President of the Regional Army Soviet in Tiflis, appealed to all units to be calm and to maintain order.[1] During the following days, scores of similar declarations were approved by the Regional Center of Soviets, the executives of the several individual soviets, and numerous civic and political societies. All pledged allegiance to the Provisional Government only, pleaded for peaceful settlement of the uprising, and demanded convocation of the All-Russian Constituent Assembly as the sole body legally authorized to arbitrate the nation's political future. The Baku Soviet alone, again choosing Stepan Shahumian as commander, recognized the Russian Sovnarkom on November 15. But even this approbation came only after most members had withdrawn in protest against the Bolshevik slogan, "All Power to the Soviets."[2]

The rest of Transcaucasia followed the lead of Tiflis. There, on the initiative of the Public Safety Committee, an emergency conference was held on November 24. Attending the noisy meeting were nearly four hundred representatives of the regional soviets, the Tiflis Duma and Executive Committee, the Public Safety Committee and Ozakom, political and civic organizations, postal-telegraph employees and professional unions, as well as Commander of the Front Przhevalskii, Chief of Staff Lebedinskii, Quartermaster General Levandovskii, military agents of France and England, and, of course, the American Consul. Presiding was Evgenii Gegechkori, who, explaining that the momentous events of the preceding weeks had severed Transcaucasia from central Russia, recommended creation of a temporary administration to deal with numerous pressing problems. Then Noi Zhordania, in his rhetorical style, summoned Transcaucasia to battle anarchy through a provisional government composed of delegates to the Constituent Assembly but suggested that, until elections could be completed, another body should rule.[3] On behalf of the Social Revolutionaries, Donskoi agreed that a regional authority was needed because of the Ozakom's resignation and the threat to the front but added quickly that this was no indication of separatism. He sponsored a resolution that was confirmed unanimously after the Bolshevik delegates had "exposed" the counterrevolutionary character of the meeting and stalked out.[4] It was decided

1) that, until completion of Constituent Assembly elections, the Committee for Public Safety—together with members of all revolutionary, democratic, civic, and national organizations—was charged with local administration;
2) that, following the elections, the chosen delegates would create a temporary government obligated
   a) to correlate regional policy with that of the All-Russian democracy to solve general questions,
   b) to make autonomous decisions in current regional matters only,
   c) to guide Transcaucasia until re-creation of the central democratic government and convocation of the Constituent Assembly,
   d) to seek support from the existing administrative bodies and local soviets.[5]

Four days later, membership of the interim body, the Commissariat, was announced. Gegechkori served concurrently as President and as Commissar for Labor and for Foreign Affairs, while his Menshevik colleague, Akakii Chkhenkeli, assumed the strategic post of Internal Affairs. Appropriately, the Social Revolutionary Donskoi was named Commissar for Military and Naval Affairs, but only after heated SR-Menshevik debates concerning agrarian policies did A. V. Neruchev of the former party emerge as Commissar for Agriculture. Portfolios of Trade and Industry, Roads and Communications, and State Control were distributed among the three Moslems on the eleven-man board. Armenians Khachatur Karjikian, Hamazasp (Hamo) Ohandjanian (Dashnaktsutiun), and Ghazar Ter Ghazarian (SD) acted as commissars for Finance, Public Welfare, and Provisions, respectively.[6] The apportionment of cabinet positions elicited Armenian criticism of Dashnaktsutiun for permitting Georgian supremacy. That the Mensheviks should lead, however, was quite natural. They had gained valuable experience in the international radical movement, had accepted commanding roles in the Russian soviets, and had even participated in the Provisional Government. The influence and fame of a Zhordania, Gegechkori, Tsereteli, or Chkheidze far surpassed that of the nationally, religiously, or territorially restricted leaders of Dashnaktsutiun and Musavat. Since the March Revolution, Menshevik views had shaped Transcaucasian policies; there was no reason for alteration after November. On the contrary, the flight or expulsion of many Georgian leaders from central Russia augmented Menshevik power beyond the Caucasus Mountains.

Publishing its first declaration on December 1, the Commissariat accounted for its own creation and revealed an ambitious program, which ranged from bolstering the economy and reinforcing the military front to abolishing class privileges, introducing the *zemstvo,* reorganizing the judicial system, and seeking a workable solution to the nationality question.[7] Actually, the Commissariat did none of these. Perhaps with premonition, Gegechkori's cabinet explained that it would rule until the convocation of the All-Russian Constituent Assembly. "If, however, the gathering of the latter becomes impossible because of circumstances in Russia, then it [the Commissariat] will retain authority until the Constituent Assembly members from Transcaucasia and the Caucasus front have conferred."[8]

The Constituent Assembly

Elections in the Caucasus and along the Turkish front for delegates to the Assembly were conducted throughout November, 1917. Though incomplete and poorly organized, it was, nonetheless, the most representative and unhindered election in Transcaucasian history. More than two million voters cast ballots in the following manner:[9]

Slate Number and Party	Votes
I. Social Democrat (Menshevik)[10]	661,934
II. Constitutional Democrat (Kadet)	25,673
III. Social Revolutionary[11]	117,522
IV. Dashnaktsutiun	558,440
V. Social Democrat (Bolshevik)[12]	93,581
X. Musavat	615,816
XI. Moslem Social Democrat (Hummet)	84,748
XII. Moslem Socialist Bloc	159,770
XIV. Moslems of Russia (Ittihad)[13]	66,504

On the basis of one delegate per sixty thousand votes, the Menshevik party was allotted eleven places; Musavat, ten; Dashnaktsutiun, nine; Social Revolutionary party, two, and so on.[14] Chosen to travel to Petrograd by the Armenian Revolutionary Federation were Rostom Zorian, Mikayel Hovhannisian, Hamo Ohandjanian, Hakob Zavriev, Kostia Hambardzumian, Avetik Shahkhatuni, Hovhannes Kachaznuni, Sirakan Tigranian, and Koriun Ghazazian.[15] Among them were two premiers and a foreign minister of the future Armenian Republic.

Many of the Transcaucasian delegates were still en route to the capital when the All-Russian Constituent Assembly convened on January 18, 1918. Because it was decidedly anti-Bolshevik in composition, the Assembly was doomed.[16] After the Sovnarkom had taken control of Petrograd, it felt too insecure to forbid the gathering, especially because Lenin's cries of prior months on behalf of that Assembly still echoed throughout the land. Unable to renege, the Bolsheviks nonetheless prepared for the likelihood of an antagonistic majority by announcing support for only a democratically represented Assembly. Clearly, an anti-Communist disposition would be nonrepresentative. Thus, after only one day's existence, the Social Revolutionary-oriented Constituent Assembly was besieged and forcibly dispersed. The "grand illusion" of the Provisional Government, the moderate socialist and liberal parties, as well as of most nationality groups, was no more.[17] The gap between Russia and Transcaucasia widened and deepened.

The Erzinjan Truce

Even before the delegates to the Constituent Assembly had left Tiflis, the Transcaucasian Commissariat grappled with the perplexing military problem. It was undoubtedly with great relief that Caucasus Front Commander Przhevalskii received Vehib Pasha's November 30 communiqué proposing a truce. The Russian general lost no time in accepting the offer and ordering a temporary cease-fire.[18] Four days later, after considering Chief of Staff Lebedinskii's report on the military situation, the Commissariat sanctioned negotiation of a truce on condition that Turkish troops not be diverted to Mesopotamia against the British, and authorized an appropriate explanation to the public. Then, while Przhevalskii called upon Vehib to respect the existing military lines pending a formal armistice, the Commissariat proclaimed to all that the truce would assuredly be superseded by a "righteous, just, and democratic peace" which the Constituent Assembly would conclude for all Russia.[19]

On December 10, several days after the Sovnarkom delegation had arrived in Brest-Litovsk to confer with the German Command, the Transcaucasian Commissariat instructed General Vyshinskii of the Caucasus Army to proceed to Erzinjan to parley with the Ottoman military authorities.[20] There, along the western perimeter of the Russian-occupied territory, the truce was signed on December 18, after three days of negotiations. In accordance with the agreement:

1) all military operations were to cease at midnight;
2) special commissions would trace the exact demarcation lines beyond which the opposing armies were not to advance;
3) aviation within seven miles of the demarcation lines was forbidden;
4) military buildup on either side was prohibited, although training would be allowed well behind the advanced positions and information on training schedules was to be exchanged;
5) transferral of Ottoman troops to the Mesopotamian front would be *casus belli;*
6) in the neutral zone between the demarcation lines, the Turks would guarantee Kurdish compliance with the truce terms; in the Russian-occupied areas, Kurds involved in hostile activities would be dealt with as ordinary bandits;
7) fourteen-day notification was mandatory for modification or abrogation of the truce.[21]

The demarcation lines detailed in annexes to the document corresponded closely to the positions held by the Russian and Turkish armies since the winter of 1916–1917.

The Second Regional Congress of the Caucasus Army

The Erzinjan Truce did not stem the tide of desertion. The approximately half-million Russian soldiers in the Caucasus at the time of the November Revolution had dwindled to only a few thousand by the approach of spring. Left behind were massive stores of supplies and a barren front stretching from the Black Sea to Lake Van. The soaring prestige of Bolshevism was evidenced in numerous soldiers' meetings, pledging allegiance to the Sovnarkom and branding as counterrevolutionary the creation of the Transcaucasian Commissariat.[22] The same disposition prevailed at the Second Regional Congress of the Caucasus Army, which met in Tiflis on December 23, 1917. Though most delegates were not Bolsheviks, they were soon enchanted by the eloquent orations of Shahumian, G. N. Korganov, and other disciples of Lenin. Resolutions recognizing the Sovnarkom as the sole legal government of all Russia and denouncing even a "defensive war" were adopted by substantial margins. In an appeal to the men at the front, the Congress promised rapid demobilization but warned that, because of transportation problems, "revolutionary self-discipline" should be imposed until the responsible committees could arrange for orderly withdrawal.[23] In elections for a new Regional Soviet, the Bolshevik-Left SR coalition won fifty-two of the one hundred positions, a significant victory for the Sovnarkom. The advantage, however, was not consolidated. The anti-

Sovnarkom minority withdrew from the meeting, held its own conference, elected a new executive, and then confiscated the buildings and property of the Regional Soldiers' Soviet. The legally elected body was compelled to seek refuge in Baku.[24] Current Soviet authors chastise the Transcaucasian Communist leadership of those days for allowing this usurpation and for pursuing an "opportunistic" policy by refusing to sanction civil war. Several non-Bolshevik writers contend that the Sovnarkom partisans were never actually a majority in the Congress, that it was they who had withdrawn, and that the present Soviet interpretation is falsification of history. In either event, while the soldier in the trenches was full of defeatism and Bolshevik sympathies, the Army Command and administration remained, legally or illegally, in the hands of the Right SR–Menshevik military oligarchy.

Even before the Congress convened, the Georgian Mensheviks had taken steps to crush their Marxist stepbrothers. When rowdy Russian troops of the Kars Division charged through the streets of Tiflis shouting Bolshevik slogans and threatening the Commissariat, the Executive Council of the Tiflis Workers' Soviet created a counterforce, the Red Guard, composed almost exclusively of Menshevik followers. On December 12, this militia surrounded the Bolshevik-held Tiflis arsenal and almost without a skirmish confiscated its twenty thousand weapons and large stores of ammunition. Fortified by this victory, the Red Guard drove the Kars Division and other retreating Russian units out of the Tiflis *guberniia*.[25] Then the Mensheviks, registering one triumph after another, blocked Bolshevik attempts to win control of the Regional Workers' Soviet and the Trade Unions' Conference.[26] Even the most ardent devotees of Lenin were forced to admit that, outside the ranks of the Russian Army and part of the Baku proletariat, Transcaucasia was decidedly anti-Bolshevik.

The Question of Bolshevik-Dashnakist Collaboration

An interesting topic never broached by Soviet historians is the secret contact between Armenian Bolsheviks and Dashnaktsutiun. Publicly, the Bolshevik press disparaged the Federation's tactics. Formation of the volunteer units, allegiance to the Provisional Government, and participation in the Commissariat were examples of its antiproletarian activity. In like manner, Dashnaktsutiun heckled the "traitorous sons" of the Armenian people. Nonetheless, the leaders of both factions had much in common. They had been nurtured by the Russian revolutionary movement, had struggled against tsarism, and had shared the deprivations of imprisonment and exile. Some had been classmates or erstwhile comrades. Thus, informal contact despite official opposition was not inconceivable. There were even members of the Sovnarkom who did not oppose a rapprochement with Dashnaktsutiun. Throughout Russia, Armenian societies associated with the National Council in Tiflis were tolerated in the first months after the

Bolshevik coup. Trotsky personally guaranteed the safety and unrestricted travel of the Dashnakist representatives in central Russia. Whereas many non-Bolsheviks fled from Petrograd, Dr. Zavriev returned to the capital from Transcaucasia and, with Liparit Nazariants, sought an agreement with the Sovnarkom.[27] Similarly, under the auspices of the Baku Armenian Council, Dashnaktsutiun dispatched first Rostom Zorian, then Artashes Chilingarian, to confer with the new masters of Russia.[28] Even in Tiflis, when the Commissariat, at Menshevik insistence, smashed Bolshevik newspapers and ordered the arrest of Shahumian, the Armenian nationalist party shielded its Bolshevik compatriots and secretly directed them to safety.[29] All the while, the two organizations officially continued to deprecate one another.

There is, of course, an explanation to the paradox. From the Armenian point of view, the most formidable problem was the threat of a Turkish offensive into the Caucasus. Measures had to be taken to escape the fate of Turkish Armenia. Dashnaktsutiun adopted two distinct tactics. It endeavored, on the one hand, to form a solid bloc with the other anti-Communist parties of Transcaucasia. United, Georgians, Tatars, and Armenians might repel the Ottomans, and, even if unsuccessful, the Armenians would suffer much less if they shared a common fate with their fellow Transcaucasians. This policy was undermined, however, by distrust of those neighbors. Joint Christian-Moslem resistance to the Ottomans was not likely, and, even assuming that it were, the Georgians and Tatars would undoubtedly abandon the Armenians if the Turkish armies were victorious. With these views, the Armenians naturally warranted the reproach and suspicion of both Tatars and Georgians. On the other hand, although Bolshevism did not offer the ideal political-economic system to most Armenians, it did in 1918 represent Great Russia. That Armenian anticipation of a brighter future was associated with a powerful Russia has repeatedly been indicated. The Armenian political mentality was so permeated by this conviction that Dashnaktsutiun groped for a modus vivendi with Bolshevism. There would be mutual advantages, for the Armenian Marxists, leaders with few followers, could then work freely to spread their doctrine into every village and every social stratum. Evidently, Dashnaktsutiun hoped that if one political tactic failed, the other would safeguard the Armenian people.

Ruben Ter Minasian, member of the Bureau, supreme body of Dashnaktsutiun, has disclosed pertinent information concerning negotiations with Stepan Shahumian and other Bolsheviks. Assertedly, Shahumian pledged to do everything in his power to reinforce the front with Russian troops, accepted the administrative repartition of Transcaucasia as proposed in the Ozakom conferences, authorized the use of Russian contingents to protect the Armenian provinces of the Caucasus and to support the local native units in the mountainous portion of Elisavetpol guberniia, and promised to reopen the communication routes from Baku to Tiflis and Erevan. Until the fulfillment of those terms, the Bolsheviks were not to incite any disturbances in western Transcaucasia and Dashnaktsutiun would continue its official anti-Communist activity and propaganda. But when the Sovnarkom had completed its share of the bargain, Dashnaktsutiun would unite with the Bolsheviks to seize control of all Transcaucasia.[30] Russian orientation among the Armenians outweighed aversion to communism. The project was neither confirmed nor enacted by the contracting sides and there is little record of Dashnakist-Bolshevik cooperation in western Transcaucasia, but the undisguised collaboration in Baku from March through July, 1918, is abundantly documented. There, the Bolsheviks possessed an influential leadership while Dashnaktsutiun controlled the Armenian masses and troops. Both parties recognized as mutual enemies the Musavat organization and the Moslem "Savage Division." To the Armenians of Baku, Bolshevism was equivalent to "Russianism," while Musavatism was synonymous with "Turkism." [31]

Formation of National Corps in Transcaucasia

Turkism was an abhorrent specter to both Ottoman and Russian Armenians. Though the Turkish armies had been decimated during three years of warfare, Enver Pasha had not forsaken the hallowed image of a united Turan. Crimea, the Volga, Turkestan awaited liberation by the armies advancing under the green banner of Islam. Disintegration of the Russian military potential beckoned Enver eastward. Armenians were not oblivious to this. Even before the November Revolution, a Turkish Armenian militia, headed by seasoned revolutionaries, attempted to fill the ever widening gaps along the front. But several hundred men were insufficient to hold the territory that had been occupied by nearly two hundred thousand Russian troops. To consider emergency measures, the Western Armenian Bureau in December, 1917, sponsored a conference which, after receiving Entente promises of limited financial support, adopted plans to form a twenty-thousand-man militia. The Defense Council selected by the conference was charged with drumming up public enthusiasm and conscripting and equipping Turkish Armenian youth from both sides of the prewar boundary. Heated arguments ensued over the designation of a commander. Despite the objection of several Russian Armenian leaders, Andranik was chosen. Already, through Zavriev's efforts, he had been promoted to Major General by the Russian Caucasus Army Command.[32] The First Brigade of his Western Armenian Division was composed of the Erzinjan and Erzerum regiments; the Second, of the Khnus and Karakilisa (Alashkert) regiments; and the Third, of the Van and mounted Zeitun regiments.[33]

Also during December, 1917, General Przhevalskii authorized the formation of the Armenian Corps. The Caucasus Army Command was now convinced that only motivated national units could save the situation.[34] General Tovmas Nazarabekov, highly decorated for his services during the Russo-Japanese War and the 1914–1917 North Persian–Van operations, was commissioned to lead the Corps.[35] Dro (Drastamat Kanayan), assassin of several high-ranking tsarist officials and commander of one of the volunteer units in 1914–1915, served as the civilian commissar.[36] The Corps comprised the First Division of General Areshov and the Second of Colonel Silikov,[37] each with four rifle regiments, the Third of Andranik with its three brigades, and a single cavalry brigade under Colonel Korganov. A few auxiliary, quartermaster, medical, and garrison units completed the structure of the Armenian "army."[38] With approximately twenty thousand men, the Corps never attained full wartime strength.

In response to urgent requests from Russian commanders who warned that the troops in the Erzinjan area were thoroughly undependable, several regiments of the Armenian Corps were immediately hustled off to the front.[39] They created a strange spectacle en route, for, to the amazement of the homeward-bound Russian soldiers, they were moving toward, not away from, the forward lines. By the end of January, 1918, Nazarabekian's divisions occupied the major posts from Erevan to Van and Erzinjan. Their disposition was as follows:[40]

First Division—General Areshian
1st Regiment   Erzerum-Erzinjan
2nd Regiment   Khnus
3rd Regiment   Erevan
4th Regiment   Erzinjan and Erevan

Second Division—Colonel Silikian
5th Regiment   Van
6th Regiment   Erevan
7th Regiment   Alexandropol
8th Regiment   Alexandropol

Third Division—General Andranik (Ozanian)
1st Brigade   Erzinjan-Erzerum
2nd Brigade   Khnus
3rd Brigade   Van

Small bands of Turkish Armenian irregulars augmented the groups around Van, Erzinjan, and Erzerum. It was indeed ironic that in many districts there were not even enough Armenian soldiers to guard the inestimable stock of food, ammunition, communication-transportation matériel, and medical supplies left by the Russian Army.[41] The Corps was worthy of laudation for its efforts, yet it had assumed the impossible task of defending the Erzinjan-Van front, a distance of nearly 250 miles. Difficulties in communication, suspicion between the Russian Armenian and Turkish Armenian, lack of experience as a regular army, and inability to maintain lasting discipline dissipated the limited strength of Nazarabekian's forces. Meanwhile, several thousand trained Armenian soldiers stood stranded in Baku and additional thousands of able-bodied men remained in the Erevan, Tiflis, Elisavetpol, and Baku guberniias, where Moslem-Armenian tensions had reached dangerous proportions. The Tatars of Transcaucasia were accused of sabotage, destroying the railway to the front lines, and attacking the villages whose male population had been drafted. In Tiflis, the Caucasus Army Command, at the insistence of the Armenian National Council, authorized the creation of special militias to guard the communication routes and protect the threatened villages. Armenian units were then formed in Shulaver, Akhalkalak, and Akhaltsikh in the Tiflis guberniia; Nukhi and Shushi in Elisavetpol; Igdir and Nakhichevan in Erevan.[42]

During sessions of the Commissariat, Armenian members charged the Moslems with obstructing legislation for broader conscription. By the time the proposal was finally approved at the end of February, precious weeks had elapsed, and, even then, the Commissar for Communications, a Moslem, purportedly jammed the roads, arranging rail transport so that movement of troops and supplies would progress at the slowest possible rate. Actually, Armenians had little need to incriminate their Commissariat colleagues, for the National Council was in full control of Armenian life. It had collected thousands of rubles for the Corps and assigned hundreds of men to the several regiments. What it seemed to desire was ex post facto confirmation of the conscription and moral support in its drive to coerce the recalcitrant "Tiflis city boys" toward the front.[43]

Armenians were not alone in their military preparations, for both Moslems and Georgians comprehended the value and necessity of national units. Because Moslems of Russia had been exempt from compulsory military service, they faced greater legal barriers in creating separate armed forces than did their Christian neighbors. Only in its final days, when restraining the Moslems was no longer possible, had the Provisional Government granted them permission to organize. But even before that, the Tatars of Transcaucasia were taking action. In November, the Moslem Council of Ganja (Elisavetpol) assumed the obligation of forming and administering Tatar units. Still, despite demands for equal treatment, the Moslems were denied the requisite matériel and weapons by the Caucasus Army.[44] Members of the Commissariat often locked in heated quarrels on the subject. In January, 1918, the Moslems broke the impasse and acquired sufficient arms by ambushing the homeward-bound 219th Russian Regiment. In this "Shamkhor Massacre," the Russian soldiers and their dependents suffered several hundred casualties while the Moslems of Elisavetpol garnered some fifteen thousand rifles, seventy machine guns, twenty cannons, and an ample supply of ammunition, food, and uniforms.[45] Soviet authors vilify the shady Moslem bands and especially castigate members of the Transcaucasian

Commissariat for their share in the tragedy.⁴⁶ Conversely, anti-Soviet Moslem sources stress that the whole affair was a matter of self-defense and that the soldiers had been the aggressors.⁴⁷ In either event, the Commissariat was embarrassingly implicated. Apparently both Zhordania, Chairman of the Soviet Regional Center, and Ramishvili, member of the Military Council, had favored disarming the Russian troops and had even informed authorities in Ganja of the proximity of the pro-Sovnarkom regiment. Ramishvili, though later refuting the accusation, seems to have ordered an armored train to participate in the confiscation of the regiment's weapons, but Military Commissar Donskoi upon learning of this immediately contravened the command. By that time, however, the "Shamkhor Massacre" had already begun. The prestige of the Commissariat was badly shaken, and the Christian populace of Transcaucasia was scandalized. The loudest protests and condemnations came from the Social Revolutionaries and Dashnaktsutiun. The reasons are obvious.

Meanwhile, the Georgians equipped their units. Besides the native troops that had been transferred from the European theater, the Georgians depended on the well-disciplined Menshevik Red Guard, which, under the command of Valiko Jugheli, patrolled the streets and held the great arsenal of Tiflis. It was not difficult to secure arms for the Georgian troops. In December, General Przhevalskii had also authorized formation of the Georgian Corps, which was assigned the defense of a relatively short front from the Black Sea west of Trebizond to a district north of Erzinjan. General Gabaev (Gabaishvili) commanded the ten-thousand-man Corps, while General Odishelidze, another Georgian, served in Erzerum as the Caucasus Army Commander, as distinct from the post held by Przhevalskii, that of Chief Commander of the Caucasus Front.⁴⁸

In the political arena, the Georgians were the last to feel the need for a national council, perhaps because the will of that people had been expressed for two decades by the Menshevik party. Thus, only at the end of November, 1917, did the Georgian National Assembly convene. Zhordania, having been chosen to preside, reviewed the stirring events of that year, explained the functions of the Commissariat, and revealed plans for the establishment of a representative regional legislature, the Transcaucasian *Seim*. He added, however, that the Georgian people should organize internally and create a standing body to deal specifically with national affairs. The Menshevik swing to the right was manifest as the fiery-tongued orator, who several weeks earlier had admonished those who favored coalition, now hailed collaboration with the Georgian Social Federalists, Social Revolutionaries, and the very national and very antisocialist National Democrats. Nevertheless, by winning most places on the newly created National Council, Zhordania and his comrades guaranteed that in Transcaucasia the terms "Menshevik" and "Georgian" would remain almost synonymous.⁴⁹

Bolsheviks favored the formation of neither national councils nor national military units. These were instruments of counterrevolutionaries, who attempted to disrupt the proletariat and to wrench the masses away from the Russian Republic. Soldiers were urged to resist induction into companies based on nationality and to defend the principle of an international army. Indeed, the Bolshevik logic was not foreign to many soldiers who crammed the Communist papers with resolutions and letters protesting the attempts to separate them from their comrades of other nationalities.[50] But most of the Russian troops, whose major concern was to get home, did not care what kind of army replaced them. Having failed to prevent the formation of Armenian, Georgian, and Moslem corps, the Bolshevik Caucasian Regional Committee then advised all units to leave the front, taking precautions against the possibility of another "Shamkhor Massacre."[51] Echoing Trotsky's "no war, no peace" tactic, Shahumian informed the soldiers in mid-February that peace was near and that demobilization had already been ordered by the Sovnarkom. He urged that the rantings of the bourgeois "defensist" journals be ignored. "There is no war and there will no longer be any war. Return to your homes and busy yourselves with the creation of a new life in that land."[52] In such statements there was not an inkling of the suggested accord between Shahumian and the Dashnakists, but it is significant that, while showering Mensheviks and Musavatists with insult and derision, the Bolshevik Central Committee member and Extraordinary Commissar for the Caucasus made no mention of his Armenian political opponents. This could scarcely have been an oversight.[53]

Consul Smith versus the Department of State

Taking an active role in the establishment of the national corps was American Consul Smith, now characterized by Soviet authors as a capitalist and imperialist of the highest degree. Long a resident in the Caucasus, he assertedly had learned to manipulate the thoughts and actions of the indigenous peoples.[54] That Smith was a rabid anti-Bolshevik is quite true, but his attempt to win active American support for Transcaucasia did not emanate so much from his aversion to communism as it did from his conviction that a bolstered native army could defend the front and even push southward to link up with General Maude's forces in Mesopotamia.[55] Prior to the November Revolution, he warned Ambassador Francis in Petrograd that the Turks were preparing a new offensive and that Tatar efforts to form military units in Transcaucasia were especially dangerous. Moreover, his endeavors to convince the Georgians to unite wholeheartedly with the Armenians were hindered by German and Turkish agents who secretly promised the Georgians immunity in the event of a military offensive. If the Georgians were assured of solid Allied backing, Smith was certain they would waver no longer and would adopt measures for active defense.[56]

However, Francis and American military officials vetoed the scheme to create a Christian army in the Caucasus and admonished Smith to refrain from becoming involved in Russian affairs.[57]

The November Revolution reinforced Smith's conviction that his views were valid and that the Department of State should promote his plan. On November 23, 1917, a day before the organizational meeting of the Commissariat, the Consul informed Secretary of State Robert Lansing of Transcaucasia's disposition and pleaded for financial assistance to the temporary government that was to be established.[58] Two days later Smith proudly reported that the November 24 conference had resolved to support the war effort, uphold democracy in Russia, and fight anarchy by creating a provisional administration. The audacious Consul, so out of tune with State Department policy, requested American de facto recognition of Transcaucasia.[59] The responses from Washington were all discouraging. On November 26, Lansing wired that the United States refused to encourage sectionalism, the disruption of Russia, or civil war.[60] Less severe on December 15, the Secretary of State promised to consult with the Allies about Smith's views, but warned, "Meanwhile, do not commit this Government."[61] Twelve days later the message was dispatched again, "Repeat. Do not commit this Government."[62]

Much more concerned with the Asiatic phase of the war, the British and French apparently did not share the qualms of the United States about involvement in Russian affairs. According to Smith's reports, the French military agents in Tiflis had 20 million rubles at their disposal for utilization by loyal indigenous forces. Several French and British military advisers were also on hand to assist.[63] Unfortunately for the Armenians and Georgians, however, the Allied officers about whom Smith wrote were too few to contribute to frontline leadership. The not-too-efficient Christian soldiers continued to man the trenches, while the Caucasus Army Command, schooled in traditional warfare and designed to regulate a force of several hundred thousand troops, proved incapable of adapting to the partisan maneuvers that were soon to be required.

As the Central Powers and Soviet Russia negotiated at Brest-Litovsk, Smith exclaimed that the Moslems of Transcaucasia were waiting impatiently for the arrival of the Turks in order to show their true colors. Reminiscent of the 1915 appeals of missionaries was his repeated cry, "Christians will be destroyed."[64] As a foreign representative of the United States government, F. Willoughby Smith was an unconventional and unprofessional diplomat. Yet his dispatches abound with accurate predictions and much common sense. What Armenian would not appreciate the candid message sent to Washington on January 7, 1918: "If we are not to give aid to the Caucasus, we should clear out, giving local Christians notice, so that they can come to an understanding with the Ottomans."[65] But what Smith did not see, or perhaps refused to accept, was that the State Department had given notice several times—"Do not commit this Government." That message Smith did not relay to the Armenian National Council or to the Transcaucasian Commissariat, which, by January, 1918, had turned temporarily from military affairs to a new sphere, often more deceptive and sometimes more tragic than warfare. The immature statesmen of Tiflis attempted to measure their acumen with the five-hundred-year tradition of adroit Ottoman diplomacy.

Transcaucasia's Inconclusive Response to Ottoman Proposals

Lieutenant General I. Z. Odishelidze received from Third Army Commander Vehib Pasha a communiqué of import in mid-January. Enver Pasha through his supreme officer on the Eastern front was inquiring about the possibility of establishing cordial relations with the "independent government of Caucasia." Permission was requested for a Turkish delegation to visit Tiflis to negotiate a mutual, just peace.[66] When the Commissariat received Vehib's message along with Odishelidze's covering report on the following day, it was obliged to reflect upon the perplexing question of whom and what the Transcaucasian government represented. Having assumed the functions of a de facto administration, that government continued to insist on the inseparability of Russia and Transcaucasia. Ostensibly, its functions were limited to preventing anarchy, safeguarding the military front, and resolving strictly regional matters. The Commissariat stubbornly maintained that the Constituent Assembly alone was authorized to define the relationship between the central government and the border provinces and to conclude peace for all Russia. Although the Commissariat had participated in negotiating the Erzinjan Truce in December, the act had been officially concluded in the name of the Russian Caucasus Army. Driven to decisions and actions reserved for sovereign states, while at the same time denying its independent status, the temporary government of Transcaucasia was riddled with inconsistencies. The Commissariat was painfully aware that in fact Transcaucasia had been severed from Russia, but that, as an independent, feeble ship of state thrown upon the turbulent waters of the World War, the Russian revolutions and civil war, and the horrifying mirages of Enver Pasha, it was destined to utter ruin. Thus, when Vehib's communiqué was relayed to Tiflis, the Commissariat found it impossible to respond clearly and decisively.

The problem was taken to the Regional Center of Soviets on January 17. There, Zhordania's resolution that only the Constituent Assembly could authorize peace negotiations was adopted. As soon as action had been taken in Petrograd, the Ottoman government would be informed. Meanwhile, the Soviet Regional Center suggested advisory conferences with other governments in Russia, including the Sovnarkom, to discuss the matter.[67] Within a few hours, however, Transcaucasia had to face the distressing fact that the Constituent Assembly had been dispersed and Vehib Pasha still awaited an answer.

The matter dragged on until January 27, when Gegechkori warned the Commissariat that its long silence could be interpreted by Turkey as a negative response to suggestions for friendship. He now proposed to reply to Vehib that, although Transcaucasia was appreciative of Turkey's concern, a definite answer would be postponed until the governments of the Ukraine and South Russia had been consulted.[68] On the following day, this course of action was confirmed in a joint session of the Commissariat, the Army Command, and political leaders. During heated debates, Chkhenkeli opposed inviting the Ukraine, for that government already was conducting separate negotiations with the Central Powers. Furthermore, should there be renewed hostilities with Turkey, only Transcaucasia and possibly its North Caucasus neighbors would be involved. However, the Armenian spokesmen, the military representatives, and most of the Mensheviks, clinging to the Russian orientation, attempted to coordinate Transcaucasia's activities with those of as much of the former Empire as possible. Karjikian called attention to the important Ukrainian naval role on the Black Sea in the event of a Turkish offensive, while Kadet-Populist Papadjanian insisted that even the Bolsheviks be invited to confer.[69] Chkhenkeli was overruled, and Commissariat President Gegechkori wired the Central Ukrainian Rada at Kiev and the South-East Union at Ekaterinodar, inviting both governments to confer at Tiflis in mid-February.[70] Gegechkori also notified the dean of foreign representatives in Tiflis, Luigi Villari, and asked that the Allied and neutral nations be informed of the Commissariat's decision.[71] Finally, on January 28, two weeks after having received Vehib's message, the Tiflis rulers responded through General Odishelidze, thanking the Ottomans for the "humanitarian desire to cease hostilities as soon as possible and to establish peace between the two sides" but requesting a three-week delay for a definite answer.[72]

Even before receipt of this inconclusive reply, Vehib wrote again, inviting the Commissariat to send delegates to Brest-Litovsk, where the Central Powers would spare no effort to obtain recognition of the Transcaucasian government.[73] The German scholar Jäschke maintains that the Commissariat committed a fatal blunder by rejecting the offer. The Ukraine, with representatives at Brest-Litovsk, was recognized by the Central Powers, which then coerced the Sovnarkom to accept the independence of that border region.[74] In February, 1918, however, the Armenian-Georgian socialist bloc should not have been expected to condone the "treacherous" Brest negotiations, which, after all, had been initiated without Constituent Assembly approval and were intended to crush the Russian democracy. Only the Georgian National Democrats accepted and approved the fact that Transcaucasia's future no longer was associated with the fate of Russia but depended on the benevolence of the Central Powers.[75]

On the day appointed for the conference of the Russian border regions, February 14, no delegates arrived from Kiev or Ekaterinodar. Earlier, the South-East Union had approved the idea but implied inability to participate because of communication and transportation problems, but the Ukrainian Rada had not even acknowledged Gegechkori's summons.[76] Anger and annoyance were shown by the Commissariat, the Soviet Regional Center, military officials, and invited leaders who met on the fourteenth to consider the situation. Papadjanian argued that there was no longer any cause to delay negotiations with Turkey, while General E. V. Lebedinskii, having replaced Przhevalskii as Chief Commander of the Front, pointed out that the Ukraine, by having withdrawn its soldiers from the Caucasus, was obviously not interested in collaboration. Still concerned about Entente opinion, Ramishvili proposed informing the Allies that Transcaucasia, with the intention of guaranteeing the inviolability of the demarcation lines established by the Erzinjan Truce, would enter negotiations with Turkey. At last it was resolved that the Seim, the legislative body still in the process of formation, would determine the bases for peace. In the interim, a special commission would prepare suggestions and the Commissariat would arrange with the Ottoman government for the time and place of negotiations. Gegechkori relayed this information to Constantinople.[77] The rather abrupt volte face of the Tiflis policy-makers was linked directly to the alarming dispatches from the front.

Turkish Violation of the Erzinjan Truce

Following the December 18 truce, the approximately four thousand Armenian soldiers along a 40-mile front near Erzinjan were constantly harassed by Kurdish tribesmen threatening to sever the outlying posts from Erzinjan and that city from its main supply base of Erzerum. The daring Kurds intensified their attacks during January, 1918, compelling the Erzinjan Commander, Colonel Morel, to dispatch several of his units from the demarcation lines in an attempt to disarm the rebels in the surrounding highlands. The small patrols had just begun their assignment when they were hastily recalled because of a reported Ottoman buildup.[78]

Turkish historians show that the condition of Vehib's forces during the winter was far from enviable and that the Ottoman Army as well as the nation was saved from an irreparable catastrophe only by the Russian revolutions and subsequent abandonment of the front.[79] Reorganizing on the Armenian Plateau soon after the Bolshevik coup, the Ottomans dissolved the joint Second-Third Army Command and sent the Second Army, minus two divisions, to the embattled Syrian theater. The 5th and 12th divisions, which remained in the Diarbekir-Mush area, were attached to the Third Army as its IV Corps, commanded by Ali Ihsan Pasha.[80] Simultaneously, Colonel Kiazım Karabekir,[81] ardent Ittihadist and experienced soldier, was appointed to lead the Army's I Caucasian Corps, which faced the Armenian troops near Erzinjan. Northward to the Black Sea stood the divisions of Yakub Shevki's II Caucasian Corps. By the end of January, 1918, Vehib Pasha's Third Army had approximately fifty thousand combat-ready troops.[82]

Scarcely a week after the conclusion of the Erzinjan Truce, General Vehib initiated a series of protests to the Caucasus Front and Army commanders, claiming that cold-blooded atrocities were being committed by Armenian bands against the peaceful Moslem population behind the Russian lines. He regretted that, after the withdrawal of the Russian troops, murder, abduction, looting, and burning had increased, and he urged the Caucasian commanders to undertake measures more forceful than simply issuing unimplemented orders.[83] In his communiqué of February 1, Vehib stated, "I am ready to give any type of assistance necessary." He described the horrors perpetrated by the Armenian revolutionary Murat, painted scenes of fifteen hundred Moslems being burned to death by that criminal, and warned that the Ottoman government could not remain indifferent to such truce violations.[84] Generals Odishelidze and Lebedinskii contended that Vehib had received faulty and exaggerated information. Certain preventive steps had been necessitated by the treacherous activity of several Moslem bands. While admitting that about two hundred people had been killed in Erzinjan, Odishelidze insisted that every precaution had been taken to secure the life, honor, and property of all Moslems and that those guilty of crimes against Turkish civilians would be punished.[85] On February 14, after Ottoman violation of the Erzinjan Truce, General Lebedinskii attempted to convince Vehib that action against Moslems in the Russian zone of occupation had been authorized only after Kurdish bands had struck repeatedly at the troops and the Christian population. He warned that renewal of hostilities would jeopardize the safety of the Moslems and protested Vehib's use of the term "Armenian bands," stressing that, although the Caucasus Army had been regrouped into national units, all men under arms were soldiers of the Russian Republic. Lebedinskii negated Ottoman justifications for violating the truce and urged that the order to advance be revoked and Turkish troops be withdrawn to the original demarcation line.[86]

The Russian general was responding to Vehib Pasha's historic note of February 12, 1918. The document was an indictment of the Armenians, who had no pity for the innocent Turkish inhabitants. Real power had slipped from the hands of Colonel Morel and the Russian troops into the clutches of Murat of Sivas, an outlaw for twenty-five years, who had been condemned to death in absentia by the Ottoman government. Vehib concluded:

> Despite my convincing appeals and your sincere promises, the crimes and atrocities in the areas evacuated by your troops, instead of ceasing, have passed all bounds and have created such a situation that it is thoroughly

impossible for me to hold my troops in the role of silent spectators, since they hear and are aware that their parents, children, wives, and relatives are doomed to annihilation. Therefore, considerations based on humanity and civilization demand the improvement and rectification of this situation by taking decisive and undelayable measures in the evacuated areas. It is only for this reason that I am compelled to push forward parts of the military units from the two armies under my command.[87] However, I hasten to add that this does not constitute an enemy act against the Russian Army. . . . I warmly and sincerely assure you that the Erzinjan temporary truce continues in force except for the paragraph respecting the demarcation lines, which, because of the withdrawal of the Russian troops, automatically loses its significance. This action is resorted to only in the name of humanity and civilization.[88]

The Ottoman armies advanced. Current Turkish authors are nearly unanimous in citing the excesses by Armenians as the prime motivation for the foremarch of the I and II corps. Not fifteen hundred, but assertedly thousands of Moslems were annihilated by the lawless bands of Christians.[89] Armenian authors and military participants maintain that every effort was made to live in peace with the Moslems. Turkish civilians were repeatedly promised security if they remained calm. That measures were taken against the Moslems is not denied, but these were adopted only after Turks and Kurds, taking advantage of the Russian evacuation, attempted to paralyze the supply routes and defensive positions.[90] Present Soviet historians, reversing earlier condemnations of both Turks and Armenians, now stress that the Ottoman notes of December–February and the rationalization of Vehib Pasha were the necessary prerequisites for violating the Erzinjan Truce.[91] It cannot be ignored that the date chosen by the Ottoman Command to launch a drive to retrieve Turkish Armenia and to conquer Transcaucasia came two days after Trotsky had delivered his "no war, no peace" declaration at Brest and a day after General von Ludendorff had sanctioned a Turkish offensive. Enver Pasha seems to have lost no time in seizing the opportunity to push toward the horizons of Turkestan.

Karabekir's corps struck at the Erzinjan defenses from the direction of Kemakh and by February 13 had nearly surrounded the city. Murat attempted to convince Colonel Morel to hold the city a day or two longer so that the Christian population could be evacuated, but the more experienced Russian officer considered the task impossible. By evening the order for retreat was given. As during the 1915 evacuation of Van, the disorganization and panic were catastrophic. The Armenian townsmen, having made no preparations for a withdrawal, now fled into the freezing night with whatever they could carry. Soldiers abandoned their units to seek their families. The disorderly throng, trudging through deep drifts of snow, was ambushed repeatedly by Kurdish bands.[92] By the time this sorry company reached Mamakhatun four days later, half the refugees had been killed, frozen to death, wounded, or frostbitten. Morel's men were ordered to regroup at Mamakhatun, but the confusion was so great that neither troops nor civilians stopped until they were a day's march from Erzerum.[93] Behind the new defense perimeter scurried thousands of refugees from lands extending westward nearly a hundred miles.

General Odishelidze seems to have committed a serious blunder when he forbade the destruction of the numerous caches of food, supplies, and armaments left in the abandoned territory. Reasoning that after a peace treaty these valuable goods would be returned to his army, he ordered their surrender to the Turks.[94] Corps Commander Karabekir later wrote that his men were nearly starved at the time of the offensive and that, had the attack been delayed another two weeks, his force would have disintegrated.[95] Throughout February and March the Turkish troops never had more than a few days' provisions, but they capitalized on the continued refusal of the Caucasus Army Command to destroy the tons of foodstuff and military matériel before retreating.

Karabekir's victory at Erzinjan earned messages of congratulation from the Ottoman Minister of War as well as from the Third Army Commander; but while the latter spoke of the necessity to liberate Erzerum, Enver's imagination had flown far beyond. In his cipher to Karabekir, the Pan-Turanic champion imparted that the Moslems of Russia had already expressed their Ottoman sympathies and that they had formed armed units in the area around Baku to free that Islamic stronghold from the Russian and Armenian usurpers. Karabekir was Enver's choice to direct Moslem military activities in Transcaucasia. The I Corps Commander and future leader of the Turkish Nationalist movement replied that only after emancipating the homeland from enemy occupation should the battle for Transcaucasia begin. He felt assured that part of the Ottoman Army could then be deployed to Baku and the North Caucasus; even if this were found to be impractical, it would not be difficult to oversee partisan warfare in those areas.[96] Logically, Karabekir listed the Ottoman objectives as first the 1914 borders, then the territories lost in 1878, and finally the expanses beyond. These were the prevailing circumstances when, in mid-February, 1918, Gegechkori informed the Ottoman government that Transcaucasia was prepared to negotiate and the Seim would soon announce conditions for an acceptable and just peace.

The Transcaucasian Seim

Formation of the Transcaucasian Seim had been contemplated as early as November, 1917, during the organizational meeting of the Commissariat. Both Zhordania and Gegechkori had spoken of the transitory character of the latter body and had sponsored a resolution entrusting the delegates elected to the Constituent Assembly with the task of establishing a more authoritative regional government. After dispersal of the Constituent Assembly on January 18, the Soviet Regional Center in Tiflis declared that the Bolsheviks had broken the final thread of Russian unity and that the Transcaucasian delegates to the Petrograd meeting, together with military representatives, should create a regional administration with sufficient power to impose revolutionary order and inaugurate needed reforms.[97] During the first week of February, 1918, these Constituent Assembly members conferred in Tiflis. A Menshevik-Musavatist resolution was introduced by Zhordania:

> Delegates to the Constituent Assembly, having examined the existing situation, found it necessary, pending the reconvening of the All-Russian Constituent Assembly, to call for the formation of the Transcaucasian Seim to exercise legislative prerogatives in all local questions.[98]

Dashnaktsutiun, dissenting from the majority opinion, proposed recognition of the Russian Democratic Federative Republic (whatever that meant in 1918) and the reorganization of Transcaucasia along federative lines. Even in the midst of the chaos, the Armenian nationalist party continued to press for territorial repartition. Finally the conference agreed that the Seim would convene on February 23 and that the number of its members would be determined by decreasing the election norms from sixty thousand, used for the Constituent Assembly, to twenty thousand votes per delegate.[99] In that manner the minor parties, which had been deprived of a voice in the Constituent Assembly, would be represented in the legislature.

Even before that decision had been made, the Bolshevik Regional Committee militated against the Seim, announcing on January 29 that the proposed body had neither the jurisdiction nor the mandate to act on behalf of the Transcaucasian peoples. Being elected to the Constituent Assembly did not make a delegate an automatic member of the Seim, as the counterrevolutionaries seemed to assume. Furthermore, that body would simply be a continuation of the Commissariat, which, in violation of the popular will, had attempted to sever Transcaucasia from the rest of Russia. The Regional Committee pledged to sabotage the Seim in every conceivable manner.[100] Concurrently, Shahumian extended his agitational activities to Tiflis. His articles and leaflets exposed the pack of scoundrels on the Commissariat and the lackeys who would fill the halls of the Seim. The Sovnarkom alone represented the legal government of all Russia. As Shahumian worked feverishly in Tiflis, his erstwhile Social Democrat Menshevik comrades searched for means to silence their rival. When they warned him to leave the bounds of Caucasia within twenty-four hours, he responded by publishing, almost under their very eyes, the single issue of a journal representing the Sovnarkom, *Kavkazskii vestnik Soveta Narodnykh Komissarov*.[101] Enraged, the Mensheviks then struck to crush the legal Bolshevik papers, *Kavkazskii rabochii, Banvori krive,* and the Georgian-language

Brzola, but almost immediately the journals reappeared with altered titles, *Kavkazskaia pravda, Banvor,* and so on.[102]

Seriously concerned about Shahumian's popularity in Tiflis, the Commissariat ordered his arrest on the day the Seim was to assemble. Utilizing the convenient hideouts of Tiflis, Shahumian avoided the police; then, with the aid of several of his anti-Bolshevik Armenian compatriots, he slipped away to Baku.[103] Later both Shahumian and Stalin claimed that Dashnaktsutiun and the Social Revolutionary party had opposed creation of the Seim and had even boycotted its opening session.[104] Though the latter contention was incorrect, Bolshevik appraisal of the Armenian psychology was not completely erroneous. Dashnakists in both Baku and Erevan were highly skeptical of the Tiflis proceedings. They often felt that the party's Bureau, located in the Transcaucasian capital, had been subordinated to the will of the Georgian Social Democrats. Several Baku Armenian delegates to the Seim did not attend a single session.[105] Aram Manukian, then chairman of the Erevan National Council, also refused to participate in the "intellectual gathering," since the future of Transcaucasia depended not upon the decisions of the Seim but on the activities at the front.[106] Even in Tiflis, the Armenian members of the legislature were not in accord with the forceful anti-Bolshevik measures of the Mensheviks. They protested vociferously when a Bolshevik-sponsored rally, remonstrating against the convening of the Seim, was fired upon in Alexandrovskii Park by the Georgian militia. At least five men were killed and fifteen wounded in this ominous event. Dashnakists and Social Revolutionaries, in an attempt to embarrass their Menshevik colleagues, demanded explanations and an investigation of the incident.[107] But the tenacity of the Mensheviks was rewarded, for, recognizing the serious threat to their physical existence, the Bolshevik leaders abandoned Tiflis. By March, 1918, their exodus toward Baku and the North Caucasus was under way.[108]

During the opening session of the Seim, on the evening of February 23, the Menshevik candidate Nikolai Chkheidze, veteran of the Petrograd Soviet, was elected president of the legislature. Following the reading of a Bolshevik boycott proclamation, Gegechkori reviewed the activities of the Commissariat whose duties he considered completed. The Seim nevertheless authorized the Commissariat to act, after some reorganization, as an executive until a government could be formed.[109] Besides listening to messages of felicitation appropriate to an inaugural session, the Seim confirmed the credentials of the delegates, affiliated politically as follows:[110]

Social Democrat, Menshevik[111]	33
Musavat-Moslem Nonpartisan Bloc	30
Dashnaktsutiun	27
Moslem Socialist Bloc	7
Social Revolutionary	5
Moslem Social Democrat (Hummet)[112]	4

Moslems of Russia (Ittihad)	3
Georgian National Democrat	1
Georgian Social Federalist	1
Constitutional Democrat[113]	1

Gegechkori, in a major foreign-policy address, monopolized proceedings of the second session. He accused the Sovnarkom of negotiating a settlement that would transform Russia into a colony of German imperialism. It was thus the sacred obligation of all disciples of democracy to shield the Transcaucasian region of Russia from that doom.[114] On February 28 the "fractions" of the Seim presented their programs. Speaking for Dashnaktsutiun, Hovhannes Kachaznuni began, "The dream of generations—the All-Russian Constituent Assembly, became a reality for one day." While mourning the recent assassination of that promising child, Transcaucasia had nonetheless to prove its stamina by facing and solving the imposing, ponderous problems. As a healthy limb, Transcaucasia would invigorate the "One All-Russian Democratic Federative Republic." The frail white-haired orator then offered his party's principles and legislative plans:

1) conclusion of warfare on the bases proclaimed by the Great Russian Democracy—a nonannexationist peace and the right to self-determination, meaning autonomy for Turkish Armenia;
2) formation of Transcaucasia's government along purely socialist lines, for only such a regime could satisfy the workers, resolve the economic crisis, and restore communications throughout every province;
3) abolition of private land ownership, followed by immediate free distribution of the fields on the principle of equal opportunity to benefit from the blessings of the soil;
4) implementation of the party's minimal economic program—an eight-hour workday, government supervision of labor, and protection of the toilers;
5) nationalization of the larger financial, industrial, and commercial establishments essential to the state for socialist production;
6) creation of just provincial boundaries within a federated Transcaucasia;
7) determination to strive and collaborate with all other democratic elements in the Seim to attain these goals.[115]

The second point was especially significant, for its adoption would have excluded the powerful nonsocialist Musavat fraction from the administration.

The pronounced Russian orientation mirrored in Kachaznuni's declaration contrasted sharply with the statement read by Musavatist Hasan Bek Aghaev. The most powerful Moslem organization of Transcaucasia maintained that the Seim had the jurisdiction of a constituent assembly and that, because the region had been severed from Russia, it must determine its own destiny without dependence upon the areas north of the Caucasus Mountains.

Agreeing to the principle of a democratic peace without annexations or indemnities, the Musavat spokesman added, with obvious reference to Turkish Armenia, "We should not mix in the internal affairs of our neighboring governments." Further, only coalition government based on proportional representation was acceptable. Aghaev passed silently over the question of provincial reorganization.[116]

Then Noi Zhordania, the personification of Menshevism, rose to the podium. He decried the Sovnarkom's shameful acceptance of the February 21 German ultimatum, which enslaved Russia politically and economically and slashed the bonds between Transcaucasia and the Russian heartlands. The benches of Dashnaktsutiun scowled when they heard the eloquent orator exclaim, "And our Seim must now shoulder the primary task of transforming with its own strength that young land, Transcaucasia, into a legally organized Transcaucasian Republic." Such words smacked too much of separatism for the Armenian palate. Peace would be negotiated with Turkey, continued Zhordania, but it would not be an ignominious settlement such as that sanctioned by the Sovnarkom. "We will not sign such a peace; we believe it is better to die in our trenches with honor than to be scandalized and subjected to the curses of generations."[117] Prudently, the Menshevik spokesman avoided the issue of the government's composition. He wished to offend neither the Soviet Regional Center and Dashnaktsutiun on the one hand nor the Moslem fractions on the other. In principle Zhordania agreed with Kachaznuni that the repartition of Transcaucasia should follow ethnic lines but noted that, except for the Georgian provinces, large national-territorial divisions were impossible. Because of the extensive racial interspersion in southern and eastern Transcaucasia, a checkerboard of small national cantons was required.

The Seim's Conditions for Peace

Before the program of any party could be considered, an urgent and vital matter demanded attention. On the day the Seim was to convene, the Commissariat had already received the Ottoman response to Transcaucasia's willingness to parley. A Turkish delegation was prepared to depart from Constantinople for Tiflis to engage in preliminary talks concerning the bases for negotiations and to agree on a meeting site for the final conference. Upon notification of the Commissariat's acceptance, the delegation would set sail for Batum.[118] The Tiflis government apparently liked to do things in a grandiose manner. In order to formulate an answer, the Commissariat invited generals, representatives from the soviets, from the political parties, and from the still-to-be-assembled Seim. Hesitant of accepting full responsibility and aware of the sharp political divergences among the Transcaucasian peoples, the temporary administration felt compelled to summon such caucuses. On this occasion, however, all were agreed that the Turks should not be allowed in Tiflis. Quartermaster General Levandovskii reasoned that accepting the Turks in the capital was tantamount to admitting defeat. According to the rules of international diplomacy, a neutral meeting place was indicated. The Seim's only Kadet, Iulii Semenov, feared German collusion in the Turkish actions and advised that the negotiations progress only with the approval of the Allies. Chkhenkeli struck a realistic chord in pointing out that, because the internal disagreements of Transcaucasia were so evident, it was wiser not to permit the Turks to witness these rivalries. Consequently, he suggested Trebizond or Constantinople as more suitable meeting sites. Sirakan Tigranian of Dashnaktsutiun felt obliged to insist on the Ottoman capital or even a ship at sea since conditions in Trebizond were as disheartening as in Tiflis. Nonetheless, the gathering finally decided on Trebizond, but added that if the Sublime Porte objected to that choice, any other "neutral zone" would be splendid. Should Trebizond be acceptable, Transcaucasia would dispatch its delegation on March 2 and would give orders to permit Turkish vessels carrying the Ottoman representatives into that Black Sea harbor. General Odishelidze relayed the message, through Vehib Pasha, to Constantinople.[119]

With the conference site selected, the Seim pondered the conditions for peace. Noi Ramishvili, chairman of a committee to prepare recommendations, reported at the evening session of March 1. He prefaced his remarks by slandering the Sovnarkom. That government was responsible for denuding the Caucasus front and was now negotiating an intolerable settlement with the Central Powers. Therefore, Transcaucasia was compelled to go to the bargaining table to defend her own interests. Ramishvili added, however, that his committee assumed the Ottoman Empire was equally desirous of a just peace. Though some committee members (presumably Armenians) had suggested postponing negotiations until Transcaucasia had time to consolidate its position, Ramishvili believed that no further delays were permissible. Then, raising the crucial question of Transcaucasia's boundaries, the Menshevik spokesman warned that it was necessary to be prudent and realistic. This required the renunciation of pretensions to territory beyond the 1914 Russo-Turkish border, for any other claims would cause reverberations on both sides of that line. "But what shall we do with the motto of the Great Russian Revolution, peace based on the self-determination of peoples?" exclaimed Ramishvili. The heart of the entire world throbbed for Turkish Armenia and certainly the Seim would strive for a happy solution. Without touching on the question of Ottoman sovereignty, the delegates of Transcaucasia would insist that Turkish Armenia be granted autonomy. And if Turkey rejected a democratic peace, Transcaucasia would rise to defend its interests.[120]

The proposed terms were bitter for the Armenians, whose pretensions to the territory long occupied by the Russian Army and for the most part still held by native troops would be shattered. Nonetheless, realizing all too well that, isolated, greater tragedy awaited the Armenians, Dashnaktsutiun sullenly voted in favor of the Seim's bases for peace:

1) The Seim was authorized to conclude peace.
2) Peace with Turkey was to be permanent.
3) The 1914 international boundaries were to be reestablished.
4) The delegation was to *try* to guarantee the right of self-determination for eastern Anatolia and, for Turkish Armenia especially, autonomy within the structure of the Ottoman state.[121]

To lead the peace delegation, the Seim selected A. I. Chkhenkeli, considered by many the most Germanophile Menshevik in Tiflis and thus the most suitable choice.

Departure was scheduled for March 2, but on that very day the astounding telegram of Lev Karakhan brought news from Brest-Litovsk that the Central Powers were forcing Soviet Russia to cede Kars, Ardahan, and Batum "under the pretext of self-determination." While the Seim chattered about Turkish Armenian autonomy, the generals at Brest-Litovsk secured not only the unconditional restoration of the eastern Ottoman *vilayets*, but also of the three *sanjaks* awarded Russia by the 1878 Treaty of Berlin. Momentarily suppressing their bewilderment, Gegechkori and Chkheidze, on behalf of the Commissariat and the Seim, wired Brest-Litovsk, the Sovnarkom, the Central Rada in Kiev, the Odessa Soviet, and the governments at London, Rome, Paris, Washington, Tokyo, Constantinople, Berlin, and Vienna, denouncing the Brest treaty, declaring it void in relation to Transcaucasia, and broadcasting that the Tiflis government had already concluded a preliminary agreement with Turkey and was sending its delegates to Trebizond.[122]

Thus, from November to March, Transcaucasia recoiled in the face of the Bolshevik victory in central Russia and the monstrous visions of Pan-Turan in the Ottoman Empire. Creating a temporary administration charged with the responsibilities of a permanent government, Transcaucasia groped for a solution to the problem of how to remain a part of Russia without recognizing its new masters. The question disturbed Moslems the least and Armenians the most. Bound in an insincere alliance with their Transcaucasian neighbors, the Armenians protested every act that drove a deeper wedge between the plains of Russia and the mountains of Caucasia. Even collaboration with the Bolsheviks was condoned if it would construct a bridge, a possible escape hatch, to Russia. On the battlefield and on the diplomatic front, Transcaucasia dangled on strings pulled by Turkey. February, in particular, had been filled with disaster. The Erzinjan Truce had been shattered and the fate of the entire Caucasus lay in the balance. Trotsky's "no war, no peace" had permitted "more war, more concessions." And on March 2, 1918, the Transcaucasian peace delegation sat in Tiflis wondering what to do.

VIII
Dilemmas
(March–April, 1918)

BATTERED BY THE GALES OF WAR, revolution, and anarchy, Transcaucasia was drawn ever deeper into the whirlpool of destruction. Efforts to avoid the catastrophe were hindered by the synchronous existence of several dilemmas, each distinctly discernible, yet all inextricably interrelated. The problems of peace negotiations with the Turks, military activities on the front, inconsistency and disunity in the Tiflis government, clashes between Moslems and Armenians in every province, as well as the establishment of Soviet order in Baku were the most salient aspects of the quandary of Transcaucasia throughout March and April, 1918.

Confusion in Trebizond and in Tiflis

Following receipt of Karakhan's telegram from Brest, the baffled Transcaucasian peace delegation remained in Tiflis until news arrived from Trebizond that Turkish negotiators were departing from Constantinople. Encouraged by this report, the Transcaucasian entourage, nearly a hundred delegates, counselors, and guards, rushed to Batum, whence, on March 7 aboard the "Korol' Karl," they set sail for Trebizond. On the overnight voyage, the ship was nearly diverted to the Crimea by order of the Bolshevik Military Committee of the Black Sea, and only by resorting to bribery did the delegation succeed in reaching its destination.[1] That episode was only the first ordeal, for upon arriving in Trebizond harbor they learned that the entire region had been occupied by Yakub Shevki's 37th Division. The Turkish *vali,* who had been reinstated, denied that Trebizond was a neutral city and refused to allow the Transcaucasian guards to disembark. Chkhenkeli's mission would be the guest of the Ottoman government and, as such, Turkish troops would provide adequate protection.[2] Added to this annoyance was the fact that the promised Turkish delegation had not yet arrived. The Transcaucasians remained aboard ship until March 12, feeling more humiliated as each day passed. In compliance with orders of the Tiflis government to return to Batum if the Turkish mission had not arrived, Chkhenkeli had already prepared to sail when a ship flying the Turkish flag and carrying the negotiators from Constantinople entered the harbor. Three hours later Husein Rauf Bey, Chief of Naval Staff and Chairman of the Ottoman delegation, boarded the "Korol' Karl" to pay his respects.[3] After the customary exchange of compliments, Rauf invited Chkhenkeli to disembark, but disconcerting news from Tiflis regarding Turkish military activities made the Georgian leader reluctant.

Two days earlier, on March 10, Vehib Pasha had invited Front Commander Lebedinskii to order the evacuation of Kars, Ardahan, and Batum, in accordance with the Brest-Litovsk settlement. At the same time he informed Army Commander Odishelidze that, because of Armenian atrocities in and around Erzerum, the Turkish Army would advance to liberate the innocent victims. Vehib warned that any resistance to this march would result in unfortunate repercussions.[4] That evening Chkheidze, as President of the Seim, wired Vehib that Transcaucasia had already repudiated all agreements concluded without its approval and that a peace delegation had departed for Trebizond. Should now the demand for Kars, Ardahan, and Batum be viewed as Ottoman disinclination to negotiate?[5] The situation became even more bewildering when Odishelidze reported to Tiflis about Vehib's March 8 communication, advising that a Turkish deputation was sailing to Trebizond on the following day to begin talks.[6]

At a special session of the Seim on the evening of the eleventh, Chkheidze and Gegechkori drew attention to the critical and perplexing state of affairs. Commissariat President Gegechkori stressed that Vehib's ultimatum did not correspond to the February 23 Turkish note proposing negotiations for peace and for recognition of the Transcaucasian government. Then Zhordania emphasized that all Transcaucasia longed for peace, but, unlike the Bolshevik traitors, it could not and would not condescend to a settlement equivalent to unconditional surrender. Batum, "the window to the West," was as vital to Transcaucasia as Petrograd was to Russia and Smyrna to Turkey. Moreover, without the great key fortress of Kars there could be no security. Alluding to what already seemed a bit of the fading past, Zhordania continued, "Defense of the boundary is defense of the Revolution!" Should Turkey attempt to justify the rape of Kars and Ajaria, the territory around Batum, by flaunting the principle of self-determination, then Transcaucasia would assert its rightful claim to Turkish Armenia.[7]

On behalf of the Dashnakist "fraction," Avetik Shahkhatuni insisted on the four-point basis for peace so reluctantly accepted by his party during the March 1 session. Fathali Khan Khoiskii, leader of the Musavat-Nonpartisan Moslem bloc, begged for a rational approach to the problem. What need was there to assume hostile attitudes, which would only embarrass the

Transcaucasian delegation at Trebizond? Only when and if the parleys were unfruitful and only after determining without any doubt that the interests of Turkey were irreconcilable with those of the Caucasus should countermeasures be contemplated. Khan Khoiskii could not refrain from pointing out that the Turkish viewpoint was quite logical. After all, the Ottoman government had offered to recognize Transcaucasia as a separate political entity and had even suggested the commissioning of envoys to Brest. Since the proposal had been rejected and a definite answer to Turkey delayed, the Sublime Porte felt compelled to regard Transcaucasia as an integral part of Russia and therefore subject to all provisions of the Brest-Litovsk treaty.[8] Social Revolutionary Ivan Lordkipanidze called for mobilization. Turning to the benches of the Musavat delegates, he asked that party to declare its readiness to stand in defense of Transcaucasia in the event of renewed hostilities. Concurring with Zhordania's appraisal, the lone Kadet, Semenov, added that the Turks were imitating the German tactic of negotiating on the one hand while preparing for invasion on the other. Khan Khoiskii, aroused to a defense of his views, exclaimed to the applause of the Moslem members that the political circumstances now necessitated a definite stand in relation to independence. As if ignoring the statement, the Seim, its ambivalence revealing helplessness, resolved to sustain the Commissariat in efforts to negotiate, on the assumption, however, that Turkey's desire for peace, expressed on several occasions, was sincere.[9]

Thus, in Trebizond, when Rauf Bey invited the Transcaucasian delegation ashore, Chkhenkeli first desired an explanation of Vehib's March 10 radiogram ordering the evacuation of Kars, Ardahan, and Batum. Rauf professed ignorance of the matter, but promised to communicate with the Third Army Commander for details. In the meantime he advised the Transcaucasians to disembark in order to avoid antagonizing the local inhabitants. Reacting to Chkhenkeli's intransigence and insistence that Ottoman intentions be clarified, Rauf stressed that the mere presence of a Turkish delegation certainly reconfirmed the Porte's willingness to establish peace and eternal friendship with Transcaucasia. He promised to answer Chkhenkeli's inquiries formally and officially as soon as the talks began.[10] Then, after quibbling about the Transcaucasian guards, the two presidents agreed that ten would remain with the delegation but the other forty would depart on the first ship to Batum.[11]

With the preliminary bargaining concluded, the Transcaucasian mission, described satirically by the local Turkish newspaper as "too small for an invading military force but much too large for a peace delegation," [12] went ashore. In sending a host of delegates, advisers, and guards, the Seim revealed its inexperience in international diplomacy and, more important, its inability to eliminate the mutual distrust of the Transcaucasians. Counselors and military attachés of each nationality were essential, for it was as impossible for an Armenian to rely on information supplied by a Moslem as it was for a Tatar to depend on statistics prepared by a Georgian. Eleven members had voting privileges:

Name[13]	Party[14]
Akakii Chkhenkeli	Menshevik (Chairman)
Haidar Abashidze[15]	Menshevik
Mahmed Hajinskii	Musavat
Khalil Khas-Mamedov	Musavat
Mir-Yakub Mehtiev	Moslems of Russia
Ibrahim Haidarov	Moslem Socialist Bloc
Akber Sheikh-ul-Islamov	Hummet
Ruben Kachaznuni[16]	Dashnaktsutiun
Alexandre Khatisian	Dashnaktsutiun
Georgii Laskhishvili	Georgian Social Federalist
Georgii Gvazava	Georgian National Democrat[17]

The interpreters were Dr. Gambashidze and Mehmed Emin Rasul-Zade, and the chief Armenian advisers, the noted historian Leo and the veteran revolutionary and representative of the militant arm of Dashnaktsutiun, Ruben Ter Minasian.[18] The Seim had bound the delegation to act as a single unit and to work within the framework of the four adopted bases for peace. Chkhenkeli was to consult with the Seim on all important questions and to keep it fully informed about the proceedings.[19] The Ottoman representatives stood out in sharp contrast to the multinational Transcaucasian aggregation. Rauf commanded complete authority over his four colleagues, Mahmed Nusret Bey of the Foreign Ministry, Colonel Tewfik Salim and Major Husrev of the Ottoman Caucasus Army, and Major Yusuf Riza of the Quartermaster Corps.[20] The Trebizond Conference finally convened on March 14, just after Chkhenkeli had received the startling news that Erzerum had fallen.

The Fall of Erzerum and All Turkish Armenia

Turkey's momentous diplomatic victory at Brest-Litovsk elicited renewed enthusiasm among the ruling circles of the Empire. On March 10, Enver Pasha triumphantly issued news of the treaty to the armed forces and instructed Vehib to take immediate steps to occupy the *sanjaks* of Kars, Ardahan, and Batum.[21] Obviously, Vehib lost no time in complying, for it was on that same day that he urged Lebedinskii to clear the three regions and apprised Odishelidze of the Turkish march on Erzerum. Prior to this official communiqué, men of Karabekir's I Corps had advanced along the main route from Erzinjan to Erzerum and had concentrated at Alaja, approximately 15 miles west of the citadel and only a few miles from the Armenian positions at Ilija.[22] Karabekir apparently carried out this move without orders from Vehib, who, even after March 10, directed the Corps Commander to delay the offensive until sufficient reinforcements could arrive. Karabekir argued that delay meant famine, for the enemy would have time to evacuate or destroy the provisions in the fortress. Without those supplies the Third Army would starve.[23] On March 11, Karabekir launched a full-scale assault on Erzerum.

A Russian unit of cannoneers and approximately four thousand Armenian troops manned the Erzerum front. In late February, Odishelidze's General Staff and Headquarters had transferred to a safer site at Sarikamish. Then, on March 3, General Andranik, entrusted with the defense of Erzerum, had reached the city with nearly a thousand men.[24] Despite his prowess as a guerrilla fighter and his legendary popularity, Andranik could not sufficiently strengthen the strategic positions, nor could he allay the fears of soldiers and civilians. Moreover, as the Ottoman Army neared, the sizable Moslem population in and around the city increased its diversionary blows and restlessly awaited the return of Ottoman suzerainty after two years of foreign rule. As Karabekir struck from the west, Kurdish units attacked from the north and south of the fortress. Unable to discipline his troops or quell the panic among the Christians, Andranik issued the order for retreat less than twenty-four hours after the Turkish offensive had begun.[25] The pandemonium of Erzinjan was repeated, only on a greater scale. Refugees poured through the Kars Gate onto the road eastward as Kurds lay in wait along this bottleneck to pluck their prey. The regulars of the Armenian Corps pushed ahead of the civilian population to save themselves. Unassisted armed bands of Turkish Armenians held the city until most of the Christians had fled. The intrepidity of such groups slightly mitigated the widespread impression of the distressing cowardice of the Armenian soldier. The frenzied troops and bands retreating from Erzerum killed any Moslems falling into their hands and burned the Turkish villages that lay in their path.[26]

According to a report prepared by General Nazarabekian, thirty-two tons of dynamite and sixty-five tons of powder in addition to vast stores of weapons, food, and uniforms were left in Erzerum. The Armenian general maintained that permission to ignite the explosives was withheld, because to grant it would have doomed the entire city and its Moslem inhabitants.[27] Army Commander Odishelidze reported, however, that preliminary arrangements had been made with the Ottoman Command to allow for the gradual withdrawal of this matériel. He complained to the Tiflis government that a similar agreement concerning the supplies abandoned in Trebizond had not been honored by the Turks.[28] Not only current Soviet authors but also some of Odishelidze's Armenian contemporaries have accused the general of treachery, of secretly corresponding with Vehib, and of inciting Armenophobia among the Georgian and Moslem leaders of Transcaucasia. In the Seim this disposition was evidenced by the

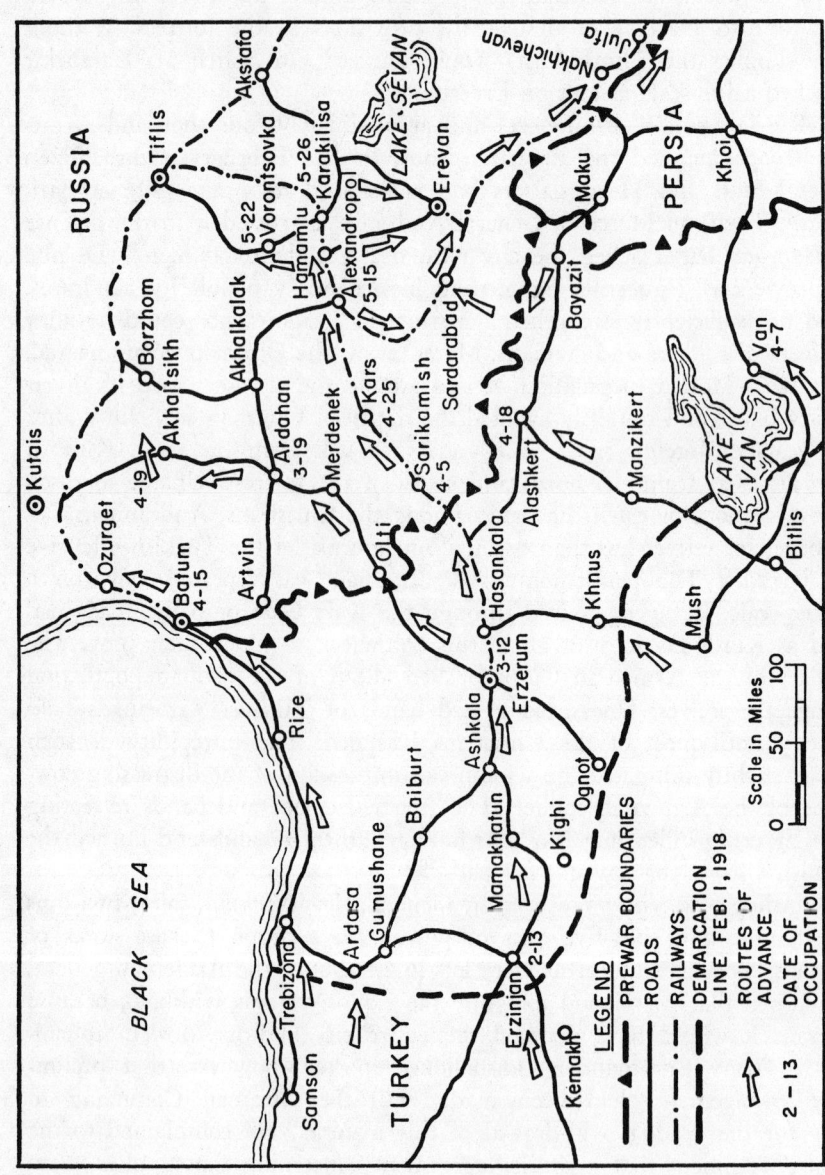

Map 8. The Turkish offensive, February–May, 1918

repeated deferment of Armenian-sponsored legislation authorizing complete mobilization and raising the age limit of men subject to military service. Only in mid-April, several weeks after the first Turkish violation of the Erzinjan Truce, did the Seim accede to a new conscription act. During that intervening period, both Moslem and Georgian members loudly criticized the several provincial Armenian councils which had inaugurated enlistment campaigns on their own initiative.[29]

Whether the Armenian assertions can be sustained or not, the fact remains that on March 12, 1918, the victorious 36th Division entered Erzerum, became master of the stockpiles, of the four hundred large fortress guns, and, more important, of the key to the entire Armenian Plateau. With the fall of Erzerum, the battle for Turkish Armenia ended. In Van and northward at Khnus and in the Alashkert Valley, Armenian units resisted a little longer before the battle for Caucasian Armenia began. In mid-March, Andranik, disgusted and dejected, resigned his command and left for Tiflis.[30] General Lebedinskii attempted to stabilize a shorter defense perimeter by entrusting to Nazarabekian the front from Maku in North Persia to Olti in the Kars *oblast,* and to General Gabaev's Georgian units the region between Olti and Batum. Meanwhile, the Caucasus Army General Staff withdrew from Sarikamish to Alexandropol, the strategic juncture of the railway running from Kars to Tiflis and to the Persian border at Julfa.[31]

Opposing the Transcaucasian forces were one Turkish division along the Black Sea coast between Trebizond and Batum and three others on the central plateau facing the Armenian positions at Sarikamish-Mejinkert and at Van. Spurred on by their near effortless victories, the shabby Ottoman units continued to advance, crossing the 1914 boundary in the last week of March.[32] In a move from the Erzerum *vilayet* into areas west and south of Sarikamish, they successfully severed communication between Van and Kars. The Caucasus Army Command, fearing a flanking movement reminiscent of Enver's 1914 strategy, recalled its feeble contingents from the Alashkert Valley and on April 5 ordered General Areshian to abandon Sarikamish and to withdraw to Novo-Selim, approximately 20 miles from the Kars fortress. Two days later units of the Turkish IV Corps entered Van, as the defenders and refugees for the third time since the outbreak of war fled over the narrow strip of Persian territory that separated the vilayet from the Erevan *guberniia.*[33] Within two months the eastern provinces of the Ottoman Empire had been retrieved. Enver, Vehib, Karabekir, and Shevki now prepared to effectuate Article IV of the Treaty of Brest-Litovsk.

Smith's Appeals for Assistance

In the midst of this dilemma, Consul Smith continued dispatching his frantic messages to Washington. He was not enthused by the decision of

Transcaucasia to parley in Trebizond and forwarded with obvious relish the Western Armenian Defense Council's declaration repudiating negotiations and pledging to continue the struggle.[34] In April, Secretary of State Lansing informed the American ambassador in Paris that Smith had on several occasions pointed out the threat of total Armenian extermination if help were not forthcoming. Smith claimed, with gross exaggeration, that the fifteen thousand Turkish Armenian and twenty-five thousand Russian Armenian defenders could be doubled with Allied support, but that, instead, the Allies were only aggravating the situation by their indifference and inactivity. Moslem bands were attacking Armenian villages in pursuance of what Smith considered a calculated German plot. He urged that two million dollars be placed at his disposal to strengthen three Russian Armenian fortresses, which could block the Turkish advance for at least six months. Moreover, he complained bitterly about the inadequate and "piteously futile" British Military Mission in the Caucasus.[35] In Paris, Ambassador William Sharp, having inquired about Anglo-French intentions, reported to Washington that the Allied War Council had recognized the value of the Armenian and Georgian units as early as December, 1917, and had authorized certain expenditures for purchase of weapons and equipment from the retreating Russian soldiers. In addition, two million rubles had been dispatched, but unfortunately the money had not reached Baghdad in time to be transmitted to Tiflis.[36]

Smith's persistence succeeded in eliciting some reserved inquiries from the Department of State, but it did not induce a modification of United States policy. On March 18 Smith received Ambassador Francis' note instructing him to adhere to the directive of November 26, 1917, prohibiting the encouragement of any measures that might lead to the segmentation of Russia or to civil war.[37] On March 30, 1918, Lansing informed Smith, "The United States is not in a position to support active military operations on the Caucasus front." Four days later he reported to Ambassador Walter Page in London that holding the Caucasus depended on the Armenians; however, "As United States is not at war with Turkey this Government is prevented from taking action. . . ."[38] By April, 1918, the Tiflis politicians should have relinquished any hope that the great democracy of the Western world would rise in defense of the "Transcaucasian Democracy."

The Trebizond Conference

Away from the theater of war but affected by the successful Turkish advance and capture of Erzerum, the Trebizond Peace Conference was called to order on March 14 by Husein Rauf Bey. The two delegations met until April 14 in six plenary sessions and several private interviews. During the opening ceremonies, Transcaucasia made its initial concession by waiving the established procedure of alternating the presidency of a conference when held on neutral ground. By allowing Rauf Bey to preside at all sessions, Chkhenkeli tacitly recognized the validity of the Turkish contention that Trebizond was an Ottoman city.[39] After the customary exchange of goodwill addresses, Rauf asked insinuatingly about the state of affairs in Transcaucasia and about the jurisdiction of the Tiflis government. Was it qualified to participate in international negotiations? The Ottoman government requested information concerning the essence, form, and civil-political administration of Transcaucasia and questioned whether the "republic" had complied with the conditions established by international law for the creation of independent nations.[40] Discussions relating to the pointed and calculated interpellation showed that Turkey held the trump cards and used them to undermine every attempt of Transcaucasia to prove it was a de facto government without officially having declared independence. One student of the subject has stated that ". . . the Seim and its delegation were trying to convince the Turks that Transcaucasia was an *almost* independent state, as though there were from the standpoint of international law such a thing as 'almost independence.' "[41]

Chkhenkeli, during the second plenary session on March 16, acknowledged Rauf's blunt inquiry by announcing that a declaration relating to the form of government soon would be made by the Seim. Indeed, Transcaucasia's repudiation of Brest-Litovsk before the nations of the world and its participation in the Trebizond Conference attested to its having already entered international diplomacy as a separate state.[42] During the third session, Rauf riddled Chkhenkeli's opposition to the acceptance of Brest-Litovsk as the basis for the current talks. As if the Transcaucasians were unaware of the facts, Rauf carefully explained that international agreements between two sovereign states could not be imposed upon a third nation if the latter had established independence and received recognition prior to the conclusion of the said accord. Consequently, since Transcaucasia had satisfied neither condition, it naturally was still considered an integral unit of the Russian Republic. That the Commissariat had refused to send delegates to Brest, that it had desired to confer with the governments of other border areas of Russia, and that the Russian Caucasus Army Command was still in charge of military activities were adequate indications that the region had not, in fact, separated from the former Romanov Empire. Now, however, learning of Transcaucasia's wish to guide its own destiny, the Sublime Porte would be pleased to enter into friendly relations founded upon the stipulations of Brest-Litovsk.[43]

The Ottoman position was quite clear and painfully logical. A commission composed of Chkhenkeli, Khatisian, Hajinskii, and Gvazava contrived countercontentions, which were delivered by the Chairman at the fourth plenary session on March 20.[44] Futilely, Chkhenkeli argued that the Brest negotiations were void because the Sovnarkom did not represent Russia, a land in the throes of civil war. He repeated that Turkey had expressed willingness to recognize Transcaucasia as early as January 14, 1918, and had reiterated this in messages of February 14 and 23. The Trebizond Conference itself testified to the desire of both governments to establish cordial relations, but this would be impossible were the Ottomans to insist upon the validity of Article IV. Chkhenkeli reassured Rauf that the Seim, prior to ratifying a treaty of peace, would fulfill all requirements for the founding of sovereign states.[45]

Rauf needed little time to prepare a rebuttal. He pointed out that civil wars had no effect on international acts unless the existing government were overthrown. Dispersal of the Constituent Assembly was sufficient proof of Bolshevik control. Therefore, agreements concluded by the Sovnarkom were binding for all parts of Russia except those, such as the Ukraine, which had proclaimed their separation and received international sanction. Then, engaging in a bit of double-talk, Rauf added that the Ottoman peace proposals had been made prior to the Brest treaty and that mere negotiations between two parties did not necessarily signify mutual recognition. The Ottoman government, he asserted, was participating in the Trebizond Conference only to clarify certain economic and commercial matters not dealt with at Brest-Litovsk. Rauf concluded decisively, "It would be desirable for Transcaucasia to declare its independence and announce the form of government before these negotiations can come to a final agreement so coveted by both sides."[46]

The conference raced toward an impasse. Since direct rapid communication with Tiflis was lacking, Kachaznuni suggested a recess so that a few members of the delegation could confer with the Seim and return to Trebizond with further instructions. Hajinskii, Khas-Mamedov, and Mehtiev objected to the proposal and insisted that the proceedings should not be interrupted.[47] The fifth plenary session proved, however, that further talks would be fruitless unless Transcaucasia made greater concessions. During the meeting, Chkhenkeli contended that the Seim had already acted positively on the subject of independence by appointing a commission to work out the necessary details in the shortest possible time. But the declaration of independence could not be made until Turkey had accepted the March 1 bases for peace. With reference to the fourth point of those terms, Rauf angrily rebuked the Transcaucasian delegation for attempting to meddle in the internal affairs of the Ottoman Empire. The "so-called question of Turkish Armenia" had no place on the agenda. In a softer tone, he added that the Imperial government was pleased to learn of Transcaucasia's decision to begin an independent life but that the mutual obligations between Russia and Turkey could not be ignored. The Sublime Porte could consider recognizing Transcaucasia only after every claim to Kars, Ardahan, and Batum had been renounced.[48] After five plenary sessions the broad gap between Ottoman and Transcaucasian views had not been bridged.

Gathering in caucus in the wake of Rauf's final statements, the Transcaucasians stooped to caustic recriminations. Hajinskii ridiculed the indecisiveness of Khatisian, who in turn accused Hajinskii of divulging secrets to the Turks in the adjoining room. Khas-Mamedov satirized the delegation of which he was a member and characterized its stand as farcical. The last semblance of even superficial unity among the delegates was shattered. In this noxious atmosphere it was finally agreed that Haidarov, Laskhishvili, and Kachaznuni would return to Tiflis for directives and that Rauf would be asked to accede to a temporary recess.[49]

Transcaucasia's Quandary

Four days later, on March 25, the Presidium of the Seim, the Commissariat, and representatives of the several political fractions studied the report of the Trebizond delegates. Kachaznuni described the quagmire created by Rauf's insinuative questions. He was convinced that Turkey honestly desired a Transcaucasian state to serve as a buffer to Russia. However, doubting Transcaucasia's ability to withstand the expansion of the new masters of the North, the Ottoman rulers deemed it imperative to annex Kars, Ardahan, and Batum. Laskhishvili verified Kachaznuni's account of the Ottoman delegation's absolute refusal to discuss the subject of Turkish Armenia. Rauf had complained that this was the same old ruse the European Powers had employed in an attempt to strangle the Ottoman Empire. Haidarov maintained that Turkey had no territorial pretensions to Transcaucasia, desired no further conquest, but simply wished to exercise the privileges she had gained at Brest-Litovsk. Transcaucasia should not expect the Sublime Porte to renounce its right to the three sanjaks, for, even if it so desired, this would be impossible in view of the popular enthusiasm elicited in Turkey by the publication of Article IV of Brest-Litovsk.[50]

No person at the emergency meeting explained more succinctly or more accurately than the Dashnakist Karjikian the reasons that compelled Transcaucasia to maintain an embarrassing ambiguity about its international status. A declaration of independence would have to be accompanied by an identification of the territorial bounds of the new state. Such a definition would, of necessity, include Kars, Ardahan, and Batum, and this, in turn, would occasion renewed hostilities with Turkey. On the other hand, were independence proclaimed without the inclusion of the three districts, Transcaucasia would not be independent at all. Thus, the declaration had to coincide with an agreement concerning the boundaries. Karjikian added that discussion of Turkish Armenia should not be viewed as involvement in Ottoman affairs, for Transcaucasia had no annexationist ambitions. Interest in the fate of the eastern vilayets arose from dedication to the principle of self-determination.[51] Social Revolutionary Lordkipanidze observed a justifiable parallel between Turkey's preoccupation with its related peoples abroad and Transcaucasia's concern for the Turkish Armenians. Disagreeing with such statements, Mehtiev, on behalf of the Seim's Moslem members, demanded unconditional acceptance of the Brest terms, warning that, if Transcaucasia did not declare independence immediately, the Moslem fractions could not support further negotiations. A foreign minister, not a large delegation, should represent Transcaucasia at Trebizond. That the meeting did not resolve the indecision of the Tiflis government was evidenced by Zhordania's motion summoning the Seim to stand firm on its conditions for peace but also to authorize the delegation president to take the necessary steps leading to an "honorable settlement."[52] In a single breath resoluteness was demanded while concessions were permitted.

During the Seim's plenary session the following evening,[53] Noi Ramishvili headed the slate of orators. Repeating Karjikian's views, the Menshevik chief explained that a declaration of independence in conformity with Transcaucasian interests would constitute a virtual ultimatum to Turkey. He saw advantages in continuing the tactic of ambiguity. It would allow the Ottomans more time to comprehend the advisability of making certain concessions, without which the buffer state they desired would never come into existence. Could the Ottoman rulers fail to understand that a consolidated Transcaucasia having no imperialistic designs was much more valuable than a score of border fortresses? In conclusion, Ramishvili urged that diplomatic tradition be respected during the negotiations in order to avoid the pitfalls experienced by Trotsky at Brest-Litovsk. The delegation president should have the freedom to make "arrangements" on secondary matters so as not to jeopardize the cardinal interests of Transcaucasia.[54] Without agreeing on the issues of independence and inclusive territory, the Seim, naming Chkhenkeli as Foreign Minister, resolved:

> Standing on the basis of our decision of March 1, 1918, on the conditions of peace with Turkey, but desiring an honorable settlement for both parties, the Seim gives to Chkhenkeli, Peace Delegation President and Minister of Foreign Affairs, extraordinary powers to take necessary steps in this direction.[55]

Except for granting broader latitude to Chkhenkeli, the Seim did nothing to clarify Transcaucasia's legal position. Armenians, though voting for the resolution, were wary of Chkhenkeli's anti-Russian orientation, while the Moslems were impatient to proclaim the separation of the Caucasus from Russia and to accept Turkish terms for friendship. The conflicting views were the natural outgrowth of contradictory aspirations.

Transcaucasia Aflame

Though the March 26 meeting of the Seim adjourned in a state of agitation, the expressions of distrust and animosity had been quite restrained in comparison to the antagonism that pervaded those sessions dealing with the internal affairs of Transcaucasia. At such times, the superficiality of cooperation was most rudely unmasked. While the "intellectuals" harangued in Tiflis, every province of Transcaucasia was aflame with anarchy and civil strife. In particular, the turmoil in the Erevan guberniia threatened to erupt into rampant interracial warfare.

From the March Revolution until the winter of 1917, civil administration in Erevan had nearly ceased to exist, but soon after the Bolshevik coup the guberniia's Russian, Armenian, and Moslem inhabitants each formed a national body wielding considerable authority.[56] The Armenian provincial council was created in December at a conference sponsored by Bishop Khoren of Erevan.[57] Yet the region lacked a strong and experienced leadership. In Tiflis, the Russian Armenian National Council delegated Aram Manukian to fill the gap. The choice was well calculated, for the hero of Van was a veteran organizer, fully aware of the strengths and shortcomings of his people. The National Council, while collaborating with the Commissariat, expected Aram to ignore and, if necessary, to counteract those directives of the Tiflis government which were deemed harmful to Armenian interests. Arriving in Erevan during the first half of January, 1918, Aram organized a committee which served as an unofficial administration. It expelled several Armenian bandit groups from the city, levied special taxes on the residents, confiscated stores of matériel abandoned by the Russian troops, and, in violation of the Commissariat's instructions, conscripted hundreds of men. With surprising unity and willingness, the Armenians of Erevan adopted almost every suggestion of "Aram Pasha."[58]

The nearly four hundred thousand Moslems of the guberniia were not oblivious of the activities of their Christian neighbors. Expropriation of the military supplies was loudly protested by the Tatars, who complained that the security of their villages was threatened by the influx of Armenian troops. Rumors that fellow Moslems were being oppressed and massacred in Turkish Armenia intensified their anxiety and antagonism. The "Shamkhor Massacre" of January, 1918, acted as a signal for concerted Moslem movements in Erevan. On the Erevan-Julfa railway, which passed near many Tatar settlements, troop trains were derailed and tracks and bridges destroyed. Armenian soldiers in transit to the Kars front were halted at the strategic juncture of Ulukhanlu, a Tatar village several miles from Erevan. To the south of Ulukhanlu in the districts of Sharur-Daralagiaz and Nakhichevan, isolated Christian villages were besieged. Throughout the province, wherever mixed Armeno-Tatar hamlets existed, the weaker national element usually fled from fear or by force. On March 5, interracial hostilities in Erevan itself claimed a hundred victims. Only immediate joint action by the Armenian and Moslem councils spared the city from going up in flames.[59]

On the same day that bullets rained down upon Erevan, a Commissariat inspection team, which had just returned from that city, presented its findings to the Seim. The Jafarov-Karjikian report painted a sad picture of anarchy and mutual Moslem-Christian atrocities. Scarcely a single depot was operative along the entire railway, which was continually sabotaged by armed bands. Armenians decried Tatar violence in one district, while, in another, Moslems bewailed the loss of hundreds of their innocent brothers at the hands of ruthless Armenians. The Kurds, on their part, had confessed to thievery and looting but asserted that these acts were essential for survival, as, unlike the Armenians and Tatars, they did not receive provisions from governmental reserves. Following the report, the Seim engaged in a round of insults, accusations, and denials. Except for the adoption of a resolution abounding with idealistic phrases, no positive action was taken to cope with the crisis.[60] No more comforting were the findings submitted two weeks later by another commission, composed of Smbat Khachatrian, former provincial commissar of Erevan; Aslan Bek Safikurdskii, an erstwhile Social Revolutionary and an organizer of the "Shamkhor Massacre"; and the chairman, Grigorii Georgadze, a Georgian Menshevik. The chairman reported that treacherous Moslem bands entrenched along the railway controlled the flow of traffic, while, on the other hand, the inhabitants of twenty Tatar villages had been killed or dispersed by regular Armenian contingents. In short, chaos reigned in Erevan. The usual Armeno-Moslem barrage in the Seim commenced even before Georgadze had completed his statements.[61]

Meanwhile, Armenian militarists had determined to "make an example" of Ulukhanlu, which, despite several warnings, still prevented the passage of troops headed for the front. On the morning of March 7, Aram, Dro, and Silikian led the bombardment and pitched combat. The battle raged until evening, when the Tatars finally broke ranks and fled. Ulukhanlu and the surrounding villages were razed and thousands of homeless Moslems scattered throughout the Sharur and Nakhichevan districts. The victorious troops reopened the railway to Alexandropol and Kars and then pushed southward to Khamarlu and Davalu, rescuing several beleaguered military units and escorting the population of isolated Christian villages to Erevan.[62] The hostilities did not cease with Ulukhanlu; on the contrary, news of the capitulation of Erzerum provoked greater turbulence. Typical of many other incidents was the ambush of an Armenian convoy by one of the six Moslem villages on the southwestern shore of Lake Sevan between Elenovka and Novo Bayazit. Armenian soldiers and peasantry responded by destroying all six villages and driving the survivors to the mountainous region east of the lake.[63]

Turkish violation of the Erzinjan Truce and the interracial friction at home fostered cohesion among the Erevan Armenians. Recognizing the need for iron discipline in order to surmount the deepening crisis, a conference of military and civil leaders in mid-March proclaimed Aram "Dictator of Erevan." Selecting directors for internal affairs, provisions, finance, and defense, Aram gave Erevan an exclusively Armenian administration for the first time in centuries. In the succeeding months, this Directorate extended its jurisdiction over much of the Plain of Ararat and, until it was relieved by the cabinet of the Armenian Republic in July, 1918, exercised the prerogatives of a de facto government.[64] It restored partial order, provided for a fraction of the refugees teeming throughout the province, and secured the transportation routes to the front. In these operations, tens of Tatar villages which "stood in the way" were not spared in what might be termed a precursor to the Moslem "treachery" and the Armenian "reprisals" that were to vex the Republic of Armenia throughout its existence.

The state of affairs in Erevan was not an exception. Events in the Kars oblast and the Elisavetpol guberniia were no more reassuring. Grigor Dsamoev, the civilian commissar of Kars, urgently wired the Seim that armed Tatars and Kurds had encircled Ardahan and Merdenek.[65] The Ardahan crisis distressed the Mensheviks in particular, for they considered the region indisputably Georgian. During the March 18 session of the Seim they vilified the "enemy within the country." That foe would no longer be tolerated. Martiros Harutunian of Dashnaktsutiun seized the opportunity to remind the Georgians that the treachery in Ardahan was no different from recent hostile acts in Elisavetpol and Erevan. He regretted that many members of the Transcaucasian legislature had chosen to ignore the grave realities until being aroused by the events in Ardahan, where the same "dark hand" was at work obstructing the government's defense efforts. Shafi Bek Rustambekov of the Musavat fraction agreed that anarchy was not permissible, especially at the critical moment when negotiations were proceeding in Trebizond. He strenuously objected, however, to the insinuative statements of Mensheviks and Dashnakists and denied the existence of a conspiracy.[66] The Musavatists and Mensheviks, having often acted in harmony, now upbraided one another. Iraklii Tsereteli shouted, "There is no difference at present between anarchy and treachery!" He contended that Transcaucasia had thus far been spared the disastrous fate of Russia only because the local democracy had not been permitted to splinter and plunge into civil war. Addressing the Musavatist legislators, the veteran Menshevik voiced astonishment that the leading Moslem organization had the audacity to rise in defense of anarchy. Was it not proper that the Seim fraction with the greatest influence on the elements causing the unrest should take active measures to restrain the transgressors?[67] As the members of the Seim bellowed at one another, Moslem insurgents captured Ardahan and disarmed soldiers of the Transcaucasian government.[68]

In Elisavetpol, the situation was equally critical. Both the province and its administrative center, called interchangeably Elisavetpol, Ganja, and Gandzak, were divided into distinct Armenian and Moslem sectors. The vital

Baku-Tiflis railway ran through the Moslem quarter of the city. Following the "Shamkhor Massacre" the relations between Tatars and Armenians had deteriorated into sporadic warfare. To arrest the strife in this strategic neighboring province, the Moslem and Armenian councils of Baku selected a mixed commission which reached Elisavetpol in mid-March. During the ensuing inquiry, local Armenians complained bitterly that they had been subjected to an economic boycott for over a month. The Moslems prohibited the movement of any provisions from the railway depot into the Armenian quarter, and the city's main market, located in the Tatar sector, was closed to Armenians. Furthermore, a group of Armenian soldiers, somehow having managed to reach Gandzak, had been ambushed on the way from the railroad to the Christian quarter. When several men were killed, the survivors retaliated by firing on any Moslem in sight. On their part, the Tatars of Ganja accused the Armenians of perfidy. The Transcaucasian Military Council in Tiflis had allotted the Moslems of Elisavetpol all goods and weapons left by the 269th Russian Regiment. Some of these supplies, mainly shells and bullets, were in the Tatar quarter of the city, but almost all rifles, uniforms, tenting, and complementary matériel were located in Armenian neighborhoods. The Christians, violating the arrangements of the Tiflis government, had refused to relinquish these goods. Armenian members of the Baku peace mission proposed a compromise whereby, except for the rifles, all stores of the 269th Regiment would be transferred to the Moslem sector and, after calm had been restored, the weapons, too, would be delivered. In return, the Tatars would lift their economic blockade and supply the Armenians with essential provisions. The plan was rejected by the Moslems and even more emphatically by the Armenians, who refused to give even a single tent peg to the "Turks." [69]

Talks had reached an impasse when a deputation of the Tiflis government arrived in the highlands. Gerasim Makharadze, controller of Transcaucasian military resources, with his Armenian and Moslem colleagues, Avetik Sahakian and Hamin Bek Shahtakhtinskii, haggled with the mountaineers for two days before a compromise was finally adopted on March 22. Makharadze promised the Moslems abundant weapons from the general reserves in Tiflis. The Armenians were to relinquish all property of the 269th Regiment except for the rifles in return for flour, sugar, and other foodstuffs. It seemed that the crisis had been surmounted, for on March 24 a train carrying Armenians traveled unhindered from Elisavetpol to Baku for the first time in over two months.[70] Coinciding with the Trebizond Conference, the bloodshed in Erevan province, Ardahan, and Elisavetpol naturally intensified the mutual distrust within the Transcaucasian peace delegation and Seim. But the greatest upheaval had not yet occurred when Kachaznuni, Laskhishvili, and Haidarov began their return voyage to Trebizond. That carnage was to burst forth in Baku.

The "March Days" in Baku

Located on the Apsheron Peninsula, Baku was the most cosmopolitan and proletarian city in Transcaucasia. No single political party was powerful enough to control the civil administration or the soviets. During the November 1917 elections to the Constituent Assembly, for example, the following returns were recorded for the leading slates:[71]

Slate number and party	Votes
I. Menshevik	5,667
II. Kadet	9,062
III. Social Revolutionary	18,789
IV. Dashnaktsutiun	20,314
V. Bolshevik	22,276
X. Musavat	21,752
XIV. Moslems of Russia	7,841

In the Workers' and Soldiers' Soviet elected in December, the Bolshevik minority was able to dominate the Executive Committee only with the indulgence of many non-Communist members. On issues such as the approval of the Sovnarkom's Brest-Litovsk policy, Musavat delegates voted with the Bolsheviks, whereas most Dashnakists and Social Revolutionaries assisted Shahumian in moves against Baku's nonsocialist organizations.[72] Shahumian, though often castigating the non-Bolshevik groups, did not renounce joint action. On more than one occasion he wrote that, since the Bolsheviks alone could not master Baku, it was necessary to rely on other elements. By mid-March, however, relations with the Moslems had reached the breaking point, for the powerful Musavat party refused to accept the Bolshevik contention that the Soviet was the only legal administrative body in Baku.[73]

While supporting the Baku Soviet, the more than seventy thousand Armenians of the city selected a national council to express their collective will. This council, formed in December, 1917, assumed the administration of the Armenian troops who, arriving daily by rail from Vladikavkaz and Petrovsk or by sea from Astrakhan, sought passage to western Transcaucasia. Stranded in Baku because of Moslem control of the railway to Tiflis, the several thousand restive Armenian soldiers threatened to disrupt the uneasy lull.[74] Moslem and Armenian councils conferred repeatedly to break the deadlock, but the roads remained closed. The Musavatists of Baku claimed to have neither jurisdiction nor influence over the bands that blocked the railway. The subsequent organization of two Armenian regiments from the nearly six thousand soldiers elicited sharp protests from the Moslem spokesmen. The explanation that the regiments had been formed to be combat-ready upon arrival at the Kars front did not satisfy the Tatars, who feverishly reinforced and augmented their own militia.[75] By February, 1918, interracial violence had erupted in several districts of the Baku guberniia. Still, a tenuous calm prevailed in the city until a feud between the Musavat party and the Executive Committee of the Soviet provoked the tempest known as the "March Days."

On March 29, a deputation from the Moslem "Savage Division," then based near Lenkoran, arrived in Baku aboard the "Evelina" to participate in the funeral of a comrade, the son of millionaire Haji Zeinal Abdin Taghiev. Returning to the ship after the services, the Moslem troops were involved in a skirmish with a detachment subject to the Bolshevik-controlled Military Revolutionary Committee.[76] When the Executive Committee of the Baku Soviet learned this, it issued orders to disarm the men from the "Evelina."[77] The Armenian Council declared its neutrality in the evolving Bolshevik-Moslem conflict and attempted to mediate between the disputants. Fortunately, partial minutes of the Council have been preserved, providing an important source for investigation into the March events, which remain the subject of vigorous controversy. According to those records, the Council sent representatives to the Moslem leaders and the Soviet Executive Committee, offering its services in reestablishing order. Those same minutes, however, reveal that the Armenian Council was aware of its inability to restrain the troops under its jurisdiction if the hostilities were to continue.[78]

Baku's Islamic population was outraged by the disarming of members of the "Savage Division" and threatened to attack the Soviet. They demanded that the Executive Committee deliver the confiscated weapons to their rightful owners and punish those responsible for the humiliation. At sunset on March 30, after several tense hours, Shahumian authorized return of the weapons through the intermediary of the Social Democrat Hummet organization.[79] But before the Moslem Marxists could implement the decision, an exchange of fire sounded from the Shemakhinka Moslem sector of the city. A battle between the Tatar units and the Red Guard of the Military Revolutionary Committee raged all night, and, although it did not spread to the Christian quarter, many Armenian soldiers hurried to join the Red Guard against the "common enemy."[80]

By the morning of March 31, the conflagration had enveloped a large part of the city. Shahumian formed the Committee for the Defense of the Revolution, which immediately sent the Tatars an ultimatum to submit to the commands of the Baku Soviet, to disband the "Savage Division" or remove it from the city, and to take effective measures to clear the rails from Baku to Tiflis and to Petrovsk. Nonetheless the strife continued and on April 1 extended into the Armenian sectors. Even those troops that had maintained neutrality now joined the swelling ranks of the Soviet's military forces.[81] The union was natural; Bolshevism signified Russia while Islam was only another name for Turkey. That which had begun as a Bolshevik-Musavat feud ended in all-out interracial warfare. Many of the Moslem neighborhoods were looted and burned as several thousand Tatars were cut down. At last the Musavat accepted Shahumian's ultimatum, but another day passed before the turbulence subsided. Joint Armenian-Tatar deputations traveled throughout the city proclaiming peace, but only after killing several of these heralds did the enraged combatants withdraw to their respective quarters.[82]

Many Armenian sources claim that every effort was made to avoid the clash and, when that had become impossible, to mitigate the suffering of the Tatar civilians. They cite the testimony of Moslem civic leaders grateful to the Armenian Council for saving the lives of thousands by protecting them in many public buildings. Musavat writers caustically refute this claim and indict the Bolshevik-Armenian entente for the death of thousands of peaceful Moslems.[83] The "March Days" strengthened the conviction of most Tatars that only with the assistance of a mighty outside power such as the Ottoman Empire could Baku, the Islamic capital of Transcaucasia, be retrieved from the usurpers. The Moslems were to wait six months to wreak an exceedingly sweet revenge.

The "usurpers" did not remain united for long. Shahumian realized that the moment was propitious for asserting undisguised Soviet control in Baku. He was assisted by Dashnaktsutiun and the Social Revolutionary party, which had swung far to the left and now supported his efforts to abolish all non-Soviet administrative bodies functioning in Baku. But, having fortified the Bolshevik position, these same collaborators were then compelled to make concessions. The Armenian Council submitted to Shahumian's demand to merge its military units, the strongest single force in Baku, with the Red Guard. Even as part of the Red forces, however, the Armenians continued to maintain distinct units headed by Dashnakist officers.[84] Elated by the turn of events, Stepan Shahumian created the Baku Council of People's Commissars. Soviet order had gained an official foothold in Transcaucasia.[85]

Concessions and Ultimatums in Trebizond

These, then, were the cleavages afflicting Transcaucasia when Kachaznuni, Laskhishvili, and Haidarov arrived in Trebizond on March 29 and informed Chkhenkeli of the extended powers granted him by the Seim.[86] As Transcaucasia was being torn asunder, the Trebizond negotiations for peace resumed. Upon notification by Chkhenkeli that the parleys could continue, Rauf suggested that Transcaucasia now rise as an independent state, but he warned that the Ottoman government was compelled to withhold recognition until the Brest boundaries were acknowledged and the question of self-determination for Armenians of the Empire dropped. The sixth plenary session of the conference was postponed for several days to give the Transcaucasians time to determine what concessions could be made to the more experienced militarists and diplomats.[87]

During that interim, the intradelegation discord was again accentuated. The Moslem members were prepared to surrender nearly all the disputed territory. Khas-Mamedov stressed that only the port of Batum, the terminal of the oil pipeline from Baku, was indispensable for Transcaucasia. The Hummetist Sheikh-ul-Islamov reminded the delegation that in the event of war the Moslems of Transcaucasia would not take arms against their Ottoman brothers. After four days of bickering, Chkhenkeli recommended offering the Turks the entire county of Olti, half of Ardahan, all Kaghisman except the northern sector, and much of the Kars *okrug*. The proposal elicited immediate retorts from Kachaznuni and Khatisian who labeled it a violation of self-determination, since Christians constituted two-thirds of the population of the Kars and Kaghisman okrugs. Bitterly, the Armenian delegates noted that not an inch of the Batum oblast, generally regarded as Georgian soil, had been included. Kachaznuni urged that the first sacrifices be made in less strategic regions, such as Artvin of the Batum oblast, Olti, and Ardahan, and that only when further concessions became inevitable should Kars and Kaghisman be mentioned. Chkhenkeli defended his suggestions by arguing that the Batum oblast (of which he was a native) was essential to the welfare of all Transcaucasia. He also maintained that the time had come for the Tiflis government to declare its unconditional independence.[88]

Utilizing the broad latitude granted him by the Seim, Chkhenkeli, on April 5, without the approval of his full delegation, presented his list of concessions to Husein Rauf Bey during the sixth and final plenary session of the Trebizond Conference. At the same time he delivered a sermon that must have sounded intolerably repetitious and barren. Reiterating the reasons that the Ottoman government should not insist on Brest-Litovsk, Chkhenkeli feebly intimated that, without at least some of the disputed territory, the economic unity of Transcaucasia would be shattered and independence could not be defended from encroachments by powerful neighbors other than Turkey. However, the attempt to frighten the Ottomans with the ghost of Imperial Russia was without effect. Turning to the problem of Turkish Armenia, Chkhenkeli advanced only an economic argument, making no mention of self-determination: the presence of thousands of refugees in Transcaucasia was paralyzing the state. This situation could not be alleviated until the Ottoman Armenians returned to their native provinces. Before repatriation could be ventured, however, certain guarantees concerning their safety and their future should be granted by the Sublime Porte.[89] After patiently listening to the Transcaucasian spokesman, Rauf Bey promised to inform his government of the proposals and then recessed the conference. Communications between Trebizond and Constantinople must have been excellent on this occasion, for within twenty-four hours

Chkhenkeli received a Turkish ultimatum to honor the Brest-Litovsk treaty. A final reply was demanded within forty-eight hours.[90]

Though the Ottoman action should not have been unexpected, the Transcaucasian delegation was unprepared to cope with the situation. The Tatars called for immediate acquiescence, but Georgian and Armenian members maintained that only the Tiflis government could act on such a momentous question. Nonetheless, most of the delegates, including Hovhannes Kachaznuni, had accepted the inevitability of bowing before the Turkish demand if the rest of Transcaucasia were to be saved.[91] Chkhenkeli wired the Seim to obtain permission to relinquish most of the Artvin okrug of the Batum oblast and the entire Kars oblast except for a minor border adjustment in favor of Transcaucasia. In pursuance of the Seim's fourth condition for peace, amnesty and permission for the refugees to repatriate were, according to Chkhenkeli, the maximum that could be expected from the Ottomans. He added pessimistically that even these concessions would probably be rejected and that it was therefore necessary to plan either on accepting the Brest provisions in toto or on breaking off the talks and declaring war.[92]

Responding on April 8, the Tiflis government sanctioned Chkhenkeli's maximum concessions but noted that Dashnaktsutiun demanded the inclusion of the Kars fortress in the strip of territory marked for the "border adjustment." No mention was made of complete acquiescence to the Brest terms or of the possibility of resuming the war.[93] By this time the last dissenter, Alexandre Khatisian, appraising the despised Brest-Litovsk treaty as less disastrous than Transcaucasia's latest concession, advised immediate acceptance of the Turkish ultimatum. After all, Article IV of Brest-Litovsk had not authorized the outright annexation of Kars, Ardahan, and Batum but had stipulated that the inhabitants, with the cooperation of neighboring governments, particularly Turkey, would determine the political future of the provinces. Yet now Transcaucasia was condoning direct Ottoman annexation of almost the entire region. Khalil Bek Khas-Mamedov was pleased that the delegation was at last unanimous. He reminded his colleagues that the incessant Turkish advance was not an invasion but was simply enforcement of the Brest-Litovsk supplementary agreement aimed at clearing the region of "armed bands."[94] The bands to which Khas-Mamedov referred were the military forces of the Transcaucasian government.

When Ottoman units pushed into Olti and Merdenek and along the Black Sea coast into the Batum oblast, Commissariat President Gegechkori instructed Chkhenkeli to protest the outrageous policy of engaging in hostilities while negotiations were in progress. Recognizing that, from the Turkish viewpoint, this tactic was neither contradictory nor illegal, Chkhenkeli begged his government to assent to the Treaty of Brest-Litovsk. Only then might the Ottomans allow certain rectifications along the new international boundary.[95] In a separate wire, Khatisian and Kachaznuni joined their chairman to urge the Seim and especially the Dashnakist fraction to respond favorably to the Turkish ultimatum.[96] On April 9, in a private interview, Chkhenkeli apprised Rauf of the Seim's maximum concessions, but the Ottoman leader was not content with nearly the entire Kars oblast and half of Batum. Instead, on the following evening, his secretary called on Chkhenkeli to receive Transcaucasia's final decision.[97] Waiting no longer for confirmation from Tiflis, Chkhenkeli notified Rauf that all further negotiations would be based on the Treaty of Brest-Litovsk. Realizing, however, that the presence of Turkey's allies would engender an atmosphere of restraint, he requested that all Central Powers now participate in the talks. Rauf coyly replied that such a step could not be seriously contemplated until Transcaucasia had officially declared independence.[98]

Menshevik Anxiety about Batum

In his role as chairman of the Transcaucasian peace mission, Akakii Chkhenkeli corresponded officially with both the Tiflis government and the Ottoman delegation. Yet he was also a Georgian political leader, and in that capacity secretly communicated with his Menshevik colleagues. The radiograms exchanged during the second week of April, 1918, were particularly relevant to the question of Batum. Chkhenkeli urged the Georgian National Council to take a clear-cut stand, pointing out that, although loss of Batum would violate the territorial unity of Georgia, it was imperative to comply with the Brest-Litovsk treaty. On April 10, Zhordania, Tsereteli, Ramishvili, and Gegechkori rejected that view, for relinquishing the area would be equivalent to suicide for Georgia and the Menshevik party. They deemed forcible enemy occupation of all Georgia preferable to renouncing claims to Batum. In separate wires, Ramishvili and Gegechkori stressed that at least the harbor district of Batum must be salvaged. Chkhenkeli contended that even this was impossible, and on April 11 warned the Menshevik quartet that, were the Turks to capture Batum through a military maneuver, they would not stop there. The road to Tiflis would beckon Vehib Pasha into the heart of Transcaucasia.[99] Chkhenkeli had formulated definite, logical convictions, but his colleagues still groped for other ways out of the quandary.

While corresponding with Rauf Bey, the Tiflis government, and the Menshevik leaders, Chkhenkeli also attempted to restrain the Turkish militarists. On April 10, he appealed to General Vehib to halt operations around Batum, at least until the Seim had made a decision about acceding to Brest-Litovsk. On the next day Chkhenkeli and Vehib Pasha jointly wired the commander of Batum, General Gedevanov, to cease all military activity, while Vehib unilaterally warned the Georgian officer that, were belligerent acts to continue after six o'clock that evening, the Turkish Army would launch an offensive. This threat was followed on April 12 by an ultimatum to Gedevanov to evacuate the city by four o'clock the next afternoon. Vehib promised that only the forts would be occupied and that men of the Georgian Corps would be permitted to retain all weapons and execute a formal withdrawal. If, however, an affirmative response were not forthcoming by noon on April 13, the responsibility for the blood of innocent victims would not rest upon the Ottoman Command, which, furthermore, would have no choice but to take prisoner all the defenders of Batum.[100] Noi Ramishvili, in Batum when the ultimatum arrived, frantically appealed to Chkhenkeli to convince the Turks that, were the city spared, every other minute detail of the Treaty of Brest-Litovsk would be honored by Transcaucasia. The reply was negative. Vehib would neither postpone nor alter his orders. Only the immediate evacuation of Batum would stay the Turkish scimitar.[101]

The Seim's Response to the Ottoman Challenge

Obviously, the Transcaucasian delegation in Trebizond was not in consonance with the Transcaucasian legislature in Tiflis. The most influential Mensheviks had not been won over to Chkhenkeli's viewpoint. As Vehib prepared to prove that his ultimatum was not an empty threat, the Commissariat, the Presidium of the Seim, and representatives of the leading fractions were engrossed in an emergency meeting to consider the latest crisis. Evgenii Gegechkori, as chairman of Transcaucasia's executive body, reported that military authorities had sustained his conviction that the enemy lacked sufficient manpower to seize Batum. The city was well fortified and prepared for a determined stand. Iraklii Tsereteli then exclaimed that it was not peace Turkey desired but the extirpation of the "Transcaucasian Democracy." Everything except Batum had already been relinquished. Now it was necessary to mobilize and "to consider all those who oppose the defense of Transcaucasia as enemies. . . ."[102] With surprising unanimity, Dashnakist, Social Revolutionary, Kadet, Moslem Socialist, and Musavatist spokesmen concurred with Tsereteli. It must have been rewarding for the Armenians and Georgians to hear Shafi Bek Rustambekov announce that the Musavat party, though heavily taxed by the decision, would stand solidly with the other democratic elements of Transcaucasia. The master draftsman, Noi Zhordania, then proposed that the Seim, scheduled to reconvene several hours later, be urged to recall the Trebizond delegation, to form a collegium of three invested with dictatorial powers, and to appeal to the peoples of Transcaucasia for support, explaining that events in Trebizond and along the front left no alternative but to acknowledge the existence of a state of war.[103]

All members of the Seim knew what was to occur when they gathered that evening. The afternoon dress rehearsal became a stirring production at night. Oratory reigned supreme. Transcaucasia, Gegechkori cried, was at the threshold of slavery and could be rescued only by the concerted joint action of all her peoples. Tsereteli likened Brest-Litovsk to a death sentence on the "Revolutionary Russia" for whom so many Seim members had dedicated their lives. That despicable imperialistic treaty, maintained only by force of German bayonets, was already beginning to crumble in the face of growing opposition of the world masses. Even the Bolshevik government had begun to criticize the treaty. On the Caucasus front, the enemy would be victorious only if disunity and anarchy, on which the Turkish armies depended, paralyzed Transcaucasia. Tsereteli concluded, "We are convinced that we will be victorious if we are not betrayed in the rear." [104] Martiros Harutunian spoke for all Armenians when he expressed doubt that the Turks would be content even if they attained the boundaries granted at Brest-Litovsk. Would not the Ottoman government pursue its scheme of uniting Baku with Constantinople and populating the lands between with a solid Islamic mass? Only two small peoples, Georgians and Armenians, along with a few Assyrians, obstructed the fulfillment of such a project. From the Ottoman point of view, there had never been such a propitious moment to effect the Turanic ideal. Scarcely disguising his insinuations, the orator for Dashnaktsutiun asserted that realization of the Turkish goals was dependent on the active collaboration of certain elements within the Caucasus. With such assistance, the Ottomans planned to occupy Baku and exterminate first the Armenian nation, then all Georgians and other Christians. Harutunian pledged that the Armenian people would fight as a single unit, and that "if we are to be defeated and if we are to die, then we Armenians will die with weapons in hand." [105]

The tone of the Moslem declarations had transformed radically since the afternoon meeting. In the name of the Musavat, Nonpartisan Moslem, and Moslems of Russia bloc, Rustambekov announced that because of racial-religious bonds with Turkey the Moslems of Transcaucasia could not actively support the proposed war and refused to accept any responsibility for the consequences. Nonetheless, he pledged that sincere efforts would be made for "all possible cooperation" with the other peoples of Transcaucasia and for "the favorable liquidation of war." [106] Valiko Jugheli, commander of the Menshevik Red Guard, rose to the podium amidst the applause of the socialist fractions. He did not refrain, as had Harutunian, from identifying Turkey's Transcaucasian collaborators. He rebuked the Moslems and their leading party, questioning how they, being fully cognizant of the plight of the peoples of Turkey, could deign to speak of neutrality! Such men were not the true representatives of the "Tatar Democracy." The Musavatists, Jugheli shouted, were double-faced intriguers. They promised to work for the favorable conclusion of war, but their spokesman "did not say for what side and for whom it should be liquidated favorably." The Musavatists supported Turkish imperialism so that, with Ottoman power, they could retrieve the rights of feudal lords, the *pomeshchiks*, and grind the Moslem peasantry under their heels.[107] What Jugheli did not state was that most Moslems in Transcaucasia were in full accord with the Musavat tactic and, if at all critical, would probably have chastised Rustambekov for his excessive moderation.

It was well after midnight when the Seim adopted the three resolutions prepared by Zhordania. Martial law was declared, and a collegium of Chief Executive Gegechkori, Interior Affairs Commissar Ramishvili, and Finance Commissar Karjikian was entrusted with unlimited powers.[108] On the same night, the Seim printed its multilingual appeal, offering the peoples of Transcaucasia "slavery or war." In a separate plea to the workers, soldiers, and peasants of Russia, the Menshevik Social Democrats called attention to the Transcaucasian struggle for survival. Acceptance of Brest-Litovsk would signify the separation of the Caucasus from Russia and would betray the Great Revolution for whose birth the peoples of both areas had shared the privations of prison, forced labor, and exile.[109] It is highly improbable that even a few workers, soldiers, or peasants in Russia ever heard the frantic voice of the Transcaucasian Social Democracy.

During the course of the entire war, the Georgians had never been so agitated and so determined as they were on the morning of April 14. The Seim had been recessed only a few hours when Zhordania and Tsereteli, rifles slung over their shoulders, departed for Batum to participate in the defense of the city, of Georgia, and of Transcaucasia.[110] Simultaneously, Gegechkori wired Trebizond to inform Chkhenkeli of the Seim's resolution, which stated: "In view of the fact that a peaceful settlement on the question of the boundaries of Transcaucasia was not reached between Turkey and Transcaucasia, the Transcaucasian delegation is instructed to depart immediately for Tiflis." [111]

The news distressed the delegation, for the confidence and enthusiasm of Tiflis were completely lacking in Trebizond. Mahmed Hasan Hajinskii angrily labeled the recall as "a scandal unequalled in history." He demanded the resignation of either the delegation or the Commissariat and Seim. Considering the latter possibility unlikely, the Musavat representative announced his immediate withdrawal from the delegation. The act initiated a round of heated recriminations, after which Hajinskii, in a near rage, exclaimed that his party had authorized him to depart for Constantinople to conclude a peace on behalf of the people it represented. Chkhenkeli took note of the statement and had it recorded in the official protocol. Finally, he begged the members to restrain themselves, for the spectacle they were creating on foreign soil would leave an unfavorable impression on the Turks.[112] Regaining a measure of composure, the delegation paid a farewell visit to Rauf Bey to leave a gift of twenty thousand rubles for the poor of Trebizond and to inform the Ottoman leader that the talks were being interrupted, not terminated. It was hoped that such a statement would expedite the resumption of negotiations if and when such were deemed necessary.[113] In a private conversation with Rauf, however, Chkhenkeli is reported to have divulged the true contents of Gegechkori's telegram. He promised to spare no efforts after reaching Tiflis to rectify the ill-advised policy of his government.[114] Before embarking, Chkhenkeli appointed a Georgian National Democrat, Grigorii Veshapeli, to serve in Trebizond as liaison with the Turks.[115] Hajinskii apparently remained behind on his own volition to fulfill his special mission.[116]

Thus, a month after the opening of the Trebizond Conference, the Transcaucasian delegates set sail for Batum, not knowing in whose hands they would find the harbor when they arrived. They were tired and agitated, angry with one another, with the Tiflis government, with the Turks, and with the Bolsheviks, and they were perturbed by the course of events. It probably would not have surprised them had they been told that several members of the delegation would be back at the bargaining table in a very short time, but not in Trebizond. And when that actually occurred, there was to be bitter irony, for Transcaucasia was to insist on and beg for application of the Treaty of Brest-Litovsk, while the Ottoman Empire was to reject categorically such a preposterous proposal.

IX
War and Independence
(*April–May, 1918*)

THE RUSSIAN SCHOLAR and statesman, P. N. Miliukov, has characterized the 1917–1918 events in the region beyond the Caucasus Mountains as the "Balkanization of Transcaucasia." This area, once a single unit within the Romanov Empire, first was wrenched from Russia and then, like the Balkans, was splintered into separate feuding districts, which some deigned to term "republics." [1] The process of division from Russia spanned the period from November, 1917, to April, 1918. The second step, the partition of Transcaucasia, was to follow a month later. To both measures, the Armenians unwillingly acquiesced. Having for several months avoided declaring independence from Russia, Transcaucasia was finally driven to action by force of Turkish arms. In vain was the Chkhenkeli delegation recalled from Trebizond, for, within two weeks, Transcaucasia was thoroughly humbled. Announcing its independent status to comply with Ottoman demands, the Tiflis government meekly sent to Batum a new delegation to establish eternal peace and friendship with the Ittihadist rulers of Turkey. The failure of that mission introduced the final phase in the "Balkanization of Transcaucasia."

War

When warfare officially resumed on April 14, the front no longer extended, as it had in February, from Trebizond to Erzinjan and Van. The Caucasus Army Command enjoined General Gabaev's Georgian troops to prevent Turkish entry into Batum and directed Nazarabekian's Corps to stand firm on the Engija–Novo-Selim–Tiknis positions west of Kars. Approximately six thousand Armenians manned that line and the Kars fortress, whose commander, General Deev, had at his disposal nearly a thousand cannons and heavy guns of various types.[2] Vehib Pasha, having transferred Third Army headquarters to Trebizond, threw the 37th Division of the II Corps against Batum and deployed twelve to fifteen thousand men from the 11th Division and from the I Corps' 9th and 36th divisions against the Armenian positions around Kars. At the same time, Enver Pasha augmented the Third Army reserves with several units from other fronts.[3]

The Seim's rejection of the Turkish ultimatum delivered by Rauf Bey alarmed the Armenians of Tiflis, for news had filtered through that the Ottomans were already marching toward the Transcaucasian capital. Many, especially the refugees from Turkish Armenia, fled to the North Caucasus, while thousands of others prepared to follow if the enemy approached the city. The calm and unconcern of the Georgians stood out in sharp contrast to the trepidation of the Armenians. Zurab Avalov, a Georgian educator and statesman who was returning from Russia in April, 1918, noted:

> Especially the Armenian population of Tiflis had reasons to fear the arrival of the Turks; many were already leaving toward the North, and we had met them along the Georgian Military Road. . . . In spite of this situation, the Tiflis crowd, I repeat, was unworried and full of joy. . . .[4]

Though the Georgian politicians appealed for a united stand against the invader, most Georgians adhered to Chkhenkeli's views and were willing to allow maximal concessions to attain immediate peace. Even the enthusiasm of the Menshevik "war party" subsided rapidly on the evening of April 14, after Turkish troops, encountering only feeble resistance, had swept into Batum and captured the three thousand Georgian troops and six hundred officers in the garrison.[5] Less than twenty-four hours after resolving to fight until the last man had fallen, the Georgian leaders recognized the hopelessness of the situation.

The plight of Transcaucasia was aggravated by the disloyalty of the Moslem populace in the war zones. Thousands of Georgian Moslems inhabiting Ajaria collaborated with the Turkish forces that moved into Batum, the district's major city. Religious identity played a much more significant role than did national origin in determining political loyalties. During the week following the capitulation of Batum, Moslem villagers in the Ozurget region of the Kutais *guberniia* and in the Abastuman district of Tiflis struck the Georgian defenders from the rear and welcomed the forward contingents of the Turkish Army. Except for a minor victory on the Cholok River, the Georgians retreated steadily along the railway from Batum to Kutais and inland through the defile of the Kur River toward Borzhom, gateway to the lowland route to Tiflis.[6]

The adverse course of events compelled the Menshevik leaders to reassess their strategy. Nevertheless, on April 20, a Zhordania-dominated conference of the party's Tiflis and Regional committees rejected a proposal to declare independence and name Chkhenkeli premier of Transcaucasia. It is not clear what transpired overnight, but the same Zhordania, as Chairman of the Georgian National Council, which met on April 21, acquiesced to the desire of the Georgian people to declare the separation of Transcaucasia from Russia and to install a "peace cabinet." The candidacy of Chkhenkeli was approved by the Council, and on the following day, in a volte-face, the Menshevik party also endorsed the proponent of peace. By April 22, the Georgians had reached a decision.[7]

Meanwhile, minor skirmishes took place on the Kars front. Generals Lebedinskii, Nazarabekian, and Deev, Colonel P. Chardigny of the French Military Mission, and several other officers personally inspected the field and satisfied themselves that the fortress could withstand an enemy assault for several months. The inspection had just ended on April 19 when a limited Turkish offensive threw the Armenians back to Begli Ahmed and three days later to Vladikars, only a few miles from the fortress.[8] The Armenian Corps Command was undaunted, however, for it was firmly convinced that Kars would hold. The Georgians may have relinquished Batum without a struggle, but Nazarabekian had no such intention for mighty Kars.

General Nazarabekian and his staff attended a special conference of Armenian political and military leaders in Alexandropol on April 20 and 21. This was the most comprehensive Armenian gathering since the National Congress of October, 1917. Among those present were members of the Bureau of Dashnaktsutiun; militarists Silikian, Dro, Ruben, Andranik; National Council delegates Aharonian, Papadjanian, Harutunian, Aghbalian, Mamikonian; Western Armenian Defense Council delegate Vahan Papazian; Kachaznuni and Khatisian, newly returned from Trebizond; and even a Bolshevik, Poghos Makintsian. Acting as a self-appointed policy-making body, the Alexandropol conclave was faced with the choice of accepting the Brest settlement together with the loss of Kars or of continuing the ravaging war. Kachaznuni described in detail the proceedings at Trebizond and implored the Armenian leaders to accede to the treaty. Former Duma and Ozakom member Mikayel Papadjanian and several others concurred with Kachaznuni, but the overwhelming majority of the political-civic leaders and all of the military representatives rejected this stand and pledged an active defense against the murderous invader. The decision was transmitted to Tiflis by the many Seim and National Council members who participated in the Alexandropol deliberations.[9]

The Democratic Federative Republic of Transcaucasia

The prevailing disposition in Tiflis differed radically from the sabre-rattling atmosphere in Alexandropol. The whole Georgian Menshevik party had been won over to the belief that it was imperative to renew negotiations immediately. The Turks had overrun the entire Batum *oblast;* it was senseless and dangerous to be adamant at such a time. Fortunately, Chkhenkeli had foreseen the necessity of resuming talks and had made provisions accordingly with Rauf Bey before leaving Trebizond. After his return to

Tiflis, he had continued to correspond with Vehib Pasha, who gave assurances that friendly negotiations could begin as soon as Transcaucasia desisted from its hostile ways and withdrew from the *sanjak*s of Kars, Ardahan, and Batum.[10] Condemned and even charged with treachery by Armenian historians for his secret dealings with the enemy, Akakii I. Chkhenkeli, nonetheless, was probably the most realistic politician in Transcaucasia. He fully comprehended the intricacies of power politics and was prepared to maneuver and bend according to the exigencies of the moment. It was not the more respected theorists or idealists, such as Zhordania or Tsereteli, who were to save Georgia from Turkish invasion. Cunning and calculating, Chkhenkeli served his people in 1918 more effectively than any other Menshevik or Georgian. The policy he had advocated for weeks, a declaration of independence, was finally adopted by the Seim on the evening of April 22.

During that historic session of the Transcaucasian legislature, Dashnaktsutiun was confronted with two alternatives. By remaining loyal to national aspirations and the Russian orientation, it could reject the Moslem and Georgian decision to separate from Russia, thus committing the Armenians to continue the war alone. On the other hand, by yielding to onerous reality, it could comply with the Ottoman demand for an independent Transcaucasia beyond the Brest boundaries. Despite the undesirability of the second course, there seemed no other feasible path. The Armenians could not stand alone against the Turks, nor could they afford to separate their fate from that of the other Transcaucasian peoples. The only possibility for the physical survival of the Russian Armenians lay in a common, at least outwardly united policy with the Georgians and, in particular, with the Moslems, the predominant element in Transcaucasia. Although espousing this strategy, the Armenian legislators were unable to feign satisfaction. The benches of Dashnaktsutiun resembled a funeral wake.

Even the Georgian Mensheviks, on whose initiative the declaration was to be made, were far from festive. On the night that Transcaucasia was to become a republic, not one of the internationally renowned Menshevik orators took the rostrum to laud independence. Colorless, second-rate politicians, who recited contradictory rationalizations, rose in the name of the Menshevik "fraction." The words of an Oniashvili, Arsenidze, and Georgadze stood in distinct contrast to the eloquent silence of Tsereteli, Zhordania, and Gegechkori. The Menshevik proxies denounced Russia for betraying Transcaucasia and argued that the region must now act as an independent state in order to gain international prestige and to unite all its peoples. They denied that separation from Russia signified espousing a Turkish orientation. The threats from both North and South necessitated the adoption of a new political formula—indepedence.[11] Rasul-Zade, on behalf of the Musavat fraction, exclaimed that the new regime in Russia was more oppressive than the former tsarist autocracy. Only independence could spare Transcaucasia from partition and domination by foreign states. Though independence would necessitate the loss of Kars, Ardahan, and Batum, it would at least give Transcaucasia the opportunity to develop into a great free nation.[12]

The most overpowering rhetorician that evening was Lev Tumanov, representing the non-Georgian members of the small Social Revolutionary fraction. Point by point, he exposed the inconsistency and hypocrisy of the lesser Menshevik spokesmen. Tumanov demanded that the Seim at least be honest with itself and admit that the question of independence had been placed on the agenda to comply with the demand of Turkish imperialism. What party represented in the Seim had ever campaigned on the platform of separation from Russia? The Mensheviks had attempted to justify the act by resorting to the claim of self-determination. Certainly, Tumanov cried, self-determination was an excellent basis. What more natural way was there to determine the people's will than to conduct a referendum? Was there doubt in anyone's mind what the popular verdict would be? Then, addressing the Musavat fraction, the tempestuous orator belittled the statement of Mehmed Emin Rasul-Zade that "conscience and not fear" was the motivation for independence. The truth was that "fear and not conscience" was prodding the Seim toward that disastrous decision. If the legislature, as was obvious, had resolved to take the step, it should at least refrain from mentioning the "will of the people," for that will remained directed toward Russia. In conclusion, Tumanov exclaimed that the Russian orientation was a revolutionary and not a Bolshevik orientation, whereas independence under the existing conditions would mean slavery to Turkey. The time would come when Transcaucasia would sorely regret the already determined strategy of the leading fractions.[13]

Ivan Lordkipanidze, speaking for the Georgian Social Revolutionaries, differed with his colleague. Russia had not come to the assistance of Transcaucasia, which now was compelled to fend for herself. As a sovereign state, Transcaucasia could negotiate with all of the Central Powers and could be assured that Germany would not permit its Turkish ally to hold Batum and Baku permanently. Even if enemy occupation could not be avoided, existence as a separate state was advantageous, for at the conference table Transcaucasia would have the international rights of a defeated nation.[14]

Iulii Semenov, as a Russian Kadet, naturally sided with Tumanov. His prediction proved accurate:

> After declaring independence, the second step will be to negotiate with Turkey about signing an alliance and you will be compelled step by step to do that which you are ordered by the Turks. . . . You will go to the aid of the Turkish troops sent to conquer Baku, and when the Turkish forces pass over Transcaucasia, there will take place the conquest of Transcaucasia by the Turco-Germanic union.[15]

Oniashvili, more animated and expressive than on his first appearance, took the podium again to lash out at Semenov. Did the Russian delegate possibly have a Kadet division that would defend Transcaucasia? The fact was that all the Semenovs would race toward Vladikavkaz and beyond the Caucasus when tragedy struck, but the Georgians and other indigenous peoples had nowhere to flee.[16]

At long last, after the loquacity of all other fractions had been expended, the silence of Dashnaktsutiun was broken. Hovhannes Kachaznuni stood before the Seim. The brevity and pungency of his single sentence left no doubt about the true feelings of his party and his people: "Citizens, members of the Seim, the fraction Dashnaktsutiun, clearly cognizant of that great responsibility which it takes upon itself at this historic moment, joins in favor of declaring a separate Transcaucasian government."[17] The speaker returned to Dashnaktsutiun's benches, some members of which had left the assembly to avoid voting in favor of the motion proposed by Oniashvili: "The Transcaucasian Seim resolves to proclaim Transcaucasia an independent democratic federative republic."[18] Only a handful of ballots was cast in opposition, but, unfortunately, events of the following month were to demonstrate that Transcaucasia was not independent, democratic, federative, or a republic.

During this same April 22 session, Chkhenkeli reported on the Trebizond Conference. With shrewdness and tact, he explained that the refusal of the Transcaucasian Moslems to take up arms against Turkey should be viewed objectively. It was as impossible for them to engage in such hostilities as it would be for the Christians to turn their weapons against Russia.[19] Having heard Chkhenkeli's account, the Seim requested its Presidium to seek means to renew the peace talks and at the same time to defend Transcaucasia. So that parleys could continue, however, it was imperative that Gegechkori's "cabinet of war" bow to a "cabinet of peace." The natural choice to head such a body was Akakii Chkhenkeli, who was delegated to form a new government. Some members of the legislature suggested that the Gegechkori-Ramishvili-Karjikian extraordinary collegium should retain authority until Chkhenkeli's cabinet had received Seim approval, but Gegechkori, feeling that his policy had been thoroughly discredited, refused to continue in office.[20] Thus, from April 23 to April 26, the day the Seim confirmed Chkhenkeli's cabinet, there was no official government in Transcaucasia. This fact could be easily omitted were it not for the momentous events that occurred during the three-day interval.

The Surrender of Kars

While still only premier-designate, Chkhenkeli assumed the functions of a legally authorized head of state and foreign minister. He communicated with Vehib Pasha, ordered the Armenian troops to halt their hostilities against the Turks, and finally commanded General Nazarabekian to relinquish Kars without firing a shot. His entire activity was kept secret from the Dashnakist fraction of the Seim and even from those Armenian leaders whom he had approached to enter his cabinet. When his moves were made known, Transcaucasia was shaken to its deepest foundations. Armenian and Soviet historians continue to execrate the "treachery" of Chkhenkeli and to impeach him for breach of faith. Though nearly half a century has passed, the Georgian leader's maneuvers still rouse the most impassioned disputations. It is difficult not to chastise Chkhenkeli for the improper and unconventional manner in which he pursued his objectives, yet in retrospect his every move can be justified on the following grounds:

1) As premier-designate, he was obliged to lead the state, for no other executive body existed. Gegechkori's cabinet had withdrawn from the political arena.
2) The Seim, during its April 22 session, had charged the Transcaucasian government with resuming negotiations in addition to preparing for defense.
3) It was clear to all that renewal of the parleys signified acceptance of the Brest-Litovsk boundaries.
4) The Armenians had voted in favor of continuing the peace talks and by that act had tacitly recognized the inevitability of relinquishing Kars and all other territory beyond the 1877 Russo-Turkish border.

Chkhenkeli's opponents can construct a more formidable case against the wisdom of evacuating Kars than against the legality of the command ordering that withdrawal. If the directive were technically illegal on April 24, it would not have been so two days later when Chkhenkeli was formally confirmed in office. There is nothing to indicate that his views might have changed in the intervening hours. For an understanding of subsequent events, it is necessary to turn to the details of the capitulation of Kars.

On the morning of April 23, a few hours after the Seim had declared the independence of Transcaucasia, Chkhenkeli wired the information to Vehib Pasha and announced acceptance of all provisions of the Treaty of Brest-Litovsk as the basis for further negotiations. He suggested that the conference between the two governments take place in Batum instead of Trebizond because it was imperative that he as chief of state be near Tiflis. As for the evacuation of Kars, Chkhenkeli promised to appoint representatives to discuss the terms of withdrawal and to direct all Transcaucasian military forces to cease fire at five o'clock that afternoon.[21] Then, without waiting for Vehib's reply, Chkhenkeli and the acting Minister of War, General Odishelidze, ordered generals Lebedinskii, Nazarabekian, and Gabaev to suspend hostilities.[22] The communiqué reached Nazarabekian's headquarters in Alexandropol at one-thirty in the afternoon. Astounded by the command, Nazarabekian attempted to contact the National Council for clarification, but the wires to Tiflis had been cut.²³ With no alternative, the Armenian Corps Commander relayed the instructions to General Silikian of the 2nd Division and through Deev in Kars to General Ter Hakobian, who had replaced Areshian as commander of the 1st Division. When Deev received the order at four in the afternoon, Armenian troops held the Samavat–Haram–Vartan–Kani Köy perimeter several miles from the city. The morale of the troops was high, for all were certain that the greatest stand of the campaign would be made there. The announcement of the cease-fire was the first devastating blow to that optimistic determination.²⁴

Complying with Chkhenkeli's directives, General Deev dispatched 1st Regiment Commander Morel to the Turkish camp. There, Colonel Kiazım Karabekir informed Morel that he had received no instructions to halt the operations against Kars. Thus, while the Transcaucasians were not permitted to fire, the Turks were under orders to advance.²⁵ The anxiety of the Kars defenders was relieved somewhat when, on the following morning, Karabekir sent word that the Third Army Command had sanctioned a temporary cessation of hostilities to permit parleys in the field. He added that during those talks the Transcaucasian troops were to withdraw to within two kilometers of Kars. Any resistance would be crushed by the Turkish troops.²⁶ Simultaneously, Vehib informed Chkhenkeli of these terms and promised to stop the advance at the 1877 Russo-Turkish border and to permit a formal evacuation of Kars. He also acknowledged that men of his 37th Division had crossed into the Kutais guberniia but assured the acting premier that they would push no farther unless provoked by Georgian troops.²⁷

On the morning of April 24, without giving General Deev enough time to receive instructions from Tiflis relating to Karabekir's stipulations, Turkish contingents advanced toward the walls of the fortress. Other units attempted a flanking maneuver to seize Mazra, a village to the east of Kars along the main road and railway to Alexandropol. General Deev ignored Karabekir's warnings and bombarded the enemy troops moving from the west, while companies of Ter Hakobian's 1st Division repelled the Turkish forces near Mazra. The Ottomans were halted.²⁸

Shortly after noon the same day, another blow from Tiflis struck. The new acting Minister of War, G. T. Georgadze, notified the defenders that he and Chkhenkeli had acceded to all Turkish conditions. Nazarabekian was informed that a misunderstanding had apparently arisen about whether it was the Transcaucasian troops who were to take positions two kilometers from Kars or the Turkish units who were to stop at that point. The Armenian Corps Commander was instructed to group behind that line to avoid any distasteful episodes.²⁹ To comply with this order would signify certain doom for Kars, because the fortress cannons, which could inflict severe damage on an enemy several kilometers distant, were useless against an opposing force within close range.

With the Armenian leaders in Tiflis still unaware of what was happening, Chkhenkeli again wired Vehib in order to account for the unfortunate attack on Turkish troops near Kars following the cease-fire. He assured Vehib that all Ottoman terms would be honored and requested one month to complete the evacuation of Kars.[30] Then Chkhenkeli, once again without awaiting an Ottoman reply, instructed Nazarabekian to communicate before midnight with the enemy commander on the Kars front to arrange the details for evacuation. News of the order spread rapidly through the Transcaucasian units and the preponderantly Christian population of Kars. Nothing more was necessary to trigger the exodus. The chaos, panic, and desertion of Van, Erzinjan, and Erzerum were fully reproduced.[31]

To execute Chkhenkeli's directive, Colonel Morel was sent once again to Karabekir's camp, but efforts to obtain liberal terms for the evacuation were futile. The confident Turks, not in a tractable mood, demanded the following:

1) clearing of the forts on the left bank of the Kars River by noon, Constantinople time, on the following day, April 25;
2) evacuation of the remaining forts and the city by nightfall, April 25;
3) withdrawal of all Transcaucasian armed units beyond the Arpachai River [the Brest boundary] by April 28.[32]

Morel begged for an extension of several days so that the thousands of civilians who wanted to leave could be assisted and the retreat could be orderly. Karabekir rejected the appeal. After learning that the Tiflis government had sent Nazarabekian a new message ordering him not to prohibit the abandonment of Kars, Morel quickly accepted the Turkish conditions.[33]

This puzzling episode, with Chkhenkeli in Tiflis, Vehib at his new headquarters in Batum, Nazarabekian at Alexandropol, Deev in Kars, Morel and Karabekir at the Turkish I Corps headquarters, finally reached a climax on April 25. Vehib must have been amused that day by Chkhenkeli's latest communiqué, which made the following requests:

1) to withdraw Turkish troops from the occupied territories in the Kutais and Tiflis guberniias at the same time that Transcaucasian forces cleared Kars;
2) to give at least seven days to evacuate the Kars oblast;
3) to allow two to three days to clear the fortress itself;
4) to grant a full month for the complete transferral of matériel from Kars to beyond the new boundaries;
5) to accede to the withdrawal of all governmental, railway, sanitary, and engineering supplies;
6) to consent to Transcaucasian control of the railway to Alexandropol during the period of evacuation;
7) to prohibit plundering by the Kurds.[34]

By the time Vehib received this appeal, the routes to Alexandropol were clogged with Christian refugees, the Armenian units were disorganized, and Kars was in flames. On the evening of April 25, the first Turkish units entered the city and, on the following day, General Deev, Colonel Morel, Military Commissar Misha Arzumanian, and several other officials formally delivered the city to Karabekir Bey.[35]

Chkhenkeli's hope to save the rich stores of war matériel, food, and governmental supplies was short-lived. The calculated Turkish refutation of the original pledge to permit a full evacuation soon arrived in Tiflis. Vehib Pasha "sadly" informed Chkhenkeli and Odishelidze that Turkish troops had been fired upon when they had approached Kars after the cease-fire. Moreover, the Ottoman forces, having encountered victims of Armenian atrocities all the way from Erzinjan, feared for the safety of Moslems in Kars. When smoke was seen rising from the city, they marched to the rescue of the populace. Therefore Turkish occupation of the fortress must be classed as an act of war. As such, the agreement to allow evacuation of all matériel was no longer valid. The captured goods were now loot belonging to the Ottoman Army.[36] Vehib Pasha, an experienced soldier, realized that permitting the enemy to take thousands of weapons and trainloads of ammunition and military supplies from Kars would be a serious blunder.

As the refugees from the Kars oblast streamed across the Arpachai (Akhurian) River into the Erevan guberniia, the military epilogue of the Kars calamity was consummated. The Tiflis government ordered Nazarabekian to explode all fortifications on the west bank of the Arpachai. The Armenian general begged that such action be delayed, for without those strongholds Alexandropol would stand defenseless. Only after the Turks had clarified their intentions and had guaranteed that the river boundary would not be violated should Transcaucasia relinquish the west-bank forts. Chkhenkeli adamantly insisted on their immediate destruction, and on April 28 Nazarabekian complied, withdrawing his remaining units into the Erevan guberniia. The enemy advance that he feared would follow near Alexandropol first occurred, however, to the south at Surmalu. When Chkhenkeli complained to Vehib about such violations, the Ottoman general replied that these minor infractions had been provoked by hostile Armenians. He assured the Transcaucasian Premier that Turkish troops would respect the international boundary.[37] The pledge was not honored.

Turmoil in Tiflis

The fall of Kars stunned the Armenian world. Refugees and undisciplined troops spilled into the Erevan province bringing anarchy, famine, and epidemic. Aram and Dro labored frantically to restore a semblance of order. By their command several Armenian deserters were executed, but the results were negligible.[38] In Tiflis the political atmosphere was lethal. Angry mobs of outraged Armenians rushed through the streets denouncing the Transcaucasian government. The most humiliated were the two Armenian delegates to Trebizond, Kachaznuni and Khatisian, who had considered themselves the close associates of Chkhenkeli and had already agreed to participate in his cabinet. They had been kept ignorant of all diplomatic and military proceedings until the secret slipped out on the night of April 24, when communication was reestablished between Armenian Corps headquarters in Alexandropol and the National Council in Tiflis. Corps Commissar Sargis Manasian relayed the unbelievable information to Council member Simon Vratzian. Now alerted, the National Council finally succeeded in speaking directly with General Nazarabekian, who dolefully announced that all was lost. He had already received orders to evacuate Kars, and it was too late to attempt a defense, for the troops and populace were fleeing and final negotiations were in progress for the surrender of the fortress.[39]

The news exploded with greater force than a score of bombs. Shouting treachery to the Georgian Mensheviks, Khatisian, Kachaznuni, and Avetik Sahakian withdrew their agreement to serve with Chkhenkeli, and Dashnaktsutiun demanded his overthrow. Chkhenkeli would not be the premier of the Transcaucasian Republic! This crisis threatened to disrupt the Republic before it was three days old. The Menshevik chiefs, Zhordania, Gegechkori, Tsereteli, and Ramishvili anxiously conferred with the Dashnakist spokesmen, Kachaznuni, Khatisian, Karjikian, and Ohandjanian. The Georgian Menshevik elite was furious with the deceitful Chkhenkeli. His actions were inexcusable. Nonetheless, for the common weal, they declared that the Armenians should display gallantry by remaining in the government. The future of Transcaucasia rested upon cooperation. When the Dashnakists refused to heed such idealistic phrases, the Mensheviks played their trump card. They would agree to topple Chkhenkeli on the condition that the new premier be a member of Dashnaktsutiun, preferably Kachaznuni. It was now the Armenians who were in a quandary. If Kachaznuni were raised to chief of state immediately after the repudiation of Chkhenkeli's policies, the move would be interpreted as the restoration of a "war cabinet," the Tatars would withdraw from the Transcaucasian Federation, and the Ottoman forces would resume an all-out offensive. With Kars already lost, the main arena of war would be the Erevan guberniia. The final stage of the Armenian decimation would be enacted in the heart of Transcaucasia. The Georgian proposal was unacceptable to Dashnaktsutiun, whose delegates insisted that any Menshevik other than Chkhenkeli should serve as premier. "Chkhenkeli or Kachaznuni" was the unalterable choice offered by the Georgian quartet. Near dawn on April 26, Dashnaktsutiun yielded. Clearly aware of the repercussions inherent in permitting an Armenian to form the new cabinet, the party leaders agreed to participate in the cabinet of the odious Chkhenkeli and consequently to subject themselves to the increased wrath of their followers.[40]

On that evening the Seim assembled to confirm the proposed cabinet. The embarrassed Armenian members heard their names presented for approval. The historian who is unaware of what had transpired during the preceding three days might be deceived by the apparent unity in the Seim. The three great fractions joined to voice their approbation of the new government, which included four Georgians, five Moslems, and four Armenians. Almost to be expected was the fact that the Armenians ran a poor third in securing strategic and influential posts. The portfolios were distributed as follows:[41]

Akakii Chkhenkeli	Premier and Foreign Affairs
Noi Ramishvili	Internal Affairs
Noi Khomeriki	Agriculture
Grigorii Georgadze	War
Fathali Khan Khoiskii	Justice
Khudadud Melik Aslanov	Transportation
Nesib Usubbekov	Enlightenment
Mahmed Hajinskii	Trade and Industry
Ibrahim Haidarov	State Control
Alexandre Khatisian	Finance
Hovhannes Kachaznuni	Welfare
Avetik Sahakian	Provisions
Aramayis Erzinkian	Labor

In his inaugural address, Chkhenkeli promised to guarantee the equality of all Transcaucasian citizens and to establish provincial boundaries within the Republic on the basis of mutual agreement and concessions. With obvious reference to the Baku Sovnarkom, he denounced dual government in Transcaucasia. To the applause of all except Dashnakists and Social Revolutionaries, Rasul-Zade stood solidly with Chkhenkeli. It was imperative that all Transcaucasia be welded into a single entity, with the neighboring district of Daghestan being invited to join the Federation.[42] According to Armenian interpretation, what Rasul-Zade was advocating was the establishment of Moslem control in Baku and the strengthening of the Moslem plurality of Transcaucasia by the incorporation of the Mountaineers of Daghestan. Khachatur Karjikian, as chairman of the fraction Dashnaktsutiun, pledged support to Chkhenkeli's government but could not refrain from adding several remarks that echoed Tumanov's sizzling speech of four days earlier. He asked the Seim to recognize that the declaration of independence had been instigated under foreign pressure and that much of the public was unenthused and skeptical. Yet the crisis could be surmounted if the government inspired faith and loyalty by concluding an honorable peace and by applying justice equally to all sections of Transcaucasia.⁴³

The polite remarks in the Seim did not satisfy the populace of Tiflis. The mobs continued to hurl insults at the traitorous government. On May 5, in an attempt to mollify the crowds, Chkhenkeli published a detailed report outlining the reasons for the fall of Kars. Included in the document were the opinions of military experts who testified that the fortress would have been unable to withstand an enemy assault.⁴⁴ The claim was unconvincing, however, for the public also knew of Nazarabekian's report to Tiflis that Kars could hold firm for at least a month and of Kars oblast Commissar Dsamoev's wire that the populace, prepared for a resolute defense, had been driven to panic by Chkhenkeli's order to evacuate. It was this order that led to the disastrous exodus and to the destruction of much of the city.⁴⁵

The Sovnarkom's Ambivalence

The catastrophe at Kars caused many supporters of Dashnaktsutiun to wonder if the strategy of the Russian Sovnarkom had not been, after all, the correct path to follow. Had Transcaucasia accepted the inevitability of yielding to the dictated terms of Brest-Litovsk, thousands of lives as well as property and provisions worth millions of rubles might have been spared. Refugees would not have been forced to flee on a moment's notice; a disciplined army could have withdrawn in orderly fashion to the new boundaries of Transcaucasia, which, like the Ukraine, would have had the integrity of her remaining lands guaranteed by all the Central Powers. It was even possible that an understanding might have been reached with the Bolshevik government of Russia. The rulers in Kiev were now engaged in such an endeavor. Having arrived at a modus vivendi with the Sovnarkom, the Transcaucasian government might have averted the growing antagonism of central Russia and of the local Communists, whose reports and suggestions bore much weight with Lenin, Trotsky, and Stalin. Although actual Soviet Russian power was still distant from the Caucasus, nearly every political maneuver of the Moscow government affected the fate of the provinces between the Caspian and Black seas.

During the first months of 1918, the Sovnarkom seems to have adopted a dualistic policy toward the Caucasus. It ratified the Treaty of Brest-Litovsk but loudly protested the cruelty of the Turkish troops as they advanced into the ceded sanjaks. It took official measures to curtail the activities of Armenian non-Communist organizations in Russia but maintained unofficial ties with those same societies and even assisted Armenian soldiers in reaching the Caucasus. It condemned the Commissariat and the Seim but did not reject the possibility of an understanding with the Tiflis government. Though the territory under the jurisdiction of the Sovnarkom was separated from the Caucasus by the land controlled by the powerful anti-Bolshevik armies of South Russia, the Soviet government tried to prohibit the Turco-Germanic occupation of Transcaucasia, for the Communists were convinced that sooner or later the region would be reunited with Russia. In mid-April, Foreign Affairs Commissar Grigorii Chicherin and his assistant Lev Karakhan complained to Germany about Turkish and Kurdish atrocities against the Armenians in Kars, Ardahan, and Batum. Though the Brest-Litovsk settlement had stipulated that the people of those regions would have the privilege of determining their own political future, the Ottoman rulers were pursuing the traditional policy of eradicating the Armenian nation. Russia had agreed to withdraw from the provinces only at the insistence of Germany. Thus the Berlin government was responsible for the actions of its Turkish ally and was obligated to take immediate measures to prohibit any further excesses.[46] Similar Soviet notes followed later that month when the Ottoman Third Army violated the borders of the Erevan and Tiflis guberniias.[47]

Communist bodies in Transcaucasia attempted to keep pace with the strategy of the Moscow government. In the first days of March, 1918, the Bolshevik Regional Committee endorsed the Sovnarkom's Brest-Litovsk policy and belittled those Transcaucasians who, imbued with "imperialistic tendencies," were scheming for the retention of Kars, Ardahan, and Batum. Enforcement of the treaty provision for the self-determination of these areas was sufficient.[48] A month later, the Committee chastised the little men in Tiflis for conducting separate negotiations with Turkey; then, following the recall of the Trebizond delegation, it denounced the Seim's decision to renew hostilities.[49] As in Moscow, inconsistencies were prevalent among the Transcaucasian Bolsheviks. On the same day that the Regional Committee demanded compliance with the Brest treaty, the Communists of Alexandropol appealed to the citizenry to defend Transcaucasia from the "Turkish barbarian imperialistic hordes" and even enlisted volunteers.[50] From Erevan, Bolshevik Makintsian, collaborating with Dashnakist leaders, traveled to Russia to solicit Sovnarkom aid.[51] In Baku, the Soviet fulminated against the Transcaucasian declaration of independence, and during its May 2 session poured insults upon the Mensheviks and the Musavat "beks." However, the participation of Dashnaktsutiun in the Seim's decision was passed over in silence. Three weeks later, Baku Sovnarkom Military Commissar Korganov claimed that declaring independence had been a Menshevik-Musavat plot to permit Turkish troops unhindered transit over Transcaucasia in their drive to "liberate Baku." Again the Armenian nationalist party was spared Bolshevik curses.[52] In fact, with Shahumian's approval, a deputation of the Baku Armenian Council had already left the city to secure arms, money, men, and diplomatic support from the Sovnarkom.[53]

Nearly every attempt to gain Russian assistance was thwarted, however, by the Soviet Commissariat for Nationalities, directed by Stalin. Soon after the establishment of the Sovnarkom, the Commissariat had created departments for specific nationalities. In January, 1918, V. A. Avanesov, secretary of the Bolshevik Central Committee, and Vahan Terian were placed in charge of the Armenian division. The initial task of the Armenian Affairs Commissariat was the translation and dissemination of Marxist literature, especially among the thousands of Turkish Armenians who had found refuge in the mountains and steppes of Russia. The suffering people were informed of the great Leninist principle, self-determination, and reassured that the Sovnarkom would guide the oppressed to freedom.[54] Soon Stalin's Armenian assistants turned their division into a militant body espousing "War Communism." All organizations associated with the Armenian National Council in Tiflis were brought under attack. In March, Terian and Avanesov convinced the Sovnarkom to liquidate the Petrograd Armenian Defense Committee, headed by tsarist General Hovhannes Bagratuni. The valuable properties and treasury of the society were transferred to the Commissariat for Nationalities. This was only the first step in destroying the broad network of Armenian newspapers and organizations operating in Russia. In June, the famed Lazarian Academy of Moscow, cradle of the Russian Armenian cultural renaissance, was expropriated. The denouement came in July when the Sovnarkom decreed that all groups and establishments associated with the Tiflis National Council were to be dissolved and their assets transferred to the Commissariat for Nationalities. In cities without an Armenian division of the Commissariat, these properties would be placed under the jurisdiction of the local soviet.[55] This decisive action in mid-1918 was taken after it was clear that a rapprochement between Dashnaktsutiun and the Sovnarkom was more remote than ever. By that time, Dashnaktsutiun not only had condoned the separation of Transcaucasia from Russia but also had taken the road to Armenian independence.

The Moscow rulers watched Transcaucasian events anxiously. Lenin usually favored a conciliatory policy toward the border regions and expressed sympathy for the Armenians. The Seim's action of April 22, however, drew angry accusations from the chief tactician of Bolshevism. Speaking before the All-Russian Soviet Executive Committee and the Moscow Soviet on May 14, Lenin attributed the perplexing situation on the Caucasus boundaries to the unforgivable indecisiveness of the Tiflis rulers. They had first repudiated the Treaty of Brest-Litovsk and then declared independence without identifying the territories they coveted. He continued:

> We have asked in numerous radio telegrams: please be kind enough to identify the territory to which you have pretensions. To claim independence is your right, but you are obliged, if speaking about independence, to say which is that territory you represent. That was a week ago. An enormous number of radiograms has been written, but there has been not a single answer. German imperialism is taking advantage of that. Thus Germany, with Turkey as a supporting government, found it possible to advance and

to advance without having to answer to anyone, without having to pay attention to anything, announcing: we will take whatever we can take; we are not violating the Brest treaty, since the Transcaucasian Army does not recognize it, because the Caucasus is independent.[56]

A week later, Stalin, too, discussed Transcaucasian affairs, but without repeating Lenin's frequent references to the right of self-determination. Instead, he stressed that the *independence* of the Tiflis Mensheviks would inevitably turn into slavish *dependence* on the Turkish and German "civilized beasts."[57] Mentioning the Transcaucasian crisis fomented by the Kars episode, Stalin reported that the Armenians had refused to participate in the Chkhenkeli cabinet and that mass demonstrations against the declaration of independence were taking place:

> All Armenia is protesting against the usurpers of the Tiflis self-appointed "government" and demanding the resignation of the Seim deputies. . . . The population of Transcaucasia is opposed to the Tiflis "government." The population of Transcaucasia is opposed to secession from Russia. The workers and peasants of Transcaucasia favor a referendum, in spite of the handful of Seim members, for nobody, absolutely nobody, has authorized the Seim to separate Transcaucasia from Russia.[58]

Foreign Affairs Commissar Chicherin likewise denounced the separation of Transcaucasia. In a note to Count Wilhelm von Mirbach, German envoy to Russia, he asserted that the Tiflis government was an unpopular clique and that, without Soviet Russia's participation, the negotiations in which Transcaucasia was now involved were illegal.[59] Chicherin was alluding to the Batum Conference.

The Batum Peace Conference

On April 28, three days after the fall of Kars, Vehib Pasha communicated to Tiflis his government's recognition of the Transcaucasian Republic. Honoring Chkhenkeli's request to resume peace talks, the Ottoman government was sending Halil Bey, the Minister of Justice, to Batum. Accompanying him would be delegates from the North Caucasus, an area that had also separated from Russia. The Sublime Porte hoped that an accord could be worked out in Batum for the unification of Transcaucasia and the North Caucasus.[60] Chkhenkeli immediately thanked Vehib for the kind consideration and reminded the general of the April 13 Turkish note stating that all the Central Powers could participate in the parleys as soon as Transcaucasia had formally declared independence. Now that this prerequisite had been fulfilled, Chkhenkeli wanted to know who would be the representatives of Turkey's allied governments.[61] The Ottomans did not reply to this inquiry until after the Batum Conference had convened.

The approximately fifty Transcaucasian delegates and counselors departed from Tiflis on May 5. Voting privileges were accorded to Akakii Chkhenkeli, Nikolai Nikoladze, Alexandre Khatisian, Hovhannes Kachaznuni, Mahmed Hasan Hajinskii, and Mehmed Emin Rasul-Zade. Among the leading advisers were the Georgians, Zurab Avalov and General I. Z. Odishelidze; Armenians, Mentor Buniatian and Simon Vratzian; and Moslems, Fathali Khan Khoiskii and Aslan Bek Safikurdskii. For the Ottomans, the only official delegate other than Halil was General Mehmed Vehib Pasha.[62] At the opening session on May 11, Chkhenkeli accepted a Turkish proposal to invite Haidar Bammat and Abdul Chermoev of the so-called North Caucasus Republic to participate. Present as observers were the Germans, General Otto von Lossow, military attaché to Turkey; Count Friedrich von der Schulenburg, former vice-consul in Tiflis; and Otto Günther von Wesendonck, adviser on Caucasian affairs.[63]

Halil Bey, erstwhile associate of Armenian leaders in Constantinople, welcomed the delegates and hailed the "beautiful star of freedom" which shone over Transcaucasia. Chkhenkeli responded with appropriate phrases and then, announcing recognition of the Treaty of Brest-Litovsk, requested an official text so that his delegation could study the provisions in detail.[64] To the Transcaucasians, the matter seemed simple. They would submit to the treaty but attempt to win certain minor territorial rectifications. The men from Tiflis were shaken, however, when Halil replied:

> The struggle between the Turkish and Transcaucasian forces was resumed and unfortunately blood was shed. Thus, in view of this, the character of our relations has changed. I cannot allow, consequently, that the Brest-Litovsk treaty be recognized as the exclusive basis for our negotiations.

Then the Ottoman Minister of Justice declared that, to facilitate matters, his government had already prepared a draft treaty to be presented to Chkhenkeli. There was little need for prolonged negotiations. Even before reading the document, the Transcaucasian Premier and Foreign Minister insisted that all four Central Powers participate in the deliberations. Halil rejected the proposal on the ground that the Treaty of Brest-Litovsk allowed any of the Central Powers to conclude agreements with other states before submitting the terms to the other three allies for approval.[65] The war of words had begun and was to intensify daily until the end of the month.

When the Transcaucasian delegation read the draft treaty, it became obvious that the Treaty of Brest-Litovsk was regarded as obsolete by the Ottoman government. In addition to Kars, Ardahan, and Batum, the Ittihadist rulers now demanded, from the Tiflis guberniia, the Akhalkalak and Akhaltsikh *uezd*s and, from the Erevan guberniia, the entire Surmalu uezd and that part of the Alexandropol and Etchmiadzin uezds through which the Kars-Julfa railway passed. A series of annexes dealt with subjects such as trade and navigation, frontier traffic, Ottoman transit rights through

Transcaucasia, and reduction of the armed forces of the Tiflis government.[66] It seemed as if Stalin was correct in predicting that *independence* would lead to obsequious *dependence*.

The Transcaucasians maneuvered desperately and vainly. Chkhenkeli cited the Brest-Litovsk proviso that indicated the necessity of a treaty between all Central Powers and the other contracting state before bilateral additional agreements could be negotiated. Halil chided Chkhenkeli for raising the point. Determining which questions on the agenda pertained to all Central Powers and which to Turkey alone was not the business of the Transcaucasian delegation, whose opinion was neither solicited nor appreciated.[67]

Following the May 11 plenary session, which proved to be the only official meeting of the two delegations, several notes were exchanged between Chkhenkeli and Halil. Transcaucasia's spokesman repeatedly insisted that the Treaty of Brest-Litovsk be honored and that all Central Powers participate in the ensuing conference. The Turkish response was a categorical rejection. Halil ridiculed Chkhenkeli's claim that the Transcaucasian delegation at Trebizond had accepted the treaty, which thus should serve as the basis for current talks. Chkhenkeli was reminded that he himself had admitted to Rauf Bey that the Seim had repudiated the treaty and had recalled the delegation. The Turkish chief delegate then warned that further obstinacy would result in deleterious consequences.[68] Halil Bey's words were not empty threats. While the bickering in Batum increased, Turkish armies rolled through Alexandropol toward the few remaining Armenian districts of Transcaucasia. Turkish Armenia had already been obliterated. It was now the turn for Russian Armenia.

Turkish Invasion of the Erevan Guberniia

The immediate need to utilize the Kars-Julfa railway served as the Ottoman excuse for advancing into the Erevan guberniia. Ostensibly, the line was to be employed to transport Turkish troops to North Persia, where the threat of concerted British activity had intensified. According to German sources, the actual motivation for the Turkish demand was not to check the still-distant Entente forces but to secure a route from Kars through Julfa to Baku. This corridor was essential for the realization of Enver's obsessive vision. Already deputations of Transcaucasian Moslems had appealed to Ottoman authorities to liberate Baku from the Bolshevik-Armenian coalition.[69] If the German thesis is accepted, the diplomatic and military incidents involving Alexandropol and the territory through which the railway passed are readily understood.

In Batum, the two delegations appointed a special commission on military affairs to consider, among other topics, the Ottoman request to place the railway from Alexandropol to Julfa at the disposal of the Turkish Army. No agreement was reached because the Transcaucasian representatives, generals Odishelidze and Korganov, firmly reiterated Chkhenkeli's stipulation that the matter be settled through a supplementary agreement to the general peace treaty.[70] Away from the commission's deliberations, Halil and Vehib urged the Armenian members of the Transcaucasian delegation to yield to the Ottoman demand. The pair claimed to represent the moderate faction of the Ittihad party and promised to do all in their power to assure the return of the railway and surrounding land at the conclusion of the World War. Should Khatisian and Kachaznuni remain adamant, the Enver-Talaat radical element would succeed in its goal of annihilating Armenia.[71] When Khatisian bitterly decried Turkish wartime policies, Halil wasted no more time on words. Late at night on May 14, he wrote Chkhenkeli that Army Commander Vehib Pasha had failed in his earnest attempt to secure a friendly agreement for use of the Kars-Alexandropol-Julfa railway. Consequently the Turkish forces would be compelled to advance on the following morning. The activity would be local and should not be labeled a violation of the truce. If the Armenians offered no resistance, they would not be harmed. Having received the note at six in the morning, the Transcaucasian delegation found it impossible to warn the Tiflis government in time for it to relay tactical instructions to General Nazarabekian.[72]

Meanwhile, toward dawn in Alexandropol, General Nazarabekian received a Turkish ultimatum to relinquish the railway running to the Persian frontier and to withdraw all forces under his command to a line 25 kilometers east of Alexandropol and the railroad. One unit of Armenian militia would be permitted to remain in the city to assist the Ottoman authorities in maintaining order. These terms were to be accepted within three hours.[73] Even before the communiqué had been translated from Turkish, parts of the I and II Caucasian corps crossed the Arpachai and stormed Alexandropol. Fortunately for the Armenians, the defenders fought stubbornly on the morning of May 15, allowing approximately twenty thousand inhabitants of the city to flee toward Erevan and Tiflis. The enemy was already in the outskirts of Alexandropol that afternoon when Nazarabekian gave the order to retreat. The entire 1st Division and two regiments of the 2nd Division withdrew eastward toward Karakilisa and, in compliance with the Turkish demand, took new positions along a line 25 kilometers from Alexandropol. Just to their rear was the village of Hamamlu, where the main road branched toward Karakilisa and Tiflis on the one hand and toward Erevan on the other. The remaining regiments of the 2nd Division together with units of militia retreated along the Julfa railway as far as the Sardarabad-Etchmiadzin zone, the western gateway to Erevan.[74] The cordon around the Armenian heartland was tightening as thousands of refugees crowded into the small area still free of Turkish troops.

On May 16, at his new headquarters in Karakilisa, General Nazarabekian received a second Turkish ultimatum, this time to permit the unhindered movement of Ottoman forces toward Julfa:

If you will ensure the security of the movement along the route, then you can be assured that this movement will be conducted honorably by us, but if you oppose us we will advance on foot and be unable to guarantee the inviolability of the population.[75]

One hour was given for a reply. Nazarabekian answered that, although only the Transcaucasian government could authorize the concession, he would, because of the time limit, take the responsibility upon himself to accept in principle the Turkish terms until final approval could arrive from Tiflis. He requested that all military activities cease at least until his government could make a decision.[76] Shevki and Karabekir did not wait. The Third Army's 5th, 9th, 11th, and 36th Caucasian divisions advanced on Hamamlu and Sardarabad. Capturing Hamamlu by May 22, the invaders blocked the communication and transportation routes between Tiflis and Erevan. Then, dividing their forces, the Ottomans pressed toward Karakilisa, approximately 75 miles from Tiflis, and toward Bash Abaran, 25 miles from Erevan.[77]

In Batum, Chkhenkeli protested the truce violations to Halil. The Turkish negotiator was reminded that even in his astonishing nighttime note of May 14–15 he had made no demand for the evacuation of Alexandropol or the 25-kilometer withdrawal. Furthermore, Halil had promised a "strictly friendly and very reserved advance." What was occurring in the Erevan guberniia was neither friendly nor reserved. Vindicating the Ottoman moves, Halil Bey replied that World War exigencies made use of the railway imperative. He feigned complete ignorance of the military activities that had taken place away from the Alexandropol-Julfa line.[78]

On May 18 Karjikian, chairman of the Seim's Dashnakist fraction, wired Khatisian and Kachaznuni instructions to try to gain German supervision over the railway and the retention of Armenian troops in the surrounding territory. If these conditions were accepted, the distraught inhabitants would be informed that their safety had been guaranteed and that there was no need to flee.[79] The presence of General von Lossow and several other German officials in Batum made intercession more likely.

Conflicting German-Turkish Interests in Transcaucasia

Transcaucasian hopes for German assistance were not unfounded, as, by the spring of 1918, the objectives of Berlin and Constantinople were more discordant than at any other time since conclusion of the secret pact of August 2, 1914. Notes exchanged between the German Foreign Ministry and its representatives abroad reveal the growing alarm over the Turkish offensive. Christians were again being massacred, and Germany was again implicated. In 1918, Christian Germany was especially sensitive to irate public opinion. It was German power, not Turkish, which had compelled Russia to sign the Treaty of Brest-Litovsk. Thus, the violent manner in which the

Ottomans pushed into Kars, Ardahan, and Batum sorely embarrassed the political and military leaders of Berlin. On April 30, before sailing for the Batum Conference, General von Lossow received instructions from the Foreign Ministry to strive for a solution favorable to the Armenians. If possible, these Asiatic Christians should receive autonomy in areas of heavy concentration in both Transcaucasia and the Ottoman Empire, and cultural-religious freedom in the remaining regions.[80]

During the opening session of the Batum Conference, the strain between the Germano-Turkish allies was evidenced in von Lossow's explanation that he was present to defend the interests of his government. On the following day, May 12, he conferred with the Armenian delegates and expressed unreserved sympathy for their cause. He doubted, however, that his influence was sufficient to restrain the Turks.[81] After promising to keep his government informed about the unbearable Ottoman attitude, von Lossow wired the Foreign Ministry and Ambassador Bernstorff in Constantinople deprecating the violations of Brest-Litovsk. As the Turkish pretensions to Akhalkalak, Alexandropol, and areas near Erevan, all solidly Armenian, were aimed at exterminating this Christian people and looting Transcaucasia, the general begged that intense German pressure be applied to the Ottoman government.[82]

Naturally, the roots of German opposition to the renewed Turkish offensive reached deeper than mere humanitarianism. It happened, as German authors attest, that concern for the Armenians coincided with the military, economic, and political interests of the Reich. The loss of Baghdad to the British and the defection of the Arab provinces of the Ottoman Empire did not overly perturb Enver Pasha and his associates, for as compensation they planned to reshape the Turkish Empire to include the Caucasus and possibly even Transcaspia and the Crimea. For the defense and economic viability of Turkey, it was necessary to transform the Caucasus into a solid Islamic stronghold and to insure the inclusion of Baku in the remolded state.[83] Already in March, 1918, Enver's half brother, Nuri Bey, had left the Mesopotamian front for Transcaucasia with instructions to organize an Islamic army that would seize control of the area and liberate Baku.[84] Some German military strategists had initially not opposed this move, for it was in the interest of the common war effort. Ludendorff had even agreed to condone Turkish territorial acquisitions beyond the frontiers established at Brest, on condition that the additional lands be occupied rapidly and their loss recognized by the Transcaucasian government.[85] The German Foreign Ministry and most members of the High Command strove, however, to limit Turkey to the sanjaks of Kars, Ardahan, and Batum. They insisted that the Ottoman armies should be concentrated on the Mesopotamian and Palestinian fronts, which had been weakened by British blows. Therefore every effort should be made to avoid conflict with Transcaucasia, which had now accepted Brest-Litovsk. Enver's acceptance would bring peace along that frontier. Even Ludendorff was soon won over to this view.[86]

Another aspect of German military strategy was the plan to utilize the Caucasus as a corridor to the Orient. The Berlin-Baghdad route to the East had been blocked by the British. By substituting the "Hamburg-Herat" line via Transcaucasia, German forces could move through Central Asia and Afghanistan toward India. With the British colonial empire placed in a vulnerable position, the London government might be constrained to sue for an armistice. Control of the Caucasus by a jealous Ottoman Empire would hinder such a project.[87] During March and April, 1918, the German Command repeatedly urged a southward concentration of Turkish power, and by May the request became a poorly disguised threat. On May 15, 20, and 25, Ludendorff appealed to General von Seeckt, the German officer serving as Ottoman Chief of Staff, to use his personal influence to prevent further Turkish advances in Transcaucasia.[88]

German suspicion of the Turks was intensified by new reports from von Lossow. On May 23 he again charged that Enver and Talaat were bent on exterminating all remaining Armenians and on annexing not only much of the Erevan and Tiflis guberniias but also Elisavetpol and Baku. They were scheming to confront Germany with a fait accompli. Von Lossow requested that a warship and a German battalion be dispatched to Transcaucasia to counteract this plot. Two days later he warned that Turkish eyes were upon the entire Caucasus and even the lands to the north. Turkey's respect for its senior ally could be restored only through a show of force.[89] Thoroughly alarmed, the German High Command had already appointed Colonel Kress von Kressenstein (von Kress) to head a military mission to Tiflis. Von Kress, elevated to the rank of acting general while serving in Transcaucasia, was quite experienced in dealing with the Turks and might succeed in upholding German interests. Enver reacted violently to the German line of action. On May 20, the Ottoman War Minister warned Berlin that all Transcaucasia was threatened by Bolshevism, and he bewailed the suffering of innocent Moslems at the hands of the vicious Armenians. A week later, through his Chief of Staff, Enver claimed that three hundred thousand men in Transcaucasia were ready and waiting to join the Turkish Army. This vast reserve would be of great assistance to the Central Powers in the difficult tasks ahead.[90] Despite this assurance, Enver Pasha failed to allay the misgivings of the German strategists.

Economic as well as political factors influenced the shaping of the Kaiser's Transcaucasian policy. Three years of warfare had depleted Germany's raw materials, and the Caucasus was an untapped reservoir that could be gainfully exploited. Both Ludendorff and Field Marshall Paul von Hindenburg have testified to German dependence on oil, copper, manganese, and cotton from this region. Ludendorff tried to justify the establishment of German control over part of Transcaucasia:

Commanders Keri, Hamazasp, Vardan

Hovhannes Kachaznuni

Alexandre Khatisian

Simon Vratzian

Boghos Nubar

Catholicos Gevorg V

Hakob Zavriev

Mikayel Papadjanian

General Andranik

General Nazarabekian

Dro Kanayan

Evgenii Gegechkori

Iraklii Tsereteli

Akakii Chkhenkeli

Noi Ramishvili

Noi Zhordania

Nikolai Chkheidze

Avetis Aharonian

Hamo Ohandjanian

Aram Manukian

Avetik Sahakian   Stepan Shahumian

Fathali Khan Khoiskii

We acquired a means to get at the raw materials of the Caucasus, independently of Turkey, and to gain influence over the operation of the railway over Tiflis. This was of decisive importance for the conduct of war in North Persia and under a management influenced by Germany was more efficient than one in which the Turks would collaborate.[91]

Supporting the military in this endeavor, the German Foreign Ministry even pondered means of depriving Turkey of Batum. German control of Batum, the terminus of the oil pipeline from Baku and the finest port of Transcaucasia, would greatly expedite the export of the raw materials to Europe.[92]

Economic considerations also affected Germany's relations with the Sovnarkom. Secret negotiations were in progress for a Caucasus settlement. Germany was plying Russia for recognition of a separate Transcaucasia, while the Sovnarkom strove to cling at least to Baku. Though full agreement was not reached until the end of August, 1918, the general provisions had already been formulated by the beginning of summer. Germany would permit Soviet Russia to retain the Baku region in return for a share of the oil and unlimited control over part of western Transcaucasia. Ottoman dominion in Caucasia naturally would abort the scheme. Aside from this consideration, Turkish seizure of Baku could provoke Russia into resuming hostilities on grounds that the action had nullified the Treaty of Brest-Litovsk. Berlin did not cherish this prospect.

If Russia were to acknowledge German interests in western Transcaucasia, it would be necessary for the Sovnarkom to arrive at a modus vivendi with the Tiflis government and to assent, directly or indirectly, to coexistence. Soon after arriving in Moscow, Count von Mirbach initiated steps for a rapprochement by suggesting German mediation. Though claiming that Transcaucasia was still legally Russian territory and protesting the Batum negotiations without Sovnarkom participation, Chicherin accepted the offer on May 13.[93] Von Mirbach informed the Foreign Commissar on May 22 that a certain Machabeli would represent Chkhenkeli's government during the conference. Kiev was suggested as the site for the parleys, because talks of a similar nature between Ukrainian, Russian, and German deputies were already in progress there. The next day, Chicherin reiterated agreement to confer but cautioned that Soviet participation did not presuppose recognition of the so-called Transcaucasian government.[94] Whether the talks would have taken place and an understanding would have been reached remains a moot question, for three days later the "so-called Transcaucasian government" was no government at all.

Attempted German Mediation and a New Ottoman Ultimatum

The strained relations between Germany and Turkey did not escape the attention of the Transcaucasian representatives at Batum. Aware that Germany favored a conciliatory policy toward the Caucasus and was attempting to circumscribe Turkey's military activities, Chkhenkeli had repeatedly insisted that the Batum negotiations include all Central Powers. For the same reasons, Kachaznuni and Khatisian had turned to von Lossow for advice and assistance. The Bavarian general recognized his limitations, however, and when the Turks demanded the railway to Julfa, advised the Armenians to comply.[95] He expressed opposition to the Ottoman advance, complained that his voice was ignored by the Turkish authorities, and again promised to inform his government of the flagrant violations of the Brest-Litovsk treaty. On May 20, the Armenian National Council sent a special deputation, Hamo Ohandjanian and Arshak Zohrabian, a well-known "internationalist" Menshevik, to confer with von Lossow. They claimed that the Turco-Tatars were plotting to crush Armenia and to snatch the very heartlands around Erevan. Two days later, their appeal for German supervision and protection was relayed by von Lossow to Ambassador Bernstorff and to the Foreign Ministry in Berlin.[96]

Meanwhile, the Batum Conference had reached an impasse. Halil insisted on acceptance of the May 11 draft treaty, while Chkhenkeli's refrain was "Brest-Litovsk." On May 19, in a note to the Transcaucasian delegation, von Lossow, presumably having received directives from his government, offered to serve as a mediator to break the deadlock.[97] Immediate Transcaucasian acceptance of the proposal would seem to have been in conformity with aspirations for a relatively favorable peace. Minutes of the delegation's May 19 caucus reveal that this was not so. The meeting was torn with dissension and accusations. While the Armenians called for instant approval of von Lossow's offer, Hajinskii and Rasul-Zade insisted that Halil be consulted on the matter for "psychological reasons." Khatisian objected, stressing that Transcaucasia was free to pursue its basic goals without soliciting the enemy's blessing. The old Georgian revolutionary, Nikoladze, defined the differences between arbitration and mediation: for the former, the sanction of both parties concerned was necessary, but for the latter, either side could act alone to authorize a third power to intercede. As the session dragged on, guarded expressions gave way to direct indictments. Hajinskii demanded information concerning Chkhenkeli's furtive activity which had led to von Lossow's proposal, and Rasul-Zade complained that the delegation president had left the members in the dark, scheming to present them with an accomplished fact. The delegates did not even know until the opening session of the Batum Conference that Chkhenkeli was to insist on the Treaty of Brest-Litovsk as the basis for further negotiations. A verbal barrage exploded when the two Moslem delegates requested a recess for at least an hour before giving a decision. Enraged, Khatisian denounced the maneuver, which would have allowed the Tatars time to inform Halil of the proceedings. Hajinskii retorted that, unless the intermission were granted, he would refuse to vote.[98] Though available records of the meeting do not indicate whether a recess was called, the delegation finally decided to accept German mediation.[99] Describing the incident, one historian of the period has written:

> During the entire length of the conference the Azerbaijani [Tatar] delegates had been keeping the Turks informed of the deliberations of the Transcaucasian delegation. Both the Georgians and the Armenians knew that, but there was nothing they could do about it. The debate over von Lossow's offer only made the picture clearer and gave additional proof of the fact that the Azerbaijanis were closer to the enemy than to the state of which they formed a part.[100]

Hajinskii and Rasul-Zade were not the only Moslems to confer with Halil Bey. From Baku, Elisavetpol, Akhalkalak, Akhaltsikh, and other areas of the Caucasus, messengers and deputations were received in Batum. Each, warning that the Moslems of Transcaucasia were threatened with destruction, pleaded for Turkish assistance. Using the principle of self-determination, the Turkic plurality of the Caucasus begged for an Ottoman foremarch. Akhalkalak and Akhaltsikh residents petitioned for direct annexation to the Ottoman Empire, while supplicants from other districts simply called for liberation and made no specific proposal concerning the final disposition of their native provinces.[101] Such expressions reinforced Enver's conviction that the golden opportunity was at hand.

Three days after von Lossow's proposal, Jemal Pasha, Minister of the Marine and junior member of the Ittihad Triumvirate, arrived in Batum to confer with the delegations. Meeting with the Transcaucasians, he warmly greeted the Georgians and Tatars but, turning toward Khatisian, coldly remarked that Armeno-Turkish animosity was of long standing and that the Armenians were unfortunately doing nothing to rectify the situation. He castigated Andranik and other partisan "bandits" who were slaughtering the peaceful Moslem population and denounced the Armenians of Baku for joining with the Bolsheviks to spill the blood of thousands of his coreligionists.[102] Two days after this scene, von Lossow informed the Transcaucasian delegation that Halil had refused to permit mediation.[103] Possibly Jemal had made the decision. In either event, it was consistent with Turkish objectives. Allowing Germany to intervene would only complicate and prolong the conference, which Turkey desired to conclude summarily. On the evening of May 25, Chkhenkeli received from von Lossow another communiqué, which startled some members of the delegation:

> I have trustworthy information that the Transcaucasian Republic and government are in the process of disintegrating. Since this was not foreseen and because I have no instructions to continue negotiations after the collapse of the Transcaucasian Federation, as my liaison relates only to those matters concerning the Transcaucasian government, it is necessary for me to communicate with and personally receive new verbal instructions from the responsible German officials. Not to lose time, I have decided to leave Batum tonight on the German steamship, the "Minna Horn."[104]

Obviously, von Lossow knew more about what was to occur in Tiflis on the following day than did several of Chkhenkeli's colleagues. Only the Georgians knew the destination of the "Minna Horn."

The full meaning of the German note had not yet become clear when, on May 26, Halil Bey abruptly halted the informal talks. In the ultimatum he delivered to Chkhenkeli, Halil expressed sorrow that, although negotiations had been in progress for over two weeks, no accord had been reached. He continued: "Hundreds of thousands of Turks and Moslems in Baku and its environs are suffering under the bloody yoke of heartless bandits, so-called revolutionaries, and the irreparable tragedy which threatens those unfortunates becomes more and more inevitable." [105] Likewise, Moslems throughout the remainder of the Caucasus were subjected to every imaginable type of criminal activity. No government could witness these atrocities with indifference, especially when the holocaust engulfed a religiously and racially related people in neighboring lands. Because of these considerations and because the exigencies of war demanded immediate utilization of the Transcaucasian railways, the Ottoman Empire now requested a definite answer regarding its terms of May 11 "as well as to the new proposal pertaining to a rectification of the boundaries, the text of which I have the honor to present herewith." Unconditional acceptance within seventy-two hours would alone guarantee a friendly settlement between the two governments. In the meantime, satisfactory relations would be maintained only if "the Turkish military activity in the south of the Caucasus meets with no resistance." [106] The boundary rectification to which Halil referred was a demand for even more territory. The Ottoman Empire would exact additional areas of the Alexandropol and Etchmiadzin uezds, nearly half of the Erevan and Sharur-Daralagiaz uezds, and, except for a small district around Ordubad, the entire Nakhichevan uezd. With ultimatum in hand, the Transcaucasians prepared to depart for Tiflis.[107]

Georgian Preparations To Abandon the Federation

During this critical period, the delegates of each nationality were of course concerned about the self-preservation of their own people. To the Tatars this betokened the need for close collaboration with the Ottomans and for a further Turkish advance. For the Armenians above all others there was ample cause to be tormented by the seemingly inevitable ruin. The only glimmer of salvation was Germany's questionable ability to restrain her Turkish ally. Germany was also the fulcrum of the Georgian pursuit of preservation. There was, however, another necessary condition—severing bonds with the Armenians, for it was clear that they were doomed and Georgia could not afford to perish with them. Consequently, it was imperative to secure German protection and to step out from the tottering Transcaucasian Federative Republic. By the time von Lossow sailed from Batum on the night of May 25, the Georgians had been assured fulfillment of the first measure, and when the Turkish ultimatum was delivered on the following evening, the second step had already been taken.

German-Georgian relations were firmly established by 1918. Although the Georgian volunteer unit serving the Central Powers during the first years of the war had been discredited and dissolved, an active group of Georgian intellectuals remained in Berlin lobbying for the restoration of the independence of their native lands. Ludendorff has written: "In the years 1915 and 1916 in Armenia, we had employed Georgian irregulars, admittedly without success. Thus we had come into contact with influential Georgians. I could only welcome these relations as I did Georgia's appeal for the protection of the German Empire."[108] It is significant that when, in mid-May, von Mirbach suggested mediation between the Sovnarkom and the Chkhenkeli government, Prince Georgii Machabeli, a member of this Georgian émigré group in Berlin, was identified as Transcaucasia's representative. The mutual advantages of a Georgian-German understanding have already been elucidated. On May 14, three days after the first session of the Batum Conference, the Georgian National Council authorized Zhordania to head a special mission to confer with von Lossow. Germany was to be requested to extend protection over Georgia, to send armed forces to the Caucasus, to release, equip, and repatriate Georgian soldiers who, as members of the Russian Tsarist Army, had been taken prisoner, and to support Georgia diplomatically.[109]

Batum became a beehive of surreptitious activities. Chkhenkeli, too, held private parleys with von Lossow and delegated the Georgian adviser, Zurab Avalov, to work with von Wesendonck to draft several agreements. Avalov's diary presents a fascinating tale of secret diplomacy. The arrangements were made under the very eyes of the Ottoman and non-Georgian Transcaucasian delegates at Batum.

According to Avalov, Zhordania was again in Batum on May 21:

> During frank conversations with members of the German delegation, Georgia's stand was prepared in anticipation of the inevitable collapse of the Transcaucasion coalition. Only a few persons knew of the secret. N. Zhordania, who had come from Tiflis, in his capacity as president of the Georgian National Council and leader of the Social Democrat party in the Seim and in Georgia, was the person on whom fell the difficult task of pushing through in Tiflis the basic acts (the declaration of Georgian independence and the self-liquidation of the Seim).[110]

Initially, the Menshevik veteran seems to have vacillated. The establishment of small national states did not conform to Marxist ideals. Despite any qualms of conscience he may have felt, Zhordania soon accepted the wisdom of Chkhenkeli's realpolitik and labored earnestly and selflessly for Georgia. While still in Batum, he and Nikoladze carefully studied the map of Transcaucasia and drew the boundaries of the Georgia to be created. They also decided what concessions could be made, if necessary, to the Turks and Tatars. They did not seriously consider relations with the Armenians, for it was doubtful that there would be any Armenia at all. Meeting with Khan Khoiskii, Safikurdskii, Khas-Mamedov, Usubbekov, Jafarov, A. D. Pepinov, and other Tatar leaders, the Menshevik representatives discussed possible future territorial boundaries. The Tatars claimed to favor the continuation of a "trio" Transcaucasia but felt that, if the Turks were to insist on absorbing one of the component areas, there should be at least a "duo" Transcaucasia.[111] There was no need to mention which of the three partners of the Federation was to be sacrificed.

Just before Zhordania departed for Tiflis on May 22, he and the Georgians of the Transcaucasian delegation approved Avalov's draft of a declaration of independence. There was now no turning back. Two days later Avalov and von Wesendonck put the finishing touches on a temporary pact. Then Chkhenkeli, in a wire coded by General Odishelidze, warned the Georgian National Council that any further delay in proclaiming independence could have disastrous consequences.[112] Only an independent Georgia protected by Germany would be spared Turkish invasion. It was already decided that Count von Schulenburg would serve as the Kaiser's representative in Tiflis.

On May 25 an aide of von Lossow's received the completed texts of the agreements and took them aboard the "Minna Horn." It was then that General von Lossow informed the Transcaucasian delegation that he had news of the impending collapse of the Republic and was departing to receive new instructions. The Georgians alone knew that the "Minna Horn" was sailing for the nearby port of Poti, where, immediately following the declaration of independence, members of their newly formed cabinet would hasten to sign the documents officially. Avalov wrote in his diary, "We are finishing the behind-the-scenes work at full speed." On the next day, May 26, he added, "The delegation begins to disperse, but the necessarily secret work has passed unnoticed. Nobody, it seems, suspects what is to happen today and tomorrow." [113]

Meanwhile, in Tiflis, the Georgian Social Democrat leaders met behind closed doors. Zhordania now championed the ideal of an independent Georgia and condoned the dissolution of the Transcaucasian Federation. He expressed his sympathy for the Armenians, who were destined for the worst possible fate. He added, however, that the responsibility for the tragedy lay with the political party which directed the Armenian people.[114] Then he departed for Batum for the final time to see that all had been properly arranged. Just after von Lossow had set sail at midnight on May 25, Zhordania met with Khatisian to explain that, because the Armenians continued to resist the Turkish forces and because of the intolerable chaos in Transcaucasia, Georgia would be obliged to declare its independence. The realities of the hour were vivid as he told his Armenian friend and associate of many years: "We cannot drown with you. Our people want to save what they can. You, too, are obligated to seek an avenue for agreement with the Turks. There is no other way!"[115] An hour later, Noi Zhordania left for Tiflis to witness the death of the Democratic Federative Republic of Transcaucasia and to assist at the birth of the independent Republic of Georgia.

The momentum of decisive Transcaucasian events increased steadily in the few weeks between April 22 and May 26. The Turks had entered Batum without a battle and had driven Transcaucasia to declare independence from Russia. The fall of Kars brought Turkey all the territories ceded by Article IV of Brest-Litovsk and opened the way toward the heartlands of Turan. The episode also intensified the mutual distrust of the Transcaucasian peoples. Attempts to negotiate with the enemy at Batum were hindered by disunity within the Transcaucasian delegation and the seemingly insatiable territorial hunger of the Ittihadist rulers of the Ottoman Empire. Georgians and Armenians realized that the narrow path that might lead to their salvation passed through Berlin. Success depended upon exploiting German-Turkish rivalry, as only a determined Germany could contain the eastward drive of Enver Pasha. By May 26 the Georgians had attained their goal. The Tatars, on their part, were not dissatisfied, for Turkish armies continued to advance over the southern regions of Transcaucasia. The Armenians, possessing neither the ports, the raw materials, nor the diplomatic astuteness of the Georgians and, unlike the Tatars, lacking strong cultural, religious, and racial bonds with the invader, were to be left in the lurch as the Transcaucasian Seim assembled to certify its own demise.

X

The Republics of Georgia, Azerbaijan, and Armenia

DURING THE LAST DAYS of May, 1918, three independent republics were born amidst the chaos and ruin of Transcaucasia. The failure to gain peace through the Batum negotiations, the Turkish drive deep into the Tiflis and Erevan *guberniia*s, and the absence of cohesion among Georgians, Armenians, and Tatars shattered the wobbling foundations of the Transcaucasian Federation. In contrast to their neighbors, the Armenians shuddered before the prospect of independence. Having been abandoned and hurled upon the mercy of the same Turkish rulers who had annihilated the Armenians of the Ottoman Empire, they searched desperately for a glimmer of hope. It was detected in the undisguised wrath of Germany against the Ittihadist rulers and in the first substantial Armenian victory on the battlefield. The Armenian National Council, basing its decision on these considerations and, more intrinsically, on the realization that there existed no other feasible alternative, timorously sanctioned the creation of the Republic of Armenia.

Collapse of the Transcaucasian Federative Republic

Just as the Mensheviks had assumed the initiative in declaring Transcaucasian independence, so, too, did they take the lead in dissolving the Federation. The preliminaries for German protection over Georgia had already been completed when, in the early afternoon of May 26, the Seim assembled for what was to be its final session. The Social Democrat "fraction" called upon Iraklii Tsereteli to defend the proposed resolution announcing the self-liquidation of the Seim. In a lengthy oration, Tsereteli accurately recounted the lack of unity in the Federative Republic, its executive body, its legislature, and its peace delegation. Each of the Transcaucasian peoples, he said, stood at a different stage of national development and was unable to reconcile its aspirations with those of the other two.¹ He chastised the Moslems for their sympathy with and assistance to the enemy. They had rejoiced as the Turks invaded Transcaucasia and had denied support to the legally constituted government of the Republic. The Armenians, on the contrary, had made every effort to withstand the foe, but had been compelled by brute force to relinquish many of their native regions.² In view of this sad reality, the Menshevik party had arrived at the following conclusion:

> That part [of Transcaucasia] which is still not occupied, that sector which is still prepared to resist occupation with all its power and which stands against the enemy, who is conducting talks with us, that part is, as we know, the Tiflis and Kutais guberniias—the Georgian people. It has been left alone, as the Armenian people were plucked from it and the Moslems have turned away from it. And the fictive existence of the Transcaucasian delegation deprives this people of the possibility of creating with the forces at its disposal a governmental organism capable of defending its interests. And we, who have always said to this people that its salvation lay in unity with the others . . . must now tell the Georgians: at the present moment you are alone, you are abandoned to your own forces; you have no government, you have no delegation in Batum, and as heavy as the loss of those allies is, you must realize that you are left to your own powers and that matters become progressively worse as you live with illusions of a united Transcaucasia, a single government, and a delegation in Batum. If you are to save yourself, then you must create your own governmental structure. . . .³

The reactions to Tsereteli's declaration varied. On behalf of the Musavat fraction, Rustambekov welcomed the Georgian decision but admonished the illustrious Menshevik spokesman that this was certainly not the time to heap unjustified abuse upon one another. He denied that the Moslems favored union with Turkey, and he pledged friendship with the other peoples of Transcaucasia. The Georgian proposal did not surprise Semenov, who had predicted this eventuality during the April 22 session of the Seim. It was all quite understandable: "The declaration of the independence of Georgia—it is the logical sequel to the separation of Transcaucasia from Russia."⁴ The Social Revolutionaries who had opposed Transcaucasian independence now condemned the Menshevik scheme. Berezov, chairman of the SR Regional Committee, accused the Georgians of turning away from the Russian Democracy and of deserting the Armenians, exclaiming, "The battle continues against the enemy, Armenian units continue to fight; they have been left alone, they are calling for aid, they search for allies!"⁵ From the opposite side of the chamber, Georgian National Democrat Gvazava expressed his party's satisfaction that the misguided Social Democrats, having always favored centralism, now stood on the correct path, which led toward the formation of a national government and the establishment of independence.⁶ Faced with an uncomfortable situation, Tsereteli rose a second time to plead for the Menshevik tactic and to refute the allegations of his critics. As if to soothe the conscience of Social Democracy, popularly recognized as the foe of nationalism, he reasoned that "national self-preservation does not contradict the work of democracy, but this survival is the best foundation for the ultimate ideal—the realization of socialism. . . ."[7] The oratory having been concluded, the legislature performed its final act by adopting the Menshevik-sponsored resolution:

> Because on the questions of war and peace there arose basic differences among the peoples who had created the Transcaucasian Republic, and because it became impossible to establish one authoritative order speaking in the name of all Transcaucasia, the Seim certifies the fact of the dissolution of Transcaucasia and lays down its powers.[8]

At three o'clock in the afternoon on May 26, 1918, the "Democratic Federative Republic of Transcaucasia" was no more. President Chkheidze wired the obituary to the capitals of eighteen nations.[9]

The Republics of Georgia and Azerbaijan

Many Georgian deputies of the now defunct Seim did not leave the chamber, for the Georgian National Council was to assemble there less than two hours later. Calling that meeting to order just before five o'clock, Council President Noi Zhordania welcomed the members and many honored guests, among whom were Count von Schulenburg and ranking clergy of the Georgian Orthodox Church. Zhordania recounted the events that had led that day to the death of one government and the imminent birth of another. Georgia was obliged to save herself from the present storm, he continued, and, having done so, would then assist others. The thousands of Armenians living in Georgia would be protected by the new republic, just as their forebears had been shielded by the Georgian kings.[10] Adhering to a carefully prepared schedule, the National Council wasted no more time on words. Instead, immediately after his introductory remarks, Zhordania called for the reading of the act of Georgian independence. The seven-point declaration established an independent democratic republic, which was to pursue a neutral course during international conflicts, foster friendly relations with all neighbors, guarantee civil and political liberties for all citizens, and provide for the unhindered development of its component nationalities.[11] Unanimously acclaiming the act, the Georgian leaders approved the temporary cabinet nominated by the Council's Executive Committee. Noi Ramishvili became the Republic's first Minister-President and Minister of Internal Affairs, while Akakii Chkhenkeli, having already proved his competence, served as Minister of Foreign Affairs.[12] Georgia was on the road to salvation. German soldiers taken prisoner and interned in Georgia during the World War had already been released and were training in the courtyard of the

Swedish Consulate. Immediately following the Georgian declaration of independence, General von Kress ordered these men to occupy strategic points in the city and to place pickets along the railway. The German flag was hoisted over Tiflis.[13]

Minister-President Ramishvili then hastily departed by train for Poti. He was joined en route by Chkhenkeli and the other Georgians returning from Batum. In Poti, General von Lossow waited aboard the "Minna Horn," where, on May 28, the "Provisional agreement for the settlement of preliminary mutual relations between Germany and Georgia" was signed. The Kaiser's government recognized the Republic and accorded it jurisdiction over an area up to the borders determined at Brest-Litovsk. Thus, the Turkish-coveted western districts of the Tiflis and Kutais guberniias were confirmed as integral parts of Georgia. In return, Germany was allowed use of the railways, with permission to transport troops and matériel of all four Central Powers and to manage the railway stations and the port of Poti. Other articles provided for the exchange of diplomatic representatives and the conclusion of a formal treaty at the earliest possible date.[14] Supplementary agreements intended to satisfy the German desire for Georgian raw materials were also signed before Chkhenkeli, Nikoladze, Avalov, and several other national leaders sailed with von Lossow toward Constanta. The general had assured them that when they reached Berlin the German government would cooperate in efforts to gain Russian recognition of the Georgian Republic.[15] Hamo Ohandjanian and Arshak Zohrabian, arriving in Poti just before departure time, were also invited by von Lossow to join the company sailing for Berlin aboard the "Minna Horn." Once there, they could plead the Armenian case before more influential authorities. Armenia, shattered by invasion, teeming with refugees, and lacking readily available raw materials, could not be given immediate German protection, but something might be gained in Berlin.[16]

The Moslems of Transcaucasia were not perturbed by the demise of the Seim. Not acting as swiftly as the Georgians, the Moslem National Council convened in Tiflis on May 27 and endorsed a proposal to declare "Eastern and Southern Transcaucasia" an independent, sovereign, democratic state. The official act establishing the Republic of Azerbaijan was proclaimed on the following day.[17] The Tatars now became "Azerbaijanis." [18] For several reasons, they enjoyed the most favorable position of the Transcaucasian peoples. They were not only the strongest numerically and the most widespread geographically, but they had nothing to fear from a Turkish invasion; on the contrary, they had much to gain. The suppression of Armenian armed bands, the assurance that Mountainous Karabagh would constitute part of Azerbaijan, and, above all, the deliverance of Baku, the Republic's natural capital, were dependent on Turkish benevolence and assistance. On June 2, Vehib Pasha reported to Enver that, in response to an Azerbaijani appeal, Turkish units would join in the struggle against the Bolsheviks.[19] Already Nuri Bey was in Ganja busily organizing hundreds of irregulars into the "Army of Islam" to conquer Baku. In the middle of June, 1918, the Moslem National Council transferred from Tiflis to Ganja, the temporary capital of Azerbaijan, and with the sanction of Nuri formed the Republic's cabinet, headed by Fathali Khan Khoiskii.[20] From June through September, the gaze of the government and its Ottoman ally was to be concentrated eastward upon the Apsheron Peninsula.

The Armenian Quandary

While Georgians and Azerbaijanis took concrete steps to strengthen the foundations of their newly proclaimed republics, the Armenian leaders were thrown into turmoil. Though they should have realized that the Transcaucasian Federation might collapse at any moment and should have planned for that eventuality, they were thoroughly unprepared to cope with the situation when it actually occurred. Bitter recrimination was the first Armenian reaction. On the night of May 26, the National Council hurled accusations of treachery at the Mensheviks and resolved to denounce the Georgian proclamation of independence.[21] The Council was unable, however, to take positive measures for determining a course of action. The Social Revolutionaries and nonpartisans insisted that the Armenian districts should not be declared independent. Would not Armenia, as a separate state, be subjected immediately to the dictates of Turkey? The Armenian Social Democrats—following the example of their Georgian colleagues—and the Populists called for independence, insisting that no alternative existed. The Dashnakists were badly split. Council Chairman Avetis Aharonian together with Ruben Ter Minasian and Artashes Babalian opposed, while Simon Vratzian and Khachatur Karjikian favored taking the momentous step. As the majority still rejected independence, the matter was deferred.[22]

That same night, a conference of Dashnakist leaders in Tiflis acted more decisively than did the National Council. They agreed that the fall of the Federative Republic and the subsequent Georgian maneuver made it necessary for the National Council to move to Erevan, where, entrusted with dictatorial powers, it would assume the functions of government.[23] This view was also shared by Kachaznuni and Khatisian, who, on the following evening, reported to the National Council on what had transpired in Batum. The two Armenian delegates stressed that the only possibility for survival required declaring independence and securing peace with Turkey, no matter what the price. Moreover, when on May 28 announcement was made of an independent Azerbaijan encompassing "Southern and Eastern Transcaucasia," the balance in the Armenian National Council tipped toward the inevitable. If the Azerbaijani claim to southern Transcaucasia passed unchallenged, those areas of the Erevan guberniia free of Ottoman occupation would also be lost. Thus, at noon on May 28, the Council appointed Khatisian, Kachaznuni, and Papadjanian to return to Batum with unlimited powers for negotiating a peace on behalf of the Armenian people or, depending on the circumstances, in the name of the independent "Republic of Armenia."[24]

Still the National Council tarried in making an official pronouncement. The matter was settled only after the dissonant leaders of Dashnaktsutiun had united. On the evening of May 29, the party's Bureau and Tiflis Central Committee and the Dashnakist members of the Seim and National Council met in emergency session. The final decision was to proclaim Armenia a republic, ruled at the start by a coalition government. The National Council would be urged to call Hovhannes Kachaznuni to the post of Minister-President.[25] With that verdict the die was cast, but that the apprehension of the nation's leaders was not dispelled is easily discerned in the Council's May 30 declaration:

> In view of the dissolution of the political unity of Transcaucasia and the new situation created by the proclamation of the independence of Georgia and Azerbaijan, the Armenian National Council declares itself the supreme and only administration for the Armenian provinces. Due to certain grave circumstances, the National Council, deferring until the near future the formation of an Armenian national government, temporarily assumes all governmental functions, in order to pilot the political and administrative helm of the Armenian provinces.[26]

In obvious and sharp contrast to the Georgian and Azerbaijani acts, the Armenian declaration made no mention of "independence," "republic," the rights of the citizenry, or relations with other states. Only after news of Armenian military successes near Erevan had been confirmed and peace had been concluded at Batum did the National Council dare to use publicly the title of Republic of Armenia.

Decisive Battles near Erevan

By the middle of May, 1918, there appeared to be no deliverance for the thousands of natives and refugees in the Erevan guberniia. They were isolated and surrounded by enemy forces. Five or six thousand shabby troops, who had retreated steadily during the preceding four months, were all that stood in the way of obliteration. W. E. D. Allen, a scholar in studies of the Caucasus, has captured the mood:

> The prospect of the ultimate victory of the western powers must have seemed at least uncertain to observers in Erevan in May 1918, and it has in fact rarely fallen to the lot of a people to confront such a desperate and seemingly hopeless situation as that which threatened the Armenians in the early summer of 1918.[27]

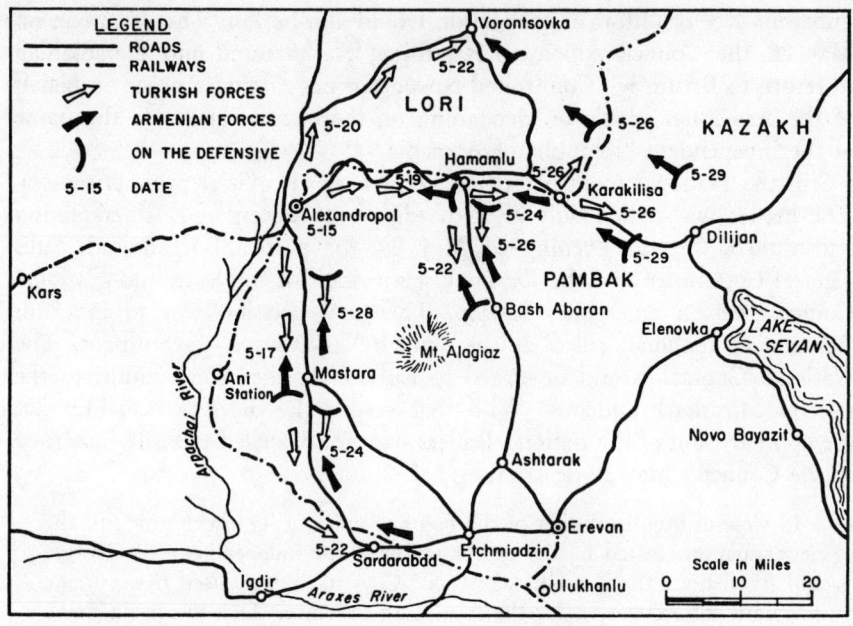

Map 9. The battles of May 16–30, 1918

Four Turkish divisions of the I and II Caucasian corps fanned out from Alexandropol in the direction of Karakilisa to the east, Bash Abaran to the southeast, and Sardarabad to the south.

To the astonishment of friend and foe alike, the unexpected came to pass. The Armenians stopped running, for there was nowhere to flee. The routes to Tiflis and Persia were sealed, the enemy advanced from north and west, and armed Tatar-Kurdish bands roamed the southern and eastern sectors of the province. As the ordeal of battle entered its final phase, the temper of defenders and populace alike transformed. Resolution supplanted panic. Sustaining the exclamation made by Harutunian several weeks earlier in the Seim, the Armenians were now ready "to die with weapons in hand." On the three fronts, the peasants and soldiers fought furiously. On May 24, General Nazarabekian ordered a counterattack from Karakilisa against Javid Bey's 11th Caucasian Division.[28] In the frenzied warfare of the next four days, thousands from both sides were killed or wounded. Then Shevki Pasha, commanding the Turkish forces on the Armenian theater, threw the 9th Division into action. In hand-to-hand combat, the Turkish regiments slowly drove Nazarabekian's men out of Karakilisa to positions just outside Dilijan. On this line the Armenians stood firm. The two Ottoman divisions avenged their heavy losses by slaying several thousand villagers who remained within the newly occupied regions.[29]

Meanwhile, to the south along the two routes leading to Erevan, there were equally rigorous encounters. General Silikian's Sardarabad group commanded by Colonel Daniel Bek Pirumian and the Bash Abaran group headed by Dro stood only three hours' march from Erevan. The Armenian soldiers were heavily outnumbered but were assisted by hundreds of civilians. Carts drawn by oxen, water buffalo, and cows jammed the roads bringing food, provisions, ammunition, and volunteers from the vicinity of Erevan. Regiments of the Turkish 5th and 11th Caucasian and of the 12th Infantry divisions struck on May 21–22, but the defenders did not retreat. Savage fighting continued until May 24, when the Ottoman troops fled for the first time since the hostilities had begun near Erzinjan. Inspired, the Armenians drove northward from Bash Abaran toward Hamamlu and from Sardarabad toward Alexandropol.[30] On the evening of May 24, Silikian made an impassioned appeal to his people. He called upon the soldiers to rescue the honor of the maidens and exhorted the women to recall the heroic determination and sacrifices of their fifth-century sisters who, assisting General Vardan Mamikonian, had defended the religion and integrity of the nation. In terms apropos of the emotions of the moment, Silikian concluded:

> In the name of the physical existence of this eternally tortured people,
> In the name of violated justice,
> Arise! On to the Holy War! [31]

By May 28, the Armenians of Erevan guberniia were certain that Alexandropol would be retrieved. Some even had visions of advancing as far as Kars. On that day Silikian again addressed the populace and troops, praising them for their unsurpassed courage and urging them "on to Alexandropol!" [32] That goal was near realization when Silikian received a startling order from Corps Commander Nazarabekian. Hostilities were to cease, for news had just arrived that a truce had been concluded in Batum, and Khatisian, Kachaznuni, and Papadjanian were negotiating for peace.[33] It would have been difficult to find an Armenian who would not have welcomed the tidings a week earlier, but now the circumstances had changed and the voices of disapproval and anger echoed throughout the land. The military leaders and Erevan's Dictator Aram received scores of appeals to ignore the order and to continue the advance to Alexandropol. Many urged Silikian to declare himself commander in chief and to save the nation by force of arms, the only language the enemy understood. Now that the Turks were running, how was it possible to cease fire and permit the invaders to maintain possession of the native soil? General Silikian, however, refused to yield to such counsel and instructed his troops to halt.[34] Though widely and caustically chastised for agreeing to a truce, the Corps Command and the National Council had been compelled to take account of the fact that the stores of ammunition were either empty or nearly exhausted and that sizable Turkish reinforcements were not distant.³⁵ If peace were not concluded and the tide of victory turned in favor of the Ottomans, the consequences would be disastrous.

The 1st and 2nd divisions of the Armenian Corps complied with the order, but Andranik, who had formed a new Turkish Armenian brigade, refused to submit. He condemned the National Council and Dashnaktsutiun for the treachery. Vowing to leave the territory of the so-called republic, which would and could be nothing more than an Ottoman vassal state, he withdrew from the Karakilisa-Dilijan area and moved along Lake Sevan, over Novo Bayazit, into Nakhichevan. His three-thousand-man force was accompanied by several thousand Turkish Armenian refugees who felt that the greatest possible security was to be found by following the general. Andranik hoped to reach North Persia in time to assist the Christian Assyrians and Armenians, who were stubbornly resisting Halil Pasha's Ottoman Sixth Army near Khoi and Lake Urmia, and to unite with British forces operating in the region. When the revenge-thirsty mass reached Khoi, however, the Christian defenders had just been defeated; some had been massacred and the others had fled.³⁶ The routes south were blocked by regular Turkish divisions. Backtracking, Andranik then pushed over Nakhichevan into Zangezur, the southernmost *uezd* of the Elisavetpol guberniia. Remaining there for the duration of the World War, Andranik's forces crushed one Tatar village after another. Thousands of homeless Moslems escaped across the Araxes River into Persia or eastward to the steppe lands of the Baku guberniia.³⁷ Many Armenians approved of Andranik's policies and shared his hatred for the humiliating and crushing treaty that was signed in Batum on June 4, 1918. It was that document which extinguished the flicker of hope that the great Plateau from the Euphrates to Karabagh would once more be Armenian. Nevertheless, under the chaotic circumstances of mid-1918, peace—even a nefarious peace—was indispensable for survival.

Final Negotiations and the Treaties of Batum

As Armenian troops were advancing toward Hamamlu and Alexandropol, Khatisian's delegation hastened to Batum. The Turkish ultimatum to the Transcaucasian Federation was to expire at eight in the evening on May 29. Arriving on that day, Khatisian immediately sought an interview with Halil Bey, during which he pointed out that the ultimatum had been sent to a government no longer existent. Halil abruptly clarified the matter by stating the ultimatum was still in effect and now pertained separately to each of the Transcaucasian states. Because of the substantial changes which had taken place, however, he agreed to extend the deadline for another twenty-four hours.³⁸ The following day Khatisian informed Halil of the National Council's decision to declare itself the supreme Armenian governing body, of his delegation's authorization to conclude peace, and of acceptance of the Turkish conditions as the basis for further discussions. Several hours later the Batum Conference between the Ottoman Empire and the "Armenian Republic" convened.[39]

During the negotiations on territorial questions, the Turkish delegates drew the boundary between Transcaucasia and the Ottoman Empire without stipulating how much of the frontier was to be shared with each of the three Republics. Nor was any consideration given to the internal divisions of Transcaucasia. Apparently the Ottoman tactic was to gain as much land as possible without becoming involved in intra-Transcaucasian conflicts. It was suggested that the republics settle that problem among themselves. Thus Khatisian's attempts to secure Ottoman support for Armenian pretensions to the southern parts of the Tiflis guberniia and the mountainous portions of the Elisavetpol guberniia were stymied from the outset. The Ottomans, by the Treaty of Brest-Litovsk, had already retrieved the three *sanjaks* ceded to Russia in 1878. Now, by insisting on possession of Akhalkalak and Akhaltsikh of the Tiflis guberniia, the Empire would extend to its 1828 boundaries. But the expansion was not to cease even at that point, for, in annexing over half of the Erevan guberniia, the Ottoman domain would stretch farther east than it had for centuries past. Halil and Vehib, the "moderate" element of Ittihad ve Terakki, offered the Armenians the uezd of Novo Bayazit and parts of the Erevan, Etchmiadzin, and Alexandropol uezds. The Republic of Armenia was to encompass an area of approximately 4,000 square miles.[40]

Vehib's explanation of the Ottoman point of view demonstrated that the dedication of Ittihadist leaders to the ideal of Pan-Turan now burned more strongly than ever:

> You see that destiny draws Turkey from the West to the East. We left the Balkans, we are also leaving Africa, but we must extend toward the East. Our blood, our religion, our language is there. And this has an irresistible magnetism. Our brothers are in Baku, Daghestan, Turkestan, and Azerbaijan. We must have a road toward those areas. And you Armenians are standing in our way. By demanding Van, you block our road to Persia. By demanding Nakhichevan and Zangezur, you obstruct our descent into the Kur Valley and our access to Baku. Kars and Akhalkalak seal our routes to Kazakh and Gandzak [Ganja]. You must draw aside and give us room. Our basic dispute rests on these grounds. We need two broad avenues which will allow us to advance our armies and to defend ourselves. One of these routes is Kars-Akhalkalak-Borchalu-Kazakh, leading to Gandzak; the other passes over Sharur-Nakhichevan-Zangezur to the Kur Valley. You may remain between these two, that is, around Novo Bayazit and Etchmiadzin.[41]

Khatisian protested that the limited territories left to the Armenians could not supply even the most elemental necessities of life, that the Armenian question, being an international problem, should not be "solved" in this manner, and that the suggested boundaries would cause eternal enmity between the two peoples. Vehib replied that Turkey would happily invite all Moslems in the Republic to emigrate in order to give the Armenians more room. He conceded that the Armenian question had been international; it was just for that reason that the Ottoman government had decided to sanction the independence of the new state. There was no need to speak of eternal enmity, for all nations began their existence in a small area and then gradually expanded. Time would take care of that problem. What was now most imperative was laying the foundations for Turco-Armenian friendship and mutual defense.[42]

On June 2, after details of the Armenian victory in the Erevan province had been received in Batum, Vehib and Halil assented to a minor territorial rectification. In the Alexandropol uezd, a strip of land between Djadjur Station and Mount Aragads (Alagiaz) in the west and the Hamamlu-Erevan road in the east, about 400 square miles, was relinquished by Turkey "for the sake of the friendly relations that have begun." This, however, was the maximum concession. Then, congratulating the Armenian delegates on the victory of Silikian, Pirumian, and Dro, General Vehib suggested that a military pact, more than anything else, would dispel the mistrust between the two peoples. He proposed that a ten-thousand-man Armenian force unite with Ottoman troops for a drive into Persia. Alexandre Khatisian, claiming that the exhausted Armenian nation could fight no more, declined the Turkish invitation.[43]

At noon on June 4, 1918, Khatisian, Kachaznuni, and Papadjanian signed the first international act on behalf of the Armenian government. "The Treaty of Peace and Friendship between the Imperial Ottoman Government and the Republic of Armenia" consisted of fourteen articles and three annexes:

> Article I announced the establishment of peace and eternal friendship.
> Article II identified the new boundary between Transcaucasia and Turkey. It ran along the eastern limits of the Akhaltsikh and Akhalkalak uezds, into the heart of the Alexandropol uezd, atop Mount Aragads, then into the Etchmiadzin uezd as far as a road 4 miles west of the village of Etchmiadzin. From there the boundary continued along a line parallel to the Alexandropol-Julfa railway until it reached a village 4 miles south of Erevan, and finally moved southeastward, leaving much of Sharur-Daralagiaz and most of Nakhichevan to Turkey, and attained the village of Alidjin, located on the Araxes River along the former Russo-Persian border.
> Article III stipulated that the Ottoman government would be informed about any Armeno-Azerbaijani agreement on the mutual boundaries of the two republics.
> Article IV bound the Ottomans to give armed assistance at the request of the Armenian government for the maintenance of law and order.
> Article V committed the Armenian government to take active measures

to prohibit the formation of armed bands on its territory and to disperse all those which sought asylum there.

Article VI provided for the unhindered religious and cultural freedom of Moslems in Armenia. The name of the Ottoman sultan would be recited in the public prayers of the Moslems.

> Annex 3 of the treaty defined these freedoms in detail.

Article VII arranged for future consular and commercial conventions. Until such time, diplomacy and commerce would be conducted on the basis of the "most-favored nation" principle.

> Annex 1 defined the privileges and obligations of the two contracting parties.

Article VIII approved low tariffs and provided for use of one another's railways.

Article IX sanctioned immediate restoration of postal and telegraph communications between the two countries.

Article X dealt with inhabitants along the frontier and border traffic.

> Annex 2 included detailed regulations on the subject.

Article XI required the Armenian government to apply every possible means to evacuate all Armenian forces from Baku and to guarantee that no clashes would occur during that operation.

Article XII certified that all Brest-Litovsk treaty provisions not incompatible with the present agreement were to be honored by both signatories.

Article XIII stipulated that troops occupying territory beyond the frontiers determined in Article II would be withdrawn after the treaty had been signed.

Article XIV specified that the treaty would come into effect upon exchange of ratifications, which was to take place in Constantinople within one month.[44]

An additional treaty and a special agreement for the exchange of war prisoners were also concluded that day.[45] It was the Batum Additional Treaty that attested to Armenia's being a vanquished nation. The government of Armenia was compelled to demobilize all troops immediately, retaining only a limited force with specified zones of operation to be determined in consultation with the Ottoman Empire. These restrictions would remain in force until the establishment of world peace. All officers and civilian representatives of nations at war with the Central Powers were to be expelled from Armenia. Ottoman troops and matériel would be transported unhindered over Armenian territory. A special mixed commission would arrange for the use of roads and railways, and the Armenian government would be held responsible for any form of obstruction. Furthermore, the Ottoman Army reserved the right to utilize its own forces if the Armenians proved incapable of maintaining order and facilitating transportation. At the behest of Turkey, other Central Powers were to be granted any or all of the privileges outlined in the Additional Treaty, which, in contrast to the primary treaty, was to take immediate effect. The heel of the Ottoman Empire pressed heavily upon the 4,500 square miles of the Republic of Armenia.[46]

Soon after the Armenian delegates had left the conference room, the Ottoman representatives greeted Mahmed Hasan Hajinskii and Mehmed Emin Rasul-Zade. With nothing to dispute, the Azerbaijani delegates, in a cordial and festive atmosphere, affixed their signatures to a preformulated treaty. Halil and Vehib assured their racial and religious brothers that Ottoman assistance would be made available immediately.[47] Georgia was the last of the Transcaucasian republics to come to terms. After signing the Germano-Georgian accord in Poti, Noi Ramishvili had come to Batum to seek a favorable settlement with Turkey. In notes to the Ottoman delegation, he had insisted on the inviolability of the Brest-Litovsk boundaries, yet had tacitly recognized the loss of Akhalkalak and most of Akhaltsikh. That, however, was the maximum Georgian concession.[48] Late at night on June 4, Halil, in an extremely agitated mood, called upon Khatisian. He was angered by Ramishvili's obduracy and counseled the Armenian delegation chairman to reason with and exert pressure on his old associate. Halil warned that thousands of Armenians in Georgia, especially in Tiflis, would be endangered should Ottoman forces be compelled to attack to bring the Georgian government to terms. Nevertheless, Ramishvili, fortified by the assurance of German support, refused to sign the treaty until almost daybreak on June 5, when Halil Bey finally agreed to strike out Turkish demands for the Abastuman district in northern Akhaltsikh.[49]

As a grand finale to the round of peacemaking, Georgian, Armenian, Azerbaijani, and Turkish delegates gathered to sign an accord affecting all four states. It was determined that the rolling stock of the Transcaucasian Railway System would be divided in proportion to the length of track falling to each of the countries.[50] Armenia was again the loser. Turkey controlled the Transcaucasian rails from Sarikamish to Julfa and throughout the Batum *oblast;* Georgia possessed the tracks radiating from Tiflis toward Baku, Batum, and Karakilisa; Azerbaijan inherited most of the Baku-Tiflis and Baku-Petrovsk railways. The Republic of Armenia had approximately 30 miles of track between Djadjur and Karakilisa; even this was still occupied by the Turks. The only rails under the actual jurisdiction of the Republic ran from Erevan to Noragavit, a distance of 4 miles. The Armenian Railway Administration began its operations with two delapidated locomotives, twenty rickety freight cars, and one passenger coach.[51]

Assessment of the Losses

On June 6, Kachaznuni, Khatisian, and Papadjanian returned to Tiflis and presented the Treaty of Batum to the National Council. Assessment of the losses showed that Transcaucasia had been sheared of over 20 percent of its territory on which nearly 19 percent of its total population had lived in 1914.[52] Nearly three-quarters of the ceded territory had been wrenched from the Kars oblast and Erevan guberniia as shown by the following figures:

Region	Territory lost (in square miles)
Batum oblast[53]	
Batum okrug	1,400
Artvin okrug	1,300
Tiflis guberniia	
Akhalkalak uezd	1,150
Akhaltsikh uezd	1,100
Kars oblast[54]	
Kars okrug	2,250
Kaghisman okrug	1,700
Ardahan okrug	2,100
Olti okrug	1,150
Erevan guberniia	
Erevan uezd	700
Alexandropol uezd	750
Etchmiadzin uezd	900
Surmalu uezd	1,400
Sharur-Daralagiaz uezd	600
Nakhichevan uezd	1,500

The Treaty of Brest-Litovsk had awarded the Ottoman Empire nearly 10,000 square miles and six hundred thousand inhabitants of Transcaucasia. By the Batum treaties, Turkey gained an additional 8,000 square miles populated by six hundred and fifty thousand people, over two-thirds of whom were Armenian.[55] The national complexion of the affected uezds was as follows:[56]

Ceded uezd or part thereof	Georgian	Moslem	Armenian	Russian
Akhalkalak	8,000	8,000	64,000[57]	8,000
Akhaltsikh	25,000[58]	18,000	27,000	540
Surmalu	—	66,000	30,000	—
Alexandropol	420	3,000	173,000	2,000
Etchmiadzin	—	42,000	76,000	400
Erevan	—	48,000	30,000	1,000
Sharur-Daralagiaz Nakhichevan[59]	—	12,000	5,000	60

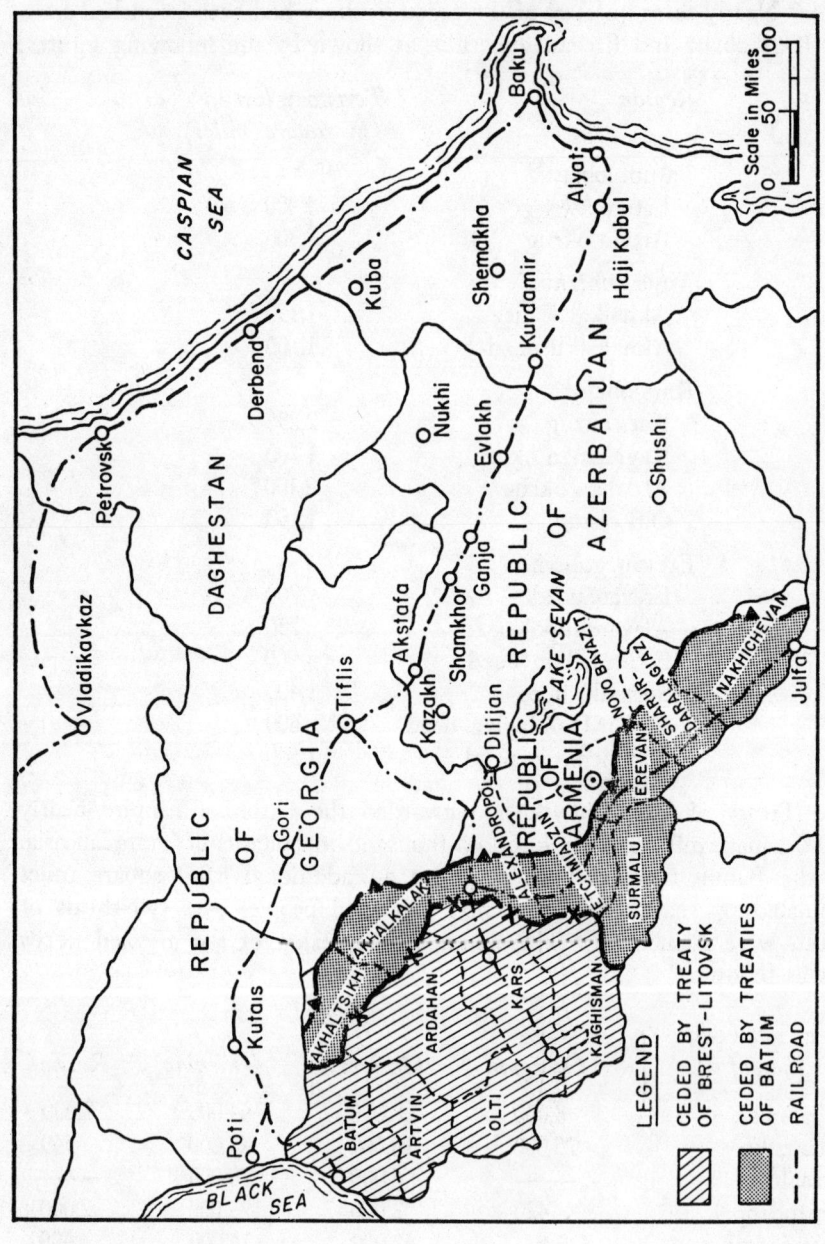

Map 10. Territorial losses of Transcaucasia

The population in the remaining districts of the Erevan guberniia, that is, in the Republic of Armenia, was composed of approximately three hundred thousand of the two million Russian Armenians and at least an equal number of refugees from Turkish Armenia and the regions surrendered at Brest-Litovsk and Batum. Even in this pitifully minute area, there were nearly a hundred thousand Moslems.[60]

Before Khatisian's delegation had departed from Batum, Vehib Pasha had given his promise that every effort would be made to exempt Armenians remaining in the ceded territories from military conscription. If unforeseen events should necessitate their services, these Armenians would not under any circumstances be removed from their native districts. Moreover, all refugees from areas between the Brest and Batum boundaries would be permitted to return home, but, pending a special arrangement, Armenians from the Kars and Batum oblasts must be denied that privilege.[61] Having received this information, the Armenian National Council named a special commission to meet in Alexandropol with Kiazım Karabekir to finalize details for repatriation, exchange of prisoners, Turkish withdrawal from the Karakilisa area, and Ottoman utilization of transportation routes over Armenia. Despite the commission's repeated requests, Karabekir would sanction neither the return of the refugees nor the withdrawal of Ottoman forces from the Pambak district of northern Armenia.[62] He and his commanding officer, General Essad Pasha, complained bitterly about violations of the Batum Treaty, as Armenian armed bands and many villagers in the ceded territories, refusing to submit peaceably to Ottoman rule, attacked Turkish officials and sabotaged the military efforts of the Central Powers.[63] The Alexandropol discussions led to no agreement, but by mid-July Ottoman troops in the southern areas of the Erevan guberniia finally attained the boundaries established by the Treaty of Batum. Turkish cannons were installed 4 miles from Etchmiadzin and 4 miles from Erevan, the capital of Armenia.[64]

Interpretations of Armenian Independence

Thus, the Republic was created under conditions so tragic as to defy adequate description. Yet, there was an Armenia. In mid-1918, even that was a remarkable accomplishment. The events surrounding the establishment of independence have been subject to divergent interpretations and acrid disputations. Dashnakist authors, in particular, insist that the heroic resistance at Sardarabad, Karakilisa, and Bash Abaran compelled the Ottomans to recognize the existence of a separate Armenia. Had it not been for these victories, the enemy would certainly have driven into Erevan, permitting Enver to annex every inch of the guberniia. However, these same authors often ignore the fact that independence, acquired willingly or unwillingly, was not the goal of most national leaders, who had consistently opposed sovereignty under the prevailing conditions. Yet, having taken the decisive step, these same leaders made the best of an unfavorable situation and, by the end of the World War in November, 1918, were to become the staunch champions of national independence. Opponents of Dashnaktsutiun, especially Soviet historians, have ridiculed and denounced as disastrous the policies of that nationalist party. They have equated the "independence" of the "Dashnakist Republic" with enslavement of the Armenian people under the yoke of "Turkish imperialism." Yet during the last decade Soviet historiography of the period has undergone basic changes. While still vilifying the Dashnakist leaders, the new generation of Soviet writers praises the defensive efforts of the "Armenian people" and contends that, indeed, it was this resistance that compelled the Ottomans to recognize Armenian independence. They stress that, to subdue Armenia completely, at least several more weeks and many more Turkish troops would have been required. The Ittihadist regime had the immediate choice of crushing Armenia or hastening the conquest of Baku. The latter alternative promised far greater rewards. Thus, until emerging victorious at Baku, the Ottomans would tolerate a helpless and harmless Armenia. Already in control of the transportation routes north and south of Erevan, Enver's armies, after having extirpated the foe in Baku, could readily resume the project of annihilating the remaining Armenians and their pitiful "republic." Approaching the question from opposing points of view, there now exists a marked correlation between Dashnakist and Soviet interpretations. Furthermore, regardless of political sympathies, almost all serious students of this topic are agreed that the rulers of Turkey, in furthering either plan, had to deal with the deepening antagonism of their German ally.

Germany's Conflict with Turkey

Refusal of the Constantinople government to halt the advance in Transcaucasia drew sharp protests from Berlin. A pact concluded between the two nations in September, 1916, had bound each to enter into no separate agreement without the participation or the consent of the other.[65] The Batum Treaty obviously stood in glaring violation of this stipulation. Conversely, had the Turks known the details of the preliminary Germano-Georgian agreements signed in Poti, they could have confronted the Reich with the same complaint. The Batum and Poti treaties were incompatible. Ramishvili had placed Georgia, her resources, and her railways at the disposal of Germany, while simultaneously consenting to Ottoman utilization and control of those same transportation routes. He would let the two Central Powers prove which was the dominant partner.

On the day that the National Council of Georgia declared independence, the German State Secretary for Foreign Affairs, Richard von Kühlmann, instructed Ambassador Bernstorff to protest the violation of allied friendship.

Bernstorff was to inform the Ottoman government that, since the advance beyond the Brest-Litovsk boundaries had destroyed the Transcaucasian Federation, Germany now

1) permitted itself a free hand in Caucasian affairs, maintaining its opposition to policies pursued in Kars, Ardahan, Batum, and beyond, which were not in accord with the Treaty of Brest-Litovsk;
2) would tolerate no further Turkish advance into Transcaucasia, or any propaganda in areas beyond the Brest boundaries;
3) granted de facto recognition to Georgia and would sanction its independence if the assent of Russia were secured;
4) urged the Ottoman rulers to deal mildly and benevolently with the Armenians in the occupied territories;
5) announced that, in accordance with existing mutual agreements, any diplomatic or military actions undertaken without German approval would be repudiated and the responsibility for these placed squarely upon the Turkish authorities; and, in particular, the Kaiser's government could not fabricate excuses for Turkish excesses against the Christian population of the Caucasus.[66]

At the same time, von Kühlmann informed the Austrian Foreign Minister that the Turks had lost their equilibrium and were obsessed with the vision of raising the Ottoman flag above Elisavetpol and Baku. The effect such strategy would have on the Palestinian and Mesopotamian theaters was obvious. He urged that Germany's decisions be relayed to Graf Johann Pallavicini, the Austrian ambassador at Constantinople, to thwart Turkish maneuvers to play one ally against the other.[67]

The German High Command was in complete accord with the Foreign Ministry. On June 8, General Ludendorff warned Enver that Turkey's treaties with the Transcaucasian states were neither condoned nor recognized. Pointing out that he had often upheld Enver's point of view, Ludendorff stressed that a guarantee of continued German support necessitated respect for the Brest-Litovsk boundaries. The following day Field Marshall von Hindenburg commanded Enver to withdraw all Turkish troops from the Caucasus, for the policy of the Central Powers was not to gain enemies in that region. In what had become a repetitive and futile message, von Hindenburg insisted that Ottoman forces be diverted to the south. Enver Pasha, in Batum to supervise the reorganization of his Caucasian divisions, scoffed at his German colleagues. Sharply, he called attention to the fact that Ludendorff himself had at one time sanctioned Turkish acquisitions beyond the Brest boundaries. Furthermore, it was not his fault that General von Lossow had chosen to leave the Batum Conference before negotiations had been concluded! In his June 10 reply to von Hindenburg, Enver emphasized that his decision to assist the Moslems of Transcaucasia was unalterable. Leaving no doubt about the intensity of his convictions, Enver pressured the supreme military commander of the Central Powers by threatening to resign as vice-generalissimo.[68]

Meanwhile, along the Transcaucasian railways, German and Turkish troops were drawing closer to armed conflict. On June 1, even before the Batum treaties had been signed, Count von Schulenburg sent Halil a denunciation of the Turkish ultimatum aimed at controlling Georgia's transportation system. That privilege was reserved for Germany. His message was reinforced by the arrival of two German battalions at Poti. On June 5, General von Kress instructed the Georgian Minister of Military Affairs to deny the Turks any information concerning the operation of the railways.[69] Two days later, Ramishvili's cabinet received a cablegram from von Lossow in Berlin, outlining directives of the German High Command. In the event of a confrontation with Turkish forces, the Georgian and German troops were to behave in a friendly manner, but at the same time were to announce that they were under orders to stand firm. Under no condition were they to relinquish their positions.[70] In the opposite camp, on June 2, General Vehib had commanded Shevki Pasha to occupy the Georgian railway and to request any German soldiers his men might encounter to withdraw. If the Germans refused to yield or offered any resistance, they were to be taken prisoner and sent to Kars.[71] A clash was thus made inevitable by these two conflicting sets of orders. On June 10, units of the Turkish 9th Caucasian Division advanced along the rails from Karakilisa into the Tiflis guberniia and fired on two companies of German station guards. Several of the guards were wounded and a number taken prisoner and sent under escort toward Alexandropol. This "scandalous incident" threatened to disrupt the alliance. Infuriated, the German High Command demanded the release of the soldiers and the cessation of the Ottoman advance. If compliance were not instantaneous, the hundreds of Germans in the service of the Turkish government and army would be recalled.[72] Turkey could not endure such a crippling blow. Enver Pasha, still in Batum, was obliged to return the German prisoners. Apparently to appease Berlin, he also removed Mehmed Vehib Pasha from command of the Third Army. Having kept the Turks out of Tiflis, Germany softened its other stipulation, and compensated Enver by permitting Turkish forces an overland avenue to Ganja. On June 17, von Kress and Ottoman officials concluded a provisional agreement defining respective transit rights in Transcaucasia and delineating German and Turkish zones of influence in the area between the Erevan and Tiflis guberniias.[73]

Compelled to compromise on several issues because of German intervention, Enver was not at all deterred from pursuing with even greater determination his basic stratagem for the East. By the end of June, new divisions from the European theater had arrived in the Caucasus, where three Ottoman armies awaited the instructions of Enver Pasha. The Third Army, now led by Essad Pasha, a cousin of Vehib, and composed of the 3rd, 5th,

36th, and 37th Caucasian divisions, was charged with maintaining order in all territories acquired by the treaties of Brest-Litovsk and Batum. The newly organized Ninth Army, made up of the 9th, 10th, and 11th Caucasian divisions and the 5th, 12th, and 15th Infantry divisions, was bestowed upon Yakub Shevki Pasha, whose temporary headquarters were in Alexandropol. Together, the Ninth Army and the Sixth Army (the latter located in North Persia) constituted the Army Group of the East, under the supreme command of Enver's uncle, General Halil Pasha. The task of liberating Baku and expelling the British from Persia and Baghdad rested upon this Group.[74] Already, Mürsel Pasha's 5th Caucasian Division was in transit to Ganja, where it was to form the nucleus of Nuri's "Army of Islam" and bolster General Ali Agha Shikhlinskii's Azerbaijani forces. The Germans, having reached a preliminary understanding with their ally, withdrew their units to a line of villages north of the Kamenka River, thus allowing Mürsel's men to pass from Alexandropol and Karakilisa into the Elisavetpol guberniia. Von Kress now counseled the Georgian government to let the Turks trespass in the southernmost *uchastok* of the Tiflis guberniia.[75] The district in question was Lori, the apple of discord between the republics of Georgia and Armenia.

The Deterioration of Armeno-Georgian Relations

Immediately after the dissolution of the Transcaucasian Federation, responsible members of the Georgian and Armenian national councils had conferred about the future status of Lori and neighboring Akhalkalak. During this meeting, Russian and Armenian sources claim, Ramishvili and Zhordania reiterated the stand that, on ethnographic grounds, both the Lori uchastok and the Akhalkalak uezd belonged rightfully to Armenia. They added, however, that application of the ethnic principle was impossible at that moment, since Turkish troops held Akhalkalak and, to block the Ottoman advance toward Tiflis, German and Georgian forces were left no alternative but to occupy Lori. With the establishment of world peace, the Menshevik party would once again rise as the champion of national self-determination.[76] On June 5, following this interview, the Georgian Minister of Military Affairs issued orders for the army to take positions along the external boundaries of the Borchalu, Tiflis, and Signakh uezds—that is, along the frontiers of the Akhalkalak uezd and the guberniias of Erevan and Elisavetpol.[77]

After returning from the round of international diplomacy in Poti and Batum, Ramishvili, in his capacity as Minister of Internal Affairs, appointed a special commission to determine the territories included within the Republic of Georgia. The group invited representatives of the Armenian National Council to participate in its June 11 session. Commission member P. Ingorokov explained to Khatisian, Karjikian, and General G. Korganov that, because of economic and strategic exigencies, it was imperative that the entire Borchalu uezd as well as the region around Karakilisa in the Erevan guberniia be included within the Republic of Georgia. The abashed Armenians then heard Tsereteli support the view that Pambak, that region of the Alexandropol uezd which had not been ceded by the Batum Treaty, was rightfully Georgian on economic, strategic, and even historic grounds. The ethnographic principle alone was not always valid. Tsereteli attempted to convince the Dashnakist leaders that Georgian suzerainty over these regions would prove advantageous to the thousands of Armenian inhabitants, for they would be accorded German protection. Moreover, the creation of a strong Christian Georgia associated with Berlin would also be beneficial to the Armenian Republic. Deeply angered, Khatisian and Karjikian pointed to the numerous Menshevik declarations recognizing most of the Borchalu uezd as an Armenian district.[78] Terming the commission's findings a flagrant violation of self-determination, the Armenian National Council representatives urged the Georgians to reconsider. The commission assented, but before the two parties could again confer, Georgian papers carried an official announcement that the Republic's jurisdiction extended over the entire Tiflis guberniia.[79] Dropping pretensions to Pambak, the Mensheviks were now determined that Lori and Akhalkalak would be Georgian. Hostilities between the two sister republics were deferred, however, because the Ottoman occupation of Lori separated Georgia and Armenia. With no common boundary until the Turkish withdrawal in late autumn, the two infant states were compelled to continue the quarrel on only an "academic" level.

Considerations other than territorial also contributed to the deterioration of Armeno-Georgian relations. Feeling betrayed, the Armenians laid part of the responsibility for their plight at the feet of their Christian neighbors, whom they envied. The Georgians had secured German protection, had contained the Turks, and had inherited the accumulated wealth of Transcaucasia, whose governmental organs, factories, rail-repair shops, arsenals, presses, storehouses, and banking, commercial, and economic establishments were concentrated in Tiflis. The Menshevik-sponsored declaration of independence now allowed the Georgian minority of the Tiflis uezd to dispossess the Armenians of their wealth, predominance in administrative positions, and overall influence. On the other hand, the Georgians felt they had ample cause to distrust the Armenians, who, in great numbers, had infiltrated the lands of ancient Kartli and Kagheti during the preceding century. As the bourgeoisie of the Caucasus, they had wrenched many estates from the Georgian aristocracy, had taken over Tiflis, and had risen to monopolize the fields of commerce, finance, and industry. They were proud, often haughty people, who mocked the carefree and fun-loving Georgians. Now thousands of their refugees were flooding the country, polluting the land, and ruining the economy. The asylum Georgia had for centuries given the Christians from the south was being exploited. It was natural and expected that any government should provide first for its native people. Now that the Armenians had their own republic, they should be told to leave Georgia.

Disposed in this manner, both Armenians and Georgians could rightfully express indignation concerning the explosive problem of refugees from Akhalkalak. When Ottoman regiments moved into that district, approximately sixty thousand Armenians fled into the mountains of Bakuriani and Tsalka, hoping to find sanctuary in the Armenian villages that lay beyond in the Borchalu uezd. The routes of descent were blocked, however, by Georgian troops under orders to permit no more refugees into the Republic. For five months, the homeless mass subsisted under the most pitiful conditions in the woods of Bakuriani, where they were repeatedly attacked by roving bandit groups. By the time these people were permitted to return home, a third of them had perished from violence, epidemic, and famine. The charge of murder was hurled against the Georgians, who in turn accused the Armenians of intentionally attempting to spread contagion throughout the Republic. Georgian self-preservation necessitated sealing the frontiers.[80] Similar occurrences along the Georgian border with Azerbaijan in July further inflamed the already heated passions. Armenian peasants, pursued by Moslem bands, forded the Alazan River into the Tiflis guberniia but were immediately thrown back by Georgian guards. Only after many had been cut down were the survivors permitted to recross the river and seek asylum in Georgia.[81] It was fortunate for the Georgians that few of their people lived in Armenia and Azerbaijan. There would otherwise have been cause for anxiety.

Organization of Armenia's Cabinet and Its Transferral to Erevan

Despite the unhealthy social and political atmosphere in Tiflis, Armenian national leaders found it difficult to tear themselves away from the city that had long served as their unofficial capital. The inevitable transfer to Erevan was not anticipated with pleasure. After Khatisian's delegation had returned to Tiflis, the National Council embarked upon the task of forming a cabinet for the "Republic of Armenia," in whose name the Treaty of Batum had been signed. On June 9, Kachaznuni was selected as the premier-designate and was enjoined to organize a coalition government, for Dashnaktsutiun had no desire to bear the grave responsibilities alone.[82] Having nearly monopolized Armenian political life for a quarter of a century, the organization now felt the disadvantages of the "one nationality—one party" system that had evolved in Transcaucasia. Scarcely 10 percent of the Russian

Armenians adhered to all the other political societies combined. Dashnaktsutiun had not been founded or shaped as a legal institution. It had been revolutionary and antigovernmental, experienced in guerrilla warfare, sabotage, political assassination, and mass provocation, and now it was uneasy at the prospect of sovereignty. Furthermore, the involvement of a revolutionary society in the functions of government would inevitably implicate it in the faults and shortcomings of the administration. Menshevik and Social Revolutionary participation in the Russian Provisional Government was a striking example of this. With such concerns and because of the importance placed upon the creation of a united Armenian front during the critical summer months of 1918, Dashnaktsutiun advocated coalition.

Kachaznuni was unable to form a cabinet until the end of June. The Armenian Social Revolutionaries, rejecting the ideal of national independence, declined the offer to participate. Nonetheless, they assured Kachaznuni that they would assume the role of loyal opposition. The Armenian Mensheviks, still in a single organization with their Georgian colleagues, agreed to serve only if granted every ministry of their choice, a demand unacceptable to the other parties. But it was the Populists who caused the greatest concern. Dashnaktsutiun valued their collaboration more than that of the SR's and SD's, for the representatives of the Armenian bourgeoisie were held in awe. Their financial, economic, commercial, and administrative acumen was believed indispensable to the welfare of the Republic. Yet the Populists were not amenable to the prospect of serving on a cabinet headed by Dashnakists. They blamed Dashnaktsutiun for the tragic state of affairs. Much of the responsibility for the devastation in Turkish Armenia, the horrendous evacuation of Kars, and the rape of most of the Erevan guberniia had to be shouldered by the party in charge of Armenian life at the time. Dashnaktsutiun, now discredited, should voluntarily remove itself from the political scene to make room for new, untainted leaders, who would build the Republic. The Populists proposed that Mikayel Papadjanian replace Kachaznuni as Premier-President.[83] There was, of course, considerable logic to the Populist position, but the "one nationality—one party" system made the suggestion impractical. The Armenian masses, who looked upon SD's, SR's, and KD's[84] as foreign creations incapable of understanding the basic strivings of the nation, would have been left leaderless. It was also necessary to recognize that the SR and SD parties, though not joining the cabinet, would assume the role of loyal opposition in a government controlled by Dashnakists but would not tolerate the formation of a bourgeois-dominated ministry. Having failed to produce the desired coalition, Kachaznuni received authorization on June 30 to select members, not according to political affiliation, but on an individual basis. Immediately thereafter, he presented the slate of his abbreviated cabinet, in which all except the nonpartisan Minister of Military Affairs were Dashnakists:[85]

Hovhannes Kachaznuni	Premier
Alexandre Khatisian	Foreign Affairs
Aram Manukian	Interior
Khachatur Karjikian	Finance
Gen. Hovhannes Hakhverdian	Military Affairs

When this cabinet was confirmed by the National Council, Armenia had been independent for a full month.[86] During that time, the actual administration of the native territories had remained in the hands of Aram and Dro. Even after Kachaznuni had formed his cabinet, Aram was not relieved of his duties, for the Armenian government tarried in Tiflis. The severance of rail service to Erevan, the presence of Turkish troops on the main line from Lori to Ulukhanlu, and the frightful activities of brigands along every road and path contributed to the delay. The primary reason for it, however, was the reluctance of many National Council members to live in the fourth-rate city that had been designated as the Republic's capital. The spokesmen for Dashnaktsutiun consistently called for transfer of both government and Council, while Populists and SR's demurred, arguing that, because the overwhelming majority of Russian Armenians lived beyond the limits of the dwarfed Republic, it was imperative that the National Council remain in Tiflis to serve as a type of supergovernment. They did not oppose the basing of Kachaznuni's "government" at Erevan to act as a regional administration, but they warned that shifting the National Council from Tiflis would result in the abandonment of over a million Armenians. In addition, the move would impose hardships on the Populists and SR's, whose leaders and party apparatus were concentrated in Tiflis and whose following in Erevan was negligible. In a rather dazzling coup de théatre, the Armenian Mensheviks sided with Dashnaktsutiun. The Transcaucasian Social Democratic organization had espoused the strategy of supporting independent national states, and the few Armenian adherents of the party now followed that line.[87]

In mid-July, the impasse was at last broken. Aram sent word from Erevan that he would no longer remain at his post unless the nation's legal administrative bodies assumed their duties in the capital. Kachaznuni also applied pressure by threatening to resign if both government and Council were not relocated. The opposition dolefully assented. Having made the decision, the Social Revolutionaries sent Arsham Khondkarian, one of their forceful and well-known leaders, to Erevan, but the Populist chiefs, refusing to budge from Tiflis, delegated in their stead inexperienced although highly patriotic junior members. Haik Azatian, a doctrinaire Marxist, was named to direct the Social Democrats of Erevan but was soon replaced by more flexible and authoritative Menshevik leaders. Having completed departure arrangements, members of the Armenian government and National Council paid farewell visits to Zhordania, who had replaced Ramishvili as Premier, and to Menshevik headquarters. They also announced that Arshak Djamalian would serve as the diplomatic envoy of the Republic of Armenia to the Republic of Georgia.[88]

On July 17, the Armenian government left for Erevan via a circuitous route, traveling the Tiflis-Baku railway to Akstafa and then by automobile to Dilijan and along Lake Sevan. No official of the Georgian government was on hand to bid adieu. On the contrary, the Armenian cabinet, denied entrance to the waiting suite in the Tiflis railway station, stood on the platform for several hours until an antiquated locomotive and a few filth-covered passenger coaches arrived. This was apparently the latest manifestation of the growing discord between the two peoples. Lieutenants von Mommsen and Eisenmann, who were to represent von Kress in Erevan, and an accompanying Turkish officer angrily protested the insulting treatment, and only through their intercession were the Armenians spared the humiliation of being searched by Georgian guards when the train reached the frontier. As the locomotive moved across the Kur River into Azerbaijani territory, the frigidness of Georgia was superseded by the felicitous reception of Tatardom. Official delegations welcomed the cabinet of the sister republic, improvised bands struck up chords of joyful music, and the short trip to the border of the Erevan guberniia was interrupted by numerous banquets. Amidst this cordial and festive atmosphere, it was impossible to discern that Armenia's territorial disputes with Azerbaijan were much more extensive and complicated than those with Georgia. As the entourage approached Erevan, General Nazarabekian, Dro, and Aram "Pasha" rode out to greet Kachaznuni. Together, on July 19, they entered the capital.[89]

The land over which Kachaznuni's cabinet began to rule was virtually sealed from the outside world. Refugees hovered in every nook and cranny. There was little food or clothing and almost no medicine. The Republic's small fertile regions still lay under Turkish occupation; mountains and rocks were all that remained. The German representatives in the Caucasus urged their government to persuade the Turks to permit the return of the refugees as far as the Brest boundaries or at least up to those demarcated in the Treaty of Batum. If the Ittihadist rulers rejected this suggestion, they must then allow Armenian men to return to their native districts for a short time to harvest the crops. Von Schulenburg and von Kress warned that, should they be denied this minimal favor, the Armenians would be annihilated by the end of winter. The two officials complained that this extermination was fervently desired by Essad Pasha, who was intent on completing the project undertaken by General Vehib.[90] Berlin failed to alter the policies of the Ottoman commanders. The crops, so vital to the Armenians, were carried away by the Turks or allowed to rot in the fields. The Republic's inhabitants subsisted on grasses and herbs throughout the summer and autumn, but by winter even these were gone. It was said that the Turks had allowed the Armenians enough room for a mass cemetery.

The appraisal did not appear exaggerated during the first months of the Republic, when more than two hundred thousand orphans and refugees perished. Cholera and typhus stalked the land, reaping victims indiscriminately. Even the seemingly invincible Aram was to succumb.[91]

Armenia's Legislature—the Khorhurd

Amidst this "formless chaos," Kachaznuni strove to build the nation's governmental apparatus. While the numerous administrative organs in Tiflis became Georgian property, there was little to inherit in Erevan. Because elections were then out of the question, the four political parties agreed that creation of a legislature could be effected most smoothly by simply tripling the National Council membership of each. Dashnaktsutiun, most willing to share the burden of government, did not object to the disproportionate number of places accorded to the opposition groups.[92] Thus, when Armenia's legislative body, the Khorhurd, convened, there were eighteen Dashnakists, six SR's, SD's, and Populists respectively, and two nonpartisans. In addition, six Moslems, a Yezidi, and a Russian represented the Republic's minorities.[93] Generals Nazarabekian and Silikian, members of the Moslem and Russian national councils of Erevan, and envoys of the Ottoman, Persian, Ukrainian, and German governments were present for the opening ceremonies. Also attending was the chief of the Austro-Hungarian mission to Transcaucasia, Baron von Frankenstein, who had arrived in Erevan with von Kress on the preceding day to pay an official visit to the Catholicos and the Armenian government. On his return to Tiflis, von Frankenstein reported to Vienna that he had been favorably impressed by the inaugural meeting of the legislature and especially by the fact that, in sharp contrast to the situation in Georgia, all minorities were represented.[94]

Gathering in the theater of the City Hall, members of the Khorhurd were called to order just before noon on August 1 by Avetik Sahakian, acting chairman of the National Council. He reviewed the tragic events that had culminated in the creation of the Republic and expressed faith in a brighter future. Armenian delegations already in Berlin and Constantinople were laboring to gain terms more favorable than those dictated by the Batum Treaty. The ideal of independence and statehood was taking root in the mind of the nation; soon it would be cherished. Stressing that every existing treaty obligation would be honored and every effort made to secure friendship with all neighboring countries, Sahakian added:

> Yes, our Republic is small and its bounds are narrow. It is deprived of its best lands, and there is not enough room for all the people. It seems as if conditions are lacking for its independent existence. But I feel that the boundaries of a state cannot remain inflexible forever. I believe that our

borders will spread with the iron force of life, with defense of our just and indisputable rights concerning the occupied lands, and with a new treaty of friendship with Turkey and its allied governments, whose representatives are here present. We have chosen the path of mutual agreement and peace, and we would like to believe that we are not mistaken in this.[95]

Following these remarks, the band played the national anthem as the red, blue, and orange tricolor was raised atop the Khorhurd. Then, turning to its agenda, the legislature elected Sahakian (Dashnakist) President, Grigor Ter Khachatrian (Populist) and Davit Zubian (SR) Vice-Presidents, and Petros Zakarian (nonpartisan, SD sympathizer) Senior Secretary.[96]

Two days later Kachaznuni presented his cabinet's platform. He explained that utter disorganization prevailed throughout the land and that even the basic apparatus essential for rule was lacking. Four years of war, the Bolshevik Revolution, Russian abandonment of the front, the unsuccessful attempt to withstand the Turks, and enemy occupation of most of Armenia had disrupted and destroyed the nation's economy. Thousands upon thousands of homeless, sick, and hungry refugees depended on the pitiful resources of the government. Only one word could describe the situation—catastrophe. Therefore, all the idealistic phrases so common to inaugural addresses would be omitted and the government's program would deal only with the bare realities. The immediate objective was to check the process of dissolution and to deliver the nation from anarchy. With this in mind, the cabinet would strive to achieve the following aims:

1) in Internal Affairs
    a) to safeguard the life and property of all residents,
    b) to restore the routes of communication and the postal-telegraph system,
    c) to mitigate the plight of the refugees;
2) in Financial Affairs
    a) to prepare for the adoption of a national monetary system,
    b) to revive trade and industry;
3) in Judicial Affairs
    a) to adjust judicial procedures to local customs and conditions,
    b) to include civilian jurists in the trial of accused criminals;
4) in Military Affairs
    a) to reorganize the nation's military forces,
    b) to build an army not large, but strong in spirit and discipline;
5) in Foreign Relations
    a) to honor all treaty obligations with the Ottoman Empire,
    b) to effect the withdrawal of Turkish troops from occupied portions of the Republic,
    c) to secure permission for refugees to return home,
    d) to determine in a friendly manner the boundaries with Georgia

and Azerbaijan, using as a guide the ethnic principle, the only one applicable in democratic states,

e) to conclude an agreement with Georgia and Azerbaijan for the liquidation and distribution of the properties and assets of the former Transcaucasian Federation.[97]

Fulfillment of these "realistic" goals in the prevailing conditions of 1918 would have been a miracle.

The reactions of the several fractions to Kachaznuni's program filled the agenda of the third and fourth sessions of the legislature.[98] Social Revolutionary Khondkarian complained that the statements included no specific proposals and no indication of how the program was to be implemented. He was especially perturbed that relations with Russia had not been mentioned. The Social Revolutionary fraction firmly championed the reestablishment of the Transcaucasian Democracy as a federative unit of the Russian Democratic Republic. Rising from the far left of the chamber, Social Democrat Azatian then declared that what Kachaznuni had proposed was reminiscent of Stolypin's tactic of "first peace, then reforms." The Armenian Marxists decried the fact that labor legislation, economics, enlightenment, and health had been ignored by the Premier. Arshavir Melikian, the lone Bolshevik of the SD fraction, used the occasion to extol world revolution and to belittle the ideal of national independence. The ideal should instead be reunion with Russia.[99] While the parties of the left objected to Kachaznuni's declarations, those of the right were content with his conservative and cautious strategy. There was nothing in the platform to indicate that for over a decade Dashnaktsutiun had been a socialist party. Populist and Moslem members of the Khorhurd joined with the Dashnakists to give Kachaznuni a vote of confidence. Even the SR's and SD's did not cast dissenting ballots. As long as Turkish armies stood in the heart of the Erevan guberniia, the fractions of the left tacitly collaborated with the Premier by abstaining rather than voting in opposition.[100]

Beacons of Hope

Although the dilemmas of the small, landlocked republic were to persist for many months, there was cause for guarded optimism by the end of summer, 1918. The tide of success in war had turned in favor of Britain, France, and the United States. The final victory of these nations would sweep the enemy out of the Caucasus and break the bonds that cut deeply into the flesh of the Republic. Locally, the Turkish intruders were moved periodically to grant minor favors. On August 16, for the first time in months, a train was permitted to pass from Erevan to Tiflis. On occasion, Mehmed Ali, the Ottoman representative in Erevan, would agree to sell Finance Minister Karjikian a carload or two of grain harvested from the

Turkish-controlled outskirts of Erevan and Etchmiadzin. In Tiflis, when Djamalian visited Abdul Kerim Pasha, the Ottoman envoy to Georgia, to offer felicitations on the Moslem holiday of Bairam, assurances were given the Armenian diplomat that everything possible was being done to permit the return of the refugees and to effect a Turkish withdrawal from the Pambak-Lori region.[101] The German government had been coaxing Enver to make these concessions for some time, but invariably the response had been, "We can't permit a half-million armed enemies to pass to the rear of our army." Enver chose to ignore the German argument that these "armed enemies" were destitute women, children, and aged.[102]

Abdul Kerim was not the only Ottoman officer to encourage the Armenians. Halil Pasha, Commander of the Army Group of the East, also promised to intercede. On August 30, accompanied by von Frankenstein, von Kress, and Djamalian, he paid his first official visit to Erevan. He announced to Kachaznuni that, in accordance with instructions received from Constantinople, refugees would be permitted to return up to a line 20 kilometers east of the Alexandropol-Julfa railway. Though the area concerned was small indeed, Halil hoped that, upon his appeal to General Essad Pasha, the officer in charge of these provinces, refugees from Akhalkalak would also be allowed home. Von Frankenstein interjected that there was some inconsistency in this remark. He had already dispatched an aide, Captain Pawlas, to discuss the question with Essad in Batum; however, the Third Army Commander had sent Pawlas away, explaining that the matter was entirely in the hands of Halil. Branding Essad a liar, Halil angrily shouted that he had always favored friendly relations with the Armenians and that, if he had failed in that endeavor, much of the blame rested with Essad, Vehib, Ali Ihsan, and Shevki pashas, who flooded Constantinople with unfavorable, provocative reports. Enver's sly uncle assured Kachaznuni that, on his return to Constantinople, he would strive to dispel the Armenophobe disposition that pervaded the political and military circles of the capital.[103]

Turning to other Transcaucasian affairs, Halil complained that Armenian belligerence in the Baku and Elisavetpol gubernias did not at all facilitate his efforts to build friendly relations. In Baku, Armenians had taken up arms against the advancing Turkish divisions, while in Zangezur and Karabagh they were slaughtering the Moslem populace. Kachaznuni attempted to prove that the Republic was not implicated in either problem. In compliance with the Treaty of Batum, his government had sent messengers toward Baku to arrange for the withdrawal of the Armenian forces, but the roads were blocked and the couriers were unable to reach the city. As for Andranik's activity in Zangezur, this, too, was out of the government's hands. The hero of the Turkish Armenians was persona non grata and would be disarmed if he entered the bounds of the Republic. Nuri Bey, whose Islamic Army headquarters were in Ganja, had refused to permit any regular Armenian units into Zangezur or Karabagh on the grounds that these were Azerbaijani territories. It was therefore unreasonable to hold the Armenian Republic responsible for events beyond its borders.[104] Halil Pasha would have been very naïve had he not doubted Kachaznuni's sincerity.

The question of Elisavetpol guberniia was broached again in a private interview between Aram, Kachaznuni, and Halil. The Premier pointed out that the population of Zangezur and Mountainous Karabagh was predominantly Armenian and that it was unjust for Azerbaijan to claim the area. Kachaznuni requested that Turkey refrain from supporting the Azerbaijani pretensions and that the final disposition of the territory be postponed until conclusion of the extraordinary conference between the Transcaucasian republics and all four Central Powers.[105] The meeting to which he referred was the Constantinople conference, which had been called to reconsider the treaties signed at Batum. Armenia, vested with the least enviable position of the three Transcaucasian states, hoped that, with German support, the Republic would be permitted to expand. At present it encompassed only those lands not seriously disputed by its neighbors. The Republic's leaders were fully aware that expansion was much more dependent on events evolving in Berlin, Vienna, and Constantinople than in Tiflis, Ganja, and Erevan. The most competent diplomats of Armenia were at work not in Transcaucasia, but in Europe.

XI

The Suppliants
(*June–October, 1918*)

UNTIL THE CONCLUSION of World War I in November, 1918, the feeble Republic of Armenia sought the benevolence of the Central Powers and Russia. Toiling for five months under difficult, often humiliating conditions, Armenian envoys, with statistics, logic, and petitions as their only weapons, tried to allay the suffering of their people and to guarantee the continued existence of the Republic, born after such a prolonged and agonizing labor. Before the representatives of Soviet Russia, these envoys argued that the Sovnarkom, unable to provide material assistance, should at least give Armenia moral support by condoning the creation of the Republic. Russian recognition would deter the Islamic plot to obliterate the Armenian nation. If Transcaucasia were transformed into a Moslem bastion, her natural bonds with Russia would be severed and future associations, possibly even federation, would be inconceivable. At the same time, in Berlin and in Vienna, the suppliants stood before the doors of German and Austrian officials to implore intercession. Seeking the same protection Georgia had secured at Poti, they strove to entice the two European states by pointing to the potential resources of Armenia. They asserted that, unless the Turks were forced to retreat, the Armenian economy would be totally destroyed, thus depriving the Central Powers of a valuable source of raw materials. The situation would be considerably alleviated by the presence in Erevan of one or two German or Austrian battalions. The humble petitioners also applied directly to the Ottoman government to permit the repatriation of several hundred thousand refugees, to foster good neighborly relations by acceding to the boundary established at Brest-Litovsk, and to support Armenia in its territorial disputes with the other states of Transcaucasia. Furthermore, were the Sublime Porte to succeed in convincing Germany to recognize the Armenian Republic, as Turkey had done at Batum, Soviet Russia would be more likely to grant recognition. Meanwhile, other envoys established political relations with the White

Armies of South Russia and with the Central Rada at Kiev. From these liaisons it was hoped that weapons and, in particular, grain would be procured for the exhausted Armenian nation. The suppliants, separated by distance and poor communication, worked with a singleness of purpose. The arguments employed varied from capital to capital and from week to week. The logic of one memorandum contradicted that of another, but every move was aimed at strengthening the foundations of the Republic of Armenia.

Armenian Diplomats in Germany

Berlin was the epicenter of Armenian activities. Already in April, 1918, National Council delegates Arshak Djamalian, Gevorg Melik Karageozian, and Liparit Nazariants had presented the German State Secretary for Foreign Affairs with an appeal for assistance. They had been received sympathetically and cordially. While still in Berlin, the trio had written their compatriots in Western Europe to cease the rampant anti-German agitation that pervaded every Armenian paper and periodical published on the Continent and in the Western Hemisphere.[1] Similar admonitions were reiterated by Ohandjanian and Zohrabian soon after they arrived on June 3 with General von Lossow and the Georgian entourage. Having lived in Germany and being well acquainted with German governmental machinery, Hamo Ohandjanian and Arshak Zohrabian were qualified envoys of the Armenian Republic. That their reception was genial is evidenced by their having been granted an interview with Foreign Ministry officials only two days after reaching Berlin. They were allowed unlimited use of the German postal-telegraph facilities and of the diplomatic pouch to Constantinople and Tiflis. At a time when the regular channels of communication were thoroughly unreliable or even nonexistent, the favor was no small consideration. They also obtained a German promise to coerce Turkey into honoring the Treaty of Brest-Litovsk.[2] On June 9, von Kühlmann told Armenian and Georgian delegates in Berlin that steps were being taken to call a general conference to reconsider the Batum treaties. The State Secretary for Foreign Affairs made no attempt to conceal his irritation with the Ottoman rulers.[3] In a sequel to this message, Count von Schulenburg in Tiflis notified the Armenian National Council that review of the Treaty of Batum would take place in Constantinople at the end of June and that Armenian delegates should leave immediately.[4] On June 14, with heightened hopes that German intervention would lead to the recovery of lands ceded by the treaty, the supreme Armenian administrative body dispatched Avetis Aharonian, Mikayel Papadjanian, and Alexandre Khatisian to the shores of the Bosporus.[5]

Throughout the summer of 1918, Ohandjanian and Zohrabian, assisted by James Greenfield, subsequently the Armenian consul-general in Berlin, drew attention to the plight of the half-million Armenian refugees in the Caucasus and warned that, were they not allowed to repatriate before the onset of winter, few would be alive in the spring of 1919. Though mentioning Kars, Ardahan, or Batum would have been highly imprudent, the Armenian delegates could safely petition for the withdrawal of Turkish troops from the Erevan and Tiflis *guberniia*s and for German approbation of Armenia's claims to the entire province of Erevan and the southwestern and southern sectors of the Elisavetpol and Tiflis guberniias respectively. Only with the inclusion of these regions would there be a viable Armenia. The scheme of provincial repartition of Transcaucasia which had been proposed at the conferences sponsored by Vorontsov-Dashkov and Grand Duke Nicholas was now laid before the German Foreign Ministry.[6] However, the guarded optimism of the delegates at Berlin declined steadily during July and August. Reports of famine, epidemic, and violence in Armenia were thoroughly demoralizing, and the promised Constantinople conference did not materialize, for the Central Powers were so much at odds that they could agree neither on the time nor on the agenda of the proposed meeting. In the Reichstag, von Kühlmann and others publicly censured the Turks for their violent acts and demanded respect for the Brest-Litovsk settlement. Ottoman leaders, on the other hand, satirized the German officials and, tenaciously clinging to the treaties of Batum, continued the drive toward Baku.[7]

Berlin was especially sensitive to the Baku problem, for negotiations with the Sovnarkom concerning the fate of the region were far advanced. Germany, having lost the military initiative on the western front, was sorely in need of the resources, particularly the oil, of the Caucasus. Soviet Russia was also hard pressed, as the anti-Bolshevik tide had engulfed most of the border provinces and was even threatening the heartlands. Thus, a Russo-German rapprochement was pursued by Count von Mirbach in Moscow and by Soviet representative Adolf Ioffe in Berlin. During talks for a supplementary treaty to Brest-Litovsk, Germany acknowledged Russian suzerainty over Baku on condition that some of the oil output be placed at Berlin's disposal and that the Sovnarkom assent to Germany's special position in Georgia. Stepan Shahumian, Chairman of Baku's Council of People's Commissars, was informed of these proceedings by Stalin, who stressed that, though certain concessions to Germany concerning Georgia would be granted, the Berlin government would be required to maintain a hands-off policy toward Armenia and Azerbaijan.[8] Thus, while the German Foreign Ministry promised Ohandjanian to help Armenia by compelling the Turks to evacuate the Erevan and Tiflis guberniias, it also assured the Sovnarkom that it would neither recognize the Armenian Republic nor interfere in the affairs of southern and eastern Transcaucasia.

The secret Russo-German parleys were soon common knowledge. The alarmed Armenian representatives in Moscow and Berlin berated the irresponsible and illogical Russian strategy. In the Kremlin, Zavriev and

Nazariants argued that Soviet failure to recognize Armenia would prove disastrous to both governments, but their voices went unheeded, for the Sovnarkom was no longer tolerant of non-Bolshevik Armenian organizations and representatives in Russia. The antagonism increased after the Russian Left Social Revolutionary collaborators broke with the Bolsheviks and, accusing the Sovnarkom of betraying the Revolution, assassinated Count Wilhelm von Mirbach, the representative of "German imperialism." Together with hundreds of other non-Communists, many Armenian leaders were arrested and imprisoned in the Bolshevik reaction to this sabotage.[9] Fortunately for Lenin, who hurriedly apologized to Germany and sanctioned the payment of a large indemnity, the Kaiser's government chose to continue talks for a supplementary agreement despite the "Mirbach incident."[10]

In Berlin, Ohandjanian labored to convince Ioffe of the justice and validity of Armenian aspirations. The Soviet delegate, expressing complete sympathy for the Armenians, promised to relay Ohandjanian's messages to the Sovnarkom. On August 8, in one such communiqué, Ohandjanian beseeched and demanded Russian recognition of Armenia. "Peace without annexation" and "self-determination" were excellent principles in the abstract and should logically have assured the Armenian people of tranquility and cultural progress, but, as it happened, abuse of those mottoes had resulted in unparalleled tragedy. The Treaty of Brest-Litovsk, to which Russia was a party, had not only betrayed Turkish Armenia but had also abandoned Kars, Ardahan, and Batum in the "supposed name of self-determination." To make matters worse, Russia, by pledging to disperse Armenian military units in those areas, had undercut efforts for self-defense. Was this the application of the Sovnarkom's "Decree about Turkish Armenia"? Ohandjanian deplored the fact that there were no longer any Armenians in Turkish Armenia and that only a few districts of Russian Armenia had been left intact. To salvage this last segment of land, an Armenian government had been created, but Azerbaijan, bolstered by Turkey, and Georgia, supported by Germany, were casting greedy glances at even this pitiful state. Under such circumstances it would seem natural, continued Ohandjanian, for the Russian Republic to give Armenia a bit more stature by granting recognition. Yet the truth was that this step had not been taken; on the contrary, if the proposed pact with Germany were accepted by the Sovnarkom, Russia's only ally in the Caucasus would be crushed.

> Thus, let Russia now aid Armenia by acknowledging her existence. Let the Russian Republic protest formally the violation of Brest by Turkey; let it send representatives to the Constantinople conference to exact recognition of the Armenian Republic and to defend your and our mutual interests.[11]

In part, the Sovnarkom had already fulfilled Ohandjanian's request. On May 31, Chicherin instructed Ioffe to protest vociferously the Turkish breach of Brest-Litovsk and the illegal use of the Transcaucasian railways to transport troops toward Baku.¹² In reply, the German government reassured the Sovnarkom that effective measures to restrain the Turks were being taken. Both parties realized that Turkish occupation of Baku would void the understanding for which they were striving. In the Turkish camp, Enver Pasha, aware of the threat posed by the negotiations of Ioffe and Paul von Hintze, successor to von Kühlmann, spurred his armies eastward to confront both Russia and Germany with a fait accompli. At the end of June, Nuri Bey's Islamic units launched an offensive against Baku's Red Army, which had just driven westward 100 miles from the Apsheron Peninsula.

The Battle for Baku

Since the establishment of Soviet order on April 25, 1918, Baku had been almost isolated.¹³ Faced with a common menace, Dashnakists and Bolsheviks continued to collaborate. When the Baku Soviet castigated the Seim for having further divided the peoples of Transcaucasia by dissolving the Federation and establishing "independent" states, it took special care to differentiate between the Baku and Tiflis factions of Dashnaktsutiun.¹⁴ The prudence of the Soviet was, of course, conditioned by the fact that the Red Army of Baku was composed largely of adherents of the Armenian nationalist party. When the Ottoman 5th Caucasian Division passed over the Armenian Republic to Ganja, the threat to Baku increased. Prompted to an attack in defense of the city, Soviet troops at the beginning of June struck out in three columns. In three weeks they had advanced as far as Karamarian, Kurdamir, and Zubovka.¹⁵ Ganja, Azerbaijan's temporary capital, was spared only by a combined Turkish and Islamic Army counterattack. Both sides suffered hundreds of casualties in savage battles during the first week of July, but the Moslem units pressed on. The Russian and Armenian troops were greatly encouraged by the arrival from North Persia of Colonel Lazar Bicherakhov's Cossack troops, who offered assistance to the Baku Sovnarkom. Bicherakhov, named commander in chief of the Red Army, fought valiantly but could not withstand the Turkish infantry and artillery in the open field and ordered a withdrawal. By August 1, the Soviet forces stood along the Balajari-Aybat line, their original positions only a few miles from Baku.¹⁶

Alarmed by the approach of Turkish regiments, the Soviet searched desperately for support. Throughout July, Shahumian kept Lenin abreast of the critical situation, but the Communist leaders of Russia could offer little help. Nonetheless, they ordered Shahumian to combat the Baku Soviet's unpardonable disposition to appeal for British aid.¹⁷ Were Baku to fall, it would be better that the Ottomans, not the experienced English colonialists, become the temporary heirs to the invaluable city and its resources. Most of the Christian population, especially the terrified Armenians, did not share this view, however. They argued that, since no real assistance was forthcoming from Russia, they had no alternative but to accept the British offer to join in the defense.

A British expeditionary group, the Dunsterforce, had already been dispatched from Baghdad to organize the anti-Ottoman elements in North Persia and the Caucasus and to block the Turkish drive toward Baku. Surmounting many difficulties, Major General Lionel C. Dunsterville, commander of the group, reached Enzeli on the south shore of the Caspian Sea in the summer of 1918. Conferring there with representatives from the Baku Soviet and the Baku Armenian Council, he promised a sizable British contingent to bolster the defense of the Apsheron Peninsula.[18] On July 25, as the Turkish troops neared Baku, the Soviet took the decisive step, defeated Shahumian's motion to deny the British entry, and implored Dunsterville to hasten the arrival of his men. Social Revolutionaries, Mensheviks, and most Dashnakists joined to override the Baku Sovnarkom Chairman and Extraordinary Commissar for the Caucasus, who, smarting under the blow, declared that the Bolshevik ministers would relinquish their posts. Just after Shahumian had concluded his denunciation of the Soviet, however, his comrade Prokopii (Alesha) Japaridze announced that the Bolsheviks would remain in the body and continue to battle the counterrevolutionaries.[19]

The question of administrative jurisdiction was especially perplexing during the following week. The Bolsheviks had withdrawn from the Sovnarkom, yet they were still at their posts. On July 28, Shahumian presided at a Communist conference that vowed the reins of government would not be surrendered without a struggle and ordered a Bolshevik mobilization. Pleas for help were wired to the Russian Sovnarkom, but on July 29 Lenin responded, "We will take measures to send you forces, however, we cannot give a definite promise."[20] Aid did not arrive and the determination of Baku's Bolsheviks dissolved into dejection. On July 31, the Baku Sovnarkom resigned officially and on the following day was replaced by the Centro-Caspian Dictatorship, a coalition dominated by Social Revolutionaries.[21] The Soviet government of Baku had fallen.

With the collapse of the Baku Sovnarkom, Bolshevik military units left the front and, to add to the city's distress, Bicherakhov's Cossack troops abandoned their positions and rode into the North Caucasus. Taking advantage of the situation, Mürsel Pasha on August 5 struck toward the center of Baku, whose armed units were now predominantly Armenian. The struggle had once again turned into an Armeno-Moslem contest. The defenders held firm and, engaging in a flanking operation, compelled Mürsel to retreat. The disappointed and demoralized Turkish division was constrained to await reinforcements, already in transit from Alexandropol. The battle of August 5, 1918, cost the Armenians several hundred men, including Murat of Sivas, the partisan leader who had faced the Third Army from Erzinjan to Baku.[22]

On the eve of Mürsel's attack, the first British contingent, led by Colonel C. B. Stokes, disembarked at Baku. Excitement in the city was great, but disillusionment was greater. Instead of the several thousand troops anticipated, fewer than a hundred soldiers came ashore. By August 17, when General Dunsterville arrived with the last unit, the British garrison was raised to barely fifteen hundred combatants.[23] Indeed, Baku's non-Communist leaders had cause to question the wisdom of their decision to invite the Dunsterforce. That action had prompted the withdrawal of at least an equal number of Bolshevik troops and was to incur the continued wrath and condemnation of the Russian government. The situation was further aggravated by the lack of rapport between the British Commander and the Centro-Caspian Dictatorship. Dunsterville and other British officers have roundly chastised the Baku government, its military strategy, and the cowardice and ill discipline of its armed forces. Conversely, the British have been charged with selfishness, deception, and treachery. Even if the suspicious partners had worked in perfect harmony, it is highly improbable that their strength would have been sufficient to withstand the joint Azerbaijani-Ottoman assault that was being prepared.[24]

With the arrival of the British, Baku's Bolsheviks decided to quit the city. Seventeen ships loaded with men of the Red Army and enormous quantities of military equipment sailed for Astrakhan on August 14. Accusing the Bolsheviks of treason, primarily for depriving the Baku defenders of supplies, the Dictatorship ordered loyal vessels of the Caspian Fleet to block the Bolshevik exodus. Three days later all but one of the fleeing ships were back in port and the former Sovnarkom members imprisoned.[25] Events in Baku were watched closely by Moscow, Berlin, Vienna, and Constantinople, and by the Armenian suppliants in each of those cities. Entrance of the British onto the scene complicated the situation. It embarrassed the Armenian envoys and threatened to nullify the nearly completed German-Russian supplementary treaty. Furthermore, it gave credence to the warnings of Enver Pasha and weakened German determination to contain the Turks.

The Brest-Litovsk Supplementary Treaty and Talaat's Mission

Despite the negative state of affairs in Baku, Soviet delegate Ioffe, German State Secretary for Foreign Affairs von Hintze, and the Foreign Ministry Judicial Department chief Johannes Kriege signed the Brest-Litovsk Supplementary Treaty on August 27, 1918. Pertaining to the Caucasus, section VI provided that

1) Russia would not oppose German recognition of Georgia;
2) Germany would refuse to assist the military operations of a third power (Turkey) in areas beyond the borders of Georgia;

3) Germany would strive to prohibit a third power from entering the Baku *uezd*;
4) Russia would deliver to Germany either one-fourth of the petroleum tapped in Baku or a certain monthly minimum to be determined later.[26]

Georgia's international status was fortified, Armenia's further weakened, and the goal of Enver Pasha seriously jeopardized. The Ottoman Minister of War ordered the 5th, 15th, and 36th divisions to strike rapidly. Despite the official Berlin policy, influential Germans now supported Enver. When he and General von Seeckt notified the German Command that the presence of the British in Baku demanded stringent countermeasures, Ambassador Bernstorff concurred, and Ludendorff urged the Foreign Ministry to accept the Turkish logic.[27] In view of the altered circumstances, the German military leaders realized that the Ottomans could not be denied entrance to Baku. The Berlin strategists now recommended that German units also participate in the campaign in order to safeguard the enormous stores of oil and to be in a position to convince the Russians that the arrangement regarding the petroleum was still in effect. General von Kress was ordered to deploy toward Baku some of the five thousand German troops under his command.[28]

The German assent to the Turkish offensive did not quell the tumult aroused by the conclusion of the August 27 agreement, which created new obstacles to Ottoman domination of Transcaucasia. Russian possession of Baku and German control over Georgia would leave as possible compensation for Turkey only the remaining unfertile and unproductive Armenian territories. It was for just that reason that the Armenian suppliants feared the von Hintze–Ioffe pact and joined the Ottomans in opposition. The Republic of Armenia, the last remaining hope, seemed about to be cast to the Turks as a paltry appeasement.

In despair, during the first days of September, Ohandjanian rushed to Vienna to implore Austrian protection. A diplomatic mission and a few hundred troops, Ohandjanian asserted, were all that was necessary. As recompense, he offered the economic wealth of Armenia. It was not difficult for the skeptical Austrians to comprehend the wisdom of noninvolvement, especially after the suppliants had painted the most pathetic scenes of conditions in Armenia. It would have been naïve for the Dual Monarchy to presume that, in return for a battalion or two, raw materials would begin to pour into Vienna. Furthermore, the exceedingly sympathetic and polite officials did not conceal that they could venture no action that might aggravate relations with their German or Turkish allies. Instead of a categorical refusal, however, the Foreign Minister agreed that, if the Armenians could induce the Ottoman rulers to sanction the participation of Austria in Caucasian affairs, more serious consideration would then be given to assisting the Armenian Republic.[29] In Constantinople, other Armenian suppliants had already met with Austrian Ambassador Graf Pallavicini and military attaché Pomiankowski and had surpassed Ohandjanian in presenting exaggerated economic data in a futile effort to entice the monarchy. Austria was in no position to act affirmatively.[30]

Thus, by the beginning of September, Armenian efforts in Moscow, Berlin, and Vienna had been frustrated. In an ironic paradox, the Republic now turned to Talaat Pasha, who was traveling to Berlin in an attempt to abrogate the August 27 treaty. Just before entraining, the Ottoman Vizier promised the Armenian delegation in Constantinople that, while in Berlin, he would demand German recognition of their republic. Certainly, from the Ittihadist point of view, a feeble and dependent Armenian state was preferable to Russian reabsorption of the area. When Talaat, accompanied by Count Bernstorff, reached Berlin on September 7, he learned that Germany and Russia had ratified the Brest-Litovsk Supplementary Treaty on the preceding day. He was enraged but found himself in an awkward position, for he had come not only to undo the pact but also to seek additional German material assistance. British forces, having broken through in Palestine, were advancing northward and, in the Balkans, Bulgaria had already taken steps to extricate itself from the war. Nonetheless, Talaat pressed the Kaiser's government to acknowledge at least Turkey's special interest in the Moslem-populated areas of Russia and to guarantee a degree of Ottoman influence in Transcaucasia by according recognition to the Armenian and Azerbaijani states, whose creation had been sanctioned by Turkey.[31] Germany's attitude was glaringly inconsistent. While the militarists defended the Turkish advance on Baku, the Foreign Ministry circle persisted in its demand that the Ottomans honor the Treaty of Brest-Litovsk and withdraw to the eastern borders of Kars and Batum. The Armenians supported both Talaat and the Berlin Foreign Ministry, as they craved both German recognition and Ottoman evacuation. Arshak Zohrabian, however, chastised his colleagues for what he termed an incongruous policy. The August 27 Supplementary Treaty placed Armenia in the Russian sphere of influence and, therefore, both the Sovnarkom and the Reich would undoubtedly compel the Ottomans to quit the Erevan guberniia. With this prospect, Zohrabian continued, insistence on the perpetuation of an "independent republic" was playing directly into the hands of the Turks. Talaat was striving to win German recognition of Armenia not because of his fondness for the Armenians, but because it would permit Turkey to retain all territories acquired by the June 4 Batum Treaty and to relegate the remainder of Armenia into a subsidiary domain.[32] Zohrabian's views were not shared by Ohandjanian or the suppliants in Russia and Constantinople, who continued to press for both recognition and evacuation.

The outcome of Talaat's mission to Berlin was the drafting of a protocol signed on September 23 by the Grand Vizier and by Foreign Secretary von Hintze. The statement of accommodations noted the following:

1) The Ottoman Empire was prepared to recognize Azerbaijan, Georgia, and Armenia.
2) Germany was prepared to recognize Georgia but regretfully could not recognize Armenia or Azerbaijan.
3) In the event of Russo-Turkish conflict arising from Ottoman recognition of the two Transcaucasian states, Germany would try to settle the dispute.
4) Turkey agreed to withdraw all military units from Azerbaijan and Armenia, after which the Kaiser's government would strive to induce the Sovnarkom to waive its objection to Ottoman recognition of the two republics.
5) The Ottoman government declared its intention to establish separate states in the North Caucasus and Turkestan and to ally with them but understood that Germany could not help in this venture.
6) The Berlin government would influence the Transcaucasian states to place all economic resources, including oil, at the disposal of all four Central Powers.
7) Germany acknowledged Turkey's interest in the Crimea. Turkey pledged to prevail upon Azerbaijan to deal favorably with German colonists in that republic.
8) Ottoman troops would evacuate Persia as soon as operations against the British had been concluded.[33]

The final German-Turkish accord of the war years was considered a victory for the Armenians. The Ottomans were to withdraw as far as the Kars *oblast*, meaning that the Republic would retrieve the ceded half of the Erevan *guberniia*, and, though not acknowledging Armenia's status itself, Germany would pressure Russia to grant indirect recognition. But the elation of the Armenian envoys was stifled by news that, a week prior to the September 23 protocol, Turkish troops had swept into Baku and massacred thousands of Armenians.

The Fall of Baku

As Talaat and von Hintze were haggling in Berlin, Enver Pasha had ordered Halil Pasha, Eastern Army Group Commander, to take charge of the Baku operation. During the first days of September, approximately fifteen thousand Ottoman and Azerbaijani troops resumed the offensive, while the 15th Division pressed toward Derbend to cut communications between Baku and the North. By September 13, the defenders had fallen back into the suburbs of the city. General Dunsterville prepared to evacuate his small British contingent and urged the Centro-Caspian Dictatorship to

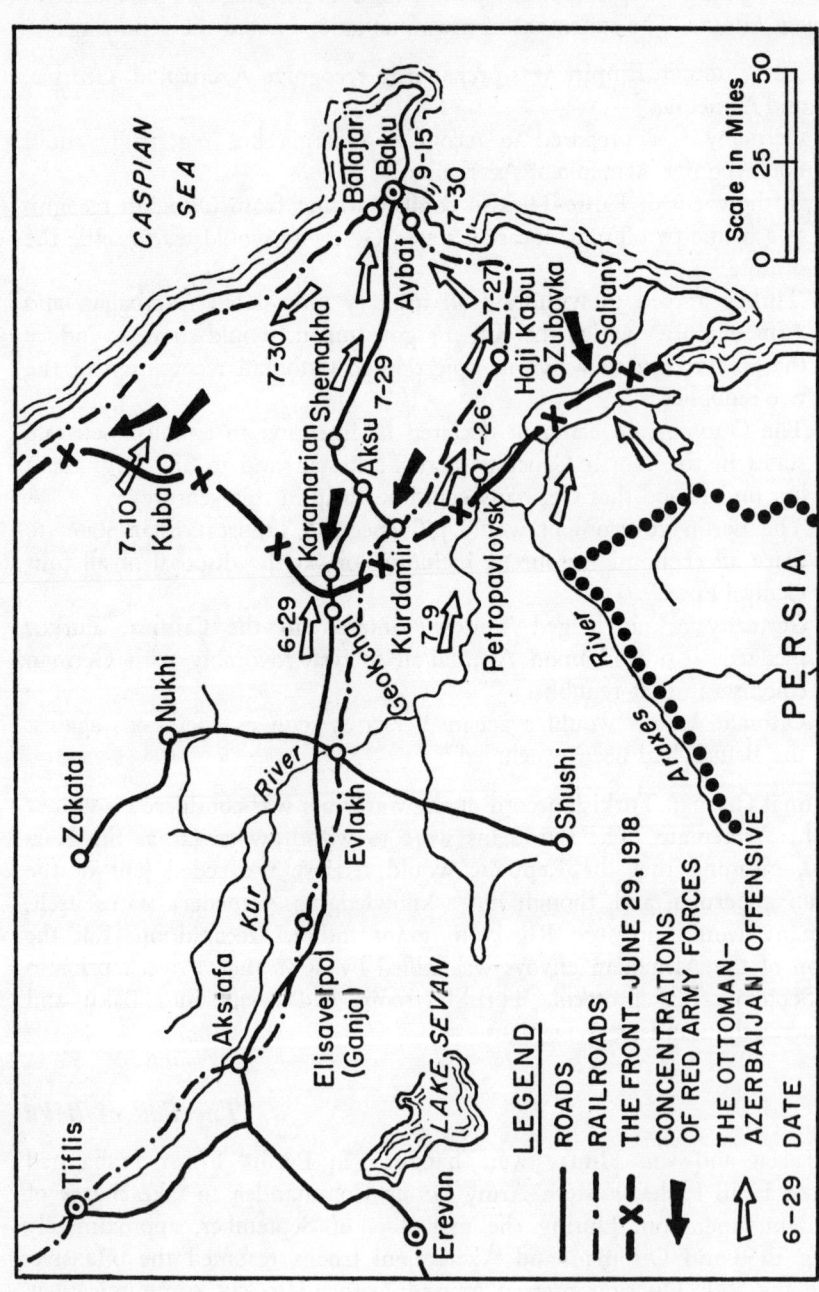

Map 11. The struggle for Baku, June–September, 1918

negotiate for the surrender of Baku. The Russian and Armenian leaders now threatened to sink every vessel of the Dunsterforce if the British attempted to desert. The situation was hopeless, however, and by the morning of September 14 few believed that Baku could hold. Restless Moslems in the city began to display greater courage and prepared for the moment of deliverance. Dunsterville, not willing to risk the loss of his entire group, rejected the Centro-Caspian appeal to hold a day or two longer so that the civilian population could be evacuated. Under cover of darkness that same evening, the British sailed unhindered toward Enzeli, whence they had appeared.[34] The panic in Baku needs no description. The Christian population rushed toward the harbor, where they crammed into every available vessel. Nearly half of Baku's seventy thousand Armenians succeeded in escaping the Turkic vengeance by sailing to Enzeli, Astrakhan, or Krasnovodsk. The remainder were abandoned. On the morning of September 15, the Armenian Council and the Centro-Caspian Dictatorship departed on one of the last ships, as the Christian quarters of Baku were already shrouded in smoke. Halil, Nuri, and Mürsel withheld the entry of regular Ottoman units into Baku so that the age-old Islamic custom of looting and pillaging defiant cities might be observed. Enver Pasha's subalterns had forbidden the participation of General von Kress's men in the attack and now ignored the entreaties for leniency from the German officers attached to the Turkish staff and from the Baku consuls of neutral nations.[35] The Moslem masses of Baku, thousands of irregular troops, and even several regular Ottoman regiments swarmed throughout the city plundering and killing. Property valued at a billion rubles was destroyed and thousands of Christians fell before the frenzied horde, which garnered sweet revenge for the humiliation and agony of the "March Days." Conservative estimates of Armenian dead are close to ten thousand, while many sources claim that from twenty to thirty thousand Christians were slaughtered.[36] On September 16, the Ottoman divisions marched into Baku in a victory parade reviewed by the Turkish Command and greeted by thousands of cheering Moslems. The despised Bolsheviks and Armenians had been expelled, and Fathali Khan Khoiskii's Azerbaijani government was now able to transfer triumphantly from Ganja to the great and natural capital of the world's first Moslem republic.[37]

The Sovnarkom-Ottoman Altercation and the Fall of the Ittihadist Government

Turkish conquest of Baku was obviously a flagrant breach of the Brest-Litovsk Supplementary Treaty. Foreign Affairs Commissar Chicherin accused the Germans of reneging on pledges to restrain the Turks and prohibit their entry to Baku. The Soviet note drew a swift retort from the German State Secretary for Foreign Affairs, who reproached Russia for violating the Supplementary Treaty clause proscribing slander.[38] The Berlin-Moscow entente of less than a month began to crumble. On September 20, Chicherin instructed Ioffe to protest in person and to deliver to Ottoman representatives in Berlin a message tantamount to abrogation of the Brest-Litovsk treaty. In that note, the Sovnarkom assailed the Turks for atrocities perpetrated while advancing through Kars, Ardahan, and Batum, and denounced the ludicrous plebiscite conducted in the three *sanjaks*, purportedly in compliance with a Brest-Litovsk stipulation.[39] In further violation of that treaty, the Ottoman Army had struck into the Caucasus. The Turkish claim that the aggressors at Baku were irregular bands was clearly contrary to fact. Because the Constantinople government had acted in bad faith and had schemed to deceive Russia, the Sovnarkom was compelled to regard the Treaty of Brest-Litovsk as never having existed.[40]

Though divulging the contents of this note, Ioffe deferred presenting it officially in order to allow the Turks time to make concessions. Striving to avoid an open confrontation with Russia, Talaat instructed the Ottoman ambassador to Berlin, Rifat Pasha, to negotiate with Ioffe. During the ensuing talks for a Caucasus arrangement, the Soviet diplomat demanded immediate withdrawal of Turkish officials and armed forces, both regular and irregular, from lands east of the Brest boundaries. Troops of the Russian Republic were to occupy the Caucasus, and the Sovnarkom was to be indemnified for damages resulting from the Ottoman march toward Baku. Prior to leaving the German capital, Talaat promised that, after conferring with the Ottoman cabinet, he would reply to the ultimatum through the person of Rifat Pasha. On October 3, Rifat informed Ioffe that the Ottoman government had agreed to honor the Brest-Litovsk boundary and withdraw its divisions from the Caucasus. However, because the Constantinople government did not state specifically that all irregulars would also be recalled, Ioffe chose to consider his ultimatum not accepted in toto and, on the same day, delivered Chicherin's September 20 denunciation of Turkey.[41] By the beginning of October it must have been obvious to the Soviet rulers that the Central Powers would soon fall, and it can be assumed that Ioffe's moves were made in anticipation of a formal annulment of Brest-Litovsk. The "Tilsit Peace" was about to be smashed.

The Soviet tactic elicited a sharp protest from Ottoman Foreign Minister Nessimi Bey. On October 6 he wired Moscow to express astonishment at the Sovnarkom's derogatory statements and to point out that Turkish action had been neither in bad faith nor illegal. The Transcaucasian government had itself repudiated the Brest boundaries, and, as for the plebiscite in the three sanjaks, Russia was not in a position to judge its validity. Furthermore, Turkish operations against Baku had been necessitated by the British tentacles which had enwrapped the area. Soviet Russia, having now gained the upper hand, refuted Nessimi's allegations on October 10. Chicherin contended that the provisions of Brest-Litovsk were flouted by Turkey from the day the treaty had been signed, that the so-called Tiflis government did not represent the masses of Transcaucasia, that even Moslems had deprecated the irregularities of the plebiscite, and that the Ottoman drive toward Baku had begun long before a single English soldier approached the Apsheron Peninsula. The Russian Foreign Commissar added that, despite Ottoman pledges to vacate the Caucasus, not a single district had been cleared nor had any such preparations been observed. Chicherin did not close the door to an accord, however, for he suggested that, were the Turkish troops to quit the illegally occupied lands, the Russian government might then consider ways of preserving the Treaty of Brest-Litovsk.[42] To be safe, Soviet Russia waited until November 13, two days after Germany had capitulated, before formally annulling the controversial treaty of March 3, 1918.[43]

Even before Chicherin's October 10 note, momentous changes had occurred in Constantinople. Returning from Berlin, Talaat told the Central Committee of the Ittihad party that Turkish interests were served by the September 23 protocol. He also notified the Armenian delegates that recognition of their republic was assured. Talaat must have been aware, however, that the days of his cabinet were numbered. Bulgaria had signed an armistice on September 29, and four days later Tsar Ferdinand abdicated. On October 1 Emir Feisal had entered Damascus with his Arab forces, and British troops pushed dangerously close to Anatolia. Constantinople itself seemed threatened by the prospect of an Allied march through the Balkans. The Central Alliance was disintegrating. The war government of the Ittihad Triumvirate was discredited, and on October 8 the Grand Vizier tendered his resignation.[44] Turkey took immediate steps to pull out of the war, as Ahmed Izzet Pasha, former Second Army Commander, succeeded Talaat on October 13 with a "peace cabinet." [45] Two days earlier, Admiral Arthur Calthorpe of the British Mediterranean Fleet set sail for the island of Lemnos to be in a position to negotiate. On October 20, General Charles Townshend, a prisoner in Turkey since the battle of Kut-el-Amara, was dispatched to Port Mudros by Izzet to act as an intermediary. Ten days later the Armistice of Mudros terminated Ottoman participation in the Great World War.[46]

The Armenian Mission to Constantinople

The Armenian representatives in Constantinople and Berlin followed the rapid course of events with near incredulity. The hopelessness of the summer months gave way to new horizons for a rewarding future. Cautiously, the suppliants first anticipated the restoration to their republic of the entire Erevan guberniia and then believed that Kars and Ardahan, too, might be retrieved. By October, 1918, it was even possible to think once again in terms of Turkish Armenia. Fortunately, the reports of the Constantinople delegation are extant as a record of the day-to-day activities of Aharonian's mission.[47] A review of the labors of the Armenian envoys during their four-month stay in the Ottoman capital indicates the great relief that must have overwhelmed them as they finally sailed for home on November 1, 1918.

Having left Tiflis on June 14, the Armenian delegation, together with a Georgian mission led by Gegechkori, arrived in Constantinople four days later. Soon they were joined by North Caucasus and Azerbaijani representatives who had also come to participate in the conference to revise the Batum treaties. Aharonian was in a quandary during the first days after arrival, because Article XV of the Batum Treaty had stipulated that ratifications were to be exchanged within a month. If the Armenians did not ratify by the July 4 deadline, the Turks could, by declaring the treaty void, use the opportunity to obliterate the infant republic. If, on the other hand, the treaty were confirmed, the Ottomans could assert that, since relations with Armenia had been determined, there was no need for a revised settlement.[48] The Armenians feared both alternatives but, as events developed, the treaty remained unratified. The prevailing impression in Constantinople was that the conference was to be a continuation of the proceedings in Batum and, as such, the clause pertaining to ratifications was not to be enforced.

With that understanding, the Armenian delegation waited week after week for the opening session. Various excuses were offered for the postponement. Enver and Talaat repeatedly blamed Berlin for the delay but on several occasions promised that the meeting would start in a day or two. Ambassador Bernstorff cited Turkish intransigence as the chief cause for the impasse, though he admitted that his government condoned deferring the sessions until a basic understanding had been reached among the four Central Powers. At the Austrian Embassy, military attaché Pomiankowski noted that the divergence between German and Turkish interests was so great that there was little likelihood a conference would take place.[49] His appraisal proved correct. As the delegates from Transcaucasia waited the entire summer for the opening of the never-to-be-convened Constantinople conference, each group worked feverishly to strengthen its own position. Khatisian reported his deep concern that the Armenians would be severely handicapped when the meetings began, for the Georgians were assured of German support and the Azerbaijanis could naturally depend on Turkish patronage, while Armenian attempts to gain the protection of Austria-Hungary had been unsuccessful. Even the Bulgarians were approached, but the diplomats from Sofia, while happy to receive memorandums from Khatisian and Aharonian, pointed out that they were themselves at odds with the Turks over possession of the Balkan province, Dobrudja, and could be of little assistance.[50] Thus the Armenian strategy was altered to deal directly with the source of affliction—the Ottoman Empire. The Ittihadist rulers controlled the means to mitigate the ordeals of the Republic. Therefore, the Armenian mission strove

1) to impress favorably the men in government and influential positions;
2) to effect Turkish withdrawal from Pambak-Lori;
3) to gain permission for refugees to return to areas ceded Turkey by the Batum Treaty;
4) to convince the Ittihadist leaders that, without a viable Armenia, there would be neither peace nor justice in Transcaucasia and that, therefore, certain lands disputed with Azerbaijan and Georgia should, with Ottoman support, be awarded to Armenia;
5) to win German recognition of the Republic through the intercession of the Sublime Porte.

Hakob Kocharian, delegation first secretary, has recorded the details of the humiliating interviews in pursuance of the first goal. In the presence of numerous Turkish officials, the suppliants proclaimed thanks to the Ottoman Empire for allowing the formation of the Armenian Republic. Khatisian and Aharonian felt the greatest revulsion to their acts of obeisance when performed before Enver and Talaat pashas. The hypocrisy began the day the delegation arrived in Constantinople. Met at the quay by Mukhtar Bey, former ambassador to Russia, Aharonian's entourage was taken to the Tokatlian Hotel as guests of the Ottoman government. There, Khatisian spoke of the new star of friendship which shone above the two neighboring lands. When the delegation called at the Sublime Porte, Talaat lamented the misfortune that had befallen the Armenians. He blamed the Kurds, the military, and irresponsible local administrators for the calamity, but the Ottoman Vizier also pointed an accusing finger at the Armenians: "Our enemies were the Russians, but when they fired on our soldiers, their bullets would strike at our feet. However, when the Armenians who were Turkish subjects began to fire and betrayed their homeland, then their bullets struck the hearts of our soldiers."[51] The petitioners hurriedly changed the topic of conversation from past to present and future relations.

The most candid official in this period of duplicity was Enver Pasha. He received the Armenian delegates coldly, gave them few hopes, and offered no sympathy. The man through whom concessions must be gained seemed the least amenable to granting them. Khatisian was impressed by the contrast between Talaat and Enver. While the first was slovenly, easily agitated, and rambling in speech, the latter was smart, shrewd, and precise. Unlike Talaat, he could not be provoked during heated discussions into disclosing a bit of secret information. During Enver's first interview with the Armenians, he rejected entreaties to permit the Republic to expand just a little. He stated clearly that his tactic was to solve the Armenian problem by condoning the establishment, on former Russian territory, of a small state which would not deter the interests of the "old or the new Turkey." All major routes east were to remain Turkish; the borders drawn in Article II of the Batum Treaty would not be altered.[52]

At the beginning of July, the delegation was granted an audience by Sultan Mehmed V and the heir apparent, Vahideddin. Abdul Hamid's successor expressed satisfaction that the Armenians now had a state of their own, and he earnestly anticipated lasting good relations. Crown Prince Vahideddin, destined to rise to the throne of Osman in a few days as Mehmed VI, left a favorable impression on Khatisian and Aharonian. He bewailed the suffering of the Armenian people and, according to a delegation report, later disclosed his dissatisfaction and impatience with the Ittihadist leaders whose contrivance had placed Turkey on the wrong path.[53] In September, during an audience to felicitate the enthronement of the Sultan, Aharonian expressed thanks for Vahideddin's good wishes and again promised that the Armenian government would not forget the Ottoman charity which had allowed the Republic to be created. With obvious satisfaction, Enver translated the laudation from French to Turkish. The Armenians acted well the role of suppliants.[54]

Interviews were also solicited with other ranking officials. Foreign Minister Nessimi, Marine Minister Rauf, and Ittihad Central Committee members Bahaeddin Shakir and Nazim Bey all enunciated the desire for friendship but pointed out that only Talaat and Enver could grant concessions. When news of the Baku massacres reached Constantinople, Shakir and Nazim claimed that the information was grossly exaggerated and that, if excesses had occurred, it was only because the Ottoman troops were too fatigued to restrain the Tatar bands. Furthermore, they complained that, while the Armenians might be subject to physical violence, the Turks were being annihilated morally. Widespread Armenian propaganda had aroused the fury of America and Europe. "The Murderous Turk" was the phrase circulating from one capital to another.[55] The same charge was repeated by Talaat and Enver. The latter stressed that in time of war the civilian population inevitably suffered. Other nations killed with cannons and rifles, while the Turks killed with scimitars and bayonets. There was no difference in the end result—it was death. Those who castigated Turkey were pharisees, for they chose to ignore the perpetrations of their own governments.[56]

The Turkish press was divided in its attitude toward the Armenian visitors. Several papers remained skeptical and critical while others, particularly *Tanin*, echoed the official government policy of favoring friendship and peace. Ahmed Emin, already a distinguished journalist, greeted the delegates enthusiastically and promised to dedicate his pen to the difficult task of championing Armeno-Turkish understanding and solidarity. In another interview, Ahmed Riza, the patriarch of the "Young Turks," recounted the long, united struggle of liberal Turks and Armenians against Abdul Hamid II. He abhorred the use of force and criticized the Enver-Talaat faction of Ittihad ve Terakki for destroying the great ideals on which that party had been founded. He warned that as long as the present clique determined Turkish politics the delegation's efforts would be in vain.[57]

Despite such advice, the Armenian mission pursued the goals for which it had been sent. One of these, Turkish withdrawal from Lori and Pambak, was complicated by Georgian pretensions to the former district. While requesting immediate clearance of Pambak, a part of the Erevan guberniia, the delegation vacillated in relation to Lori. Khatisian wrote Ohandjanian of his fear that the Georgians with German backing would occupy Lori as soon as the Turks evacuated the *uchastok*. He urged his colleague to convince the Berlin government that Lori, though in the Tiflis guberniia, constituted an integral part of Armenia. With that accomplished, the matter could be pressed more forcefully in Constantinople.[58] At the end of July, Khatisian reported that the Ottoman authorities had finally agreed to clear the two areas and permit Armenian troops to occupy them. He doubted Ottoman sincerity, however, for until mid-July the Turks had continued to advance near Erevan and had conscripted several thousand young men from Pambak for forced labor in the Erzerum *vilayet*.[59] Khatisian's misgivings notwithstanding, it was logical that were the Turks to leave Lori-Pambak they should uphold Armenian claims. Inclusion of the areas within Georgia would add rich copper mines and another strip of railway to the German protectorate, whereas annexation by a subservient Armenian state would best protect Turkish interests. The question remained academic, however, for Third Army regiments stood firm in Lori-Pambak. Even when, in October, they were compelled to retreat as a precursor to surrender, the Turks succeeded in prolonging the turbulence in the Caucasus by inflaming Armeno-Georgian relations. While Ottoman envoy Abdul Kerim informed Zhordania's government of the evacuation and gave permission for the Georgians to enter Lori, Mehmed Ali made the same announcement in Erevan and invited Armenian troops to occupy the abandoned districts. The result was an immediate and inevitable Armeno-Georgian confrontation.[60]

As vital as, and more urgent than, clearing Lori-Pambak was the repatriation of refugees. From Erevan and Tiflis came sporadic reports of famine and epidemic. Thousands died monthly, and before winter's end it was expected that all would be swept away by the "white massacre." The torment of the Akhalkalak fugitives was the most appalling. Khatisian appealed for their return, arguing that Vehib Pasha had given assurances in Batum that the Ottoman government would authorize this. Throughout June and July, Enver refused to consider the subject, pointing out that Moslems in the region were so agitated by Armenian atrocities that the safety of the refugees could not be guaranteed were they to descend from the Bakuriani heights. Furthermore, it was presumptive of the Armenians to make such a request when Moslems were being oppressed in Baku and when, in Zangezur, Andranik was pillaging, burning, and massacring![61] In August, Enver made a minor concession by stating that Armenians could soon return as far as 20 kilometers east of the Alexandropol-Julfa railway. Khatisian complained that few villages existed in that specific narrow mountainous strip, whereas thousands of the refugees were natives of the adjacent river valley through which the railway passed. It would be a great favor if the latter group were allowed to go home.[62] Permission was not granted, but in September, while Talaat was being pressured in Berlin by von Hintze, Enver made a verbal concession relating to Akhalkalak. The Armenian delegates were informed that Essad Pasha had received instructions to supervise the repatriation of inhabitants from one hundred villages in the uezd and to take measures to relocate the Moslems who had recently settled there.[63] Despite the good news, the Armenian refugees, whether from Akhalkalak, the ceded half of the Erevan guberniia, or lands extending farther to the west, remained refugees until the conclusion of World War I.

The need for bread was closely related to the refugee problem. Armenia was starving. As a unit of the Romanov Empire, Transcaucasia had received wheat from the rich grainlands north of the Caucasus Mountains. This source was no longer available. Aggravating the situation was the Turkish occupation of the Erevan guberniia's best cropland. Even on the remaining soil, there was little to harvest because of wartime devastation and the countless refugees who trod over the fields. Aharonian and Khatisian begged Ottoman officials to intercede by persuading Azerbaijan to sell a small share of the abundant cereal crops of eastern Transcaucasia to the Armenian government. Rasul-Zade and Ali Mardan Topchibashev, in the Ottoman capital to seek Turkish support, would certainly accede were the request to come from Enver Pasha. Transportation of the vital goods could be easily arranged by Halil, Mürsel, Nuri, and Essad. Yet the suppliants must have known that their entreaty could not be considered seriously, for, while Ottoman and Azerbaijani troops were battling the Armenians of Baku, it would have been ironic at the least were the Armenians of Erevan to be fed by Moslems. The Ottoman officials regretted that they could not intervene in the internal affairs of another nation and suggested that the Armenians attempt direct negotiations with the Azerbaijanis.[64]

A more likely source for economic relief was the Ukraine, which, having established bonds with the Central Powers, had sent representatives to Constantinople.[65] Mentor Buniatian, economic adviser to the Armenian mission, conferred with the Kievan delegates and proposed that from the Ukrainian grain, which was sufficient to feed millions, a small fraction be exported via the Black Sea to Batum or Poti, whence with Turkish or German beneficence it would be transferred to Erevan.[66] The Ukrainians promised to urge favorable action by their government, and, in fact, the Armenian diplomatic representative to Kiev, Grigor Dsamoev, did succeed in negotiating the sale of 200 tons of sugar and 1,000 tons of wheat.[67] There is, however, nothing to indicate that the foodstuffs were ever shipped. Undoubtedly, transportation problems and political changes caused by the defeat of the Central Powers precluded delivery.[68]

Amidst its other activities, the Aharonian delegation strove to convince the officials of Turkey and the other Central Powers that the Republic could not prosper or even survive on the 4,500 square miles of Transcaucasia's most barren land. Statistical expert Gevorg Khatisian prepared numerous impressive charts and graphs to bolster Armenia's claim to an additional 16,000 square miles, not including the ceded territories of Kars and Ardahan. This goal could be realized if the Turks were to return Akhalkalak and the half of the Erevan guberniia acquired by the Treaty of Batum and if parts of the Elisavetpol and Tiflis guberniias were joined to the Republic. While the Armenians revived the ghost of their *zemstvo* scheme, Georgian and Azerbaijani delegates were equally active in disproving the presented evidence and even extending the pretensions of their nations to the small area under the actual jurisdiction of Kachaznuni's government. From the southern half of the Erevan guberniia, Rasul-Zade and Topchibashev demanded all land not annexed by Turkey. Azerbaijan coveted 500 square miles of Sharur-Daralagiaz, 193 of Nakhichevan, and 202 of Novo Bayazit, with a combined population ratio of three Moslems to one Armenian. Moreover, if Turkey waived her right to much of the Erevan guberniia, Azerbaijan would annex over half of that area's 5,000 square miles. Armenian counterclaims included the entire Erevan guberniia and over 6,000 square miles of Elisavetpol. In the latter region, Armenians outnumbered Moslems three to one. The Armeno-Georgian contest centered around the Lori-Pambak-Kazakh districts, approximately 3,500 square miles populated by 30,000 Moslems, scarcely 1,000 Georgians, and more than 150,000 Armenians. If the Turks cleared neighboring Akhalkalak and Tsalka, the dispute would naturally extend to that district as well. In the total contested area there were, according to the prewar Russian statistics cited by the delegation, 940,000 Armenians, 470,000 Moslems, 7,500 Georgians, and 34,000 others.[69]

The envoys of the Erevan government contended that, were Georgia and Azerbaijan to have their way, Armenia could expand very little even if the Ottoman Empire relinquished the lands outside the Brest-Litovsk boundaries. Though Transcaucasia's 1,800,000 Armenians represented 29 percent of the total population, the area and ethnic composition of the three republics would then be as shown in Schedule A in the accompanying table.[70] Alexandre and Gevorg Khatisian, Aharonian, and Papadjanian argued that inclusion in the Armenian Republic of the Erevan guberniia, mountainous Elisavetpol, and the Akhalkalak-Lori districts would establish balance and equity among the three states. With such a settlement, the figures in Schedule A would be altered to those shown in Schedule B.[71]

Republic	Square Miles	Percentage of Transcaucasia*	Inhabitants			
			Armenian	Georgian	Moslem	Other
		SCHEDULE A				
Armenia	6,000	8	470,000	—	168,000	41,000
Georgia	29,000	41	535,000	1,607,000	200,000	510,000
Azerbaijan	36,000	51	653,000	—	2,138,000	304,000
		SCHEDULE B				
Armenia	20,600	29	1,169,000	7,000	546,000	75,000
Georgia	23,400	33	275,000	1,600,000	160,000	480,000
Azerbaijan	27,000	38	214,000	—	1,800,000	300,000

* Excluding the oblasts of Kars, Batum, and Daghestan.

On the basis of Schedule B, Georgia's population would be 64 percent Georgian, Armenia's 65 percent Armenian, and Azerbaijan's 78 percent Moslem.

The flow of statistics had no overt effect on the Turkish authorities until the autumn of 1918, when, for reasons other than validity of the Armenian thesis, they indicated willingness to offer limited support to the "Erevan Republic." After conclusion of the Soviet-German Supplementary Treaty, Enver confidentially informed Khatisian and Aharonian that Turkey would champion the Armenian right to Lori-Pambak and that he was confident a satisfactory arrangement could be worked out with Azerbaijan. It was even possible that the boundaries of the Erevan Republic might be extended to the shore of the Arpachai River, the western limit of the guberniia. Turkish patronage was conditional, however, upon the willingness of the Armenians to act as allies, turning their backs once and for all on Britain and Russia, and possibly entering an Azerbaijani-Armenian-Ottoman confederation. The latter project was the subject of several interviews, but the Armenian delegates remained as noncommittal as the occasion would permit. The prospect was frightening, yet a decisive negative response was not given.[72]

After Talaat returned from Berlin, more sweeping promises were made. The Grand Vizier stated that his government was prepared to grant the Armenians more than they themselves had requested during the preceding months. Khatisian wrote Ohandjanian that the change in Turkish heart was undoubtedly prompted by the unfavorable course of the war. Yet he advised extreme caution, stressing that, even at this late date, if the Ottomans were to propose a workable agreement, he would favor immediate acceptance. To wait for the Western Allies to establish a viable Armenian state would be foolish. True, Lloyd George, Clemenceau, and Wilson had made certain pledges and commitments. They spoke of liberation and justice, but "what do such statements mean?" asked Khatisian. "We must create our own government and effect a fait accompli, and this must be done with the assistance of Turkey." On a personal note the Armenian Foreign Minister reported that his wife had just given birth to their first child and that the delegation considered the boy a symbol of improved future Armeno-Turkish relations.[73] In retrospect, it may be said that, if the birth of a son was a good omen, his death from pneumonia nine days later might have been interpreted as signifying continued and violent animosity between the two peoples.

Following formation of Izzet Pasha's cabinet in the second week of October, the new Grand Vizier and War Minister conferred several times with the Aharonian mission. He knew that his task was to lead Turkey out of the war and that the Armenians would soon be knocking on the doors of the Allies. Those governments had repeatedly indicated that the Armenians would be indemnified at the expense of the Ottoman Empire. Izzet, now the suppliant, urged Aharonian and Khatisian to inform the victors that Turks and Armenians were in accord. In return, the Ottoman government would recall all troops from Transcaucasia, release and compensate those Armenians seized for forced labor,[74] condone the repatriation of all refugees, and assist in retrieving Armenian women and children unwillingly converted to Islam.[75] Still, there was no mention of Turkish Armenia. On October 24, Aharonian wrote Izzet suggesting the recall of Shevki and Nuri pashas. The two militarists had caused the Armenian people much agony, and it was not in Turkey's interest that they remain in the Caucasus. Aharonian also requested that Armenians still in Baku be permitted to leave by rail and sea.[76] On the following day the Ottoman government replied that all its troops would be evacuated from the Caucasus in the shortest possible time.[77] On October 27, notifying the Grand Vizier that his delegation was returning to Transcaucasia, Aharonian again urged the immediate withdrawal of Ottoman forces, adding that no rolling stock should be taken from Armenia to Turkey.[78] Izzet then disclosed that Shevki Pasha had already received orders to complete the evacuation within six weeks of October 24 and, in the meantime, to facilitate the return of refugees.[79]

As the Armenian envoys prepared to depart for home, Rauf Bey called on Khatisian. During March and April the two men had sat together at the Trebizond Conference, but now the wheel of fortune had turned. Rauf was to leave for Port Mudros the following day to negotiate an armistice. Like Izzet, he exhorted the Armenian representatives to accompany him as evidence that enmity no longer existed between Turks and Armenians. For this favor, the Ottoman government was willing to relinquish Kars and Ardahan, reestablish the 1914 international boundary, and even cede a part of the Alashkert Valley.[80] Ironically, the Seim's March 1 bases for peace were now being advanced by the Ottoman rulers. This time it was the Armenians who considered the concessions insufficient. Khatisian and

Aharonian did not sail with Rauf to Lemnos. Instead, after appointing Ferdinand Tahtadjian diplomatic representative at Constantinople, they embarked for Batum aboard the "Reshid Pasha" on November 1, two days following Turkey's surrender.[81]

In one of his last letters to Ohandjanian, the Armenian Foreign Minister again expressed concern about the vagueness of the Allied pledges, especially in light of the secret Entente treaties. The fate of Armenia was far from determined. Moreover, the Allied commitment to reestablish a united Russia after the anticipated overthrow of the Bolsheviks would pose another obstacle to the Armenian Republic. Khatisian understood well the turbulent political waters through which his nation was to pass. He concluded his long correspondence with the Armenian envoy to Berlin with the following words:

> Our being here for four months has greatly strengthened our conviction that Armenia must be independent. Otherwise we must always conform to the psychology of our masters, whoever they may be and these contortions ruin our national character. . . . We must consolidate into one united Armenian government from Van to Sevan. This and the benevolent protection of the United States should be our motto as we attend the general conference of peace. There cannot be a confederation of Armenians with either Turks or Russians, for assuredly there will be another Russo-Turkish War, and again it will come crashing down upon our heads.[82]

By November, 1918, independence no longer meant subservience to the Central Powers. The end of the war, the withdrawal of Ottoman troops, the return of the refugees, the expansion of the boundaries of the Republic, all advanced the possibility of an independent state, not only in name, but in fact. The Armenian delegation would soon cross the borders of the Armenian Republic for the first time, report on the proceedings in Constantinople, and urge that a new delegation be sent immediately to defend Armenian interests at the world congress of peace. During the first days of November, Ohandjanian would leave Berlin for Geneva to shift the supplications from the Central Powers to the agents of the Allied nations. His departure was to be followed by Germany's capitulation on November 11. The tragic war of four years was over.

Misgivings Arising from the Mudros Armistice

The October 30 Ottoman-Allied Armistice was greeted with rejoicing throughout the Armenian world. Services of thanksgiving were held on every continent, but to the Armenian politicians there was cause for serious misgivings. The Armistice was, in general, lenient, and the clauses dealing with Armenia were as vague as the Allied pledges toward that nation. The Armenians were directly affected by the following articles:

IV.   All Allied prisoners of war and Armenian interned persons and prisoners to be collected in Constantinople and handed over unconditionally to the Allies.

V.   Immediate demobilization of the Turkish army, except for such troops as are required for surveillance of the frontiers and for the maintenance of internal order.

VII.   The Allies to have the right to occupy any strategic points in the event of any situation arising which threatens the security of the Allies.

XI.   Immediate withdrawal of the Turkish troops from North-West Persia to behind the pre-war frontier has already been ordered and will be carried out. Part of Trans-Caucasia has already been ordered to be evacuated by Turkish troops; the remainder to be evacuated if required by the Allies after they have studied the situation there.

XV.   Allied Control Officers to be placed on all railways including such portions of the Trans-Caucasian Railways as are now under Turkish control, which must be placed at the free and complete disposal of the Allied authorities, due consideration being given to the needs of the population. This clause to include Allied occupation of Batum. Turkey will raise no objections to the occupation of Baku by the Allies.

XVI.   . . . the withdrawal of [Ottoman] troops from Cilicia, except those necessary to maintain order, as will be determined under Clause V.

XXIV.   In case of disorder in the six Armenian vilayets, the Allies reserve to themselves the right to occupy any part of them.[83]

During the course of negotiations aboard the "SS Agamemnon," Admiral Calthorpe had made certain concessions to Rauf, Reshad Hikmet, and Colonel Saadullah, the Ottoman conferees. The original draft of Article XXIV had included "Sis, Hadjin, Zeitun, and Aintab" with the "six Armenian vilayets" the Allies might occupy in the event of disorder. Turkish success in erasing the four districts from the article was highly significant, for Cilicia was thus disassociated from the Armenian provinces. Equally important was the modification of Article XI. In the original draft, the Ottomans were required to withdraw their forces from North Persia and *all* Transcaucasia, which, of course, included the Kars and Batum oblasts. On this point especially, the Ottoman delegates were obdurate. Izzet Pasha wired Rauf at Mudros that the three sanjaks should remain under Turkish control at least until conclusion of the general peace. Calthorpe compromised with the defeated enemy by requiring evacuation of only "part of Trans-Caucasia." Thus, on the Caucasus front, the Armistice permitted Ottoman armies to retain territories that had been seized during the war.[84]

Understandably, then, Armenian leaders were wary of the October 30 terms. The Turks had not been compelled to vacate Kars and Ardahan, as might have been expected. Not even the 1914 Russo-Turkish frontier had been restored. No effective provisions had been included in the document for supervision to assure a rapid Turkish demobilization. As for the Turkish Armenian provinces, what was meant by "the Allies reserve to themselves the right to occupy any part of them"? The statement seemed to imply that Turkey would be permitted to retain control there. Moreover, how could there be "disorders" when the entire native Armenian population had been deported or massacred? There was absolutely nothing to force the Ottomans to leave the Armenian Plateau. Although the war had ended in Allied victory and Armenia had often been dubbed "the Little Ally," the shortcomings and dangers of the Mudros Armistice seemed to cast doubt upon both facts.

Had the Armenians been aware of several orders issued by the Ottoman War Ministry during the last week of hostilities, they would have had reason for even greater concern. Izzet Pasha had commanded the Turkish units to withdraw to the Brest-Litovsk boundaries and had so apprised the Armenian and Georgian representatives. He nevertheless issued a circular on October 27 permitting all Turkish officers to enter the service of the North Caucasus or Azerbaijani republics.[85] A month later, when Izzet had relinquished his post of Grand Vizier to Tewfik Pasha and the Ministry of War to Abdullah, this order was revoked and all Ottoman divisions were recalled to Kars. The command was ineffective, however, for already on November 4 Nuri Pasha had informed Turkish soldiers in the Caucasus of an agreement with the government of Azerbaijan. All Ottoman enlisted men and officers who so desired could join the Azerbaijani Army and become Azerbaijani citizens. They would retain their current rank, and if they were eligible for promotion, the Azerbaijani government would confer upon them a still higher rank. Each officer was to be granted two months' furlough every year with pay in advance. Turkish soldiers who accepted the offer were to serve for at least a year, but should they be forced to leave for reasons of health, compensation would be made, and should the Azerbaijani Army annul the contract, six months' pay would be granted. In addition, certain provisions would be made for the soldiers' families in Turkey.[86] Hundreds of Ottoman instructors, officers, and soldiers remained in Azerbaijan throughout its independent existence and became the object of numerous Armenian complaints and accusations.

By the beginning of December, 1918, the regular Ottoman divisions had vacated the Erevan guberniia, leaving the abandoned territory completely denuded. A few hundred more Armenians met death in this last Ottoman wartime operation. Some of the loot was transferred to the southern districts of the guberniia where Turkish officers and troops voluntarily remained to organize and direct the efforts of the Moslem-populated Araxes Valley in resisting submission to the Armenian government. For two years these *askiar*s were to aid their coreligionists and to strive for the area's annexation to Turkey or Azerbaijan. Local councils, *shura*s, organized just 10 miles from Erevan, remained resolutely hostile to the Armenian Republic. During

1919 the lands to the south of the Armenian capital were to serve as a passageway between Turkey and Azerbaijan, and in 1920 their importance vaulted, for it was across this route that Mustafa Kemal and Lenin were to extend the hand of friendship.

The British in Transcaucasia

To implement Article XV of the Mudros Armistice, British troops moved into Transcaucasia, supplanting Russians, Germans, and Ottomans as the dominant power. On November 14, 1918, General William M. Thomson, Commander of British forces in North Persia, ordered the last Turkish contingents out of Baku, and, three days later, with several companies of the 39th Infantry Brigade, disembarked on the wharves abandoned by Dunsterville two months earlier. Initially, Thomson withheld recognition of the Azerbaijani government and announced that his troops were there to secure the area in the name of democratic Russia. Soon, however, the British tactic changed, and in December the general acknowledged Khan Khoiskii's government as the only legally constituted local administrative body.[87] Later that month, the British 27th Division landed at Batum, where, much to the chagrin of Zhordania's cabinet, Brigadier General Cooke-Collis established a British military governorship. On December 25, after a series of strained and hostile exchanges between Zhordania and British officials, English troops under General G. T. Forestier-Walker entered Tiflis to supersede the Germans. Now the Union Jack waved above the Georgian capital.[88]

The coming of the British to Transcaucasia was welcomed by most Armenians but was to have a definite negative effect on Erevan's claims to the mountainous sector of the Elisavetpol guberniia. Throughout the summer of 1918 the Armenians of Mountainous Karabagh had resisted the Turks. Even after Shushi, the administrative center, was finally occupied in the last days of September, the rural areas continued to hold out.[89] When the Ottomans were forced to withdraw in November, the partisans of Karabagh implored Andranik in neighboring Zangezur to march on Shushi, the district's major center of Moslem strength. This would assure Mountainous Karabagh's inclusion within Armenia. Andranik accepted the challenge and had, on December 1, just broken through the Tatar-Kurdish vale of Zabukh separating Zangezur from Karabagh, when a telegram from Thomson was delivered by special courier. The British general informed Andranik of the Armistice and the forthcoming conference of peace and warned that, in order not to jeopardize Armenian interests, all hostilities must cease immediately. The Allies would arrange a lasting settlement. The Armenians were thrown into a new dilemma. Ahead lay the unobstructed road to Shushi; they could be there in a day. But Andranik, as many other Armenians, had not yet learned that a British command could be flouted. Faith in the Allies still burned strongly, and Andranik, yielding to Thomson's personal envoys who arrived the following day, withdrew to Zangezur to await world justice.[90] Yet, even before the Paris Peace Conference had assembled, Thomson announced from his Baku headquarters that jurisdiction not only over Karabagh but also over Zangezur belonged to Azerbaijan. The Armenian blunder had been so monumental that it could never be rectified.[91]

The history of the Armenian Republic entered a new phase with the conclusion of World War I. From despair rose hope, from tragedy rose the possibility of existing as a modern nation state. The final miles on the road to independence had been the most agonizing. Most of historic Armenia had been depopulated and the remainder denied the protection it had found as part of the Romanov Empire. Events from November, 1917, through May, 1918, had drawn the Armenians progressively deeper into the abyss. And when independence finally arrived at the end of May, few recognized it as the desirable culmination of the path begun a century before. The humiliations and ordeals of the Republic of Armenia during its first five months were many and severe. Internally, chaos prevailed and death and destruction were the rule; externally, supplication and political exigency were the tactics espoused. It is difficult to judge the worth of the role played by the suppliants in Moscow, Berlin, and Constantinople during those months. Perhaps in some small way they helped the Republic to survive, and from May to November survival was the maximum that could have been expected.

When the Central Powers sued for peace, there was in existence an Armenian Republic. Around this small state Armenian aspirations were to be concentrated for the next two years. This was the core onto which it was hoped Turkish Armenia would be added, and this was the organism that could most logically request admission to the family of independent nations. The realization of both aspirations was dependent on the benevolence of the victors in war. Would they fulfill their pledges?[92] Would they be willing to use force if necessary to assure the Armenians the justice they had been promised? These were the troublesome questions that weighed upon the leaders in Erevan, the suppliants as they returned home, and the Republic's representatives in Western Europe. There was cause both for optimism and for pessimism. In November, 1918, there were hopes for a brilliant future and there were fears of continued torment and oppression. Independence had been attained. The key to determining the course of that independence was in the hands of the nations of Europe and America. Would they turn the key or would the door to fulfillment remain locked?

XII
In Conclusion

THE ROAD to independence, like so much of the history of the Armenian people, was filled with tragedy. The Republic was a goal neither anticipated nor coveted. Yet both domestic and external factors drove the Armenians relentlessly toward sovereignty. Living for centuries under foreign domination, they had learned to adjust to many inequalities, but when the wind of nationalism swept the Armenian Plateau, they turned to protest, foreign intercession, and revolution. The rise of nationalism, coupled with the Russian conquest of Transcaucasia, constituted the beginning of a new epoch in Armenian history. Within the Romanov Empire, the Armenians surmounted the bureaucratic obstacles and rediscovered their heritage, gradually repopulated their native provinces, and extended the hand of assistance and the voice of exhortation to their brothers across the border. It was on the very territory of the *Armianskaia oblast,* established in 1828, that the Republic was to emerge in 1918.

In their national development, the Armenians faced many obstacles. Both in Transcaucasia and in the Ottoman eastern *vilayet*s they were widely dispersed and were a numerical minority in all but a few districts. They were separated by international boundaries and deep-seated particularism. They suffered from the mentality of a subject people. By the latter half of the nineteenth century, however, this people was drawn together in a renaissance, expressed through a drive toward mass education, revived national pride, and the demand for reform and even self-government. With disillusionment in European-sponsored Ottoman reforms and with resentment against the tsarist policies toward minorities, the Armenians turned increasingly to the opposition movements in both empires. On the eve of the Great World War, after many bitter experiences, it seemed as if their primary aspiration, unhindered autonomous development, was on the verge of fruition. Tsar Nicholas had effected a rapprochement with his Armenian subjects, and the European Powers had at last settled upon a functional arrangement for improved administration in "Turkish Armenia."

IN CONCLUSION

The fires of war both crushed and exacerbated Armenian hopes. On the one hand, Western Armenia was depopulated and devastated, eliminating the possibility of implementing the reform plan. On the other hand, the Allied pledges and the Russian advance to the western limits of the Plateau elicited visions of a promising future. This goal seemed one step nearer to realization when the Romanov dynasty, branded with the stamp of oppressor, was overthrown by "democratic Russia." Western and Eastern Armenia, united into an autonomous state within the great Russian federation, was now the plausible recompense for the sacrifice of half the nation. The November Revolution, however, dealt a crippling blow to such expectations. The Bolshevik application of "self-determination" stood in sharp contraposition to Armenian interests. The front was denuded by the Russian Army, and Transcaucasia was betrayed by the Sovnarkom's action at Brest-Litovsk. By that treaty, Turkey retrieved the eastern vilayets and gained the Kars and Batum oblasts, Eastern Armenia was exposed to annihilation, and Transcaucasia was propelled toward separation from Russia.

The Russian Armenians, represented primarily by Dashnaktsutiun, strove to join with Georgians and Moslems in formulating a common policy to defend Transcaucasia and to uphold the principles of the "democratic" Russian Revolution. The failure to achieve these goals has been the subject of much of the present study. The basic motivations and aspirations of the three peoples contrasted too greatly to allow for earnest collaboration. In the midst of Turkish invasion, the Transcaucasian provinces were aflame with civil strife and interracial warfare. From the village level to the Commissariat and the Seim, the incompatibility was glaringly revealed. While Armenians clung desperately to Russia as the only means of salvation, the Moslems looked expectantly toward Turkey as the source of deliverance and welcomed Transcaucasia's separation from Russia. When, on Georgian initiative, the Transcaucasian Federation crumbled, only the Armenians expressed bitter indignation and vacillated before the unwelcome prospect of independence—a synonym for defeat.

Once the National Council had taken the decisive step, the Armenians strove to salvage what they could. The belated military successes in the heart of the Erevan *guberniia* inspired a glow of faith, and Germany's anger with its Ottoman ally kindled a flicker of hope. For five months, the Armenian suppliants had only faith and hope to sustain them. And while the petitioners humbled themselves before the Sublime Porte, the crude wheels of government began to grind in Erevan. With each rotation, the ideal of independence drove deeper into the Armenian mentality. By the end of the war it had an electrifying effect on Armenians and their sympathizers the world over. It was now possible for the Republic to expand, to reclaim the entire Armenian Plateau, and to exist as a veritable independent nation. Possibility could become reality if the Allied victors would deliver a rapid deathblow to the Ottoman Empire and if a modus vivendi could be arranged with Russia, whether royalist, republican, or communist. The struggle to transform possibility into reality, the subject of a subsequent study, constitutes the second phase in the history of the Republic of Armenia.

Appendix
The Allies and Armenia

THE CONCLUSION of World War I and the return of Aharonian's delegation to Transcaucasia completed the road to Armenia's independence. Still, there is an aspect that, though touched upon throughout this study, requires greater amplification if the picture is to be placed in full perspective. The Allied declarations affecting the Armenians have not yet been examined.

The Armenian tragedy of 1915–1918 created a sensation of horror throughout the world. Thousands of articles condemned the Ottoman government, described the viciousness of the Turk, portrayed the history of Armenian martyrdom, and demanded restitution. On several occasions the Entente had warned the ruling Turkish clique that it would be held personally responsible for these crimes against mankind and civilization. Allied declarations left little doubt that, following victory, the Ottoman Empire would undergo sweeping structural and territorial alterations. Thus when, in December, 1918, the Republic of Armenia dispatched a new delegation to Europe, this time to the Paris Peace Conference, there were grounds to believe that the map of Western Asia would be redrawn in fulfillment of those pledges. Indeed, those glowing promises seemed to dispel the pessimism that had arisen after publication of the secret wartime agreements of the Entente.[1]

British Words

In January of 1916, the London *Times* reported that Arthur Henderson, Laborite leader and member of the Allied War Council, had declared the determination of the working class, deeply stung by the Turkish atrocities, that never again should a Christian people be bound by the odious Ottoman shackles.[2] This view was reiterated hundreds of times before the end of the year, when the *Manchester Guardian* summarized the feelings of the British people:

Another word remains—Armenia—a word of ghastly horror, carrying the memory of deeds not done in the world since Christ was born—a country swept clear by the wholesale murder of its people. To Turkey that country must never and under no circumstances go back. . . .³

The invective against the Ottomans intensified during 1917. Men in public office spoke longer and more frequently on the subject. On November 6, Foreign Secretary Arthur J. Balfour announced in the House of Commons that, although Britain did not intend to terminate the rule of the Turk over Turks, it was pledged to liberate those peoples whose progress had been impeded by the Ottomans and who would flourish as a separate governmental organism.⁴ Six weeks later, on December 20, Premier David Lloyd George, speaking in Commons, repeated one of his declarations:

What will happen to Mesopotamia must be left to the Peace Congress when it meets, but there is one thing which will never happen. It will never be restored to the blasting tyranny of the Turk. . . . That same observation applies to Armenia, the land soaked with the blood of innocence [innocents] and massacred by the people who were bound to protect them.⁵

Throughout 1918, the British continued to imply, without specifically enunciating, that Armenia would be established as a separate state. On January 5, during a historic address to the Trade Unions Conference, the Premier listed the British war aims, one of which read:

While we do not challenge the maintenance of the Turkish Empire in the homelands of the Turkish race with its capital at Constantinople—the passage between the Mediterranean and the Black Sea being internationalised and neutralised—Arabia, Armenia, Mesopotamia, Syria and Palestine are in our judgment entitled to a recognition of their separate national condition.⁶

In answering opposition-leader Ramsay Macdonald's queries as to whether the government was keeping abreast of the Armenian struggle against the Turks and whether the Allies were pledged to settle Armenia's future on the principle of self-determination, Foreign Secretary Balfour stated on July 11:

Yes, Sir; His Majesty's Government are following with earnest sympathy and admiration the gallant resistance of the Armenians in defence of their liberties and honour, and are doing everything they can to come to their assistance. As regards the future of Armenia, I would refer the hon. Member to the public statements made by leading statesmen among the Allied Powers in favour of a settlement upon the principles he indicates.⁷

A month later, Lloyd George assured a deputation from the Manchester Armenian community, "Britain will not forget its responsibilities towards your martyred race."⁸ Subsequently, when the end of war was in sight, Lord Robert Cecil, Assistant Secretary for Foreign Affairs, wrote Viscount James Bryce⁹ that the "Charter for Armenian Justice" stemmed from the following considerations:

1) In the autumn of 1914, the national Congress of the Ottoman Armenians, then sitting at Erzerum, was offered autonomy by the Turkish emissaries, if it would actively assist Turkey in the war, but it replied that while they would do their duty individually as Ottoman subjects, they could not, as a nation, work for the cause of Turkey and her allies.

2) Following this courageous refusal, the Ottoman Armenians were systematically murdered by the Turkish Government in 1915, more than 700,000 people being exterminated by the most cold-blooded and fiendish methods.

3) From the beginning of the war, that half of the Armenian nation under Russian sovereignty organized volunteer forces and, under their heroic leader, General Andranik, bore the brunt of some of the heaviest fighting in the Caucasus campaign.

4) After the Russian army's breakdown at the end of last year, these Armenian forces took over the Caucasus front and for five months delayed the Turks' advance, thus rendering important services to the British Army in Mesopotamia, these operations in the Alexandropol and Erivan region being, of course, unconnected with those of Baku.

Armenian soldiers are still fighting in the ranks of the allied forces in Syria. They are to be found serving alike in the British, the French, and in the American armies, and have borne their part in General Allenby's great victory in Palestine.[10]

The Mudros Armistice aroused discontent in the British Parliament. In mid-November members of both Houses voiced concern about the laxity of the terms and advocated the use of force to effect immediate Turkish evacuation of the Armenian *vilayet*s and even Allied occupation of the region if it should prove necessary.[11] In defense of the government's actions, Cecil assured Parliament that the official policy was to foster the unification of Western and Eastern Armenia:

I recognize fully the strength of the observations that we must not allow the misdeeds of the Turks to diminish the patrimony of the Armenians. That is the general principle. I recognize the great force of what the hon. Member said—that there ought to be no division of Armenia and that it ought to be treated as one whole. . . . As far as I am concerned—and I believe in this matter I am speaking for the Government—I should be deeply disappointed if any shred or shadow of Turkish government were left in Armenia.[12]

Already, on November 8, an Anglo-French declaration of Middle East objectives pledged the two Entente powers to assure

. . . the complete and final emancipation of all those peoples so long oppressed by the Turks, and to establish national governments and administrations which shall derive their authority from the initiative and free will of the peoples themselves.[13]

French Words

The French declarations were more stirring than those of the English. In April of 1916, many French political, civic, and cultural leaders gathered at the Sorbonne to participate in the "Hommage à l'Arménie," where, to resounding applause, Anatole France exclaimed:

> L'Arménie expire, mais elle renaîtra. La peu de sang qui lui reste est un sang précieux dont sortira une postérité héroïque. Un peuple qui ne veut pas mourir ne meurt pas. Après la victoire de nos armées, qui combattent pour la liberté, les Alliés auront de grands devoirs à remplir. Et le plus sacré de ces devoirs sera de rendre la vie aux peuples martyrs, à la Belgique, à la Serbie. Alors ils assureront la sureté et l'indépendance de l'Arménie. Penchés sur elle, ils lui diront: "Ma soeur, lève toi! ne souffre plus. Tu es désormais libre de vivre selon ton génie et foi!"[14]

Aristide Briand, Premier and Foreign Minister, wrote Senator Louis Martin during the first week of November, 1916:

> When the hour for legitimate reparation shall have struck, France will not forget the terrible trials of the Armenians, and in accord with her Allies, she will take the necessary measures to ensure for Armenia a life of peace and progress.[15]

Two months later in conjunction with the other Allied governments, he announced that the "high war aims" included "the liberation of peoples who now lie beneath the murderous tyranny of the Turks, and the expulsion from Europe of the Ottoman Empire, which has proved itself so radically alien to Western civilization."[16]

On December 27, 1917, soon after Georges Clemenceau had accepted the reins of government, Foreign Minister Stéphan Pichon declared to the Chamber of Deputies:

> An adherence to the policy of the rights of nationalities has been the honor of our traditions and of our history. It applies, as we view it, to the Armenians, Syrian and Lebanese populations, as it does to all peoples who suffer, against their will, the yoke of the oppressor, be he who he may. Such peoples have a right to our sympathy, to our help. All of them should be given an opportunity of deciding their fate.[17]

In a letter to Boghos Nubar on July 14, 1918, Premier Clemenceau reaffirmed the determination of France to settle the fate of the Armenians according to the supreme laws of humanity and justice:

> France, the victim of the most unjust of aggressions, has included in her peace terms the liberation of oppressed nations. The traditional defender of such peoples, she on many occasions has expressed sympathy for the Armenians. She has done all possible to extend aid to them.

The spirit of self-abnegation of the Armenians, their loyalty towards the Allies, their contributions to the Foreign Legion, to the Caucasus front, to the Légion d'Orient, have strengthened the ties that connect them with France.

I am happy to confirm to you that the government of the Republic, like that of Great Britain, has not ceased to place the Armenian nation among the peoples whose fate the Allies intend to settle according to the supreme laws of Humanity and Justice.[18]

Italian Words

Though Italian sympathy was not so overwhelming, many newspapers and officials by the end of 1918 urged the victors to do the Armenians justice. On November 8, former premier Luigi Luzzatti wired Wilson, Clemenceau, Lloyd George, and Italian Prime Minister Vittorio Orlando to relay the resolution of a mass rally of governmental, intellectual, and political leaders. Only the creation of a free and independent Armenia, especially in view of the martyrdom for the Allied cause, would constitute a just settlement.[19] Ten days later Orlando replied, "Say to the Armenians that I make their cause my cause."[20] The Italian Chamber of Deputies also called for Armenian independence, and Foreign Minister Sidney Sonnino declared, "I am very happy of the occasion offered me to express once more the sentiments of heartfelt sympathy with which the Royal Government follows the constant and noble efforts of Armenia for her independence and unity."[21] On that point the European Allies seemed unanimous.

American Words

Incredulity and outrage were the reactions of the United States to the Turkish atrocities. Overcoming its initial bewilderment, the nation rallied to assist the "Starving Armenians." In September, 1915, many officials, led by James L. Barton, Charles R. Crane, Samuel T. Dutton, and Cleveland H. Dodge, formed the American Relief Committee and within a short time solicited more than 100,000 dollars.[22] President Woodrow Wilson set aside two days in October, 1916, for a nationwide drive for Armenian relief. The result of such activities was that by early 1918 over 11 million dollars in currency and goods had been gathered.[23]

American public opinion in 1918 turned to the question of the postwar settlement. The unanimous verdict was that the Turkish yoke should never again press upon the people of the Armenian Plateau. Many Americans backed Boghos Nubar's request of May, 1917, that the United States supervise an autonomous Armenia extending over the six vilayets and Cilicia with outlets on the Black and Mediterranean seas.[24] On January 8, 1918, President Wilson, champion of the oppressed, pronounced his famed Fourteen Points, the twelfth of which was applicable to the Armenians:

> The Turkish portions of the present Ottoman Empire should be assured a secure sovereignty, but the other nationalities which are now under Turkish rule should be assured an undoubted security of life and an absolutely unmolested opportunity of autonomous development. . . .[25]

Armenophiles argued that "autonomous development" was conceivable only in an independent state, and later in the year the President himself declared, "I feel very strongly that the Armenians should be given their independence."[26]

On December 22, 1917, two weeks prior to Wilson's delivery of the Fourteen Points, the Inquiry,[27] the special body appointed by the President to formulate the American position on issues that would arise at the peace conference, submitted its preliminary recommendations, among which was the following:

> . . . we must secure a guaranteed autonomy for the Armenians, not only as a matter of justice and humanity but in order to re-establish the one people in Asia Minor capable of preventing economic monopolization of Turkey by the Germans.

And further:

> It is necessary to free the subject races of the Turkish Empire from oppression and misrule. This implies at the very least autonomy for Armenia and the protection of Palestine, Syria, Mesopotamia, and Arabia by the civilized nations.[28]

Throughout 1918 the Inquiry continued to prepare the United States in some measure for the postwar role it was obliged to play. In September, the Department of State, having utilized scores of Inquiry reports, issued a memorandum to guide the American peace delegation. Point 17 of those instructions read:

> Armenia and Syria to be created into protectorate of such Government or Governments as seem expedient from domestic as well as international point of view, with guarantees that they to be self governing as soon as possible and that open door in commercial-economic fields to be strictly observed.[29]

In January, 1919, the Inquiry, now operating as the American delegation's Division of Territorial and Economic Intelligence, elaborated on its recommendations. An Armenian state encompassing the six vilayets, the Black Sea coast around Trebizond, and the Mediterranean Sea coast around Adana should be established. The Taurus and Anti-Taurus mountain chains should constitute the southern and western boundaries of the state. Moreover, the Armenians of Transcaucasia should be guaranteed permanent independence, and the provinces of Erevan and Kars, together with the adjoining districts of Akhalkalak and Akhaltsikh, should be united with the Armenian areas to be detached from the Ottoman Empire. The new state would be placed under the aegis of a mandatory power that would, in turn, be under the supervision of the League of Nations.³⁰ A shadow of ambiguity could be discerned in the plan, however, for, although recommending complete and permanent independence for Russian Armenia, the Inquiry only implied the same for Turkish Armenia.

While the Inquiry had left certain questions unanswered, the powerful American Committee for the Independence of Armenia persistently advanced its steadfast convictions. The bipartisan organization, composed of many members of Congress, leading educators and clergy, philanthropists and industrialists, with former ambassador to Germany James W. Gerard as chairman, called upon the United States government to recognize the Armenian Republic, champion its right to the six vilayets and Cilicia, grant it military, economic, and cultural assistance, and reject the excessive territorial claims of the European Allies. Strongly backed by President Wilson, the American Committee was to occasion much discomfort and distress to Secretary of State Robert Lansing, who advocated a "rational" approach in pursuance of a lasting world settlement.³¹

The Committee's Congressional members were very active on behalf of Armenia. On October 14, 1918, Congressman Edward C. Little introduced Joint Resolution 336, which read:

> Resolved, That the Armenian people are entitled to be a free and independent nation with access to the sea and to secure the advantages of that Christian civilization for which they have been martyred. The Republic of Ararat [the Erevan government] should be given universal recognition.³²

Two months later, on December 10, influential Republican Senator Henry Cabot Lodge introduced Senate Resolution 378:

> Resolved, That in the opinion of the Senate, Armenia, including the six vilayets of Turkish Armenia and Cilicia, Russian Armenia, and the northern part of the Province of Azerbaijan, Persian Armenia, should be independent and that it is the hope of the Senate that the peace conference will make arrangements for helping Armenia to establish an independent republic.³³

Russian Armenia, Turkish Armenia, and Cilicia combined into an "independent Armenia from Sea to Sea" was the solution demanded by the American Committee for the Independence of Armenia.

It was against such a backdrop of Allied pronouncements that the Armenian delegation traveled toward Paris. Yet there loomed the disturbing wartime agreements of the Entente. Avetis Aharonian, chairman of the delegation, knew that those secret agreements had not been repudiated. On the contrary, Premier Briand had announced in the Chamber of Deputies on December 27, 1918, that they would be enforced if both the legislature and the Peace Conference sanctioned them,³⁴ and two days later Foreign Minister Pichon spoke of French rights in Armenia, Syria, Lebanon, and Palestine based on "historic contentions and recent contracts." [35] Thus, it remained for the Paris Peace Conference to determine whether the fate of the Armenians would be determined by "historic contentions and recent contracts" or according to the "supreme laws of Humanity and Justice."

Transliteration Key

Russian

The Library of Congress system of transliteration has been used, but without diacritical marks and ligatures. The transliteration of several proper names varies slightly from this system—thus *Kerensky*, not *Kerenskii*.

А а	a		Р р	r
Б б	b		С с	s
В в	v		Т т	t
Г г	g		У у	u
Д д	d		Ф ф	f
Е е	e		Х х	kh
Ё ё	e		Ц ц	ts
Ж ж	zh		Ч ч	ch
З з	z		Ш ш	sh
И и	i		Щ щ	shch
І і	i		Ъ ъ	''[1]
Й й	i		Ы ы	y
К к	k		Ь ь	'[1]
Л л	l		Ѣ ѣ	e
М м	m		Э э	e
Н н	n		Ю ю	iu
О о	o		Я я	ia
П п	p			

[1] Transliterated in titles only.

Armenian

The transliteration system is based on the phonetic values of Classical and Eastern Armenian. Diacritical marks have not been used. The transliteration of several proper names varies slightly from this system—thus *Kachaznuni,* not *Kadjaznuni,* and *Alexandropol,* not *Aleksandropol.*

Ա ա	a		Մ մ	m
Բ բ	b		Յ յ	h[1], y or —[2]
Գ գ	g		Ն ն	n
Դ դ	d		Շ շ	sh
Ե ե	e		Ո ո	vo[1] or o
Զ զ	z		Չ չ	ch
Է է	e		Պ պ	p
Ը ը	e		Ջ ջ	dj
Թ թ	t		Ռ ռ	r
Ժ ժ	zh		Ս ս	s
Ի ի	i		Վ վ	v
Լ լ	l		Տ տ	t
Խ խ	kh		Ր ր	r
Ծ ծ	ds		Ց ց	ts
Կ կ	k		Ւ ւ	v
Հ հ	h		Փ փ	p
Ձ ձ	dz		Ք ք	k
Ղ ղ	gh		Օ օ	o
Ճ ճ	j		Ֆ ֆ	f

DIPHTHONGS

Ու ու	—u, v[3]		Յու յու	—iu[4]
Ոյ ոյ	—ui, oy[3] or o[2]		Եա եա	—ia or ya[5]
Այ այ	—ai, ay[3] or a[2]		Յա յա	—ia[4] or ya[4,5]
Իւ իւ	—iu			

[1] In initial position only.
[2] The letter Յ is not transliterated in final position.
[3] When followed by a vowel.
[4] In Soviet Armenian orthography only.
[5] When preceded by a vowel.

Notes

Note: English titles given in brackets following Armenian titles are translations for the convenience of the reader. Authors' names are listed as they are found on title pages of works cited, thus accounting for variations.

Notes to Chapter I

[1] For questions relating to the origins of the Armenian people, consult the following works: Hakob Manandian, *Knnakan tesutiun hai zhoghovrdi patmutian* [A Critical History of the Armenian People], Vol. I (Erevan, 1944); Nicholas Adontz, *Histoire d'Arménie: Les origines du Xe siècle au VIe (av. J. C.)* (Paris, 1946); H. Zhamkochian, *Hayastane nakhnadarian-hamainakan hasarakutian ev strkatirutian shrdjanum* [Armenia during the Epoch of Prehistoric-Communal Society and Slave Ownership] (Erevan, 1961), Gr. Kapantsian, *Khaiasa—kolybel' armian: Etnogenez armian i ikh nachal'naia istoriia* (Erevan, 1947). According to the national epic, the Plateau was the homeland of the Armenians as early as the third millennium B.C.

[2] Levon Lisitzyan, "Physiographic Armenia," *Armenian Review,* VIII (Spring, 1955), 93-95.

[3] The Anti-Taurus Range to the west of the Euphrates is considered by some historians and geographers as the natural division between the Plateau and the adjacent Anatolian lowlands.

[4] T. Kh. Hakobian, *Urvagdser Hayastani patmakan ashkharhagrutian* [Outlines of Armenia's Historical Geography] (Erevan, 1960), pp. 16-17, 40-52; Lisitzyan, *op. cit.,* p. 96; H. Pasdermadjian, *Histoire de l'Arménie depuis les origines jusqu'au traité de Lausanne* (Paris, 1949), pp. 11, 18-19.

[5] The fifteen provinces as recorded by seventh-century historians were Upper Haik, Fourth Haik (Sophena), Aghdznik, Turuberan, Mokk, Gorjaik, Parskahaik, Vaspurakan, Siunik, Artsakh, Paitakaran, Utik, Gugark, Taik, and Airarat. For detailed studies of each province, consult Hakobian, *op. cit.,* pp. 120-257; and S. T. Eremian, *Hayastane est "Ashkharhatsuits"i* [Armenia according to the "Atlas"] (Erevan, 1963), pp. 7-120.

[6] Kévork-Mesrob, *L'Arménie au point de vue géographique, historique, statistique et cultural* (Constantinople, 1919), pp. 18-21; Artashes Abeghian, *Hayastan ev dratsi erkirner* [Armenia and Neighboring Countries] (Stuttgart, n.d.) [map].

[7] Arshak Alboyajian, *Patmakan Hayastani sahmannere* [The Boundaries of Historic Armenia] (Cairo, 1950), p. 3, cited hereafter as Alboyajian, *Sahmannere;* Armenian SSR, Akademiia Nauk, *Haikakan Sovetakan Sotsialistakan Respublikayi Atlas* [Atlas of the Armenian Soviet Socialist Republic] (Erevan-Moscow, 1961), p. 104.

[8] Consult Manandian, *op. cit.,* I, 114–303; Zhamkochian, *op. cit.,* pp. 186–250; René Grousset, *Histoire de l'Arménie des origines à 1071* (Paris, 1947), pp. 79–104.

[9] For a critical study of the Arsacid dynasty, consult Manandian, *op. cit.,* Vol. II, pt. 1 (1957); also consult A. Abrahamian, *Hayastane vagh feodalizmi shrdjanum* [Armenia during the Period of Early Feudalism] (Erevan, 1959).

[10] N. Adontz, *Patmakan usumnasirutiunner* [Historical Studies] (Paris, 1948), pp. 49–92; Leo [A. Babakhanian], *Hayots patmutiun* [History of the Armenians], II (Erevan, 1947), 520–637; Grousset, *op. cit.,* pp. 394–520.

[11] S. Poghosian, *Hayastane zargatsads feodalizmi shrdjanum, IX–XIII darer* [Armenia during the Period of Advanced Feudalism, 9th–13th Centuries] (Erevan, 1958), pp. 80–94; Grousset, *op. cit.,* pp. 553–630; J. Laurent, *Byzance et les Turcs seldjoucides dans l'Asie occidentale jusqu'en 1081* (Paris and Nancy, 1913), pp. 20–24, 43–44, 91–109.

[12] Ghevond Alishan, *Sisvan* (Venice, 1885); N. Iorga, *Brève histoire de la Petite Arménie: L'Arménie cilicienne* (Paris, 1930); Édouard Dulaurier "Étude sur l'organization politique, religieuse et administrative du Royaume de la Petite Arménie," *Journal Asiatique,* 5th series, XVII (April-May, 1861), 377–437, and XVIII (October-November, 1861), 289–357; Sirarpie Der Nersessian, "The Kingdom of Cilician Armenia," *A History of the Crusades,* ed. by Kenneth M. Setton, *et al.,* II (Philadelphia, [1962]), 630–659.

[13] For studies of the Armenian emigration, consult the following: A. G. Abrahamian, *Hamarot urvagids hai gaghtavaireri patmutian* [Concise Outline of the History of the Armenian Colonies] (Erevan, 1964); V. A. Mikayelian, *Ghrimi haikakan gaghuti patmutiun* [History of the Armenian Community of the Crimea] (Erevan, 1964); Arshak Alboyajian, *Patmutiun hai gaghtakanutian* [History of Armenian Emigration], Vol. II (Cairo, 1955).

[14] For recent studies of these changes, consult S. Poghosian, *Hayastane XIII–XVII darerum* [Armenia during the 13th–17th Centuries] (Erevan, 1960); L. H. Babayan, *Hayastani sotsial-tntesakan ev kaghakakan patmutiune XIII–XIV darerum* [The Socio-Economic and Political History of Armenia during the 13th–14th Centuries] (Erevan, 1964).

[15] A. Kh. Safrastian, comp., *Turkakan aghbiurnere Hayastani, hayeri, ev Andrkovkasi mius zhoghovurdneri masin* [Turkish Sources about Armenia, the Armenians, and the Other Peoples of Transcaucasia], I (Erevan, 1961), 210–212, a valuable work translating pertinent sections of sixteenth- through nineteenth-century Ottoman documents. For an English translation of the 1639 treaty, consult J. C. Hurewitz, *Diplomacy in the Near and Middle East: A Documentary Record,* I, *1535–1914* (Princeton, New York, Toronto, and London, [1956]), 21–23.

[16] H. A. Anasian, *XVII dari azatagrakan sharzhumnern Arevmtian Hayastanum* [The 17th Century Liberation Movements in Western Armenia] (Erevan, 1964), pp. 14–20. The author uses several sources to compile his version of the Ottoman administrative units. Consult also A. Kh. Safrastian and M. K. Zulalian, *Osmanian orenknere Arevmtian Hayastanum (XVI–XVII dd.), Kanunnamener* [Ottoman Laws in Western Armenia (16th–17th Centuries), *Kanunnames*] (Erevan, 1964), pp. 19–34, 45–48, 53–55, 73–76.

[17] For a discussion of these *khanate*s and their respective subdivisions, the *mahal*s, consult V. R. Grigorian, *Erevani khanutiune XVIII dari verdjum, 1780–1800* [The Khanate of Erevan at the End of the 18th Century, 1780–1800] (Erevan, 1958), pp. 33–48; and Alboyajian, *Sahmannere,* pp. 376–379, 385–386.

18 In the eighteenth century, Karabagh was established as a separate khanate, with its administrative center at Shushi. Consult Alboyajian, *Sahmannere,* pp. 382-384.
19 Grigorian, *op. cit.,* pp. 31-32; Hakobian *op. cit.,* pp. 348-357. During the eighteenth century, the district of Shuragial was taken from Georgia and added to the Erevan khanate. Much valuable information on the administrative history of Transcaucasia is compiled in *Akty sobrannye Kavkazskoiu Arkheograficheskoiu Kommissieiu* (the Archives of the Viceroy for the Caucasus) (Tiflis, 1866-1904), 12 vols.

Notes to Chapter II

1 The phrase is attributed to S. S. Uvarov, the influential Minister of Education during the reign of Nicholas I. For biographical sketches of Uvarov, consult *Bol'shaia Entsiklopediia,* XVIII (St. Petersburg, n.d.), 711-712; *Entsiklopedicheskii Slovar',* XXXIV (St. Petersburg, 1902), 419-420.
2 The following works include much material on this subject: G. A. Ezov, ed., *Snosheniia Petra Velikago s armianskim narodom* (St. Petersburg, 1898); Ashot Hovhannisian, *Drvagner hai azatagrakan mtki patmutian* [Episodes from the History of Armenian Liberation Thought], Vol. II (Erevan, 1959); Joseph Emin, *Life and Adventures of Emin Joseph Emin, 1726-1809: Written by Himself* (2d ed., Calcutta, 1918), 2 vols.; Leo [A. Babakhanian], *Hayots patmutiun* [History of the Armenians], III (Erevan, 1946), 512-821; Z. T. Grigorian, *Prisoedinenie Vostochnoi Armenii k Rossii v nachale XIX veka* (Moscow, 1959), cited hereafter as Grigorian, *Prisoedinenie.*
3 Boris Nolde, *La formation de l'Empire russe: Études, notes et documents,* II (Paris, 1953), 364-384; John F. Baddeley, *The Russian Conquest of the Caucasus* (New York and London, 1908), pp. 59-61; David Marshall Lang, *The Last Years of the Georgian Monarchy, 1658-1832* (New York, 1957), pp. 181-185, 242-245.
4 T. Iuzefovich, ed., *Dogovory Rossii s Vostokom: Politicheskie i torgovye* (St. Petersburg, 1869), p. 53; Baddeley, *op. cit.,* pp. 65-82; A. V. Fadeev, *Rossiia i Kavkaz pervoi treti XIX v.* (Moscow, 1960), pp. 100-169.
5 J. C. Hurewitz, *Diplomacy in the Near and Middle East: A Documentary Record,* II, *1914-1956* (Princeton, New York, Toronto, and London, [1956]), 84-86; Iuzefovich, *op. cit.,* pp. 208-210; Grigorian, *Prisoedinenie,* pp. 66-93; V. Parsamian, *Hayastane XIX dari aradjin kesin* [Armenia during the First Half of the 19th Century] (Erevan, 1960), pp. 18-30.
6 The role of the Armenian volunteers is the subject of a study by Z. T. Grigorian, *Rus ev hai zhoghovurdneri razmakan hamagordsaktsutiune XIX dari skzbin* [The Military Collaboration of the Armenian and Russian Peoples at the Beginning of the 19th Century] (Erevan, 1957). The most thorough work pertaining to the Russian wars in the Caucasus is that of V. Potto, *Kavkazskaia voina v otdel'nykh ocherkakh, epizodakh, legendakh i biografiiakh* (St. Petersburg and Tiflis, 1885-1889), 4 vols. in 16 parts.
7 *Polnoe sobranie zakonov Rossiiskoi imperii,* 2d ser., Vol. III (St. Petersburg, 1830), no. 1794; Iuzefovich, *op. cit.,* pp. 214-217; Hurewitz, *op. cit.,* II, 92-102; Fadeev, *op. cit.,* pp. 213-214.
8 This emigration was allowed by Article XV of the Treaty of Turkmanchai. Potto, *op. cit.,* Vol. III, pt. 4 (1887), p. 732, states that 8,249 Armenian families left North Persia within the stipulated time. Also consult Parsamian, *op. cit.,* pp. 57-62; and Iuzefovich, *op. cit.,* pp. 221-222.
9 Great Britain, Foreign Office, *British and Foreign State Papers, 1828-1829,* [XVI] (London, 1831), 647-657, cited hereafter as GB, *BFSP;* Edward Hertslet, *The Map of Europe by Treaty,* II (London, 1875), 813-823.
10 Leo [A. Babakhanian], *Hayots hartsi vaveragrere* [The Documents concerning the

Armenian Question] (Tiflis, 1915), pp. 40–41; Parsamian, *op. cit.,* pp. 78–81; Fadeev, *op. cit.,* pp. 277–279; Grigorian, *Prisoedinenie,* p. 160. Potto, *op. cit.,* Vol. IV, pt. 4 (1888), pp. 486–490, states that more than 14,000 families migrated from the regions of Erzerum, Kars, and Bayazit. Article XIII, which pertains to the exchange of populations, is found in Hertslet, *op. cit.,* II, 821–822; GB, *BFSP,* p. 653; and Iuzefovich, *op. cit.,* p. 79.

11 Of the 7,300 families from Erzerum, most settled in Akhaltsikh, whereas the majority of the emigrants from Kars and Bayazit moved into the districts of Erevan and Karabagh. Consult Potto, *op. cit.,* Vol. IV, pt. 4, p. 492; and A. N. Nersisian, *Arevmtahayeri tntesakan ev kaghakakan vijake ev nrants rusakan orientatsian XIX dari aradjin kesin* [The Economic and Political Situation of the Western Armenians and Their Russian Orientation in the First Half of the 19th Century] (Erevan, 1962), p. 164.

12 Statistics in the United States National Archives, *Record Group 256: Records of the American Commission to Negotiate Peace,* Class 867B.00, Document 10, give 107,200 as the population of Akhalkalak at the beginning of the twentieth century; 82,800—or 77.2 percent—of these were Armenians. (*Record Group 256* is cited hereafter as US Archives, *RG 256.*) These figures correspond closely to those given by A. Shakhatuni, *Administrativnyi peredel Zakavkazskago kraia* (Tiflis, 1918), p. 71, showing that, of the 108,500 inhabitants, 84,275—or 77.6 percent—were Armenians.

13 *Polnoe sobranie zakonov,* 2d ser., Vol. III, no. 1888; T. Kh. Hakobian, *Erevani patmutiune (1801–1879 tt.* [The History of Erevan (1801–1879)] (Erevan, 1959), pp. 364–365; Grigorian, *Prisoedinenie,* p. 141; Kavkazskaia Arkheograficheskaia Kommissiia, *Akty sobrannye Kavkazskoiu Arkheograficheskoiu Kommissieiu* (the Archives of the Viceroy for the Caucasus), VII (Tiflis, 1878), 487, cited hereafter as *AKAK.*

14 I. Shopen [Chopin], *Istoricheskii pamiatnik Armianskoi oblasti v epokhu ee prisoedineniia k Rossiiskoi imperii* (St. Petersburg, 1852), in Hakobian, *op. cit.,* p. 369; Parsamian, *op. cit.,* p. 95; *Entsiklopedicheskii Slovar',* XLI (1904), 14; *AKAK,* VIII (1881), 961–962.

15 Art. Abeghian, "Menk ev mer harevannere—Azgayin kaghakakanutian khndirner" [We and Our Neighbors—Problems of National Policy], *Hairenik Amsagir,* VI (December, 1927), 144.

16 *Ibid.,* pp. 144–145. Grigorian, *Prisoedinenie,* p. 161, states that, on the eve of its annexation to Russia, the territory that entered the *oblast* had only 25,151 Armenians, while in 1831 the number had risen to 82,377.

17 *Polnoe sobranie zakonov,* 2d ser., Vol. XV (1841), no. 13368; Hakobian, *op. cit.,* pp. 380–381.

18 Potto, *op. cit.,* Vol. III, pt. 4, pp. 736–746.

19 S. Esadze, *Istoricheskiia zapiski ob upravlenii Kavkazom,* I (Tiflis, 1907), 65, lists the several administrative variants in the Caucasus prior to 1840. Also consult Hakobian, *op. cit.,* pp. 371–372.

20 *Polnoe sobranie zakonov,* 2d ser., Vol. XV, nos. 13368 and 13413; Shakhatuni, *op. cit.,* p. 86; Hakobian, *op. cit.,* p. 381.

21 Shamil's saga is the subject of Lesley Blanch's *The Sabres of Paradise* (New York, 1960). Much additional information is included in Baddeley, *op. cit.,* pp. 361–482. For short biographical sketches of Shamil, consult *Entsiklopedicheskii Slovar',* XXXIX (St. Petersburg, 1903), 125–132; *Bol'shaia Entsiklopediia,* XX (St. Petersburg, 1909), 159; *Bol'shaia Sovetskaia Entsiklopediia,* XLVII (n.p., 1957), 506–508.

22 Mikhail Semenovich Vorontsov (1782–1856). Consult *Sovetskaia Istoricheskaia Entsiklopediia,* III (Moscow, 1963), 711; and *Entsiklopedicheskii Slovar',* VII (1892), 222–223.

23 Esadze, *op. cit.,* p. 86; Hakobian, *op. cit.,* p. 383; Shakhatuni, *op. cit.,* p. 87.

24 *AKAK,* X (1885), 875–876; *Obzor Erivanskoi gubernii za 1886 god,* p. 1, in Hakobian, *op. cit.,* p. 384; Grigorian, *Prisoedinenie,* p. 145. The Erevan *guberniia* was initially composed of the *uezds* of Ordubad, Nakhichevan, Erevan, Novo Bayazit, and Alexandropol.
25 Shakhatuni, *op. cit.,* p. 94.
26 Hakobian, *op. cit.,* p. 384; Shakhatuni, *op. cit.,* pp. 94, 98.
27 Shakhatuni, *op. cit.,* p. 99. Hakobian, *op. cit.,* p. 384, using as his source *Materialy dlia voennago obozreniia Erivanskoi gubernii,* Vol. I, pt. 1, pp. 15–16, gives 1874 as the date for the administrative reorganization of the province.
28 Hertslet, *op. cit.,* IV (1891), 2672–2692; Great Britain, Parliament, House of Commons, *Preliminary Treaty of Peace between Russia and Turkey, Signed at San Stefano 19th February/3rd March, 1878,* in Sessional Papers, 1878, LXXXIII (Accounts and Papers) c. 1973, Turkey No. 22 (1878). This series is cited hereafter as GB, Sess. (A and P).
29 GB, *Treaty between Great Britain, Germany, Austria, France, Italy, Russia and Turkey . . ., Signed at Berlin, July 13, 1878,* Sess., 1878, LXXXIII (A and P) c. 2108, Turkey No. 44 (1878).
30 H. Pasdermadjian, *Histoire de l'Arménie depuis les origines jusqu'au traité de Lausanne* (Paris, 1949), p. 344. Numerous reports of panic among the Christian population are included in GB, *Further Correspondence respecting the Affairs of Turkey,* Sess., 1878, LXXXI (A and P) c. 1905, Turkey No. 1 (1878).
31 Shakhatuni, *op. cit.,* p. 96.
32 B. Ishkhanian, *Narodnosti Kavkaza* (Petrograd, 1916), p. 35; Shakhatuni, *op. cit.,* pp. 72–73.
33 Abeghian, *op. cit.* (February, 1928), p. 100; Shakhatuni, *op. cit.,* p. 73.
34 US Archives, *RG 256,* 867.00/10; Abeghian, *op. cit.* (February, 1928), p. 99, and (March, 1928), p. 139.
35 US Archives, *RG 256,* 867.00/10 and 867.00/11; Ishkhanian, *op. cit.,* pp. 25–26, 34; Abeghian, *op. cit.* (February, 1928), p. 99.
36 US Archives, *RG 256,* 867.00/11.
37 Shakhatuni, *op. cit.,* pp. 61–68.
38 For the background, accomplishments, and limitations of the *zemstvo* movement, consult Boris Veselovskii, *Istoriia Zemstva za sorok let* (St. Petersburg, 1909–1911), 4 vols. [Vols. III and IV entitled *Istoriia Zemstva*]; George Fischer, *Russian Liberalism: From Gentry to Intelligentsia* (Cambridge, Mass., 1958).
39 G. M. Tumanov, *K vvedeniiu na Kavkaz zemskago samoupravleniia* (Tiflis, 1905), pp. 59–68; Shakhatuni, *op. cit.,* pp. 107–152.
40 For the Moslem viewpoint concerning the zemstvo in Transcaucasia, consult P. Kara-Murza, *Nakanune zemskoi reformy na Kavkaze* (Baku, 1919). Also consult D. Ananun, *Rusahayeri hasarakakan zargatsume,* III, *1901–1918* [The Social Development of the Russian Armenians: 1901–1918] (Venice, 1926), 441–442.
41 The period is described and analyzed in the study of Ashot Hovhannisian, *Nalbandiane ev nra zhamanake* [Nalbandian and His Times] (Erevan, 1955–1956), 2 vols. Also consult Mesrop Djanachian, *Patmutiun ardi hai grakanutian* [History of Modern Armenian Literature] (Venice, 1953); Garegin Zarbhanalian, *Patmutiun hayeren dprutian* [History of Armenian Literature], Vol. II (Venice, 1905); Armenian SSR, Akademiia Nauk, Institut Literatury, *Hai nor grakanutian patmutiun* [History of Modern Armenian Literature] (Erevan, 1962–1964), I, 5–94; II, 5–66; III, 5–95.
42 The "new hero" is best portrayed in the novels of Raffi (Hakob Melik-Hakobian, 1835–1888), still one of the most widely read Armenian authors. Discussion of several of the first societies dedicated to the liberation of Turkish Armenia is included in

V. A. Parsamian, *Hai azatagrakan sharzhumneri patmutiunits: Usumnasirutiun ev pastatghter* [From the History of the Armenian Liberation Movements: Study and Documents] (Erevan, 1958), pp. 111–243.

[43] The history of the formation and early activities of the Hnchakist party is found in its central committee's publication, *Hisnamiak Sots. Dem. Hnchakian Kusaktsutian, 1887–1937* [Fiftieth Anniversary of the Soc. (Social) Dem. (Democrat) Hnchakist Party, 1887–1937] (Providence, 1937); and in the articles of a founder, R. Khan-Azat, "Hai heghapokhakani husherits" [From the Memoirs of an Armenian Revolutionary], *Hairenik Amsagir*, V–VII (June, 1927–May, 1929). Also consult Louise Nalbandian, *The Armenian Revolutionary Movement* (Berkeley and Los Angeles, 1963), pp. 104–131.

[44] The organization was formed by the merger of several already existing societies. It was first named Hai Heghapokhakanneri Dashnaktsutiun ("Federation of Armenian Revolutionaries"), but soon acquired the attributes of a single party and was renamed Hai Heghapokhakan Dashnaktsutiun ("Armenian Revolutionary Federation"). The organization's first manifesto is reprinted in *Divan H. H. Dashnaktsutian* [Archives of the A. (Armenian) R. (Revolutionary) Federation], I (Boston, 1934), 88–89.

[45] *H. H. D. Vatsunamiak (1890–1950)* [Sixtieth Anniversary of the A. R. F.], ed. by S. Vratzian (Boston, 1950), pp. 97–109; *Divan*, I, 95–102.

[46] Opposed ideologically to the Marxists, these organizations believed that individuals could and did shape the course of history. Consequently, the elimination of evil influential persons was a service to humanity. On this premise, "terror," assassination, became a vital tactic of the related parties.

[47] Mikayel Varandian, *H. H. Dashnaktsutian patmutiun* [History of the A. (Armenian) R. (Revolutionary) Federation], I (Paris, 1932), 52–284. Written by one of the leading ideologues of Dashnaktsutiun, this work presents an important survey of the party's activities during the last decade of the nineteenth century and the beginning years of the twentieth. For biographical sketches of the leaders of Dashnaktsutiun and other revolutionary societies, consult *Hushapatum H. H. Dashnaktsutian, 1890–1950* [Historical Recollections of the A. (Armenian) R. (Revolutionary) Federation, 1890–1950], publication of the Bureau of the Armenian Revolutionary Federation (Boston, 1950), pp. 345–555; Gabriel Lazian, *Heghapokhakan demker (mtavorakanner ev haidukner* [Revolutionary Figures (Intellectuals and Guerrilla Fighters)] (Cairo, 1945), and his *Demker hai azatagrakan sharzhumen* [Figures of the Armenian Liberation Movement] (Cairo, 1949).

[48] Golitsyn was appointed Governor-General in December, 1896.

[49] The Catholicos was Mkrtich Khrimian, native of Van, delegate to the Congress of Berlin, former Patriarch of Constantinople.

[50] Ananun, *op. cit.*, pp. 25–27; Gabriel Lazian, *Hayastan ev Hai Date: Hai-ev-rus haraberutiunneru luisin tak* [Armenia and the Armenian Question: Under the Light of Armeno-Russian Relations] (Cairo, 1957), pp. 90–96, 121–123, cited hereafter as Lazian, *Hayastan;* Victor Bérard, *The Russian Empire and Czarism*, trans. by G. Fox Davies and G. O. Pope (London, 1905), pp. 201–204.

[51] Ananun, *op. cit.*, pp. 45–48, lists the leading tsarist officials who were assassinated between 1905–1907. Golitsyn was stabbed in October, 1903, by three Hnchakists. He was well enough to leave the Caucasus in mid-1904 and was officially relieved of his duties several months later.

[52] Mik. Hovhannisian [Varandian], *Dashnaktsutiun ev nra hakarakordnere* [Dashnaktsutiun and Its Opponents] (Tiflis, 1907), pp. 168–169; Ananun, *op. cit.*, pp. 128–129; H. H. Dashnaktsutiun, *Kaghvadsner Errord Endh. Zhoghovi atenagrutiunnere* [Excerpts from the Minutes of the Third Gen. (General) Congress] (Geneva, 1905).

In 1904, the party accepted the tactic of "self-defense" but a year later adopted the "Caucasian Project," which committed it to joining the general revolutionary movement against the Russian autocracy. For the decision to move from the defensive to the offensive, consult H. H. Dashnaktsutiun, *Nakhagids kovkasian gordsuneutian* [Preliminary Project of Caucasian Activity] (2d ed.; Geneva, 1906), p. 2; Varandian, *op. cit.*, I, 353–356; V. Navasardian, "H. H. D. gaghaparabanutiune" [The Ideology of the A. R. F.], *Hushapatum,* pp. 181–182.

53 Ds. P. Aghayan, *Revoliutsion sharzhumnere Hayastanum 1905–1907 tt.* [The Revolutionary Movements in Armenia, 1905-1907] (Erevan, 1955), pp. 74–77; St. Shahumian, *Erker* [Works], I (Erevan, 1955), 48–52, 290; G. Abov, *Dashnaktsutiunn antsialum ev aizhm* [Dashnaktsutiun in the Past and Present] (2d printing; Erevan, 1930), pp. 20–33, 46–48; G. M. Mneyan, *Stepan Shahumiani partiakan ev petakan gordsuneutiune (1900–1918)* [Stepan Shahumian's Party and Governmental Activity (1900–1918)] (Erevan, 1958), p. 56.

54 G. Harutunian, *Revoliutsion sharzhumnere Hayastanum 1905–1907 tt.* [The Revolutionary Movements in Armenia, 1905–1907] (Erevan, 1956), pp. 29, 31; Mneyan, *op. cit.*, p. 26; Georgii Sokolovskii, "Erevani kaghaki sotsial-demokratakan kazmakerputian patmutian hamarot aknark 1904–10 tt." [A Cursory View of the History of the Social-Democratic Organization of the City of Erevan, 1904–1910], *Hin bolshevikneri hishoghutiunner* [Memoirs of Veteran Bolsheviks] (Erevan, 1958), pp. 110–113.

55 Ananun, *op. cit.*, pp. 91–98; *Nakhagids-Dsragir Kovkasian Sotsial-Demokratiakan Banvorakan Kazmakerputiunneri* [Preliminary Project and Program of the Caucasian Social-Democratic Workers Organizations] (Geneva, 1903).

56 Harutunian, *op. cit.*, pp. 43–45; Mneyan, *op. cit.*, pp. 113–122; M. V. Arzumanian, *Bolshevikneri gordsuneutiune ev revoliutsion sharzhumnere Hayastanum 1907–1917 tvakannerin* [Bolshevik Activity and the Revolutionary Movements in Armenia, 1907–1917] (Erevan, 1959), pp. 203–212; Artashes Voskerchian, *Hai marksistakan knnadatutian himnadirnere, Stepan Shahumian, Suren Spandarian* [Stepan Shahumian and Suren Spandarian, Founders of Armenian Marxist Criticism] (Erevan, 1962), pp. 55–56.

57 Varandian, *op. cit.*, I, 352–353; Lazian, *Hayastan,* pp. 131–133; Fischer, *op. cit.*, pp. 168–170; Paul Miliukov, *Russia and Its Crisis* (New York, 1962), pp. 381–384; Michael T. Florinsky, *Russia: A History and an Interpretation* (New York, 1953), I, 1169–1170. The agreement of the opposition societies was published by Dashnaktsutiun in the brochure, *Heghapokhakan Dashn* [Revolutionary Alliance] (Geneva, 1905).

58 Soviet literature about the 1905 Revolution is voluminous. The most complete set of documents relating to the period was issued under the auspices of the Academy of Sciences of the USSR. The thirteen volumes edited by A. M. Pankratova and, later, A. L. Sidorov between 1955 and 1963 have various subtitles and inconsistent numbering but are listed under the general heading, *Revoliutsiia 1905–1907 g.g. v Rossii: Dokumenty i materialy.*

59 Soviet Armenian studies of the 1905 Revolution are quite repetitive and tend to exaggerate the role played by the Marxist societies, but because these publications include much archival material they are of significant value. In addition to the cited works of Mneyan, Shahumian, Aghayan, and Harutunian, consult Kh. A. Barsegian, *Istoriia armianskoi bol'shevistskoi periodicheskoi pechati, 1900–1920* (Erevan, 1958), pp. 73–122. Also consult the collection of articles published by the Armenian SSR Academy of Sciences, *Revoliutsion sharzhumnere Hayastanum rusakan aradjin revoliutsiayi tarinerin (hodvadsneri zhoghovadsu)* [The Revolutionary Movements in Armenia during the Years of the First Russian Revolution (Collection of Articles)] (Erevan, 1955); and by the University of Erevan, *Revoliutsion sharzhumnere Hayastanum, 1905–1907 (hodvadsneri zhoghovadsu)* [The Revolutionary Movements in Armenia, 1905–1907 (Collection of Articles)] (Erevan, 1955); As. Asatrian, *Hai*

grakanutiune ev rusakan aradjin revoliutsian [Armenian Literature and the First Russian Revolution] (Erevan, 1956).

60 Fortunately, some of the correspondence between Vorontsov-Dashkov and St. Petersburg has been published, providing an important insight into Russian imperial policy toward the peoples of the Caucasus. Included in Vorontsov-Dashkov's reports is much information concerning the confiscation of the Church properties, local nationality problems, Armeno-Tatar antagonism, and, from 1912–1914, the Viceroy's recommendations that Russia champion the "cause of the Turkish Armenians." Consult Vorontsov-Dashkov's *Vsepoddanneishaia zapiska po upravleniiu Kavkazskim kraem generala ad"iutanta grafa Vorontsova-Dashkova* (St. Petersburg, 1907), and his *Vsepoddanneishii otchet za vosem' let upravleniia Kavkazom* (St. Petersburg, 1913). Also consult "Pis'ma I. I. Vorontsova-Dashkova Nikolaiu Romanovu (1905–1915)," foreword by V. Semennikov, *Krasnyi Arkhiv*, XXVI (1928), 97–126.

61 Lazian, *Hayastan,* pp. 129–131; Ananun, *op. cit.,* pp. 359–361. In his *Vsepoddanneishaia zapiska,* pp. 8–10, Vorontsov-Dashkov pointed out the harmful effects of confiscation of the Armenian Church properties. He asserted that Dashnaktsutiun, which had been formed to free the Turkish Armenians, had, as a result of the imprudence of tsarist officials, spread into every village and city of Transcaucasia and was supported in its terroristic activity against Romanov functionaries by all Armenian classes.

62 Ananun, *op. cit.,* pp. 365–367.

63 For descriptions of the "Armeno-Tatar War" and the culpability of tsarist officials, consult Luigi Villari, *Fire and Sword in the Caucasus* (London, 1906); and Bérard, *op. cit.,* pp. 204–213. In his *Vsepoddanneishaia zapiska,* pp. 10–14, Vorontsov-Dashkov reviewed the problem and confirmed the charge that officials and military contingents were inactive or indifferent during the hostilities. For accounts of participants, consult A. Giulkhandanian, *Hai-tatarakan endharumnere* [The Armeno-Tatar Clashes] (Paris, 1933); and Aramayis, *Mi kani glukh hai-trkakan endharumnerits* [A Few Chapters from the Armeno-Turkish Clashes] (Tiflis, 1907), 2 pts.

64 Filip Makharadze, *Ocherki revoliutsionnogo dvizheniia v Zakavkaz'e* (Tiflis, 1927), pp. 300, 307, gives the number killed in Baku in February, 1905, as more than 1,000, most of whom were Armenian, while he contends that the total losses for 1905–1907 were more than 10,000 killed and 15,000 uprooted. E. Aknouni, *Political Persecutions: Armenian Prisoners of the Caucasus* (New York, 1911), p. 30, states that 128 Armenian and 158 Tatar villages were sacked and ruined. Ananun, *op. cit.,* p. 180, calculates that no fewer than 1,500 Armenians and 1,600 Tatars were killed, and that the Armenians sustained more than 75 percent of the property damage.

65 Varandian, *op. cit.,* I, 493–494; Ananun, *op. cit.,* p. 325.

66 H. H. Dashnaktsutiun, *Dsragir* [Program] (Geneva, [1908]), pp. 18–19; *Programma armianskoi revoliutsionnoi i sotsialisticheskoi partii Dashnaktsutiun* (Geneva, 1908).

67 Stolypin criticized Vorontsov-Dashkov for being too lenient with the revolutionaries. He became even more convinced of this after receiving police reports that Dashnaktsutiun had more than 100,000 members, operated schools and arsenals, and schemed to create an independent Armenia. Consult "Bor'ba s revoliutsionnym dvizheniem na Kavkaze v epokhu stolypinshchiny: Iz perepiski P. A. Stolypina s Gr. I. I. Vorontsovym-Dashkovym," introduction by S. Fuks, *Krasnyi Arkhiv,* XXXIV (1928), 200–202, and XXXV (1929), 144–150.

68 Aknouni, *op. cit.,* pp. 15–25, 35–39; Ananun, *op. cit.,* pp. 326–327; A. Khatisian, "Kaghakapeti me hishataknere" [The Memoirs of a Mayor], *Hairenik Amsagir,* X (June, 1932), 124–127; Varandian, *op. cit.,* II (Cairo, 1950), 116–132. The chief prosecutor, Legine, called more than 500 witnesses to the stand and compiled an incriminating report of more than 20,000 pages, entitled "The Affair of Dashnaktsutiun."

Many of the future officials of the Armenian Republic were among those tried. Vorontsov-Dashkov was firmly opposed to the trial and labeled it a parody. Consult his *Vsepoddanneishii otchet*, p. 7.

[69] The events of 1894–1896 are discussed in chapter iii.

Notes to Chapter III

[1] For discussions and documents relating to the nineteenth century Ottoman reform movement, consult the following: Roderic H. Davison, *Reform in the Ottoman Empire, 1856–1876* (Princeton, 1963); A. Schopoff, *Les réformes et la protection des Chrétiens en Turquie, 1673–1904* (Paris, 1904), pp. 17–24, 48–65; Bernard Lewis, *The Emergence of Modern Turkey* (London, 1961), pp. 73–126; Éd. Engelhardt, *La Turquie et le tanzimat: Ou, Histoire des réformes dans l'empire Ottoman depuis 1826 jusqu'à nos jours*, I (Paris, 1882), 35–146; Great Britain, Parliament, House of Commons, *Firman and Hatti Sherif by the Sultan relative to Privileges and Reforms in Turkey*, in Sessional Papers, 1856, LXI (Accounts and Papers) command 2040, Eastern Papers, pt. 17; and *Correspondence respecting Christian Privileges in Turkey*, command 2069, Eastern Papers, pt. 18. This series is cited hereafter as GB, Sess. (A and P).

[2] For the establishment and development of the Armenian Patriarchate of Constantinople, consult the study of Archbishop Maghakia Ormanian, *Azgapatum* [National History], Vol. II (Constantinople, 1914), and Vol. III (Jerusalem, 1927).

[3] In the publication of the Armenian Patriarchate of Constantinople, *Atenagrutiunk Azgayin Zhoghovo* [Minutes of the National Assembly], 1870–1914, hundreds of irregularities and excesses against the Armenians in the interior provinces are recorded. These documents have been utilized by A. O. Sarkissian in his monograph, *History of the Armenian Question to 1885* (Urbana, Ill., 1938). For British documents of the period, consult GB, *Reports by Her Majesty's Diplomatic and Consular Agents in Turkey respecting Conditions of the Christian Subjects of the Porte 1868–1875*, Sess., 1877, CXII (A and P) c. 1739, Turkey No. 16 (1877).

[4] Davison, *op. cit.*, pp. 358–403; Schopoff, *op. cit.*, pp. 191–210; Great Britain, Foreign Office, *British and Foreign State Papers, 1875–1876*, LXVII (London, 1883), 683–698, cited hereafter as GB, *BFSP*. Useful works relating to the reign of Abdul Hamid II include: Sir Edwin Pears, *Life of Abdul Hamid* (New York, 1917); Paul Fesch, *Constantinople aux derniers jours d'Abdul Hamid* (Paris, [1907]); Gilles Roy, *Abdul-Hamid, le sultan rouge* (Paris, 1936).

[5] Duke of Argyll [George Douglas Campbell, Eighth Duke], *Our Responsibilities for Turkey: Facts and Memories of Forty Years* (London, 1896), p. 74.

[6] Sarkissian, *op. cit.*, pp. 89–90; Leo [A. Babakhanian], *Hayots hartsi vaveragrere* [The Documents concerning the Armenian Question] (Tiflis, 1915), pp. 113–133, cited hereafter as Leo, *Vaveragrere*.

[7] GB, *Further Correspondence respecting the Affairs of Turkey*, Sess., 1878–1879, LXXIX (A and P) c. 2204, Turkey No. 53 (1879); *Correspondence respecting the Conditions of the Population in Asia Minor and Syria*, Sess., 1878–1879, LXXX (A and P) c. 2432, Turkey No. 10 (1879); *Correspondence respecting . . .*, Sess., 1880, LXXX (A and P) c. 2537, Turkey No. 4 (1880); *Further Correspondence . . .*, Sess., 1880, LXXXII (A and P) c. 2712, Turkey No. 23 (1880); Sarkissian, *op. cit.*, pp. 92–93.

[8] For texts and interpretations of the several notes, consult Sarkissian, *op. cit.*, pp. 92–113; Leo, *Vaveragrere*, pp. 173–187; Pears, *op. cit.*, pp. 220–225. From official British sources, the following are pertinent: *BFSP, 1877–1878*, LXIX, 1313–1347; *BFSP, 1880–1881*, LXXII, 1196–1207; *Despatch from Her Majesty's Ambassador at Constantinople forwarding a Copy of the Identic Note Addressed to the Porte on the 11th June 1880*, Sess., 1880, LXXXI (A and P) c. 2611, Turkey No. 9 (1880); *Correspondence respect-*

ing the Affairs of Turkey, Sess., 1880, LXXXI (A and P) c. 2574, Turkey No. 7 (1880); Turkey No. 23 (1880), nos. 154–155.

[9] GB, *Further Correspondence respecting the Conditions of the Populations of Asia Minor and Syria,* Sess., 1881, C (A and P) c. 2986, Turkey No. 6 (1881), nos. 147, 148, 160, 166.

[10] Victor Bérard, "La politique du Sultan," *La Revue de Paris,* 39th yr. (December 15, 1896), pp. 880–889; Maurice Leveyre, "Les massacres des Sasounkh," *La Revue de Paris,* 38th yr. (September 1, 1895), pp. 79–86; Ruben [Ter Minasian], *Hai heghapokhakani me hishataknere* [The Memoirs of an Armenian Revolutionary], III (Los Angeles, 1951), 103–116.

[11] The events of Sassun and details of the Commission of Inquiry's activities and findings are in the official publications of the major European nations. Consult, especially, France, Ministère des Affaires Étrangères, *Documents diplomatiques: Affaires arméniennes: Projets de réformes dans l'empire Ottoman, 1893–1897* (Paris, 1897), cited hereafter as France, *Af. Armén.;* GB, *Correspondence relating to the Asiatic Provinces of Turkey,* Sess., 1895, CIX (A and P), pt. 1, c. 7894, *Events at Sassoun and Commission of Inquiry at Moush,* pt. 2, c. 7894–1, *Commission of Inquiry at Moush: Procès-verbaux and Separate Dispositions,* Turkey No. 1 (1895); Germany, Auswärtiges Amt, *Die grosse Politik der europäischen Kabinette, 1871–1914,* IX (Berlin, 1924), nos. 2184–2189, cited hereafter as Germany, *Politik.*

[12] Schopoff, *op. cit.,* pp. 475–492; France, *Af. Armén.,* nos. 43, 57; Atom [H. Shahrikian], *Barenorogumneru hartse* [The Question of Reforms] (Constantinople, 1914), pp. 42–51; GB, *Correspondence respecting the Introduction of Reforms in the Armenian Provinces of Asiatic Turkey,* Sess., 1896, XCV (A and P) c. 7923, Turkey No. 1 (1896), no. 45.

[13] The entire two hundred and four documents of GB, Turkey No. 1 (1896), deal with the question of Armenian reforms. For the negotiations of May-October, 1895, consult nos. 46–198. A despatch reporting acceptance of the reform program by Abdul Hamid is in no. 199, and the text of the reform is enclosed in no. 204. Consult also Schopoff, *op. cit.,* pp. 493–526; and Germany, *Politik,* IX, nos. 2203–2212, X (1924), nos. 2394–2444.

[14] It is of interest that British consular reports of 1892–1895 relating to excesses committed against the Armenians were not published until 1896, after world opinion had been roused once more against the Turk. Hundreds of documents concerning the massacres of 1895–1896 and their antecedents are included in the British "Blue Books," the most pertinent of which are the following: *Correspondence relating to the Asiatic Provinces of Turkey, 1892–1893,* Sess., 1896, XCV (A and P) c. 8015, Turkey No. 3 (1896) [includes documents from December, 1891, to December, 1893]; *Correspondence relating . . ., 1894–1895,* Sess., 1896, XCVI (A and P) c. 8108, Turkey No. 6 (1896) [documents from December, 1893, to September, 1895]; *Correspondence relative to the Armenian Question and Reports from Her Majesty's Consular Officers in Asiatic Turkey,* Sess., 1896, XCV (A and P) c. 7927, Turkey No. 2 (1896) [events of September, 1895–February, 1896]; *Further Correspondence relating to the Asiatic Provinces of Turkey,* Sess., 1896, XCVI (A and P) c. 8273, Turkey No. 8 (1896) [to August, 1896]. Also consult France, *Af. Armén.,* nos. 116–235, and *(Supplément) 1895–1896* (Paris, 1897), nos. 1–178; Germany, *Politik,* X, nos. 2410, 2424, 2425, 2428–2430, 2433, 2435, 2437, 2444, 2447, 2448, 2450, 2456–2459, 2470, 2471, 2476; XII, pt. 1 (1924), nos. 2891–2893, 2909, 3071.

[15] Hundreds of books and articles, overwhelmingly Turcophobe, were written on the subject during the last years of the century. With final statistics not yet gathered, Johannes Lepsius presented the following count of losses:

People killed	88,243
Towns and villages plundered	2,493
Churches and monasteries plundered	645
Villages forcibly Islamized	646
Churches transformed into mosques	328
Victims left destitute	546,000

Taken from his *Armenia and Europe: An Indictment* (London, 1897), pp. 330–331. Also consult Pears, *op. cit.*, pp. 235–243; Georges Clemenceau, *Les massacres d'Arménie: Témoignages des victimes* (Paris, 1896); Augustus Warner Williams and M. S. Gabriel, *Bleeding Armenia: Its History and Horrors under the Curse of Islam* (Chicago, 1896); J. Rendel and Helen B. Harris, *Letters from the Scenes of the Recent Massacres in Armenia* (New York, Chicago, and Toronto, 1897); Félix Charmetant, *Martyrologe Arménien: Tableau officiel des massacres d'Arménie* (Paris, 1896); Roy, *op. cit.*, pp. 125–134, 157–175.

16 Concerning the failure of the reform plan and the European abandonment of the question, consult, in addition to GB, Turkey No. 2 and Turkey No. 8 (1896), *Further Correspondence respecting the Asiatic Provinces of Turkey and Events in Constantinople*, Sess., 1897, CI (A and P) c. 8305, Turkey No. 3 (1897); Germany, *Politik*, X, nos. 2445, 2448–2449, 2461, 2472–2479, XII, nos. 2883–2890, 2908, 2910, 3065, 3068, 3071–3104, 3111, 3113; France, Ministère des Affaires Étrangères, Commission de Publication des Documents Relatifs aux Origines de la Guerre de 1914, *Documents diplomatiques français (1871–1914)*, 1re série *(1871–1900)*, XIII (Paris, 1943). Most related correspondence is included between nos. 1 and 252; cited hereafter as France, *1871–1914*.

17 Lobanov's reserve in the projects for Armenian reforms was expressed many times during the negotiations of 1895 and in the diplomatic exchanges of the following year. He warned the British ambassador to Russia that the Armenian committees were directing an international plot to create an independent Armenian kingdom. For representative views of the Russian Foreign Ministry until the death of Lobanov-Rostovskii in the summer of 1896, consult GB, Turkey No. 1 (1896), nos. 14, 44, 65, 71, 76, 78, 83, 94, 110, 120, 136, 138–140, 174, 192; Germany, *Politik*, IX, nos. 2208, 2212, X, nos. 2436, 2443, 2445, 2455, XII, nos. 2883–2884, 2887. Also Bérard in *La Revue de Paris*, 40th yr. (January 15, 1897), pp. 441–446.

18 The decision was made at the party's Third General Congress, held at Sofia in 1904. Consult Mikayel Varandian, *H. H. Dashnaktsutian patmutiun* [History of the A. (Armenian) R. (Revolutionary) Federation], I (Paris, 1932), 436–445.

19 A. Aharonian, *Kristapor Mikayelian* (Boston, 1926), pp. 155–165; Varandian, *op. cit.*, I, 436–445; Gabriel Lazian, *Hayastan ev Hai Date: Hai-ev-rus haraberutiunneru luisin tak* [Armenia and the Armenian Question: Under the Light of Armeno-Russian Relations] (Cairo, 1957), pp. 140–151.

20 An excellent study of these men and their ideals is Ernest Edmondson Ramsaur's *The Young Turks: Prelude to the Revolution of 1908* (Princeton, 1957). Also consult Ernest Jackh, *The Rising Crescent: Turkey Yesterday, Today and Tomorrow* (New York and Toronto, [1944]), pp. 93–94; and Fesch, *op. cit.*, pp. 332–341.

21 Ramsaur, *op. cit.*, pp. 47–74; Fesch, *op. cit.*, pp. 342–375; B. Lewis, *op. cit.*, pp. 197–199; Leo [A. Babakhanian], *Tiurkahai heghapokhutian gaghaparabanutiune* [The Ideology of the Turkish Armenian Revolution], II (Paris, 1935), 44, cited hereafter as Leo, *Tiurkahai*.

22 John MacDonald, *Turkey and the Eastern Question* (London, [1913]), p. 55.

23 Ramsaur, *op. cit.*, pp. 122–128; Abraham Galanté, *Turcs et Juifs: Étude historique, politique* (Istanbul, 1932), pp. 38–39; Leo, *Tiurkahai*, p. 54. By 1907, joint Armeno-

Turkish demonstrations against the regime of Abdul Hamid II had occurred in Erzerum, Van, and Bitlis. At the 1907 Vienna Congress of Dashnaktsutiun, the party reaffirmed its program of active collaboration with other opposition societies as well as its dedication to the principle of federative government and an inviolable Ottoman Empire. Consult Varandian, *op. cit.*, II (Cairo, 1950), 5.

[24] For accounts of the "Young Turk" revolution, consult Alma Wittlin, *Abdul Hamid, the Shadow of God,* trans. by Norman Denny (London, [1940]), pp. 261–284; Ramsaur, *op. cit.*, pp. 130–137; Charles Roden Buxton, *Turkey in Revolution* (London, 1909), pp. 55–73; Great Britain, Foreign Office, *British Documents on the Origins of the War, 1898–1914,* ed. by G. P. Gooch and Harold Temperley, V (London, 1928), nos. 196–217, cited hereafter as GB, *Origins.*

[25] Varandian, *op. cit.*, II, 18–24, cites several such publications of Dashnaktsutiun. Also consult Leo, *Tiurkahai,* pp. 61–65.

[26] B. Lewis, *op. cit.*, pp. 211–212; A. Sarrou, *La Jeune-Turquie et la Révolution* (Paris and Nancy, 1912), pp. 77–90, 99–162; W. M. Ramsay, *The Revolution in Constantinople and Turkey* (London, 1909), pp. 94–134; Pears, *op. cit.*, pp. 311–322; GB, *Origins,* V, nos. 218–219.

[27] The "Adana Massacre" was followed by a governmental inquiry, the findings of which were presented to the Ottoman Parliament and subsequently published in Armenian and French. In the report of Hakob Papikian, member of Parliament and the Inquiry, the number of victims given is 21,000, of whom 19,479 were Armenian, 850 Syrian, 422 Chaldean, and 250 Greek. Consult his *Adanayi egherne* [The Atrocity of Adana] (Constantinople, 1919), p. 48. Details of the massacres and inquiry are found also in Hakob H. Terzian, *Kilikio aghete* [The Calamity of Cilicia] (Constantinople, 1912); M. Seropian, *Les Vêpres ciliciennes: Les responsabilités, faits et documents* (Alexandria, 1909). For invectives against the Turks by foreigners, consult Duckett Z. Ferriman, *The Young Turks and the Truth about the Holocaust at Adana in Asia Minor, during April, 1909* (London, 1913); Georges Brézol, *Les Turcs ont passé là: Recueil de documents . . . sur les massacres d'Adana en 1909* (Paris, 1911); René Pinon, *L'Europe et la Jeune Turquie* (Paris, 1911).

[28] B. Lewis, *op. cit.*, pp. 212–213. Dashnaktsutiun was criticized by many Armenians for continuing to collaborate with the "Young Turks" even after the affair of Adana. The Fifth General Congress of Dashnaktsutiun, meeting in 1909, pledged continued support to the Ittihad government and again rejected all moves toward separatism. A proclamation to that effect was issued. Consult Varandian, *op. cit.*, II, 19–21.

[29] B. Lewis, *op. cit.*, p. 214; Pinon, *op. cit.*, pp. 92–102. In 1911, Ittihad ve Terakki adopted a resolution to forbid the existence of separate, non-Turkish political societies. Consult Vahan Papazian, *Im hushere* [My Memoirs], II (Beirut, 1952), 151–152; and X., "Les courants politiques dans la Turquie contemporaine," *Revue du monde musulman,* XXI (September, 1912), 198. For the development of "Turkism," consult Uriel Heyd, *Foundations of Turkish Nationalism: The Life and Teachings of Ziya Gökalp* (London, 1950), especially pp. 71–81, 104–148. For the negative aspects of this movement and for the growth of Ittihadist intolerance, consult Victor Bérard, *La mort de Stamboul: Considérations sur le gouvernement des Jeunes-Turcs* (Paris, 1913), pp. 259–398; and A. J. Toynbee, *Turkey: A Past and a Future* (New York, 1917), pp. 15–40.

[30] Geoffrey Lewis, *Turkey* (London, [1960]), pp. 44–45; André Mandelstam, *Le sort de l'empire Ottoman* (Paris, 1917), pp. 35–42; Bérard, *La mort . . .*, pp. 342–351; Wilhelm Feldmann, *Kriegstage in Konstantinopel* (Strassburg, 1913), pp. 106–117, 167–171.

[31] Roderic H. Davison, "The Armenian Crisis (1912–1914)," *The American Historical Review,* LIII (April, 1948), 482–484, cited hereafter as Davison, *Crisis;* Mandelstam, *op. cit.*, pp. 30, 206–213.

³² The Sixth General Congress of Dashnaktsutiun, meeting in 1911, accused Ittihad ve Terakki of retreating from the goal of constitutional government, and adopted the tactic of collaborating with other societies still dedicated to that ideal.
³³ Davison, *Crisis,* pp. 486–487; Germany, *Politik,* XXXVIII (1926), nos. 15284, 15349, 15397, 15398.
³⁴ Serge Sazonov, *Fateful Years, 1909–1916* (New York, 1928), pp. 140–141.
³⁵ E. A. Adamov, ed., *Sbornik dogovorov Rossii s drugimi gosudarstvami 1856–1917* ([Moscow], 1952), pp. 386–389; GB, *BFSP, 1906–1907,* C (1911), 555–560; Davison, *Crisis,* p. 487.
³⁶ D. Ananun, *Rusahayeri hasarakakan zargatsume,* III, *1901–1918* [The Social Development of the Russian Armenians: 1901–1918] (Venice, 1926), 530–531.
³⁷ "Pis'ma I. I. Vorontsova-Dashkova Nikolaiu Romanovu, 1905–1915," *Krasnyi Arkhiv,* XXVI (1928), 118–120; A. Khondkarian, "Varantsov-Dashkovi namaknere Tsarin" [Vorontsov-Dashkov's Letters to the Tsar], *Hairenik Amsagir,* VII (May, 1929), 95–97; Lazian, *op. cit.,* pp. 150–153.
³⁸ Leo, *Tiurkahai,* pp. 86–87; Lazian, *op. cit.,* p. 155. Members of the nine-man bureau were Alexandre Khatisian, Samson Harutunian, Alexandre Kalantar, Hambardzum Arakelian, Avetis Poghosian, Hovhannes Tumanian, Nikol Aghbalian, Karapet Stepanian, and Arshak Djamalian.
³⁹ Lazian, *op. cit.,* p. 155; Leo, *Tiurkahai,* pp. 91–92.
⁴⁰ Nubar Pasha (1825–1899). For a brief biographical sketch, consult *Encyclopaedia of Islam,* III (Leiden, 1936), 946–948.
⁴¹ Ananun, *op. cit.,* pp. 523–525; Leo, *Tiurkahai,* p. 88.
⁴² Lazian, *op. cit.,* pp. 155–157; Leo, *Tiurkahai,* pp. 90–91, 93.
⁴³ Papazian, *op. cit.,* pp. 543–583; Lazian, *op. cit.,* pp. 160–162.
⁴⁴ Davison, *Crisis,* pp. 491–492, 495–496; Mandelstam, *op. cit.,* pp. 214–216, 225–234; Papazian, *op. cit.,* pp. 241–253; GB, *Origins,* X, pt. 1 (1936), nos. 486, 493, 498, 505, 507, 521, 558, 560; France, *1871–1914,* 3ᵉ série (*1911–1914*), VII (1934), nos. 30, 45, 76, 86, 102; Germany, *Politik,* XXXVIII, nos. 15283, 15299, 15312, 15317, 15321–15322, 15326, 15331, 15345; Russia, Ministerstvo Inostrannykh Del, *Sbornik diplomaticheskikh dokumentov: Reformy v Armenii, 26 noiabria 1912 goda—10 maia 1914 goda* (Petrograd, 1915), nos. 42–43, cited hereafter as Russia, *Reformy.*
⁴⁵ Mandelstam, *op. cit.,* pp. 218–222; Russia, *Reformy,* nos. 48, 50, 52, 57; France, *1871–1914,* 3ᵉ série, VII, nos. 176, 185, 331; Germany, *Politik,* XXXVIII, nos. 15337, 15344, 15347.
⁴⁶ Russia, *Reformy,* nos. 15, 46, 53, 54; France, *1871–1914,* 3ᵉ série, VII, nos. 229, 232, 270, 289, 298; GB, *Origins,* X, pt. 1, nos. 533–535, 538–540, 543, 573–574, 579–587, 589; Germany, *Politik,* XXXVIII, nos. 15318, 15338, 15341, 15346, 15354, 15357, 15363, 15401; Papazian, *op. cit.,* pp. 254–258.
⁴⁷ Details of these negotiations are found in the following sources: Mandelstam, *op. cit.,* pp. 234–245; Davison, *Crisis,* pp. 498–504; France, *1871–1914,* 3ᵉ série, VII, nos. 105, 112, 131, 140, 171, 187, 191, 227; VIII, nos. 31, 99, 118, 124, 135, 144, 171, 176, 191, 208, 213, 240, 296, 385, 393, 473, 514, 674, 688; IX (1936), nos. 25, 56, 78, 91, 96, 107, 108, 156, 202, 225, 333; GB, *Origins,* X, pt. 1, nos. 487–488, 499, 510–511, 515–516, 518, 532, 537, 546, 548, 550, 553, 555, 560, 561–563, 571, 579–583; Germany, *Politik,* XXXVIII, nearly all documents from no. 15333 to no. 15423; Russia, *Reformy,* nearly all documents from no. 55 to no. 145.
⁴⁸ B. Lewis, *op. cit.,* pp. 381–382; Engelhardt, *op. cit.,* pp. 193–198; Schopoff, *op. cit.,* pp. 114–130.
⁴⁹ The Armenian Delegation to the Paris Peace Conference presented this information in 1919. The voluminous archives of that delegation include, in addition to materials pertaining to the Peace Conference, thousands of documents and copies of documents

relating to the foreign and domestic policy of the Republic of Armenia, 1918–1920. In recent years the archives of the delegation have been integrated into those of Dashnaktsutiun, located in Boston, Massachusetts. As this is the largest single collection of the Republic's official papers, it will be cited hereafter as Rep. of Arm. Archives. The delegation's memorandum concerning the sixteenth-century geographers is in File 118/11, *H. H. Pat. 1920, Hashtutian Konferens* [Rep. of Arm. Del. 1920, Peace Conference].

[50] Joseph von Hammer, *Geschichte des osmanischen Reiches*, IV (Pest, 1829), 237–238, states that at the end of the sixteenth century, the Empire was divided into forty provinces, among which were Sivas, Van, Childer, Kars, Erzerum, and Diarbekir. Similar administrative divisions are described by Paul Rycaut, *Histoire de l'état présent de l'Empire Ottoman*, trans. by Briot (2d ed.; Paris, 1670), pp. 165–171.

[51] Rep. of Arm. Archives, File 118/11; Z. Khanzadian, *Rapport sur l'unité géographique de l'Arménie: Atlas historique* (Paris, 1920), p. 28 and map 21.

[52] [Armenian Delegation], *Réponse au mémoire de la Sublime-Porte en date du 12 février 1919* (Constantinople, 1919), p. 15, cited hereafter as *Réponse au mémoire;* Rep. of Arm. Archives, File 118/11; Khanzadian, *op. cit.*, pp. 31–32.

[53] Schopoff, *op. cit.*, p. 476.

[54] Rep. of Arm. Archives, File 104a/3a, *H. H. Patvirakutiun, 1919* [Rep. of Arm. Delegation, 1919]; *Réponse au mémoire*, p. 16.

[55] Sarkissian, *op. cit.*, p. 30.

[56] [J. H.] A. Ubicini, *Lettres sur la Turquie: Ou, Tableau statistique religieux, politique, administratif, militaire, commercial, etc., de l'Empire ottoman, depuis le khatti-cherif de Gulkhanè, (1839)* (2d ed., Paris, 1853–1854), I, 22, and II, 294–296.

[57] *Réponse au mémoire*, Annex C, p. 43.

[58] *Ibid.*, Annex D, pp. 44–45; Kévork-Mesrob, *L'Arménie au point de vue géographique, historique, statistique et cultural* (Constantinople, 1919), p. 72.

[59] *Réponse au mémoire*, Annex E, p. 46; [Armenian Delegation], *The Armenian Question before the Peace Conference* ([Paris, 1919]), Schedule No. 1; Rep. of Arm. Archives, File 107/6, *H. H. Patvirakutiun, 1919* [Rep. of Arm. Delegation, 1919].

[60] On the eve of World War I, the Armenian world population was estimated to be 4,500,000. The figure was obtained by adding the 1,800,000 Armenians of the Caucasus and the 825,000 abroad to the 2,000,000 assertedly within the Ottoman Empire. Consult Rep. of Arm. Archives, File 104a/3a; and Kévork-Mesrob, *op. cit.*, p. 77.

[61] [Turkey], *Memorandum of the Sublime Porte Communicated to the American, British, French, and Italian High Commissioners on the 12th February 1919* (Constantinople, 1919), p. 7. Also United States, The National Archives, Record Group 256: *Records of the American Commission to Negotiate Peace*, Class 867.00, Document 18. *Record Group 256* is cited hereafter as US Archives, *RG 256*.

[62] Statistics used by the American delegation to the Paris Peace Conference in 1919 show that prior to the World War there were, at the very least, 1,600,000 Armenians in the Ottoman Empire. Consult US Archives, *RG 256*, 867.00/31.

[63] Vital Cuinet, *La Turquie d'Asie* (Paris, 1890–1895), 4 vols. Chapters on the *vilayets* of Trebizond, Erzerum, and Sivas are in Vol. I, published in 1890, while those relating to the vilayets of Kharput, Diarbekir, Bitlis, and Van are in Vol. II, published in 1891.

[64] *Réponse au mémoire*, pp. 17–20, 40–43; Kévork-Mesrob, *op. cit.*, pp. 56–59. Armenian sources often quote Cuinet, *op. cit.*, I, p. iii: "... et si nous insistons sur ce mot *statistiques*, c'est pour bien préciser que cette science a été jusqu'ici totalement négligée, soit parce que les authorités administratives n'en ressentent pas l'utilité, soit plutôt parce que si elles possèdent quelques données relatives au dénombrement de la population, aux productions et aux besoins du pays par quantité et valeurs, elles se font un devoir de refuser systématiquement toute communication de cette nature."

⁶⁵ For reports and discussions pertinent to the final agreement, consult the following: Germany, *Politik*, XXXVIII, no. 15425; Russia, *Reformy*, nos. 122, 146–149; GB, *Origins*, X, pt. 1, nos. 568, 590–591; France, *1871–1914*, 3ᵉ série, IX, nos. 240, 362; Leo, *Vaveragrere*, pp. 333–340; Mandelstam, *op. cit.*, pp. 236–238.

⁶⁶ Lazian, *op. cit.*, pp. 166–168.

⁶⁷ For negotiations leading up to the appointment of Hoff and Westenenk, consult Russia, *Reformy*, nos. 150–157, 159; Germany, *Politik*, XXXVIII, nos. 15426–15434; GB, *Origins*, X, pt. 1, nos. 592–595; France, *1871–1914*, 3ᵉ série, IX, no. 156. Also consult Papazian, *op. cit.*, pp. 289–292; and Davison, *Crisis*, p. 504.

⁶⁸ Leo, *Vaveragrere*, pp. 342–357.

Notes to Chapter IV

¹ Diplomatic exchanges leading to the agreement are included in Ernest Jackh's *The Rising Crescent: Turkey Yesterday, Today and Tomorrow* (New York and Toronto, [1944]), pp. 10–21. Also consult Kurt Ziemke, *Die neue Türkei: Politische Entwicklung, 1914–1929* (Stuttgart, 1930), pp. 21–22; and Carl Mühlmann, *Das deutsch-türkische Waffenbündnis im Weltkrieg* (Leipzig, [1940]), pp. 15–16.

² This provision was not included in the final draft but had been verbally accepted. On August 6, Ambassador von Wangenheim agreed that Germany would support Turkey in its quest for the return of Kars, Ardahan, and Batum. Consult Bernadotte E. Schmitt, *The Coming of the War, 1914* (New York and London, 1930), II, 437; and Harry N. Howard, *The Partition of Turkey: A Diplomatic History, 1913–1923* (Norman, Okla., 1931), p. 87.

³ Mühlmann, *op. cit.*, p. 23; Howard, *op. cit.*, p. 110.

⁴ M. Larcher, *La guerre turque dans la guerre mondiale* (Paris, 1926), p. 43; Howard, *op. cit.*, pp. 110–111; Iu. N. Danilov, *Rossiia v mirovoi voine 1914–1915 g.g.* (Berlin, 1924), p. 267.

⁵ Edward Reginald Vere-Hodge, *Turkish Foreign Policy, 1914–1948* (Geneva, 1950), p. 13; Howard, *op. cit.*, p. 113.

⁶ Gotthard Jäschke, "Der Turanismus der Jungtürken: Zur osmanischen Aussenpolitik im Weltkriege," *Die Welt des Islams*, XXIII (bk. 1–2, 1941), 12.

⁷ E. K. Sargsian, *Ekspansionistskaia politika Osmanskoi imperii v Zakavkaz'e nakanune i v gody pervoi mirovoi voiny* (Erevan, 1962), p. 181; Felix Guse, *Die Kaukasusfront im Weltkrieg bis zum Frieden von Brest* (Leipzig, [1940]), pp. 14–15, 27. Larcher, *op. cit.*, p. 73, estimates the force of the Third Army at the end of 1914 to have been 150,000.

⁸ Leo [A. Babakhanian] *Tiurkahai heghapokhutian gaghaparabanutiune* [The Ideology of the Turkish Armenian Revolution], II (Paris, 1935), 76–77; G. Sassuni, *Tajkahayastane rusakan tirapetutian tak (1914–1918)* [Turkish Armenia under Russian Domination (1914–1918)] (Boston, 1927), pp. 20–24. For Turkish interpretations and documents relating to the conference, consult *Aspirations et agissements révolutionnaires des comités arméniens avant et après la proclamation de la constitution ottomane* (Constantinople, 1917), pp. 199–203; Esat Uras, *Tarihte Ermeniler ve Ermeni Meselesi* [The Armenians in History and the Armenian Question] (Ankara, 1950), pp. 589–590; Yusuf Hikmet Bayur, *Türk Inkılâbı Tarihi*, III, *1914–1918 Genel Savaşı*, pt. 3, *1915–1917 vuruşmaları ve bunların siyasal tepkileri* [History of the Turkish Revolution: The 1914–1918 World War: The Battles of 1915–1917 and Their Political Effects] (Ankara, 1957), pp. 11–12.

⁹ Decisions of the meeting at Erzerum and negotiations with the Ittihad leaders are described in considerable detail by V. Minakhorian, *1915 tvakane* [The Year 1915] (Venice, 1949), pp. 66–71. Consult also Johannes Lepsius, *Der Todesgang des Ar-*

menischen Volkes (Potsdam, 1930), pp. 178–179, cited hereafter as Lepsius, *Todesgang;* M. Philips Price, *War and Revolution in Asiatic Russia* (New York, [1918]), pp. 243–244; René Pinon, *La suppression des Arméniens: Méthode allemande—travail turc* (7th ed.; Paris, 1916), pp. 24–25, quoting *La Gazette de Lausanne* of February 16, 1916; Leo, *op. cit.,* pp. 77–78.

10 The noted German scholar of modern Turkish history, Gotthard Jäschke, *op. cit.,* p. 14, believes that an unconditional positive response from the leaders at Erzerum could have altered the tragic fate of the Armenians of the Ottoman Empire. Turkish publications during the World War referred to Armenian decisions at Erzerum as proof of disloyalty.

11 Lepsius, *Todesgang,* p. 160; Leo, *op. cit.,* p. 139.

12 Lepsius, *Todesgang,* pp. 160, 183–184; Leo, *op. cit.,* pp. 118–119.

13 Gr. Tchalkhouchian, *Le livre rouge* (Paris, 1919), pp. 11–12; Edvard Choburian, *Meds paterazme ev hai zhoghovurde* [The Great War and the Armenian People] (Constantinople, 1920), pp. 5–6; A. Khatisian, "Kaghakapeti me hishataknere" [The Memoirs of a Mayor], *Hairenik Amsagir,* X (September, 1932), 123–124. Gabriel Lazian, *Hayastan ev Hai Date (Vaveragrer)* [Armenia and the Armenian Question (Documents)] (Cairo, 1946), pp. 194–196, cited hereafter as Lazian, *Vaveragrer.*

14 Gabriel Lazian, *Hayastan ev Hai Date: Hai-ev-rus haraberutiunneru luisin tak* [Armenia and the Armenian Question: Under the Light of Armeno-Russian Relations] (Cairo, 1957), p. 174, cited hereafter as Lazian, *Hayastan.*

15 Leo, *op. cit.,* pp. 113–116; Lazian, *Hayastan,* pp. 170–173.

16 D. Ananun, *Rusahayeri hasarakakan zargatsume,* III, *1901–1918* [The Social Development of the Russian Armenians: 1901–1918] (Venice, 1926), 543; Khatisian, *op. cit.* (October, 1932), p. 156.

17 *Zapiska ob Armianskom voprose i Armianskikh druzhinakh,* quoted in Ananun, *op. cit.,* pp. 543–544, 549; Khatisian, *op. cit.* (October, 1932), pp. 156–157; S. Vratzian, *Kianki ughinerov: Depker, demker, aprumner* [Along Life's Ways: Episodes, Figures, Experiences], III (Beirut, 1963), 27–28, cited hereafter as Vratzian, *Ughinerov.*

18 Leo, *op. cit.,* p. 120; Vratzian, *Ughinerov,* III, 21, 28. Others opposed to the volunteer movement included Sahak Torosian, future representative of the Armenian Republic to South Russia.

19 Ananun, *op. cit.,* pp. 549–550; Vratzian, *Ughinerov,* III, 31–34; Lazian, *Vaveragrer,* pp. 186–187; Choburian, *op. cit.,* p. 20.

20 The most comprehensive account of the volunteer activities is the study of General G. Korganoff, *La participation des Arméniens à la guerre mondiale sur le front du Caucase, 1914–1918* (Paris, 1927).

21 Archives of the Republic of Armenia Delegation to the Paris Peace Conference [now integrated into the archives of Dashnaktsutiun, Boston, Massachusetts], File 1/1, *Hayastani Hanrapetutiun, 1918 t.* [Republic of Armenia, 1918], cited hereafter as Rep. of Arm. Archives; Tchalkhouchian, *op. cit.,* p. 26; Vratzian, *Ughinerov,* III, 33–37; Khatisian, *op. cit.* (October, 1932), p. 157. The commanders were known to all by a single given or assumed name. Their full names were Andranik Ozanian, Drastamat Kanayan (Dro), Hamazasp Srvandztian, and Arshak Gafavian (Keri).

22 The figure quoted by many Armenian sources is 200,000. H. Pasdermadjian, *Histoire de l'Arménie depuis les origines jusqu'au traité de Lausanne* (Paris, 1949), p. 454, states that 120,000 were recruited in 1914 and 60,000 more during the remaining years of the war. Using the Georgian SSR Central State Historical Archives, Fund 2(g), work 3595, pp. 25–28, A. N. Mnatsakanian states that there were, in all, 120,000 Armenian regulars and 10,000 volunteers in the Tsarist Army. Consult his *V. I. Lenine ev hai zhoghovrdi azatagrakan paikare* [V. I. Lenin and the Armenian People's Struggle for Freedom] (Erevan, 1963), pp. 214–216. According to statistics in File 1/1, Rep.

of Arm. Archives, 13 percent of all Russian Armenians, or 180,000, were participants in the war.
[23] Khatisian, *op. cit.*, XI (November, 1932), 135–137; Leo, *op. cit.*, p. 125; Vratzian, *Ughinerov*, III, 38–40.
[24] *Horizon* (Tiflis), November 30, 1914, quoted in *Hairenik Taregirk* [Hairenik Yearbook], V (Boston, 1947), 126.
[25] Tchalkhouchian, *op. cit.*, pp. 14–15; Leo, *op. cit.*, pp. 125–126; Lazian, *Vaveragrer*, pp. 197–198.
[26] Tchalkhouchian, *op. cit.*, p. 15.
[27] N. Korsun, *Sarykamyshskaia operatsiia na Kavkazskom fronte mirovoi voiny v 1914–1915 godu* (Moscow, 1937), pp. 19–20, 56; Guse, *op. cit.*, pp. 35, 37; Mühlmann, *op. cit.*, p. 64; A. M. Poghosian, *Sotsial-tntesakan haraberutiunnere Karsi marzum, 1878–1920* [The Social-Economic Relations in the Province of Kars, 1878–1920] (Erevan, 1961), pp. 221–222; W. E. D. Allen and Paul Muratoff, *Caucasian Battlefields: A History of the Wars on the Turco-Caucasian Border, 1828–1921* (Cambridge, 1953), pp. 251–253.
[28] E. V. Maslovskii, *Mirovaia voina na Kavkazskom fronte, 1914–1917 g.* (Paris, [1933]), p. 31; Allen and Muratoff, *op. cit.*, pp. 240–241; Korsun, *op. cit.*, p. 25; Danilov, *op. cit.*, p. 268.
[29] Larcher, *op. cit.*, pp. 385–387; Guse, *op. cit.*, pp. 39–41; Allen and Muratoff, *op. cit.*, pp. 256–269; Korsun, *op. cit.*, pp. 32–62; Poghosian, *op. cit.*, pp. 222–226; Maslovskii, *op. cit.*, pp. 113–114.
[30] Allen and Muratoff, *op. cit.*, pp. 270–272; Korsun, *op. cit.*, pp. 78–93.
[31] Guse, *op. cit.*, pp. 46, 52; Korsun, *op. cit.*, p. 81; Allen and Muratoff, *op. cit.*, p. 258.
[32] Sargsian, *op. cit.*, p. 195; Allen and Muratoff, *op. cit.*, pp. 270–276; Maslovskii, *op. cit.*, pp. 123–126.
[33] Allen and Muratoff, *op. cit.*, pp. 276–277.
[34] Larcher, *op. cit.*, p. 389; Sargsian, *op. cit.*, pp. 196–197; Poghosian, *op. cit.*, pp. 226–227.
[35] [Otto] Liman von Sanders, *Five Years in Turkey* (Annapolis, 1928), p. 40.
[36] Joseph Pomiankowski, *Der Zusammenbruch des Ottomanischen Reiches: Erinnerungen an die Türkei aus der Zeit des Weltkrieges* (Leipzig, 1928), pp. 103–104. Allen and Muratoff, *op. cit.*, pp. 283–284, estimate that Enver lost 75,000 of his original 95,000 men. Almost all survivors belonged to the XI Corps. In the course of the Sarikamish operation, the Russians suffered 16,000 killed or wounded, and nearly 12,000 frostbitten.
[37] Korganoff, *op. cit.*, p. 20.
[38] Choburian, *op. cit.*, pp. 28–30; Tchalkhouchian, *op. cit.*, pp. 30–31; Korganoff, *op. cit.*, pp. 16, 19–20. Copies of numerous citations are in the Rep. of Arm. Archives, File 1/1.
[39] Tchalkhouchian, *op. cit.*, p. 29; Korganoff, *op. cit.*, pp. 20–21; S. Vratzian, *Hayastani Hanrapetutiun* [Republic of Armenia] (2d ed.; Beirut, 1958), p. 10, cited hereafter as Vratzian, *Hanrapetutiun*.
[40] Choburian, *op. cit.*, pp. 26–29; Ananun, *op. cit.*, p. 552. The unit was first commanded by Djanpolatian and later by Grigor Avsharian.
[41] Ananun, *op. cit.*, pp. 587–588; Sassuni, *op. cit.*, pp. 45–47; Khatisian, *op. cit.* (November, 1932), p. 139.
[42] Korsun, *op. cit.*, p. 78; Khatisian, *op. cit.* (November, 1932), p. 137.
[43] Vratzian, *Ughinerov*, III, 47–49. The Georgian Social Democrats had organized in 1892. Adhering overwhelmingly to the Menshevik faction of the Marxist movement, these Social Democrats monopolized Georgian politics.
[44] Guse, *op. cit.*, p. 74; Jäschke, *op. cit.*, pp. 13–14; Liman von Sanders, *op. cit.*, p. 130; P. G. La Chesnais, *Les peuples de la Transcaucasie pendant la guerre et devant la*

paix (Paris, 1921), pp. 32–36; Pomiankowski, *op. cit.*, p. 225. For a romantic saga of a Georgian collaborator of the Central Powers, consult H. C. Armstrong, *Unending Battle* (New York and London, 1934).

[45] Jäschke, *op. cit.*, p. 16; Guse, *op. cit.*, p. 73.

[46] Pomiankowski, *op. cit.*, pp. 146–147; Guse, *op. cit.*, pp. 61–62. The role of the Armenian volunteers in this operation is described in considerable detail by Sebouh [Arshak Nersesian], *Edjer im husheren* [Pages from My Memoirs], I (Boston, 1925), 188–253.

[47] That the massacres and deportations were premeditated and thoroughly planned has been verified by numerous documents as well as by testimony of Ottoman officials. Aram Andonian has compiled pertinent governmental communiqués and documents in the following three works: *The Memoirs of Naim Bey: Turkish Official Documents Relating to the Deportations and Massacres of Armenians* (London, 1920); *Meds vojire: Haikakan verdjin kotoradsnere ev Talaat Pasha: Pashtonakan heragirner, bnagirneru storagrutiamb* [The Great Crime: The Recent Armenian Massacres and Talaat Pasha: Official Telegrams, with Signed Originals] (Boston, 1921), pp. 19–238; *Documents officiels concernant les massacres arméniens* (Paris, 1920). Among the most revealing works is that of a former Ittihadist, Mevlan Zade Rifat, who in his *Türkiye inkilabının iç yüzü* [The Inner Aspects of the Turkish Revolution] (Aleppo, 1929), relates the discussions and decisions of the Ittihad Central Committee about the complete annihilation of the Armenian people. Consult especially pp. 84–93, and, in the Armenian translation (Beirut, 1938), pp. 159–166.

[48] Altemur Kilic, *Turkey and the World* (Washington, [1959]), pp. 18, 22.

[49] Talaat, "Posthumous Memoirs of Talaat Pasha," *Current History*, XV (November, 1921), 294–295.

[50] *Aspirations et agissements révolutionnaires des comités arméniens avant et après la proclamation de la constitution ottomane* (Constantinople, 1917); the same in Turkish, *Ermeni komitelerinin âmâl ve harekâtı ihtilâliyesi ilanı meşrutiyetten evvel ve sonra* (Istanbul, 1333 [1916]); *Vérité sur le mouvement révolutionnaire arménien et les mesures gouvernementales* (Constantinople, 1916); *Hai heghapokhakan kusaktsutiunnere ev Osm. karavarutiune* [The Armenian Revolutionary Parties and the Ottoman Government] (Constantinople, 1916).

[51] April 24, 1915, is accepted as the inaugural date of the Armenian deportations, although massacres, deportations, and forced conversions to Islam had begun several months earlier. For a résumé of these cases prior to the "Revolt of Van" on April 20 and before the mass arrest of the leaders of Constantinople, consult On. Mkhitarian, *Vani herosamarte* [The Heroic Battle of Van] (Sofia, 1930), pp. 14–25; and Johannes Lepsius, *Deutschland und Armenien, 1914–1918: Sammlung diplomatischer Aktenstücke* (Potsdam, 1919), pp. xxxiv–xxxxv, cited hereafter as Lepsius, *Deutschland*.

[52] Bayur, *op. cit.*, pp. 37–38.

[53] *Ibid.*, pp. 40–42.

[54] *Ibid.*, p. 39.

[55] *Ibid.*, p. 40; *Aspirations et agissements*, p. 316.

[56] Uras, *op. cit.*, p. 618; *Aspirations et agissements*, pp. 317–318.

[57] Uras, *op. cit.*, pp. 618–622, 624–625; Bayur, *op. cit.*, pp. 42–43; Lepsius, *Todesgang*, pp. 200–215.

[58] Ahmed Rustem Bey, *La guerre mondiale et la question turco-arménienne* (Berne, 1918), p. 64.

[59] Henry Morgenthau, *Ambassador Morgenthau's Story* (Garden City, N.Y., 1919), pp. 337–338.

[60] *Ibid.*, pp. 346, 351–352.

[61] For representative literature describing the cruel tortures and deaths of hundreds

of thousands of Armenians, consult, in addition to the works of Lepsius and Pinon cited in this chapter, Great Britain, Parliament, *The Treatment of the Armenians in the Ottoman Empire, Miscellaneous No. 31 (1916)* (London, 1916), cited hereafter as *Miscellaneous No. 31;* Herbert Adams Gibbons, *The Blackest Page of Modern History: Events in Armenia in 1915* (New York and London, 1916); Émile Doumergue, *L'Arménie: Les massacres et la question d'Orient* (2d ed. rev.; Paris, 1920); J. de Morgan, *Essai sur nationalités* (Paris and Nancy, 1917), pp. 92–115; André Mandelstam, *Le sort de l'empire Ottoman* (Paris, 1917), pp. 245–284; Dj. S. Kirakosian, *Aradjin hamashkharhayin paterazme ev Arevmtahayutiune, 1914–1916* [The First World War and the Western Armenians, 1914–1916] (Erevan, 1965); Arnold J. Toynbee, *Armenian Atrocities: The Murder of a Nation* (London, New York, and Toronto, 1915).

62 Morgenthau, *op. cit.*, pp. 301–304; *Miscellaneous No. 31,* p. 638. Sargsian, *op. cit.*, p. 234, states that in April, 1915, there were approximately 120 work battalions, each composed of 300 to 500 Armenian men.

63 Lepsius, *Todesgang,* pp. 161–162.

64 For a description of the Van episode by an officer in the Turkish Army, consult Rafael de Nogales, *Four Years beneath the Crescent,* trans. by Muna Lee (New York and London, 1926), pp. 56–97. Discussing the events in one of the villages of Van *vilayet,* he exclaims, "Judge of my amazement to discover that the aggressors had not been the Armenians, after all, but the civil authorities themselves! Supported by the Kurds and the rabble of the vicinity, they were attacking the Armenian quarter." When ordering the chief man of the village to desist, "he astounded me by replying that he was doing nothing more than carry out an unequivocal order emanating from the Governor-General of the province . . . *to exterminate all Armenian males of twelve years of age and over*" (p. 60).

65 *Miscellaneous No. 31,* pp. 32–47, 627–628; Morgenthau, *op. cit.*, pp. 296–300; Lepsius, *Todesgang,* p. 234; Mandelstam, *op. cit.*, pp. 248–251.

66 Arnold Toynbee, "A Summary of Armenian History up to and including the Year 1915," *Armenian Review,* XII (Autumn, 1959), 68–69, cited hereafter as Toynbee, "Summary"; Lepsius, *Todesgang,* pp. 232–233; Mandelstam, *op. cit.*, pp. 287–294.

67 *Miscellaneous No. 31,* p. 632; Toynbee, "Summary," p. 70.

68 Lepsius, *Todesgang,* pp. 215–216.

69 A. J. Toynbee, *Turkey: A Past and a Future* (New York, 1917), pp. 20–27, 30–31, 36, and "Summary," pp. 71–72; *Miscellaneous No. 31,* pp. 633–636; Lepsius, *Todesgang,* pp. 217–229; Harry Stuermer, *Two War Years in Constantinople* (New York, [1917]), pp. 151–175.

70 Jäschke, *op. cit.*, p. 18, concurs with this view.

71 Erich Ludendorff, *Meine Kriegserinnerungen, 1914–1918* (Berlin, 1919), p. 136; Pomiankowski, *op. cit.*, p. 165; Mühlmann, *op. cit.*, p. 277; Guse, *op. cit.*, p. 101.

72 Consult, for example, C. A. Bratter, *Die Armenische Frage* (Berlin, 1915), and Emil Daniels, "England und Russland in Armenien und Persien," *Preussische Jahrbücher,* CLXIX (July-September, 1917), 237–267.

73 *New York Times,* September 28 and 29, 1915.

74 J. Ellis Barker, "Germany, Turkey, and the Armenian Massacres," *Quarterly Review,* CCXXXIII (April, 1920), 394; Pinon, *op. cit.*, pp. 59–75; Mandelstam, *op. cit.*, pp. 301–331. One of the strongest invectives against the Kaiser's government was written by a German correspondent, Harry Stuermer, who, in his *Two War Years in Constantinople,* pp. 65, 68, states, "The attitude of Germany was . . . one of boundless *cowardice*. For we had the Turkish Government firmly enough in hand, from the military as well as the financial and political point of view to insist upon the observance of the simplest principles of humanity if we wanted to. . . . And cases have actually been proved to have occurred, from the testimony of German doctors and Red Cross nurses

returned from the Interior, of German officers light-heartedly taking the initiative in exterminating and scattering the Armenians when the less-zealous local authorities who still retained some remnants of human feeling, scrupled to obey the instructions of the 'Nur-el Osmanieh' (the headquarters of the Committee at Stamboul)."

[75] Morgenthau, op. cit., pp. 374-375; Barker, op. cit., pp. 390-392. In 1916, Gottlieb von Jagow, German State Secretary for Foreign Affairs expressed the official position of the government: "Much as we deplore the fate of the Armenians from the point of view of pure humanity, our sons and brothers are nearer to us than the Armenians. They [our sons and brothers] are spilling their precious blood in terrible battles and they depend for their security upon Turkey's support. The Turks are rendering us a valuable service by protecting the flanks of our military position. You, gentlemen, will agree with me that we could not break off our alliance on account of the Armenian question."

[76] Ziemke, op. cit., pp. 272-273; Johannes Lepsius, "The Armenian Question," *Muslim World*, X (1920), 352-355, and his *Deutschland und Armenien*. The latter work includes 295 documents [1915-1917] of German correspondence, consular reports, government inquiries, and protests concerning the deportations and massacres.

[77] Pomiankowski, op. cit., p. 164.

[78] Price, op. cit., pp. 61-62; Allen and Muratoff, op. cit., p. 298.

[79] Tchalkhouchian, op. cit., p. 29; Korganoff, op. cit., p. 23; Rep. of Arm. Archives, File 1/1.

[80] Larcher, op. cit., p. 394; Guse, op. cit., p. 62; Sargsian, op. cit., p. 274; Mkhitarian, op. cit., pp. 211-213. The Turks had deserted Van on May 16 and in the two-day interlude before the arrival of the first Armenian volunteer unit, the Armenians of Van burned the fortress and public buildings of the city. It is important to note the change in Soviet historiography relating to armed resistance of the Turkish Armenians and to the role of the volunteer units. Earlier belittled and condemned, the volunteers now win the praise of Soviet authors. Consult, for example, G. Stepanian, "Hai zhoghovrdi herosakan inknapashtpanutiune 1915 t." [The Heroic Self-Defense of the Armenian People in 1915], and Armen Hatsagordsian, "Drvagner Vani herosamartits" [Episodes from the Heroic Battle of Van], both in *Sovetakan grakanutiun*, XXXI (April, 1965), 82-93, 100-102.

[81] Rep. of Arm. Archives, File 1/1; Tchalkhouchian, op. cit., p. 32.

[82] Sassuni, op. cit., pp. 67-72; Arshak Alboyajian, "Ankakh Hayastan" [Independent Armenia], *Amenun Taretsuitse* [Everyone's Almanac], XV ([Constantinople], 1921), 107-108.

[83] Aram was confirmed in office on May 20 and given instructions to appoint only Armenian officials and militia. His government, which lasted seventy days, was as follows:

Aram Manukian	Governor
Sirakan Tigranian	Vice-Governor
Paruir Levonian	Assistant Governor
Artak Darbinian	Chancellor
Karapet Ajemian	Controller
Tigran Terlemezian	Treasurer
Onnik Mkhitarian	Secretary

The province was partitioned into fourteen regions, each with an Armenian administrator. Consult Mkhitarian, op. cit., pp. 213-218.

[84] Korganoff, op. cit., pp. 26-27; Allen and Muratoff, op. cit., p. 301; Tchalkhouchian, op. cit., pp. 32-33; Rep. of Arm. Archives, File 1/1.

[85] Maslovskii, op. cit., pp. 173-177; Guse, op. cit., p. 69; Pomiankowski, op. cit., p. 147; Sassuni, op. cit., pp. 75-81; Allen and Muratoff, op. cit., pp. 303-309.

86 Lepsius, *Todesgang*, pp. 101–102; Guse, *op. cit.*, p. 69; Mkhitarian, *op. cit.*, p. 220.
87 Kirakosian, *op. cit.*, p. 273, and other Armenian sources estimate that approximately 40,000 civilians perished during the retreat. Consult also Mkhitarian, *op. cit.*, p. 221; Sassuni, *op. cit.*, p. 90; Sargsian, *op. cit.*, p. 279.
88 Georgian SSR Central State Historical Archives, Fund 2c, folder 3198, p. 101, in Sargsian, *op. cit.*, p. 280; *Miscellaneous No. 31*, pp. 83–95; Lepsius, *Todesgang*, pp. 116–123; Sisak Nalbandian, *Tarono inknapashtpanutiune u djarde, 1914–1915* [The Self-Defense and Massacre of Taron, 1914–1915] (Fresno, Calif., 1920). For an excellent account of the final days of the Armenians of Mush and Sassun, consult Vahan Papazian, *Im hushere* [My Memoirs], II (Beirut, 1952), 384–417.
89 Allen and Muratoff, *op. cit.*, pp. 367–368; Korganoff, *op. cit.*, pp. 33–43; Larcher, *op. cit.*, p. 404. After the reoccupation of Mush and Bitlis, Armenian societies of Transcaucasia offered rewards for the deliverance of women and children forcibly Islamized and taken into Turkish and Kurdish homes. The "one piece of gold for an Armenian" fund retrieved between 5,000 and 6,000 persons. Consult Sebouh, *op. cit.*, pp. 270–274.
90 Leo, *op. cit.*, pp. 163–167; Lazian, *Hayastan*, pp. 187–189; Tchalkhouchian, *op. cit.*, pp. 57–59.
91 Leo, *op. cit.*, pp. 167–173; Lazian, *Hayastan*, p. 186.
92 Consult the Appendix for a résumé of Entente declarations about the future of the Armenians.
93 Lazian, *Vaveragrer*, pp. 199–200; Khatisian, *op. cit.* (October, 1932), p. 160; Tchalkhouchian, *op. cit.*, pp. 54–55.
94 Ashot Hovhannisian, compiler, *Hayastani avtonomian ev Antantan: Vaveragrer imperialistakan paterazmi shrdjanits* [Armenia's Autonomy and the Entente: Documents from the Period of the Imperialistic War] (Erevan, 1926), pp. 77–79. Also consult Ministerstvo Inostrannykh Del, *Razdel Aziatskoi Turtsii po sekretnym dokumentam b. ministerstva inostrannykh del*, ed. by E. A. Adamov (Moscow, 1924), Appendix III, pp. 360–362, cited hereafter as *Razdel*.
95 The secret messages, negotiations, and agreements are included in *Razdel* and in *Konstantinopol' i Prolivy po sekretnym dokumentam b. ministerstva inostrannykh del*, ed. by E. A. Adamov (Moscow, 1925–1926), 2 vols., cited hereafter as *Konstantinopol'*.
96 *Razdel*, pp. 135–136; Hovhannisian, *op. cit.*, pp. 10–11.
97 *Razdel*, p. 136; Hovhannisian, *op. cit.*, p. 11.
98 Great Britain, *Documents on British Foreign Policy, 1919–1939*, 1st Series, ed. by E. L. Woodward and Rohan Butler, IV (London, 1952), 635–636; *Konstantinopol'*, I, 252.
99 Woodward and Butler, *op. cit.*, pp. 636–638; *Konstantinopol'*, I, 275–277.
100 *Razdel*, p. 127; C. Jay Smith, *The Russian Struggle for Power, 1914–1917* (New York, [1956]), p. 233.
101 *Konstantinopol'*, I, 295; Smith, *op. cit.*, pp. 237–238. For a concise article on these proceedings, consult R. J. Kerner, "Russia, the Straits, and Constantinople, 1914–1915," *The Journal of Modern History*, I (September, 1929), 400–415.
102 For negotiations and final agreement, consult Smith, *op. cit.*, pp. 243–270; *Konstantinopol'*, I, 305–335; and R. W. Seton-Watson, "Italian Intervention and the Secret Treaty of London," *The Slavonic Review*, V (December, 1926), 271–297.
103 *Razdel*, pp. 154–157; Smith, *op. cit.*, pp. 359–362.
104 During the first year of the war, the tsarist government Russified the name of the capital by changing St. Petersburg to Petrograd.
105 "Dnevnik Ministerstva Inostrannykh Del za 1915–1916 g.g.," *Krasnyi Arkhiv*, XXXII (1929), 19–20, cited hereafter as "Dnevnik."
106 *Razdel*, p. 157.
107 *Ibid.*, p. 158.

108 Hovhannisian, *op. cit.*, pp. 27–28; *Razdel*, p. 159.
109 *Razdel*, pp. 163–164.
110 "Dnevnik," pp. 26–28; *Razdel*, pp. 172–174.
111 *Razdel*, pp. 170–171, 185–188, 199–200; Smith, *op. cit.*, p. 371; Woodward and Butler, *op. cit.*, pp. 244–247.
112 Ananun, *op. cit.*, p. 552; Lazian, *Vaveragrer*, p. 187.
113 Rep. of Arm. Archives, File 1/1; Sassuni, *op. cit.*, pp. 108–109.
114 *Hamarot teghekagir H. Azgayin Biuroyi gordsuneutian, 1915–1917* [Brief Report about the Activity of the Armenian National Bureau, 1915–1917] (Tiflis, [1917]), pp. 8–9, in Ananun, *op. cit.*, pp. 552–553.
115 Leo, *op. cit.*, pp. 192–193; Tchalkhouchian, *op. cit.*, pp. 55–56.
116 *Razdel*, pp. 207–209.
117 *Ibid.*, pp. 211–212; Leo, *op. cit.*, pp. 193–194.
118 Larcher, *op. cit.*, pp. 399–402; Price, *op. cit.*, pp. 64–86; Guse, *op. cit.*, pp. 75–76; Maslovskii, *op. cit.*, pp. 267–275; Allen and Muratoff, *op. cit.*, pp. 331–362; Bayur, *op. cit.*, p. 63.
119 Pomiankowski, *op. cit.*, p. 190; Sargsian, *op. cit.*, p. 216; Maslovskii, *op. cit.*, pp. 277–293.
120 Guse, *op. cit.*, p. 77; Larcher, *op. cit.*, pp. 403–404.
121 Liman von Sanders, *op. cit.*, pp. 125–126; Guse, *op. cit.*, p. 82; Mühlmann, *op. cit.*, p. 66; Pomiankowski, *op. cit.*, pp. 190–191; Maslovskii, *op. cit.*, pp. 362–365.
122 Among well-known works pertaining to the Gallipoli campaign are Liman von Sanders, *op. cit.*, pp. 57–105; Ian Hamilton, *Gallipoli Diary* (New York, 1920), 2 vols.; Winston Churchill, *The World Crisis*, II, *1915* (New York, 1929); C. E. Callwell, *The Dardanelles* (London, 1919); Trumbull Higgins, *Winston Churchill and the Dardanelles* (New York, 1963).
123 Allen and Muratoff, *op. cit.*, pp. 378–383; Maslovskii, *op. cit.*, pp. 326–330.
124 Korganoff, *op. cit.*, pp. 57–61; Maslovskii, *op. cit.*, pp. 369–396; Rep. of Arm. Archives, File 1/1. Bayur, *op. cit.*, p. 65, states that Erzinjan fell on July 25.
125 The XVI Corps, operating in the Mush-Bitlis area, was commanded by Mustafa Kemal.
126 Guse, *op. cit.*, pp. 87–88; Maslovskii, *op. cit.*, pp. 400–403; Allen and Muratoff, *op. cit.*, pp. 420–427. Liman von Sanders, *op. cit.*, p. 132, concludes his description of the plight of the Turkish Army by stating, "The balance sheet for 1916 on the Caucasus was anything but gratifying."
127 Aram Turabian, *L'éternelle victime de la diplomatie européenne* (Paris, 1919), pp. 58–82; Lazian, *Vaveragrer*, pp. 188–191; Rep. of Arm. Archives, File 1/1.
128 Hovhannisian, *op. cit.*, pp. 91–93; Georgian SSR Central State Historical Archives, Fund 154, folder 1, 1917, pp. 3–43, in Mnatsakanian, *op. cit.*, pp. 224–225.
129 Hovhannisian, *op. cit.*, pp. 92–93.
130 Vratzian, *Ughinerov*, III, 120.
131 Rep. of Arm. Archives, File 118/11; Ananun, *op. cit.*, pp. 591–592; *Miscellaneous No. 31*, pp. 194–218.
132 Ananun, *op. cit.*, pp. 593–595.
133 The Armenian branch of the Social Revolutionary party had been formed in 1907, attracting its small membership from that element of Dashnaktsutiun which felt that the organization had failed to emphasize socialist goals and to participate sufficiently in the Russian revolutionary movement. Dashnaktsutiun, unhappy with its stepchild, attempted, but without success, to convince its Russian SR allies not to recognize the Armenian SR branch. Dashnaktsutiun argued that in Armenian life it was the sole representative of the Social Revolutionary movement.
134 Vratzian, *Hanrapetutiun*, pp. 12–14; Tchalkhouchian, *op. cit.*, p. 67.

135 Vratzian, *Ughinerov*, III, 111–113.
136 Khatisian, *op. cit.* (December, 1932), pp. 138–141.
137 *Ibid.* (February, 1933), p. 124; Vratzian, *Ughinerov*, III, 143–145.

Notes to Chapter V

1 *Horizon* (Tiflis), May 1, 1917, as quoted in S. Vratzian, *Hayastani Hanrapetutiun* [Republic of Armenia] (2d ed.; Beirut, 1958), p. 24, cited hereafter as Vratzian, *Hanrapetutiun*. All dates in this study are given according to the Gregorian calendar, although the Julian calendar, which in the twentieth century is thirteen days behind the Gregorian, was used in Russia until 1918. Exceptions will be made when citing newspaper articles and when dates appear in direct quotations.
2 It is important to distinguish between the original meaning of *soviet* ("council") and the current use of the term. Until the eve of the Communist seizure of power in November, 1917, most soviets of Russia were pronouncedly anti-Bolshevik.
3 William H. Chamberlin, *The Russian Revolution, 1917–1921* (New York, 1935), I, 73–98, 429–431; Jesse D. Clarkson, *A History of Russia* (3d printing; New York, [1963]), pp. 436–441.
4 S. E. Sef, *Revoliutsiia 1917 goda v Zakavkaz'i (dokumenty, materialy)* ([Tiflis], 1927), pp. 57–63; Mamiia Orakhelashvili, *Zakavkazskie bol'shevistskie organizatsii v 1917 godu* ([Tiflis], 1927), p. 34.
5 S. Vratzian, *Kianki ughinerov: Depker, demker, aprumner* [Along Life's Ways: Episodes, Figures, Experiences], III (Beirut, 1963), 150, cited hereafter as Vratzian, *Ughinerov*.
6 Sef, *op. cit.*, p. 63.
7 A. Khatisian, "Kaghakapeti me hishataknere" [The Memoirs of a Mayor], *Hairenik Amsagir*, XI (February, 1933), 125–126; *Kavkazskoe slovo* (Tiflis), March 8 and 9, 1917, in Sef, *op. cit.*, pp. 66–67; Marxism-Leninism Institute, Armenian Filial Archive, Fund 33, folder 2, work 3, p. 7, in S. Vartanian, *Pobeda sovetskoi vlasti v Armenii* (Erevan, 1959), p. 48.
8 G. M. Mneyan, *Stepan Shahumiani partiakan ev petakan gordsuneutiune (1900–1918)* [Stepan Shahumian's Party and Governmental Activity (1900–1918)] (Erevan, 1958), p. 153; Sef, *op. cit.*, pp. 70–71; L. A. Khurshudian, *Stepan Shahumian: Petakan ev partiakan gordsuneutiune 1917–1918 tvakannerin* [Stepan Shahumian: Governmental and Party Activity, 1917–1918] (Erevan, 1959), pp. 18–19.
9 Sef, *op. cit.*, p. 140.
10 *Ibid.*, pp. 94–97, 112–114, 124.
11 Vratzian, *Hanrapetutiun*, p. 19.
12 *Ibid.*, p. 20.
13 Among the organization's founders were former members of the Social Democratic *Hummet* ("Energy") party which had been formed on the eve of the 1905 Russian Revolution to propagate Marxism among the Moslems. Soviet authors differ about the date of the formation of Hummet, some stating that it was in existence as early as 1903, while others maintain, probably incorrectly, that only after the Revolution had begun was the party organized. An official publication of the Institute of Party History of the Central Committee of the Communist Party of Azerbaijan and of the Azerbaijani Filial of the Marxism-Leninism Institute, *Istoriia Kommunisticheskoi partii Azerbaidzhana*, pt. 1 (Baku, 1958), p. 66, states that the Hummet was organized in the fall of 1904 but had existed as a circle (*kruzhok*) since 1903.
14 Mirza-Davud Guseinov, *Tiurkskaia Demokraticheskaia Partiia Federalistov "Musavat" v proshlom i nastoiashchem* ([Tiflis], 1927), pp. 14–15.
15 *Ibid.*, pp. 71–73.

16 *Ibid.*, pp. 20, 30.
17 Rasul-Zade states that the Musavat party was organized after the March Revolution of 1917. Consult M. E. Rassoul-Zadé, *L'Azerbaidjan en lutte pour l'Indépendance* (Paris, 1930), p. 17.
18 Vratzian, *Hanrapetutiun*, p. 21. For a slightly different version of the resolutions, consult Robert Paul Browder and Alexander F. Kerensky, eds., *The Russian Provisional Government, 1917: Documents* (Stanford, 1961), I, 417–419; also B. Baikov, "Vospominaniia o revoliutsii v Zakavkaz'i (1917–1920 g.g.)," *Arkhiv Russkoi Revoliutsii*, IX ([Berlin], 1933), 103–104.
19 Vratzian, *Hanrapetutiun*, pp. 31–32.
20 D. Ananun, *Rusahayeri hasarakakan zargatsume*, III, *1901–1918* [The Social Development of the Russian Armenians: 1901–1918] (Venice, 1926), 605–606.
21 Though favoring the administrative reorganization of Transcaucasia, the Armenian middle class was vitally concerned with the rights of minorities. In any territorial redivision, there was no doubt that Tiflis, the stronghold of the Armenian bourgeoisie, would be included in the Georgian districts. The city's 198,000 Armenians out of a total population of 428,000 were in danger of becoming "second-class citizens." In 1916, only 62,000 Georgians lived in Tiflis. Consult United States, The National Archives, *Record Group 256: Records of the American Commission to Negotiate Peace*, Class 867B.00, Document 10. *Record Group 256* is cited hereafter as *RG 256*.
22 This article referred primarily to the confiscations of 1903 but was also intended to alter the 1836 tsarist arrangements, the *Polozhenie*, which limited the prerogatives of the Armenian Church. Moreover, the professional-middle-class representatives were concerned about the efforts of Dashnaktsutiun to dominate all Church councils. Charging that Dashnaktsutiun was attempting to master the Church, the Armenian Constitutional Democrats had withdrawn from such a council in 1906 before it was dispersed by order of Viceroy Vorontsov-Dashkov.
23 Ananun, *op. cit.*, pp. 604–605.
24 Leonard Schapiro, *The Origin of the Communist Autocracy* (London, 1956), pp. 26–27; Edward Hallett Carr, *The Bolshevik Revolution, 1917–1923*, I (London, 1950), 74–77; Merle Fainsod, *How Russia Is Ruled* (Cambridge, Mass., 1953), pp. 62–63.
25 V. I. Lenin, *Polnoe sobranie sochinenii*, XXXI (5th ed.; Moscow, 1962), 103–112; Clarkson, *op. cit.*, p. 461.
26 *Protokoly i stenograficheskie otchety s"ezdov i konferentsii Kommunisticheskoi partii Sovetskogo Soiuza: Sed'maia (Aprel'skaia) Vserossiiskaia konferentsiia RSDRP (bol'shevikov): Petrogradskaia obshchegorodskaia konferentsiia RSDRP (bol'shevikov), 1917 goda: Protokoly*, prepared by the Institute of Marxism-Leninism (Moscow, 1958), pp. 241–260; Carr, *op. cit.*, pp. 83–84.
27 A basic shortcoming of Soviet authors is their habitual use of the words "and others." It is extremely difficult to ascertain the full membership of the various Communist bodies discussed. It should be noted, however, that, as many purged Bolsheviks are being rehabilitated, the list of names preceding the "and others" is constantly growing.
28 A. M. Poghosian, *Sotsial-tntesakan haraberutiunnere Karsi marzum, 1878–1920* [The Social-Economic Relations in the Province of Kars, 1878–1920] (Erevan, 1961), p. 261; M. V. Arzumanian, *Bolshevikneri gordsuneutiune ev revoliutsion sharzhumnere Hayastanum 1907–1917 tvakannerin* [Bolshevik Activity and the Revolutionary Movements in Armenia, 1907–1917] (Erevan, 1959), pp. 552–553.
29 The Baku Soviet voiced confidence in the Provisional Government by a vote of 166 to 9, with 8 abstaining. New president of the combined Soviet of Workers' and Soldiers' Deputies was Sako (Sargis) Sahakian, a Social Revolutionary.
30 Kh. A. Barsegian, *Istoriia armianskoi bol'shevistskoi periodicheskoi pechati* (Erevan, 1958), pp. 191–200. The paper was printed in fifteen issues from May through August, 1917.

31 Khurshudian, *op. cit.,* pp. 33–34; Mneyan, *op. cit.,* pp. 162–163.
32 A. N. Mnatsakanian, *Revoliutsian Andrkovkasum ev Rusastani patviraknere, 1917–1921* [The Revolution in Transcaucasia and the Envoys of Russia, 1917–1921] (Erevan, 1961), pp. 28–29, cited hereafter as Mnatsakanian, *Patviraknere;* Barsegian, *op. cit.,* pp. 200–208, 212–215.
33 S. H. Melkonian, *Bagrat Gharibdjanian, 1890–1920* (Erevan, 1954), pp. 44–48, 53–59; G. B. Gharibdjanian, *Hayastani komunistakan kazmakerputiunnere sovetakan ishkhanutian haghtanaki hamar mghvads paikarum* [The Communist Organizations of Armenia in the Struggle for Victory of the Soviet Order] (Erevan, 1955), pp. 77–80, 92–96, cited hereafter as Gharibdjanian, *Paikarum; Revoliutsion kocher ev trutsikner, 1902–1921* [Revolutionary Appeals and Circulars, 1902–1921], compiled by the Institute of Party History of the Central Committee of the Communist Party of Armenia and the Armenian Filial of the Institute of Marxism-Leninism (Erevan, 1960), pp. 405–412, cited hereafter as *Kocher.*
34 Vratzian, *Hanrapetutiun,* pp. 17–18.
35 Browder and Kerensky, *op. cit.,* p. 425.
36 The Georgian Social Federalist party was founded in 1904. Opposed to the expansion of capitalism in Russia, the party advocated the distribution of the land to the peasantry and espoused general socialist principles. As its name implies, the organization considered federation the solution to the nationality question in Russia. Consult Al. Stavrovskii, *Zakavkaz'e posle Oktiabria* (Moscow-Leningrad, [1925]), p. 6.
37 There is some discrepancy about the original composition of the Ozakom. A. M. Elchibekian, *Velikaia Oktiabr'skaia sotsialisticheskaia revoliutsiia i pobeda sovetskoi vlasti v Armenii* (Erevan, 1957), p. 13, and Firuz Kazemzadeh, *The Struggle for Transcaucasia (1917–1921)* (New York and Oxford, [1951]), p. 34, state that Pereverzev was a member. Elchibekian incorrectly adds that Chkhenkeli later replaced Abashidze, while Kazemzadeh is equally mistaken in stating that Chkheidze, Georgian Menshevik and leader of the Petrograd Soviet, subsequently was appointed. P. N. Pereverzev remained in Petrograd all the while and served as Minister of Justice in the Russian coalition government formed in May, while N. S. Chkheidze presided in the Petrograd Soviet and had no position on the Ozakom. The composition of the Ozakom as stated in the text of this work corresponds, for example, with the findings of Ds. Aghayan, *Hoktemberian revoliutsian ev hai zhoghovrdi azatagrume* [The October Revolution and the Liberation of the Armenian People] (Erevan, 1957), p. 35; and Vartanian, *op. cit.,* p. 49.
38 G. I. Uratadze, *Obrazovanie i konsolidatsiia Gruzinskoi Demokraticheskoi Respubliki* (Munich, 1956), p. 20.
39 Sef, *op. cit.,* pp. 78–80.
40 Vratzian, *Hanrapetutiun,* p. 18.
41 This was an aftermath to the Kornilov "Mutiny." See pp. 83–84, this volume.
42 Sef, *op. cit.,* pp. 80–83.
43 *Ibid.,* pp. 82–83.
44 V. A. Mikayelian, *Hayastani giughatsiutiune sovetakan ishkhanutian hamar mghvads paikari zhamanakashrdjanum (1917–1920 t.t.)* [The Peasantry of Armenia in the Period of Struggle for the Establishment of Soviet Order (1917–1920)] (Erevan, 1960), pp. 14–15.
45 The flexibility of Bolshevik tactics was an important factor in the party's ultimate victory. Adopted Bolshevik formulas concerning the peasantry and the land were often taken from the Social Revolutionaries and applied to meet the prevailing situation. Consult David Mitrany, *Marx against the Peasant: A Study in Social Dogmatism* (2d printing; London, [1952]), pp. 71–81. A leading Social Revolutionary, Victor Chernov, discusses the agrarian problem in his *The Great Russian Revolution,* trans. by Philip E. Mosely (New Haven, 1936), pp. 233–263.

46 Aghayan, *op. cit.*, pp. 41–42.

47 *Velikaia Oktiabr'skaia sotsialisticheskaia revoliutsiia i pobeda sovetskoi vlasti v Armenii: Sbornik dokumentov,* ed. by A. N. Mnatsakanian, A. M. Akopian, and G. M. Dallakian (Erevan, 1957), pp. 18–20, cited hereafter as *Velikaia revoliutsiia.*

48 Armenian SSR Central State Historical Archives, Fund 541, folder 1, work 75, p. 1, in G. Galoyan, *Bor'ba za sovetskuiu vlast' v Armenii* (Moscow, 1957), p. 22.

49 *Bol'sheviki v bor'be za pobedu sotsialisticheskoi revoliutsii v Azerbaidzhane: Dokumenty i materialy 1917–1918 g.g.,* ed. by Z. I. Ibragimov and M. S. Iskenderov (Baku, 1957), pp. 69–72, cited hereafter as *Revoliutsii v Azerbaidzhane.*

50 *Hoktemberian sotsialistakan meds revoliutsian ev sovetakan ishkhanutian haghtanake Hayastanum: Pastatghteri ev niuteri zhoghovadsu* [The Great October Socialist Revolution and the Victory of the Soviet Order in Armenia: Collection of Documents and Materials], ed. by A. N. Mnatsakanian, *et al.* (Erevan, 1960), pp. 41–42, 62–64, 67–70. This work includes many documents found in *Velikaia revoliutsiia.* Cited hereafter as *Meds revoliutsian.*

51 Georgian SSR Central State Archives of the October Revolution, Fund 1472, work 382, p. 75, in Mikayelian, *op. cit.,* p. 30; *Meds revoliutsian,* pp. 35, 65–66.

52 Vahan Papazian, *Im hushere* [My Memoirs], II (Beirut, 1952), 439. G. Sassuni, *Tajkahayastane rusakan tirapetutian tak (1914–1918)* [Turkish Armenia under Russian Domination (1914–1918)] (Boston, 1927), p. 137, states there were sixty-four delegates, of whom forty-one adhered to Dashnaktsutiun.

53 Papazian, *op. cit.*, pp. 439–440; Sassuni, *op. cit.*, p. 138.

54 The Sahmanadir Ramkavar ("Constitutional Democrat") party, organized at Constantinople in 1908, adopted liberal, antirevolutionary, and laissez-faire principles. Like the Armenian Populists of Transcaucasia, the Ramkavars reflected middle-class opinion but enjoyed more public support than did the Populists. For a résumé of the founding of the Sahmanadir Ramkavar party and its initial program, consult Manuk G. Jizmejian, *Patmutiun amerikahai kaghakakan kusaktsutiants, 1890–1925* [History of the Armenian-American Political Parties, 1890–1925] (Fresno, Calif., 1930), pp. 168–172.

55 Papazian, *op. cit.*, p. 440; Sassuni, *op. cit.*, p. 139. The latter author, omitting Terzipashian, states that the Bureau was composed of five members.

56 Arshak Alboyajian, "Ankakh Hayastan" [Independent Armenia], *Amenun Taretsuitse* [Everyone's Almanac], XV ([Constantinople], 1921), 109–110.

57 Vratzian, *Hanrapetutiun,* p. 26; Papazian, *op. cit.*, p. 442.

58 See pp. 66–67, this volume.

59 Vratzian, *Hanrapetutiun,* pp. 24–25; paraphrased in Papazian, *op. cit.*, pp. 441–442.

60 Sassuni, *op. cit.*, pp. 141–143. The administrative-territorial divisions of Turkish Armenia and the duties of the officials are found in Georgian SSR Central State Archives of the October Revolution, Fund 154, work 1, 1917, pp. 3–43, in A. N. Mnatsakanian, *V. I. Lenine ev hai zhoghovrdi azatagrakan paikare* [V. I. Lenin and the Armenian People's Struggle for Freedom] (Erevan, 1963), pp. 224–225.

61 Joseph Pomiankowski, *Der Zusammenbruch des Ottomanischen Reiches: Erinnerungen an die Türkei aus der Zeit des Weltkrieges* (Leipzig, 1928), p. 225; W. E. D. Allen and Paul Muratoff, *Caucasian Battlefields: A History of the Wars on the Turco-Caucasian Border, 1828–1921* (Cambridge, 1953), p. 436.

62 Carl Mühlmann, *Das deutsch-türkische Waffenbündnis im Weltkrieg* (Leipzig, [1940]), p. 184.

63 M. Larcher, *La guerre turque dans la guerre mondiale* (Paris, 1926), p. 411, states that the Third Army dwindled to 36,000 men.

64 Pomiankowski, *op. cit.*, p. 224; Allen and Muratoff, *op. cit.*, p. 437. Felix Guse, *Die Kaukasusfront im Weltkrieg bis zum Frieden von Brest* (Leipzig, [1940]), p. 93, is apparently mistaken in stating that the reorganization occurred in 1915.

65 Larcher, *op. cit.*, p. 415; Allen and Muratoff, *op. cit.*, p. 437. The joint command was dissolved at the end of the year.
66 Mühlmann, *op. cit.*, p. 133; Larcher, *op. cit.*, p. 415.
67 Mühlmann, *op. cit.*, p. 134.
68 Allen and Muratoff, *op. cit.*, p. 450; Larcher, *op. cit.*, pp. 412–413.
69 In May, 1917, Lvov had formed a coalition cabinet that included Social Revolutionary and Menshevik representatives. Because of a serious crisis in Russian politics, the two parties had compromised their decision not to participate in the government. Popular demonstrations against Foreign Minister Miliukov's declarations about "war to decisive victory" and the conquest of Constantinople had compelled Miliukov and Minister of War Guchkov to resign. The Petrograd Soviet agreed to coalition government in order to save the country from the spreading political anarchy but allowed its members to take only secondary positions in Lvov's cabinet. For documents and discussions of the period, consult Frank Alfred Golder, *Documents of Russian History, 1914–1917* (New York and London, [1927]), pp. 320–358; Donald W. Treadgold, *Twentieth Century Russia* (2d ed.; Chicago, [1964]), pp. 128–129, 131; Chamberlin, *op. cit.*, pp. 143–148.
70 G. Pasdermadjian, *Why Armenia Should Be Free* (Boston, 1918), p. 35. Bertha Papazian, *The Tragedy of Armenia* (Boston and Chicago, 1918), p. 124, claims that 35,000 troops had been transferred by November, 1917, but this seems a gross exaggeration.
71 Archives of the Republic of Armenia Delegation to the Paris Peace Conference [now integrated into the archives of Dashnaktsutiun, Boston, Massachusetts], File 379/1, *H. H. Vashingtoni Nerkayatsutsich ev H. Amerikian Karavarutiune, 1917–1918* [R. (Republic) of A. (Armenia) Washington Representative and the Government of North America, 1917–1918], cited hereafter as Rep. of Arm. Archives. In this memorandum sent to Secretary of State Robert Lansing, the Armenian diplomatic representative stated that there were 18,000 Armenian troops in Transcaucasia.
72 The Baku Soviet did not assume full control of the city's administration until April, 1918. See chapter viii.
73 Allen and Muratoff, *op. cit.*, pp. 442–453, discuss Russian attempts in the first half of 1917 to unite with the British forces in Mesopotamia.
74 Rep. of Arm. Archives, File 1/1.
75 General G. Korganoff, *La participation des Arméniens à la guerre mondiale sur le front du Caucase, 1914–1918* (Paris, 1927), pp. 63–69.
76 United States, The National Archives, *Record Group 59: General Records of the Department of State*, Class 861.00, Document 621.
77 *Ibid.*, 861.00/734.
78 *Ibid.*, 861.00/796.
79 *Ibid.*, 861.00/2319. See also *Record Group 84: Records of the Foreign Service Posts of the Department of State*, C46(C8).1, Correspondence, American Consulate, Tiflis, 1917, 1918, 1919, Class 711.
80 Golder, *op. cit.*, pp. 425–434; Treadgold, *op. cit.*, p. 132; Nicholas Golovine, *The Russian Army in the World War* (New Haven and London, 1931), pp. 272–274.
81 Michael T. Florinsky, *Russia: A History and an Interpretation* (New York, 1953), II, 1430–1433; Golder, *op. cit.*, pp. 444–462; Chamberlin, *op. cit.*, pp. 167–177.
82 *Protokoly i stenograficheskie . . .: Shestoi s"ezd RSDRP (bol'shevikov), Avgust 1917 goda: Protokoly*, prepared by Institute of Marxism-Leninism (Moscow, 1958), pp. 241–257; Schapiro, *op. cit.*, pp. 49–50.
83 Golder, *op. cit.*, pp. 470–479. In this August 6 coalition, Kerensky also continued as minister of War and the Navy.
84 Sef, *op. cit.*, pp. 191–196.
85 Clarkson, *op. cit.*, pp. 467–469. Kerensky's account of the event and justification of

his actions are in his *The Prelude to Bolshevism: The Kornilov Rebellion* (London, [1919]). For a critical view of the Premier's moves, consult Leonid I. Strakhovsky, "Kerensky Betrayed Russia," in *The Russian Revolution and Bolshevik Victory: Why and How?*, ed. by Arthur E. Adams (Boston, [1960]), pp. 85–96; and Florinsky, *op. cit.*, pp. 1436–1441.

86 Sef, *op. cit.*, pp. 211–214, 217–228.

87 M. Gorky, V. Molotov, K. Voroshilov, *et al.*, eds., *The History of the Civil War in the U.S.S.R.*, II, *The Great Proletarian Revolution*, ed. by G. F. Alexandrov (London, 1947), 165; Mnatsakanian, *Patviraknere*, p. 33; Vartanian, *op. cit.*, p. 79.

88 Soviet sources differ on the number of delegates attending. There were fifty-two according to *Meds revoliutsian*, p. 618; Aghayan, *op. cit.*, p. 56; Gharibdjanian, *Paikarum*, p. 120; and R. Movsisian, *Kovkasian bolshevikian kazmakerputiunneri Erkrayin aradjin hamagumare ev Stepan Shahumian* [The First Regional Conference of Caucasian Bolshevik Organizations and Stepan Shahumian] (Erevan, 1955), p. 27. Gharibdjanian, in another work, *V. I. Lenine ev Andrkovkasi zhoghovrdneri azatagrume* [V. I. Lenin and the Liberation of the Peoples of Transcaucasia] (Erevan, 1960), p. 50, agrees with Vartanian, *op. cit.*, p. 84, who states that there were twenty-nine voting delegates representing 8,626 Bolsheviks from the North Caucasus, Transcaucasia, and the Caucasus Military Front. The latter study of Gharibdjanian is cited hereafter as *V. I. Lenine*.

89 St. Shahumian, *Erker* [Works], II (Erevan, 1957), 509–514, 517–520.

90 Movsisian, op. cit., pp. 67–77.

91 *Revoliutsii v Azerbaidzhane*, pp. 156–157; *Velikaia revoliutsiia*, pp. 80–81; Movsisian, *op. cit.*, pp. 37–42.

92 Elchibekian, *op. cit.*, pp. 21–22.

93 Of the several sources consulted, each gives a different list of members. One of the longer lists is found in *Hayastani Komunistakan partiayi patmutian urvagdser* [Outlines of the History of the Communist Party of Armenia], ed. by Hr. Margarian, A. Mnatsakanian, Kh. Barseghian (Erevan, 1958), p. 220. This source does not include Feoletov. Gharibdjanian, *V. I. Lenine*, p. 51, adds D. P. Shahverdian.

94 Mneyan, *op. cit.*, pp. 171–172; Gharibdjanian, *Paikarum*, pp. 129–131.

95 Vratzian, *Ughinerov*, IV (Beirut, 1965), 56–58; Ananun, *op. cit.*, p. 654.

96 Interview, June 12, 1965, in Los Angeles, with Artashes Chilingarian [Reuben Darbinian], delegate from Baku to the National Congress.

97 Ananun, *op. cit.*, pp. 654–655.

98 Vratzian, *Hanrapetutiun*, p. 34. There are considerable discrepancies regarding the number and the political affiliation of the delegates. Ananun, *op. cit.*, p. 655, states that there were 99 Dashnakists, 11 Populists, 28 Social Democrats, and 23 Social Revolutionaries. According to Alboyajian, *op. cit.*, p. 121, there were 115 Dashnakists, 44 Populists, 24 Social Democrats, 23 Social Revolutionaries, and 19 nonpartisans.

99 Anastas Mikoyan sent notification of the Bolshevik boycott to the Congress. Found in the Armenian SSR Central State Historical Archives, Fund 222, work 5, p. 71, in Gharibdjanian, *Paikarum*, pp. 122–123.

100 *Kavkazskii rabochii* (Tiflis), September 25, 1917, in *Meds revoliutsian*, pp. 73–74, and *Velikaia revoliutsiia*, pp. 69–70.

101 *Kavkazskii rabochii*, October 3, 1917, in Aghayan, *op. cit.*, p. 65; *Kocher*, pp. 415–417.

102 S. Masurian, "Rusahayots Azgayin Hamagumare" [The National Congress of the Russian Armenians], in *Mayis 28* [May 28], publication of the Paris Regional Committee of H. H. Dashnaktsutiun (Paris, 1926), pp. 7–8.

103 *Ibid.*, pp. 9–10.

104 Vratzian, *Hanrapetutiun*, pp. 39–40.

105 Masurian, *op. cit.*, pp. 14–16.
106 *Ibid.*, p. 18.
107 Ananun, *op. cit.*, p. 655. Vratzian, *Ughinerov*, IV, 68, states there were fifty members in the National Assembly, while Alboyajian, *op. cit.*, p. 122, asserts that there were forty-five.
108 Vratzian, *Hanrapetutiun*, p. 47. In the following weeks, several members were replaced. Ananun, *op. cit.*, p. 656, seems to be mistaken in stating that original council members included Abraham Giulkhandanian and Koriun Ghazazian in place of Manukian and Babalian (Dashnaktsutiun), H. Aivazian in place of Papadjanian (Populist), Aramayis Erzinkian in place of Gharabekian (SD), and Levon Atabekian in place of Stamboltsian (SR).
109 Vratzian, *Hanrapetutiun*, p. 45; Ananun, *op. cit.*, p. 639.
110 Brother of Alexandre Khatisian.
111 Art. Abeghian, "Menk ev mer harevannere—Azgayin kaghakakanutian khndirner" [We and Our Neighbors—Problems of National Policy], *Hairenik Amsagir*, VI (February, 1928), 96–98; A. Shakhatuni, *Administrativnyi peredel Zakavkazskago kraia* (Tiflis, 1918), pp. 61–71.
112 Masurian, *op. cit.*, p. 20. For criticisms by the Armenian Social Democrats, consult Ananun, *op. cit.*, pp. 623–639.
113 Shakhatuni, *op. cit.*, pp. 61, 68, 72, 73; US Archives, *RG 256*, 867B.00/4.
114 In the Tiflis *guberniia* there were 642,000 (43.5 percent) Georgians. It was fortunate for the Georgians that, unlike Armenians and Moslems, they were not scattered throughout every Transcaucasian province. US Archives, *RG 256*, 867B.00/10, includes the following statistics for the Tiflis guberniia: Georgian, 580,000; Armenian, 411,000; Russian, 150,000; other Christian, 40,000; Yezidi, 56,000; Georgian Moslem, 67,700; Sunni Moslem, 67,500; Shia Moslem, 39,000.
115 This number does not include approximately 70,000 Kurds. D. S. Zavriev, *K noveishei istorii severo-vostochnykh vilaetov Turtsii* (Tbilisi, 1947), p. 17, accounting for the Kurds, gives the Moslem population of the Kars *oblast* in 1916 as 42 percent. The Christian ratio was strengthened by more than 65,000 Russian *Molokan* religious sectarians and Greeks.
116 Rep. of Arm. Archives, File 65/1, *Vrastani Divanagitakan Nerkayatsutsich ev Vrastani Karavarutiun, 1918* [Diplomatic Representative to Georgia and the Georgian Government, 1918]; Arshak Djamalian, "Hai-vratsakan knjire" [The Armeno-Georgian Entanglement], *Hairenik Amsagir*, VI (April, 1928), 88.
117 The project which was sent to the Ozakom appeared in the Tiflis journal, *Kavkazskoe slovo*, nos. 227 and 229, 1917, paraphrased in Ananun, *op. cit.*, pp. 617–623, and analyzed in detail by Shakhatuni, *op. cit.*, pp. 124–135, 139–144. For excerpts of the minutes of Avalov's committee, consult the Baku Armenian National Council publication, *Armiano-gruzinskii vooruzhennyi konflikt: Na osnovanii fakticheskikh dannykh i podlinnykh dokumentov* (Baku, 1919), pp. 7–9, cited hereafter as *Arm-Gruz konflikt*.
118 Rep. of Arm. Archives, File 65/1; Djamalian, *op. cit.*, p. 89.
119 Ananun, *op. cit.*, pp. 641–646.
120 Rep. of Arm. Archives, File 65/1; *Arm-Gruz konflikt*, pp. 9–10; Djamalian, *op. cit.*, pp. 86, 89. Using Russian statistics of 1912–1913, Djamalian computed the Armenian population of Akhalkalak-Lori at 144,594, and the Georgian at 14,111.

Notes to Chapter VI

1 *Proletarskaia Revoliutsiia*, no. 10, 1922, quoted in William H. Chamberlin, *The Russian Revolution, 1917–1921* (New York, 1935), I, 465.

² Merle Fainsod, *How Russia Is Ruled* (Cambridge, Mass., 1953), pp. 80–83; Chamberlin, *op. cit.*, pp. 306–314.
³ Jane Degras, ed., *Soviet Documents on Foreign Policy*, I, *1917–1924* (London, 1951), 1–3.
⁴ Frank Alfred Golder, *Documents of Russian History, 1914–1917* (New York and London, [1927]), pp. 619–620; James Bunyan and H. H. Fisher, *The Bolshevik Revolution, 1917–1918: Documents and Materials* (Stanford, 1934), p. 133.
⁵ M. A. Melikian, *K voprosu o formirovanii armianskoi natsii i ee sotsialisticheskogo preobrazovaniia* (Erevan, 1957), pp. 93–94; Bunyan and Fisher, *op. cit.*, pp. 282–283.
⁶ Alfred G. Meyer, *Leninism* (Cambridge, Mass., 1957), pp. 145–160.
⁷ I. V. Stalin, *Sochineniia*, IV, *Noiabr' 1917–1920* (Moscow, 1947), 31–32.
⁸ *Ibid.*, p. 354.
⁹ *Ibid.*, p. 372.
¹⁰ *Ibid.*, p. 226.
¹¹ A. N. Mnatsakanian, *V. I. Lenine ev hai zhoghovrdi azatagrakan paikare* [V. I. Lenin and the Armenian People's Struggle for Freedom] (Erevan, 1963), pp. 228–229.
¹² V. I. Lenin, *Polnoe sobranie sochinenii* XXXII, *Mai-iiul' 1917* (5th ed.; Moscow, 1962), 11.
¹³ *Ibid.*, p. 16.
¹⁴ *Ibid.*, XXXI, *Mart-aprel' 1917* (1962), 347–348.
¹⁵ *Ibid.*, p. 436.
¹⁶ *Ibid.*, XXXII, 287–288.
¹⁷ *Ibid.*, pp. 289–290.
¹⁸ B. A. Borian, *Armeniia, mezhdunarodnaia diplomatiia i SSSR*, II (Moscow-Leningrad, 1929), 263, 277.
¹⁹ Ministerstvo Inostrannykh Del SSSR, *Dokumenty vneshnei politiki SSSR*, I, *7 noiabria 1917 g.–31 dekabria 1918 g.* (Moscow, 1957), 34–35, cited hereafter as *Vnesh. pol. SSSR*. Ivar Spector, *The Soviet Union and the Muslim World, 1917–1958* (Seattle, 1959), pp. 33–34, dates the document December 5, that is, when published in *Izvestiia*. December 7 is given by many authors who use as a basic source Iu. V. Kliuchnikov and A. Sabanin, *Mezhdunarodnaia politika noveishego vremeni v dogovorakh, notakh i deklaratsiiakh*, II (Moscow, 1926), 94. Most Armenian sources, in accord with *Vnesh. pol. SSSR*, date the decree November 20 [old style].
²⁰ Lenin, *op. cit.*, XXXIV, *Iiul'-oktiabr' 1917* (1962), 232.
²¹ *Ibid.*, p. 379.
²² S. T. Alikhanian, *Haikakan Gordseri Komisariati gordsuneutiune (1917–1921)* [Activity of the Commissariat of Armenian Affairs (1917–1921)] (Erevan, 1958), pp. 7–13.
²³ S. Vratzian, *Hayastane bolshevikiun murji ev trkakan sali midjev* [Armenia between the Bolshevik Hammer and the Turkish Anvil] (Beirut, 1953), pp. 15–16; St. Shahumian, *Erker* [Works], III (Erevan, 1958), 37–39; Mnatsakanian, *op. cit.*, p. 272.
²⁴ Borian, *op. cit.*, pp. 260–261, claims that the final provisions of the decree did not at all resemble those suggested by the Armenians. He feels that Terian had little to do with adoption of the proclamation, which was necessitated by considerations of Soviet Eastern policy.
²⁵ *Pravda*, no. 227, December 31, 1917, in Stalin, *op. cit.*, pp. 25–26.
²⁶ *Vnesh. pol. SSSR*, I, 74–75.
²⁷ United States, Department of State, *Papers Relating to the Foreign Relations of the United States, 1918, Russia*, I (Washington, D.C., 1931), 588, cited hereafter as *US, FRUS, Russia*. Also consult *Vnesh. pol. SSSR*, I, 93–94.
²⁸ Henry Barby, . . . *Le débâcle russe: Les extravagances bolcheviques et l'épopée arménienne* (Paris, [1919]), p. 30.
²⁹ Borian, *op. cit.*, p. 262.

30 Degras, *op. cit.*, pp. 3–4; Bunyan and Fisher, *op. cit.*, p. 233.
31 John W. Wheeler-Bennett, *Brest-Litovsk: The Forgotten Peace, March 1918* (London, 1938), pp. 74–75, 83–93; *Vnesh. pol. SSSR*, I, 47–51.
32 Degras, *op. cit.*, p. 20, quoting Kliuchnikov and Sabanin, *op. cit.*, p. 100.
33 Wheeler-Bennett, *op. cit.*, pp. 117–118; *Soviet Union and Peace*, intro. by Henri Barbuesse (New York, [1929]), pp. 33–35; Judah L. Magnes, *Russia and Germany at Brest Litovsk: A Documentary History of the Peace Negotiations* (New York, [1919]), p. 31; Bunyan and Fisher, *op. cit.*, pp. 477–478.
34 Degras, *op. cit.*, p. 23. Slightly different in Magnes, *op. cit.*, p. 36. Also Bunyan and Fisher, *op. cit.*, p. 483.
35 Gotthard Jäschke, "Der Turanismus der Jungtürken: Zur osmanischen Aussenpolitik im Weltkriege," *Die Welt des Islams*, XXIII (bk. 1–2, 1941), pp. 23–24.
36 Degras, *op. cit.*, p. 26.
37 Chamberlin, *op. cit.*, pp. 396–399; Bunyan and Fisher, *op. cit.*, pp. 498–500.
38 United States, Department of State, *Proceedings of the Brest-Litovsk Peace Conference: The Peace Negotiations between Russia and the Central Powers, 21 November, 1917–3 March, 1918* (Washington, D.C., 1918), pp. 172–173.
39 Wheeler-Bennett, *op. cit.*, p. 256. Slightly different translation in *Proceedings . . .*, p. 176, and Magnes, *op. cit.*, pp. 154–155.
40 Carl Mühlmann, *Das deutsch-türkische Waffenbündnis im Weltkrieg* (Leipzig, [1940]), p. 194.
41 Jäschke, *op. cit.*, p. 24.
42 Mühlmann, *op. cit.*, p. 190.
43 G. V. Chicherin, *Stat'i i rechi po voprosam mezhdunarodnoi politiki* (Moscow, 1961), p. 26.
44 Degras, *op. cit.*, p. 49. Slightly different in *Proceedings . . .*, p. 186.
45 Wheeler-Bennett, *op. cit.*, pp. 405–406; Degras, *op. cit.*, p. 53. Slightly different in US, *FRUS, Russia*, I, 443.
46 *Vnesh. pol. SSSR*, I, 199–200.
47 *Ibid.*, p. 200. See also US, *FRUS, Russia*, I, 472.
48 On March 12, 1918, the Sovnarkom decreed that Moscow was henceforth the capital of Russia. This move was confirmed by the Fourth Soviet Congress. Consult Kliuchnikov and Sabanin, *op. cit.*, p. 134, and Bunyan and Fisher, *op. cit.*, pp. 529–530.
49 V. G. Trukhanovskii, ed., *Istoriia mezhdunarodnykh otnoshenii i vneshnei politiki SSSR, 1917–1939 gg.*, I (Moscow, 1961), 55. Bunyan and Fisher, *op. cit.*, pp. 523–524, estimate that by the Brest-Litovsk treaty Russia sustained the following losses: territory, 25 percent; population, 44 percent; croplands, 33 percent; state income, 27 percent; sugar refineries, 80 percent; iron ore, 73 percent; and coal, 75 percent.
50 For resolutions and decisions of the Russian Social Democrat Bolshevik Seventh Congress, meeting March 6–8 in Petrograd, consult Lenin, *op. cit.*, XXXVI, *Mart-iiul' 1918* (1962), 1–76.

Notes to Chapter VII

1 [Republic of Georgia], *Dokumenty i materialy po vneshnei politike Zakavkaz'ia i Gruzii* (Tiflis, 1919), pp. 1–4, cited hereafter as *Dokumenty i materialy*.
2 G. M. Mneyan, *Stepan Shahumiani partiakan ev petakan gordsuneutiune (1900–1918)* [Stepan Shahumian's Party and Governmental Activity (1900–1918)] (Erevan, 1963), p. 174; V. L. Avakian, *Edjer Andrkovkasum otarerkria interventsiayi patmutiunits (1918 t.)* [Pages from the History of Foreign Intervention in Transcaucasia (1918)] (Erevan, 1957), p. 18. That the Bolsheviks were still not the masters of Baku political life was evidenced in the December elections for a new Soviet. Chosen were

85 Social Revolutionaries, 48 Bolsheviks, 36 Dashnakists, 18 Musavatists, and 13 Mensheviks. Consult B. H. Lalabekian, *V. I. Lenine ev sovetakan kargeri hastatumn u amrapndumn Andrkovkasum* [V. I. Lenin and the Establishment and Strengthening of Soviet Order in Transcaucasia] (Erevan, 1961), pp. 31–32.

[3] *Dokumenty i materialy,* pp. 4–5; N. Zhordania, *Za dva goda* (Tiflis, 1919), pp. 51–52.

[4] For the Bolshevik position and statement of noncollaboration, consult *Velikaia Oktiabr'skaia sotsialisticheskaia revoliutsiia: Dokumenty i materialy,* ed. by A. L. Sidorov, et al., II (Moscow, 1963), 151, cited hereafter as *Oktiabr'skaia Revoliutsiia.* Also S. E. Sef, *Revoliutsiia 1917 goda v Zakavkaz'i (dokumenty, materialy)* ([Tiflis], 1927), pp. 277–278; S. Vartanian, *Pobeda sovetskoi vlasti v Armenii* (Erevan, 1951), pp. 100–101.

[5] Al. Khatisian, *Hayastani Hanrapetutian dsagumn u zargatsume* [The Creation and Development of the Republic of Armenia] (Athens, 1930), p. 17; G. I. Uratadze, *Obrazovanie i konsolidatsiia Gruzinskoi Demokraticheskoi Respubliki* (Munich, 1956), p. 28.

[6] *Dokumenty i materialy,* pp. 7–8; Uratadze, *op. cit.,* pp. 28–29. The three Moslem commissars were Mohammed Iusuf Jafarov, Khudadud Melik Aslanov, and Khalil Bek Khas-Mamedov.

[7] Khatisian, *op. cit.,* p. 18; [Republic of Azerbaijan], *Le 28 Mai 1919* ([Baku, 1919]), pp. 5–6.

[8] *Dokumenty i materialy,* pp. 8–9.

[9] D. Ananun, *Rusahayeri hasarakakan zargatsume,* III, *1901–1918* [The Social Development of the Russian Armenians: 1901-1918] (Venice, 1926), 672.

[10] According to Oliver Henry Radkey, *The Election to the Russian Constituent Assembly of 1917* (Cambridge, Mass., 1950), Appendix, the Mensheviks received 569,362 of the 1,887,453 votes cast in Transcaucasia, whereas the total Menshevik vote for all Russia was only 1,364,826.

[11] Wladimir Woytinsky, *La démocratie géorgienne* (Paris, 1921), p. 113, gives the Social Revolutionary party only 97,612. His figures for the other major slates are 660,216 for the Menshevik party; 419,887 for Dashnaktsutiun; 402,917 for the Musavat party; and 228,889 for other Moslem organizations combined.

[12] The Bolshevik vote came primarily from the Russian soldiers in Transcaucasia. For example, of the 9,316 soldiers voting in Alexandropol, 7,311 cast Bolshevik ballots. Consult *Hayastani Komunistakan partiayi patmutian urvagdser* [Historical Outlines of the Communist Party of Armenia], ed. by Hr. Margarian, A. Mnatsakanian, Kh. Barseghian (Erevan, 1958), p. 232. L. A. Khurshudian, *Stepan Shahumian: Petakan ev partiakan gordsuneutiune 1917–1918 tvakannerin* [Stepan Shahumian: Governmental and Party Activity, 1917–1918] (Erevan, 1959), states that nearly 8,000 soldiers in Baku cast ballots for slate no. V.

[13] The other slates, which received few votes, were no. VI, Georgian Social Federalist; no. VII, Armenian Populist; no. VIII, Georgian National Democrat; no. IX, Peoples Socialist; no. XIII, Transcaucasian Moslem; no. XV, Zionist.

[14] Ananun, *op. cit.,* pp. 672–673. Radkey, *op. cit.,* pp. 19–20, seems to be mistaken in stating that Transcaucasia sent fourteen Mensheviks and ten Dashnakists to the Constituent Assembly.

[15] S. Vratzian, *Hayastani Hanrapetutiun* [Republic of Armenia] (2d ed.; Beirut, 1958), p. 33, cited hereafter as Vratzian, *Hanrapetutiun.*

[16] Radkey, *op. cit.,* p. 21, states that there were 703 delegates, of whom 380 were Social Revolutionary; 39, Left Social Revolutionary; 168, Bolshevik; 18, Menshevik; 15, Kadet; and 77 from the nationality groups.

[17] For preliminaries, proceedings, and dispersal of the Constituent Assembly, consult James Bunyan and H. H. Fisher, *The Bolshevik Revolution, 1917–1918: Documents and*

Materials (Stanford, 1934), pp. 338–386; and M. V. Vishniak, *Vserossiiskoe Uchreditel'noe Sobranie* (Paris, 1932), pp. 98–116.

[18] *Oktiabr'skaia Revoliutsiia*, p. 163; D. Enukidze, *Krakh imperialisticheskoi interventsii v Zakavkaz'e* (Tbilisi, 1954), p. 20.

[19] *Dokumenty i materialy*, pp. 11–13, 15–16.

[20] *Ibid.*, pp. 16–18. The delegation included two army officers and three civilians, Smirnov and Tevzaia (SD) and Djamalian (Dashnaktsutiun). Consult S. T. Arkomed, *Materialy po istorii otpadeniia Zakavkaz'ia ot Rossii* (Tiflis, 1923), p. 13.

[21] *Dokumenty i materialy*, pp. 18–23; Ministerstvo Inostrannykh Del SSSR, *Dokumenty vneshnei politiki SSSR*, I, *7 noiabria 1917 g.–31 dekabria 1918 g.* (Moscow, 1957), 53–56, cited hereafter as *Vnesh. pol. SSSR;* Armenian SSR Central State Historical Archives, Fund 190/507, work 7, pp. 1–2, in A. M. Poghosian, *Sotsial-tntesakan haraberutiunnere Karsi marzum, 1878–1920* [The Social-Economic Relations in the Province of Kars, 1878–1920] (Erevan, 1961), pp. 277–278.

[22] Examples in *Velikaia Oktiabr'skaia sotsialisticheskaia revoliutsiia i pobeda sovetskoi vlasti v Armenii: Sbornik dokumentov*, ed. by A. N. Mnatsakanian, A. M. Akopian, and G. M. Dallakian (Erevan, 1957), pp. 116–118, 125–128, cited hereafter as *Velikaia revoliutsiia; Hoktemberian sotsialistakan meds revoliutsian ev sovetakan ishkhanutian haghtanake Hayastanum: Pastatghteri ev niuteri zhoghovadsu* [The Great October Socialist Revolution and the Victory of the Soviet Order in Armenia: Collection of Documents and Materials], ed. by A. N. Mnatsakanian, *et al.* (Erevan, 1960), pp. 151–152, 165–167, cited hereafter as *Meds revoliutsian;* Ds. Aghayan, *Hoktemberian revoliutsian ev hai zhoghovrdi azatagrume* [The October Revolution and the Liberation of the Armenian People] (Erevan, 1957), pp. 109–111; Poghosian, *op. cit.*, pp. 268–270, 283–284.

[23] G. Khachapuridze, *Bol'sheviki Gruzii v boiakh za pobedu sovetskoi vlasti* (2d ed.; [Moscow], 1951), pp. 139–140; *Oktiabr'skaia revoliutsiia*, pp. 178–179; Vartanian, *op. cit.*, pp. 107–108; Lalabekian, *op. cit.*, pp. 32–34.

[24] *Bol'sheviki v bor'be za pobedu sotsialisticheskoi revoliutsii v Azerbaidzhane: Dokumenty i materialy 1917–1918 g.g.*, ed. by Z. I. Ibragimov and M. S. Iskenderov (Baku, 1957), pp. 235–236, cited hereafter as *Revoliutsii v Azerbaidzhane;* Lalabekian, *op. cit.*, pp. 34–36.

[25] Uratadze, *op. cit.*, p. 41; Mamiia Orakhelashvili, *Zakavkazskie bol'shevistskie organizatsii v 1917 godu* ([Tiflis], 1927), pp. 50–53.

[26] Firuz Kazemzadeh, *The Struggle for Transcaucasia (1917–1921)* (New York and Oxford, [1951]), pp. 62–64; Khurshudian, *op. cit.*, pp. 134–135; A. M. Elchibekian, *Velikaia Oktiabr'skaia sotsialisticheskaia revoliutsiia i pobeda sovetskoi vlasti v Armenii* (Erevan, 1957), pp. 34–35.

[27] Gabriel Lazian, *Hayastan ev Hai Date: Hai-ev-rus haraberutiunneru luisin tak* [Armenia and the Armenian Question: Under the Light of Armeno-Russian Relations] (Cairo, 1957), pp. 214–216. For an analysis of the Armenian psychology, consult B. Ishkhanian, *Kontr-revoliutsiia v Zakavkaz'e* (Baku, 1919), pp. 77–80; H. Kachaznuni, *H. H. Dashnaktsutiune anelik chuni ailevs* [The Armenian Revolutionary Federation Has Nothing More To Do] (Vienna, 1923), p. 19; and Ruben [Ter Minasian], *Hai heghapokhakani me hishataknere* [The Memoirs of an Armenian Revolutionary], VII (Los Angeles, 1952), 136–140, 260–263.

[28] S. Vratzian, *Hin tghter nor patmutian hamar* [Old Papers for New History] (Beirut, 1962), p. 263; Reuben Darbinian, "A Mission to Moscow: Memoirs," *Armenian Review*, I (Spring, 1948), 23, 26.

[29] Khatisian, *op. cit.*, pp. 11–12.

[30] Ruben [Ter Minasian], *op. cit.*, pp. 142–143.

[31] B. Baikov, "Vospominaniia o revoliutsii v Zakavkaz'i (1917–1920 g.g.)," *Arkhiv*

Russkoi Revoliutsii, IX ([Berlin], 1923), 122, 191. Because Moslems in the Romanov Empire were exempt from compulsory military service, those who wished to see action during the World War entered the ranks of the volunteer "Savage Division" (*Dikaia Diviziia*), which served in the European theater. After the collapse of the Russian front, parts of the "Savage Division" returned to Transcaucasia, where they formed the nucleus of a Moslem army.

[32] Edvard Choburian, *Meds paterazme ev hai zhoghovurde* [The Great War and the Armenian People] (Constantinople, 1920), pp. 90–91; G. Sassuni, *Tajkahayastane rusakan tirapetutian tak (1914–1918)* [Turkish Armenia under Russian Domination (1914–1918)] (Boston, 1927), pp. 146–151; Vahan Papazian, *Im hushere* [My Memoirs], II (Beirut, 1952), 452–455.

[33] Vardges Aharonian, *Andranik, marde ev razmike* [Andranik, the Man and the Warrior] (Boston, 1957), p. 147.

[34] Archives of the Republic of Armenia Delegation to the Paris Peace Conference [now integrated into the archives of Dashnaktsutiun, Boston, Massachusetts], File 1/1, cited hereafter as Rep. of Arm. Archives; General G. Korganoff, *La participation des Arméniens à la guerre mondiale sur le front du Caucase, 1914–1918* (Paris, 1927), pp. 77–78.

[35] Nazarabekov was born in Tiflis in 1855, attended military academy in Moscow, participated in the 1877–1878 Russo-Turkish War. During the Russo-Japanese War, he was decorated with the medal of St. George, and, during World War I, with one of the two French military medals awarded to Russian officers. For an unfavorable appraisal of his leadership qualities, consult W. E. D. Allen and Paul Muratoff, *Caucasian Battlefields: A History of the Wars on the Turco-Caucasian Border, 1828–1921* (Cambridge, 1953).

[36] Korganoff, *op. cit.,* p. 78; Rep. of Arm. Archives, File 1/1.

[37] Silikov was soon promoted to the rank of general. Many Armenian officers in tsarist service had substituted the suffix "ov" or "ev" for the "ian" used in Armenian family names. Returning to Transcaucasia and entering Armenian service, officers such as Nazarabekov and Silikov reverted again to Nazarabekian, Silikian, and so forth.

[38] Rep. of Arm. Archives, File 1/1; Allen and Muratoff, *op. cit.,* p. 458; E. K. Sargsian, *Ekspansionistskaia politika Osmanskoi imperii v Zakavkaz'e nakanune i v gody pervoi mirovoi voiny* (Erevan, 1962), p. 337. Serving in the Armenian Corps was a company composed of three hundred Russian officers who had refused to retreat with their regular units.

[39] Korganoff, *op. cit.,* pp. 80–83.

[40] A. Poidebard, "Rôle militaire des Arméniens sur le front du Caucase après la défection de l'armée russe (décembre 1917–novembre 1918)," *Revue des études arméniennes,* I (pt. 2, 1920), 150–151; Allen and Muratoff, *op. cit.,* p. 462. Corps headquarters were first in Tiflis, then Alexandropol. The 1st Division's headquarters were in Alexandropol, and the 2d Division's, in Erevan.

[41] Choburian, *op. cit.,* p. 94; Aram Amirkhanian, *Rus ev turk zinadadare: Patmakan antsker* [The Russo-Turkish Truce: Historical Events] (Fresno, Calif., 1921), p. 23.

[42] Rep. of Arm. Archives, File 103/2, *H. H. Patvirakutiun 1919 t.* [Rep. of Arm. Delegation, 1919], Report no. 11 of 1918; Khatisian, *op. cit.,* pp. 20–21. For recriminations against the Tatars by non-Armenians, consult Henry Barby, . . . *Le débâcle russe. Les extravagances bolcheviques et l'épopée arménienne* (Paris, 1919), pp. 8–20, 32–40; and Consul Smith's dispatches in United States, The National Archives, *Record Group 59: General Records of the Department of State,* 861.00/872, 861.00/1094, and 867.22/22. Record Group 59 is cited hereafter as US, *RG 59.*

[43] Khatisian, *op. cit.,* pp. 20–21.

[44] Ishkhanian, *op. cit.,* pp. 49–51. Consult also Delegation of the Republic of Azerbaijan

to the Paris Peace Conference, *Economic and Financial Situation of Caucasian Azerbaijan* (Paris, 1919), pp. 15–16.

⁴⁵ St. Shahumian, *Erker* [Works], III (Erevan, 1958), 103; Aghayan, *op. cit.*, p. 148; G. B. Gharibdjanian, *Hayastani komunistakan kazmakerputiunnere sovetakan ishkhanutian haghtanaki hamar mghvads paikarum* [The Communist Organizations of Armenia in the Struggle for Victory of the Soviet Order] (Erevan, 1955), p. 175.

⁴⁶ For example, Ia. M. Shafir, *Grazhdanskaia voina v Rossii i men'shevistskaia Gruziia* (Moscow, 1921), pp. 20–26; I. V. Stalin, *Sochineniia*, IV, *Noiabr' 1917–1920* (Moscow, 1947), 55–59; Shahumian, *op. cit.*, pp. 80–89; *Meds revoliutsian*, pp. 167–169.

⁴⁷ Adil Khan Ziatkhan, *Aperçu sur l'histoire, la littérature et la politique de l'Azerbeidjan* (Baku, 1919), pp. 57–62.

⁴⁸ Allen and Muratoff, *op. cit.*, p. 462; Sargsian, *op. cit.*, p. 338.

⁴⁹ Uratadze, *op. cit.*, pp. 37–40; Zhordania, *op. cit.*, pp. 52–54; P. G. La Chesnais, *Les peuples de la Transcaucasie pendant la guerre et devant la paix* (Paris, 1921), pp. 39–43.

⁵⁰ *Revoliutsii v Azerbaidzhane*, pp. 236–238; Gharibdjanian, *op. cit.*, pp. 176–182; Sargsian, *op. cit.*, pp. 328–332; H. N. Karapetian, *Hayastani Komeritmiutian dsnunde* [The Birth of the Communist Youth Union of Armenia] (Erevan, 1956), pp. 70–73.

⁵¹ *Revoliutsion kocher ev trutsikner, 1902–1921* [Revolutionary Appeals and Circulars, 1902–1921], compiled by the Institute of Party History of the Central Committee of the Communist Party of Armenia and the Armenian Filial of the Institute of Marxism-Leninism (Erevan, 1960), p. 445, cited hereafter as *Kocher; Velikaia revoliutsiia*, pp. 174–176; *Meds revoliutsian*, pp. 180–181.

⁵² Shahumian, *op. cit.*, III, 94–95; *Kocher*, p. 447; *Meds revoliutsian*, p. 183.

⁵³ On many other occasions, Shahumian cursed the Menshevik "lords" and Musavat "beks" but, when referring to his Armenian opponents, avoided the term "Dashnaktsutiun," by using such phrases as "nationalists," "bourgeois," and so on.

⁵⁴ Givi Gambashidze, *Iz istorii politiki S.Sh.A. v otnoshenii Gruzii, 1917–1920* (Tbilisi, 1960), pp. 10–20; G. Galoyan, *Bor'ba za sovetskuiu vlast' v Armenii* (Moscow, 1957), pp. 38–40; Vartanian, *op. cit.*, pp. 114–115.

⁵⁵ US Archives, *RG 59*, 861.00/871, and *Record Group 84: Foreign Service Posts of the Department of State*, C46(C8).1, Class 711, Smith to Secretary of State, November 2, 1917. *Record Group 84* is cited hereafter as *RG 84*.

⁵⁶ *Ibid.*, *RG 59*, 861.00/796; *RG 84*, C46(C8).1, Class 711, Smith to Francis, October 5, 1917.

⁵⁷ *Ibid.*, *RG 84*, C46(C8).1, Class 711, Francis to Smith, October 5, 1917.

⁵⁸ *Ibid.*, *RG 59*, 861.00/711.

⁵⁹ *Ibid.*, 861.00/719; *RG 84*, C46(C8).1, Class 711, telegram, November 25, 1917.

⁶⁰ United States, Department of State, *Papers Relating to the Foreign Relations of the United States, 1918, Russia*, II (Washington, D.C., 1932), 582, cited hereafter as US, *FRUS, Russia;* US Archives, *RG 84*, C46(C8).1, Class 711, Francis to Smith, January 18, 1918.

⁶¹ US Archives, *RG 59*, 861.00/807; US, *FRUS, Russia*, II, 590.

⁶² US Archives, *RG 59*, 861.00/848.

⁶³ *Ibid.*, Enclosure, December 22, 1917, telegram of Smith.

⁶⁴ *Ibid.*, *RG 84*, C46(C8).1, Class 711, Smith to Francis, January 3, 1918.

⁶⁵ *Ibid.*, January 7, 1918, Consular report.

⁶⁶ *Dokumenty i materialy*, pp. 11–15; Korganoff, *op. cit.*, p. 103; US Archives, *RG 84*, C46(C8).1, Class 711, Gegechkori to Villari, January 17, 1918 [old style].

⁶⁷ *Dokumenty i materialy*, pp. 25–27.

⁶⁸ *Ibid.*, pp. 28–29.

⁶⁹ *Ibid.*, pp. 29–35; Uratadze, *op. cit.*, pp. 33–34.

⁷⁰ *Dokumenty i materialy*, pp. 35–37.
⁷¹ US Archives, *RG 84*, C46(C8).1, Class 711, Gegechkori to Villari, January 17, 1918 [old style]; *Dokumenty i materialy*, pp. 37–40.
⁷² US Archives, *RG 84*, C46(C8).1, Class 711, Smith to Washington and London, January 30, 1918; *Dokumenty i materialy*, pp. 35–36.
⁷³ Woytinsky, *op. cit.*, p. 121; Khatisian, *op. cit.*, p. 23.
⁷⁴ Gotthard Jäschke, "Der Turanismus der Jungtürken: Zur osmanischen Aussenpolitik im Weltkriege," *Die Welt des Islams*, XXIII (bk. 1–2, 1941), 29.
⁷⁵ Khatisian, *op. cit.*, p. 23.
⁷⁶ *Dokumenty i materialy*, p. 40.
⁷⁷ *Ibid.*, pp. 52–57, 60.
⁷⁸ Korganoff, *op. cit.*, pp. 90–93.
⁷⁹ Sabahettin Selek, *Millî Mücadele: Anadolu İhtilâli* [The National Struggle: Anatolian Rebellion] (Istanbul, 1963), p. 14.
⁸⁰ M. Larcher, *La guerre turque dans la guerre mondiale* (Paris, 1926), p. 416; Joseph Pomiankowski, *Der Zusammenbruch des Ottomanischen Reiches: Erinnerungen an die Türkei aus der Zeit des Weltkrieges* (Leipzig, 1928), p. 329; Sargsian, *op. cit.*, pp. 336–337; Allen and Muratoff, *op. cit.*, p. 459.
⁸¹ Karabekir had participated in the Balkan wars and during the World War, prior to joining the Third Army, served as chief of staff of the First and Sixth armies and as a corps commander of the Second Army. He was destined to become the chief Turkish antagonist to the Armenian Republic.
⁸² Allen and Muratoff, *op. cit.*, p. 460. There is considerable discrepancy among military historians about the corps commanders. Allen and Muratoff, p. 478, and Larcher, *op. cit.*, p. 418, state that I Corps Commander was Yakub Shevki Pasha, but, contradicting himself, Larcher, p. 667, identifies Karabekir as the commander. It seems that Sargsian, *op. cit.*, p. 338, and the biographer of Karabekir, F. Kandemir, *Kâzım Karabekir* (Istanbul, 1948), p. 136, are correct in naming the Turkish Colonel as head of the I Corps. Kandemir states that the order for Karabekir's appointment was dated December 13, 1917.
⁸³ *Dokumenty i materialy*, pp. 41–43.
⁸⁴ *Ibid.*, pp. 43–44, 44–46.
⁸⁵ *Ibid.*, pp. 46–47.
⁸⁶ *Ibid.*, pp. 50–51.
⁸⁷ Vehib apparently considered the attached IV Corps as still a component of the Second Army.
⁸⁸ *Dokumenty i materialy*, pp. 48–49.
⁸⁹ [Turkey], *Memorandum of the Sublime Porte Communicated to the American, British, French, and Italian High Commissioners on the 12th February 1919* (Constantinople, 1919), pp. 13–20; Esat Uras, *Tarihte Ermeniler ve Ermeni Meselesi* [The Armenians in History and the Armenian Question] (Ankara, 1950), pp. 655–666; Kandemir, *op. cit.*, pp. 142–145.
⁹⁰ Sassuni, *op. cit.*, pp. 155–158; Amirkhanian, *op. cit.*, pp. 35–60.
⁹¹ O. Minasian, "Vneshniaia politika zakavkazskoi kontrrevoliutsii v pervoi polovine 1918 goda," *Istorik marksist* (no. 6, 1938), p. 59; Sargsian, *op. cit.*, p. 336; Avakian, *op. cit.*, p. 39.
⁹² Amirkhanian, *op. cit.*, pp. 105–120; Korganoff, *op. cit.*, pp. 94–98.
⁹³ *Dokumenty i materialy*, pp. 59–61; Allen and Muratoff, *op. cit.*, pp. 461–462.
⁹⁴ Armenian SSR Central State Historical Archives, Fund 200, work 99, pp. 42–44, in Sargsian, *op. cit.*, p. 339.
⁹⁵ Kandemir, *op. cit.*, pp. 153–154. In a message to the Department of State, Smith

reported that one of the primary purposes of the Turkish offensive was to seize vital supplies. Consult US Archives, *RG 59*, 861.00/1102.

96 Kandemir, *op. cit.*, pp. 145–146.
97 *Dokumenty i materialy*, pp. 27–28.
98 Ananun, *op. cit.*, p. 673.
99 *Ibid.*, pp. 673–674.
100 *Revoliutsii v Azerbaidzhane*, p. 258; *Velikaia revoliutsiia*, pp. 173–174.
101 Khurshudian, *op. cit.*, pp. 153–155, 158–160; Vartanian, *op. cit.*, p. 113.
102 Kh. A. Barsegian, *Istoriia armianskoi bol'shevistskoi periodicheskoi pechati* (Erevan, 1958), pp. 221–223; A. N. Mnatsakanian, *Revoliutsian Andrkovkasum ev Rusastani patviraknere, 1917–1921* [The Revolution in Transcaucasia and the Envoys of Russia, 1917–1921] (Erevan, 1961), p. 45.
103 Khachapuridze, *op. cit.*, p. 156; Khurshudian, *op. cit.*, pp. 184–185; Mneyan, *op. cit.*, p. 188; Sergei Melik-Yolchian, "Bakvi herosamarte" [The Heroic Battle of Baku], *Hairenik Amsagir*, III (May, 1925), 113–114.
104 Stalin, *op. cit.*, pp. 64–65; *Revoliutsii v Azerbaidzhane*, pp. 272–273.
105 Vratzian, *Hanrapetutiun*, pp. 71–72. As early as November, 1917, part of the Social Revolutionary and Dashnakist fractions of the Baku Soviet had voted in favor of recognizing the Russian Sovnarkom. Consult Lalabekian, *op. cit.*, p. 54.
106 Hovakim Melikian, "Arian janaparhov" [On the Bloody Path], *Hairenik Amsagir*, III (January, 1925), 119.
107 *Kocher*, pp. 453–454; Stalin, *op. cit.*, pp. 62–63; *Meds revoliutsian*, p. 188; Khurshudian, *op. cit.*, pp. 177–183.
108 [Communist Party of Armenia], *Hayastani Komunistakan Kusaktsutian nerkayatsutsichi zekutsume errord Komunistakan Internatsionalin* [Report of the Representative of the Armenian Communist Party to the Third Communist International] (Moscow, 1919), pp. 18–20.
109 Uratadze, *op. cit.*, p. 45.
110 Ananun, *op. cit.*, p. 674.
111 In addition to the Georgians in this fraction, there were two Russians, a German, and four Armenians: Arshak Zohrabian, Hovhannes Bekzadian, Ghazar Ter Ghazarian, and Simeon Pirumian.
112 During different periods of Soviet historiography, Hummet is alternately considered Menshevik and Bolshevik. Minasian, *op. cit.*, p. 60, and Khurshudian, *op. cit.*, p. 114, label the party as Menshevik. At times there seem to have been both Bolshevik and Menshevik Hummetist factions.
113 Kazemzadeh, *op. cit.*, p. 87, allots the Mensheviks and Musavatists thirty each, the Social Revolutionaries six, and the Hummetists three places in the Seim. This seems to be incorrect, however, for by tripling the eleven Menshevik and ten Musavat Constituent Assembly delegates, the figures given by Ananun prove more valid.
114 *Dokumenty i materialy*, pp. 67–69.
115 *Zakavkazskii Seim, Stenograficheskii otchet: Sessiia pervaia, zasedanie tret'e* (Tiflis, 1918), p. 15, cited in Vratzian, *Hanrapetutiun*, pp. 72–74; Shahan, *Tiurkizm Angoraen Baku ev trkakan orientatsion* [Turkism from Angora to Baku and the Turkish Orientation] (Athens, 1928), p. 131.
116 Vratzian, *Hanrapetutiun*, p. 74.
117 *Ibid.*, pp. 74–75.
118 *Dokumenty i materialy*, p. 62.
119 *Ibid.*, pp. 62–66.
120 *Ibid.*, pp. 73–83.
121 *Ibid.*, pp. 83–84; Arkomed, *op. cit.*, p. 17; Korganoff, *op. cit.*, p. 106.
122 *Dokumenty i materialy*, pp. 85–86.

Notes to Chapter VIII

[1] Al. Khatisian, *Hayastani Hanrapetutian dsagumn u zargatsume* [The Creation and Development of the Republic of Armenia] (Athens, 1930), pp. 28–29.

[2] [Republic of Georgia], *Dokumenty i materialy po vneshnei politike Zakavkaz'ia i Gruzii* (Tiflis, 1919), pp. 107–108, cited hereafter as *Dokumenty i materialy;* O. Minasian, "Vneshniaia politika zakavkazskoi kontrrevoliutsii v pervoi polovine 1918 goda," *Istorik marksist* (no. 6, 1938), p. 64.

[3] Khatisian, *op. cit.,* pp. 29–30.

[4] *Dokumenty i materialy,* pp. 86–87; V. Minakhorian, "Karsi ankume" [The Fall of Kars], *Hairenik Amsagir,* XIII (August, 1935), 84.

[5] *Dokumenty i materialy,* pp. 87–88.

[6] *Ibid.,* p. 90.

[7] G. I. Uratadze, *Obrazovanie i konsolidatsiia Gruzinskoi Demokraticheskoi Respubliki* (Munich, 1956), pp. 48–49; Minakhorian, *op. cit.* (August, 1935), p. 86.

[8] *Dokumenty i materialy,* pp. 98–99; Uratadze, *op. cit.,* pp. 50.

[9] *Stenograficheskii otchet zasedaniia Seima,* pp. 93–106, in Uratadze, *op. cit.,* pp. 50–52; *Dokumenty i materialy,* pp. 100–106.

[10] Minakhorian, *op. cit.* (September, 1935), pp. 85–87; Minasian, *op. cit.,* p. 64; *Dokumenty i materialy,* pp. 113–116.

[11] Khatisian, *op. cit.,* p. 30.

[12] *Ibid.,* p. 28.

[13] Armenian SSR Central State Historical Archives, Fund 68/200, work 7, p. 158, in Kh. H. Badalian, *Germana-turkakan okupantnere Hayastanum 1918 tvakanin* [The Germano-Turkish Occupants in Armenia, 1918] (Erevan, 1962), pp. 87–89; *Dokumenty i materialy,* p. 107.

[14] S. Vratzian, *Hayastani Hanrapetutiun* [Republic of Armenia] (2d ed., Beirut, 1958), p. 79.

[15] Khatisian, *op. cit.,* p. 24, states that Abashidze was a Georgian Moslem. Several authors confuse Haidar (Gaidar) Bey Abashidze with Prince Kita Abashidze, a Georgian Social Federalist and member of the Ozakom.

[16] Ruben H. Kachaznuni preferred the use of his patronymic and was thus known as Hovhannes to most Armenians. The latter name is used in this study.

[17] There is considerable discrepancy about the party affiliation of the delegates. Firuz Kazemzadeh, *The Struggle for Transcaucasia (1917–1921)* (New York and Oxford, [1951]), p. 93, states that Haidarov was a Musavatist and that Mehtiev and Sheikh-ul-Islamov were Moslem Mensheviks. He omits Khas-Mamedov from the list of delegates. D. Enukidze, *Krakh imperialisticheskoi interventsii v Zakavkaz'e* (Tbilisi, 1954), p. 30, agrees with Vratzian, *op. cit.,* that Haidarov was from the Moslem Socialist Bloc but labels Khas-Mamedov, Mehtiev, and Sheikh-ul-Islamov as Moslem Mensheviks. The party affiliations suggested by Vratzian seem most accurate, for they correspond to an official government report which states that on the delegation there were two places each for the Mensheviks, Musavatists, and Dashnakists, and one place each for the Moslem Socialists, Hummetists, Moslems of Russia, Georgian Social Federalists, and Georgian National Democrats. Consult *Dokumenty i materialy,* p. 107.

[18] Badalian, *op. cit.,* p. 88; Archives of the Republic of Armenia Delegation to the Paris Peace Conference [now integrated into the archives of Dashnaktsutiun, Boston, Massachusetts], File 1406a/26a, H. H. D. *Amerikayi Kedronakan Komite, 1918* [A. (Armenian) R. (Revolutionary) F. (Federation) Central Committee of America, 1918], cited hereafter as Rep. of Arm. Archives.

[19] S. T. Arkomed, *Materialy po istorii otpadeniia Zakavkaz'ia ot Rossii* (Tiflis, 1923), p. 17; Vratzian, *op. cit.,* p. 79.

20 Badalian, *op. cit.*, p. 87.
21 Joseph Pomiankowski, *Der Zusammenbruch des Ottomanischen Reiches: Erinnerungen an die Türkei aus der Zeit des Weltkrieges* (Leipzig, 1928), p. 334.
22 F. Kandemir, *Kâzım Karabekir* (Istanbul, 1948), pp. 152–153.
23 *Ibid.*, pp. 153–154.
24 General G. Korganoff, *La participation des Arméniens à la guerre mondiale sur le front du Caucase, 1914–1918* (Paris, 1927), p. 108; Aram Amirkhanian, *Rus ev turk zinadadare: Patmakan antsker* [The Russo-Turkish Truce: Historical Events] (Fresno, Calif., 1921), pp. 128, 145.
25 Rep. of Arm. Archives, File 1406a/26a and 1/1; W. E. D. Allen and Paul Muratoff, *Caucasian Battlefields: A History of the Wars on the Turco-Caucasian Border, 1828–1921* (Cambridge, 1953), pp. 462–463.
26 Amirkhanian, *op. cit.*, pp. 187–188; Rep. of Arm. Archives, File 1406a/26a.
27 Rep. of Arm. Archives, File 1/1, "Opérations militaires sur le front du Caucase." According to statistics in the USSR Central State Archives of the October Revolution, Fund 1318, work 40, p. 52, there were left, in addition to the fortress cannons, eleven thousand rifles, two million cartridges, and a year's supply of food. Consult Ds. Aghayan, *Hoktemberian revoliutsian ev hai zhoghovrdi azatagrume* [The October Revolution and the Liberation of the Armenian People] (Erevan, 1955), p. 160.
28 *Dokumenty i materialy*, p. 93.
29 Vratzian, *op. cit.*, p. 93. The conscription act of April, 1918, authorized drafting men up to twenty-eight years of age first, and then those up to thirty-three years.
30 Kandemir, *op. cit.*, p. 157; Vardges Aharonian, *Andranik, marde ev razmike* [Andranik, the Man and the Warrior] (Boston, 1957), pp. 148–149; Rep. of Arm. Archives, File 1406a/26a.
31 Korganoff, *op. cit.*, p. 114; Rep. of Arm. Archives, File 1/1.
32 Korganoff, *op. cit.*, p. 117; Rep. of Arm. Archives, File 1/1.
33 E. K. Sargsian, *Ekspansionistskaia politika Osmanskoi imperii v Zakavkaz'e nakanune i v gody pervoi mirovoi voiny* (Erevan, 1962), pp. 349–350; Rep. of Arm. Archives, File 1406a/26a; Korganoff, *op. cit.*, pp. 120–123; Allen and Muratoff, *op. cit.*, pp. 463–464.
34 United States, The National Archives, *Record Group 84: Foreign Service Posts of the Department of State*, C46(C8).1, Class 711, Smith to Secretary of State, April 10, 1918. *Record Group 84* is cited hereafter as *RG 84*.
35 *Ibid.*, March 12 telegram, and *Record Group 59: General Records of the Department of State*, 867.22/22 and 867.48/77. *Record Group 59* is cited hereafter as *RG 59*. A similar message of Lansing to Ambassador Page in London is in United States, Department of State, *Papers Relating to the Foreign Relations of the United States, 1918, Russia*, II (Washington, D.C., 1932), 623–624, cited hereafter as *US, FRUS, Russia*.
36 US Archives, *RG 59*, 867.22/22.
37 *Ibid.*, *RG 84*, C46(C8).1, Class 711, Wright to Smith, January 18, 1918.
38 *Ibid.*, *RG 59*, 763.72/9295 and 763.72/9405a; *US, FRUS, Russia*, II, 623–624.
39 *Dokumenty i materialy*, p. 108; Khatisian, *op. cit.*, p. 30.
40 Arkomed, *op. cit.*, p. 16; *Dokumenty i materialy*, p. 116.
41 Kazemzadeh, *op. cit.*, p. 95.
42 Minakhorian, *op. cit.* (September, 1935), p. 89; *Dokumenty i materialy*, pp. 109–110; Sargsian, *op. cit.*, p. 347.
43 *Dokumenty i materialy*, pp. 109, 118–119.
44 Arkomed, *op. cit.*, p. 27.
45 *Ibid.*, pp. 27–28; *Dokumenty i materialy*, pp. 132–134.
46 Armenian SSR Central State Historical Archives, Fund 200, work 7, pp. 178–181, in Sargsian, *op. cit.*, pp. 347–348; *Dokumenty i materialy*, pp. 111, 134–136, 141.

47 Arkomed, *op. cit.*, p. 33.
48 *Ibid.*, pp. 34–35; *Dokumenty i materialy*, pp. 111, 137–139.
49 Minasian, *op. cit.*, pp. 66–67; Arkomed, *op. cit.*, pp. 36–39.
50 *Dokumenty i materialy*, pp. 139–142; Minakhorian, *op. cit.* (October, 1935), p. 79.
51 Uratadze, *op. cit.*, p. 54; *Dokumenty i materialy*, p. 144; Minakhorian, *op. cit.* (October, 1935), p. 80.
52 *Dokumenty i materialy*, pp. 145–146; Uratadze, *op. cit.*, p. 55.
53 There exists a minor discrepancy as to the date of the plenary session of the Seim. *Dokumenty i materialy*, p. 146, gives March 25, 1918, while the resolution prepared by Zhordania states that the Seim would meet the following night. March 26 is also the date recorded in the minutes of the Seim and by Arkomed, *op. cit.*, p. 40.
54 *Dokumenty i materialy*, pp. 147–151.
55 Arkomed, *op. cit.*, p. 40; *Dokumenty i materialy*, p. 146.
56 Hovakim Melikian, "Arian janaparhov" [On the Bloody Path], *Hairenik Amsagir*, III (November, 1924), 77–81, presents a résumé of events in Erevan between the March and November revolutions.
57 Vratzian, *op. cit.*, p. 120; Melikian, *op. cit.* (December, 1924), p. 91.
58 Gabriel Lazian, *Heghapokhakan demker (mtavorakanner ev haidukner)* [Revolutionary Figures (Intellectuals and Guerrilla Fighters)] (Cairo, 1954), p. 197; Melikian, *op. cit.* (December, 1924), pp. 92–95, and (February, 1925), p. 85.
59 Rep. of Arm. Archives, File 103/2, "Teghekagir no. 11"; John Elder, "Memories of the Armenian Republic," *Armenian Review*, VI (Spring, 1953), 7; Melikian, *op. cit.* (December, 1924), pp. 96–99.
60 Quoted in Vratzian, *op. cit.*, pp. 130–133.
61 Melikian, *op. cit.* (January, 1925), pp. 120–124, depicts the activities of the special commission while it was in the Erevan *guberniia*.
62 Vratzian, *op. cit.*, pp. 127–129.
63 Melikian, *op. cit.* (February, 1925), pp. 85–87.
64 *Ibid.*, pp. 87–88; Vratzian, *op. cit.*, pp. 136–137. Arshaluis Astvadsatrian, "Arame," *Vem*, III (January-April, 1935), 57–60.
65 *Dokumenty i materialy*, pp. 119–120; Minakhorian, *op. cit.* (September, 1935), pp. 88–89.
66 *Dokumenty i materialy*, pp. 121–127.
67 *Ibid.*, pp. 128–131.
68 Armenian SSR Central State Historical Archives, Fund 56/120, work 15, p. 5, in A. M. Poghosian, *Sotsial-tntesakan haraberutiunnere Karsi marzum, 1878–1920* [The Social-Economic Relations in the Province of Kars, 1878–1920] (Erevan, 1961), pp. 292–293; Minasian, *op. cit.*, p. 65; *Dokumenty i materialy*, p. 132.
69 M. Shatirian, "Drvagner motik antsialits" [Episodes from the Recent Past], *Hairenik Amsagir*, I (May, 1923), 114–122; Sergei Melik-Yolchian, "Bakvi herosamarte" [The Heroic Battle of Baku], *Hairenik Amsagir*, III (May, 1925), 115–116.
70 Shatirian, *op. cit.*, pp. 122–123; Melik-Yolchian, *op. cit.*, p. 116. A slightly different account of the episode is presented by A. Giulkhandanian, "Bakvi herosamarte" [The Heroic Battle of Baku], *Hairenik Amsagir*, XIX (September-October, 1941), 87–92.
71 *Izvestiia Bakinskogo Soveta*, no. 199, 1917, in L. A. Khurshudian, *Stepan Shahumian: Petakan ev partiakan gordsuneutiune 1917–1918 tvakannerin* [Stepan Shahumian: Governmental and Party Activity, 1917–1918] (Erevan, 1959), p. 114.
72 B. Ishkhanian, *Kontr-revoliutsiia v Zakavkaz'e* (Baku, 1919), pp. 67–68, 78–81; Kazemzadeh, *op. cit.*, pp. 66–67.
73 Khurshudian, *op. cit.*, pp. 212–217; Melik-Yolchian, *op. cit.*, p. 115. Until the spring of 1918, the Baku City Duma, composed of representatives of all political shades, was generally considered the legal administration.
74 Giulkhandanian, *op. cit.* (July, 1941), pp. 98–101; Vratzian, *op. cit.*, p. 157. Official

1912 Russian statistics for the Baku guberniia show 1,175,000 inhabitants, of whom 300,000 were Christians. Over half of the Christian element was Armenian. Within the city limits there were 378,000 residents, of whom 176,000 were Moslems; 103,000, Russians; 73,000, Armenians; and 25,000, Europeans and Jews. Approximately 60,000 of the Armenians were concentrated in the city proper, while the other 13,000, mostly laborers, lived near the oil fields.

[75] Melik-Yolchian, *op. cit.*, p. 119; Shatirian, *op. cit.*, p. 114; Khurshudian, *op. cit.*, p. 191. Nariman Narimanov, Hummetist and later premier of Soviet Azerbaijan, accused the Musavatists of bringing interracial bloodshed one step closer by blocking the exit routes of the Armenian soldiers. Consult his *Stat'i i pis'ma* (Moscow, 1925), pp. 7-8. Abraham Giulkhandanian, chairman of the Baku Armenian Council, gives a valuable account of the Armeno-Moslem negotiations of January–March, 1918. Consult his study, *op. cit.* (August, 1941), pp. 108-113.

[76] This was the group that had left Tiflis at the beginning of the year after the Menshevik-Right Social Revolutionary coalition had seized the property of the Regional Army Soviet. The Military *Revkom* claimed jurisdiction over the Russian Caucasus Army.

[77] Korganoff, *op. cit.*, p. 176; Melik-Yolchian, *op. cit.*, p. 119; Vratzian, *op. cit.*, p. 162. There are many versions of the immediate cause for the outbreak of hostilities. Richard Pipes, *The Formation of the Soviet Union* (rev. ed.; Cambridge, Mass., 1964), pp. 199-200, states that the men were disarmed before being allowed to disembark, thus triggering a Moslem reaction. Most Soviet sources claim that the men from the "Savage Division" were already in Baku recruiting warriors to assist in the squelching of the Soviet administration that had been established in Lenkoran. Therefore, the Baku Soviet Executive Committee took measures to assist Lenkoran by forbidding the departure of these armed men. For the Soviet viewpoint, consult, for example, Aghayan, *op. cit.*, pp. 163-164; and B. H. Lalabekian, *V. I. Lenine ev sovetakan kargeri hastatumn u amrapndumn Andrkovkasum* [V. I. Lenin and the Establishment and Strengthening of Soviet Order in Transcaucasia] (Erevan, 1961), p. 55.

[78] Melik-Yolchian, *op. cit.*, pp. 120-121; Vratzian, *op. cit.*, pp. 162-164; M. Shatirian, "Edj me hai-trkakan krivneren" [A Page from the Armeno-Turkish Battles], *Hairenik Amsagir*, I (September, 1923), 96, cited hereafter as Shatirian, "Edj."

[79] Narimanov, *op. cit.*, p. 6; Khurshudian, *op. cit.*, pp. 200-201.

[80] Shatirian, "Edj," p. 96; Melik-Yolchian, *op. cit.*, p. 120. Reuben Darbinian, "A Mission to Moscow: Memoirs," *Armenian Review*, I (Spring, 1948), 23, justifies Armenian participation, stating that without Armenian aid the Bolsheviks would have been crushed by the Musavat, who would then have turned on the Christians of the area. Shahumian admitted that without Armenian assistance Baku and its oil would have been seized by the Moslems. Consult Pipes, *op. cit.*, p. 201.

[81] Gr. Tchalkhouchian, *Le livre rouge* (Paris, 1919), pp. 85-86; Lalabekian, *op. cit.*, pp. 57-58; Khurshudian, *op. cit.*, p. 202; *Bol'sheviki v bor'be za pobedu sotsialisticheskoi revoliutsii v Azerbaidzhane: Dokumenty i materialy 1917-1918 g.g.*, ed. by Z. I. Ibragimov and M. S. Iskenderov (Baku, 1957), pp. 333-334, cited hereafter as *Revoliutsii v Azerbaidzhane*.

[82] Melik-Yolchian, *op. cit.*, pp. 123-126. Kazemzadeh, *op. cit.*, p. 75, asserts that the Soviet provoked the civil war, which turned into a massacre of Moslems by Armenians. He is in accord with Azerbaijani sources, which report thousands were killed. The Azerbaijani delegation at Paris in 1919 claimed that during the "March Days" twelve thousand Moslems were slaughtered. Shahumian wrote on April 13, 1918, that there had been three thousand fatalities from the two opposing sides combined. Consult *Revoliutsii v Azerbaidzhane*, p. 347. Pipes, *op. cit.*, p. 200, accepts Shahumian's figures but stresses that the majority of the victims were Moslems.

[83] Armenian claims of protecting Moslem civilians are included in Tchalkhouchian,

op. cit., pp. 86–87, and Shatirian, "Edj," pp. 97–98. Moslem condemnations of the Bolshevik-Dashnakist entente are in memorandums to the Paris Peace Conference, copies found in the Rep. of Arm. Archives, Files 70/2, 104/3, and 132/31. Also in [Republic of Azerbaijan Peace Conference Delegation], *La République de l'Azerbaidjan du Caucase* (Paris, 1919), pp. 14–22.

[84] St. Shahumian, *Erker* [Works], III (Erevan, 1958), 154–155; *Revoliutsii v Azerbaidzhane*, p. 361; Khurshudian, *op. cit.*, pp. 208–210; Melik-Yolchian, *op. cit.* (June, 1925), p. 105. Vratzian, *op. cit.*, p. 166, gives the text of the agreement between the Armenian Council and the Military *Revkom* of the Soviet. Armenian troops remained under the command of Hamazasp, while the commander in chief of the Soviet forces was G. N. Korganov (Korganian).

[85] *Revoliutsii v Azerbaidzhane*, p. 381; Khurshudian, *op. cit.*, pp. 218–219; Lalabekian, *op. cit.*, p. 68.

[86] Arkomed, *op. cit.*, p. 41; Minasian, *op. cit.*, p. 68.

[87] Arkomed, *op. cit.*, pp. 41–42.

[88] Minakhorian, *op. cit.*, XIV (December, 1935), 81; Minasian, *op. cit.*, p. 68; *Zhurnal zasedaniia delegatsii*, in Arkomed, *op. cit.*, pp. 42–44.

[89] Al. Stavrovskii, *Zakavkaz'e posle Oktiabria* (Moscow-Leningrad, [1925]), p. 18; *Protokol 6-go zasedaniia mirnoi konferentsii*, in Arkomed, *op. cit.*, pp. 45–46.

[90] Armenian SSR Central State Historical Archives, Fund 68/200, work 7, p. 152, in Badalian, *op. cit.*, p. 90; Sargsian, *op. cit.*, p. 350; Khatisian, *op. cit.*, p. 34; *Dokumenty i materialy*, pp. 112, 155–156.

[91] Arkomed, *op. cit.*, pp. 47–48.

[92] *Dokumenty i materialy*, pp. 156–157.

[93] Armenian SSR Central State Historical Archives, Fund 200, work 7, pp. 178–181, in Sargsian, *op. cit.*, p. 350; *Dokumenty i materialy*, pp. 158–159.

[94] Minakhorian, *op. cit.* (December, 1935), pp. 84–85; Arkomed, *op. cit.*, p. 48; Armenian SSR Central State Historical Archives, Fund 200, work 7, pp. 140–141, in Sargsian, *op. cit.*, p. 348.

[95] *Dokumenty i materialy*, p. 158; Arkomed, *op. cit.*, pp. 49–50.

[96] Rep. of Arm. Archives, File 1406*a*/26*a*; Khatisian, *op. cit.*, p. 35; *Dokumenty i materialy*, p. 160.

[97] Arkomed, *op. cit.*, p. 51.

[98] Armenian SSR Central State Historical Archives, Fund 68/200, work 7, p. 152, in Badalian, *op. cit.*, p. 91; *Dokumenty i materialy*, pp. 112, 160, 162.

[99] Arkomed, *op. cit.*, pp. 51, 53–54.

[100] Minasian, *op. cit.*, p. 71; Stavrovskii, *op. cit.*, p. 21; Minakhorian, *op. cit.* (December, 1935), pp. 89–90; *Dokumenty i materialy*, pp. 161–162.

[101] Arkomed, *op. cit.*, p. 56; Minakhorian, *op. cit.* (December, 1935), p. 90.

[102] *Dokumenty i materialy*, pp. 163–164.

[103] *Ibid.*, p. 165.

[104] Arkomed, *op. cit.*, p. 60; Vratzian, *op. cit.*, p. 98; *Dokumenty i materialy*, p. 174.

[105] Uratadze, *op. cit.*, p. 59; Minakhorian, *op. cit.* (December, 1935), pp. 91–92; *Dokumenty i materialy*, pp. 174–177.

[106] Stavrovskii, *op. cit.*, p. 26; V. Stankevich, *Sud'by narodov Rossii* (Berlin, 1921), p. 244; *Dokumenty i materialy*, pp. 177–179.

[107] Uratadze, *op. cit.*, pp. 60–61; *Dokumenty i materialy*, pp. 179–182.

[108] Khatisian, *op. cit.*, p. 36; *Dokumenty i materialy*, pp. 183–184.

[109] Stavrovskii, *op. cit.*, p. 29; *Dokumenty i materialy*, pp. 185–187.

[110] Vratzian, *op. cit.*, p. 102.

[111] Armenian SSR Central State Historical Archives, Fund 68/200, work 7, p. 152, in Badalian, *op. cit.*, pp. 91–92; Khatisian, *op. cit.*, p. 36.

¹¹² *Zhurnal zasedaniia delegatsii,* in Arkomed, *op. cit.,* pp. 62–63.
¹¹³ Khatisian, *op. cit.,* p. 36; Arkomed, *op. cit.,* pp. 63–64.
¹¹⁴ Minakhorian, *op. cit.* (December, 1935), p. 134; Arkomed, *op. cit.,* p. 64.
¹¹⁵ Vratzian, *op. cit.,* p. 97; Arkomed, *op. cit.,* p. 65.
¹¹⁶ Kazemzadeh, *op. cit.,* p. 100.

Notes to Chapter IX

¹ Paul Miliukov, "The Balkanization of Transcaucasia," *The New Russia,* II (June 24, July 1, July 8, 1920), 236–241, 269–274, 299–303.
² Archives of the Republic of Armenia Delegation to the Paris Peace Conference [now integrated into the archives of Dashnaktsutiun, Boston, Massachusetts], File 1406a/26a, cited hereafter as Rep. of Arm. Archives; General G. Korganoff, *La participation des Arméniens à la guerre mondiale sur le front du Caucase, 1914–1918* (Paris, 1927), p. 122; A. B. Kadishev, *Interventsiia i grazhdanskaia voina v Zakavkaz'e* (Moscow, 1960), p. 53.
³ Rep. of Arm. Archives, File 1/1. W. E. D. Allen and Paul Muratoff, *Caucasian Battlefields: A History of the Wars on the Turco-Caucasian Border, 1828–1921* (Cambridge, 1953), p. 470, state that the Turks had from 55,000 to 60,000 troops for the Caucasus campaign. The 37th and 5th Caucasian divisions of the II Corps were in the Batum-Olti area, while the Corps' 11th Division as well as the 9th, 10th, and 36th Caucasian divisions of the I Corps were in the regions of Kars and Ardahan. Operating in the Diadin–Bayazit–North Persian sector were the 5th and 12th divisions of the IV Corps.
⁴ Z. Avalov, *Nezavisimost' Gruzii v mezhdunarodnoi politike, 1918–1921 g.g.* (Paris, 1924), p. 28. The author uses his Georgian name, Zourab Avalishvili, in the English translation, *The Independence of Georgia in International Politics, 1918–1921.*
⁵ Rep. of Arm. Archives, File 1406a/26a; Allen and Muratoff, *op. cit.,* p. 465; Al. Khatisian, *Hayastani Hanrapetutian dsagumn u zargatsume* [The Creation and Development of the Republic of Armenia] (Athens, 1930), p. 38.
⁶ [Republic of Georgia], *Dokumenty i materialy po vneshnei politike Zakavkaz'ia i Gruzii* (Tiflis, 1919), pp. 197–198, cited hereafter as *Dokumenty i materialy.*
⁷ S. T. Arkomed, *Materialy po istorii otpadeniia Zakavkaz'ia ot Rossii* (Tiflis, 1923), p. 66; Vahan Minakhorian, "Batumi Khorhrdazhoghove" [The Batum Conference], *Hairenik Amsagir,* XIV (March, 1936), 94, cited hereafter as Minakhorian, "Batum."
⁸ Rep. of Arm. Archives, File 1406a/26a and 1/1; Vardges Aharonian, *Andranik, marde ev razmike* [Andranik, the Man and the Warrior] (Boston, 1957), p. 151; Korganoff, *op. cit.,* pp. 123–128.
⁹ Khatisian, *op. cit.,* p. 39; S. Vratzian, *Hayastani Hanrapetutiun* [Republic of Armenia] (2d ed.; Beirut, 1958), pp. 102–104. H. Kachaznuni, *H. H. Dashnaktsutiune anelik chuni ailevs* [The A. (Armenian) R. (Revolutionary) Federation Has Nothing More To Do] (Vienna, 1923), p. 27.
¹⁰ V. Minakhorian, "Karsi ankume" [The Fall of Kars], *Hairenik Amsagir,* XIV (January, 1936), 146–147, cited hereafter as Minakhorian, "Kars"; *Dokumenty i materialy,* p. 199; Khatisian, *op. cit.,* p. 39.
¹¹ *Dokumenty i materialy,* pp. 200–204, 216–218.
¹² *Ibid.,* pp. 204–206.
¹³ *Ibid.,* pp. 207–210; Al. Stavrovskii, *Zakavkaz'e posle Oktiabria* (Moscow-Leningrad, [1925]), pp. 43–46.
¹⁴ *Dokumenty i materialy,* pp. 211–214.
¹⁵ Vratzian, *op. cit.,* p. 105.
¹⁶ *Dokumenty i materialy,* pp. 219–220.

17 *Mshak* (Tiflis), no. 76, 1918, in Kh. H. Badalian, *Germana-turkakan okupantnere Hayastanum 1918 tvakanin* [The Germano-Turkish Occupants in Armenia, 1918] (Erevan, 1962), p. 12; Stavrovskii, *op. cit.*, p. 47; Vratzian, *op. cit.*, p. 105.
18 *Dokumenty i materialy*, p. 221.
19 Vratzian, *op. cit.*, pp. 105–106.
20 Khatisian, *op. cit.*, p. 41; *Dokumenty i materialy*, p. 222; Arkomed, *op. cit.*, p. 67.
21 Minakhorian, "Kars" (January, 1936), p. 147; Stavrovskii, *op. cit.*, pp. 51–52; Arkomed, *op. cit.*, pp. 68–69; *Dokumenty i materialy*, p. 224.
22 O. Minasian, "Vneshniaia politika zakavkazskoi kontrrevoliutsii v pervoi polovine 1918 goda," *Istorik marksist* (no. 6, 1938), p. 75; Aharonian, *op. cit.*, pp. 155–156; *Dokumenty i materialy*, p. 225.
23 Rep. of Arm. Archives, File 1/1, Report of Nazarabekian, "Opérations militaires. . . ."
24 *Ibid.*; Korganoff, *op. cit.*, p. 143.
25 Armenian SSR Central State Historical Archives, Fund 45, work 42, in Badalian, *op. cit.*, pp. 101–102, 144; Korganoff, *op. cit.*, pp. 145–146.
26 Armenian SSR Central State Historical Archives, Fund 45, work 30, p. 14, in Badalian, *op. cit.*, pp. 107–108; Korganoff, *op. cit.*, p. 146.
27 *Dokumenty i materialy*, p. 227; Minakhorian, "Kars" (January, 1936), p. 148.
28 Rep. of Arm. Archives, File 1/1, Report of Nazarabekian; Korganoff, *op. cit.*, pp. 146–147; Badalian, *op. cit.*, p. 146.
29 *Dokumenty i materialy*, p. 245; Minakhorian, "Kars" (January, 1936), p. 149.
30 *Dokumenty i materialy*, pp. 247–248; Korganoff, *op. cit.*, p. 149.
31 Rep. of Arm. Archives, File 1/1, Report of Nazarabekian; Minakhorian, "Kars" (January, 1936), p. 147; Hovakim Melikian, "Arian janaparhov" [On the Bloody Path], *Hairenik Amsagir*, III (April, 1925), 132–133; *Dokumenty i materialy*, p. 246.
32 Ds. Aghayan, *Hoktemberian revoliutsian ev hai zhoghovrdi azatagrume* [The October Revolution and the Liberation of the Armenian People] (Erevan, 1957), pp. 171–172; Georgian SSR Central State Historical Archives, Fund 1005, work 17, p. 23, in A. M. Poghosian, *Sotsial-tntesakan haraberutiunnere Karsi marzum, 1878–1920* [The Social-Economic Relations in the Province of Kars, 1878–1920] (Erevan, 1961), p. 299; Badalian, *op. cit.*, pp. 104–106.
33 Korganoff, *op. cit.*, pp. 150–151; Armenian SSR Central State Historical Archives, Fund 45, work 42, in Badalian, *op. cit.*, p. 149.
34 *Dokumenty i materialy*, pp. 247–248; Minakhorian, "Kars" (January, 1936), p. 150.
35 Badalian, *op. cit.*, p. 153. Javid Bey, leader of the Turkish 11th Caucasian Division, replaced General Deev as commander of Kars fortress.
36 Stavrovskii, *op. cit.*, pp. 60–61; *Dokumenty i materialy*, pp. 251–252.
37 Arkomed, *op. cit.*, p. 70; Korganoff, *op. cit.*, p. 152; *Dokumenty i materialy*, pp. 248, 259–261, 265.
38 Rep. of Arm. Archives, File 1406a/26a and 100/1, *H. H. Patvirakutiun, 1918: H. Ohandjaniani tghtere* [Rep. of Arm. Delegation, 1918: H. Ohandjanian's Papers].
39 Vratzian, *op. cit.*, pp. 110, 112–113. Khatisian, *op. cit.*, p. 42, states that only on April 25 did Chkhenkeli inform the Armenian cabinet members about his activities relating to Kars.
40 Vratzian, *op. cit.*, p. 113; Khatisian, *op. cit.*, pp. 42–44.
41 *Dokumenty i materialy*, p. 229; Khatisian, *op. cit.*, p. 45. Since Erzinkian was a Social Democrat, the Mensheviks had five posts, the Musavat-Moslems, five, and the Dashnakists, three.
42 *Dokumenty i materialy*, pp. 229–233.
43 *Ibid.*, pp. 240–241; Khatisian, *op. cit.*, pp. 45–47.
44 *Dokumenty i materialy*, pp. 261–267.

45 Stavrovskii, *op. cit.*, p. 59; Arkomed, *op. cit.*, p. 70.
46 The protest was sent by radio on April 12 according to Ministerstvo Inostrannykh Del SSSR, *Dokumenty vneshnei politiki SSSR*, I (Moscow, 1957), 240–241, cited hereafter as *Vnesh. pol. SSSR*. Most other sources give April 13 or May 15 as the date of the protest. Consult also P. G. La Chesnais, *Les peuples de la Transcaucasie pendant la guerre et devant la paix* (Paris, 1921), pp. 144–145; *Hoktemberian sotsialistakan meds revoliutsian ev sovetakan ishkhanutian haghtanake Hayastanum: Pastatghteri ev niuteri zhoghovadsu* [The Great October Socialist Revolution and the Victory of the Soviet Order in Armenia: Collection of Documents and Materials], ed. by A. N. Mnatsakanian, *et al.* (Erevan, 1960), pp. 211–212, cited hereafter as *Meds revoliutsian;* *Velikaia Oktiabr'skaia sotsialisticheskaia revoliutsiia i pobeda sovetskoi vlasti v Armenii: Sbornik dokumentov,* ed. by A. N. Mnatsakanian, A. M. Akopian, and G. M. Dallakian (Erevan, 1957), p. 195, cited hereafter as *Velikaia revoliutsiia.*
47 Armenian SSR Central State Historical Archives, Fund 244, work 10, pp. 13–16, in Badalian, *op. cit.*, p. 22.
48 *Bol'sheviki v bor'be za pobedu sotsialisticheskoi revoliutsii v Azerbaidzhane: Dokumenty i materialy 1917–1918 g.g.,* ed. by Z. I. Ibragimov and M. S. Iskenderov (Baku, 1957), p. 310, cited hereafter as *Revoliutsii v Azerbaidzhane: Revoliutsion kocher ev trutsikner, 1902–1921* [Revolutionary Appeals and Circulars, 1902–1921], compiled by the Institute of Party History of the Central Committee of the Communist Party of Armenia and the Armenian Filial of the Institute of Marxism-Leninism (Erevan, 1960), p. 461, cited hereafter as *Kocher.*
49 Marxism-Leninism Institute, Armenian Filial Archive, Fund 33, work 720, in *Meds revoliutsian,* pp. 212–214, and *Velikaia revoliutsiia,* pp. 195–198.
50 Marxism-Leninism Institute, Armenian Filial Archive, Fund 33, work 754, p. 1, in A. N. Mnatsakanian, *Revoliutsian Andrkovkasum ev Rusastani patviraknere, 1917–1921* [The Revolution in Transcaucasia and the Envoys of Russia, 1917–1921] (Erevan, 1961), pp. 49–50; *Velikaia revoliutsiia,* pp. 195–198; G. B. Gharibdjanian, *Hayastani komunistakan kazmakerputiunnere sovetakan ishkhanutian haghtanaki hamar mghvads paikarum* [The Communist Organizations of Armenia in the Struggle for Victory of the Soviet Order] (Erevan, 1955), pp. 207–208.
51 Ruben [Ter Minasian], *Hai heghapokhakani me hishataknere* [The Memoirs of an Armenian Revolutionary], VII (Los Angeles, 1952), 143.
52 *Revoliutsii v Azerbaidzhane,* pp. 392–393, 418.
53 Reuben Darbinian, "A Mission to Moscow: Memoirs," *Armenian Review,* I (Spring, 1948), 24–25.
54 S. T. Alikhanian, *Haikakan Gordseri Komisariati gordsuneutiune (1917–1921)* [Activity of the Commissariat of Armenian Affairs (1917–1921)] (Erevan, 1958), pp. 27–32.
55 *Velikaia revoliutsiia,* p. 192; Alikhanian, *op. cit.*, pp. 75, 103, 142–146.
56 V. I. Lenin, *Polnoe sobranie sochinenii,* XXXVI (5th ed.; Moscow, 1962), 339–340.
57 I. V. Stalin, *Sochineniia,* IV (Moscow, 1947), 95.
58 *Ibid.*, p. 96.
59 Marxism-Leninism Institute, Armenian Filial Archive, Fund 13, work 15, p. 2, in V. L. Avakian, *Edjer Andrkovkasum otarerkria interventsiayi patmutiunits (1918 t.)* [Pages from the History of Foreign Intervention in Transcaucasia (1918)] (Erevan, 1957), pp. 48–49; *Vnesh. pol. SSSR,* I, 285, 302–303. V. G. Trukhanovskii, ed., *Istoriia mezhdunarodnykh otnoshenii i vneshnei politiki SSSR, 1917–1939 gg.,* I (Moscow, 1961), 58, states that Mirbach was officially received in Moscow on April 26, 1918.
60 *Dokumenty i materialy,* p. 253.
61 Georgian SSR Central State Archives of the October Revolution, Fund 1, work 176, p. 98, telegraph fund, in *Velikaia revoliutsiia,* p. 198.

[62] Avalov, *op. cit.*, p. 34. Vratzian, *op. cit.*, p. 113, includes Rasul-Zade among the advisers and names Khan Khoiskii as a voting delegate.

[63] Avalov, *op. cit.*, p. 40. Bammat, Chermoev, and two other "Mountaineers," Kantemirov and Temir-Khanov, had arrived in Trebizond during the Ottoman-Transcaucasian negotiations there. Subsequently, they accompanied Rauf Bey to Constantinople in order to win Turkish support and recognition. Consult Arkomed, *op. cit.*, p. 71, and Haidar Bammate, *Le Caucase et la révolution russe* (Paris, 1929), pp. 38–39. Joseph Pomiankowski, *Der Zusammenbruch des Ottomanischen Reiches: Erinnerungen an die Türkei aus der Zeit des Weltkrieges* (Leipzig, 1928), p. 337, states that he sent Captain Pawlas to Transcaucasia to represent the Austro-Hungarian Empire and that Colonel Kableshkoff attended the Batum parleys for Bulgaria. No available records of the conference indicate that either officer was present.

[64] Vratzian, *op. cit.*, p. 114; *Dokumenty i materialy*, pp. 313–314.

[65] Khatisian, *op. cit.*, p. 52; *Dokumenty i materialy*, pp. 314–316.

[66] Rep. of Arm. Archives, Copy of draft treaty in File 100/1; Allen and Muratoff, *op. cit.*, p. 467; Arkomed, *op. cit.*, p. 72; Minakhorian, "Batum" (April, 1936), pp. 123–124.

[67] Rep. of Arm. Archives, File 100/1; Avalov, *op. cit.*, pp. 45–47.

[68] *Dokumenty i materialy*, pp. 268–269, 272–277, 288–290; Rep. of Arm. Archives, File 100/1, nos. 300, 327.

[69] Kurt Ziemke, *Die neue Türkei: Politishche Entwicklung, 1914–1929* (Stuttgart, 1930), pp. 54–55; Pomiankowski, *op. cit.*, pp. 367–368; Johannes Lepsius, *Deutschland und Armenien, 1914–1918: Sammlung diplomatischer Aktenstücke* (Potsdam, 1919), pp. 374–375, 390.

[70] Vratzian, *op. cit.*, p. 115. General Korganov is not to be confused with G. N. Korganov, Military Commissar of the Baku Sovnarkom.

[71] Khatisian, *op. cit.*, pp. 55–56.

[72] Rep. of Arm. Archives, File 100/1; E. K. Sargsian, *Ekspansionistskaia politika Osmanskoi imperii v Zakavkaz'e nakanune i v gody pervoi mirovoi voiny* (Erevan, 1962), p. 360; Jean Loris-Melicof, *La révolution russe et les nouvelles républiques transcaucasiennes* (Paris, 1920), pp. 120–121.

[73] Korganoff, *op. cit.*, p. 158; Rep. of Arm. Archives, File 1/1, Report of Nazarabekian.

[74] Melikian, *op. cit.* (April, 1925), pp. 134–135; Rep. of Arm. Archives, File 1406a/26a.

[75] *Dokumenty i materialy*, p. 287; Rep. of Arm. Archives, File 100/1, no. 327, annex 1.

[76] Minasian, *op. cit.*, p. 80; *Dokumenty i materialy*, pp. 287–288.

[77] Allen and Muratoff, *op. cit.*, pp. 472–475; Korganoff, *op. cit.*, pp. 159–160.

[78] Rep. of Arm. Archives, File 100/1, nos. 20a, 312; Stavrovskii, *op. cit.*, pp. 72–73; *Dokumenty i materialy*, pp. 278–280, 282–283.

[79] Khatisian, *op. cit.*, p. 57.

[80] Lepsius, *op. cit.*, pp. 383–384.

[81] Minakhorian, "Batum" (March, 1936), pp. 97, 99; Stavrovskii, *op. cit.*, p. 98; Khatisian, *op. cit.*, pp. 53–54; *Dokumenty i materialy*, p. 316.

[82] Lepsius, *op. cit.*, p. 381.

[83] Gotthard Jäschke, "Der Turanismus der Jungtürken: Zur osmanischen Aussenpolitik im Weltkriege," *Die Welt des Islams*, XXIII (bk. 1–2, 1941), 22, 28; Pomiankowski, *op. cit.*, pp. 367–368.

[84] Jäschke, *op. cit.*, p. 39; Erich Ludendorff, *Meine Kriegserinnerungen, 1914–1918* (Berlin, 1919), p. 499.

[85] Carl Mühlmann, *Das deutsch-türkische Waffenbündnis im Weltkrieg* (Leipzig, [1940]), p. 196.

[86] Ludendorff, *op. cit.*, pp. 498–500; Mühlmann, *op. cit.*, pp. 196–197.

[87] Pomiankowski, *op. cit.*, p. 336; Ziemke, *op. cit.*, p. 53.

⁸⁸ Mühlmann, *op. cit.*, p. 198.
⁸⁹ *Ibid.*, p. 199; Lepsius, *op. cit.*, pp. 388–389.
⁹⁰ Mühlmann, *op. cit.*, pp. 197, 199.
⁹¹ Ludendorff, *op. cit.*, p. 500.
⁹² Ziemke, *op. cit.*, p. 51.
⁹³ *Vnesh. pol. SSSR*, I, 296, 317–318.
⁹⁴ *Ibid.*, pp. 317–318; G. V. Chicherin, *Stat'i i rechi po voprosam mezhdunarodnoi politiki* (Moscow, 1961), p. 46; Stavrovskii, *op. cit.*, pp. 105–106.
⁹⁵ Armenian SSR Central State Historical Archives, Fund 68/200, work 23, pp. 111–112, in A. M. Elchibekian, *Velikaia Oktiabr'skaia sotsialisticheskaia revoliutsiia i pobeda sovetskoi vlasti v Armenii* (Erevan, 1957), p. 68.
⁹⁶ Khatisian, *op. cit.*, pp. 58–59; Lepsius, *op. cit.*, p. 389.
⁹⁷ Armenian SSR Central State Historical Archives, Fund 200, folder 1, work 11, p. 22, in Badalian, *op. cit.*, p. 157; Stavrovskii, *op. cit.*, p. 107.
⁹⁸ *Dokumenty i materialy*, pp. 293–301; Minakhorian, "Batum" (May, 1936), pp. 113–118.
⁹⁹ *Dokumenty i materialy*, pp. 301–302.
¹⁰⁰ Firuz Kazemzadeh, *The Struggle for Transcaucasia (1917–1921)* (New York and Oxford, [1951]), p. 114.
¹⁰¹ Khatisian, *op. cit.*, p. 58; Vratzian, *op. cit.*, p. 146; *Dokumenty i materialy*, pp. 310–312.
¹⁰² Khatisian, *op. cit.*, p. 59.
¹⁰³ *Ibid.*, p. 62; Stavrovskii, *op. cit.*, p. 107.
¹⁰⁴ *Dokumenty i materialy*, p. 307; Minakhorian, "Batum" (May, 1936), p. 119.
¹⁰⁵ Vratzian, *op. cit.*, p. 149; *Dokumenty i materialy*, p. 309.
¹⁰⁶ Stavrovskii, *op. cit.*, pp. 108–110; *Dokumenty i materialy*, pp. 309–310.
¹⁰⁷ Rep. of Arm. Archives, File 100/1, Draft treaty with annexes; Sargsian, *op. cit.*, p. 362.
¹⁰⁸ Ludendorff, *op. cit.*, p. 500.
¹⁰⁹ Marxism-Leninism Institute, Georgian Filial Archive, Fund 7, work 1, p. 70, in D. Enukidze, *Krakh imperialisticheskoi interventsii v Zakavkaz'e* (Tbilisi, 1954), pp. 48–49; Minasian, *op. cit.*, p. 82.
¹¹⁰ Avalov, *op. cit.*, p. 56.
¹¹¹ *Ibid.*, p. 57.
¹¹² *Ibid.*, pp. 58–59.
¹¹³ *Ibid.*, pp. 59–60.
¹¹⁴ Arkomed, *op. cit.*, p. 75.
¹¹⁵ Khatisian, *op. cit.*, p. 65. A similar statement is in Armenian SSR Central State Historical Archives, Fund 190/507, work 23, p. 101, in Sargsian, *op. cit.*, p. 363.

Notes to Chapter X

¹ Critics of Tsereteli point out that the conditions described were not new but were used as an excuse to dissolve the Transcaucasian Federation only after the Georgians had secured German protection.
² Irakly Tsérételli, *Séparation de la Transcaucasie et de la Russie et indépendance de la Géorgie: Discours prononcés à la Diète transcaucasienne* (Paris, 1919), pp. 31–40.
³ [Republic of Georgia], *Dokumenty i materialy po vneshnei politike Zakavkaz'ia i Gruzii* (Tiflis, 1919), p. 323, cited hereafter as *Dokumenty i materialy*.
⁴ G. I. Uratadze, *Obrazovanie i konsolidatsiia Gruzinskoi Demokraticheskoi Respubliki* (Munich, 1956), pp. 71–72.

5 Arsham Khondkarian, "Opozitsian Hanrapetakan Hayastanum" [The Opposition in Republican Armenia], *Vem,* I (November–December, 1933), 78.
6 Uratadze, *op. cit.,* p. 73.
7 *Dokumenty i materialy,* p. 329. This official Georgian publication gives only Tsereteli's speeches. The views of the non-Menshevik fractions can be ascertained only by studying Tsereteli's rebuttal or by consulting other sources.
8 S. Vratzian, *Hayastani Hanrapetutiun* [Republic of Armenia] (2d ed.; Beirut, 1958), p. 151; Uratadze, *op. cit.,* p. 74.
9 [Republic of Azerbaijan], *Le 28 Mai 1919* ([Baku, 1919]), p. 7, cited hereafter as *Le 28 Mai 1919; Dokumenty i materialy,* pp. 330–331.
10 Mikael Varandian, *Le conflit arméno-géorgien et la guerre du Caucase* (Paris, 1919), p. 72; *Dokumenty i materialy,* pp. 332–334.
11 United States, The National Archives, *Record Group 256: Records of the American Commission to Negotiate Peace,* 861G.00/74. *Record Group 256* is cited hereafter as *RG 256. Dokumenty i materialy,* pp. 336–338.
12 S. T. Arkomed, *Materialy po istorii otpadeniia Zakavkaz'ia ot Rossii* (Tiflis, 1923), pp. 77–78; *Dokumenty i materialy,* p. 335. The following men completed the membership of the Georgian cabinet:

Grigorii Georgadze	Military
Georgii Zhuruli	Finance, Trade, and Industry
Georgii Laskhishvili	Public Enlightenment
Noi Khomeriki	Agriculture and Labor
Shavla Meskhishvili	Justice
Ivan Lordkipanidze	Roads and Communications

On June 24, 1918, this temporary government was superseded by a cabinet headed by Noi Zhordania. Consult Uratadze, *op. cit.,* p. 84.
13 Paul Miliukov, "The Balkanization of Transcaucasia," *The New Russia,* II (July 8, 1920), 300; P. G. La Chesnais, *Les peuples de la Transcaucasie pendant la guerre et devant la paix* (Paris, 1921), pp. 58–59; Joseph Pomiankowski, *Der Zusammenbruch des Ottomanischen Reiches: Erinnerungen an die Türkei aus der Zeit des Weltkrieges* (Leipzig, 1928). According to Gotthard Jäschke, "Der Turanismus der Jungtürken: Zur osmanischen Aussenpolitik im Weltkriege," *Die Welt des Islams,* XXIII (bk. 1–2, 1941), 36, von Kress did not arrive in Tiflis until the end of June, but apparently this information is incorrect. Von Kress was dispatched to the Caucasus in April, 1918, and, according to almost all Armenian and Russian sources, reached Batum during the second half of May.
14 Z. Avalov, *Nezavisimost' Gruzii v mezhdunarodnoi politike, 1918–1921 g.g.* (Paris, 1924), pp. 65–66; James Bunyan, *Intervention, Civil War and Communism in Russia, April–December, 1918* (Baltimore, 1936), p. 53.
15 Avalov, *op. cit.,* pp. 66–67; A. Sanders [Nikuradze], *Kaukasien: Nordkaukasien, Aserbeidschan, Armenien, Georgien* (Munich, [1944]), p. 304.
16 Vratzian, *op. cit.,* p. 149; Archives of the Republic of Armenia Delegation to the Paris Peace Conference [now integrated into the archives of Dashnaktsutiun, Boston, Massachusetts], File 100/1, Report of June 16, 1918, cited hereafter as Rep. of Arm. Archives.
17 *Le 28 Mai 1919,* pp. 7–9; M. E. Rassoul-Zadé, *L'Azerbaidjan en lutte pour l'Indépendance* (Paris, 1930), p. 18. Most of the territory of Azerbaijan had comprised part of historic Atropatene. In recent centuries the North Persian province around Tabriz had been known as "Azerbaijan." It has been suggested that in selecting the same name for their republic, the Moslem leaders of Transcaucasia hoped to pave the way to the unification of the racially and linguistically related regions extending to the north and south of the Araxes River.

[18] Several historians and philologists have pointed out that, in identifying the dominant Moslem element of Transcaucasia, the term "Tatar" or "Tartar" is a misnomer. "Azeri" or "Azeri Turk" is given as the accurate scientific name. Nonetheless, use of "Azeri" or "Azerbaijani" in this study has thus far been avoided, because prior to 1918 the people in question referred to themselves as "Tatar," "Turk," or, more commonly, as "Moslem."

[19] Jäschke, *op. cit.*, p. 39.

[20] A cabinet originally proposed by the National Council was rejected by Nuri Bey until several of his nominees were included. Consult E. A. Tokarzhevskii, *Iz istorii inostrannoi interventsii i grazhdanskoi voiny v Azerbaidzhane* (Baku, 1957), p. 88, and the publication of the Azerbaijani SSR Academy of Sciences, *Istoriia Azerbaidzhana*, ed. by I. A. Guseinov, *et al.*, Vol. III, pt. 1 (Baku, 1963), 138. The Azerbaijani cabinet, as constituted in Ganja, was as follows:

Fathali Khan Khoiskii	Minister-President, and Justice
Mahmed Hasan Hajinskii	Foreign Affairs, and acting State Controller
Behbut Djevanshir	Internal Affairs
Khudadud Melik Aslanov	Ways and Communications, and acting in Post and Telegraph
A. Amirjanov	Finance
Nesib Usubbekov	Public Instruction and Religion
Agha Ashurov	Commerce and Industry, and acting in Provisions
Kh. Sultanov	Agriculture
Khudadud Rafibekov	Public Welfare and Assistance
Ali Marden Topchibashev Khalil Khas-Mamedov M. Rafiev	Ministers without Portfolio

Consult *Le 28 Mai 1919*, pp. 9–10.

[21] A. Babalian, *Edjer Hayastani ankakhutian patmutiunits* [Pages from the History of Armenia's Independence] (Cairo, 1959), p. 6; Vratzian, *op. cit.*, p. 152. Yielding to the insistence of its Social Democrat members, the Armenian National Council did not deliver the protest note to the Georgian government.

[22] Vratzian, *op. cit.*, p. 152; Babalian, *op. cit.*, p. 6.

[23] Vratzian, *op. cit.*, p. 152.

[24] Khondkarian, *op. cit.*, II (January-February, 1934), 88–89; Al. Khatisian, *Hayastani Hanrapetutian dsagumn u zargatsume* [The Creation and Development of the Republic of Armenia] (Athens, 1930), p. 76. The first anniversary of the Republic of Armenia was celebrated on May 28, 1919. May 28 is now accepted as the founding date of the Republic.

[25] Vratzian, *op. cit.*, p. 153.

[26] D. Ananun, *Rusahayeri Hasarakakan zargatsume*, III, *1901–1918* [The Social Development of the Russian Armenians: 1901-1918] (Venice, 1926), 683; Babalian, *op. cit.*, pp. 6–7; Rep. of Arm. Archives, File 8/8, *H. H., 1919* [Rep. of Arm., 1919].

[27] W. E. D. Allen and Paul Muratoff, *Caucasian Battlefields: A History of the Wars on the Turco-Caucasian Border, 1828–1921* (Cambridge, 1953), pp. 469–470.

[28] G. Sassuni, "Erku jakatamart vor vjretsin hayutian bakhte" [Two Decisive Battles That Determined the Fate of the Armenians], *Miatsial ev Ankakh Hayastan* [United and Independent Armenia], publication of H. H. Dashnaktsutiun (Constantinople, 1919), pp. 29–31, cited hereafter as *Miatsial Hayastan;* Rep. of Arm. Archives, File 1/1, "Opérations militaires . . ." ; Hovakim Melikian, "Arian janaparhov" [On the Bloody Path], *Hairenik Amsagir,* III (May, 1925), 75–76.

[29] A. M. Elchibekian, *Velikaia Oktiabr'skaia sotsialisticheskaia revoliutsiia i pobeda*

sovetskoi vlasti v Armenii (Erevan, 1957), pp. 73-74; Ds. Aghayan, *Hoktemberian revoliutsian ev hai zhoghovrdi azatagrume* [The October Revolution and the Liberation of the Armenian People] (Erevan, 1957), p. 177; V. A. Mikayelian, *Hayastani giughatsiutiune sovetakan ishkhanutian hamar mghvads paikari zhamanakashrdjanum (1917-1920 tt.)* [The Peasantry of Armenia in the Period of Struggle for the Establishment of Soviet Order (1917-1920)] (Erevan, 1960), pp. 58-60; A. Poidebard, "Rôle militaire des Arméniens sur le front du Caucase après la défection de l'armée russe (décembre 1917-novembre 1918)," *Revue des études arméniennes,* I (pt. 2, 1920), 155.

[30] General G. Korganoff, *La participation des Arméniens à la guerre mondiale sur le front du Caucase, 1914-1918* (Paris, 1927), pp. 168-169; G. Shahinian, "Herosakan shabate" [The Week of Heroism], *Miatsial Hayastan,* pp. 23-25; Allen and Muratoff, *op. cit.,* pp. 475-476; Rep. of Arm. Archives, File 1/1; Armenian SSR Central State Historical Archives, Fund 68/200, work 132, pp. 940-941, in E. K. Sargsian, *Ekspansionistskaia politika Osmanskoi imperii v Zakavkaz'e nakanune i v gody pervoi mirovoi voiny* (Erevan, 1962), p. 399, and work 19, pp. 99-102, in Elchibekian, *op. cit.,* p. 72.

[31] Rep. of Arm. Archives, File 1/1; *Miatsial Hayastan,* pp. 33-35.

[32] *Mayis 28* [May 28], publication of the Paris Regional Committee of H. H. Dashnaktsutiun (Paris, 1926), p. 24.

[33] Rep. of Arm. Archives, File 157/56 and 1/1; Melikian, *op. cit.* (May, 1925), p. 75.

[34] Vratzian, *op. cit.,* pp. 143-144; Rep. of Arm. Archives, File 1406a/26a.

[35] During the battle for Karakilisa, Nazarabekian had wired the National Council, "Victory is escaping me; I have fired my last cartridge." Consult Poidebard, *op. cit.,* p. 154. At least three other Turkish divisions were close enough to the Erevan *guberniia* to be utilized by the Ottoman Command.

[36] US Archives, *RG 256,* 861K.00/5; Vardges Aharonian, *Andranik, marde ev razmike* [Andranik, the Man and the Warrior] (Boston, 1957), pp. 163-164; *General Andranik: Haikakan Arandzin Harvadsogh Zoramase* [General Andranik: The Armenian Separate Striking Division], transcribed by Eghishe Kadjuni (Boston, 1921), pp. 29-55.

[37] For a description of Andranik's activities in Nakhichevan and Zangezur from June through October, 1918, consult the above work, *General Andranik,* pp. 57-137.

[38] Armenian SSR Central State Historical Archives, Fund 68/200, work 79, p. 2, in Kh. H. Badalian, *Germana-turkakan okupantnere Hayastanum 1918 tvakanin* [The Germano-Turkish Occupants in Armenia, 1918] (Erevan, 1962), pp. 162-163.

[39] Khatisian, *op. cit.,* p. 69. In his work, Khatisian does not mention the twenty-four-hour extension granted by Halil.

[40] *Ibid.* For comparison, the state of Connecticut is 5,000 and Belgium is 11,775 square miles in area.

[41] Khatisian, *op. cit.,* p. 70.

[42] *Ibid.*

[43] Vratzian, *op. cit.,* p. 154; *Mayis 28,* p. 42.

[44] Rep. of Arm. Archives, File 1/1, includes both Armenian and French texts. The original or a copy is also in Armenian SSR Central State Historical Archives, Fund 68/200, work 11. For a published French version, consult A. Poidebard, "Le Transcaucase et la République d'Arménie dans les textes diplomatiques du Traité de Brest-Litovsk au Traité de Kars, 1918-1921," *Revue des études arméniennes,* IV (no. 1, 1924), 37-50. Russian and Armenian published texts are in Badalian, *op. cit.,* pp. 172-185.

[45] Rep. of Arm. Archives, File 1/1. The draft agreement for the exchange of prisoners had been prepared on May 15, with General Odishelidze acting on behalf of the Transcaucasian Federation. The same draft was used by the Ottomans in treaties with the three republics. Consult also *Dokumenty i materialy,* pp. 361-363.

[46] Elchibekian, *op. cit.,* pp. 76-77; Rep. of Arm. Archives, File 1/1; Armenian SSR

Central State Historical Archives, Fund 68/200, work 11, pp. 120–121, in Badalian, *op. cit.*, pp. 185–193.

[47] D. Z. T., "La première République musulmane: L'Azerbaidjan," *Revue du monde musulman*, XXXVI (1918–1919), 254–255; Avalov, *op. cit.*, p. 95; Rüştü, *Büyük Harpte Bakü Yollarında 5. Kafkas Piyade Fırkası* [The 5th Caucasian Infantry Division on the Road to Baku during the Great War] (Istanbul, 1934), p. 21.

[48] *Dokumenty i materialy*, pp. 340–342.

[49] Khatisian, *op. cit.*, pp. 73–74. For the Ottoman-Georgian Treaty of Batum, consult Al. Stavrovskii, *Zakavkaz'e posle Oktiabria* (Moscow-Leningrad, [1925]), pp. 112–116, and *Dokumenty i materialy*, pp. 343–368. Ramishvili was also compelled to sign an additional treaty similar to the one concluded between the Armenians and Ottomans. Georgia promised to expel all representatives of the Allied nations. Already, Smith and members of the British and French military missions had departed for Russia. From Moscow, Smith continued to keep the State Department informed on affairs in the Caucasus. In 1919, he returned to Tiflis to resume his consular duties.

[50] Armenian SSR Central State Historical Archives, Fund 68/200, work 74, p. 34, in Badalian, *op. cit.*, pp. 203–204; *Dokumenty i materialy*, p. 365.

[51] Rep. of Arm. Archives, File 22/22, *H. H., 1919* [Rep. of Arm., 1919]. A. M. Poghosian, *Sotsial-tntesakan haraberutiunnere Karsi marzum, 1878–1920* [The Social-Economic Relations in the Province of Kars, 1878–1920] (Erevan, 1961), p. 307, shows that the Ottomans took 868 kilometers of Transcaucasian railway from Sarikamish to Julfa. D. S. Zavriev, *K noveishei istorii severo-vostochnykh vilaetov Turtsii* (Tbilisi, 1947), p. 71, states that the Turks acquired 24 percent of the total railway mileage of Transcaucasia.

[52] A. B. Kadishev, *Interventsiia i grazhdanskaia voina v Zakavkaz'e* (Moscow, 1960), p. 64; Zavriev, *op. cit.*, p. 71.

[53] Figures for the Batum *oblast* and Tiflis guberniia have been compiled from information supplied by Zavriev, *op. cit.*, p. 70, and *Entsiklopedicheskii Slovar'* (7th ed., Moscow, 1909–1926).

[54] Figures for the Kars oblast and Erevan guberniia have been compiled from Ananun, *op. cit.*, p. 685, and Rep. of Arm. Archives, File 1/1 and File 74/1, *H. H. Patvirakutiun ev Divanagitakan Nerkayatsutschutiun Tajkastanum, 1914–1918 t.t.* [Rep. of Arm. Delegation and Diplomatic Representation in Turkey, 1914–1918].

[55] B. H. Lalabekian, *V. I. Lenine ev sovetakan kargeri hastatumn u amrapndumn Andrkovkasum* [V. I. Lenin and the Establishment and Strengthening of Soviet Order in Transcaucasia] (Erevan, 1961), p. 194; Zavriev, *op. cit.*, p. 70; Kadishev, *op. cit.*, p. 64; Georgian SSR Central State Archives of the October Revolution, Fund 13, work 26, p. 42, in Poghosian, *op. cit.*, p. 307.

[56] Zavriev, *op. cit.*, p. 70.

[57] Most Armenian and prerevolutionary Russian sources give the Armenian population of Akhalkalak at that time as more than 80,000.

[58] This figure includes 19,000 Moslems of Georgian origin.

[59] The Soviet studies consulted do not account for the six-sevenths of Nakhichevan ceded to Turkey. Figures in the US Archives, *RG 256,* 867B.00/10, give for the entire *uezd* 136,000 inhabitants, of whom 81,000 were Moslem and 54,000 Armenian. Using Russian statistics of 1914, Artashes Abeghian substantiates this information. Consult Abeghian's "Menk ev mer harevannere—Azgayin kaghakakanutian khndirner" [We and Our Neighbors—Problems of National Policy], *Hairenik Amsagir*, VI (February, 1928), 99. By the time Turkish forces actually occupied the area, most Christians had already fled.

[60] Rep. of Arm. Archives, File 107/6 and 100/1. Aghayan, *op. cit.*, p. 195, shows the distribution of refugees in Armenia during 1918 as follows:

Erevan	75,000	Daralagiaz	36,000
Ashtarak	30,000	Bash Abaran	35,000
Akhta-Elenovka	22,000	Etchmiadzin	70,000
Bashgarni	15,000	Karakilisa	16,000
Novo Bayazit	38,000	Dilijan	13,000

[61] Rep. of Arm. Archives, File 74/1 and 100/1.
[62] Melikian, *op. cit.* (July, 1925), pp. 94–96; Vratzian, *op. cit.*, p. 144.
[63] Armenian SSR Central State Historical Archives, Fund 68/200, work 79, p. 67, and work 33, p. 4, in Badalian, *op. cit.*, pp. 210–211, 235–236. Also, work 20 and work 79, in Sargsian, *op. cit.*, pp. 403–405. For the role of Essad Pasha, see pp. 204–205, above.
[64] Rep. of Arm. Archives, File 1/1, Report of March 25, 1919; Arshak Djamalian, "Hai-vratsakan knjire" [The Armeno-Georgian Entanglement], *Hairenik Amsagir*, VI (September, 1928), 119–120; Korganoff, *op. cit.*, pp. 170–171.
[65] Kurt Ziemke, *Die neue Türkei: Politische Entwicklung, 1914–1929* (Stuttgart, 1930), p. 41; Jäschke, *op. cit.*, p. 42.
[66] Johannes Lepsius, *Deutschland und Armenien, 1914–1918: Sammlung diplomatischer Aktenstücke* (Potsdam, 1919), pp. 391–392.
[67] *Ibid.*, p. 392.
[68] Carl Mühlmann, *Das deutsch-türkische Waffenbündnis im Weltkrieg* (Leipzig, [1940]), pp. 200–203; Lepsius, *op. cit.*, pp. 393–394.
[69] Georgian SSR Central State Archives of the October Revolution, Fund 13, work 8, p. 1, and work 6, p. 6, in D. Enukidze, *Krakh imperialisticheskoi interventsii v Zakavkaz'e* (Tbilisi, 1954), pp. 93–94. Allen and Muratoff, *op. cit.*, p. 477, state that two German companies arrived in Georgia on June 3, 1918.
[70] *Dokumenty i materialy*, p. 367.
[71] Jäschke, *op. cit.*, pp. 36–37.
[72] Allen and Muratoff, *op. cit.*, pp. 477–478; Pomiankowski, *op. cit.*, p. 365.
[73] Allen and Muratoff, *op. cit.*, p. 478; Jäschke, *op. cit.*, p. 37.
[74] Jäschke and M. Larcher, *La guerre turque dans la guerre mondiale* (Paris, 1926), give this composition for the Third and Ninth armies, but Allen and Muratoff state that the 10th and 37th Caucasian divisions constituted the Third Army, and the 5th, 9th, 11th, and 36th Caucasian divisions and the 5th and 12th Infantry divisions made up the Ninth Army. Pomiankowski's information differs, showing the 3d, 11th, 36th, and 37th Caucasian divisions as components of the Third Army, and the 9th, 10th, and 15th Caucasian and the 5th and 12th Infantry divisions as those of the Ninth Army.
[75] Tokarzhevskii, *op. cit.*, p. 87; Enukidze, *op. cit.*, p. 121; Larcher, *op. cit.*, p. 422; Republic of Georgia, *Iz istorii armiano-gruzinskikh otnoshenii: 1918 god* (Tiflis, 1919), pp. 12–13, cited hereafter as Georgia, *Iz istorii*.
[76] Rep. of Arm. Archives, File 65/1; Varandian, *op. cit.*, p. 74; Miliukov, *op. cit.*, p. 303; Djamalian, *op. cit.* (April, 1928), p. 90.
[77] Enukidze, *op. cit.*, p. 120; Georgia, *Iz istorii*, p. 10.
[78] Enukidze, *op. cit.*, pp. 120–121; Djamalian, *op. cit.* (April, 1928), p. 91; Georgia, *Iz istorii*, pp. 10–11; A. I. Denikin, *Ocherki russkoi smuti*, III (Berlin, 1924), 51.
[79] Rep. of Arm. Archives, File 65/1; Djamalian, *op. cit.* (April, 1928), p. 91.
[80] Henri Barbusse, *Voici ce qu'on a fait de la Géorgie* (Paris, 1929), pp. 28, 114, states that 80,000 refugees were in the Bakuriani region and that 30,000 of them perished. Consult also Varandian, *op. cit.*, pp. 72–73, and Rep. of Arm. Archives, File 230/129, *H. H. Patvirakutiun, 1919* [Rep. of Arm. Delegation, 1919].
[81] Varandian, *op. cit.*, p. 73; Djamalian, *op. cit.* (April, 1928), p. 78.
[82] Khondkarian, *op. cit.* (January-February, 1934), p. 92.
[83] *Ibid.*, pp. 92–96; Vratzian, *op. cit.*, p. 178.

NOTES TO PP. 208–213   309

84 The Armenian Populists often were not differentiated from the Russian Kadets and were thus referred to by many as "KD's."
85 Babalian, *op. cit.*, pp. 9–10; Vratzian, *op. cit.*, pp. 178–179.
86 Grigor Petrosian, a nonpartisan, subsequently entered the cabinet as Minister of Justice, and in November, 1918, five Populists also joined the cabinet to form a coalition government.
87 Vratzian, *op. cit.*, p. 180.
88 Khondkarian, *op. cit.* (January-February, 1934), p. 97, and (May-June, 1934), pp. 42–46; Babalian, *op. cit.*, pp. 8, 10.
89 Djamalian, *op. cit.* (September, 1928), pp. 120–121; Babalian, *op. cit.*, pp. 8–9; Vratzian, *op. cit.*, pp. 180–181.
90 Lepsius, *op. cit.*, pp. 402–404, 410, 414–415.
91 Babalian, *op. cit.*, pp. 19–20; Vratzian, *op. cit.*, p. 192.
92 Rep. of Arm. Archives, File 71/1, *H. H. Nerkayatsutschutiun Ukrayinayum, 1918–1928 t.t.* [Rep. of Arm. Representation in the Ukraine, 1918–1928]; *Miatsial Hayastan*, pp. 43–44; Khondkarian, *op. cit.* (May-June, 1934), pp. 46–47.
93 *Khorhurd* is the Armenian word for *Sovet* or Council. Members of the Khorhurd were the following:

Populists: S. Malkhasian, A. Mkhitarian, G. Ter Khachatrian, H. Melikian, G. Engibarian, S. Ter Martirosian.
Nonpartisans: S. Mamikonian, P. Zakarian.
Moslems: S. Mir Babaev, M. Mamedov, A. Ismailov, M. Mir Babaev, M. Mahmedbekov, A. Aghababekov.
Russian: I. Zorin.
Yezidi: Iu. Temurov.
Dashnakists: A. Sahakian, S. Tigranian, S. Khachatrian, S. Torosian, A. Babalian, E. Sargsian, R. Ter Minasian, H. Ter Mikayelian, A. Ghazarian, D. Kanayan, H. Budaghian, T. Rashmajian, T. Toshian, H. Ter Hakobian, H. Sargsian, A. Vantsian, A. Astvadsatrian.
Social Revolutionaries: G. Ter Hakobian, D. Zubian, A. Khondkarian, G. Ter Ohanian, T. Musheghian, A. Avetikian.
Social Democrats: A. Melikian, H. Azatian, T. Avtalbekian, M. Gharabekian, A. Melik-Aghadjanian, H. Zakarian.

Consult "Hayastani Khorhrdi Ardzanagrutiunnere" [Minutes of the Khorhurd of Armenia], *Vem*, II (July-August, 1934), 115, cited hereafter as "Ardzanagrutiunnere."
94 Lepsius, *op. cit.*, pp. 421–422.
95 Rep. of Arm. Archives, File 71/1; Babalian, *op. cit.*, pp. 14–15; "Ardzanagrutiunnere," pp. 117–118.
96 Arshak Alboyajian, "Ankakh Hayastan" [Independent Armenia], *Amenun Taretsuitse* [Everyone's Almanac], XV ([Constantinople], 1921), 122; *Miatsial Hayastan*, pp. 46–47.
97 "Ardzanagrutiunnere," pp. 120–122; Rep. of Arm. Archives, File 71/1, Bulletin no. 15.
98 The Khorhurd fractions occupied the following positions in the chamber:

Far Right	Populists
Right	Russian delegate and Moslems
Right Center	Yezidi delegate and nonpartisans
Center and Left Center	Dashnakists
Left	Social Revolutionaries
Far Left	Social Democrats

⁹⁹ Khondkarian, *op. cit.* (July-August, 1934), pp. 80–82; "Ardzanagrutiunnere" (September-October, 1934), pp. 92–93, 96.
¹⁰⁰ Khondkarian, *op. cit.* (July-August, 1934), pp. 82–83; "Ardzanagrutiunnere" (September-October, 1934), pp. 93–96, 102.
¹⁰¹ Rep. of Arm. Archives, File 65/1, Reports of September 19 and 25, 1918.
¹⁰² Lepsius, *op. cit.*, p. 433.
¹⁰³ Rep. of Arm. Archives, File 65/1, Report of September 23, 1918; Lepsius, *op. cit.*, pp. 432–434.
¹⁰⁴ Rep. of Arm. Archives, File 65/1, Reports of September 23 and 26, 1918.
¹⁰⁵ *Ibid.*, Report of September 26, 1918.

Notes to Chapter XI

¹ Archives of the Republic of Armenia Delegation to the Paris Peace Conference [now integrated into the archives of Dashnaktsutiun, Boston, Massachusetts], File 1378/9, *H. H. D. Germania, 1916–1920* [A. (Armenian) R. (Revolutionary) F. (Federation), Germany, 1916–1920], Nazariants to Armenian Committee of Geneva, April 27, 1918, cited hereafter as Rep. of Arm. Archives.
² *Ibid.*, Ohandjanian and Zohrabian to Avetis Isahakian, Geneva, June 18, 1918, and File 100/1, Ohandjanian report of June 16, 1918.
³ Z. Avalov, *Nezavisimost' Gruzii v mezhdunarodnoi politike, 1918–1921 g.g.* (Paris, 1924), p. 98; D. Enukidze, *Krakh imperialisticheskoi interventsii v Zakavkaz'e* (Tbilisi, 1954), pp. 94–95; Rep. of Arm. Archives, File 100/1, Ohandjanian to German State Secretary for Foreign Affairs, June 10, 1918.
⁴ Al. Khatisian, *Hayastani Hanrapetutian dsagumn u zargatsume* [The Creation and Development of the Republic of Armenia] (Athens, 1930), p. 77, states that von Kress, not von Schulenburg, relayed the message.
⁵ Rep. of Arm. Archives, File 100/1, Khatisian to Ohandjanian, and Report of Kocharian, June 26, 1918. According to Kh. H. Badalian, *Germana-turkakan okupantnere Hayastanum 1918 tvakanin* [The Germano-Turkish Occupants in Armenia, 1918] (Erevan, 1962), p. 48, the delegation departed on June 13, 1918, and arrived in Constantinople a week later.
⁶ Several of the appeals have been published by Johannes Lepsius in *Deutschland und Armenien, 1914–1918: Sammlung diplomatischer Aktenstücke* (Potsdam, 1919), pp. 401–402, 404–408, 411–412. Others are in Rep. of Arm. Archives, File 100/1, Ohandjanian and Zohrabian to German State Secretary for Foreign Affairs, June 15, July 2, 8, and 15, 1918.
⁷ Avalov, *op. cit.*, p. 90 n.; Rep. of Arm. Archives, File 103/2, Report no. 13, 1918, and File 65/1.
⁸ Ministerstvo Inostrannykh Del SSSR, *Dokumenty vneshnei politiki SSSR*, I (Moscow, 1957), 381, cited hereafter as *Vnesh. pol. SSSR;* L. A. Khurshudian, *Stepan Shahumian: Petakan ev partiakan gordsuneutiune 1917–1918 tvakannerin* [Stepan Shahumian: Governmental and Party Activity, 1917–1918] (Erevan, 1959), pp. 321–322; Enukidze, *op. cit.*, p. 64.
⁹ Zavriev and Nazariants were imprisoned in August, 1918.
¹⁰ Count von Mirbach was assassinated on July 6, 1918. Lenin himself hurried to the German Embassy to extend apologies. Consult V. G. Trukhanovskii, ed., *Istoriia mezhdunarodnykh otnoshenii i vneshnei politiki SSSR, 1917–1939 gg.*, I (Moscow, 1961), 59. In a settlement concluded in August, Russia agreed to pay Germany six billion marks in goods and negotiables. For eyewitness accounts of the assassination and the testimony of Social Revolutionary leaders, consult James Bunyan, *Intervention, Civil War and Communism in Russia, April–December, 1918* (Baltimore, 1936), pp. 213–220.

[11] Rep. of Arm. Archives, File 100/1, Memorandum to the Sovnarkom.
[12] *Vnesh. pol. SSSR*, I. 338.
[13] Because the overland routes remained virtually sealed, the food shortage became very acute. Limited provisions arrived by sea from Astrakhan, in return for which Baku sent Soviet Russia nearly 1.5 million tons of petroleum products. Consult G. B. Gharibdjanian, *V. I. Lenine ev Andrkovkasi zhoghovurdneri azatagrume* [V. I. Lenin and the Liberation of the Peoples of Transcaucasia] (Erevan, 1960), p. 72; and A. B. Kadishev, *Interventsiia i grazhdanskaia voina v Zakavkaz'e* (Moscow, 1960), p. 99.
[14] *Bol'sheviki v bor'be za pobedu sotsialisticheskoi revoliutsii v Azerbaidzhane: Dokumenty i materialy 1917–1918 g.g.*, ed. by Z. I. Ibragimov and M. S. Iskenderov (Baku, 1957), pp. 505–506, cited hereafter as *Revoliutsii v Azerbaidzhane*.
[15] General G. Korganoff, *La participation des Arméniens à la guerre mondiale sur le front du Caucase, 1914–1918* (Paris, 1927), pp. 184–188; W. E. D. Allen and Paul Muratoff, *Caucasian Battlefields: A History of the Wars on the Turco-Caucasian Border, 1828–1921* (Cambridge, 1953), pp. 486–488; Kadishev, *op. cit.*, pp. 109–112.
[16] E. A. Tokarzhevskii, *Iz istorii inostrannoi interventsii i grazhdanskoi voiny v Azerbaidzhane* (Baku, 1957), pp. 118–123; Korganoff, *op. cit.*, pp. 190–196; Allen and Muratoff, *op. cit.*, pp. 488–489; Kadishev, *op. cit.*, pp. 117–120.
[17] *Vnesh. pol. SSSR*. I, 401–402; B. H. Lalabekian, *V. I. Lenine ev sovetakan kargeri hastatumn u amrapndumn Andrkovkasum* [V. I. Lenin and the Establishment and Strengthening of Soviet Order in Transcaucasia] (Erevan, 1961), pp. 112–114; Khurshudian, *op. cit.*, pp. 322–325.
[18] Ds. Aghayan, *Hoktemberian revoliutsian ev hai zhoghovrdi azatagrume* [The October Revolution and the Liberation of the Armenian People] (Erevan, 1957), p. 183.
[19] V. L. Avakian, *Edjer Andrkovkasum otarerkria interventsiayi patmutiunits (1918 t.)* [Pages from the History of Foreign Intervention in Transcaucasia (1918)] (Erevan, 1957), pp. 100–101; Khurshudian, *op. cit.*, p. 326; G. M. Mneyan, *Stepan Shahumiani partiakan ev petakan gordsuneutiune (1900–1918)* [Stepan Shahumian's Party and Governmental Activity (1900–1918)] (Erevan, 1963), p. 205.
[20] *Revoliutsii v Azerbaidzhane*, p. 598; *Vnesh. pol. SSSR*, I, 411–412; Khurshudian, *op. cit.*, pp. 327–329; Lalabekian, *op. cit.*, pp. 123–127; Institute of Marxism-Leninism, *V. I. Lenin ob Azerbaidzhane* (Baku, 1959), p. 91.
[21] Avakian, *op. cit.*, p. 109; A. M. Elchibekian, *Velikaia Oktiabr'skaia sotsialisticheskaia revoliutsiia i pobeda sovetskoi vlasti v Armenii* (Erevan, 1957), p. 81; Institute of Party History and Azerbaijani Filial of the Institute of Marxism-Leninism, *Istoriia Kommunisticheskoi partii Azerbaidzhana*, I (Baku, 1958), 309–311.
[22] Rep. of Arm. Archives, File 1/1 and 71/1, Bulletin no. 12; Korganoff, *op. cit.*, pp. 197–202; Allen and Muratoff, *op. cit.*, pp. 490, 492; Sergei Melik-Yolchian, "Bakvi herosamarte" [The Heroic Battle of Baku], *Hairenik Amsagir*, III (July, 1925), 72–74.
[23] Rep. of Arm. Archives, File 1/1; Lalabekian, *op. cit.*, pp. 131–134; Allen and Muratoff, *op. cit.*, p. 492; Melik-Yolchian, *op. cit.* (August, 1925), p. 100.
[24] For accounts of the defense of Baku from the British viewpoint, consult the following works: Major General L. C. Dunsterville, *The Adventures of Dunsterforce* (London, 1920); Lt. Col. F. J. F. French, *From Whitehall to the Caspian* (London, 1920), pp. 83–106; A. Rawlinson, *Adventures in the Near East, 1918–1922* (London and New York, 1923), pp. 72–94; Ranald MacDonell, "... *And Nothing Long*" (London, [1938]), pp. 201–268. For an invective against the British, consult Henry Barby, ... *Le débâcle russe: Les extravagances bolcheviques et l'épopée arménienne* (Paris, 1919), pp. 160–230.
[25] *Revoliutsii v Azerbaidzhane*, pp. 627–628; Khurshudian, *op. cit.*, p. 333; Mneyan, *op. cit.*, p. 211.
[26] John W. Wheeler-Bennett, *Brest-Litovsk: The Forgotten Peace, March 1918* (London, 1938), p. 433; Jane Degras, ed., *Soviet Documents on Foreign Policy*, I, *1917–1924*

(London, 1951), 97; *Vnesh. pol. SSSR,* I, 443–445; Alfred L. P. Dennis, *The Foreign Policies of Soviet Russia* (New York, 1924), p. 204.

27 Carl Mühlmann, *Das deutsch-türkische Waffenbündnis im Weltkrieg* (Leipzig, [1940]), pp. 208–209.

28 E. K. Sargsian, *Ekspansionistskaia politika Osmanskoi imperii v Zakavkaz'e nakanune i v gody pervoi mirovoi voiny* (Erevan, 1962), p. 372; Mühlmann, *op. cit.,* pp. 209–210.

29 Rep. of Arm. Archives, File 100/1, Ohandjanian to Austrian Foreign Minister, September 7, 1918, and Report of September 20, 1918.

30 Joseph Pomiankowski, *Der Zusammenbruch des Ottomanischen Reiches: Erinnerungen an die Türkei aus der Zeit des Weltkrieges* (Leipzig, 1928), p. 369; Rep. of Arm. Archives, File 100/1, Khatisian reports of August 16, 27, and September 24, and Kocharian reports of September 3 and 23, 1918.

31 Pomiankowski, *op. cit.,* p. 373; Gotthard Jäschke, "Der Turanismus der Jungtürken: Zur osmanischen Aussenpolitik im Weltkriege," *Die Welt des Islams,* XXIII (bk. 1–2, 1941), 44–45.

32 Rep. of Arm. Archives, File 100/1, Zohrabian letters of September 8 and 11, and Khatisian reports of September 14 and 21, 1918.

33 Mühlmann, *op. cit.,* pp. 212–213; Jäschke, *op. cit.,* pp. 45–47.

34 Dunsterville, *op. cit.,* pp. 309–311; Rawlinson, *op. cit.,* p. 94; Melik-Yolchian, *op. cit.* (August, 1925), pp. 111–112.

35 Lepsius, *op. cit.,* pp. 441–445; Pomiankowski, *op. cit.,* p. 374; Rep. of Arm. Archives, File 1/1, Protest of the Danish, Norwegian, Persian, and Dutch consuls in Baku to Nuri Pasha.

36 Allen and Muratoff, *op. cit.,* p. 495, give the number killed as 9,000, Pomiankowski, *op. cit.,* p. 374, as 10,000, M. Larcher, *La guerre turque dans la guerre mondiale* (Paris, 1926), p. 423, as 15,000, and Tokarzhevskii, *op. cit.,* p. 160, as between 30,000 and 35,000. The most thorough statistical study of the September massacre is B. Ishkhanian's *Velikie uzhasy v gor. Baku: Anketnoe izsledovanie sentiabr'skikh sobytii 1918 g.* (Tiflis, 1920). He shows that, during the struggle for Baku and immediately following the city's capitulation, 20,000 Armenians perished. Among the refugee population, the number of fatalities from famine, epidemic, and violence subsequently rose to 10,000.

37 Just before the fall of Baku, the Bolshevik prisoners were released, largely through the endeavors of Anastas Mikoyan. Twenty-six of the former Baku commissars sailed aboard the "Turkmen" for Astrakhan, but en route the captain changed course and anchored at Krasnovodsk, on the eastern shore of the Caspian Sea. The Social Revolutionaries, in control of Transcaspia, sent the commissars by rail toward Ashkhabad. Before reaching that city, the twenty-six commissars were taken from the train, forced to dig their own graves, and shot. British Captain Teague-Jones was implicated in the bloody deed, which finds a place in every history of the Soviet Union. Stepan Shahumian and his comrades, as martyrs and victims of the "imperialistic interventionists," still serve their party and ideology.

38 *Vnesh. pol. SSSR,* I, 492–493, 494–497.

39 The plebiscite was held on July 14, 1918, resulting in 83,000 favoring union with Turkey and only 2,000 opposing. The rigged election drew the protest of the Georgian, Russian, and German governments. Consult Pomiankowski, *op. cit.,* p. 370, and [Republic of Georgia], *Dokumenty i materialy po vneshnei politike Zakavkaz'ia i Gruzii* (Tiflis, 1919), pp. 377–378, cited hereafter as *Dokumenty i materialy.* Kars, Ardahan, and Batum were annexed officially to the Ottoman Empire in August and on September 11 were combined to form the Batum *vilayet.* Consult Sabahettin Selek, *Millî Mücadele: Anadolu İhtilâli* [The National Struggle: Anatolian Rebellion] (Istanbul, 1963), p. 49.

40 *Vnesh. pol. SSSR,* I, 490–492; Degras, *op. cit.,* I, 109–110; Kurt Ziemke, *Die neue Türkei: Politische Entwicklung, 1914–1929* (Stuttgart, 1930), p. 56.

⁴¹ *Vnesh. pol. SSSR,* I, 509–510; Pomiankowski, *op. cit.,* pp. 383–384; Ziemke, *op. cit.,* p. 56.
⁴² *Vnesh. pol. SSSR,* I, 514–516.
⁴³ By decision of the Central Executive Committee of the All-Russian Soviet. See Degras, *op. cit.,* I, 124–125, and *Vnesh. pol. SSSR,* I, 565–567.
⁴⁴ Cemal Kutay, *Atatürk-Enver Paşa hadiseleri* [The Atatürk-Enver Pasha Incidents] (Istanbul, [1956]), p. 15. Most authorities state that Talaat's cabinet fell on October 8 or October 9; however, Tarik Z. Tunaya, *Türkiyede siyasî partiler, 1859–1952* [Political Parties in Turkey, 1859–1952] (Istanbul, 1952), p. 180, claims that Talaat was in power until October 27, 1918.
⁴⁵ Mühlmann, *op. cit.,* p. 237; Pomiankowski, *op. cit.,* p. 386.
⁴⁶ Turkey, Ministry of Interior, *La Guerre de l'Indépendance Turque* ([Istanbul], 1937), p. 7, cited hereafter as Turkey, *La Guerre;* Frederick Maurice, *The Armistice of 1918* (London, 1943), pp. 16, 20.
⁴⁷ M. Papadjanian, the third member of the delegation, was often absent from Constantinople and participated but little in the mission's activities.
⁴⁸ Rep. of Arm. Archives, File 1/1, Khatisian to Ohandjanian, June 25, 1918.
⁴⁹ *Ibid.,* Delegation reports of July 20 and 30, August 6 and 16, and Kocharian minutes of July 13, 1918.
⁵⁰ Rep. of Arm. Archives, File 74/1 and 100/1, Khatisian to Ohandjanian, July 6 and August 16, 1918.
⁵¹ Khatisian, *op. cit.,* p. 82.
⁵² *Ibid.,* p. 83.
⁵³ Rep. of Arm. Archives, File 100/1, Report of July 3, 1918.
⁵⁴ *Ibid.,* Khatisian report of September 7, and Kocharian minutes of September 6, 1918.
⁵⁵ Khatisian, *op. cit.,* p. 90.
⁵⁶ *Ibid.,* p. 91; Rep. of Arm. Archives, File 100/1, Khatisian report of August 24, and Kocharian minutes of August 23, 1918.
⁵⁷ Khatisian, *op. cit.,* pp. 86–87.
⁵⁸ Rep. of Arm. Archives, File 100/1, Khatisian to Ohandjanian, July 13, 1918.
⁵⁹ *Ibid.,* Khatisian to Ohandjanian, July 30, 1918.
⁶⁰ Enukidze, *op. cit.,* p. 122; Rep. of Arm. Archives, File 71/1, Bulletin no. 18, 1918.
⁶¹ Rep. of Arm. Archives, File 100/1, Report of July 30, 1918. Also File 353, *H. H. Berlini Nerkayatsutschutiun, 1918–1919* [Rep. of Arm. Berlin Representation, 1918–1919], Report of July 29, 1918.
⁶² *Ibid.,* File 100/1, Report of Khatisian, August 24, and Report of Ohandjanian, August 17, 1918; Lepsius, *op. cit.,* pp. 418–420.
⁶³ Rep. of Arm. Archives, File 100/1, Kocharian minutes of September 23, and Khatisian to Ohandjanian, September 24, 1918.
⁶⁴ *Ibid.,* File 74/1.
⁶⁵ In Kiev, an Armenian Commissariat headed by former tsarist officers, Colonel Mikayel Lomiza, Lt. Colonel Makar Papov, and Captain Ashot Toniev, was granted official recognition by Ukrainian Foreign Minister D. I. Doroshenko. The Commissariat was permitted to issue passports to Armenians, to send stranded Armenian soldiers to Erevan, and to solicit among the Ukraine's Armenian communities money for the Republic of Armenia. Branches were established in Kharkov, Odessa, the Crimea, and Bessarabia. A rich source for materials relating to the activities of the Ukrainian Armenian Commissariat is Rep. of Arm. Archives, File 71/1.
⁶⁶ Rep. of Arm. Archives, File 100/1, Kocharian reports of September 3, 11, and 21, 1918.
⁶⁷ *Ibid.,* File 71/1, Report of September 2, 1918.
⁶⁸ At the same time that Dsamoev was negotiating in Kiev, another envoy, Simon Vratzian, was in the Don Basin at General M. V. Alekseev's "Volunteer Army" head-

quarters to seek assistance for the Republic. Alekseev allotted Armenia several carloads of grain and three million bullets. However, because Georgia denied transit privileges, the goods were never delivered. Both Georgia and Azerbaijan were suspicious of Armenia's association with the "Volunteer Army," which had pretensions to territories of the two states. The bonds between Armenia and the anti-Bolshevik forces of South Russia aggravated the strained relations between the Erevan government and its Transcaucasian neighbors.

[69] Rep. of Arm. Archives, File 74/1, and 104/3.
[70] *Ibid.*, File 74/1.
[71] *Ibid.*
[72] Rep. of Arm. Archives, File 100/1, Khatisian to Ohandjanian, September 7, 10, and 21, 1918.
[73] *Ibid.*, Kocharian minutes of October 1, and Khatisian report of October 5, 1918.
[74] Of the eight thousand youths taken from the Pambak district for labor in the Erzerum vilayet, only six hundred were alive at the end of the war. Consult Armenian SSR Central State Historical Archives, Fund 70/202, work 1271, p. 47, in Elchibekian, *op. cit.*, p. 74. Also Sargsian, *op. cit.*, pp. 390–391.
[75] Rep. of Arm. Archives, File 100/1, Khatisian to Ohandjanian, and Kocharian report of October 22, 1918.
[76] *Ibid.*, File 74/1, and 100/1, Communiqué of October 24, 1918, no. 214. Nuri received the title of Pasha for his participation in the conquest of Baku.
[77] *Ibid.*, File 100/1, Foreign Affairs Ministry to Aharonian, October 25, 1918.
[78] *Ibid.*, File 74/1, Aharonian to Izzet, October 27, 1918, no. 216.
[79] *Ibid.*, File 100/1,'War Ministry to Aharonian, October 28, 1918.
[80] Khatisian, *op. cit.*, p. 94.
[81] *Ibid.*, p. 95. On November 2, several members of the Ittihad Central Committee, including Jemal, Talaat, and Enver pashas, fled to Odessa aboard a German vessel, the "Lorelei." Consult Kutay, *op. cit.*, p. 22.
[82] Rep. of Arm. Archives, File 100/1, Khatisian to Ohandjanian.
[83] Turkey, *La Guerre,* pp. 7–10; Maurice, *op. cit.*, pp. 85–87; H. W. V. Temperley, *A History of the Peace Conference of Paris,* I (London, 1920), 495–497.
[84] G. Jäschke, "Die Südwestkaukasische Regierung von Kars," *Die Welt des Islams,* n.s., II (no. 1, 1952), 47.
[85] Selek, *op. cit.*, p. 151.
[86] *Ibid.*, p. 155.
[87] French, *op. cit.*, pp. 126–128; Adil Khan Ziatkhan, *Aperçu sur l'histoire, la littérature, et la politique de l'Azerbeidjan* (Baku, 1919), p. 74; M. E. Rassoul-Zadé, *L'Azerbaidjan en lutte pour l'Indépendance* (Paris, 1930), pp. 114–116; United States, The National Archives, *Record Group 256,* 861.00/2; A. Raevskii, *Angliiskaia interventsiia i Musavatskoe pravitel'stvo* (Baku, 1927), pp. 33–35; 46–47; G. P. La Chesnais, *Les peuples de la Transcaucasie pendant la guerre et devant la paix* (Paris, 1921), pp. 114–116.
[88] United States, The National Archives, *Record Group 59,* 861.00/6583; *Dokumenty i materialy,* pp. 426–427; Kadishev, *op. cit.*, pp. 164–165; F. Kostiaeff, "Intervention des puissances étrangères en Russie méridionale et dans les régions du Caucase et du Turkestan de 1918 à 1920," *Les Alliés contre la Russie avant, pendant et après la guerre mondiale (faits et documents)* (Paris, [1926]), p. 259.
[89] For a résumé of events in Mountainous Karabagh from November, 1917, until November, 1918, consult E. Ishkhanian, "Depkere Gharabaghum: Jshtumner ev ditoghutiunner" [The Events in Karabagh: Corrections and Observations], *Hairenik Amsagir,* XI (September, 1933), 85–92.
[90] *General Andranik: Haikakan Arandzin Harvadsogh Zoramase* [General Andranik: The Armenian Separate Striking Division], transcribed by Eghishe Kadjuni (Boston,

NOTES TO PP. 242–251   315

1921), pp. 131–159; La Chesnais, *op. cit.*, p. 161; Sarur, "Gharabaghi ktsume Adrbedjani" [The Annexation of Karabagh to Azerbaijan], *Hairenik Amsagir*, VII (June, 1929), 128–129.
⁹¹ Ishkhanian, *op. cit.* (October, 1933), p. 121; Sarur, *op. cit.*, p. 134; United States, The National Archives, *Record Group 84*, C46(C8).1, Tiflis Consulate, 1919, pt. 4, Class 711, *Dokladnaia zapiska* of the Karabagh National Council, March 13, 1919.
⁹² See Appendix for résumé of Allied pledges.

Notes to Appendix

[1] For a résumé of the pertinent agreements, see pp. 59–62.
[2] Quoted in A. P. Hacobian, *Armenia and the War* (London, New York, and Toronto, 1917), p. 52.
[3] Reprinted in the London *Times*, December 30, 1916.
[4] Great Britain, *The Parliamentary Debates, House of Commons*, 5th Series, XCVII (1917), columns 2041–2042, cited hereafter as GB, *Parl. Deb., HC*. Also Archives of the Republic of Armenia Delegation to the Paris Peace Conference [now integrated into the archives of Dashnaktsutiun, Boston, Massachusetts], File 331/1, *H. H. Londoni Nerkayatsutschutiun ev Britanakan Karavarutiune, 1917* [Rep. of Arm. London Representation and the British Government, 1917].
[5] GB, *Parl. Deb., HC*, C (1917), col. 2220.
[6] Carnegie Endowment for International Peace, *Official Statements of War Aims and Peace Proposals, December 1916 to November 1918*, supervised by James Brown Scott (Washington, D.C., 1921), p. 231, cited hereafter as *Official Statements*. Also David Lloyd George, *War Memoirs*, V (Boston, 1936), 70.
[7] GB, *Parl. Deb., HC*, CVIII (1918), col. 473.
[8] Rep. of Arm. Archives, File 331/1; *Armenia's Charter: An Appreciation of the Services of Armenians to the Allied Cause by the Rt. Hon. David Lloyd George, M. Georges Clemenceau, the Rt. Hon. A. J. Balfour, the Rt. Hon. Lord Robert Cecil, the Rt. Hon. Viscount Bryce, General Sir Edmund Allenby* (London 1918), p. 9, cited hereafter as *Armenia's Charter*.
[9] Bryce was the leading Armenophile who initiated and supervised the preparation of *The Treatment of the Armenians in the Ottoman Empire*, the British Blue Book published in 1916.
[10] *Armenia's Charter*, pp. 6–7; Armenian National Union of America, *The Case of Armenia* ([New York, 1919]), p. 8. Also consult André Mandelstam, *La Société des Nations et les Puissances devant le Problème Arménien* (Paris, 1926), pp. 311–312.
[11] GB, *Parl. Deb., HC*, CX (1918), cols. 3239–3267, and *House of Lords*, 5th Series, XXXII (1919), cols. 34–41.
[12] GB, *Parl. Deb., HC*, CX, col. 3268.
[13] United States, Department of State, *Papers Relating to the Foreign Relations of the United States, 1919: The Paris Peace Conference*, II (Washington, D.C., 1942), 274. The Department of State series of *Papers* is cited hereafter as US, *FRUS*, and those volumes entitled *The Paris Peace Conference* are cited as *PPC*. Also consult Seth P. Tillman, *Anglo-American Relations at the Paris Peace Conference of 1919* (Princeton, 1961), p. 220.
[14] Hacobian, *op. cit.*, p. 51.
[15] Rep. of Arm. Archives, File 1/1; *Le Temps*, November 7, 1916.
[16] Lloyd George, *op. cit.*, III (Boston, 1934), 64.
[17] Rep. of Arm. Archives, File 1/1.
[18] *Ibid.*, File 65/1 and 1/1; *Armenia's Charter*, pp. 14–15; Mandelstam, *op. cit.*, p. 310.
[19] US, *FRUS*, *PPC*, II, 272.

20 Rep. of Arm. Archives, File 344/1, *H. H. Hromi Nerkayatsutschutiun ev Italakan Karavarutiune, 1918* [Rep. of Arm. Rome Representation and the Italian Government, 1918].

21 James Gerard, *England and France in Armenia* ([New York, 1920]), p. 2.

22 James L. Barton, *Story of Near East Relief (1915–1930)* (New York, 1930), pp. 5–6, 12.

23 US, *FRUS, 1918,* Supplement 1, *The World War* (Washington, D.C., 1933), I, 892.

24 United States, The National Archives, *Record Group 59: General Records of the Department of State,* 867.48/713; Barton, *op. cit.,* pp. 86–88.

25 *Official Statements,* p. 238; US, *FRUS, 1918,* Supplement 1, I, 16; H. W. V. Temperley, ed., *A History of the Peace Conference,* VI (London, 1926), 24.

26 "The United States and Armenia," *Armenian Bulletin* (no. 2, 1945), pp. 3–4.

27 Colonel Edward M. House was delegated by President Wilson to organize the Inquiry. By the end of 1917, House had selected an impressive array of historians, economists, and experts in military and cultural affairs to fulfill the President's instructions. The Inquiry was headed by Sidney E. Mezes, president of the City College of New York. Most questions relating to the Armenians were considered by the Western Asian and Russian sectors. For details relating to the personnel, plans, administration, and operation of the Inquiry, consult US, *FRUS, PPC,* I (1942), 9–118, and Lawrence E. Gelfand, *The Inquiry: American Preparations for Peace, 1917–1919* (New Haven and London, 1963).

28 US, *FRUS, PPC,* II, 43, 52.

29 Robert Lansing, *The Peace Negotiations: A Personal Narrative* (Boston and New York, 1921), pp. 195–196.

30 David Hunter Miller, *My Diary at the Conference of Paris, with Documents* ([New York, 1928]), IV, 229, 259–260; United States, The National Archives, *Record Group 256: Records of the American Commission to Negotiate Peace,* 185.112/1.

31 The following men constituted the executive board of the Committee (ACIA): Charles Evans Hughes, James W. Gerard, Elihu Root, Henry Cabot Lodge, John Sharp Williams, Alfred E. Smith, Frederic Courtland Penfield, Charles W. Eliot, and Cleveland H. Dodge. Among the organization's members were over twenty governors and such distinguished leaders as William Jennings Bryan, Nicholas Murray Butler, Samuel Gompers, William H. King, Albert Bushnell Hart, Oscar S. Straus, and Rabbi Stephen S. Wise.

32 Rep. of Arm. Archives, File 379/1. Reference to the resolution is in the *Congressional Record,* 65th Cong., 2d sess., LVI, pt. 11 (October 14, 1918), 11264.

33 *Congressional Record,* 65th Cong., 3d sess., LVII, pt. 1 (December 10, 1918), 237.

34 Harry N. Howard, *The King-Crane Commission* (Beirut, 1963), p. 9.

35 *New York Times,* January 2, 1919.

Bibliography

Note: English titles given in brackets following Armenian titles are translations for the convenience of the reader. Authors' names are listed as they are found on title pages of works cited. Where several works by the same author are listed, the name is given as it is printed in the first of these works.

Archival Materials

Archives of the Republic of Armenia Delegation to Paris. (Now integrated into the Archives of Dashnaktsutiun, Boston, Massachusetts.)

File 1/1. *Hayastani Hanrapetutiun, 1918* [The Republic of Armenia, 1918].
File 2/2. *Hayastani Hanrapetutiun, 1918* [The Republic of Armenia, 1918].
File 8/8. *Hayastani Hanrapetutiun, 1919* [The Republic of Armenia, 1919].
File 22/22. *Hayastani Hanrapetutiun, 1920* [The Republic of Armenia, 1920].
File 65/1. *Vrastani Divanagitakan Nerkayatsutsich ev Vrastani Karavarutiun, 1918* [Diplomatic Representative to Georgia and the Georgian Government, 1918].
File 66/2. *Vrastani Divanagitakan Nerkayatsutsich ev Vrastani Karavarutiun, 1919* [Diplomatic Representative to Georgia and the Georgian Government, 1919].
File 69/1. *H. H. Adrbedjani Divanagitakan Nerkayatsutsich ev Adrbedjani Karavarutiun, 1918 t.* [R. (Republic) of A. (Armenia) Diplomatic Representative in Azerbaijan and the Azerbaijani Government, 1918].
File 70/2. *H. H. Adrbedjani Divanagitakan Nerkayatsutsich ev Adrbedjani Karavarutiun, 1920 t.* [R. (Republic) of A. (Armenia) Diplomatic Representative in Azerbaijan and the Azerbaijani Government, 1920].
File 71/1. *H. H. Nerkayatsutschutiun Ukrayinayum, 1918-1928 t.t.* [R. (Republic) of A. (Armenia) Representation in the Ukraine, 1918-1928].
File 74/1. *H. H. Patvirakutiun ev Divanagitakan Nerkayatsutschutiun Tajkastanum, 1914-1918 t.t.* [R. (Republic) of A. (Armenia) Delegation and Diplomatic Representation in Turkey, 1914-1918].
File 100/1. *H. H. Patvirakutiun, 1918. H. Ohandjaniani tghtere* [R. (Republic) of A. (Armenia) Delegation, 1918. H. Ohandjanian's Papers].

File 103/2. *H. H. Patvirakutiun, 1919 t.* [R. (Republic) of A. (Armenia) Delegation, 1919].
File 104/3. *H. H. Patvirakutiun, 1919 t.* [R. (Republic) of A. (Armenia) Delegation, 1919].
File 104a/3a. *H. H. Patvirakutiun, 1919 t.* [R. (Republic) of A. (Armenia) Delegation, 1919].
File 107/6. *H. H. Patvirakutiun, 1919 t.* [R. (Republic) of A. (Armenia) Delegation, 1919].
File 118/11. *H. H. Pat., 1920. Hashtutian Konferens* [R. (Republic) of A. (Armenia) Del. (Delegation), 1920. Peace Conference].
File 132/31. *H. H. Patvirakutiun, 1920* [R. (Republic) of A. (Armenia) Delegation, 1920].
File 157/56. *H. H. Pat., 1921* [R. (Republic) of A. (Armenia) Del. (Delegation), 1921].
File 230/129. *H. H. Patvirakutiun, 1919* [R. (Republic) of A. (Armenia) Delegation, 1919].
File 241/140. *H. H. Patvirakutiun: Azgayin Patvirakutiun* [R. (Republic) of A. (Armenia) Delegation: National Delegation].
File 283/182. *H. H. Pat. Hayaserner* [R. (Republic) of A. (Armenia) Del. (Delegation). Armenophiles].
File 331/1. *H. H. Londoni Nerkayatsutschutiun ev Britanakan Karavarutiune, 1917* [R. (Republic) of A. (Armenia) London Representation and the British Government, 1917].
File 344/1. *H. H. Hromi Nerkayatsutschutiun ev Italakan Karavarutiune, 1918* [R. (Republic) of A. (Armenia) Rome Representation and the Italian Government, 1918].
File 353. *H. H. Berlini Nerkayatsutschutiun, 1918–1919* [R. (Republic) of A. (Armenia) Berlin Representation, 1918–1919].
File 379/1. *H. H. Vashingtoni Nerkayatsutsich ev H. Amerikian Karavarutiune, 1917–1918* [R. (Republic) of A. (Armenia) Washington Representative and the Government of North America, 1917–1918].
File 503. *Kamavorakan Gnder, 1914–1918* [Volunteer Units, 1914–1918].
File 504. *Azgayin Miutiun Kilikio ev Siurio, 1919–1924* [The National Union of Cilicia and Syria, 1919–1924].
File 1378/9. *H. H. D. Germania, 1916–1920* [A. (Armenia) R. (Revolutionary) F. (Federation). Germany, 1916–1920].
File 1406a/26a. *H. H. D. Amerikayi Kedronakan Komite, 1918* [A. (Armenian) R. (Revolutionary) F. (Federation) Central Committee of America, 1918].
United States of America. The National Archives (Washington, D.C.).
Record Group 59. *General Records of the Department of State.*
Record Group 84. *Foreign Service Posts of the Department of State.*
Record Group 256. *Records of the American Commission to Negotiate Peace.*

Official Publications

Austria. Bundesministerium für Heereswesen und Kriegsarchiv. *Österreich-Ungarns letzter Krieg, 1914–1918.* Vienna, 1930–1938. 8 vols.

———. Staatsamt für Aüsseres. *Diplomatische Aktenstücke zur Vorgeschichte des Krieges 1914.* Vienna, 1919. 3 vols.
[France]. Ministère des Affaires Étrangères. *Documents diplomatiques. Affaires arméniennes. Projets de réformes dans l'empire Ottoman, 1893–1897.* Paris, 1897.
———. ———. ———. *(Supplément) 1895–1896.* Paris, 1897.
———. ———. Commission de Publication des Documents Relatifs aux Origines de la Guerre de 1914. *Documents diplomatiques français (1871–1914).* 1re série *(1871–1900).* Paris, 1929–1954. 16 vols.
———. ———. ———. ———. 3e série *(1911–1914).* Paris, 1929–1936. 11 vols.
Germany. Auswärtiges Amt. *Die deutschen Dokumente zum Kriegsausbruch 1914.* Berlin, 1919. 4 vols.
———. ———. *Die grosse Politik der europäischen Kabinette, 1871–1914.* Berlin, 1922–1927. 40 vols.
———. Reichsarchiv. *Der Weltkrieg 1914 bis 1918.* Berlin, 1925–1956. 14 vols.
Great Britain. Foreign Office. *British and Foreign State Papers.* Vols. XVI-C. London, 1831–1911.
———. ———. *British Documents on the Origins of the War, 1898–1914.* Edited by G. P. Gooch and Harold Temperley. London, 1926–1938. 11 vols.
———. ———. *The Treatment of the Armenians in the Ottoman Empire.* Miscellaneous No. 31 (1916). London, 1916.
———. ———. Historical Section. *Peace Handbooks.* Vol. IX, *The Russian Empire.* No. 54, *Caucasia.* London, 1920.
———. ———. ———. *Peace Handbooks.* Vol. XI, *Turkey in Asia.* No. 62, *Armenia and Kurdistan.* London, 1920.
———. Parliament. House of Commons. *Sessional Papers (Accounts and Papers),* 1856–1897. The following Command Papers have been used in this study: 2040, 2069, 2854, 3944 [unprefixed series]; C. 1641, 1738, 1739, 1806, 1860, 1905, 1973, 1975, 1995, 2057, 2059, 2081, 2083, 2108, 2204, 2205, 2432, 2537, 2611, 2712, 2986, 3030, 7894, 7894-1, 7923, 7927, 8015, 8018, 8273, 8305.
———. ———. ———. *The Parliamentary Debates.* 5th Series. Vols. C, CVIII, CX. London, 1917–1919.
———. ———. House of Lords. *The Parliamentary Debates.* 5th Series. Vol. XXXII. London, 1919.
Hai Heghapokhakan Dashnaktsutiun [Armenian Revolutionary Federation]. *Dsragir* [Program]. Geneva, [1908].
———. *Heghapokhakan Dashn* [Revolutionary Alliance]. Geneva, 1905.
———. *Kaghvadsner Errord Endh. Zhoghovi atenagrutiunnere* [Excerpts from the Minutes of the Third Gen. (General) Congress]. Geneva, 1905.
———. *Miatsial ev Ankakh Hayastan* [United and Independent Armenia]. Constantinople, 1919.
———. *Nakhagids kovkasian gordsuneutian* [Preliminary Project of Caucasian Activity]. 2d ed. Geneva, 1906.
———. *Programma armianskoi revoliutsionnoi i sotsialisticheskoi partii Dashnaktsutiun.* Geneva, 1908.
———. The Bureau. *Hushapatum H. H. Dashnaktsutian, 1890–1950* [Historical Recollections of the A. (Armenian) R. (Revolutionary) Federation, 1890–1950]. Boston, 1950.

———. Central Committee of America. *Divan H. H. Dashnaktsutian* [Archives of the A. (Armenian) R. (Revolutionary) Federation]. Boston, 1934–1938. 2 vols.

———. *H. H. D. Vatsunamiak (1890–1950)* [Sixtieth Anniversary of the A. R. F. (1890–1950)]. Edited by S. Vratzian. Boston, 1950.

———. Paris Regional Committee. *Mayis 28* [May 28]. Paris, 1926.

Hisnamiak Sots. Dem. Hnchakian Kusaktsutian, 1887–1937 [Fiftieth Anniversary of the Soc. (Social) Dem. (Democrat) Hnchakist Party, 1887–1937]. Publication of the Central Committee of America. Providence, 1937.

Nakhagids-Dsragir Kovkasian Sotsial-Demokratiakan Banvorakan Kazmakerputiunneri [Preliminary Project and Program of the Caucasian Social-Democratic Workers Organizations]. Geneva, 1903.

Republic of Armenia Delegation to the Conference of Peace. *The Armenian Question before the Peace Conference.* [Paris, 1919].

———. *L'Arménie transcaucasienne. Territoires, frontières, ethnographie, statistique.* Paris, 1919.

———. *Données statistiques des populations de la Transcaucasie.* Paris, 1920.

———. *Réponse au mémoire de la Sublime-Porte en date 12 février 1919.* Constantinople, 1919.

———. *La République Arménienne et ses Voisins. Questions territoriales.* Paris, 1919.

———. *Tableau approximatif des réparations et indemnités pour les dommages subis par la nation arménienne en Arménie de Turquie et dans la République Arménienne du Caucase.* Paris, 1919.

[Republic of Azerbaijan]. *Le 28 Mai 1919.* [Baku, 1919].

———. Delegation to the Paris Peace Conference. *Claims of the Peace Delegation of Caucasian Azerbaijan Presented to the Peace Conference in Paris.* Paris, 1919.

———. ———. *Composition anthropologique et ethnique de la population de l'Azerbaidjan du Caucase.* Paris, 1919.

———. ———. *Economic and Financial Situation of Caucasian Azerbaijan.* Paris, 1919.

———. ———. *L'Azerbaidjan en chiffres.* [Paris, 1919].

———. ———. *La République de l'Azerbaidjan du Caucase.* Paris, 1919.

[Republic of Georgia]. *Documents Presented by the Government of the Republic of Georgia to the First Assembly of the League of Nations Relative to the Admission of Georgia to the Said League.* London, 1920.

———. *Dokumenty i materialy po vneshnei politike Zakavkaz'ia i Gruzii.* Tiflis, 1919.

———. *Iz istorii armiano-gruzinskikh otnoshenii, 1918 god. Pogranichnye konflikty, peregovory, voina, soglashenie.* Tiflis, 1919.

Russia [Imperial]. *Polnoe sobranie zakonov Rossiiskoi imperii.* 2d series. St. Petersburg, 1830–1885, 58 vols.

———. Kavkazskaia Arkheograficheskaia Kommissiia. *Akty sobrannye Kavkazskoiu Arkheograficheskoiu Kommissieiu* (Archives of the Viceroy for the Caucasus). Tiflis, 1866–1904. 12 vols.

———. Ministerstvo Inostrannykh Del. *Sbornik diplomaticheskikh dokumentov.*

Reformy v Armenii. 26 noiabria 1912 goda—10 maia 1914 goda. Petrograd, 1915.

[Turkey]. *Aspirations et agissements révolutionnaires des comités arméniens avant et après la proclamation de la constitution ottomane.* Constantinople, 1917.

———. *Ermeni komitelerin âmâl ve harekâtı ihtilaliyesi ilanı meşrutiyetten evvel ve sonra* (The Turkish version of *Aspirations et agissements* . . .). Istanbul, 1333 [1916].

———. *Hai heghapokhakan kusaktsutiunnere ev Osm. karavarutiune* [The Armenian Revolutionary Parties and the Ott. (Ottoman) Government]. Constantinople, 1916.

———. *Memorandum of the Sublime Porte Communicated to the American, British, French, and Italian High Commissioners on the 12th February 1919.* Constantinople, 1919.

———. *Vérité sur le mouvement révolutionnaire arménien et les mesures gouvernementales.* Constantinople, 1916.

———. Ministry of Interior. *La Guerre de l'Indépendance Turque.* [Istanbul], 1937.

Union of Soviet Socialist Republics. Akademiia Nauk SSSR—Glavnoe Arkhivnoe Upravlenie. *Revoliutsiia 1905–1907 g.g. v Rossii. Dokumenty i materialy.* Chief editor A. M. Pankratova, later A. L. Sidorov. Moscow, 1955–1963. 13 vols.

———. ———. *Velikaia Oktiabr'skaia sotsialisticheskaia revoliutsiia. Dokumenty i materialy.* Edited by A. L. Sidorov, et al. Vol. II. Moscow, 1963.

———. Institut Marksizma-Leninizma [Formerly Marx-Engels-Lenin-Stalin Institute]. *Protokoly i stenograficheskie otchety s"ezdov i konferentsii Kommunisticheskoi partii Sovetskogo Soiuza. Sed'maia (Aprel'skaia) Vserossiiskaia konferentsiia RSDRP (bol'shevikov). Petrogradskaia obshchegorodskaia konferentsiia RSDRP (bol'shevikov), 1917 goda. Protokoly.* Moscow, 1958.

———. ———. *Protokoly i stenograficheskie . . . Shestoi s"ezd RSDRP (bol'shevikov), Avgust 1917 goda. Protokoly.* Moscow, 1958.

———. ———. Armianskii Filial i Institut Istorii Partii. *Hoktemberian sotsialistakan meds revoliutsian ev sovetakan ishkhanutian haghtanake Hayastanum. Pastatghteri ev niuteri zhoghovadsu* [The Great October Socialist Revolution and the Victory of the Soviet Order in Armenia. Collection of Documents and Materials]. Edited by A. N. Mnatsakanian, et al. Erevan, 1960.

———. ———. ———. *Revoliutsion kocher ev trutsikner, 1902–1921* [Revolutionary Appeals and Circulars, 1902–1921]. Erevan, 1960.

———. ———. ———. *Velikaia Oktiabr'skaia sotsialisticheskaia revoliutsiia i pobeda sovetskoi vlasti v Armenii. Sbornik dokumentov.* Edited by A. N. Mnatsakanian, A. M. Akopian, and G. M. Dallakian. Erevan, 1957.

———. ———. Azerbaidzhanskii Filial i Institut Istorii Partii. *Bol'sheviki v bor'be za pobedu sotsialisticheskoi revoliutsii v Azerbaidzhane. Dokumenty i materialy, 1917–1918 gg.* Edited by Z. I. Ibragimov and M. S. Iskenderov. Baku, 1957.

———. ———. ———. *V. I. Lenin ob Azerbaidzhane.* Edited by Dzh. B. Kultsev, et al. Baku, 1959.

———. ———. Gruzinskii Filial i Akademiia Nauk. *Bor'ba za pobedu sovetskoi vlasti v Gruzii. Dokumenty i materialy (1917–1921).* Edited by G. V. Khachapuridze, et al. Tbilisi, 1958.

———. Ministerstvo Inostrannykh Del. *Dokumenty vneshnei politiki SSSR.* Vol. I. Moscow, 1957.

———. ———. *Konstantinopol' i Prolivy po sekretnym dokumentam b. ministerstva inostrannykh del.* Edited by E. A. Adamov. Moscow, 1925–1926. 2 vols.

———. ———. *Razdel Aziatskoi Turtsii po sekretnym dokumentam b. ministerstva inostrannykh del.* Edited by E. A. Adamov. Moscow, 1924.

United States. Congress. *Congressional Record.* 65th Cong., 2d sess. Washington, D.C. Vol. LVI, pt. 11 (1918). 3d sess. Vol. LVII, pt. 1. (1918).

———. Department of State. *Papers Relating to the Foreign Relations of the United States, 1917.* Supplement 2, *The World War.* Washington, D.C., 1932. 2 vols.

———. ———. ———. *1918.* Washington, D.C., 1931. 3 vols.

———. ———. ———. *1918.* Supplement 1, *The World War.* Washington, D.C., 1933. 2 vols.

———. ———. ———. *1919. The Paris Peace Conference.* Washington, D.C., 1942–1947. 13 vols.

———. ———. ———. *1918. Russia.* Washington, D.C., 1931–1932. 3 vols.

———. ———. ———. *1919. Russia.* Washington, D.C., 1937.

———. ———. *Proceedings of the Brest-Litovsk Peace Conference. The Peace Negotiations between Russia and the Central Powers, 21 November, 1917–3 March, 1918.* Washington, D.C., 1918.

Collections of Published Documents, Speeches, and Papers

Adamov, E. A., ed. *Sbornik dogovorov Rossii s drugimi gosudarstvami (1856–1917).* Moscow, 1952.

Andonian, Aram, ed. *Documents officiels concernant les massacres arméniens.* Paris, 1920.

———. *Meds vojire. Haikakan verdjin kotoradsnere ev Talaat Pasha. Pashtonakan heragirner, bnagirneru storagrutiamb* [The Great Crime. The Recent Armenian Massacres and Talaat Pasha. Official Telegrams, with Signed Originals]. Boston, 1921.

———. *The Memoirs of Naim Bey. Turkish Official Documents Relating to the Deportations and Massacres of Armenians.* London, 1920.

Armenia's Charter. An Appreciation of the Services of Armenians to the Allied Cause by the Rt. Hon. David Lloyd George, M. Georges Clemenceau, the Rt. Hon. A. J. Balfour, the Rt. Hon. Lord Robert Cecil, the Rt. Hon. Viscount Bryce, General Sir Edmund Allenby. London, 1918.

Badalian, Kh. H. *Germana-turkakan okupantnere Hayastanum 1918 tvakanin* [The Germano-Turkish Occupants in Armenia, 1918]. Erevan, 1962.

Baker, Ray Stannard. *Woodrow Wilson. Life and Letters.* Vol. VII. New York, 1939.

Baku Armenian National Council. *Armiano-gruzinskii vooruzhennyi konflikt. Na osnovanii fakticheskikh dannykh i podlinnykh dokumentov.* Baku, 1919.

"Bor'ba s revoliutsionnym dvizheniem na Kavkaze v epokhu stolypinshchiny (Iz perepiski P. A. Stolypina s Gr. I. I. Vorontsovym-Dashkovym)," Introduction by S. Fuks, *Krasnyi Arkhiv*, XXXIV (no. 3, 1929), 184–221, and XXXV (no. 4, 1929), 128–150.

Browder, Robert Paul, and Alexander F. Kerensky, eds. *The Russian Provisional Government, 1917. Documents*. Vol. I. Stanford, 1961.

Carnegie Endowment for International Peace. *Official Statements of War Aims and Peace Proposals, December 1916 to November 1918*. Prepared under supervision of James Brown Scott. Washington, D.C., 1921.

Chicherin, G. V. *Stat'i i rechi po voprosam mezhdunarodnoi politiki*. Moscow, 1961.

———. *Two Years of Foreign Policy*. New York, 1920.

Degras, Jane, ed. *Soviet Documents on Foreign Policy*, Vol. I, *1917–1924*. London, 1951.

"Dnevnik Ministerstva Inostrannykh Del za 1915–1916 g.g.," *Krasnyi Arkhiv*, XXXI (1928), 3–50, and XXXII (1929), 3–87.

Eudin, Xenia Joukoff, and Robert C. North. *Soviet Russia and the East, 1920–1927. A Documentary Survey*. Stanford, 1957.

Golder, Frank Alfred. *Documents of Russian History, 1914–1917*. New York and London, [1927].

"Hayastani Khorhrdi Ardzanagrutiunnere" [Minutes of the Khorhurd of Armenia], *Vem*, II (nos. 4–6, 1934), and III (nos. 1–3, 1935).

Hayastani Komunistakan kusaktsutian nerkayatsutsichi zekutsume errord Komunistakan Internatsionalin [Report of the Representative of the Armenian Communist Party to the Third Communist International]. Moscow, 1919.

Hertslet, Edward. *The Map of Europe by Treaty*. London, 1875–1891. 4 vols.

Holland, Erskine, ed. *The European Concert in the Eastern Question. A Collection of Treaties and Other Public Acts*. Oxford, 1885.

Hovhannisian, Ashot, comp. *Hayastani avtonomian ev Antantan. Vaveragrer imperialistakan paterazmi shrdjanits* [Armenia's Autonomy and the Entente. Documents from the Period of the Imperialistic War]. Erevan, 1926.

Hurewitz, J. C. *Diplomacy in the Near and Middle East. A Documentary Record*. Princeton, New York, Toronto, and London, [1956]. 2 vols.

Iuzefovich, T., ed. *Dogovory Rossii s Vostokom. Politicheskie i torgovye*. St. Petersburg, 1869.

Khondkarian, A. "Varantsov-Dashkovi namaknere Tsarin" [Vorontsov-Dashkov's Letters to the Tsar], *Hairenik Amsagir*, VII (May, 1929), 81–98.

Kirov, S. M. *Stat'i, rechi, dokumenty*. Vol. I. Moscow, 1935.

Kliuchnikov, Iu. V., and A. Sabanin. *Mezhdunarodnaia politika noveishego vremeni v dogovorakh, notakh i deklaratsiiakh*. Vol. II. Moscow, 1926.

Lazian, Gabriel. *Hayastan ev Hai Date. Hai-ev-rus haraberutiunneru luisin tak* [Armenia and the Armenian Question. Under the Light of Armeno-Russian Relations]. Cairo, 1957.

———. *Hayastan ev Hai Date. (Vaveragrer)* [Armenia and the Armenian Question. (Documents)]. Cairo, 1946.

Léart, Marcel [Zohrab, G.]. *La question arménienne à la lumière des documents*. Paris, 1913.

Lenin, V. I. *Polnoe sobranie sochinenii.* 5th ed. Prepared by the Institute of Marxism-Leninism. Vols. XXX-XXXVI. Moscow, 1962.

Leo [Babakhanian, A.]. *Hayots hartsi vaveragrere* [The Documents concerning the Armenian Question]. Tiflis, 1915.

Lepsius, Johannes. *Deutschland und Armenien, 1914-1918. Sammlung diplomatischer Aktenstücke.* Potsdam, 1919.

Miller, David Hunter. *My Diary at the Conference of Paris. With Documents.* Vols. I-IV. [New York, 1928].

Minakhorian, Vahan. *Tragediia Turtsii.* Baku, 1919.

Narimanov, N. *Stat'i i pis'ma.* Moscow, 1925.

Noradounghian, Gabriel. *Recueil d'actes internationaux de l'empire Ottoman.* Paris, 1897-1903. 4 vols.

Ordzhonikidze, G. K. *Izbrannye stat'i i rechi, 1911-1937.* [Moscow], 1939.

Petrosian, Sh. N. *Sovetakan petakanutian hastatume ev amrapndume Hayastanum 1920 t. noyember-1922 t. petrvar* [The Establishment and Strengthening of the Soviet Governmental Organism in Armenia, November, 1920-February, 1922]. Erevan, 1958.

"Pis'ma I. I. Vorontsova-Dashkova Nikolaiu Romanovu, 1905-1915," foreword by V. Semennikov, *Krasnyi Arkhiv,* XXVI (1928), 97-126.

Poidebard, A. "Le Transcaucase et la République d'Arménie dans les textes diplomatiques du Traité de Brest-Litovsk au Traité de Kars, 1918-1921," *Revue des études arméniennes,* III (1923), 64-78, and IV (pt. I, 1924), 31-103.

Safrastian, A. Kh., comp. *Turkakan aghbiurnere Hayastani, hayeri ev Andrkovkasi mius zhoghovurdn'eri masin* [Turkish Sources about Armenia, Armenians, and the Other Peoples of Transcaucasia]. Erevan, 1961-1964. 2 vols.

Safrastian, A. Kh., and M. K. Zulalian, comps. and trans. *Osmanian orenknere Arevmtian Hayastanum (XVI-XVII dd.) Kanunnamener* [Ottoman Laws in Western Armenia (16th-17th Centuries) *Kanunnames*]. Erevan, 1964.

Sef, S. E. *Revoliutsiia 1917 goda v Zakavkaz'i (dokumenty, materialy).* [Tiflis], 1927.

Seymour, Charles, ed. *The Intimate Papers of Colonel House.* Vol. IV. Boston and New York, 1928.

Shahumian, St. *Erker* [Works]. Erevan, 1955-1958. 3 vols.

Stalin, I. V. *Sochineniia.* Vol. IV. Moscow, 1947.

Temperley, H. W. V., ed. *A History of the Peace Conference of Paris.* London, 1920-1926. 6 vols.

Traité conclu en 1783 entre Catherine II, impératrice de Russie, et Irakly II, roi de Géorgie. Preface by Paul Moriaud and commentaries by A. Okoumeli. Geneva, 1919.

Tsérételli, Irakly. *Séparation de la Transcaucasie et de la Russie et indépendance de la Géorgie. Discours prononcés à la Diète transcaucasienne.* Paris, 1919.

Vorontsov-Dashkov, I. I. *Vsepoddanneishaia zapiska po upravleniiu Kavkazskim kraem generala ad"iutanta grafa Vorontsova-Dashkova.* St. Petersburg, 1907.

———. *Vsepoddanneishii otchet za vosem' let upravleniia Kavkazom.* St. Petersburg, 1913.

Vratzian, S. *Hin tghter nor patmutian hamar* [Old Papers for New History]. Beirut, 1963.

Zhordania, N. *Za dva goda.* Tiflis, 1919.

Memoirs and Travel Documents

Aramayis. *Mi kani glukh hai-trkakan endharumnerits* [A Few Chapters from the Armeno-Turkish Clashes]. Tiflis, 1907. 2 pts.
Armen Garo [Pasdermadjian, G.]. *Aprvads orer* [Bygone Days]. Boston, 1948.
Avalov, Z. *Nezavisimost' Gruzii v mezhdunarodnoi politike, 1918–1921 g.g. Vospominaniia. Ocherki.* Paris, 1924.
Baikov, B. "Vospominaniia o revoliutsii v Zakavkaz'i (1917–1920 g.g.)," *Arkhiv Russkoi Revoliutsii.* [Berlin], IX (1923), 91–194.
Chernov, Victor. *The Great Russian Revolution.* Translated by Philip E. Moseley. New Haven, 1936.
Darbinian, Reuben. "A Mission to Moscow: Memoirs," *Armenian Review,* I (Spring, 1948–Autumn, 1948), and II (Winter, 1948–Summer, 1949).
Djemal Pasha. *Memories of a Turkish Statesman, 1913–1919.* New York, 1922.
Donohoe, M. H. *With the Persian Expedition.* London, 1919.
Dunsterville, L. C. *The Adventures of Dunsterforce.* London, 1920.
Elder, John. "Memories of the Armenian Republic," *Armenian Review,* VI (Spring, 1953), 3–27.
Emin, Joseph. *Life and Adventures of Emin Joseph Emin, 1726–1809. Written by Himself.* 2d ed. Calcutta, 1918. 2 vols.
Falkenhayn, General [Erich] von. *The German General Staff and Its Decisions, 1914–1916.* New York, 1920.
French, F. J. F. *From Whitehall to the Caspian.* London, 1920.
General Andranik. *Haikakan Arandzin Harvadsogh Zoramase* [General Andranik. The Armenian Separate Striking Division]. Transcribed by Eghishe Kadjuni. Boston, 1921.
Giulkhandanian, A. "Bakvi herosamarte" [The Heroic Battle of Baku], *Hairenik Amsagir,* XIX (July, 1941–September/October, 1941), 89–102, 101–115, 81–92.
Guse, Felix. *Die Kaukasusfront im Weltkrieg bis zum Frieden von Brest.* Leipzig, [1940].
Hamilton, Ian. *Gallipoli Diary.* New York, 1920. 2 vols.
Hoover, Herbert. *The Memoirs of Herbert Hoover.* Vol. I. New York, 1952.
Karabekir, Kâzım. *İstiklâl Harbimiz* [Our War of Independence]. Istanbul, [1960].
———. *İstiklâl Harbimizin esasları* [The Basic Principles of Our War of Independence]. Istanbul, 1957.
Kerensky, Alexander. *The Prelude to Bolshevism. The Kornilov Rebellion.* London, [1919].
Khan-Azat, R. "Hai heghapokhakani husherits" [From the Memoirs of an Armenian Revolutionary], *Hairenik Amsagir,* Vols. V–VII (June, 1927–May, 1929).
Khatisian, Al. *Hayastani Hanrapetutian dsagumn u zargatsume* [The Creation and Development of the Republic of Armenia]. Athens, 1930.
———. "Kaghakapeti me hishataknere" [The Memoirs of a Mayor], *Hairenik Amsagir,* Vol. X (May, 1932–October, 1932), and Vol. XI (November, 1932–March, 1933).

Lansing, Robert. *The Peace Negotiations. A Personal Narrative.* Boston and New York, 1921.
Liman von Sanders, [Otto]. *Five Years in Turkey.* Annapolis, 1928.
Lloyd George, David. *War Memoirs.* Boston, 1933–1937. 6 vols.
Ludendorff, Erich. *Meine Kriegserinnerungen, 1914–1918.* Berlin, 1919.
Lynch, H. F. B. *Armenia. Travels and Studies.* London, 1901. 2 vols.
MacDonell, Ranald. *". . . And Nothing Long."* London, [1938].
Melikian, Hovakim. "Arian janaparhov" [On the Bloody Path], *Hairenik Amsagir,* III (November, 1924–July, 1925).
Melik-Yolchian, Sergei. "Bakvi herosamarte" [The Heroic Battle of Baku], *Hairenik Amsagir,* III (May, 1925–October, 1925), 105–128, 104–118, 68–74, 97–113, 68–78, 125–129.
Mkhitarian, On. *Vani herosamarte* [The Heroic Battle of Van]. Sofia, 1930.
Morgenthau, Henry. *Ambassador Morgenthau's Story.* Garden City, N.Y., 1919.
Nogales, Raphael de. *Four Years beneath the Crescent.* Translated by Muna Lee. New York and London, 1926.
Paléologue, Maurice. *An Ambassador's Memoirs.* Translated by F. A. Holt. 6th ed. New York, [1924–1925]. 3 vols.
Papazian, Vahan. *Im hushere* [My Memoirs]. Boston [Vol. I] and Beirut [Vols. II–III], 1950–1957. 3 vols.
Pears, Edwin. *Forty Years in Constantinople.* New York, 1916.
Poidebard, A. *Voyages. Au carrefour des routes de Perse.* Paris, 1923.
Pomiankowski, Joseph. *Der Zusammenbruch des Ottomanischen Reiches. Erinnerungen an die Türkei aus der Zeit des Weltkrieges.* Leipzig, 1928.
Ramsay, W. M. *The Revolution in Constantinople and Turkey. A Diary.* London, 1909.
Rawlinson, A. *Adventures in the Near East, 1918–1922.* London and New York, 1923.
Rifat, Mevlan Zade. *Türkiye inkilabının iç yüzü* [The Inner Aspects of the Turkish Revolution]. Aleppo, 1929.
Ruben [Ter Minasian, Ruben]. *Hai heghapokhakani me hishataknere* [The Memoirs of an Armenian Revolutionary]. Los Angeles, 1951–1952. 7 vols.
Rüştü. *Büyük Harpte Baku Yollarında 5. Kafkas Piyade Fırkası* [The 5th Caucasian Infantry Division on the Road to Baku during the Great War]. Istanbul, 1934.
Sazonov, Serge. *Fateful Years, 1909–1916.* New York, 1928.
Sebouh [Nersesian, Arshak]. *Edjer im husheren* [Pages from My Memoirs]. Boston, 1925–1929. 2 vols.
Stuermer, Harry. *Two War Years in Constantinople. Sketches of German and Young Turkish Ethics and Politics.* New York, [1917].
Talaat. "Posthumous Memoirs of Talaat Pasha," *Current History,* XV (November, 1921), 287–295.
Vratzian, S. *Kianki ughinerov: Depker, demker, aprumner* [Along Life's Ways: Episodes, Figures, Experiences]. Cairo [Vol. I] and Beirut [Vols. II–VI], 1955–1967. 6 vols. to date.

Reference Materials

Abeghian, Artashes. *Hayastan ev dratsi erkirner* [Armenia and Neighboring Countries]. Stuttgart, n.d. [Map.]
Amenun Taretsuitse [Everyone's Almanac]. [Constantinople]. Edited by Teodik. Vol. XV. (1921).
Armenian SSR. Akademiia Nauk. *Haikakan Sovetakan Sotsialistakan Respublikayi Atlas* [Atlas of the Armenian Soviet Socialist Republic]. Erevan-Moscow, 1961.
Birge, John Kingsley. *A Guide to Turkish Area Study*. Washington, D.C., 1949.
Bol'shaia Entsiklopediia. St. Petersburg, 1896–1909. 22 vols.
Bol'shaia Sovetskaia Entsiklopediia. 1st ed. Moscow, 1926–1947. 65 vols. 2d ed. [Moscow, 1950–1958]. 51 vols.
Encyclopaedia of Islam. Leiden, 1913–1936. 4 vols.
Entsiklopedicheskii Slovar'. St. Petersburg, 1890–1904. 41 vols.
Entsiklopedicheskii Slovar'. 7th ed. [Granat]. Moscow, 1909–1926. 37 vols.
Eremian, S. T. *Hayastane est "Ashkharhatsuits"i* [Armenia according to the "Atlas"]. Erevan, 1963.
Hairenik Taregirk [Hairenik Yearbook] [Boston]. Edited by S. Vratzian. V. (1947).
Khanzadian, Z. *Rapport sur l'unité géographique de l'Arménie. Atlas historique*. Paris, 1920.
Koray, Enver. *Türkiye tarih yayınları bibliyografyası, 1729–1955* [Bibliography of Turkish Historical Publications, 1729–1955]. Istanbul, 1959.
Russkii Biograficheskii Slovar'. St. Petersburg, 1896–1918. 25 vols.
Salmaslian, A. *Bibliographie de l'Arménie*. Paris, 1946.
Sovetskaia Istoricheskaia Entsiklopediia. Moscow, 1961–1965. 7 vols. to date.

Newspapers

Bor'ba (Tiflis). 1917–1918.
Droshak (Geneva). 1902–1915.
Ertoba (Tiflis). 1918–1919.
Horizon (Tiflis). 1917–1918.
Kavkazskoe slovo (Tiflis). 1918–1919.
Manchester Guardian. 1916–1918.
New York Times. 1915–1919.
Pravda (Petrograd and Moscow). 1917–1918.
Sotsial-Demokrat (Baku). 1917.
Temps (Paris). 1917–1918.
Times (London). 1916–1918.

Documented Studies and General Works

Abeghian, Manuk. *Hayots hin grakanutian patmutiun* [History of Ancient Armenian Literature]. Erevan, 1944–1946. 2 vols.
Abov, G. *Dashnaktsutiunn antsialum ev aizhm* [Dashnaktsutiun in the Past and Present]. 2d printing. Erevan, 1930.

Abrahamian, A. G. *Hamarot urvagids hai gaghtavaireri patmutian* [Concise Outline of the History of the Armenian Colonies]. Erevan, 1964.

———. *Hayastane vagh feodalizmi shrdjanum* [Armenia during the Period of Early Feudalism]. Erevan, 1959.

Adontz, Nicholas. *Histoire d'Arménie. Les origines du Xe siècle au VIe (av. J. C.)*. Paris, 1946.

———. *Patmakan usumnasirutiunner* [Historical Studies]. Paris, 1948.

Aghayan, Ds. *Hoktemberian revoliutsian ev hai zhoghovrdi azatagrume* [The October Revolution and the Liberation of the Armenian People]. Erevan, 1957.

———. *Revoliutsion sharzhumnere Hayastanum 1905–1907 tt.* [The Revolutionary Movements in Armenia, 1905–1907]. Erevan, 1955.

Aharonian, A. *Kristapor Mikayelian* [written in Armenian]. Boston, 1926.

Aharonian, Vardges. *Andranik, marde ev razmike* [Andranik, the Man and the Warrior]. Boston, 1957.

Aknouni, E. *Boghoki dzain (tsarakan haladsanki mi edj)* [The Voice of Protest (A Page from Tsarist Persecutions)]. Boston, 1911.

———. *Political Persecutions. Armenian Prisoners of the Caucasus*. New York, 1911.

Alboyajian, Arshak. *Patmakan Hayastani sahmannere* [The Boundaries of Historic Armenia]. Cairo, 1950.

———. *Patmutiun hai gaghtakanutian* [History of Armenian Emigration]. Vol. II. Cairo, 1955.

Alikhanian, S. T. *Haikakan Gordseri Komisariati gordsuneutiune (1917–1921)* [Activity of the Commissariat of Armenian Affairs (1917–1921)]. Erevan, 1958.

Alishan, Ghevond. *Sisvan* [written in Armenian]. Venice, 1885.

Allen, W. E. D., and Paul Muratoff. *Caucasian Battlefields. A History of the Wars on the Turco-Caucasian Border, 1828–1921*. Cambridge, 1953.

Amirkhanian, Aram. *Rus ev turk zinadadare. Patmakan antsker, 1917–1918* [The Russo-Turkish Truce. Historical Events, 1917–1918]. Fresno, Calif., 1921.

Ananun, D. *Rusahayeri hasarakakan zargatsume* [The Social Development of the Russian Armenians]. Vol. III, *1901–1918*. Venice, 1926.

Anasian, H. S. *XVII dari azatagrakan sharzhumnern Arevmtian Hayastanum (patmakan hetazotutiun)* [The Seventeenth-Century Liberation Movements in Western Armenia (Historical Investigation)]. Erevan, 1961.

Argyll, Duke of [Campbell, George Douglas]. *Our Responsibilities for Turkey. Facts and Memories of Forty Years*. London, 1896.

Arkomed, S. T. *Materialy po istorii otpadeniia Zakavkaz'ia ot Rossii*. Tiflis, 1923.

Armenian National Union of America. *The Case of Armenia* [New York, 1917].

Armenian SSR. Akademiia Nauk. Institut Istorii. *Revoliutsion sharzhumnere Hayastanum rusakan aradjin revoliutsiayi tarinerin (hodvadsneri zhoghovadsu)* [The Revolutionary Movements in Armenia during the Years of the First Russian Revolution (Collection of Articles)]. Erevan, 1955.

———. ———. Institut Literatury. *Hai nor grakanutian patmutiun* [History of Modern Armenian Literature]. Erevan, 1962–1964. 3 vols. to date.

———. University of Erevan. *Revoliutsion sharzhumnere Hayastanum, 1905–1907 (hodvadsneri zhoghovadsu)* [The Revolutionary Movements in Armenia, 1905–1907 (Collection of Articles)]. Erevan, 1955.

Armstrong, H. C. *Unending Battle*. New York and London, 1934.
Arzumanian, M. V. *Bolshevikneri gordsuneutiune ev revoliutsion sharzhumnere Hayastanum 1907-1917 tvakannerin* [Bolshevik Activity and the Revolutionary Movements in Armenia, 1907-1917]. Erevan, 1959.
Asatrian, As. *Hai grakanutiune ev rusakan aradjin revoliutsian* [Armenian Literature and the First Russian Revolution]. Erevan, 1956.
Aslan, Kévork. *Études historiques sur le peuple arménien*. Paris, 1928.
Atom [Shahrikian, H.]. *Barenorogumneru hartse* [The Question of Reforms]. Constantinople, 1914.
Avakian, V. L. *Edjer Andrkovkasum otarerkria interventsiayi patmutiunits (1918 t)*. [Pages from the History of Foreign Intervention in Transcaucasia (1918)]. Erevan, 1957.
Azerbaijan SSR. Akademiia Nauk. *Istoriia Azerbaidzhana*. Edited by I. A. Guseinov, *et al*. Vol. III, pt. 1. Baku, 1963.
———. Institut Istorii Partii i Azerbaidzhanskii Filial Instituta Marksizma-Leninizma. *Istoriia Kommunisticheskoi partii Azerbaidzhana*. Pt. 1. Baku, 1958.
Babalian, A. *Edjer Hayastani ankakhutian patmutiunits* [Pages from the History of Armenia's Independence]. Cairo, 1959.
Babayan, L. H. *Hayastani sotsial-tntesakan ev kaghakakan patmutiune XIII-XIV darerum* [The Socio-Economic and Political History of Armenia during the 13th-14th Centuries]. Erevan, 1964.
Baddeley, John F. *The Russian Conquest of the Caucasus*. London, New York, Bombay, and Calcutta, 1908.
Bagirov, M. D. *Bakvi ev Adrbedjani bolshevikian kazmakerputian patmutiunits* [From the History of the Bolshevik Organization of Baku and Azerbaijan]. Erevan, 1944.
Baker, Ray Stannard. *Woodrow Wilson and World Settlement*. Vol. I. Garden City, N.Y., 1923.
Bammate, Haidar. *Le Caucase et la révolution russe*. Paris, 1929.
Barbusse, Henri. *Voici ce qu'on a fait de la Géorgie*. Paris, 1929.
Barby, Henry. . . . *Le débâcle russe. Les extravagances bolcheviques et l'épopée arménienne*. Paris, 1919.
Barsegian, Kh. A. *Istoriia armianskoi bol'shevistskoi periodicheskoi pechati*. Erevan, 1958.
Barton, James. *Story of Near East Relief (1915-1930)*. New York, 1930.
Bayur, Yusuf Hikmet. *Türk İnkılâbı Tarihi*. Vol. III. *1914-1918 genel savaşı*. Pt. 3. *1915-1917 vuruşmaları ve bunların siyasal tepkileri* [History of the Turkish Revolution. The 1914-1918 World War. The Battles of 1915-1917 and Their Political Effects]. Ankara, 1957.
Beliaev, I. I. *Russko-turetskaia voina 1877-1878 g.g*. Moscow, 1956.
Bérard, Victor. *La mort de Stamboul. Considérations sur le gouvernement des Jeunes-Turcs*. Paris, 1913.
———. *La révolution turque*. Paris, 1909.
———. *The Russian Empire and Czarism*. Translated by G. Fox Davies and G. O. Pope. London, 1905.
Biurat, Smbat. *Arevelian Khndir ev Haikakan Harts* [The Eastern Problem and the Armenian Question]. Constantinople, 1919.
Blanch, Lesley. *The Sabres of Paradise*. New York, 1960.

Bliss, E. M. *Turkey and the Armenian Atrocities. A Reign of Terror.* N.p., 1896.
Borian, B. A. *Armeniia, mezhdunarodnaia diplomatiia i SSSR.* Moscow-Leningrad, 1928–1929. 2 vols.
Bratter, C. A. *Die Armenische Frage.* Berlin, 1915.
Brézol, Georges. *Les Turcs ont passé là. Recueil de documents . . . sur les massacres d'Adana en 1909.* Paris, 1911.
Buchan, John, ed. *The Baltic and Caucasian States. The Nations of To-Day.* Boston and New York, [1923].
Bunyan, James. *Intervention, Civil War and Communism in Russia, April–December, 1918.* Baltimore, 1936.
Bunyan, James, and H. H. Fisher. *The Bolshevik Revolution, 1917–1918. Documents and Materials.* Stanford, 1934.
Buxton, Charles Roden. *Turkey in Revolution.* London, 1909.
Callwell, C. E. *The Dardanelles.* London, 1919.
Carr, Edward Hallett. *The Bolshevik Revolution, 1917–1923.* Vol. I. London, 1950.
Chamberlin, William Henry. *The Russian Revolution, 1917–1921.* New York, 1935. 2 vols.
Charmetant, Félix. *Martyrologe arménien. Tableau officiel des massacres d'Arménie.* Paris, 1896.
Choburian, Edvard. *Meds paterazme ev hai zhoghovurde* [The Great War and the Armenian People]. Constantinople, 1920.
Churchill, Winston. *The World Crisis.* Vol. II, *1915.* New York, 1929.
Clarkson, Jesse D. *A History of Russia.* 3d printing. New York, [1963].
Clemenceau, Georges. *Les massacres d'Arménie. Témoignages des victimes.* Paris, 1896.
Cuinet, Vital. *La Turquie d'Asie. Géographie administrative, statistique, descriptive et raisonnée de chaque province de l'Asie-Mineure.* Paris, 1890–1895. 4 vols.
Danilov, Iu. N. *Rossiia v mirovoi voine 1914–1915 g.g.* Berlin, 1924.
Davison, Roderic H. *Reform in the Ottoman Empire, 1856–1876.* Princeton, 1963.
Denikin, A. I. *Ocherki russkoi smuti.* Vol. III. Berlin, 1924.
Dennis, Alfred L. P. *The Foreign Policies of Soviet Russia.* New York, 1924.
Der Nersessian, Sirarpie. *Armenia and the Byzantine Empire.* Cambridge, Mass., 1945.
Djanachian, Mesrop. *Patmutiun ardi hai grakanutian* [History of Modern Armenian Literature]. Venice, 1953.
Dorys, Georges. *The Private Life of the Sultan of Turkey.* Translated by Arthur Hornblow. New York, 1909.
Doumergue, Émile. *L'Arménie. Les massacres et la question d'Orient.* 2d. ed., rev. Paris, 1920.
Driault, Édouard. *La question d'Orient depuis ses origines jusqu'à nos jours.* 5th ed. Paris, 1912.
Dubner, A. *Bakinskii proletariat v gody revoliutsii (1917–1920).* Baku, 1931.
Duda, Herbert W. *Vom Kalifat zur Republik.* Vienna, 1948.
Edib, Halidé. *Turkey Faces West. A Turkish View of Recent Changes and Their Origin.* New Haven, 1930.

Elchibekian, A. M. *Velikaia Oktiabr'skaia sotsialisticheskaia revoliutsiia i pobeda sovetskoi vlasti v Armenii.* Erevan, 1957.

Elchibekian, H[A]. M., and A. M. Hakobian. *Urvagdser Sovetakan Hayastani patmutian* [Outlines of the History of Soviet Armenia]. Vol. I. Erevan, 1954.

Emin, Ahmed [Yalman]. *Turkey in the World War.* New Haven and London, 1930.

Engelhardt, Éd. *La Turquie et le tanzimat: Ou, Histoire des réformes dans l'empire Ottoman depuis 1826 jusqu'à nos jours.* Paris, 1882–1884. 2 vols.

Enukidze, D. *Krakh imperialisticheskoi interventsii v Zakavkaz'e.* Tbilisi, 1954.

Esadze, S. *Istoricheskaia zapiska ob upravlenii Kavkazom.* Vol. I. Tiflis, 1907.

Etmekjian, James. *The French Influence on the Western Armenian Renaissance, 1843–1915.* New York, 1964.

Ezov, G. A. *Snosheniia Petra Velikago s armianskim narodom.* St. Petersburg, 1898.

Fadeev, A. V. *Rossiia i Kavkaz pervoi treti XIX v.* Moscow, 1960.

Fainsod, Merle. *How Russia Is Ruled.* Cambridge, Mass., 1953.

Feldmann, Wilhelm. *Kriegstage in Konstantinopel.* Strassburg, 1913.

Ferriman, Duckett Z. *The Young Turks and the Truth about the Holocaust at Adana in Asia Minor during April, 1909.* London, 1913.

Fesch, Paul. *Constantinople aux derniers jours d'Abdul-Hamid.* Paris, [1909].

Fischer, George. *Russian Liberalism. From Gentry to Intelligentsia.* Cambridge, Mass., 1958.

Florinsky, Michael T. *Russia: A History and an Interpretation.* New York, 1953. 2 vols.

Galanté, Abraham. *Turcs et Juifs. Étude historique, politique.* Istanbul, 1932.

Galoyan, G. *Bor'ba za sovetskuiu vlast' v Armenii.* Moscow, 1957.

———. *Sotsialisticheskaia revoliutsiia v Zakavkaz'e v osveshchenii burzhuaznoi istoriografii.* Moscow, 1960.

Gambashidze, Givi. *Iz istorii politiki S.Sh.A. v otnoshenii Gruzii, 1917–1920.* Tbilisi, 1960.

Gelfand, Lawrence E. *The Inquiry. American Preparations for Peace, 1917–1919.* New Haven and London, 1963.

Gentizon, Paul. *La résurrection géorgienne.* Paris, 1921.

Gerard, James W. *England and France in Armenia* [New York, 1920].

Gharibdjanian, G. B. *Hayastani komunistakan kazmakerputiunnere sovetakan ishkhanutian haghtanaki hamar mghvads paikarum* [The Communist Organizations of Armenia in the Struggle for Victory of the Soviet Order]. Erevan, 1955.

———. *V. I. Lenine ev Andrkovkasi zhoghovurdneri azatagrume* [V. I. Lenin and the Liberation of the Peoples of Transcaucasia]. Erevan, 1960.

Gibbons, Herbert Adams. *The Blackest Page of Modern History. Events in Armenia in 1915. The Facts and the Responsibilities.* New York and London, 1916.

Giulkhandanian, A. *Hai-tatarakan endharumnere* [The Armeno-Tatar Clashes]. Tiflis, 1907.

———. *Hai-trkakan endharumnere* [The Armeno-Turkish Clashes]. Vol. I. Paris, 1933.

Golovine, Nicholas. *The Russian Army in the World War.* New Haven and London, 1931.

Gorky, M., V. Molotov, K. Voroshilov, *et al.*, eds. *The History of the Civil War in the U.S.S.R.* Volume II, *The Great Proletarian Revolution*, ed. by G. F. Alexandrov. London, 1947.

Grigorian, V. R. *Erevani khanutiune 18rd dari verdjum (1780–1800)* [The Khanate of Erevan at the End of the 18th Century (1780–1800)]. Erevan, 1958.

Grigorian, Z. T. *Prisoedinenie Vostochnoi Armenii k Rossii v nachale XIX veka.* Moscow, 1959.

———. *Rus ev hai zhoghovurdneri razmakan hamagordsaktsutiune XIX dari skzbin* [The Military Collaboration of the Armenian and Russian Peoples at the Beginning of the 19th Century]. Erevan, 1957.

Grousset, René. *Histoire de l'Arménie des Origines à 1071.* Paris, 1947.

Gulanian, Kh. G. *Marksistakan tntesagitakan mtki taradsume hai irakanutian medj, 1890–1920* [The Spread of Marxist Economic Thought on the Armenian Scene, 1890–1920]. Erevan, 1961.

———. *Urvagdser hai tntesagitakan mtki patmutian* [Outlines of the History of Armenian Economic Thought]. Erevan, 1959.

Guseinov, Mirza-Davud. *Tiurkskaia Demokraticheskaia Partiia Federalistov "Musavat" v proshlom i nastoiashchem.* [Tiflis], 1927.

Guseinov, T. *Oktiabr' v Azerbaidzhane.* Baku, 1927.

Hacobian, A. P. *Armenia and the War.* London, New York, and Toronto, 1917.

Hakobian, T. Kh. *Erevani patmutiune (1801–1879)* [The History of Erevan (1801–1879)]. Erevan, 1959.

———. *Urvagdser Hayastani patmakan ashkharhagrutian* [Outlines of Armenia's Historical Geography]. Erevan, 1960.

Hammer, Joseph von. *Geschichte des osmanischen Reiches.* Vol. IV. Pest, 1829.

Harris, J. Rendel and Helen B. *Letters from the Scenes of Recent Massacres in Armenia.* New York, Chicago, and Toronto, 1897.

Harutunian, G. *Revoliutsion sharzhumnere ev Bolshevikneri gordsuneutiune Andrkovkasum 1910–1912 tvakannerin* [The Revolutionary Movements and the Activity of the Bolsheviks in Transcaucasia, 1910–1912]. Erevan, 1959.

———. *Revoliutsion sharzhumnere Hayastanum 1905–1907 tt.* [The Revolutionary Movements in Armenia, 1905–1907]. Erevan, 1956.

Harutunian, Varazdat. *Ani kaghake* [The City of Ani]. Erevan, 1964.

Hecquard, Charles. *La Turquie sous Abdul-Hamid II.* Brussels, 1901.

Heyd, Uriel. *Foundations of Turkish Nationalism. The Life and Teachings of Ziya Gökalp.* London, 1950.

Higgins, Trumbull. *Winston Churchill and the Dardanelles.* New York and London, [1963].

Hovhannisian, Ashot. *Drvagner hai azatagrakan mtki patmutian* [Episodes from the History of Armenian Liberation Thought]. Erevan, 1957–1959. 2 vols.

———. *Nalbandiane ev nra zhamanake* [Nalbandian and His Times]. Erevan, 1955–1956. 2 vols.

Hovhannisian [Varandian], Mikayel. *Dashnaktsutiun ev nra hakarakordnere* [Dashnaktsutiun and Its Opponents]. Tiflis, 1907.

———. *Kovkasian Vandean (turk-haikakan endharumnere: Nrants patjarnere)* [The Caucasian Vendée. (The Turco-Armenian Clashes: Their Causes)]. Tiflis, 1907.

Howard, Harry N. *The King-Crane Commission. An American Inquiry in the Middle East.* Beirut, 1963.
———. *The Partition of Turkey. A Diplomatic History, 1913–1923.* Norman, Okla., 1931.
Ioannisian [Hovhannisian], A. R. *Prisoedinenie Zakavkaz'ia k Rossii i mezhdunarodnye otnosheniia v nachale XIX stoletiia.* Erevan, 1958.
Iorga, N. *Brève histoire de la Petite Arménie. L'Arménie cilicienne.* Paris, 1930.
Ishkhanian, B. *Kontr-revoliutsiia v Zakavkaz'e.* Baku, 1919.
———. *Narodnosti Kavkaza.* Petrograd, 1916.
———. *Velikie uzhasy v gor. Baku. Anketnoe izsledovanie sentiabr'skikh sobytii 1918 g.* Tiflis, 1920.
Iskenderov, M. S. *Iz istorii bor'by Kommunisticheskoi partii Azerbaidzhana za pobedu sovetskoi vlasti.* Baku, 1958.
Jackh, Ernest. *The Rising Crescent. Turkey Yesterday, Today and Tomorrow.* New York and Toronto, [1944].
Jizmejian, Manuk G. *Patmutiun amerikahai kaghakakan kusaktsutiants, 1890–1925* [History of the Armenian-American Political Parties, 1890–1925]. Fresno, Calif., 1930.
Kachaznuni, H. *H. H. Dashnaktsutiune anelik chuni ailevs* [The Armenian Revolutionary Federation Has Nothing More To Do]. Vienna, 1923.
Kadishev, A. B. *Interventsiia i grazhdanskaia voina v Zakavkaz'e.* Moscow, 1960.
Kandemir, F. *Kâzım Karabekir* [written in Turkish]. Istanbul, 1948.
Kapantsian, Gr. *Khaiasa—kolybel' armian. Etnogenez armian i ikh nachal'naia istoriia.* Erevan, 1947.
Kara-Murza, P. *Nakanune zemskoi reformy na Kavkaze.* Baku, 1919.
Karapetian, H. N. *Hayastani Komeritmiutian dsnunde* [The Birth of the Communist Youth Union of Armenia]. Erevan, 1956.
Karapetian, S. Kh. *Kommunisticheskaia partiia v bor'be za pobedu Oktiabr'skoi Revoliutsii v Armenii.* Erevan, 1959.
Kazemzadeh, Firuz. *The Struggle for Transcaucasia (1917–1921).* New York and Oxford, [1951].
Kedourie, Elie. *England and the Middle East (The Destruction of the Ottoman Empire, 1914–1921).* [London, 1956].
Kévork-Mesrob. *L'Arménie au point de vue géographique, historique, statistique et cultural.* Constantinople, 1919.
Khachapuridze, G. *Bol'sheviki Gruzii v boiakh za pobedu sovetskoi vlasti.* 2d ed. [Moscow], 1951.
Khurshudian, L. A. *Stepan Shahumian. Petakan ev partiakan gordsuneutiune 1917–1918 tvakannerin* [Stepan Shahumian. Governmental and Party Activity in 1917–1918]. Erevan, 1959.
Kilic, Altemur. *Turkey and the World.* Washington, D.C., [1959].
Kirakosian, Dj. S. *Aradjin hamashkharhayin paterazme ev Arevmtahayutiune, 1914–1916 t.t.* [The First World War and the Western Armenians, 1914–1916]. Erevan, 1965.
Koms [Papazian, Vahan]. *Khonar herosner* [Humble Heroes]. Beirut, 1949–1956. 3 vols.
Korganoff, G. *La participation des Arméniens à la guerre mondiale sur le front du Caucase, 1914–1918.* Paris, 1927.

Korsun, N. G. *Pervaia mirovaia voina na Kavkazskom fronte.* Moscow, 1946.

———. *Sarykamyshskaia operatsiia na Kavkazskom fronte mirovoi voiny v 1914–1915 godu.* Moscow, 1937.

Krischtschian, M. *Deutschland und die Ausrottung der Armenier in der Türkei.* Potsdam, 1930.

Kutay, Cemal. *Atatürk-Enver Paşa hadiseleri* [The Atatürk-Enver Incidents]. Istanbul, [1956].

———. *Milli Mücadelede öncekiler ve sonrakiler* [Those Who Came before and after in the National Struggle]. Istanbul, [1963].

La Chesnais, P. G. *Les peuples de la Transcaucasie pendant la guerre et devant la paix.* Paris, 1921.

Lalabekian, B. H. *V. I. Lenine ev sovetakan kargeri hastatumn u amrapndumn Andrkovkasum* [V. I. Lenin and the Establishment and Strengthening of Soviet Order in Transcaucasia]. Erevan, 1961.

Lamouche, Colonel. *Histoire de la Turquie depuis les origines jusqu'à nos jours.* Paris, 1953.

Lang, David Marshall. *The Last Years of the Georgian Monarchy, 1658–1832.* New York, 1957.

Langer, William L. *The Diplomacy of Imperialism, 1890–1902.* 2d ed. New York, 1951.

Larcher, M. *La guerre turque dans la guerre mondiale.* Paris, 1926.

Laurent, J. *L'Arménie entre Byzance et l'Islam depuis la conquête arabe jusqu'en 886.* Paris, 1919.

———. *Byzance et les Turcs seldjoucides dans l'Asie occidentale jusqu'en 1081.* Paris and Nancy, 1913.

Lazian, Gabriel. *Demker hai azatagrakan sharzhumen* [Figures of the Armenian Freedom Movement]. Cairo, 1949.

———. *Heghapokhakan demker (mtavorakanner ev haidukner)* [Revolutionary Figures (Intellectuals and Guerrilla Fighters)]. Cairo, 1945.

Leo [Babakhanian, A.]. *Ani* [written in Armenian]. Erevan, 1963.

———. *Hayots patmutiun* [History of the Armenians]. Tiflis, 1917 [Vol. I]. Erevan, 1946–1947 [Vols. II–III]. 3 vols.

———. *Tiurkahai heghapokhutian gaghaparabanutiune* [The Ideology of the Turkish Armenian Revolution]. Paris, 1934–1935. 2 vols.

Lepsius, Johannes. *Armenia and Europe. An Indictment.* London, 1897.

———. *Der Todesgang des Armenischen Volkes.* 4th ed. Potsdam, 1930.

Lewis, Bernard. *The Emergence of Modern Turkey.* London, New York, and Toronto, 1961.

Lewis, Geoffrey. *Turkey.* London, [1960].

Loris-Melicof, Jean. *La révolution russe et les nouvelles républiques transcaucasiennes.* Paris, 1920.

Loti, Pierre. *Turquie agonisante.* Paris, 1913.

Luke, Harry. *The Making of Modern Turkey. From Byzantium to Angora.* London, 1936.

MacDonald, John. *Turkey and the Eastern Question.* London and Edinburgh, [1913].

Magnes, Judah L. *Russia and Germany at Brest-Litovsk. A Documentary History of the Peace Negotiations.* New York, [1919].

Makharadze, Filip. *Ocherki revoliutsionnogo dvizhennia v Zakavkaz'e*. Tiflis, 1927.
Manandian, Hakob. *Knnakan tesutiun hai zhoghovrdi patmutian* [A Critical History of the Armenian People]. Erevan, 1944-1952. 3 vols.
Mandelstam, André. *La Société des Nations et les Puissances devant le Problème Arménien*. Paris, 1926.
―――. *Le sort de l'empire Ottoman*. Paris and Lausanne, 1917.
Margarian, Hr., A. Mnatsakanian, and Kh. Barseghian, eds. *Hayastani Komunistakan partiayi patmutian urvagdser* [Outlines of the History of the Communist Party of Armenia]. Erevan, 1958.
Marriott, H. A. R. *The Eastern Question. An Historical Study in European Diplomacy*. 4th ed. Oxford, 1951.
Maslovskii, E. V., *Mirovaia voina na Kavkazskom fronte, 1914-1917 g.* Paris, [1933].
Maurice, Frederick, *The Armistice of 1918*. London, 1943.
Mears, Eliot Grinnell. *Modern Turkey. A Politico-Economic Interpretation, 1908-1923 Inclusive*. New York, 1924.
Medlicott, W. N. *The Congress of Berlin and After. A Diplomatic History of the Near Eastern Settlement, 1878-1880*. London, [1938].
Melik-Bakhshian, St. *Hayastane VII-IX darerum* [Armenia in the 7th-9th Centuries]. Erevan, 1958.
Melikian, M. A. *K voprosu o formirovanii armianskoi natsii i ee sotsialisticheskogo preobrazovaniia*. Erevan, 1957.
Melkonian, S. H. *Bagrat Gharibdjanian, 1890-1920* [written in Armenian]. Erevan, 1954.
Meyer, Alfred G. *Leninism*. Cambridge, Mass., 1957.
Mikayelian, V. A. *Ghrimi haikakan gaghuti patmutiun* [History of the Armenian Community of the Crimea]. Erevan, 1964.
―――. *Hayastani giughatsiutiune sovetakan ishkhanutian hamar mghvads paikari zhamanakashrdjanum (1917-1920 tt.)* [The Peasantry of Armenia in the Period of Struggle for the Establishment of Soviet Order (1917-1920)]. Erevan, 1960.
Miliukov, Paul. *Russia and Its Crisis*. New York, 1962.
Miller, A. F. *Ocherki noveishei istorii Turtsii*. Moscow and Leningrad, 1948.
Miller, William. *The Ottoman Empire and Its Successors, 1801-1922*. Cambridge, 1923.
Minakhorian, V. *1915 tvakane* [The Year 1915]. Venice, 1949.
Mitrany, David. *Marx against the Peasant. A Study in Social Dogmatism*. 2d printing. London, 1952.
Mnatsakanian, A. N. *Hai zhoghovrdi voghbergutiune. Rus ev hamashkharhayin hasarakakan mtki gnahatmamb* [The Tragedy of the Armenian People. As Appraised by Russian and Worldwide Public Opinion]. Erevan, 1965.
―――. *Revoliutsian Andrkovkasum ev Rusastani patviraknere, 1917-1921* [The Revolution in Transcaucasia and the Envoys of Russia, 1917-1921]. Erevan, 1961.
―――. *V. I. Lenine ev hai zhoghovrdi azatagrakan paikare* [V. I. Lenin and the Armenian People's Struggle for Freedom]. Erevan, 1963.
Mneyan, G. M. *Stepan Shahumiani partiakan ev petakan gordsuneutiune (1900-*

1918) [Stepan Shahumian's Party and Governmental Activity (1900–1918)]. Erevan, 1963.

Morgan, Jacques de. *Essai sur les nationalités.* Paris and Nancy, 1917.

———. *Histoire du peuple arménien depuis les temps les plus reculés de ses annales jusqu'à nos jours.* Paris and Nancy, 1919.

Movsisian, R. *Kovkasian bolshevikian kazmakerputiunneri Erkrayin aradjin hamagumare ev Stepan Shahumian* [The First Regional Conference of Caucasian Bolshevik Organizations and Stepan Shahumian]. Erevan, 1955.

Mühlmann, Carl. *Das deutsch-türkische Waffenbündnis im Welkrieg.* Leipzig, [1940].

Nalbandian, Louise. *The Armenian Revolutionary Movement. The Development of Armenian Political Parties through the Nineteenth Century.* Berkeley and Los Angeles, 1963.

Nalbandian, Sisak. *Tarono inknapashtpanutiune u djarde, 1914–1915* [The Self-Defense and Massacre of Taron, 1914–1915]. Fresno, Calif., 1920.

Navasardian, Vahan. *Bolshevizme ev Dashnaktsutiune* [Bolshevism and Dashnaktsutiun]. Cairo, 1949.

Nersisian, A. N. *Arevmtahayeri tntesakan u kaghakakan vijake ev nrants rusakan orientatsian XIX dari aradjin kesin* [The Economic and Political Situation of the Western Armenians and Their Russian Orientation in the First Half of the 19th Century]. Erevan, 1962.

———. *Hayeri masnaktsutiune 1877–78 tt. rus-turkakan paterazmin* [The Participation of the Armenians in the Russo-Turkish War of 1877–78]. Erevan, 1958.

Nersisian, M. *Dekabristnere Hayastanum* [The Decembrists in Armenia]. Erevan, 1958.

Nolde, Boris. *La formation de l'Empire russe. Études, notes et documents.* Paris, 1952–1953. 2 vols.

Orakhelashvili, Mamiia. *Zakavkazskie bol'shevistskie organizatsii v 1917 godu.* [Tiflis], 1927.

Ormanian, Malachia. *Azgapatum* [National History]. Constantinople [Vols. I–II] and Jerusalem [Vol. III], 1913–1927. 3 vols.

———. *The Church of Armenia. Her History, Doctrine, Rule, Discipline, Liturgy, Literature, and Existing Conditions.* Translated by G. Marcar. London, 1955.

Papazian, Bertha. *The Tragedy of Armenia.* Boston and Chicago, 1918.

Papikian, Hakob. *Adanayi egherne* [The Atrocity of Adana]. Constantinople, 1919.

Parsamian, V. A. *Hai azatagrakan sharzhumneri patmutiunits. Usumnasirutiun ev pastatghter* [From the History of the Armenian Liberation Movements. Study and Documents]. Erevan, 1958.

———. *Hayastane XIX dari aradjin kesin* [Armenia during the First Half of the 19th Century]. Erevan, 1960.

Pasdermadjian, G. *Why Armenia Should Be Free.* Boston, 1918.

Pasdermadjian, H. *Histoire de l'Arménie depuis les origines jusqu'au traité de Lausanne.* Paris, 1949.

Pears, Edwin. *Life of Abdul Hamid.* New York, 1917.

Pernot, Maurice. *La question turque.* Paris, 1923.

Pinon, René. *L'Europe et la Jeune Turquie*. Paris, 1911.

——. *La suppression des Arméniens. Méthode allemande—travail turc*. 7th ed. Paris, 1916.

Pipes, Richard. *The Formation of the Soviet Union. Communism and Nationalism 1917–1923*. Revised ed. Cambridge, Mass., 1964.

Poghosian, A. M. *Sotsial-tntesakan haraberutiunnere Karsi marzum, 1878–1920* [The Social-Economic Relations in the Province of Kars, 1878–1920]. Erevan, 1961.

Poghosian, S. *Hayastane XIII–XVII darerum* [Armenia during the 13th–17th Centuries]. Erevan, 1958.

——. *Hayastane zargatsads feodalizmi shrdjanum, IX–XIII darer* [Armenia during the Period of Advanced Feudalism, 9th–13th Centuries]. Erevan, 1958.

Potto, V. *Kavkazskaia voina v otdel'nykh ocherkakh, epizodakh, legendakh i biografiiakh*. St. Petersburg [Vols. I–III] and Tiflis [Vol. IV], 1885–1888. 4 vols. [Vol. I is 2d ed.]

Price, M. Philips. *War and Revolution in Asiatic Russia*. New York, [1918].

Radkey, Oliver Henry. *The Election to the Russian Constituent Assembly of 1917*. Cambridge, Mass., 1950.

Raevskii, A. *Angliiskaia interventsiia i Musavatskoe pravitel'stvo*. Baku, 1927.

Rassoul-Zadé, M. E. *L'Azerbaidjan en lutte pour l'Indépendance*. Paris, 1930.

Ratgauzer, Ia. *Revoliutsiia i grazhdanskaia voina v Baku*. Pt. 1. *1917–1918 g.g.* Baku, 1927.

Robinson, Richard D. *The First Turkish Republic. A Case Study in National Development*. Cambridge, Mass., 1963.

Ross, Frank A., Luther C. Fry, and Elbridge Sibler. *The Near East and American Philanthropy. A Survey Conducted under the Guidance of the General Committee of the Near East Survey*. New York, 1929.

Roy, Gilles. *Abdul-Hamid, le sultan rouge*. Paris, 1936.

Rshtuni, V. *Hai hasarakakan hosankneri patmutiunits* [From the History of Armenian Social Currents]. Erevan, 1956.

Rustem Bey, Ahmed. *La guerre mondiale et la question turco-armén enne*. Berne, 1918.

Rycaut, Paul. *Histoire de l'état présent de l'Empire Ottoman*. Translated by Briot. 2d ed. Paris, 1670.

Sanders [Nikuradze], A. *Kaukasien. Nordkaukasien, Aserbeidschan, A menien, Georgien*. Munich, [1944].

Sargsian, E. K. *Ekspansionistskaia politika Osmanskoi imperii v Zakavkaz'e nakanune i v gody pervoi mirovoi voiny*. Erevan, 1962.

Sarkissian, A. O. *History of the Armenian Question to 1885*. Urbana, Ill., 1938.

Sarrou, A. *La Jeune-Turquie et la Révolution*. Paris and Nancy, 1912.

Sassuni, G. *Tajkahayastane rusakan tirapetutian tak (1914–1918)* [Turkish Armenia under Russian Domination (1914–1918)]. Boston, 1927.

Schapiro, Leonard. *The Origin of the Communist Autocracy*. London, [1956].

Schmitt, Bernadotte, E. *The Coming of the War, 1914*. New York and London, 1930. 2 vols.

Schopoff, A. *Les réformes et la protection des Chrétiens en Turquie, 1673–1904*. Paris, 1904.

Selek, Sabahettin. *Millî Mücadele. Anadolu İhtilâli* [The National Struggle. Anatolian Rebellion]. Istanbul, 1963.

Seropian, M. *Les Vêpres ciliciennes. Les responsabilités, faits et documents.* Alexandria, 1909.

Seton-Watson, R. W. *Disraeli, Gladstone and the Eastern Question. A Study in Diplomacy and Party Politics.* London, 1935.

Setton, Kenneth H., et al., eds. *A History of the Crusades,* Vol. II. Philadelphia, [1962].

Shabanov, F. Sh. *Razvitie sovetskoi gosudarstvennosti v Azerbaidzhane.* Moscow, 1959.

Shafir, Ia. M. *Grazhdanskaia voina v Rossii i men'shevistskaia Gruziia.* Moscow, 1921.

Shahan. *Tiurkism Angoraen Baku ev trkakan orientatsion* [Turkism from Angora to Baku and the Turkish Orientation]. Athens, 1928.

Shakhatuni, A. *Administrativnyi peredel Zakavkazskago kraia.* Tiflis, 1918.

Shcherbatov, Kniaz'. *General-Fel'dmarshal Kniaz' Paskevich. Ego zhizn' i deiatel'nost', po neizdannym istochnikam.* St. Petersburg, 1884–1904. 7 vols.

Shopen [Chopin], I. *Istoricheskii pamiatnik Armianskoi oblasti v epokhu ee prisoedineniia k Rossiiskoi imperii.* St. Petersburg, 1852.

Smirnov, N. A. *Politika Rossii na Kavkaze v XVI–XIX vekakh.* Moscow, 1958.

Smith, C. Jay. *The Russian Struggle for Power, 1914–1917. A Study of Russian Foreign Policy during the First World War.* New York, [1956].

Soviet Union and Peace. Introduction by Henri Barbuesse. New York, [1929].

Spector, Ivar. *The Soviet Union and the Muslim World, 1917–1958.* Seattle, 1959.

Stankevich, V. B. *Sud'by narodov Rossii.* Berlin, 1921.

Stavrianos, L. S. *The Balkans Since 1453.* New York, 1958.

Stavrovskii, Al. *Zakavkaz'e posle Oktiabria. Vzaimo-otnosheniia s Turtsiei v pervoi polovine 1918 goda.* Moscow-Leningrad, [1925].

Taeschner, Franz, and Gotthard Jäschke. *Aus der Geschichte des islamischen Orients.* Tübingen, 1949.

Tchalkhouchian, Gr. *Le livre rouge.* Paris, 1919.

Terzian, Hakob H. *Kilikio aghete* [The Calamity of Cilicia]. Constantinople, 1912.

Tigranian, S. *Dashnaktsakan patkamavornere Erkrord Pet. Dumaum* [The Dashnakist Delegates in the Second St. (State) Duma]. Tiflis, 1907.

Tillman, Seth P. *Anglo-American Relations at the Peace Conference of 1919.* Princeton, 1961.

Tokarzhevskii, E. A. *Iz istorii inostrannoi interventsii i grazhdanskoi voiny v Azerbaidzhane.* Baku, 1957.

Toynbee, Arnold J. *Armenian Atrocities. The Murder of a Nation.* London, New York and Toronto, 1915.

———. *Turkey. A Past and a Future.* New York, 1917.

Treadgold, Donald W. *Twentieth Century Russia.* 2d ed. Chicago, [1964].

Trukhanovskii, V. G., ed. *Istoriia mezhdunarodnykh otnoshenii i vneshnei politiki SSSR, 1917–1939 gg.* Vol. I. Moscow, 1961.

Tumanov, G. M. *K vvedeniiu na Kavkaz zemskago samoupravleniia.* Tiflis, 1905.

Tunaya, Tarik Z. *Türkiyede siyasî partiler, 1859–1952* [Political Parties in Turkey, 1859–1952]. Istanbul, 1952.
Turabian, Aram. *L'éternelle victime de la diplomatie européenne.* [Paris], 1929.
Ubicini, A. [J. H.]. *Lettres sur la Turquie: Ou, Tableau statistique religieux, politique, administratif, militaire, commercial, etc. de l'Empire ottoman, depuis le khatti-cherif de Gulkhanè (1839).* 2d ed. Paris, 1853–1854. 2 vols.
Uras, Esat. *Tarihte Ermeniler ve Ermeni Meselesi* [The Armenians in History and the Armenian Question]. Ankara, 1950.
Uratadze, G. I. *Obrazovanie i konsolidatsiia Gruzinskoi Demokraticheskoi Respubliki.* Munich, 1956.
Varandian, Mikayel. *Le conflit arméno-géorgien et la guerre du Caucase.* Paris, 1919.
——. *Haikakan sharzhman nakhapatmutiun* [Prehistory of the Armenian Movement]. Geneva, 1912–1914. 2 vols.
——. *H. H. Dashnaktsutian patmutiun* [History of the A. (Armenian) R. (Revolutionary) Federation]. Paris [Vol. I], 1932, and Cairo [Vol. II], 1950. 2 vols.
——. *Hosankner* [Currents]. Geneva, 1910.
Vartanian, S. *Pobeda sovetskoi vlasti v Armenii.* Erevan, 1959.
Véchapeli, G. *La Géorgie turque. Lasistan, Trébizonde et contrée du Tchorokh.* Berne, 1919.
Vere-Hodge, Edward Reginald. *Turkish Foreign Policy, 1914–1948.* Geneva, 1950.
Veselovskii, Boris. *Istoriia Zemstva za sorok let.* St. Petersburg, 1909–1911. 4 vols. [Vols. III–IV entitled *Istoriia Zemstva*].
Villari, Luigi. *Fire and Sword in the Caucasus.* London, 1906.
Vishniak, M. V. *Vserossiiskoe Uchreditel'noe Sobranie.* Paris, 1932.
Voskerchian, Artashes. *Hai marksistakan knnadatutian himnadirnere, Stepan Shahumian, Suren Spandarian* [Stepan Shahumian and Suren Spandarian, Founders of Armenian Marxist Criticism]. Erevan, 1962.
Vratzian, S. *Hayastane bolshevikian murji ev trkakan sali midjev* [Armenia between the Bolshevik Hammer and the Turkish Anvil]. Beirut, 1953.
——. *Hayastani Hanrapetutiun* [Republic of Armenia]. 2d ed. Beirut, 1958.
Wheeler-Bennett, John W. *Brest-Litovsk. The Forgotten Peace, March 1918.* London, 1938.
Williams, August Warner, and M. S. Gabriel. *Bleeding Armenia. Its History and Horrors under the Curse of Islam.* Chicago, 1896.
Wittlin, Alma. *Abdul Hamid, the Shadow of God.* Translated by Norma Denny. London, [1940].
Woytinsky, Wladimir. *La démocratie géorgienne.* Paris, 1921.
Zarbhanalian, Garegin. *Patmutiun hayeren dprutian* [History of Armenian Literature]. Vol. II. Venice, 1905.
Zavriev, D. S. *K noveishei istorii severo-vostochnykh vilaetov Turtsii.* Tbilisi, 1947.
Zeine, Zeine N. *Arab-Turkish Relations and the Emergence of Arab Nationalism.* Beirut, [1958].
Zhamkochian, H. *Hayastane nakhnadarian-hamainakan hasarakutian ev strka-*

tirutian shrdjanum [Armenia during the Epoch of Prehistoric-Communal Society and Slave Ownership]. Erevan, 1961.

Zhamkochian, H. G., A. G. Abrahamian, and St. T. Melik-Bakhshian. *Hai zhoghovrdi patmutiun* [History of the Armenian People]. Vol. I. Erevan, 1963.

Ziatkhan, Adil Khan. *Aperçu sur l'histoire, la littérature, et la politique de l'Azerbeidjan*. Baku, 1919.

Ziemke, Kurt. *Die neue Turkei. Politische Entwicklung, 1914–1929*. Stuttgart, Berlin, and Leipzig, 1930.

Articles

Abeghian, Art. "Menk ev mer harevannere—Azgayin kaghakakanutian khndirner" [We and Our Neighbors—Problems of National Policy], *Hairenik Amsagir*, VI (December, 1927–October, 1928), and VII (November, 1928–January, 1929).

Alboyajian, Arshak. "Ankakh Hayastan" [Independent Armenia], *Amenun Taretsuitse* [Constantinople], XV (1921), 107–129.

Astvadsatrian, Arshaluis. "Arame," *Vem*, II (no. 6, 1934), 23–35, and III (no. 1, 1935), 57–71.

Barker, J. Ellis. "Germany, Turkey, and the Armenian Massacres," *Quarterly Review*, CCXXXIII (April, 1920), 385–400.

Bérard, Victor. "La politique du Sultan," *La Revue de Paris*, 39th yr. (December 15, 1896), pp. 865–899; 40th yr. (January 1 and 15, 1897), pp. 57–94, 421–458.

Castagné, Joseph. "Le Bolchevisme et l'Islam," pt. 1, *Revue du monde musulman*, LI (October, 1922), 1–254. Pt. 2, LII (December, 1922), includes articles by several authors.

Daniels, Emil. "England und Russland in Armenien und Persien," *Preussische Jahrbücher*, CLXIX (July-September, 1917), 237–267.

Davison, Roderic H. "The Armenian Crisis (1912–1914)," *The American Historical Review*, LIII (April, 1948), 481–505.

Djamalian, Arshak. "Hai-vratsakan knjire" [The Armeno-Georgian Entanglement], *Hairenik Amsagir*, Vol. VI (April, 1928–October, 1928), and Vol. VII (November, 1928–April, 1929).

Dulaurier, Édouard. "Étude sur l'organisation politique, religieuse et administrative du Royaume de la Petite-Arménie," *Journal Asiatique*, 5th Series, XVII (April–May, 1861), 377–437, and XVIII (October–November, 1861), 289–357.

D.Z.T. "La première République musulmane: L'Azerbaidjan," *Revue du monde musulman*, XXXVI (1918–1919), 229–265.

Hatsagordsian, Armen. "Drvagner Vani herosamartits" [Episodes from the Heroic Battle of Van], *Sovetakan grakanutiun*, XXXI (April, 1965), 100–102.

Ishkhanian, E. "Depkere Gharabaghum: Jshtumner ev ditoghutiunner" [The Events in Karabagh: Corrections and Observations], *Hairenik Amsagir*, XI (September, 1933–October, 1933), 85–93, 111–127.

Jäschke, Gotthard. "Beiträge zur Geschichte des Kampfes der Türkei um ihre Unabhängigkeit," *Die Welt des Islams*, n.s., V (no. 1–2, 1958), 1–64.

———. "Entwurf zu einem Friedens-und Freundschaftsvertrag zwischen dem

Osmanischen Reich und der Föderativen Transkaukasischen Republik," *Die Welt des Islams,* XXIII (bk. 3-4, 1941), 170-174.

———. "Der Freiheitskampf des türkischen Volkes," *Die Welt des Islams,* XIV (1932), 6-21.

———. "Gliederung des osmanischen Heeres am 15. Mai 1918," *Die Welt des Islams,* XXIII (bk. 3-4, 1941), 184-185.

———. "Die Republik Aserbeidschan," *Die Welt des Islams,* XXIII (bk. 1-2, 1941), 55-69.

———. "Die Südwestkaukasische Regierung von Kars," *Die Welt des Islams,* n.s., II (no. 1, 1952), 47-51.

———. "Der Turanismus der Jungtürken. Zur osmanischen Aussenpolitik im Weltkriege," *Die Welt des Islams,* XXIII (bk. 1-2, 1941), 1-54.

Kamsarakan, Peter. "Republik Armenien," *Mitteilungen der Geographischen Gesellschaft in Wien,* LXXXI (1938), 198-214.

Kasparian, Hamo. "Bakvi 26 Komisarnere" [The 26 Commissars of Baku], *Sovetakan Hayastan* (no. 9, 1949), pp. 32-34.

Kerner, R. J. "Russia, the Straits, and Constantinople, 1914-1915," *The Journal of Modern History,* I (September, 1929), 400-415.

Khatisian, Al. "Batumi Dashnagire" [The Treaty of Batum], *Mayis 28* (Paris, 1926), pp. 35-43.

Khondkarian, Arsham. "Opozitsian Hanrapetakan Hayastanum" [The Opposition in Republican Armenia], *Vem,* I (nos. 1-2, 1933), and II (nos. 1-4, 1934).

———. "Tsarakan Rusastane ev Kovkasahayutiune" [Tsarist Russia and the Caucasian Armenians], *Hairenik Amsagir,* VIII (March, 1930-April, 1930), 80-91, 143-155.

Kocharian, S. "Soviet National Policy in Armenia," *Caucasian Review* (no. 1, 1956), pp. 81-92.

Kostiaeff, F. "Intervention des puissances étrangères en Russie méridionale et dans les régions du Caucase et du Turkestan de 1918 à 1920," *Les Alliés contre la Russie avant, pendant et après la guerre mondiale. (faits et documents).* Paris, [1926], pp. 249-303.

Lepsius, Johannes. "The Armenian Question," *Muslim World,* X (1920), 341-355.

Leveyre, Maurice. "Les massacres des Sasounkh," *La Revue de Paris,* 38th yr. (September 1, 1895), pp. 73-91.

Lisitzyan, Levon. "Physiographic Armenia," *Armenian Review,* VIII (Spring, 1955), 92-100.

Macler, Frédéric. "Armenia," *The Cambridge Medieval History,* IV [New York, 1923], 156-181.

Masurian, S. "Rusahayots Azgayin Hamagumare" [The National Congress of the Russian Armenians], *Mayis 28,* pp. 4-22.

Miliukov, Paul. "The Balkanization of Transcaucasia," *The New Russia,* II (June 24, July 1, July 8, 1920), 236-241, 269-274, 299-303.

Minakhorian, Vahan. "Batumi Khorhrdazhoghove" [The Batum Conference], *Hairenik Amsagir,* XIV (March, 1936-May, 1936), 91-99, 123-131, 112-120.

———. "Karsi ankume" [The Fall of Kars], *Hairenik Amsagir,* XIII (August, 1935-October, 1935), 79-87, 83-96, 79-92, and XIV (December, 1935-January, 1936), 133-139, 145-152.

Minasian, O. "Vneshniaia politika zakavkazskoi kontrrevoliutsii v pervoi polovine 1918 goda," *Istorik marksist* (no. 6, 1938), pp. 53–86.

Navasardian, V. "H. H. D. gaghaparabanutiune" [The Ideology of the A. R. F.], *Hushapatum* (Boston, 1950), pp. 167–259.

Piotrovski, B. "Concerning the Origin of the Armenian Nation," *Armenian Affairs*, I (Summer–Fall, 1950), 287–292.

Poidebard, A. "Rôle militaire des Arméniens sur le front du Caucase après la défection de l'armée russe (décembre 1917–novembre 1918)," *Revue des études arméniennes*, I (pt. 2, 1920), 143–161.

Rasulzade, M. E. "The Meaning of a Certain Historical Act," *United Caucasus* (no. 3–4, 1953), pp. 7–10.

Ruben [Ter Minasian, R.]. "Gandzak-Gharabaghi veje" [The Gandzak-Karabagh Dispute], *Droshak*, XXVI (no. 2, 1926), 46–52.

——. "Tashiri gavarin brnagravume" [The Forceful Seizure of the County of Tashir], *Droshak*, XXVI (no. 3, 1926), 67–71.

Sarur. "Gharabaghi ktsume Adrbedjani" [The Annexation of Karabagh to Azerbaijan], *Hairenik Amsagir*, VII (June, 1929), 128–146.

Sassuni, G. "Erku jakatamart vor vjretsin hayutian bakhte" [Two Decisive Battles That Determined the Fate of the Armenians], *Miatsial ev Ankakh Hayastan* (Constantinople, 1919), pp. 29–31.

Seton-Watson, R. W. "Italian Intervention and the Secret Treaty of London," *The Slavonic Review*, V (December, 1926), 271–297.

Shahinian, G. "Herosakan shabate" [The Week of Heroism], *Miatsial ev Ankakh Hayastan*, pp. 23–25.

Shatirian, M. "Drvagner motik antsialits" [Episodes from the Recent Past], *Hairenik Amsagir*, I (May, 1923), 111–123.

——. "Edj me hai-trkakan krivneren" [A Page from the Armeno-Turkish Battles], *Hairenik Amsagir*, I (September, 1923), 96–100.

Sokolovskii, Georgii. "Erevani kaghaki sotsial-demokratakan kazmakerputian patmutian hamarot aknark 1904–10 tt." [A Cursory View of the History of the Social-Democratic Organization of the City of Erevan, 1904–1910], *Hin bolshevikneri hishoghutiunner* [Memoirs of Veteran Bolsheviks] (Erevan, 1958), pp. 110–113.

Stepanian, G. "Hai zhoghovrdi herosakan inknapashtpanutiune 1915 t." [The Heroic Self-Defense of the Armenian People in 1915], *Sovetakan grakanutiun*, XXXI (April, 1965), 82–93.

Strakhovsky, Leonid I. "Kerensky Betrayed Russia," *The Russian Revolution and Bolshevik Victory: Why and How?* Edited by Arthur E. Adams. Boston, [1960], pp. 85–96.

Torosian, S. "Soviet Policy in the Armenian Question," *Armenian Review*, XI (Summer, 1958), 27–39.

Toynbee, Arnold. "A Summary of Armenian History up to and including the Year 1915," *Armenian Review*, XII (Summer, Autumn, Winter, 1959–1960), 78–97, 59–74, 137–150.

"The United States and Armenia," *Armenian Bulletin*, (no. 2, 1945), pp. 3–5.

Vardanian, H. G. "Arevmtahayeri sotsialakan ev azgayin jnshman uzheghatsume Berlini Kongresits heto" [Intensification of the Social and National Suppression of the Western Armenians after the Congress of Berlin], *Patma-Banasirakan handes* (no. 3, 1964), pp. 69–78.

Vratzian, S. "H. H. Dashnaktsutian dsnunde ev himnadirnere" [The Birth and the Founders of the Armenian Revolutionary Federation], *Hushapatum*, pp. 61–140.

X. "Les courants politiques dans la Turquie contemporaine," *Revue du monde musulman*, XXI (September, 1912), 158–221.

Zarzecki, S. "La question kurdo-arménienne," *La Revue de Paris*, 31st yr. (April 15, 1914), pp. 873–894.

Index

Abashidze, Haidar (Gaidar) Bey, 134, 294 n. 15
Abashidze, Prince Kita, 76, 294 n. 15
Abastuman, 158, 198
Abbasid Caliph, 4
Abbas Mirza, Crown Prince, 8
Abdul Hamid II, Sultan, 12, 17, 20, 26, 28, 29, 30, 53, 232
Abdul Kerim Pasha, 56, 214, 233
Abdullah (Ottoman war minister), 240
Abkhazia, 8
Achaemenids, 2
Acre, 59
Adalia *vilayet*, 59
Adana, 50, 252, 268 n. 27
Adrianople, 30; Treaty of, 8–9, 259–260 n. 10
Adriatic, 59
Afghanistan, 100, 178
Africa, 195
"Agamemnon," 239
Aghaev, Hasan (Gasan) Bek, 127–128
Aghbalian, Nikol, 89, 90, 159, 269 n. 38
Aharonian, Avetis, 90, 159, 190, 217, 247, 253; heads Constantinople mission, 230–238 *passim*
Ahmed Izzet Pasha. *See* Izzet Pasha, Ahmed
"Aims of the Revolution," 98. *See also* Lenin
Aintab, 239
Aivazian, H., 285 n. 108
Ajaria, 132, 158
Ajemian, Karapet, 276 n. 83
Ajemian (Ajemov), M. S., 68

Akhalkalak, 9, 10, 11, 115, 181, 252; Armenian claims to, 9, 15, 91, 92, 205, 206, 207, 235, 252; population of, 92, 199, 260 n. 12; Ottoman occupation of, 173, 177, 195, 196, 198, 199; Armenian refugees from, 207, 214, 233, 234
Akhaltsikh, 35, 115, 181, 252, 260 n. 11; *pashalik*, 5, 9; Ottoman occupation of, 173, 195, 196, 198, 199
Akhta, 307–308 n. 60
Akhurian River. *See* Arpachai River
Aknuni, E. (Khachatur Malumian), 41, 42
Akstafa, 210
Alagiaz, Mount, 196
Alaja, 134
Alashkert, 9, 12, 57–58, 137, 237; Regiment, 113
Alaverdi, 86
Alazan River, 207
Albanian, 29
Alekseev, General M. V., 66, 313–314 n. 68
Aleppo *vilayet*, 5, 50
Alexander I, Tsar, 8
Alexander II, Tsar, 12, 17
Alexandretta, Gulf of, 59
Alexandropol, 44, 71, 91, 114, 137, 144, 164, 170, 204, 205, 221, 249; *uezd*, 11, 173, 182, 195, 196, 199, 206, 261 n. 24; Shahumian in, 75, 86; Armenian conference in, 159; Armenian Corps headquarters in, 163–167 *passim;* Ottoman occupation of, 173–176, 177, 182, 192–194, 199, 201. *See also* Kars-Alexandropol-Julfa Railway

INDEX

Alexandrovskii Park "episode," 126
Alidjin, 196
Allen, W. E. D., 191
Allenby, General Edmund, 66, 249
Allied War Council, 138, 247
Allies, 59, 66, 121, 229; and Armenians, 51, 59–62, 117–118, 138, 236, 237, 238–240, 241, 244, 247–254. *See also* Entente, Triple
America, 27, 36, 47, 49, 66, 232, 242, 249, 251–253. *See also* United States
American Committee for Independence of Armenia, 253, 316 n. 31
American Relief Committee, 251
Amirjanov, A., 305 n. 20
Anatolia, 24, 35, 52, 54, 55, 59, 229, 257 n. 3; eastern, 1, 38, 103, 104, 130. *See also* Ottoman Empire, eastern *vilayets*
Andranik (Ozanian), General, 82, 159, 181; as volunteer corps commander, 44, 56, 63, 249; as commander of Western Armenian Division, 113–114, 135, 137; in Zangezur, 194, 214, 234, 241
Ani, 4
Antakya, 50
Anti-Taurus Mountains, 252, 257 n. 3
Apostolic Church. *See* Armenian Church
"April Theses," 74–75. *See also* Lenin
Apsheron Peninsula, 147, 190, 220, 221, 229
Arab, 2, 4, 29, 177, 229
Arabia, 59, 96, 248, 252
Aragadz (Alagiaz), Mount, 196
Arakelian, Hambardzum, 89, 269 n. 38
Aram (Manukian), 90, 126; at Van, 56, 276 n. 83; as Erevan "dictator," 143–145, 166, 193; as Armenian interior minister, 209, 210, 211, 215
Ararat: Plain, 10, 145; Legion, 55–56; Republic, 253
Araxes River, 1, 2, 5, 8, 58, 194, 196; Valley, 10, 240
Ardahan *okrug*, 13, 35, 46, 150, 229, 235, 237, 239; Russian annexation of, 11–13; Ottoman strategy in and occupation of, 45, 132, 133, 134, 140, 141, 160, 173, 177, 199, 271 n. 2; and Brest-Litovsk treaty, 103, 104, 130, 151, 161, 170, 203, 218, 219, 228; Moslem insurgents in, 145, 146
Ardahan *sanjak*. *See* Ardahan *okrug*
Areshian (Areshov), General, 114, 137, 164

Arghutian, Hovsep, 47
Argyll, Duke of, 26
Armen Garo (Garegin Pasdermadjian), 44, 54, 81
Armenia, 10, 56, 175, 180, 184, 189, 218; early history of, 1–6, 16; tsarist Russian plans for, 56–67 *passim*; in Bolshevik-Soviet declarations, 96–98, 99, 101, 102, 172; in Allied declarations, 247–254 *passim*. *See also* Armenia, Republic of; Russian (Eastern) Armenia; Turkish (Western) Armenia
Armenia, Greater (Major), 2, 5; provinces of, 257 n. 5
Armenia, Lesser (Minor), 2, 5, 34, 60
Armenia, Republic of, 2, 9, 11, 13, 19, 37, 40, 90, 91, 109, 145, 186, 190–191, 194–225 *passim*, 230–245 *passim*, 247, 251, 253, 305 n. 24, 307–308 n. 60, 313–314 n. 68
Armenia, Russian. *See* Russian (Eastern) Armenia
Armenia, Turkish. *See* Turkish (Western) Armenia
Armenian Affairs Commissariat, 171
Armenian Agrarian Society, 79
Armenian Army Corps, 113–115, 135, 157, 159, 164, 167, 193, 194, 290 n. 40
Armenian Bolsheviks. *See* Social Democrat Bolsheviks (Armenian)
Armenian Central Committee for Self-Defense, 18
Armenian Church, 7, 37; crisis of 1903–1905, 17–21, 28; under Ottoman rule, 25; after Russian Revolution, 74, 78; *Polozhenie* of, 280 n. 22. *See also* Armenian Patriarchate of Constantinople
Armenian Commissariat of the Ukraine, 313 n. 65
Armenian Committee of Moscow, 67, 79, 81, 88
Armenian Committee of Petrograd, 66, 81
Armenian Constitutional Democrats. *See* Constitutional Democrats (Armenian); Populists (Armenian)
Armenian Council of Baku. *See* Baku Armenian Council
Armenian Council of Erevan, 126, 143
Armenian Defense Committee of Petrograd, 171
Armenian Justice, Charter for, 248–249
Armenian legislature. *See* Khorhurd of Armenia

INDEX 347

Armenian literary movement, 15–16
Armenian Mensheviks. *See* Social Democrat Mensheviks (Armenian)
Armenian National Assembly, 33
Armenian National Bureau, 67, 68, 87; formation of, 32, 269 n. 38; directs Armenian volunteer movement, 42–45, 47, 57, 63
Armenian National Congress, 85, 86–91, 159, 284 n. 98
Armenian National Council, 115, 119, 143, 159, 180; formation of, 90, 285 n. 108; and Soviet Russia, 111, 171; and fall of Kars, 163, 167; proclaims Armenian independence, 186, 190, 191, 244; and peace with Ottoman Empire, 191, 193, 194, 198, 199, 201, 217; and Georgian Republic, 205–206, 209–210, 305 n. 21; forms Armenia's cabinet, 207–209, 211
Armenian *oblast*, 9–10, 11, 243, 260 n. 16
Armenian Patriarchate of Constantinople: creation of, 25; and Ottoman reforms, 26, 27, 30, 33, 36, 37; in World War I, 42, 53
Armenian Plateau: geography of, 1–2, 257 n. 3; early history of, 1–6, 257 n. 1; Armenian aspirations for, 7, 16, 23, 47, 55, 80, 194, 243, 244, 251; Russian expansion to, 7–12 *passim*, 16; under Ottoman jurisdiction, 24, 26, 28, 31, 34–35, 37; in World War I, 41, 44, 46, 57, 60, 62, 64, 66–67, 80, 81, 96, 98, 121, 137, 240
Armenian political societies. *See* Dashnaktsutiun; Hnchakists; Populists (Armenian); Social Democrat Bolsheviks (Armenian); Social Democrat Mensheviks (Armenian); Social Revolutionaries (Armenian)
Armenian Populist party. *See* Populists (Armenian)
"Armenian Question," 19, 26–39 *passim*, 43, 63, 100, 140, 195–196
Armenian Railway Administration, 198
Armenian Revolutionary Federation. *See* Dashnaktsutiun
Armenian Rifle battalions, 63, 66, 81–82
Armenians of Ottoman Empire. *See* Turkish (Western) Armenians
Armenians of Russia. *See* Russian (Eastern) Armenians
Armenian volunteer movement, 42–43, 46–47, 49, 53–54, 55–57, 62–63, 66, 67, 81, 87, 249

Armeno-Tatar "War," 21, 73, 264 nn. 63 and 64
Armianskaia oblast, 9–10, 11, 243, 260 n. 16
Army of Islam, 177, 190, 205, 214, 220
Arpachai River, 165, 166, 175, 236
Arsacid (Arshakuni) dynasty, 2
Arsenidze, 160
Artaxiad (Artashesian) dynasty, 2
Artvin *okrug*, 150, 151, 199
Arzumanian, Misha, 166
Ashkhabad, 312 n. 37
Ashtarak, 307–308 n. 60
Ashurov, Agha, 305 n. 20
Asia Minor, 31, 58, 252
Asiatic Turkey, 59, 62, 66. *See also* Anatolia
Assyrians, 154, 194
Astrakhan, 147, 222, 227, 311 n. 13, 312 n. 37
Atabekian, Levon, 285 n. 108
Austria-Hungary: and Armenians, 26, 27, 33, 55, 203, 211, 216, 223–224, 230; in World War I, 40, 53, 59, 83, 97, 101, 102
Avalov (Avalishvili), Zurab, 92, 158, 173, 183, 184, 189
Avanesov, V. A., 171
Averianov, General P., 80
Avsharian, Grigor, 47, 273 n. 40
Aybat, 220
Azatamart (Constantinople), 42
Azatian, Haik, 209, 213, 309 n. 93
Azerbaijan, Republic of, 11, 48, 198, 207, 218, 230, 234; formation of, 189–190, 191, 304 n. 17; boundaries with Armenia, 196, 210, 212–213, 214–215, 231, 234–236, 241–242; Ottoman assistance to, 198, 205, 219, 220–222, 224, 225–227, 240; and Great Britain, 241–242; cabinet of, 305 n. 20
Azerbaijan (Persian), 47, 48, 55, 60, 62, 86, 195, 253. *See also* North Persia

Babalian, Artashes, 90, 190, 309 n. 93
Baghdad, 59, 138, 177, 178, 205, 207, 221
Bagratid (Bagratuni) kingdom, 4, 5
Bagratuni, General Hovhannes, 171
Bahaeddin Shakir, 41, 232
Baiburt, 64
Baku, 16, 48, 70, 71, 72, 73, 76, 86, 91, 111, 126, 146, 150, 154, 168, 189, 198, 210, 237, 239, 249; *khanate*, 8; *guberniia*, 11, 15, 73, 91, 92, 194, 195; popula-

tion of, 15, 92, 296–297 n. 74; Armenian troops in, 81, 115, 147–148, 197; Armenian-Moslem strife in, 81, 115, 148–149, 181, 182, 214, 221, 227, 232, 233, 234, 312 n. 36; Armenian-Bolshevik collaboration in, 112, 113, 124, 147–149, 170, 174, 181, 220, 297 n. 80; Ottoman conquest of, 124, 161, 174, 177, 181, 202, 205, 220–222, 225–227, 228, 229, 312 n. 36; German-Ottoman competition for, 178, 179, 203, 218, 222–223, 224; British in, 220–222, 225–227, 241, 242
Baku Armenian Council, 81, 112, 146, 147, 148, 149, 170, 221, 227, 298 n. 84
Baku Centro-Caspian Dictatorship. *See* Centro-Caspian Dictatorship
Baku City Duma, 298 n. 73
Baku Council of People's Commissars. *See* Baku Sovnarkom
Baku "March Days," 147–149, 227, 297 nn. 77, 80, and 82
Baku Military Revolutionary Committee (Revkom), 148, 297 n. 76, 298 n. 84
Baku Moslem Council, 146, 147
Baku Red Army and Red Guard, 148, 149, 220–222
Bakuriani, 207, 233, 308 n. 80
Baku Soviet: and Provisional Government, 71, 75, 280 n. 29; conflict of, with Moslems, 81, 147–149; and Soviet Russia, 106, 170, 220–222; on Transcaucasian independence, 170, 220; appeals to British, 220–221; elections to, 287–288 n. 2
Baku Sovnarkom, 131, 149, 168, 170, 218, 220–222, 311 n. 13, 312 n. 37
Balajari, 220
Balfour, Arthur J., 248
Balkans, 12, 25, 26, 32, 34, 35, 47, 157, 195, 224, 229, 230
Balkan wars, 22, 29, 30, 42, 44, 72
Bammat, Haidar, 173, 302 n. 63
Banvor (Tiflis), 126
Banvori krive (Tiflis), 75, 125
Barby, Henry, 100
Barduz, 45
Barton, James L., 251
Bash Abaran, 176, 192, 193, 201, 307–308 n. 60
Bashgarni, 307–308 n. 60
Batum, 128, 131, 132, 137, 150, 156, 165, 174, 181–191 *passim,* 196, 198, 203, 204, 214, 234, 236, 238

Batum *oblast,* 15, 35, 198, 201, 224; Russian annexation of, 11–13; Ottoman strategy in and occupation of, 45, 103, 104, 132, 133, 134, 140, 141, 152–153, 157–158, 159–160, 199; Soviet policy in, 103, 104, 130, 170, 219, 228, 244, 312 n. 39; and concessions by Transcaucasia, 150, 151, 152, 161, 173; and Georgian Mensheviks, 152–153, 155, 159, 183; German policy in, 177, 179, 203, 218, 271 n. 2; and Mudros Armistice, 239, 241
Batum Peace Conference, 163, 172–185 *passim,* 186, 203
Batum *sanjak. See* Batum *oblast*
Batum Treaty, 202–218 *passim,* 224; negotiations, 191, 193, 194–196, 302 nn. 62 and 63; terms of, 196–201, 306 n. 45; proposed revision of, 211, 215, 217, 230–236 *passim*
Bayazit Valley, 12, 36, 57–58, 77, 259–260 nn. 10 and 11
Bayur, Hikmet, 51
Begli Ahmed, 159
Beirut, 59
Bekzadian, Hovhannes, 293 n. 111
Bekzadian, Tigran, 90
Belgium, 97, 101, 250
Belon, Pierre, 34
Berezov, 187
Berlin, 54, 55, 102, 103, 130, 170, 176–185 *passim,* 202, 204, 206, 215, 216, 218, 225, 228, 230, 234, 236; Armenian mission to, 189, 211, 215, 217–219, 222, 223–224, 229, 233, 238, 242
Berlin Congress and Treaty, 12, 26, 130
Bernstorff, Count Johann, 54, 170, 177, 180, 202–203, 223, 224, 230
Beylan, 50
Bicherakhov, Colonel Lazar, 220, 221
Bitlis *vilayet,* 27, 34, 38, 42; population of, 36, 37; massacres in, 50, 51, 52, 56, 67; military activity in, 56, 57, 64, 80, 81; Russian policy in, 58, 60, 79, 80
Black Sea, 2, 5, 40, 120, 169, 234, 248, 251; coastal areas, 1, 8, 9, 58, 129, 252; Ottoman fleet, 40; Russian fleet, 40, 64; front along, 41, 64, 66, 80, 110, 116, 122, 137, 151; Bolshevik Military Committee of, 131
"Bloody Sunday." *See* Russian Revolution of 1905
Boghos Nubar, 32, 66, 250, 251

INDEX 349

Bolshevik. *See* Social Democrat party, Bolshevik
Bolshevik Revolution. *See* Russian Revolution of November, 1917
Borchalu (Borchalo) *uezd,* 11, 195, 205, 206, 207
Borian, B. A., 97, 100
Borzhom, 158
Bosnia-Herzegovina, 29
Bosporus, 45, 59, 217
Brest-Litovsk, Treaty of, 106, 109, 118, 142, 156, 165, 197, 201, 216, 218, 235, 240, 287 n. 49; and Soviet policy, 101–104, 131, 147, 154, 169, 170, 171, 172, 219, 228–229, 244; and German-Ottoman relations, 102, 103, 176, 177, 179, 189, 203–205, 210, 217, 224; and Transcaucasian-Ottoman relations, 103, 104, 105, 120, 123, 130, 132–142 *passim,* 149–156 *passim,* 159, 160, 163, 169, 170, 171, 173, 174, 180, 195, 198, 199; Article IV of, 104, 137, 140, 141, 151, 185; Supplementary Treaty, 218, 222–223, 224, 227–228, 236
Briand, Aristide, 250, 253
British Mediterranean Fleet, 229
British military forces: in Mesopotamia, 82, 109, 117, 177, 249; in Persia, 174, 194, 205, 225, 241; in Baku, 220–228 *passim,* 241–242; in Palestine, 224, 249
British Military Mission in Caucasus, 82, 118, 138, 307 n. 49
Brotherly Aid Committee, 79
Brusa, 25
Bryce, Viscount James, 48, 248
Brzola (Tiflis), 126
Buchanan, George, 59, 62
Bucharest, Treaty of, 8
Bukhara, 97, 103
Bulgaria, 28, 29, 30, 44, 60, 101, 102, 224, 229, 230, 302 n. 63
Buniatian, Mentor, 173, 234
Byzantine Empire, 2, 4

Calthorpe, Admiral Arthur, 229, 239
Caspian Fleet (Russian), 222
Caspian *oblast,* 10–11
Caspian Sea, 2, 5, 169, 221
Catherine II, Tsarina, 8, 92
Catholicos (Armenian), 7, 18, 32, 56, 211. *See also* Gevorg V, Catholicos
Caucasia, 86, 119, 125, 130, 179

Caucasian Armenian Benevolent Society, 79
Caucasian Union, 19
Caucasus, 23, 42, 60, 70–82 *passim,* 91, 121, 130, 133, 142, 162, 191, 213; Russian conquest of, 7–9; tsarist Russian policies in, 10–11, 18, 20–22, 44–45, 46, 68; Armenians of, 36, 45, 49, 62, 66, 112, 118, 138, 206, 218; Ottoman strategy in, 45–46, 103, 119, 154, 177, 178, 181, 182, 203, 204, 233, 237, 240; and Soviet Russia, 99, 103, 104, 108, 110, 112, 155, 169, 170, 171–172, 179, 218, 219, 222–223, 228; German strategy in, 103, 104, 171–172, 178, 179, 180, 210, 218, 222–223. *See also* Caucasus front; North Caucasus; Transcaucasia
Caucasus Army. *See* Russian Caucasus Army
Caucasus front, 79, 108, 154, 239, 249; 1914–1917 campaigns on, 44–47, 64–66, 80–82, 109–110; Soviet Russian policy on, 97, 99, 102, 106; Russia abandons, 101, 110, 129, 212, 244, 249; National Corps on, 113–117, 135, 137, 152–153, 157–159, 249, 251; 1918 campaigns on, 121–124, 134–138, 221–222, 299 n. 3
Caucasus Mountains, 2, 5, 70, 84, 108, 127, 157, 162, 234
Caucasus Union of Cities, 68
Cecil, Lord Robert, 248, 249
Central Alliance, 229. *See also* Central Powers
Central Asia, 178
Central Powers: and Armenians, 42, 54, 55, 197, 201, 216, 235, 238, 242; and Georgians, 48, 183, 189, 202; and Soviet Russia, 101–105, 118, 129, 130, 228; and Ukraine, 120, 169, 234; and proposed negotiations with Transcaucasia, 152, 161, 169, 172, 173, 174, 180, 215, 230; mutual relations of, 177–179, 202–204, 217–218, 224–225, 230. *See also* Austria-Hungary; Brest-Litovsk, Treaty of; Germany; Ottoman Empire
Centro-Caspian Dictatorship, 221, 222, 225, 227
Chardigny, Colonel P., 159
Chermoev, Abdul, 173, 302 n. 63
Chicherin, Grigorii V., 103, 170, 172, 179, 219, 227–228, 229
Childer, 5, 36
Chilingarian, Artashes, 112

China, 97
Chkheidze, Nikolai S., 68, 69, 108, 281 n. 37; as president of Seim, 126, 130, 132, 188
Chkhenkeli, Akakii I.: as Ozakom member, 76, 92, 281 n. 37; as Commissariat minister, 107, 120, 129; as Trebizond delegation chairman, 130–134 *passim,* 139–140, 142, 149–156 *passim,* 157; as Transcaucasian premier, 158–160, 162, 169; and fall of Kars, 162–169, 300 n. 39; at Batum Peace Conference, 172–176 *passim,* 179–184 *passim;* as Georgian foreign minister, 188–189
Cholok River, 158
Chorokh River, 2
Church of Armenia. *See* Armenian Church
Cilicia, 2, 5, 16, 33, 62, 66, 239; Armenian kingdom of, 4, 60–62; deportations from and massacres in, 30, 51–54 *passim,* 268 n. 27; Armenian population of, 36, 37; French pretensions to, 58–62 *passim;* American proposals for, 251–253
Circassian, 29
Clemenceau, Georges, 236, 250, 251
Committee for Public Safety (Tiflis), 84, 85, 107
Committee of Union and Progress. *See* Ittihad ve Terakki; "Young Turks"
Communists, 85, 106, 111, 117, 169, 170, 220, 221. *See also* Social Democrat party, Bolshevik
Congress of Cities, All-Russian, 68
Congress of Soviets, All-Russian: First, 75, 95, 97; Second, 95; Third, 100; Fourth, 104, 287 n. 48; Central Executive Committee of, 102, 103, 171
Constanta, 189
Constantinople (Istanbul), 4, 12, 25, 27, 31, 33, 34, 40, 41, 52, 59, 64, 66, 154, 155, 173, 176, 177, 202, 203, 214, 217, 228, 229, 238, 239, 248; Armenians in, 16, 24, 50, 51, 67; Ittihadist coup in, 29, 30; and Transcaucasia, 121, 128–132 *passim,* 150, 197
Constantinople conference (1918), 215, 218, 219, 230; Armenian delegation to, 211, 217, 222, 224, 229–238, 242
Constantinople–Straits Agreement, 59. *See also* Entente, Triple
Constituent Assembly, All-Russian, 94, 127; and Transcaucasia, 71, 73, 77, 92, 106, 107, 119, 120, 124–125; elections in Caucasus for, 85, 108–109, 147, 288 nn. 10–14 and 16; dispersal of, 109, 120, 140
Constitutional Democrat party (Kadets), 67, 69, 73, 74, 76, 84, 89, 97, 108, 127, 129, 133, 147, 153, 161, 162, 208
Constitutional Democrats (Armenian), 31, 67, 73, 76, 89, 120, 208, 280 n. 22, 309 n. 84. *See also* Populists (Armenian)
Cooke-Collis, General W. J. N., 241
Cossacks, 58, 220, 221
Council of People's Commissars (Sovnarkom). *See* Russia, Soviet
Courland, 102
Crane, Charles R., 251
Crete, 29
Crimea, 4, 113, 131, 177, 225, 313 n. 65
Crusaders, 4
Cuinet, Vital, 37
Cyprus, 5

Daghestan, 11, 15, 168, 195, 236
Damascus, 229
Daralagiaz, 78, 307–308 n. 60. *See also* Sharur-Daralagiaz *uezd*
Darbinian, Artak, 79, 276 n. 83
Dardanelles, 45, 59
Dashnaktsutiun, 47, 68, 69, 70, 76, 78–79, 84, 85, 116, 206, 244; formation and programs of, 16–17, 18, 21–22, 73, 88, 127, 262 nn. 44 and 46; in tsarist Russia, 17–18, 19, 20–21, 22–23, 43, 44, 67, 262–263 n. 52, 264 n. 67; and Bolsheviks, 19, 75, 83, 86, 97, 99, 111–113, 117, 147–149, 169, 170, 171, 220–221, 293 n. 105; and Ottoman government, 27, 28, 29, 31, 38, 41–42, 249, 267 n. 18, 267–268 n. 23, 268 n. 28, 269 n. 32; Erzerum Congress of, 41–42, 249; in National Congress, 85, 86–91 *passim;* Bureau of, 88, 112, 126, 159, 191; members of, on Commissariat, 108; Constituent Assembly votes for, 108–109, 147; in Seim, 125–130 *passim,* 132, 134, 145, 151–154 *passim,* 176; on Transcaucasian independence, 141, 160, 162, 168–169; and fall of Kars, 159, 163, 167, 168–169; role of, in Armenian independence, 190–191, 194, 201–202; and Armenian Republic, 207–213 *passim*
Daulphine, Nicholas du, 34
Davalu, 144
Decembrists, 8
Deev, General, 157, 159, 164, 165, 166

Derbend, 11, 225
Diadin, 58
Diarbekir, 36, 60, 64, 121; *vilayet,* 34, 36, 38
Dikaia Diviziia. See "Savage Division"
Dilijan, 192, 194, 210, 307–308 n. 60
Djadjur, 198; Station, 196
Djamalian, Arshak, 210, 214, 217, 269 n. 38, 289 n. 20
Djanpolatian, 273 n. 40
Djugashvili, I. V. *See* Stalin
Dobrudja, 230
Dodecanese Islands, 59
Dodge, Cleveland H., 251, 316 n. 31
Don region, 58, 313–314 n. 68
Donskoi, D., 106, 107, 116
Doroshenko, D. I., 313 n. 65
Dro (Drastamat Kanayan), 44, 114, 144, 159, 166, 193, 196, 209, 210, 272 n. 21, 309 n. 93
Dsamoev, Grigor, 145, 169, 234
Dual Monarchy, 223. *See also* Austria-Hungary
Dukhonin, General N. N., 101
Dulaurier, Édouard, 35
Dunsterforce, 221, 222, 227
Dunsterville, General Lionel C., 221, 222, 225, 227, 241
Dutton, Samuel T., 251

Eghine, 51
Egypt, 4, 32, 66, 96
Eisenmann, Lieutenant, 210
Ekaterinodar, 120, 121
Elenovka, 144, 307–308 n. 60
Elisavetpol *guberniia,* 10, 15, 73, 78, 178, 203, 205; formation of, 11; Armenian claims to, 15, 91–92, 112, 195, 218, 235, 241; Moslems of, 48, 72, 92, 115, 181; hostilities in, 115, 145–146, 194, 214, 215. *See also* Gandzak; Ganja
Emin, Ahmed, 232
Engija, 157
England, 58, 107. *See also* Great Britain
English, 30, 54, 220, 229, 241, 250. *See also* British
Enos-Midia line, 59
Entente, Triple, 34, 42, 52, 64, 88, 101, 113, 121, 174; declarations of, 51–52, 247–249; secret agreements of, 57–62, 66, 68, 95, 97, 238, 253. *See also* Allies
Enver Pasha, 30, 119, 134, 137, 189, 314 n. 81; and Germany, 40, 48, 103, 178, 185, 202–203, 204, 214, 220, 222–223, 225, 230; Pan-Turanic views of, 41, 103, 113, 123–124, 174–175, 177, 178, 181, 201–202; role of, in Armenian massacres, 42, 52–55 *passim,* 67; military strategy of, 45–48, 64, 66, 80, 123–124, 158, 201–202, 204–205; directs Baku offensive, 220, 222–223, 225, 227; and Armenian suppliants, 230–234
Enzeli, 221, 227
Erevan, 8, 44, 47, 55, 78, 87, 113, 114, 126, 190, 196, 198, 201, 202, 216, 241, 242, 244, 249, 253; Armenian government moves to, 209–215 *passim*
Erevan Armenian Council, 126, 143
Erevan *guberniia,* 15, 19, 44, 48, 71, 73, 75, 78, 91, 137, 166, 167, 196, 204, 205, 206, 244, 252; formation of, 11, 261 n. 24; population of, 13, 15, 23, 92, 199, 201, 260 n. 11; Moslems of, 13, 92, 143, 196, 201, 211; Villagers' Congress, 73; hostilities in, 115, 143–145, 146; Ottoman pretensions to and invasion of, 170, 173, 174–176, 177, 178, 182, 186, 191–194, 195, 213, 233; Ottoman occupation of and withdrawal from, 197–201, 208, 218, 224, 225, 229, 234, 235, 236, 240
Erevan *khanate,* 5, 8, 10, 259 n. 19
Ermeni Millet, 25. *See also* Armenian Patriarchate of Constantinople
Ermenistan, 34
Erzerum, 8, 12, 41, 45, 46, 62, 116, 121, 165, 249; *eyalet,* 5, 9, 34, 36; Armenians of, 12, 34, 36, 42, 50, 51, 52, 67, 259–260 nn. 10 and 11; *vilayet,* 34, 38, 42, 50, 58, 60, 137, 233; Russian occupation of, 64, 66, 79, 80; Regiment, 113, 114; Ottoman recapture of, 124, 132, 134–137, 138, 144
Erzerum Congress. *See* Dashnaktsutiun
Erzinjan, 64, 109, 134, 157, 165, 166, 193, 221; front, 66, 80, 113, 114, 116, 121–122; Ottoman recapture of, 123–124, 135
Erzinjan Truce, 109–110, 119, 121, 289 n. 20; Ottoman violation of, 121–123, 130, 137, 144
Erzinkian, Aramayis, 90, 91, 168, 285 n. 108, 300 n. 41
Essad Pasha, General, 201, 204, 210, 214, 234
Etchmiadzin, 16, 175, 201, 214, 307–308 n. 60; *uezd,* 11, 173, 182, 195, 196, 199
Euphrates River, 1, 2, 58, 194, 257 n. 3
Europe, 16, 25, 29, 32, 41, 101, 102, 179,

215, 250; and Armenians, 4, 6, 23, 24, 27, 30, 36, 53, 66, 98, 232, 247, 251, 253; Western, 12, 25, 88, 217, 242; and Ottoman reforms, 26, 28, 33–39 *passim,* 141, 243; front in, 44, 46, 81, 116, 204
"Evelina," 148

Feisal, Emir, 229
Feoletov, I. T., 86
Ferdinand, Tsar (Bulgaria), 229
Finland and Finns, 19, 97, 98, 100
Forestier-Walker, General G. T., 241
Fourteen Points, 251–252. *See also* Wilson, Woodrow
France, 107, 213; and Armenians, 27, 28, 30, 33–34, 54, 58, 59, 250–251; and Entente agreements, 58–62, 63, 253; Légion d'Orient of, 66, 251; Chamber of Deputies of, 250, 253
France, Anatole, 250
Francis, David, 82, 117, 118, 138
Frankenstein, Baron von, 211, 214
French Armenia, 62
French Military Mission in Caucasus, 107, 118, 159, 307 n. 49
French Revolution, 24

Gabaev (Gabaishvili), General, 116, 137, 157, 163
Galicia, 97
Galikian, Hrand, 79
Gallipoli, 64
Gambashidze, Dr., 134
Gandzak, 91, 145, 146, 195. *See also* Elisavetpol; Ganja
Ganja, 72, 116, 145, 146, 190, 195, 204, 205, 214, 215, 220, 227; *khanate* of, 5, 8, 10; Moslem Council of, 115. *See also* Elisavetpol; Gandzak
Gedevanov, General, 152–153
Gegechkori, Evgenii P., 84, 230; as Commissariat president, 107, 108, 120, 121, 124, 126, 127, 130, 132, 151–156 *passim;* on Transcaucasian independence, 160, 162, 163, 167
Geneva, 16, 28, 38, 238
Georgadze, Grigorii T., 144, 160, 164, 168, 304 n. 12
Georgia, 4, 5, 8, 72, 87, 152, 155, 160, 182–185, 188, 259 n. 199
Georgia, Republic of, 9, 11, 47, 72, 185, 203, 204, 211, 216, 218, 219, 222; formation of, 186–189; and Armenia, 191, 205–207, 209–210, 212–213, 231, 233, 235, 236; and Ottoman Empire, 198–199, 214, 222, 225, 230, 233, 307 n. 49; cabinet of, 304 n. 12
Georgian Army Corps, 116, 117, 137, 153, 157
Georgian Bagratid kingdom, 5
Georgian-Imeretian *guberniia,* 10–11
Georgian Military Road, 158
Georgian National Assembly, 116
Georgian National Council, 116, 152, 158–159, 183, 184, 188, 202, 205
Georgian National Democrat party, 72, 92, 116, 120, 127, 134, 156, 187, 288 n. 13
Georgian Orthodox Church, 188
Georgians, 13, 15, 41–42, 47–48, 68, 70, 71–72, 76, 82, 84, 89, 91, 93, 107–108, 111, 112, 116–117, 135, 137, 145, 152–160 *passim,* 181–189 *passim,* 202–207 *passim,* 209–210, 233, 235–236, 241, 244
Georgian Social Federalist party, 76, 116, 127, 134, 281 nn. 13 and 36
Gerard, James, 253, 316 n. 31
Germany, 31, 43, 60, 80–81, 83, 161, 238, 244, 252, 253; and Armenians, 26, 27, 33–34, 54–55, 103–104, 176, 177, 178, 180, 182, 186, 210, 214, 215, 216–220 *passim,* 275–276 n. 74, 276 n. 75; and Georgians, 48, 117, 178–179, 182–185, 188–189, 198, 202–205 *passim,* 218, 222–223, 225; and Soviet Russia, 97–98, 101–104, 109, 169–170, 171–172, 178, 179, 218–229 *passim,* 236. *See also* Central Powers; Ottoman Empire, and Germany
Gevorg V, Catholicos, 32, 43, 45, 56
Gevorgian Academy, 16
Gharabekian, Misha (Mikayel), 90, 309 n. 93
Ghazazian, Koriun, 109, 285 n. 108
Gibbons, Herbert A., 49
Giers, M. N., 31, 34, 38
Giulkhandanian, Abraham, 285 n. 108
Golitsyn, Prince Grigorii, 18, 20, 28, 32, 262 nn. 48 and 51
Gracey, G. F., 82
Great Britain, 12, 31, 213, 236; and Armenian reforms, 24–28 *passim,* 30–31, 33–34, 38–39; and Entente agreements, 59–62; wartime declarations of, 51–52, 247–249, 251; Parliament of, 248, 249
Greater Armenia (Major), 2, 5; provinces of, 257 n. 5
Greece and Greeks, 13, 26, 29, 36, 101, 268 n. 27, 285 n. 115

INDEX 353

Greek Orthodox *Millet,* 25
Greenfield, James, 217
Guchkov, A. I., 69, 283 n. 69
Gulf of Alexandretta, 59
Gulistan, Treaty of, 8
Gulkevich, K. N., 38
Gummet party. *See* Hummet party
Guria, 8
Gvazava, Grigorii, 134, 139, 187

Hadjin, 60, 239
Haghpat, 86
Haidarov (Gaidarov), Ibrahim: as Trebizond delegation member, 134, 141, 146, 149, 294 n. 17; as Transcaucasian minister, 168
Haifa, 59
Hai Heghapokhakan Dashnaktsutiun. *See* Dashnaktsutiun
Hai Zhoghovrdakan Kusaktsutiun. *See* Populists (Armenian)
Hajinskii (Gadjinskii), Mahmed Hasan: as Trebizond delegation member, 134, 139, 141, 155, 156; as Transcaucasian minister, 168; at Batum Peace Conference, 173, 180, 181, 198; as Azerbaijani cabinet member, 305 n. 20
Hakhverdian, General Hovhannes, 209
Hakki, Ismail, 103
Hakki Bey, Colonel, 46
Halil Bey (Justice minister): at Batum Peace Conference, 172–176 *passim,* 180, 181, 182; and Batum treaties, 194, 195, 198, 204
Halil Pasha, General, 48, 55, 194, 214, 215, 225, 227, 234
Hamamlu, 175, 176, 193, 194, 196
Hamazasp (Srvandztian), 44, 272 n. 21, 298 n. 84
Hambardzumian, Kostia, 109
"Hamburg-Herat" line, 178
Hamdi Bey, 35
Hamid II. *See* Abdul Hamid II
Hamidiye corps, 17, 27, 33
Hammer-Purgstall, Joseph von, 34
Haram-Vartan (Garam-Vartan), 164
Harutunian, Martiros, 145, 154, 192
Harutunian, Samson, 45, 57, 62, 90, 159, 269 n. 38
Hasankala, 64
Hekkiari, 34, 36
Henderson, Arthur, 247
Hilmi Bey, 41

Hindenburg, Field Marshall Paul von, 178, 203
Hintze, Paul von, 220, 222, 223, 225, 234
Hnchakists (Armenian Social Democrats), 47, 54, 262 n. 51; formation and program of, 16; and Turkish Armenia, 16, 27, 31, 78, 79
Hoff, Major, 38, 39
Hoffman, General Max von, 102
Holy Lands, 59
Horizon (Tiflis), 69
House, Colonel Edward M., 316 n. 27
Hovhannisian (Varandian), Mikayel, 109
Hummet party (Moslem Social Democrat), 108, 126, 134, 148, 150, 279 n. 13, 293 n. 112
Husein Rauf Bey. *See* Rauf Bey, Husein
Huseinov (Guseinov), Mirza-Davud, 72
Husrev, Major, 134

Ianushkevich, General Nicholas, 63, 78
Igdir, 44, 115
Ignatiev, Count N. P., 12
Ihsan Pasha, Ali, 121, 214
Ilija, 134
Imeretia, 8, 10–11
India, 96, 178
Ingorokov, P., 205
Ioffe, Adolf A., 101, 102, 218–223 *passim,* 228
Iraklii II, Tsar (Georgia), 8, 48, 92
Ishkhan of Van, 53
Iskenderum, 50
Islam, 4, 7, 25, 27, 49, 72, 73, 113, 148, 237. *See also* Army of Islam
Istanbul, 46. *See also* Constantinople
Italy, 27, 29, 33, 59, 251
Ittihad ve Terakki, 29, 30, 40, 41, 52, 175, 195, 229, 232, 233, 269 n. 32. *See also* "Young Turks"; Dashnaktsutiun, and Ottoman government
Iudenich, General N. N., 46, 57, 64, 66, 81
Izvolskii, A. P., 58
Izzet Pasha, Ahmed, 64, 66, 80, 229, 237, 239, 240

Jafarov, Mohammed Iusuf, 76, 144, 184, 288 n. 6
Jagow, Gottlieb von, 276 n. 75
Japan, 20, 22, 83
Japaridze, Prokopii (Alesha), 86, 221
Jäschke, Gotthard, 120
Javid Bey, 192, 300 n. 35

Jebelibereket, 50
Jemal Pasha, 30, 181, 314 n. 81
Jevdet Bey, 53, 55, 56
Jewish *Millet,* 25
Jews, 7, 29, 52
Jisr-i Shuur, 50
Jugheli, Valiko, 116, 154–155
Julfa, 137, 175, 180, 198. *See also* Kars–Alexandropol–Julfa Railway
"July Days," 83, 85. *See also* Russia, Provisional Government of

Kableshkoff, Colonel, 302 n. 63
Kachaznuni, Hovhannes, 44, 109; in Seim, 127, 128, 162; as Trebizond delegation member, 134, 140, 141, 146, 149, 150, 151, 294 n. 16; at Alexandropol conference, 159; and Transcaucasian independence, 162, 167, 168; at Batum Peace Conference, 173, 175, 176, 180; negotiates Batum Treaty, 190, 191, 193, 196, 198; as Armenian premier, 207, 208–215 *passim,* 235
Kachaznuni, Ruben I. *See* Kachaznuni, Hovhannes
Kagheti, 206
Kaghisman *okrug,* 13, 150, 199
Kalantar, Alexandre, 269 n. 38
Kalitin, General, 46
Kamenev, L. B., 94
Kamenka River, 205
Kamsarakan, Stepan, 90, 91
Kanayan, Drastamat. *See* Dro
Kani Köy, 164
Kantemirov, 302 n. 63
Karabagh: Mountainous, 1, 5, 10, 15, 189, 194, 214, 215, 241, 242, 260 n. 11; Steppe of, 1, 11; *khanate* of, 8, 259 n. 18
Karabekir Bey, Colonel Kiazım, 201, 292 n. 81; and Erzinjan campaign, 121–124; and Erzerum campaign, 134–137; and Kars campaign, 164–166; and Alexandropol campaign, 176
Karakhan, Lev M., 105, 130, 131, 170
Karakilisa (Alashkert) Regiment, 113, 114
Karakilisa (Erevan *guberniia*), 11, 175, 176, 192, 194, 198, 201, 204, 205, 206, 307–308 n. 60
Karamarian, 220
Karjikian, Khachatur: as National Council member, 90, 190, 205, 206; on Commissariat and in Seim, 108, 120, 141, 142, 144, 155, 162, 176; and Transcaucasian independence, 167, 168; as Armenian finance minister, 209, 213
Kars, 35, 36, 75, 135, 145, 150, 161, 172, 173, 193, 201, 204, 229, 235, 237, 252; *pashalik,* 5, 9, 259–260 nn. 10 and 11; *oblast,* 12–13, 15, 44, 91, 92, 165, 166, 199, 236, 285 n. 115; Ottoman strategy in, 44, 45, 46, 103, 104, 132, 133, 134, 140, 141, 160, 176, 195; front, 64, 137, 143, 144, 148, 157, 158, 159, 169; Soviet policy in, 103, 104, 130, 170, 172, 219, 228, 244; German policy in, 103, 104, 177, 203, 218, 224, 225, 271 n. 2; Transcaucasian concessions in, 150–152, 173; fall of, 162–166, 169, 185, 208; and Mudros Armistice, 239–240
Kars–Alexandropol–Julfa Railway, 137, 143, 144, 164, 173, 174, 175, 176, 180, 196, 198, 214, 234, 307 n. 51
Kars Division, 111
Kars River, 165
Kars *sanjak. See* Kars *oblast*
Kartli, 206
Kavkazskaia pravda (Tiflis), 126
Kavkazskii krai, 11
Kavkazskii rabochii (Tiflis), 125
Kavkazskii vestnik Soveta Narodnykh Komissarov (Tiflis), 125
Kavtaradze, S. I., 86
Kazakh, 10, 195, 235
Kazan, 103
Kemakh, 80, 123
Kemal, Mustafa, 80, 81, 241, 278 n. 125
Kerensky, Alexander F.: and Armenians, 22, 81, 99; in Provisional Government, 69, 76, 83–84, 94–95, 191, 283 n. 83
Keri (Arshak Gafavian), 44, 272 n. 21
Khachatrian, Smbat, 144, 309 n. 93
Khamarlu, 144
Khan Khoiskii, Aslan, 48
Khan Khoiskii, Fathali: in Seim, 132–133; as Transcaucasian minister, 168; at Batum Peace Conference, 173, 184, 302 n. 62; as Azerbaijani premier, 190, 227, 241, 305 n. 20
Khanoyan, Sargis, 75
Kharlamov, V. A., 76
Kharput (Mamuret-ul-Aziz), 41, 64, 66, 80; *vilayet,* 34, 36, 38, 60
Khas-Mamedov, Khalil Bek, 184; as Trebizond delegation member, 134, 140, 141, 150, 151, 294 n. 17; as Commissariat

minister, 288 n. 6; as Azerbaijani minister, 305 n. 20
Khatisian, Alexandre, 159, 269 n. 38; as mayor of Tiflis, 43, 57, 62, 68, 70; as Trebizond delegation member, 134, 139, 141, 150, 151; and Transcaucasian independence, 167, 168; at Batum Peace Conference, 173, 175, 176, 180, 181, 184–185; negotiates Batum Treaty, 190–198 *passim*, 201; parleys with Georgians, 205, 206; as Armenian foreign minister, 207, 209, 217, 230–238 *passim*
Khatisian, Gevorg, 91, 235
Khnus, 137; Regiment, 113, 114
Khoi, 194
Khomeriki, Noi, 168, 304 n. 12
Khondkarian, Arsham, 209, 213, 309 n. 93
Khoren, Bishop of Erevan, 143
Khorhurd of Armenia, 211–213, 309 nn. 93 and 98
Khram River, 11
Khrimian, Catholicos Mkrtich, 262 n. 49
Kiamil, Mahmud, 64
Kiev, 120, 121, 130, 169, 179, 217, 234, 313 n. 65. *See also* Ukraine
Kievan Russia, 4
Kighi, 66, 80
Kizilbash, 36, 37
Kocharian, Hakob, 231
Korganov, Colonel, 114
Korganov (Korganian), General Gabriel, 175, 205
Korganov (Korganian), G. N., 86, 110, 170, 298 n. 84
Kornilov, General L. G., 83–84
Kornilovshchina, 83–84, 85
"Korol' Karl," 131, 132
Kozan, 50
Krasnovodsk, 227, 312 n. 37
Kremlin, 218
Kress (Kressenstein), Colonel Kress von, 178, 189, 204, 205, 210, 211, 214, 223, 227, 304 n. 13
Kriege, Johannes, 222
Krilenko, N. V., 101
Krivoshein, A. V., 58
Kuba, *khanate* of, 8
Kuban region, 58
Kühlmann, Richard von, 202, 203, 217, 218, 220
Kurdamir, 220
Kurdistan, 36
Kurds, 13, 29, 36, 57, 58, 59, 60, 63, 110, 165, 231, 285 n. 115; armed bands of, 27, 30, 33, 41, 45, 51, 56, 57, 77–78, 121, 122, 123, 135, 144, 145, 170, 192
Kur River, 2, 158, 210; valley, 195
Kutais *guberniia*, 11, 13, 15, 158, 164, 165, 187, 189
Kut-el-Amara, 229

Lake Sevan, 1, 144, 194, 198, 210, 238
Lake Urmia, 1, 82, 194
Lake Van, 5, 56, 64, 80, 110
Lansing, Robert, 118, 138, 253
Laskhishvili, Georgii, 134, 141, 146, 149, 304 n. 12
Latvian, 19
Lazarev, General I. I., 12
Lazarian Academy, 16, 171
Lazes, 60
Lazistan, 86
League of Nations, 253
Lebanon, 59, 250, 253
Lebedinskii, General E. V., 107, 109, 121, 122, 132, 134, 137, 139, 163
Left Social Revolutionaries, 84, 94, 95, 110, 219. *See also* Social Revolutionary party
Légion d'Orient, 66, 251
Lemnos, 229, 238. *See also* Mudros
Lenin (Vladimir Ulianov), 19, 104, 109, 110, 219, 241, 310 n. 10; and Provisional Government, 74, 83, 85, 94, 95; and Armenia, 94–104 *passim;* on Transcaucasian government, 169, 171–172; and Baku Sovnarkom, 220, 221
Lenkoran, 148, 297 n. 77
Leo (A. Babakhanian), 134
Leon V, King, 4
Lepsius, Johannes, 49, 53, 54
Lesser Armenia (Minor), 2, 5, 34, 60
Levandovskii, General, 107, 129
Levasseur, 34
Levonian, Paruir, 276 n. 83
Liakhov, General V., 64
Liberal Union (Ottoman), 30
Libya (Tripolitania), 29, 42
Liman von Sanders, General Otto, 46, 278 n. 126
Lithuania, 102
Little, Edward C., 253
Lloyd George, David, 236, 248, 251
Lobanov-Rostovskii, B. A., 28, 31, 32, 67, 267 n. 17
Lodge, Henry Cabot, 253, 316 n. 31
Lomiza, Colonel Mikayel, 313 n. 65

London, 59, 130, 138, 178; Conference, 32; *Times,* 247
Lordkipanidze, Ivan, 133, 141, 161, 304 n. 12
Lori, 10, 19, 78, 86; Armenian pretensions to, 11, 15, 91, 92, 205, 206, 235, 236; Ottoman occupation of, 205, 209, 214, 231, 233
Loris-Melikov, General M. T., 12
Lossow, General Otto von, 173, 176–184 *passim,* 189, 203, 204, 217. *See also* Batum Peace Conference
Ludendorff, General Erich von, 80, 103, 123, 177, 178, 183, 203, 223. *See also* Ottoman Empire, and Germany
Lukashin, Sargis, 99
Luzzatti, Luigi, 251
Lvov, Prince G. E., 69, 70, 75, 79, 83, 97, 283 n. 69

Macdonald, Ramsay, 248
Macedonian Army (Ottoman), 29
Macedonian Empire, 2
Machabeli, Prince Georgii, 179, 183
Makharadze, F. I., 86
Makharadze, Gerasim, 146
Makintsian, Poghos, 159, 170
Maku, 137
Malatia, 34, 64
Mamakhatun, 64, 66, 123–124
Mamikonian, General Vardan, 193
Mamikonian, Stepan, 88, 90, 159, 309 n. 93
Mamluks, 2, 4
Mamuret-ul-Aziz. *See* Kharput
Manasian, Sargis, 167
Manchester Guardian, 247
Mandelstam, André, 33
Manukian, Aram. *See* Aram
Manzikert, 4, 55, 56
Marash, 5, 37, 50
Marmora, Sea of, 59
Martin, Louis, 250
Marxists, 16, 18, 19, 22, 31, 73, 83, 111, 112, 148, 171, 183, 209, 213. *See also* Social Democrat party; Social Democrats
Maude, General, 117
Mazra, 164
Mediterranean Sea, 58, 248, 251; ports, 59
Mehmed Ali (envoy to Erevan), 213, 233
Mehmed II, Sultan, 25
Mehmed V, Sultan, 232
Mehmed VI, Sultan, 232
Mehtiev, 142

Mehtiev, Mir-Yakub, 134, 140, 294 n. 17
Mejinkert, 137
Melik Aslanov, Khudadad, 168, 288 n. 6, 305 n. 20
Melikian, Arshavir, 213, 309 n. 93
Melik Karageozian, Gevorg, 217
Menshevik. *See* Social Democrat Mensheviks; Social Democrat party, Menshevik
Merdenek, 145, 151
Mersin, 50, 58
Meskhishvili, Shavla, 304 n. 12
Mesopotamia, 1, 2, 59; front in, 82, 109, 110, 117, 177, 203, 249; future of, 248, 252
Mesrop, Bishop of Tiflis, 43, 57
Michael Romanov, Grand Duke, 69
Middle East, 31, 249
Mikayelian, Kristapor, 28
Mikoyan, Anastas, 75, 85, 86, 312 n. 37
Miliukov, Pavel N., 22, 63, 69, 79, 96, 157, 283 n. 69
Mingrelia, 8
"Minna Horn," 181, 182, 184, 189
Mirbach, Count Wilhelm von, 172, 179, 183, 218, 219, 301 n. 59, 310 n. 10
Mkhitarian, Onnik, 276 n. 83
Mommsen, Lieutenant von, 210
Mongols, 2, 4, 5
Morel, Colonel, 121–124 *passim,* 164, 165, 166
Morgenthau, Henry, 49, 52, 55
Morocco, 96
Moscow, 16, 67, 68, 104, 169, 170, 171, 179, 218, 222, 224, 228, 242, 287 n. 48; Armenian Committee, 67, 79, 81, 88; Soviet, 171
Moslem Council: of Ganja, 115; of Erevan, 143; of Baku, 146, 147
Moslem Democratic Party Musavat. *See* Musavat party
Moslem National Council, 189, 190
Moslems, Transcaucasian Conference of, 72–73
Moslem Social Democrat Hummet party. *See* Hummet party
Moslem Socialist Bloc, 108, 126, 134, 153
Moslems of Russia and the East, Appeal to, 98
Moslems of Russia (Ittihad) party, 108, 127, 134, 147, 154
Moslems of Transcaucasia. *See* Tatars of Transcaucasia
Mosul, 50

Mountainous Karabagh. *See* Karabagh
Mount Aragadz (Alagiaz), 196
Moush. *See* Mush
Mravian, Askanaz A., 75, 86
Mudros: Port of, 229, 237; Armistice of, 229, 238–240, 241, 249
Mughan, Steppe of, 1
Mukhtar Bey, 231
Murat of Sivas, 122, 123, 221
Mürsel Pasha, 205, 221, 222, 227, 234
Musavat party: formation and program of, 72–73, 280 n. 17; Constituent Assembly votes for, 108–109, 147; in Baku, 113, 117, 147–149; in Seim, 125–133 *passim,* 145, 153, 154, 160–161, 168, 170, 187; Trebizond delegation members of, 134, 139–141, 150, 151, 155, 156
Mush, 36, 51, 56, 57, 62, 64, 66, 80, 81, 121
Mustafa Kemal, 80, 81, 241, 278 n. 125
Myshlaevskii, General, 46

Nabokov, A., 76
Naji, Omer, 41
Nakhichevan, *khanate* of, 5, 8, 10
Nakhichevan *uezd,* 11, 194, 235, 261 n. 24; interracial hostilities in, 115, 143, 144; Ottoman occupation of, 182, 195, 196, 199
Narimanov, Nariman, 297 n. 75
Narodnaia Volia, 17
National Congress of Russian Armenians. *See* Armenian National Congress
Nazarabekian (Nazarabekov), General Tovmas, 135, 137, 157, 159, 210, 211, 290 n. 35; as Corps commander, 114, 115; and fall of Kars, 163–169 *passim;* in battles of May, 1918, 175, 176, 192, 193
Nazaretian, H., 86
Nazariants, Liparit, 112, 217, 219
Nazarov, 84
Nazim Bey, 232
Nerses, Patriarch, 26
Nersisian Academy, 16
Neruchev, A. V., 107
Nessimi Bey, Ahmed, 228, 232
Nestorians, 36
Nicholas I, Tsar, 8, 9, 10, 11
Nicholas II, Tsar, 62, 97; and 1903–1905 church crisis, 17–18, 19–21; Armenian policy of, 31, 32, 42–43, 44–45, 58, 60, 243; abdication of, 40, 69, 70, 97
Nicholas Nicholaevich Romanov, Grand Duke, 66, 70, 92, 218; appointed Viceroy, 62; restrictive measures of, 62–64, 78; dismissal of, 75
Nikoladze, Nikolai, 173, 180, 183, 189
Nikolaev, General, 55
Nikolskii, N. V., 62
Noragavit, 198
Nor kiank (Alexandropol), 75
North Caucasus, 35, 47, 103, 120, 126, 158, 172, 221, 230; and Ozakom, 76, 84; and Ottoman Empire, 124, 225; Republic, 173, 240
North Persia, 48, 60, 220, 241; Armenian emigration from, 8, 9, 10, 259 n. 8; front in, 44, 64, 70, 82, 114, 137, 174, 179, 194, 205, 221, 239
Novo Bayazit, 144, 194; *uezd,* 11, 195, 235, 261 n. 24, 307–308 n. 60
Novorossiisk, 41
Novo-Selim, 137, 157
Nubar, Boghos, 32, 66, 250, 251
Nukhi (Nukha), 115
Nuri Bey. *See* Nuri Pasha
Nuri Pasha, 177, 190, 205, 214, 220, 227, 234, 237, 240, 305 n. 20
Nusret Bey, Mahmed, 134

Odessa, 41, 313 n. 65; Soviet, 130
Odishelidze, General I. Z., 116, 119, 120, 122, 124, 129, 132, 134, 135, 163, 166, 173, 175, 184
Oganovskii, General, 56
Ognot, 66
Ohandjanian, Hamazasp (Hamo), 108, 109, 167, 180, 189; in Berlin and Vienna, 217–219, 223, 224, 233, 236, 238
Olti, 44, 45, 47, 137, 151; *okrug,* 13, 150, 199
Oniashvili, 160, 162
Orakhelashvili, M. D., 86
Ordubad, 182, 261 n. 24
Orenburg, 103
Orlando, Vittorio, 251
Orlov, Prince, 70
Osobyi Zakavkazskii Komitet. *See* Ozakom
Ottoman Army Group of the East, 205, 215; Baku campaign, 205, 220–221, 223, 225–227
Ottoman Empire (Turkey), 5, 7, 23, 84, 148, 149, 161, 162, 244; Armenians of, 1, 8, 10, 16–17, 22, 24–28, 29, 32, 33, 35–37, 42–44, 45–55 *passim,* 67, 130, 140,

141, 149, 150; in nineteenth century, 7–9, 11–12, 13, 25–28; and tsarist Russia, 7–9, 11–12, 31, 40–41, 43, 44, 64–67; eastern *vilayet*s of, 16, 24, 27, 30–36 *passim,* 40, 43, 49, 52, 57, 66, 103–104, 130, 141, 239, 243, 244, 249, 251, 252, 253; government of, 16, 25, 29–30, 33–34, 42, 44, 49, 50–53, 154, 195, 229; and Germany, 26–27, 33–34, 40, 54–55, 80–81, 103, 123, 161, 176–181 *passim,* 185, 186, 202–204, 210, 214, 217, 218, 220, 222–225 *passim,* 227, 230, 271 n. 2; reforms in, 26–28, 32–34, 38–39; and Allies, 51–52, 57–62 *passim,* 68, 224, 229, 237, 239–240, 241, 245, 247–252 *passim;* and Soviet Russia, 96–105 *passim,* 169–170, 171, 195, 219–220, 225, 227–229; negotiates with Transcaucasia, 119–121, 128–130, 131–134, 138–142, 149–152, 157, 171–174, 175, 179–182; and Armenian Republic, 190–191, 194–202 *passim,* 211–215 *passim,* 222–225 *passim,* 230–238 *passim*
Ottoman liberals, congress of, 29
Ottoman Macedonian Army, 29
Ottoman Ninth Army, 205
Ottoman Second Army, 64, 66, 80, 121, 228
Ottoman Sixth Army, 205
Ottoman Third Army: composition of, 41, 80, 121–122, 157–158, 204–205, 299 n. 3, 308 n. 74; 1914–1918 campaigns of, 45–47, 55–56, 64–66, 80, 81, 121–124, 134–138, 214, 278 n. 126, 282 n. 63; occupies Kars, Ardahan, and Batum, 132, 133, 152–153, 154, 157–159, 163–166, 185; invades Erevan *guberniia,* 166, 170, 174–176, 180, 191–194, 233; withdraws from Transcaucasia, 225, 236–240 *passim*
Ozakom, 80, 107, 112, 159; formation and activity of, 75–78, 92–93; criticism of, 78, 84, 85, 88–89, 281 n. 37
Ozanian, Andranik. *See* Andranik
Ozurget, 158

Page, Walter, 138
Paikar (Tiflis), 75
Paléologue, Maurice, 59, 62
Palestine: front in, 66, 177, 203, 224, 249; future of, 248, 252, 253
Pallavicini, Graf Johann, 203–204, 244
Pampak district, 201, 206, 214; Ottoman occupation of, 206, 231, 233, 235, 236, 314 n. 74
Pan-Turan, 41, 46, 54, 55, 72, 124, 130, 195

Papadjanian, Mikayel I., 90, 120, 121, 159, 208; as Ozakom member, 76, 78, 89; negotiates Batum Treaty, 191, 193, 196, 198; in Constantinople, 217, 235, 313 n. 47
Papazian, Vahan, 79, 159
Papov, Colonel Makar, 313 n. 65
Paris, 19, 20, 28, 29, 58, 59, 60, 130, 138, 253
Paris Peace Conference, 242, 247, 248, 253, 254, 269–270 n. 49
Pasdermadjian, Garegin. *See* Armen Garo
Paskevich, General I. F., 8
Paul, Tsar, 8
Pawlas, Captain, 214, 302 n. 63
Pepinov, A. D., 184
Pereverzev, P. N., 281 n. 37
Persia, 4, 5, 13, 31, 48, 137, 175, 192, 194, 195, 196, 205, 211, 225; Caucasian *khanate*s of, 5, 9; Russian annexations from, 7–10 *passim;* and Entente agreements, 31, 59–60; Soviet policy in, 96–102 *passim. See also* Azerbaijan (Persian); North Persia
Persian Armenia, 253
Persian Empire, 2, 5
Persian Gulf, 1, 59
Peshkov, General, 67
Peter the Great, 8, 45
Petrograd, 60, 63, 67–87 *passim,* 92, 93, 94, 102, 109, 112, 117, 119, 125, 132. *See also* St. Petersburg
Petrograd Armenian Committee, 66, 81
Petrograd Soviet, 69, 71, 74, 76, 83, 84, 85, 94, 95, 126, 283 n. 69; Executive Committee, 83; Red Guard, 84; Military Revolutionary Committee, 94
Petrosian, Grigor, 309 n. 86
Petrovsk, 147, 148, 198
Pichon, Stéphen, 250, 253
Picot, Georges, 59–62
Pinon, René, 48
Pirumian, Colonel Daniel Bek, 193
Pirumian, Simeon, 89, 196, 293 n. 111
Plehve, V. K., 18, 19, 83
Poghosian, Avetis, 269 n. 38
Poland and Poles, 7, 10, 19, 53–54, 97, 101, 102
Pomiankowski, Joseph, 46, 55, 224, 230
Pontus Mountains, 1, 2
Popov, D., 70
Populists (Armenian), 97, 120, 190, 288 n. 13; formation and program of, 73–74; at

National Congress, 87–91 *passim;* and Armenian Republic, 208–213 *passim,* 309 nn. 86, 93, and 98
Populists (Russian), 69
Port Mudros, 229, 237
Poti, 184, 189, 198, 202, 204, 205, 216, 234
Pravda, 83, 96, 99
Przhevalskii, General, 46, 81, 82, 107, 109, 113, 116, 121

Qajar dynasty, 8
Quadruple Alliance, 102. *See also* Central Powers

Raffi (Hakob Melik-Hakobian), 261 n. 42
Rafibekov, Khudadud, 305 n. 20
Rafiev, M., 305 n. 20
Ramishvili, Noi: and Armenians, 47–48, 92, 205, 209; in Transcaucasian government, 116, 121, 129, 142, 152, 153, 155, 162, 167, 168; as Georgian premier, 188, 189, 198, 202, 204, 307 n. 49
Ramkavar party, 78, 79–80, 282 n. 54. *See also* Populists (Armenian)
Rasputin, 68
Rasul-Zade, Mehmed Emin, 73; as Trebizond delegation member, 134, 160, 161; and Transcaucasian independence, 160–161, 168; at Batum Peace Conference, 173, 180, 181, 302 n. 62; as Azerbaijani envoy, 198, 234, 235
Rauf Bey, Husein: at Trebizond Peace Conference, 132, 133, 138, 139, 140, 141, 149, 150, 152, 155–156, 158, 159, 174, 302 n. 63; negotiates Mudros Armistice, 232, 237, 238, 239
Red Guard: in Petrograd, 84; in Tiflis, 111, 116, 154; in Baku, 148, 149
Reshad Hikmet, 239
"Reshid Pasha," 238
Rifat Pasha, 228
Riza, Ahmed, 29, 232
Riza, Major Yusuf, 134
Rize, 64
Rodzianko, M. V., 70
Roman Empire, 2
Romanov: dynasty, 7, 9, 15, 20, 22, 23, 28, 57, 62, 68, 69, 244; Empire, 7, 11, 32, 67, 95, 139, 157, 234, 242, 243
Rome, 130
Rostom (Stepan Zorian), 41, 70, 109, 112
Ruben. *See* Ter Minasian, Ruben
Rumania, 101

Russia, Provisional Government of, 69, 82–84, 94, 95, 109, 111, 208, 283 n. 69; and Transcaucasia, 70–78 *passim,* 82, 84, 85, 88, 92–93, 106, 108, 115; and Turkish Armenia, 79–80, 81, 82, 96
Russia, Soviet: Commissariat for Foreign Affairs, 95, 101, 102, 103, 170, 172, 179, 227; Commissariat for Nationalities, 95, 99–100, 170–171; Council of People's Commissars (Sovnarkom), 95–111 *passim,* 116, 117, 119, 120, 125–132 *passim,* 140, 147, 169–172, 179, 183, 216, 218–220, 221, 224, 225, 244; nationality policy of, 95–101 *passim;* and Armenians, 96–101 *passim,* 111–113, 160, 169–172 *passim,* 213, 216, 218–219, 224, 244, 245; decree of, "About Turkish Armenia," 98–101; and Brest-Litovsk treaty, 101–105 *passim,* 118, 120, 125–130 *passim,* 132, 140, 147, 154, 169–170, 218–229 *passim,* 244; and Transcaucasia, 106–112 *passim,* 117, 119, 120, 127–132 *passim,* 139, 140, 142, 155, 169–172, 179, 186, 203, 218–225 *passim,* 227–229; partisans of, in Caucasus, 107, 110–111, 116, 117, 125–126, 147–149, 179, 218, 220–221; and Constituent Assembly, 108–109, 119–120, 125, 140
Russia, Tsarist, 1, 15, 100, 150; annexes Transcaucasia, 5–6, 7–9, 11–13; nationality policies of, 7, 10–11, 17–23 *passim,* 28, 57–58, 62, 63, 67–68; administrative policies of, 9–11; Viceroy for the Caucasus, 11, 15, 18, 20–21, 31, 32, 43–44, 57, 62, 63, 66, 70, 75, 76, 77; and Turkish Armenia, 24, 26–28 *passim,* 30–34, 38–39, 64–67; and Entente, 31, 34, 43, 57–62 *passim;* in World War I, 40–48 *passim,* 54, 55–57, 64–66; collapse of, 69. *See also* Romanov; Russian Empire
Russian (Eastern) Armenia, 7–23 *passim,* 42, 137, 174, 219, 244, 249, 253. *See also* Armenia
Russian (Eastern) Armenians, 9, 16, 20, 21, 23, 24, 31–32, 40, 42–44, 47, 55, 56, 60, 67, 73, 78, 93, 111–115, 138, 160, 171, 201, 207–208, 209; Congress of, 87–91
Russian Caucasus Army, 8, 45–47, 55–57, 63, 66, 70, 81–82, 85, 109–124 *passim,* 129, 137, 139, 157; Second Regional Congress of, 110–111
Russian Communist Party, 140. *See also* Social Democrat party, Bolshevik

Russian "Democratic Republic," 70, 72, 73, 102, 122, 123, 125, 127, 213, 241, 244
Russian Empire, 1, 7, 9, 16–18, 42, 44, 57, 67, 68, 87, 96
Russian Revolution of 1905, 20, 21, 22, 31, 73
Russian Revolution of March, 1917, 66, 68, 69–74 *passim,* 78, 79, 80, 93, 108, 129, 143, 155
Russian Revolution of November, 1917, 84, 85, 93, 94–96, 98, 101, 106, 112, 113, 117, 118, 119, 121, 143, 212, 244
Russian Senate, 22, 31
Russian Social Democrat Labor party. *See* Social Democrat party, Bolshevik; Social Democrat party, Menshevik
Russian Social Revolutionary party. *See* Social Revolutionary party
Russian State Duma, 63, 67, 68, 69, 70, 76, 159; Temporary Committee, 69, 70, 71
Russo-Turkish boundary of 1877, 102, 163, 164
Russo-Turkish boundary of 1914, 41, 44, 47, 58, 124, 129, 137, 237, 239
Russo-Turkish War of 1828–1829, 8–9
Russo-Turkish War of 1877–1878, 11–12, 26, 57
Rustambekov, Shafi Bek, 145, 153, 154, 155, 187
Rustem, Ahmed, 52

Saadullah, Colonel, 239
Safavids, 5
Safikurdskii, Aslan Bek, 144, 173, 184
Sahakian, Avetik, 146, 167, 168, 211, 212, 309 n. 93
Sahakian, Sako (Sargis), 280 n. 29
Said Halim, 38, 40
St. Petersburg, 10, 20, 23, 31, 32. *See also* Petrograd
Sakarya River, 59
Samavat, 164
San Stefano, Treaty of, 12, 26
Sardarabad, 175, 176, 192, 193, 201
Sarikamish, 44, 135, 137, 198; campaign, 45–48, 53, 55, 64, 81, 273 n. 36
Sassanid Persia, 4
Sassun, 27, 51, 56
Sassuni, Garo, 79
"Savage Division," 113, 148, 289–290 n. 31, 297 n. 77
Savinkov, Boris, 82
Sazonov, S. D., 31, 58–63 *passim*

Schulenburg, Count Friedrich von der, 173, 184, 188, 204, 210, 217
Sebastia. *See* Sivas
Second International, 22
Seeckt, General Hans von, 103, 178, 223
Seert, 34
Seleucids, 2
Seljuk Turks, 4
Semenov, Iulii, 129, 133, 161, 162, 187
Serbia, 40, 41, 97, 101, 250
Sevan, Lake, 1, 144, 194, 198, 210, 238
Sevastopol, 41
Shabin Karahisar, 5, 53, 54
Shahkhatuni, Avetik, 91, 109, 132
Shahtakhtinskii, Hamim Bek, 146
Shahumian, Stepan G., 85–86; and Dashnaktsutiun, 19, 110, 112–113, 117, 126, 147–149, 170, 221, 297 n. 80; leads Baku Soviet and Sovnarkom, 71, 75, 106, 147–149, 218, 220–221; as Extraordinary Commissar for Caucasus, 99–100, 117, 125–126, 221; execution of, 312 n. 37
Shamil, 11
"Shamkhor Massacre," 115–116, 117, 143, 144, 146
Sharp, William, 138
Sharur, 144, 195
Sharur-Daralagiaz *uezd,* 11, 143, 182, 196, 199, 235
Shemakh *guberniia,* 11
Sheikh-ul-Islamov, Akber, 92, 134, 150, 294 n. 17
Shevki Pasha, Yakub, 122, 131, 137, 176, 192, 204, 205, 214, 237
Shikhlinskii, General Ali Agha, 205
Shirak, 91
Shore, General Offley, 82
Shulaver, 115
Shuragial, 259 n. 19
Shushi (Shusha), 78, 115, 241, 259 n. 18
Signakh *uezd,* 205
Silikian, General, 114, 144, 159, 164, 193, 196, 211, 290 n. 37
Silikov, Colonel. *See* Silikian, General
Sis, 2, 50, 239
Sivas (Sebastia), 2, 5, 34, 38, 60, 66
Smirnov, 289 n. 20
Smith, F. Willoughby, 80, 82, 107, 117–118, 137–138, 307 n. 49
Smyrna, 132
Social Democrat Bolsheviks (Armenian), 74–75, 85, 87, 88, 98, 99, 111, 112, 159, 170, 213

INDEX 361

Social Democratic Workers Armenian Organization (Specifist), 19, 74
Social Democrat Mensheviks (Armenian), 83, 84, 89, 90, 97, 108, 180, 208–213 *passim*
Social Democrat Mensheviks (Georgian), 47, 68, 69, 70, 71–72, 152–153, 273 n. 43; and Bolsheviks, 75, 83, 85, 111, 112, 117, 125–126, 170, 172; and Ozakom, 76, 77, 84, 89, 92; and Armenians, 84, 89, 92, 108, 120, 126, 167, 190, 205–206, 209–210; on Commissariat and in Seim, 107, 108, 116, 119–121, 125–130 *passim*, 132–134, 141–142, 144, 145, 153–155, 186–188; Constituent Assembly votes for, 108–109, 288 n. 10; Red Guard, 111, 116, 154; on Transcaucasian and Georgian independence, 142, 158, 159, 160–162, 182–188 *passim;* Regional Committee of, 158
Social Democrat party, Bolshevik, 58, 72, 120, 156, 161, 169, 178, 190, 222, 238; and Dashnaktsutiun, 19, 22, 83, 86, 87, 88, 97, 98, 99, 111–113, 116, 117, 130, 147–149, 170–171, 174, 219, 220, 221, 227, 293 n. 105, 297 n. 80; Central Committee of, 74, 85, 94, 102, 117; and Provisional Government, 74–75, 83, 84, 85–86, 94–95; tactics of, 74–86 *passim*, 95, 98–100 *passim*, 107, 116–117, 125–126; Conference of May, 1917, 75, 97; Sixth Congress of, 83, 85; coalition of, with Left SR's, 84, 94, 95, 110, 219; and Constituent Assembly, 85, 108–109, 140, 147, 280 n. 12; Caucasian Regional Conference of, 85–86, 284 n. 88; Caucasian Regional Committee of, 86, 117, 125, 170; Tiflis Committee of, 87; Seventh Congress of, 104
Social Democrat party, Menshevik, 69, 74–75, 84, 85, 108–109, 120, 147, 208, 221, 283 n. 69
Social Democrats (Armenian), 18–19, 22, 31–32, 67, 74, 78, 83, 85, 108, 190, 305 n. 21; at National Congress, 87–91 *passim;* and Armenian Republic, 208–213 *passim*, 309 nn. 93 and 98
Social Federalist party. *See* Georgian Social Federalist party
Social Revolutionaries (Armenian), 67, 74, 97, 190; at National Congress, 87–91 *passim;* and Armenian Republic, 208–213 *passim*, 309 nn. 93 and 98; organization of, 278 n. 133
Social Revolutionaries (Georgian), 116, 133, 141, 161
Social Revolutionary party (SR), 71, 84, 111, 144, 293 n. 105, 312 n. 37; and Dashnaktsutiun, 17, 19, 73, 278 n. 133; and Provisional Government, 83, 84, 208, 283 n. 69; on Commissariat and in Seim, 107, 116, 126, 133, 141, 153, 161, 168, 187; Constituent Assembly votes for, 108–109, 147; in Baku, 147, 149, 221; Transcaucasian Regional Committee of, 187
Sofia, 230, 267 n. 18
Sonnino, Sidney, 251
Sotsial-Demokrat (Baku), 75
Souchon, Admiral Wilhelm, 40
South-East Union, 120, 121
South Russia, 16, 67, 101, 120, 170, 216, 217
Soviet historiography, 20, 97–98, 100, 111, 115–116, 117, 123, 135, 163, 202, 276 n. 80
Soviet Russia. *See* Russia, Soviet
Soviets, All-Russian Congress of. *See* Congress of Soviets, All-Russian
Sovnarkom. *See* Russia, Soviet
Spartak, 88
Stalin (Djugashvili), I. V., 74, 95–96, 99, 126, 169–174 *passim*, 218
Stamboltsian, Anushavan, 90
Stepanian, Karapet, 269 n. 38
Stokes, Colonel C. B., 222
Stolypin, P. A., 22, 43, 213, 264 n. 67
Straits, 59, 97; Agreement, 62
Sublime Porte, 26, 27, 38, 51, 54, 55, 129, 133, 140, 172, 231, 244
Sultanov, Kh., 305 n. 20
Surmalu *uezd*, 11, 166, 173, 199
Sykes, Sir Mark, 59–62
Sykes-Picot Agreement, 59–62
Syria, 2, 50, 52, 55, 59, 66, 82, 121, 248–253 *passim*

Taghiev, Haji Zeinal-Abdin, 148
Tahtadjian, Ferdinand, 238
Takvim-i Vekayi (Constantinople), 51
Talaat Pasha, 30, 40, 42, 49–52 *passim*, 67, 103, 175, 178, 222–236 *passim*, 314 n. 81
Tanin (Constantinople), 232
Tatars (Moslems) of Transcaucasia, 8–15 *passim*, 21, 41–42, 47–48, 70, 72–73, 76, 81, 89, 91–93, 112–118 *passim*, 124, 127–128, 132–133, 137, 138, 142–151 *passim*,

154, 162, 168, 170, 174, 180–185 *passim,* 190, 192, 194, 198–203 *passim,* 207, 210, 211, 214–215, 220, 225–227, 232, 233, 234–235, 240–242, 244
Taurus Mountains, 1, 59, 60, 252
Teague-Jones, Captain, 312 n. 37
Temir-Khanov, 302 n. 63
Terdjan, 51
Ter Ghazarian, Ghazar, 90, 108, 293 n. 111
Ter Gukasov, General A. A., 12
Ter Hakobian, General, 164
Terian, Vahan, 99, 171, 286 n. 24
Ter Khachatrian, Grigor, 212, 309 n. 93
Terlemezian, Tigran, 276 n. 83
Ter Minasian, Ruben, 90, 112, 134, 159, 190, 309 n. 93
Ter Ohanian, Haik, 90
Ter Zakarian, Hakob, 79
Terzipashian, Avetis, 79
Tevzaia, 289 n. 20
Tewfik Pasha, 240
Tewfik Salim, Colonel, 134
Theodosia, 41
Third International, 74–75
Thomson, General William M., 241, 242
Thrace, 59
Tiflis, 16, 32, 42–47 *passim,* 57, 62, 68, 69–87 *passim,* 91, 92, 106–116 *passim,* 125–132 *passim,* 138–143 *passim,* 146, 150–185 *passim,* 189, 190, 192, 198, 205, 207, 213, 214, 215, 217, 220, 230, 241; Armenians in, 42–44, 47, 74, 91, 158, 198, 280 n. 21; soviets in, 70–71, 76, 83, 106, 111, 125; Armenian National Congress in, 87–91; government, 105, 107–108, 118–139 *passim,* 142, 150, 151, 153, 157, 165, 171, 172, 174, 175, 179, 229; Armenian cabinet leaves, 209–211
Tiflis City Duma, 70, 76, 84, 107
Tiflis *guberniia,* 91, 92, 111, 165, 207; formation of, 11; Georgians of, 13, 47, 111, 187, 199, 206, 235, 285 n. 114; Armenians of, 15, 73, 92, 115, 119, 199, 206, 235, 285 n. 114; Moslems of, 92, 158, 199, 285 n. 114; Ottoman pretensions to and partial occupation of, 170, 173, 178, 186, 189, 195, 204, 205, 218, 233
Tigranes, Emperor, 2
Tigranian, Sirakan, 109, 129, 276 n. 83, 309 n. 93
Tigris River, 1, 60
Tiknis, 157
Tireboli, 80

Tokyo, 130
Toniev, Captain Ashot, 313 n. 65
Topchibashev, Ali Marden, 234, 235, 305 n. 20
Torosian, Sahak, 272 n. 18, 309 n. 93
Townshend, General Charles, 229
Toynbee, Arnold, 48, 53
Transcaspia, 54, 177, 312 n. 37
Transcaucasia: in Romanov Empire, 7–15, 21–23, 44–48, 68; from March to November, 1917, 69–93; from November Revolution to independence, 106–156; independence of, 157–185; creation of three republics in, 186–215. *See also* Armenia; Azerbaijan; Caucasus; Georgia
Transcaucasian Commissariat, 106–133 *passim,* 139, 141, 143, 151, 153, 155, 169, 244
Transcaucasian Conference of Moslems, 72–73
Transcaucasian Federative Republic, 167, 194, 205, 213, 244; formation of, 159–162; cabinet of, 168; Ottoman recognition of and negotiations with, 168, 172–174, 180–182; dissolution of, 181, 182–185 *passim,* 186–188, 190, 203
Transcaucasian Regional Center of Soviets, 84, 106, 116, 119, 121, 125, 128
Transcaucasian Regional Soviets, 71, 110–111
Transcaucasian Seim, 116, 121, 159, 176, 183, 185, 191, 192, 244; formation of, 124–128, 293 nn. 111 and 113; bases for peace, 128–130, 132, 237; negotiates with Ottoman Empire, 131–134, 138–142, 149–156 *passim,* 158, 172–174; discord in, 135, 137, 144, 145, 146; on independence, 160–162, 167–169; and Soviet Russia, 169–171, 220; dissolution of, 186–188, 189
Trebizond, 28, 64, 67, 82, 116, 131, 135, 137, 140, 142, 146, 155, 156, 157, 159, 163, 167, 252; *vilayet,* 38, 60, 79, 80; Peace Conference, 129, 130, 131–134, 138–141, 145, 146, 149–152, 153, 155–156, 162, 170, 174, 237, 294 n. 17
Triple Alliance, 27, 33, 34. *See also* Central Powers
Tripolitania (Libya), 29
Trotsky, L. D., 94, 95, 102, 103, 112, 117, 123, 130, 142, 169
Trukhin, General, 56
Tsalka, 207, 235

Tsereteli, Iraklii, 108, 145, 152–155 *passim*, 160, 167, 186, 206
Tskhakaia, M. G., 86
Tumanian, Hovhannes, 269 n. 38
Tumanov, Lev, 161, 168
Turan, 113, 154, 185
Turkestan, 103, 113, 123, 195, 225
Turkey. *See* Ottoman Empire
Turkic Federalistic Party, 72
Turkic Federalistic Party of Musavat. *See* Musavat party
Turkish (Western) Armenia, 24–39 *passim*, 47, 63, 70, 73, 77, 78, 79, 112, 132, 141, 143, 158, 174, 201, 208, 229, 237, 240, 242, 244, 249, 253; Russian policy in, 31–32, 44–45, 62–67 *passim*, 79–80, 96; proposed autonomy for, 22, 23, 37–39, 45, 56, 58, 64, 68, 93, 127–128, 129–130, 140, 141, 149–150; Ottoman reoccupation of, 80, 81, 104, 121–124, 134–137. *See also* Ottoman Empire, eastern *vilayet*s
Turkish (Western) Armenians, 20, 24, 31, 38, 40, 42, 63, 80, 135, 138, 214; emigration of, 9, 10, 12–13, 26; concern for, 16, 30, 31–32, 43, 44, 55–56; deportations and massacres of, 27–28, 30, 44, 48–55, 89, 244, 249; population statistics for, 35–37; refugees, 47, 67, 78–79, 89, 150, 158, 166, 171, 194, 201, 210–211; militia of, 113–115, 135, 138, 194. *See also* Western Armenian Council
Turkish front. *See* Caucasus front
Turkmanchai, Treaty of, 8, 9, 259 n. 8
"Turkmen," 312 n. 37

Ubicini, 35–36
Ukraine, 97, 98, 101, 120, 121, 140, 169, 179, 211, 234, 313 n. 65
Ukrainian Central Rada, 120, 121, 130, 217
Ulukhanlu, 143, 144, 209
United States, 67, 213; and Armenians, 55, 238, 251–253; Transcaucasian policy of, 117–119, 138; Inquiry, 252, 253, 316 n. 27
Urfa, 50, 53
Urmia, Lake, 1, 82, 194
Usubbekov, Nesib, 168, 184, 305 n. 20
Uvarov, S. S., 259 n. 1

Vahideddin (Mehmed VI), 232
Van, 39, 44, 82, 113, 114, 143, 157, 195, 238; *eyalet*, 5; *vilayet*, 34, 36, 38, 42, 58, 60, 137; Ottoman Army in, 41, 55–56, 137; "Revolt of," 48, 53, 54, 55, 275 n. 64; deportations from and massacres in, 50, 51, 52, 275 n. 64; Russian capture and evacuation of, 55–57, 123, 165, 276 n. 87; Armenian government in, 56, 79, 80, 276 n. 83
Vardan, Commander, 47, 55
Vardan Mamikonian, 193
Varzhapetian, Patriarch Nerses, 26
Vehib Pasha, General Mehmed, 66, 119–120, 189–190, 210, 214; commands Third Army, 64; occupies Turkish Armenia, 121–124, 132–138; captures Batum and Kars, 152–153, 157, 160–166 *passim;* at Batum Peace Conference, 172, 173, 175, 195, 196, 198, 201, 233; dismissed, 204
Vekilov, 78
Vermishian, Kristapor, 88
Veselovskii, Boris, 92
Veshapeli, Grigorii, 156
Vestnik Vremennago pravitel'stva (Petrograd), 79
Viceroy for the Caucasus. *See* Russia, Tsarist
Vienna, 22, 130, 211, 215, 216, 222, 223, 224
Villari, Luigi, 120
Vladikars, 159
Vladikavkaz, 147, 162
Volga region, 113
Volinskii Guard Regiment, 69
Vorontsov, Prince M. S., 11
Vorontsov-Dashkov, Count I. I., 15, 20, 21, 92, 218; and Russian Armenians, 20, 32, 43, 44, 57, 264 nn. 60, 61, 63, and 67; relieved, 62
Vostan, 56, 57
Vramian, Arshak, 41, 53
Vratzian, Simon, 44, 88, 167, 173, 190, 313–314 n. 38
Vyshinskii, General, 109

Wangenheim, Freiherr Hans von, 33, 34, 40, 271 n. 2
War Communism, 171
Washington, D.C., 49, 52, 54, 118, 130, 137, 138
Wesendonck, Otto G. von, 173, 183, 184
Westenenk, Inspector-General, 38, 39
Western Armenian Council, 78–79; Executive Bureau, 79, 113
Western Armenian Defense Council, 113, 138, 159

Western Armenians, First Congress of, 78–79
Western Asia, 2, 4, 5, 59, 247
White Armies, 216–217. *See also* South Russia
Wilhelm II, Kaiser, 55, 97
Wilson, Woodrow, 236, 251, 252, 253
Winter Palace, 95, 106
World War I, 40–68 *passim*. *See also* Caucasus front

Yakub Shevki Pasha. *See* Shevki Pasha, Yakub
Yarrow, Ernest, 82
Yerevan. *See* Erevan
Yezidis, 36, 211, 285 n. 114, 309 nn. 93 and 98
"Young Turks," 28–29, 49, 54, 232, 268 n. 29. *See also* Ittihad ve Terakki

Zabukh, Vale of, 241
Zakarian, Petros, 90, 212, 309 n. 93
Zangezur *uezd*, 194, 195, 214, 215, 234, 241, 242
Zavriev, Dr. Hakob, 109; and tsarist Russia, 43, 58, 59, 68; and Provisional Government, 79–81, 113; and Soviet Russia, 112, 218
Zazas, 36
Zeitun, 51, 54, 60, 239; Regiment, 113
Zekki Pasha, General, 102
Zemstvo: proposed for Transcaucasia, 15, 73, 77, 88, 92, 108, 235
Zemstvo Union, 69
Zhordania, Noi, 108, 155; expresses Georgian Menshevik views, 70, 71–72, 116, 152, 158–159; and Ozakom, 76, 84, 89, 92; and Armenians, 89, 92, 167, 185, 188, 205, 209; and Commissariat, 107, 116, 119; as Georgian National Council chairman, 116, 160, 183–184, 188; as Menshevik spokesman in Seim, 124–125, 128, 132, 133, 142, 153; and Georgian Republic, 183–185, 188, 209, 241, 304 n. 12
Zhuruli, Georgii, 304 n. 12
Zinoviev, G. E., 94
Zohrabian (Zurabov), Arshak, 84, 180, 189, 217, 224, 293 n. 111
Zorian, Stepan. *See* Rostom
Zor *sanjak*, 50
Zubian, Davit, 212, 309 n. 93
Zubovka, 220

Library and Learning
Resources Center
Bergen Community College
400 Paramus Road
Paramus, N.J. 07652-1595

Return Postage Guaranteed